Lecture Notes in Computer Science 9048

Commenced Publication in 1973
Founding and Former Series Editors:
Gerhard Goos, Juris Hartmanis, and Jan van Leeuwen

T0210452

More information about this series at http://www.springer.com/series/7410

Kaisa Nyberg (Ed.)

Topics in Cryptology – CT-RSA 2015

The Cryptographers' Track at the RSA Conference 2015
San Francisco, CA, USA, April 21–24, 2015
Proceedings

 Springer

Editor
Kaisa Nyberg
Aalto University School of Science
Espoo
Finland

ISSN 0302-9743   ISSN 1611-3349   (electronic)
Lecture Notes in Computer Science
ISBN 978-3-319-16714-5   ISBN 978-3-319-16715-2   (eBook)
DOI 10.1007/978-3-319-16715-2

Library of Congress Control Number: 2015934581

LNCS Sublibrary: SL4 – Security and Cryptology

Springer Cham Heidelberg New York Dordrecht London

Printed on acid-free paper

Springer International Publishing AG Switzerland is part of Springer Science+Business Media
(www.springer.com)

Preface

The RSA conference has been a major international event for information security experts since its inception in 1991. It is an annual event that attracts hundreds of vendors and thousands of participants from industry, government, and academia. Since 2001, the RSA conference has included the Cryptographers' Track (CT-RSA), which provides a forum for current research in cryptography. CT-RSA has become a major publication venue in cryptography. It covers a wide variety of topics from public-key to symmetric-key cryptography and from cryptographic protocols to primitives and their implementation security.

This volume represents the proceedings of the 2015 RSA Conference Cryptographers' Track which was held in San Francisco, California, during April 21–24, 2015. A total of 111 full papers were submitted for review out of which 26 papers were selected for presentation. As Chair of the Program Committee, I heartily thank all the authors who contributed the results of their innovative research and all the members of the Program Committee and their designated assistants who carefully reviewed the submissions. In the thorough peer-review process that lasted 2 months, each submission had three independent reviewers. The selection process was completed at a discussion among all members of the Program Committee.

In addition to the contributed talks, the program included a panel discussion moderated by Bart Preneel on *Post-Snowden Cryptography* featuring Paul Kocher, Adi Shamir, and Nigel Smart.

February 2015   Kaisa Nyberg

Organization

The RSA Cryptographers' Track is an independently managed component of the annual RSA Conference.

Steering Committee

Josh Benaloh	Microsoft Research, USA
Ed Dawson	Queensland University of Technology, Australia
Kaisa Nyberg	Aalto University School of Science, Finland
Ron Rivest	Massachusetts Institute of Technology, USA
Moti Yung	Google, USA

Program Chair

Kaisa Nyberg	Aalto University School of Science, Finland

Program Committee

Frederik Armknecht	University of Mannheim, Germany
Josh Benaloh	Microsoft Research, USA
John Black	University of Colorado, USA
Jean-Sebastien Coron	University of Luxembourg, Luxembourg
Orr Dunkelman	University of Haifa, Israel
Steven Galbraith	University of Auckland, New Zealand
Henri Gilbert	ANSSI, France
Jens Groth	University College London, UK
Helena Handschuh	Cryptography Research, Inc., USA
Thomas Johansson	Lund University, Sweden
Marc Joye	Technicolor, USA
John Kelsey	National Institute of Standards and Technology, USA
Dmitry Khovratovich	University of Luxembourg, Luxembourg
Kwangjo Kim	Korea Advanced Institute of Science and Technology, Republic of Korea
Lars R. Knudsen	Technical University of Denmark, Denmark
Anna Lysyanskaya	Brown University, USA
María Naya-Plasencia	Inria, France
Kaisa Nyberg (chair)	Aalto University School of Science, Finland
Elisabeth Oswald	University of Bristol, UK
Kenneth Paterson	Royal Holloway University of London, UK

David Pointcheval   École Normal Supérieure, France
Rei Safavi-Naini   University of Calgary, Canada
Kazue Sako   NEC, Japan
Palash Sarkar   Indian Statistical Institute, India
Ali Aydin Selçuk   TOBB University of Economics and Technology,
                            Turkey
Nigel Smart   University of Bristol, UK
Vanessa Teague   University of Melbourne, Australia
Dominique Unruh   University of Tartu, Estonia
Serge Vaudenay   École Polytechnique Fédérale de Lausanne,
                            Switzerland
Huaxiong Wang   Nanyang Technological University, Singapore

External Reviewers

Mohamed Ahmed	Essam Ghadafi	Kerry McKay
Abdelraheem	Jorge Guajardo	Kazuhiko Minematsu
Divesh Aggarwal	Florian Hahn	Khoa Nguyen
Murat Ak	Mike Hamburg	Kazuma Ohara
James Alderman	Ghaith Hammouri	Adam O'Neill
Elena Andreeva	Haruna Higo	Ray Perlner
Diego Aranha	Daniel Hutchinson	Leo Perrin
Shi Bai	Toshiyuki Isshiki	Thomas Peters
Foteini Baldimtsi	Christian Janson	Christophe Petit
Subhadeep Banik	Angela Jäschke	Duong Hieu Phan
Larry Bassham	Mahavir Jhawar	Rachel Player
Sanjay Bhattacherjee	Orhun Kara	Jérôme Plût
Sonia Bogos	Ferhat Karakoc	Emmanuel Prouff
Christina Boura	Hak Ju Kim	Somindu C. Ramanna
Florian Bourse	Stefan Koelbl	Jean-René Reinhard
Beyhan Çalışkan	Alptekin Küpçü	Christian Reuter
Andrea Cerulli	Adeline Langlois	Reza Reyhanitabar
Pyrros Chaidos	Martin Lauridsen	Thomas Roche
Debrup Chakraborty	Hyung Tae Lee	Arnab Roy
Rakyong Choi	Anthony Leverrier	Sumanta Sarkar
Ashish Choudhury	Gaëtan Leurent	Peter Scholl
Geoffroy Couteau	Kaitai Liang	Yannick Seurin
Gareth Davies	Fuchun Lin	Siamak Shahandashti
Angelo De Caro	Zhen Liu	Dale Sibborn
Huseyin Demirci	Atul Luykx	Shashank Singh
Alexandre Duc	Ceyda Mangir	Isamu Teranishi
Sebastian Faust	Joana Marim	Cihangir Tezcan
Jun Furukawa	Dan Martin	Nicolas Theriault
Shishay Gebregiyorgis	Alexander May	Susan Thomson

Tyge Tiessen

Elmar Tischhauser

Meltem Sonmez Turan

Joop van de Pol

Damien Vergnaud

Damian Vizár

Pengwei Wang

Guomin Yang

Hongbo Yu

Emre Yuce

Liangfeng Zhang

Contents

Authenticated Encryption

Detecting and Tracing Malicious Activities

Implementation Attacks on Exponentiation Algorithms

Homomorphic Encryption and Its Applications

Timing Attacks

Just a Little Bit More

Joop van de Pol[1]([✉]), Nigel P. Smart[1], and Yuval Yarom[2]

[1] Department Computer Science, University of Bristol, Bristol, UK
joop.vandepol@bristol.ac.uk, nigel@cs.bris.ac.uk
[2] School of Computer Science, The University of Adelaide, Adelaide, Australia
yval@cs.adelaide.edu.au

Abstract. We extend the FLUSH+RELOAD side-channel attack of Benger et al. to extract a significantly larger number of bits of information per observed signature when using OpenSSL. This means that by observing only 25 signatures, we can recover secret keys of the **secp256k1** curve, used in the Bitcoin protocol, with a probability greater than 50 percent. This is an order of magnitude improvement over the previously best known result.

The new method of attack exploits two points: Unlike previous partial disclosure attacks we utilize all information obtained and not just that in the least significant or most significant bits, this is enabled by a property of the "standard" curves choice of group order which enables extra bits of information to be extracted. Furthermore, whereas previous works require direct information on ephemeral key bits, our attack utilizes the indirect information from the wNAF double and add chain.

1 Introduction

The Elliptic Curve Digital Signature Algorithm (ECDSA) is the elliptic curve analogue of the Digital Signature Algorithm (DSA). It has been well known for over a decade that the randomization used within the DSA/ECDSA algorithm makes it susceptible to side-channel attacks. In particular a small leakage of information on the ephemeral secret key utilized in each signature can be combined over a number of signatures to obtain the entire key.

Howgrave-Graham and Smart [14] showed that DSA is vulnerable to such partial ephemeral key exposure and their work was made rigorous by Nguyen and Shparlinski [21], who also extended these results to ECDSA [22]. More specifically, if, for a polynomially bounded number of random messages and ephemeral keys about $\log^{1/2} q$ least significant bits (LSBs) are known, the secret key α can be recovered in polynomial time. A similar result holds for a consecutive sequence of the most significant bits (MSBs), with a potential need for an additional leaked bit due to the paucity of information encoded in the most significant bit of the ephemeral key. When an arbitrary sequence of consecutive bits in the ephemeral key is known, about twice as many bits are required. The attack works by constructing a lattice problem from the obtained digital signatures and side-channel information, and then applying lattice reduction techniques such as LLL [16] or BKZ [23] to solve said lattice problem.

K. Nyberg (ed.): CT-RSA 2015, LNCS 9048, pp. 3–21, 2015.
DOI: 10.1007/978-3-319-16715-2_1

Brumley and co-workers employ this lattice attack to recover ECDSA keys using leaked LSBs (in [4]) and leaked MSBs (in [5]). The former uses a cache side-channel to extract the leaked information and the latter exploits a timing side-channel. In both attacks, a fixed number of bits from each signature is used and signatures are used only if the values of these bits are all zero. Signatures in which the value of any of these bits are one are ignored. Consequently, both attacks require more than 2,500 signatures to break a 160-bit private key.

More recently, again using a cache based side-channel, Benger et al. [2] use the LSBs of the ephemeral key for a wNAF (a.k.a. sliding window algorithm) multiplication technique. By combining a new side-channel called the FLUSH+RELOAD side-channel [26, 27], and a more precise lattice attack strategy, which utilizes all of the leaked LSBs from every signature, Benger et al. are able to significantly reduces the number of signatures required. In particular they report that the full secret key of a 256-bit system can be recovered with about 200 signatures in a reasonable length of time, and with a reasonable probability of success.

In this work we extend the FLUSH+RELOAD technique of Benger et al. to reduce the number of required signatures by an order of magnitude. Our methodology abandons the concentration on extraction of bits in just the MSB and LSB positions, and instead focuses on all the information leaked by all the bits of the ephemeral key. In particular we exploit a property of many of the standardized elliptic curves as used in OpenSSL. Our method, just as in [2], applies the FLUSH+RELOAD side-channel technique to the wNAF elliptic curve point multiplication algorithm in OpenSSL.

ECDSA Using Standard Elliptic Curves: The domain parameters for ECDSA are an elliptic curve E over a field $\mathbb{F}$, and a point G on E, of order q. Given a hash function h, the ECDSA signature of a message m, with a private key $0 < \alpha < q$ and public key $Q = \alpha G$, is computed by:

- Selecting a random ephemeral key $0 < k < q$
- Computing $r = x(kG) \pmod{q}$, the X coordinate of kG.
- Computing $s = k^{-1}(h(m) + \alpha \cdot r) \pmod{q}$.

The process is repeated if either $r = 0$ or $s = 0$. The pair (r, s) is the signature.

To increase interoperability, standard bodies have published several sets of domain parameters for ECDSA [1, 7, 20]. The choice of moduli for the fields used in these standard curves is partly motivated by efficiency arguments. For example, all of the moduli in the curves recommended by FIPS [20] are generalised Mersenne primes [24] and many of them are pseudo-Mersenne primes [10]. This choice of moduli facilitates efficient modular arithmetic by avoiding a division operation which may otherwise be required.

A consequence of using pseudo-Mersenne primes as moduli is that, due to Hasse's Theorem, not only is the finite-field order close to a power of two, but so is the elliptic-curve group order.

That is, q can be expressed as $2^n - \epsilon$, where $|\epsilon| < 2^p$ for some $p \approx n/2$. We demonstrate that such curves are more susceptible to partial disclosure of ephemeral keys than was hitherto known. This property increases the amount of information that can be used from partial disclosure and allows for a more effective attack on ECDSA.

Our Contribution: We demonstrate that the above property of the standardized curves allows the utilization of far more leaked information, in particular some arbitrary sequences of consecutive leaked bits. In a nutshell, adding or subtracting q to or from an unknown number is unlikely to change any bits in positions between $p + 1$ and n. Based on this observation we are able to use (for wNAF multiplication algorithms) all the information in consecutive bit sequences in positions above $p + 1$. Since in many of the standard curves $p \approx n/2$, a large amount of information is leaked per signature. (Assuming one can extract the sequence of additions and doubles in an algorithm.) As identified by Ciet and Joye [8] and exploited by Feix et al. [11], the same property also implies that techniques for mitigating side-channel attack, such as the scalar blinding suggested in [4,18], do not protect bits in positions above $p + 1$.

Prior works deal with the case of partial disclosure of consecutive sequences of bits of the ephemeral key. Our work offers two improvements: It demonstrates how to use partial information leaked from the double and add chains of the wNAF scalar multiplication algorithm [13,19]. In most cases, the double and add chain does not provide direct information on the value of bits. It only identifies sequences of repeating bits without identifying the value of these bits. We show how to use this information to construct a lattice attack on the private key. Secondly, our attack does not depend on the leaked bits being consecutive. We use information leaked through the double and add chain even though it is spread out along the ephemeral key.

By using more leaked information and exploiting the above property of the elliptic curves, our attack only requires a handful of leaked signatures to fully break the private key. Our experiments show that the perfect information leaked on double and add chains of only 13 signatures is sufficient for recovering the 256 bit private key of the **secp256k1** curve with probability greater than 50 percent. For the 521 bit curve **secp521r1**, 40 signatures are required. We further demonstrate that for the **secp256k1** case observing 25 signatures is highly likely to recover 13 perfect double and add chains. Hence, by observing 25 Bitcoin transactions using the same key, an attacker can expect to recover the private key. For most of the paper we discuss the case of perfect side channels which result in perfect double and add chains, then in Section 6 we show how this assumption can be removed in the context of a real FLUSH+RELOAD attack.

2   Background

In this section we discuss three basic procedures we will be referring to throughout. Namely the FLUSH+RELOAD side-channel attack technique, wNAF scalar multiplication method and the use of lattices to extract secret keys from triples. The side-channel information we obtain from executing the wNAF algorithm produces instances of the Hidden Number Problem (HNP) [3]. Since the HNP is traditionally studied via lattice reduction it is therefore not surprising that we are led to lattice reduction in our analysis.

2.1   The FLUSH+RELOAD Side-Channel Attack Technique

FLUSH+RELOAD is a recently discovered cache side-channel attack [26,27]. The attack exploits a weakness in the Intel implementation of the popular X86 architecture, which allows a spy program to monitor other programs' read or execute access to shared regions of memory. The spy program only requires read access to the monitored memory.

Unlike most cache side-channel attacks, FLUSH+RELOAD uses the Last-Level Cache (LLC), which is the cache level closest to the memory. The LLC is shared by the execution cores in the processor, allowing the attack to operate when the spy and victim processes execute on different cores. Furthermore, as most virtual machine hypervisors (VMMs) actively share memory between co-resident virtual machines, the attack is applicable to virtualized environment and works cross-VM.

```
Input: adrs—the probed address
Output: true if the address was accessed by the victim
begin
      evict(adrs)
      wait_a_bit()
      time ← current_time()
      tmp ← read(adrs)
      readTime ← current_time()-time
      return readTime < threshold
end
```

Algorithm 1. FLUSH+RELOAD Algorithm

To monitor access to memory, the spy repeatedly evicts the contents of the monitored memory from the LLC, waits for some time and then measures the time to read the contents of the monitored memory. See Algorithm 1 for a pseudo-code of the attack. FLUSH+RELOAD uses the X86 `clflush` instruction to evict contents from the cache. To measure time the spy uses the `rdtsc` instruction which returns the time since processor reset measured in processor cycles.

As reading from the LLC is much faster than reading from memory, the spy can differentiate between these two cases. If, following the wait, the contents of memory is retrieved from the cache, it indicates that another process has accessed the memory. Thus, by measuring the time to read the contents of memory, the spy can decide whether the victim has accessed the monitored memory since the last time it was evicted.

To implement the attack, the spy needs to share the monitored memory with the victim. For attacks occurring within the same machine, the spy can map files used by the victim into its own address space. Examples of these files include the victim program file, shared libraries or data files that the victim accesses. As all mapped copies of files are shared, this gives the spy access to memory pages accessed by the victim. In virtualized environments, the spy does not have access to the victim's files. The spy can, however, map copies of the victim files to its own address space, and rely on the VMM to merge the two copies using page de-duplication [15,25]. It should be pointed that, as the LLC is physically tagged, the virtual address in which the spy maps the files is irrelevant for the attack. Hence, FLUSH+RELOAD is oblivious to address space layout randomization [17].

This sharing only works when the victim does not make private modifications to the contents of the shared pages. Consequently, many FLUSH+RELOAD attacks target executable code pages, monitoring the times the victim executes specific code. The spy typically divides time into fixed width time slots. In each time slot the spy monitors a few memory locations and records the times that these locations were accessed by the victim. By reconstructing a trace of victim access, the spy is able to infer the data the victim is operating on. Prior works used this attack to recover the private key of GnuPG RSA [27] as well as for recovering the ephemeral key used in OpenSSL ECDSA signatures either completely, for curves over binary fields [26], or partially, for curves over prime fields [2].

2.2 The wNAF Scalar Multiplication Method

Several algorithms for computing the scalar multiplication kG have been proposed. One of the suggested methods is to use the *windowed nonadjacent form* (wNAF) representation of the scalar k, see [13]. In wNAF a number is represented by a sequence of digits k_i. The value of a digit k_i is either zero or an odd number $-2^w < k_i < 2^w$, with each pair of non-zero digits separated by at least w zero digits. The value of k can be calculated from its wNAF representation using $k = \sum 2^i \cdot k_i$. See Algorithm 2 for a method to convert a scalar k into its wNAF representation. We use $|\cdot|_x$ to denote the reduction modulo x into the range $[-x/2, \ldots, x/2]$.

Input: Scalar k and window width w
Output: k in wNAF: $k_0, k_1, k_2 \ldots$
begin
    $e \leftarrow k$
    $i \leftarrow 0$
    while $e > 0$ do
        if $e \bmod 2 = 1$ then
            $k_i \leftarrow |e|_{2^{w+1}}$
            $e \leftarrow e - k_i$
        else
            $k_i \leftarrow 0$
        end
        $e \leftarrow e/2$
        $i \leftarrow i + 1$
    end
end

Algorithm 2. Conversion to Non-Adjacent Form

Let $\overline{k_i}$ be the value of the variable e at the start of the ith iteration in Algorithm 2. From the algorithm, it is clear that

$$k_i = \begin{cases} 0 & \overline{k_i} \text{ is even} \\ |\overline{k_i}|_{2^{w+1}} & \overline{k_i} \text{ is odd} \end{cases} \tag{1}$$

Furthermore:

$$k = 2^i \cdot \overline{k_i} + \sum_{j < i} 2^j \cdot k_j \tag{2}$$

Let m and $m + l$ be the position of two consecutive non-zero wNAF digits, i.e. $k_m, k_{m+l} \neq 0$ and $k_{m+i} = 0$ for all $0 < i < l$. We now have

$$-2^{m+w} < \sum_{i \leq m} k_i \cdot 2^i < 2^{m+w}, \tag{3}$$

and because $l > w$, we get $-2^{m+l-1} < \sum_{i \leq m+l-1} k_i \cdot 2^i < 2^{m+l-1}$. Substituting m for $m + l$ gives

$$- 2^{m-1} < \sum_{i \leq m-1} k_i \cdot 2^i < 2^{m-1} \tag{4}$$

We note that for the minimal m such that $k_m \neq 0$ we have $\sum_{i \leq m-1} k_i \cdot 2^i = 0$. Hence (4) holds for every m such that $k_m \neq 0$.

Because k_m is odd, we have $-(2^w - 1) \leq k_m \leq 2^w - 1$. Adding $k_m \cdot 2^m$ to (4) gives a slightly stronger version of (3):

$$- (2^{m+w} - 2^{m-1}) < \sum_{i \leq m} k_i \cdot 2^i < 2^{m+w} - 2^{m-1} \tag{5}$$

One consequence of subtracting negative wNAF components is that the wNAF representation may be one digit longer than the binary representation of the number. For n-digits binary numbers Möller [19] suggests using $k_i \leftarrow \lfloor k \rfloor_{2^w}$ when $i = n - w - 1$ and e is odd, where $\lfloor \cdot \rfloor_x$ denotes the reduction modulo x into the interval $[0, \ldots, x)$. This avoids extending the wNAF representation in half the cases at the cost of weakening the non-adjacency property of the representation.

2.3   Lattice Background

Before we describe how to get the necessary information from the side-channel attack, we recall from previous works what kind of information we are looking for. As in previous works [2,4,5,14,21,22], the side-channel information is used to construct a lattice basis and the secret key is then retrieved by solving a lattice problem on this lattice. Generally, for a private key α and a group order q, in previous works the authors somehow derive triples (t_i, u_i, z_i) from the side-channel information such that

$$- q/2^{z_i+1} < v_i = |\alpha \cdot t_i - u_i|_q < q/2^{z_i+1}. \tag{6}$$

Note that for arbitrary α and t_i, the values of v_i are uniformly distributed over the interval $[-q/2, q/2)$. Hence, each such triple provides about z_i bits of information about α. The use of a different z_i per equation was introduced in [2]. If we take d such triples we can construct the following lattice basis

$$
B = \begin{pmatrix}
2^{z_1+1} \cdot q & & & \\
& \ddots & & \\
& & 2^{z_d+1} \cdot q & \\
2^{z_1+1} \cdot t_1 & \cdots & 2^{z_d+1} \cdot t_d & 1
\end{pmatrix},
$$

whose rows generate the lattice that we use to retrieve the secret key. Now consider the vector $\mathbf{u} = (2^{z_1+1} \cdot u_1, \ldots, 2^{z_d+1} \cdot u_d, 0)$, which consists of known quantities. Equation (6) implies the existence of integers $(\lambda_1, \ldots, \lambda_d)$ such that for the vectors $\mathbf{x} = (\lambda_1, \ldots, \lambda_d, \alpha)$ and $\mathbf{y} = (2^{z_1+1} \cdot v_1, \ldots, 2^{z_d+1} \cdot v_d, \alpha)$ we have

$$\mathbf{x} \cdot B - \mathbf{u} = \mathbf{y}.$$

Again using Equation (6), we see that the 2-norm of the vector $\mathbf{y}$ is at most $\sqrt{d \cdot q^2 + \alpha^2} \approx \sqrt{d+1} \cdot q$. Because the lattice determinant of $L(B)$ is $2^{d+\sum z_i} \cdot q^d$, the lattice vector $\mathbf{x} \cdot B$ is heuristically the closest lattice vector to $\mathbf{u}$. By solving the Closest Vector Problem (CVP) on input of the basis B and the target vector $\mathbf{u}$, we obtain $\mathbf{x}$ and hence the secret key α.

There are two important methods of solving the closest vector problem: using an exact CVP-solver or using the heuristic embedding technique to convert it to a Shortest Vector Problem (SVP). Exact CVP-solvers require exponential time in the lattice rank ($d + 1$ in our case), whereas the SVP instance that follows from the embedding technique can sometimes be solved using approximation methods that run in polynomial time. Because the ranks of the lattices in this work become quite high when attacking a 521 bit key, we mostly focus on using the embedding technique and solving the associated SVP instance in this case.

The embedding technique transforms the previously described basis B and target vector $\mathbf{u}$ to a new basis B', resulting in a new lattice of dimension one higher than that generated by B:

$$B' = \begin{pmatrix} B & 0 \\ \mathbf{u} & q \end{pmatrix},$$

Following the same reasoning as above, we can set $\mathbf{x}' = (\mathbf{x}, -1)$ and obtain the lattice vector $\mathbf{y}' = \mathbf{x}' \cdot B' = (\mathbf{y}, -q)$. The 2-norm of $\mathbf{y}'$ is upper bounded by approximately $\sqrt{d+2} \cdot q$, whereas this lattice has determinant $2^{d+\sum z_i} \cdot q^{(d+1)}$. Note, however, that this lattice also contains the vector

$$(-t_1, \ldots, -t_d, q, 0) \cdot B' = (0, \ldots, 0, q, 0)$$

which will most likely be the shortest vector of the lattice. Still, our approximation algorithms for SVP work on bases and it is obvious to see that any basis of the same lattice must contain a vector ending in $\pm q$. Thus, it is heuristically likely that the resulting basis contains the short vector $\mathbf{y}'$, which reveals α.

To summarize, we turn the side-channel information into a lattice and claim that, heuristically, finding the secret key is equivalent to solving a CVP instance. Then, we claim that, again heuristically, solving this CVP instance is equivalent to solving an SVP instance using the embedding technique. In Section 5 we will apply the attack to simulated data to see whether these heuristics hold up.

3   Using the wNAF Information

Assuming we have a side channel that leaks the double and add chain of the scalar multiplication. We know how to use the leaked LSBs [2]. These leaked LSBs carry, on average, two bits of information.

Given a double and add chain, the positions of the add operations in the chain correspond to the non-zero digits in the wNAF representation of the ephemeral key k. Roughly speaking, in half the cases the distance between consecutive non-zero digits is $w + 1$. In a quarter of the cases it is $w + 2$ and so on. Hence, the average distance between consecutive non-zero digits is $w + \sum_i i/2^i = w + 2$. Since there are 2^w non-zero digits, we expect that the double and add chain carries two bits of information per each non-zero digit position.

Reducing this information to an instance of the HNP presents three challenges:

- The information is not consecutive, but is spread along the scalar.
- Due to the use of negative digits in the wNAF representation, the double and add chain does not provide direct information on the bits of the scalar
- Current techniques lose half the information when the information is not at the beginning or end of the scalar.

As described in [2], the OpenSSL implementation departs slightly from the descriptions of ECDSA in Section 1. As a countermeasure to the Brumley and Tuveri remote timing attack [5], OpenSSL adds q or $2 \cdot q$ to the randomly chosen ephemeral key, ensuring that k is $n+1$ bits long. While the attack is only applicable to curves defined over binary fields, the countermeasure is applied to all curves. Consequently, our analysis assumes that $2^n \leq k < 2^{n+1}$.

To handle non-consecutive information, we extract a separate HNP instance for each consecutive set of bits, and use these in the lattice. The effect this has on the lattice attack is discussed in Section 4.

To handle the indirect information caused by the negative digits in the wNAF representation we find a linear combination of k in which we know the values of some consecutive bits, we can use that to build an HNP instance.

Let m and $m+l$ be the positions of two consecutive non-zero wNAF digits where $m + l < n$. From the definition of the wNAF representation we know that $k = \overline{k_{m+l}} 2^{m+l} + \sum_{i \leq m} k_i 2^i$. We can now define the following values:

$$a = \frac{\overline{k_{m+l}} - 1}{2}$$

$$c = \sum_{i \leq m} k_i \cdot 2^i + 2^{m+w}$$

By (5) we have

$$2^{m-1} < c < 2^{m+w+1} - 2^{m-1} \tag{7}$$

From (2) we have

$$k - 2^{m+l} + 2^{m+w} = a \cdot 2^{m+l+1} + c$$

where $0 \leq a < 2^{n-m-l}$ and because $l \geq w+1$ there are $l - w$ consecutive zero bits in $k - 2^{m+l} + 2^{m+w}$.

In order to extract this information, we rely on a property of the curve where the group order q is close to a power of two. More precisely, $q = 2^n - \epsilon$ where $|\epsilon| < 2^p$ for $p \approx n/2$. We note that many of the standard curves have this property.

Let $K = A \cdot 2^n + C$, with $0 \leq A < 2^{L_1}$ and $2^{p+L_1} \leq C < 2^{L_1+L_2} - 2^{p+L_1}$, note that this implies $L_2 > p$. Because $q = 2^n - \epsilon$ we get $K - A \cdot q = K - A \cdot 2^n + A \cdot \epsilon = C + A \cdot \epsilon$. Now, $|\epsilon| < 2^p$. Consequently, $0 \leq K - A \cdot q < 2^{L_1+L_2}$ and we get

$\left| K - 2^{L_1+L_2-1} \right|_q < 2^{L_1+L_2-1}$. For $p + 1 < m < n - l$ we can set

$$L_1 = n - m - l$$
$$L_2 = m + w$$
$$C = c \cdot 2^{n-m-l-1} = c \cdot 2^{L_1-1}$$
$$K = (k - 2^{m+l} + 2^{m+w}) \cdot 2^{n-m-l-1} = (k - 2^{m+l} + 2^{m+w}) \cdot 2^{L_1-1} = a \cdot 2^n + C$$

From (7) we obtain $2^{L_1+m-2} < C < 2^{L_1+L_2} - 2^{L_1+m-2}$ which, because $m \geq p-2$, becomes $2^{p+L_1} < C < 2^{L_1+L_2} - 2^{p+L_1}$. Thus, we have

$$\left| (k - 2^{m+l} + 2^{m+w}) \cdot 2^{n-m-l-1} - 2^{n-l+w-1} \right|_q < 2^{n-l+w-1}$$

Noting that $k = \alpha \cdot r \cdot s^{-1} + h \cdot s^{-1}$ (mod q), we can define the values

$$t = \lfloor r \cdot s^{-1} \cdot 2^{n-m-l-1} \rceil_q,$$
$$u = \lfloor 2^{n+w-l-1} - (h \cdot s^{-1} + 2^{m+w} - 2^{m+l}) \cdot 2^{n-m-l-1} \rceil_q,$$
$$v = |\alpha \cdot t - u|_q.$$

$|v| \leq 2^{n-l+w-1} \approx q/2^{l-w+1}$, which gives us an instance of the HNP which carries $l - w$ bits of information.

4   Heuristic Analysis

Now we know how to derive our triples t_i, u_i and z_i that are used to construct the lattice. The next obvious question is: How many do we need before we can retrieve the private key α? Because the lattice attack relies on several heuristics, it is hard to give a definitive analysis. However, we will give heuristic reasons here, similar to those for past results.

Each triple (t_i, u_i, z_i) gives us z_i bits of information. If this triple comes from a pair (m, l) such that $p + 1 < m < n - l$, then $z_i = l - w$. In Section 3 we know that on average $l = w + 2$. Since the positions of the non-zero digits are independent of p, on average we lose half the distance between non-zero digits, or $(w + 2)/2$ bits, before the first usable triple and after the last usable triple, which leaves us with $n - 1 - (p + 2) - (w + 2)$ bits where our triples can be. The average number of triples is now given by $(n - p - 3 - (w + 2))/(w + 2)$ and each of these triples gives us $l - w = 2$ bits on average. Combining this yields $2 \cdot (n - p - 3 - (w+2))/(w+2) = 2 \cdot (n - p - 3)/(w + 2) - 2$ bits per signature. For the **secp256k1** curve we have that $n = 256, p = 129$ and $w = 3$, leading to 47.6 bits per signature on average. Our data obtained from perfect side-channels associated to 1001 signatures gives us an average of 47.6 with a 95% confidence interval of ± 0.2664. For the **secp521r1** curve, we have that $n = 521, p = 259$ and $w = 4$, which suggests 84.33 bits per signature on average. The data average here is 84.1658 with a 95% confidence interval of ± 0.3825. See also the $Z = 1$ cases of Figures 1 and 2, which show the distribution of the bits leaked per signature in the 256-bit and 521-bit cases, respectively.

This formula suggests that on average, six signatures would be enough to break a 256-bit key (assuming a perfect side channel), since $47.6 \cdot 6 = 285.6 > 256$. However, in our preliminary experiments the attack did not succeed once when using six or even seven signatures. Even eight or nine signatures gave a minimal success probability. This indicates that something is wrong with the heuristic. In general there are two possible reasons for failure. Either the lattice problem has the correct solution but it was too hard to solve, or the solution to the lattice problem does not correspond to the private key α. We will now examine these two possibilities and how to deal with them.

4.1   Hardness of the Lattice Problem

Generally, the lattice problem becomes easier when adding more information to the lattice, but it also becomes harder as the rank increases. Since each triple adds information but also increases the rank of the lattice, it is not always clear whether adding more triples will solve the problem or make it worse. Each triple contributes z_i bits of information, so we would always prefer triples with a higher z_i value. Therefore, we set a bound $Z \geq 1$ and only keep those triples that have $z_i \geq Z$. However, this decreases the total number of bits of information we obtain per signature. If Z is small enough, then roughly speaking we only keep a fraction 2^{1-Z} of the triples, but now each triple contributes $Z + 1$ bits on average. Hence, the new formula of bits per signature becomes

$$2^{1-Z} \cdot (Z + 1) \cdot ((n - p - 3)/(w + 2) - 1).$$

Our data reflects this formula as well as can be seen in Figures 1 and 2 for the 256-bit and the 521-bit cases, respectively. In our experiments we will set an additional bound d on the number of triples we use in total, which limits the lattice rank to $d+1$. To this end, we sort the triples by z_i and then pick the first d triples to construct the lattice. We adopt this approach for our experiments and the results can be found in Section 5.

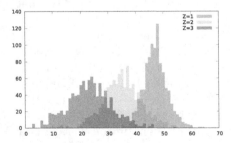

Fig. 1. Number of signatures against bits per signature in the 256 bit case

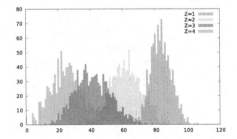

Fig. 2. Number of signatures against bits per signature in the 521 bit CASE

4.2   Incorrect Solutions

The analysis of Nguyen and Shparlinski [22] requires that the t_i values in the triples are taken uniformly and independently from a distribution that satisfies some conditions. However, it is easy to see that when two triples are taken from the same signature, the values for the $t_i = \lfloor r \cdot s^{-1} \cdot 2^{n-m_i-l_i-1} \rfloor_q$ and $t_j = \lfloor r \cdot s^{-1} \cdot 2^{n-m_j-l_j-1} \rfloor_q$ are not even independent, as they differ $\bmod q$ by a factor that is a power of 2 less than 2^n.

Recall from Sections 2.3 and 3 how the triples are used and created, respectively. Consider a triple (t_{ij}, u_{ij}, z_{ij}) corresponding to a signature (r_i, s_i, h_i). The corresponding $v_{ij} = |\alpha \cdot t_{ij} - u_{ij}|_q$ satisfies

$$|v_{ij}| = \left||\alpha \cdot (r_i \cdot s_i^{-1} \cdot 2^{n-m_j-l_j-1}) - 2^{n+w-l_j-1}\right.$$
$$\left. + (h_i \cdot s_i^{-1} + 2^{m_j+w} - 2^{m_j+l}) \cdot 2^{n-m_j-l_j-1}|_q\right|$$
$$\leq q/2^{z_{ij}+1},$$

which is equivalent to

$$|v_{ij}| = \left||(\alpha \cdot r_i + h_i) \cdot s_i^{-1} \cdot 2^{n-m_j-l_j-1} - 2^{n-1}|_q\right| \leq q/2^{z_{ij}+1},$$

where $p + 1 < m_j < n - l_j$ and $z_{ij} = l - w$. Now $(\alpha \cdot r_i + h_i) \cdot s_i^{-1} = k_i \bmod q$ and we know that the previous statement holds due to the structure of k_i, specifically due to its bits $m_j + w, \ldots, m_j + l_j - 1$ repeating, with bit $m_j + l_j$ being different than the preceding bit. But the map $x \mapsto (x \cdot r_i + h_i) \cdot s_i^{-1}$ is a bijection $\bmod q$, and hence for each i there will be many numbers X such that for all j

$$|v_{ij}(X)| = \left||(X \cdot r_i + h_i) \cdot s_i^{-1} \cdot 2^{n-m_j-l_j-1} - 2^{n-1}|_q\right| \leq q/2^{z_{ij}+1}.$$

Let $S_i = \{X : |v_{ij}(X)| \leq q/2^{z_{ij}+1} \text{ for all } j\}$. If we now have that there exists an $X \in \bigcap_i S_i$ such that

$$X^2 + \sum_{i,j} (2^{z_{ij}} \cdot v_{ij}(X))^2 < \alpha^2 + \sum_{i,j} (2^{z_{ij}} \cdot v_{ij}(\alpha))^2,$$

then it is very unlikely that the lattice algorithm will find α, because X corresponds to a better solution to the lattice problem. Note that this problem arises when fewer signatures are used, because this leads to fewer distinct values for (r_i, s_i, h_i) and hence fewer sets S_i that need to intersect. This suggests that increasing the number of signatures could increase the success probability.

Assuming that the S_i are random, we want to determine what is the probability that their intersection is non-empty. First we consider the size of the S_i. Recall that S_i consists of all $X \bmod q$ such that $v_{ij}(X)$ has 'the same structure as k_i'. This means that for each triple specified by m_j and l_j, the bits $m_j + w, \ldots, m_j + l_j - 1$ repeat, and bit $m_j + l_j$ is the opposite of the preceding bits. There are approximately $2^{n-(l_j-w+1)+1}$ numbers $\bmod q$ that have this structure. Let f_i be the number of triples of signature i and $g_{ij} = (l_j - w + 1)$ be the number of bits fixed by triple j of signature i. Then, because the triples do not overlap and because $v_{ij}(.)$ is a bijection, we have that

$$\log_2(|S_i|) = n - \sum_{j=1}^{f_i}(1 - g_{ij}) = n - f_i + \sum_{j=1}^{f_i} g_{ij}.$$

Let $s_i = |S_i|$ and assume that the S_i are chosen randomly and independently from all the subsets of integers in the range $[0, \ldots, N-1]$ (of size s_i), where $N = 2^n$. Consider the following probability

$$p_i = \mathbb{P}(0 \in S_i) = s_i/N,$$

since S_i is randomly chosen. Now, because the S_i are also chosen independently, we have

$$\mathbb{P}\left(0 \in \bigcap_i S_i\right) = \prod_i p_i.$$

Finally, since this argument holds for any $j \in [0, \ldots, N-1]$, we can apply the union bound to obtain

$$p_{\text{fail}} = \mathbb{P}\left(\bigcup_j\left(j \in \bigcap_i S_i\right)\right) \leq \sum_j \mathbb{P}\left(0 \in \bigcap_i S_i\right) = N \cdot \prod_i p_i. \tag{8}$$

Recall that each signature has $f_i = 2^{1-Z} \cdot ((n - p - 3)/(w + 2) - 1)$ triples on average and each triple contributes $Z + 1$ bits on average, which means $g_{ij} = Z + 2$ on average. If we plug in the numbers $n = 256$, $p = 129$, $w = 3$ and $Z = 3$, we get that $f_i \approx 6$, $g_{ij} = 5$ and hence $p_i \approx 2^{-6\cdot(5-1)} \approx 2^{-24}$ if we assume an average number of triples and bits in each signature. This in turn gives us an upper bound of $p_{\text{fail}} \leq N/2^{24\cdot k}$. If $k \geq 11$, this upper bound is less than one, so this clearly suggests that from about eleven signatures and up, we should succeed with some probability, which is indeed the case from our experiments.

Repeating this for $n = 521$, $p = 259$, $w = 4$ and $Z = 4$, we obtain $f_i \approx 5$, $g_{ij} = 6$ and hence $p_i \approx 2^{-5\cdot(6-1)} \approx 2^{-25}$. Consequently, $p_{\text{fail}} \leq N/2^{25\cdot k}$, which is less than one when $k \geq 21$. However, in our experiments we require at least 30 signatures to obtain the secret key with some probability. Thus the above analysis is only approximate as the secret key length increases.

5   Results With a Perfect Side-Channel

Subsection 2.3 outlined our (heuristic) approach to obtain the secret key from a number of triples (t_i, u_i, z_i) using lattices and Section 3 outlined how to generate these triples from the side-channel information. In this section we will look at some experimental results to see if our heuristic assumptions are justified.

As per Section 4, we used the following approach for our experiments. First, we fix a number of signatures s, a lattice rank d and a bound Z. We then take s signatures at random from our data set and derive all triples such that $z_i \geq Z$, sorting them such that the z_i are in descending order. If we have more than d triples, we only take the first d to construct the lattice. Finally we attempt to solve the lattice problem and note the result. All executions were performed in single thread on an Intel Core i7-3770S CPU running at 3.10 GHz.

When solving the CVP instances there are three possible outcomes. We obtain either no solution, the private key or a wrong solution. No solution means that the lattice problem was too hard for the algorithm and constraints we used, but spending more time and using stronger algorithms might still solve it. When a 'wrong' solution is obtained, this means that our heuristics failed: the solution vector was not unique, in the sense that there were other lattice vectors within the expected distance from our target vector.

When solving the SVP instance there are only two outcomes. Either we obtain the private key or not. However, in this case it is not as clear whether a wrong solution means that there were other solutions due to the additional heuristics involved. The complete details of our experimental data are given in the Appendix.

5.1   256 Bit Key

For the 256 bit case, we used BKZ with block size 20 from fplll [6] to solve the SVP instances, as well as to pre-process the CVP instances. To solve the CVP, we applied Schnorr-Euchner enumeration [23] using linear pruning [12] and limiting the number of enumerated nodes to 2^{29}.

The CVP approach seems the best, as the lattice rank $(d+1)$ remains quite small. We restrict our triples to $Z = 3$ to keep the rank small, but a smaller Z would not improve our results much. See the appendix for details. We observed that failures are mostly caused by 'wrong' solutions in this case, rather than the lattice problem being too hard. In all cases we found that using 75 triples gave the best results. Table 2 in the Appendix lists the runtimes and success probabilities of the lattice part of the attack for varying s. The results are graphically presented in Figures 4 and 5 in the Appendix.

5.2   521 Bit Key

For the 521 bit case, we used BKZ with block size 20 from fplll [6] to solve the SVP instances. Due to the higher lattice ranks in this case, solving the CVP instances proved much less efficient, even when restricting the triples to $Z = 4$.

With 30 signatures we get a small probability of success in the lattice attack whereas with 40 signatures we can obtain the secret key in more than half of the cases. It should be noted that as the number of signatures increases, the choice of d becomes less important, because the number of triples with more information increases. See the Appendix for Table 4 details and Figures 6 and 7 for a graphical representation.

6 Results in a Real-Life Attack

So far our discussion was based on the assumption of a perfect side-channel. That is, we assumed that the double-and-add chains are recovered without any errors. Perfect side-channels are, however, very rare. In this section we extend the results to the actual side-channel exposed by the FLUSH+RELOAD technique.

The attack was carried on an HP Elite 8300, running CentOS 6.5. The victim process runs OpenSSL 1.0.1f, compiled to include debugging symbols. These symbols are not used at run-time and do not affect the performance of OpenSSL. We use them because they assist us in finding the addresses to probe by avoiding reverse engineering [9]. The spy uses a time slot of 1,200 cycles ($0.375\mu s$). In each time slot it probes the memory lines containing the last field multiplication within the group add and double functions. (ec_GFp_simple_add and ec_GFp_simple_dbl, respectively.) Memory lines that contain function calls are accessed both before and after the call, reducing the chance of a spy missing the access due to overlap with the probe. Monitoring code close to the end of the function eliminates false positives due to speculative execution. See Yarom and Falkner [27] for a discussion of overlaps and speculative execution.

Fig. 3. FLUSH+RELOAD spy output. Vertical bars indicate time-slot boundaries; 'A' and 'D' are probes for OpenSSL access to add and double; dashes indicate missed time-slots.

Figure 3 shows an example of the output of the spy when OpenSSL signs using **secp256k1**. The double and three addition operations at the beginning of the captured sequence are the calculation of the pre-computed wNAF digits. Note the repeated capture of the double and add operations due to monitoring a memory line that contains a function call. The actual wNAF multiplication starts closer to the end of the line, with 7 double operations followed by a group addition.

In this example, the attack captures most of the double and add chain. It does, however, miss a few time-slots and consequently a few group operations in the chain. The spy recognises missed time-slots by noting inexplicable gaps in the processor cycle counter. As we do not know which operations are missed, we lose the bit positions of the operations that precede the missed time-slots. We believe that the missed time-slots are due to system activity which suspends the spy.

Occasionally OpenSSL suspends the calculation of the scalar multiplication to perform memory management functions. These suspends confuse our spy program, which assumes that the scalar multiplication terminated. This, in turn, results in a short capture, which cannot be used for the lattice attack.

To test prevalence of capture errors we captured 1,000 scalar multiplications and compared the capture results to the ground truth. 342 of these captures contained missed time-slots. Another 77 captures contains less than 250 group operations and are, therefore, too short. Of the remaining 581 captures, 577 are perfect while only four contain errors that we could not easily filter out.

Recall, from Section 5, that 13 perfectly captured signatures are sufficient for breaking the key of a 256 bits curve with over 50% probability. An attacker using FLUSH+RELOAD to capture 25 signatures can thus expect to be able to filter out 11 that contain obvious errors, leaving 14 that contain no obvious errors. With less than 1% probability that each of these 14 captures contains an error, the probability that more than one of these captures contains an error is also less than 1%. Hence, the attacker only needs to test all the combination of choosing 13 captures out of these 14 to achieve a 50% probability of breaking the signing key.

Several optimisations can be used to improve the figure of 25 signatures. Some missed slots can be recovered and the spy can be improved to correct short captures. Nevertheless, it should be noted that this figure is still an order of magnitude than the previously best known result of 200 signatures [2], where 200 signatures correspond to a 3.5% probability of breaking the signing key, whereas 300 signatures were required to get a success probability greater than 50%.

Acknowledgements. The authors would like to thank Ben Sach for helpful conversations during the course of this work. The first and second authors work has been supported in part by ERC Advanced Grant ERC-2010-AdG-267188-CRIPTO, by EPSRC via grant EP/I03126X, and by Defense Advanced Research Projects Agency (DARPA) and the Air Force Research Laboratory (AFRL) under agreement number FA8750-11-2-0079[1]. The third author wishes to thank Dr Katrina Falkner for her advice and support and the Defence Science and Technology Organisation (DSTO) Maritime Division, Australia, who partially funded his work.

---

[1] The US Government is authorized to reproduce and distribute reprints for Government purposes notwithstanding any copyright notation thereon. The views and conclusions contained herein are those of the authors and should not be interpreted as necessarily representing the official policies or endorsements, either expressed or implied, of Defense Advanced Research Projects Agency (DARPA) or the U.S. Government.

A   Experimental Results

A.1   256 Bit Keys

Table 1. Results for d triples taken from s signatures with a 256-bit key ($Z = 3$)

		SVP		CVP	
s	d	Time (s)	p_{succ} (%)	Time (s)	p_{succ} (%)
10	60	1.47	0.0	1.56	0.5
10	65	1.42	1.0	1.90	2.5
10	70	1.44	1.5	2.45	4.0
10	75	1.50	1.5	2.25	7.0
11	60	1.28	0.0	1.63	0.5
11	65	1.68	5.0	2.35	6.5
11	70	1.86	2.5	3.15	19.0
11	75	2.05	7.5	4.66	25.0
11	80	2.12	6.0		
12	60	1.27	2.0	1.69	7.0
12	65	1.71	2.5	2.45	10.5
12	70	2.20	7.5	3.99	29.5
12	75	2.57	10.5	7.68	38.5
12	80	2.90	13.0		
12	85	3.12	8.5		
12	90	3.21	15.5		
13	60	1.30	3.5	1.92	8.5
13	65	1.77	6.0	2.79	25.5
13	70	2.39	11.0	4.48	46.5
13	75	3.16	19.0	11.30	54.0
13	80	3.67	18.5		
13	85	3.81	21.5		
13	90	4.37	25.0		

Table 2. CVP results for 75 triples taken from s signatures with a 256-bit key ($Z = 3$)

s	Time (s)	p_{succ} (%)
10	2.25	7.0
11	4.66	25.0
12	7.68	38.5
13	11.30	54.0

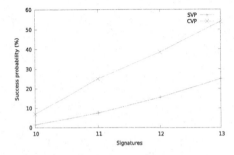

Fig. 4. Success probability per number of signatures against a 256 bit key

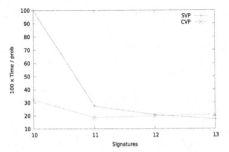

Fig. 5. Expected running time per number of signatures against a 256 bit key

A.2   521 Bit Keys

Table 3. SVP results for d triples taken from s signatures with a 521-bit key ($Z = 4$)

s	d	Time (s)	p_{succ} (%)
30	130	50.10	4.0
30	135	58.80	3.0
30	140	66.65	3.5
30	145	69.68	2.5
32	130	50.15	6.5
32	135	58.07	6.5
32	140	62.55	4.0
32	145	67.46	5.0
32	150	70.77	9.5
34	130	50.00	15.5
34	135	55.93	10.5
34	140	62.83	16.0
34	145	64.41	14.0
34	150	70.50	16.0
34	155	71.07	11.5
36	130	48.71	24.5
36	135	54.74	21.0
36	140	59.25	22.5
36	145	62.32	29.0
36	150	65.60	29.0
36	155	68.57	24.5
38	130	49.04	38.5
38	135	53.86	36.0
38	140	57.14	38.5
38	145	61.31	42.5
38	150	66.75	36.5
38	155	66.52	36.5
40	130	47.73	53.0
40	135	50.80	49.0
40	140	54.88	52.0
40	145	60.47	47.0
40	150	64.77	53.0
40	155	64.95	52.5

s	d	Time (s)	p_{succ} (%)
31	130	48.50	7.5
31	135	59.91	3.5
31	140	67.35	6.0
31	145	69.96	5.5
33	130	49.70	8.0
33	135	56.52	11.5
33	140	60.31	11.5
33	145	66.39	8.5
33	150	70.54	13.5
33	155	75.49	8.5
35	130	49.76	12.0
35	135	55.33	24.5
35	140	59.50	15.5
35	145	65.59	19.5
35	150	66.93	24.0
35	155	69.67	20.0
37	130	48.20	24.0
37	135	54.79	23.5
37	140	58.60	28.0
37	145	60.05	29.0
37	150	63.40	27.5
37	155	69.14	34.5
39	135	50.99	45.5
39	140	58.81	46.0
39	145	57.08	47.5
39	150	62.35	41.5
39	155	64.99	42.5

Table 4. SVP results for d triples taken from s signatures with a 521-bit key ($Z = 4$)

s	d	Time (s)	p_{succ} (%)
30	130	50.10	4.0
31	130	48.50	7.5
32	150	70.77	9.5
33	150	70.54	13.5
34	140	62.83	16.0
35	135	55.33	24.5
36	145	62.32	29.0
37	155	69.14	34.5
38	145	61.31	42.5
39	145	57.08	47.5
40	130	47.73	53.0

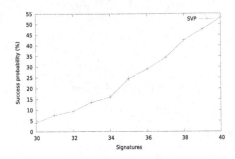
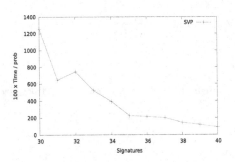

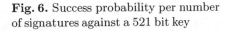

Fig. 6. Success probability per number of signatures against a 521 bit key

Fig. 7. Expected running time per number of signatures against a 521 bit key

References

1. American National Standards Institute. ANSI X9.62, Public Key Cryptography for the Financial Services Industry: The Elliptic Curve Digital Signature Algorithm (1999)
2. Benger, N., van de Pol, J., Smart, N.P., Yarom, Y.: "Ooh aah.. just a little bit" : a small amount of side channel can go a long way. In: Batina, L., Robshaw, M. (eds.) CHES 2014. LNCS, vol. 8731, pp. 75–92. Springer, Heidelberg (2014)
3. Boneh, D., Venkatesan, R.: Hardness of computing the most significant bits of secret keys in diffie-hellman and related schemes. In: Koblitz, N. (ed.) CRYPTO 1996. LNCS, vol. 1109, pp. 129–142. Springer, Heidelberg (1996)
4. Brumley, B.B., Hakala, R.M.: Cache-timing template attacks. In: Matsui, M. (ed.) ASIACRYPT 2009. LNCS, vol. 5912, pp. 667–684. Springer, Heidelberg (2009)
5. Brumley, B.B., Tuveri, N.: Remote timing attacks are still practical. In: Atluri, V., Diaz, C. (eds.) ESORICS 2011. LNCS, vol. 6879, pp. 355–371. Springer, Heidelberg (2011)
6. Cadé, D., Pujol, X., Stehlé, D.: FPLLL-4.0.4 (2013). http://perso.ens-lyon.fr/damien.stehle/fplll/
7. Certicom Research. SEC 2: Recommended Elliptic Curve Domain Parameters, Version 2.0, January 2010
8. Ciet, M., Joye, M.: (Virtually) free randomization techniques for elliptic curve cryptography. In: Qing, S., Gollmann, D., Zhou, J. (eds.) ICICS 2003. LNCS, vol. 2836, pp. 348–359. Springer, Heidelberg (2003)
9. Teodoro Cipresso and Mark Stamp. Software reverse engineering. In: Peter Stavroulakis and Mark Stamp, editors, Handbook of Information and Communication Security, chapter 31, pp. 659–696. Springer (2010)
10. Crandall, R.E.: Method and apparatus for public key exchange in a cryptographic system. US Patent 5,159,632, October 1992
11. Feix, B., Roussellet, M., Venelli, A.: Side-channel analysis on blinded regular scalar multiplications. In: Meier, W., Mukhopadhyay, D. (eds.) Progress in Cryptology – INDOCRYPT 2014. LNCS, pp. 3–20. Springer, Heidelberg (2014)
12. Gama, N., Nguyen, P.Q., Regev, O.: Lattice enumeration using extreme pruning. In: Gilbert, H. (ed.) EUROCRYPT 2010. LNCS, vol. 6110, pp. 257–278. Springer, Heidelberg (2010)
13. Gordon, D.M.: A survey of fast exponentiation methods. Journal of Algorithms **27**(1), 129–146 (1998)

14. Howgrave-Graham, N., Smart, N.P.: Lattice attacks on digital signature schemes. Designs, Codes and Cryptography **23**(3), 283–290 (2001)
15. Kivity, A., Kamay, Y., Laor, D., Lublin, U., Liguori, A.: kvm: the Linux virtual machine monitor. In: Proceedings of the Linux Symposium. volume one, pp. 225–230. Ottawa, Ontario, Canada (2007)
16. Lenstra, A.K., Lenstra, H.W., Lovász, L.: Factoring polynomials with rational coefficients. Mathematische Annalen **261**(4), 515–534 (1982)
17. Li, L., Just, J.E. Sekar, R.: Address-space randomization for Windows systems. In: Proceedings of the 22nd Annual Computer Security Applications Conference, pp. 329–338, Miami Beach, Florida, United States, December 2006
18. Möller, B.: Parallelizable elliptic curve point multiplication method with resistance against side-channel attacks. In: Chan, A.H., Gligor, V.D. (eds.) ISC 2002. LNCS, vol. 2433, p. 402. Springer, Heidelberg (2002)
19. Möller, B.: Improved techniques for fast exponentiation. In: Lee, P.J., Lim, C.H. (eds.) ICISC 2002. LNCS, vol. 2587, pp. 298–312. Springer, Heidelberg (2003)
20. National Institute of Standards and Technology. FIPS PUB 186–4 Digital Signature Standard (DSS) (2013)
21. Nguyen, P.Q., Shparlinski, I.E.: The insecurity of the digital signature algorithm with partially known nonces. Journal of Cryptology **15**(3), 151–176 (2002)
22. Nguyen, P.Q., Shparlinski, I.E.: The insecurity of the elliptic curve digital signature algorithm with partially known nonces. Designs, Codes and Cryptography **30**(2), 201–217 (2003)
23. Schnorr, C.-P., Euchner, M.: Lattice basis reduction: Improved practical algorithms and solving subset sum problems. In: Budach, L. (ed.) FCT 1991. LNCS, vol. 529, pp. 68–85. Springer, Heidelberg (1991)
24. Solinas, J.A.: Generalized Mersenne numbers. Technical Report CORR-39, University of Waterloo (1999)
25. Waldspurger, C.A.: Memory resource management in VMware ESX Server. In: Culler, D.E., Druschel, P., (eds), Proceedings of the Fifth Symposium on Operating Systems Design and Implementation, pp. 181–194. Boston, Massachusetts, United States, December 2002
26. Yarom, Y., Benger, N.: Recovering OpenSSL ECDSA nonces using the Flush+Reload cache side-channel attack. Cryptology ePrint Archive, Report 2014/140, February 2014. http://eprint.iacr.org/
27. Yarom, Y., Falkner, K.: Flush+Reload: a high resolution, low noise, L3 cache side-channel attack. In: Proceedings of the 23rd USENIX Security Symposium, pp. 719–732. San Diego, California, United States, August 2014

Cache Storage Attacks

Billy Bob Brumley$^{(\boxtimes)}$

Department of Pervasive Computing, Tampere University of Technology,
Tampere, Finland
billy.brumley@tut.fi

Abstract. Covert channels are a fundamental concept for cryptanalytic
side-channel attacks. Covert timing channels use latency to carry data,
and are the foundation for timing and cache-timing attacks. Covert storage channels instead utilize existing system bits to carry data, and are not
historically used for cryptanalytic side-channel attacks. This paper introduces a new storage channel made available through cache debug facili-
ties on some embedded microprocessors. This channel is then extended
to a cryptanalytic side-channel attack on AES software.

Keywords: Side-channel attacks · Covert channels · Storage channels ·
Timing attacks · Cache-timing attacks

1 Introduction

In one of the seminal computer security works, Schaefer et al. [12] define a covert
channel as follows.

> Covert channels are [data] paths not meant for communication but that
> can be used to transmit data indirectly.

They go on to define both storage and timing channels:

> Storage channels consist of variables that are set by a system process on
> behalf of the sender, e.g., interlocks, thresholds, or an ordering. In timing
> channels, the time variable is controlled: resource allocations are made
> to a receiver at intervals of time controlled by the sender. In both cases,
> the state of the variable ("on" or "off", "time interval is 2 seconds") is
> made to represent information, e.g., digits or characters.

Continuing this line of research, a team of researchers at DEC in the 1990s wrote
a number of influential papers regarding covert channels [4–6,13], in particular
those enabled by caching technologies.

Traditional cryptanalysis views cryptosystems as mathematical abstractions
and develops attacks using theoretical models consisting of only inputs and outputs of the cryptosystem. In the case of e.g. a block cipher, the input would be
the plaintext and output the ciphertext, and cryptanalysis tasked with recovering the key using sets of these inputs and outputs.

© Springer International Publishing Switzerland 2015
K. Nyberg (ed.): CT-RSA 2015, LNCS 9048, pp. 22–34, 2015.
DOI: 10.1007/978-3-319-16715-2_2

In contrast, side-channel cryptanalysis exploits implementation aspects to aid in key recovery. What constitutes a side-channel is technically ill-defined, but generally speaking it is an implementation-dependent signal procured during the execution of a cryptographic primitive. This is where the fields of covert channels and side-channel analysis intersect: identifying some microarchitecture or software feature within a cryptosystem implementation that can be used to transfer data between two legitimate parties, then developing it into a cryptanalytic side-channel attack when one party is legitimate and one illegitimate.

Cache-timing attacks exploit the varying latency of data load instructions to carry out cryptanalytic side-channel attacks. These attacks are recognized by both academia and industry as a serious threat to security-critical software: from Page's seminal work [9], to Bernstein's attack on AES [2], to Percival's attack on RSA [11], to Osvik et al.'s attack on AES [8], to Brumley and Hakala's attack on ECDSA [3], to Aciiçmez et al.'s attack on DSA [1]. Arguably the most recent example of cache-timing attacks affecting real-world systems and software is Yarom and Benger's work [14] that led to CVE-2014-0076 and induced changes[1] in OpenSSL's Montgomery ladder implementation.

Placing cache-timing attacks within the covert timing channel framework, it is fair to say that utilizing covert timing channels for cryptanalytic side-channel attacks is a popular, well-established paradigm. Covert storage channels, however, are essentially ignored due to lack of application.

This paper introduces a novel, practical covert storage channel. The basis for the channel is that many caches have hardware support for per-cache line privilege separation. The access control enforced by this separation creates a storage channel that can be used to violate the system security policy. As with most covert channels, it is then possible to extend this particular covert storage channel to a cryptanalytic side-channel attack.

The organization of this paper is as follows. Section 2 provides necessary background on popular AES software and existing cache-timing attacks against such software implementations. Then Sec. 3 describes the new covert storage channel, including the prerequisite hardware differences in the cache implementation compared to a traditional cache (Sec. 3.1), why such differences exist in modern caches (Sec. 3.2), how this feature leads to a covert storage channel (Sec. 3.3), how this channel extends to a cryptanalytic side-channel (Sec. 3.4), and what practical architectures this applies to (Sec. 3.5). Final thoughts and conclusions are drawn in Sec. 4.

2   Background

Applications of covert channels and subsequently side-channels are important aspects from the practicality perspective. To this end, Sec. 2.1 gives some background on typical high-performance AES software implementation, and Sec. 2.2 on cache-timing attacks on such software. While this background is important

---

[1] https://www.openssl.org/news/secadv_20140605.txt

to show the immediate applicability of the results in this paper, keep in mind the underlying main results of this paper is the covert channel itself, and not its application to any one cryptosystem in particular. That is, the covert channel described in this paper will absolutely have applications outside of AES, but at the same time AES serves as a good example of its application.

2.1   AES Software

Viewing the 16-byte AES state as a 4×4 matrix, the first nine AES rounds are identical and consist of steps SubBytes, ShiftRows, MixColumns, and AddRoundKey. The last round omits the MixColumns step. SubBytes $\gamma : \mathcal{M}_{4\times4}[\mathbb{F}_{2^8}] \rightarrow \mathcal{M}_{4\times4}[\mathbb{F}_{2^8}]$ is a fixed non-linear substitution $S : \mathbb{F}_{2^8} \rightarrow \mathbb{F}_{2^8}$ (S-box) using finite field inversion applied to all state bytes.

$$\gamma(a) = b \Leftrightarrow b_{ij} = S[a_{ij}], \ 0 \le i,j < 4$$

MixColumns $\theta : \mathcal{M}_{4\times4}[\mathbb{F}_{2^8}] \rightarrow \mathcal{M}_{4\times4}[\mathbb{F}_{2^8}]$ is a fixed linear transformation.

$$\theta(a) = b \Leftrightarrow b = M \cdot a$$

Here M is the following 4×4 matrix.

$$M = \begin{bmatrix} 2 & 3 & 1 & 1 \\ 1 & 2 & 3 & 1 \\ 1 & 1 & 2 & 3 \\ 3 & 1 & 1 & 2 \end{bmatrix}$$

Traditional AES software is heavily lookup table based. The reason for this is that many of the low-level finite field operations, such as multiplications in θ and inversions in γ, are simply not natively supported on mainstream microprocessors. To compensate for the understandable lack of Instruction Set Architecture (ISA) support for such operations, a 32-bit processor leverages the linearity property of the MixColumns step to improve performance. Consider the following four tables, each containing 256 4-byte words.

$$T_0[x] = (2 \cdot S[x], S[x], S[x], 3 \cdot S[x])$$
$$T_1[x] = (3 \cdot S[x], 2 \cdot S[x], S[x], S[x])$$
$$T_2[x] = (S[x], 3 \cdot S[x], 2 \cdot S[x], S[x])$$
$$T_3[x] = (S[x], S[x], 3 \cdot S[x], 2 \cdot S[x])$$

That is, each T_i maps one byte for a particular component through the nonlinear layer input to the linear layer output. With these tables in hand, one AES round amounts to 16 table lookups and 16 bitwise XORs, illustrated in Fig. 1.

Since the last round omits the MixColumns step, its implementation differs. One popular way to implement the last round is as follows. Consider the following table, containing 256 4-byte words.

$$T_4[x] = (S[x], S[x], S[x], S[x])$$

```
y0 = T0[x0 & 0xFF] ^ T1[(x1 >> 8) & 0xFF] ^ T2[(x2 >> 16) & 0xFF] ^ T3[x3 >> 24] ^ rk0;
y1 = T0[x1 & 0xFF] ^ T1[(x2 >> 8) & 0xFF] ^ T2[(x3 >> 16) & 0xFF] ^ T3[x0 >> 24] ^ rk1;
y2 = T0[x2 & 0xFF] ^ T1[(x3 >> 8) & 0xFF] ^ T2[(x0 >> 16) & 0xFF] ^ T3[x1 >> 24] ^ rk2;
y3 = T0[x3 & 0xFF] ^ T1[(x0 >> 8) & 0xFF] ^ T2[(x1 >> 16) & 0xFF] ^ T3[x2 >> 24] ^ rk3;
```

Fig. 1. One AES round with the T tables approach. 32-bit unsigned integers x_i hold state column i and rk_i are words of the particular round key.

Duplicating the S-box output across the word means that no shifting is necessary to place the S-box output in the proper component. Instead, the redundant bytes in the output get masked off with a bitwise AND operation after the lookup. Implementation of the last round otherwise follows the computation in Fig. 1, with the lookups into all T_i replaced with lookups into T_4.

As a final note, there are countless strategies for implementing AES software, but the preceding description is accurate for the popular C reference implementation `rijndael-alg-fst.c` by P. Barreto et al. used already in the AES competition.

2.2 Cache-Timing Attacks

This T tables implementation approach potentially exposes the AES software to cache-timing attacks. Lookups into the memory-resident T tables cause data cache lines to be populated and evicted. Consider a typical data cache line size of 64 bytes. Each T table is 1kB, hence spans 16 lines in the cache. For one particular lookup of the $10 \times 16 = 160$ lookups in an AES encryption (or decryption), the latency of the lookup depends on the state of the cache and hence the state of the AES algorithm. Amongst the plentiful AES cache-timing results over the past decade that leverage this varying latency to carry out cryptanalytic side-channel attacks, two are particularly relevant to this paper and are discussed below.

Prime and Probe. Osvik et al. [8] devise a number of cache-timing attacks against T table based implementations of AES. For the purposes of this paper, the most important part of their work is the strategy they devise to procure the timings called "Prime+Probe". In this strategy, the attacker first brings the cache to a known state by either filling the entire cache or relevant cache sets by performing loads and stores, inducing cache line population and eviction. The attacker then submits a plaintext block. After the encryption completes, the attacker, cache set-wise, measures the time required to re-read the data in the cache sets, obtaining a latency measurement for each set. High latency implies cache misses and that the victim accessed data mapping to the cache set, and low latency the opposite.

Targeting the Last Round. Considering the first 9 AES rounds, each T table has 4 lookups into it per round for a total of 36 lookups. Assuming each table spans 16 cache lines, the amount of state information that can be learned from these lookups is limited because the order of the lookups is not (necessarily) known w.r.t. the trace timing data. For example, after the probe step the attacker knows which lines were evicted, but not what exact lookup caused the eviction. Neve and Seifert [7] instead target the last round, specifically the T_4 table. The authors devise two attacks that seek to recover the last round key. The most important for the purposes of this paper is the "elimination method" summarized below.

The average number of cache sets accessed in the last round is 10.3 [7, Sec. 5] and not accessed is 5.7 [7, Sec. 7.2]. This method keeps a set of candidate bytes for each round key byte. An unreferenced set implies the corresponding upper four bits of state are not possible for *any* state byte. Use the corresponding ciphertext to compute the resulting impossible key bytes. This eliminates up to sixteen key byte candidates from each key byte, or 256 candidates total. The attack proceeds iteratively through the traces in this fashion, trimming the candidate sets. Naturally as more traces are processed less trims are made as collisions start occurring, i.e., eliminating bytes that have already been eliminated, but the authors show that roughly 20 queries suffices to recover the key using this method [7, Sec. 7.2].

3   Cache Storage Attacks

Consider the following hypothetical, simple data cache. There are 16 lines and each line is 64 bytes. Assume wlog the cache is direct mapped. Whether the cache is virtually/physically indexed/tagged is irrelevant to this paper. With respect to the cache, a 32 bit address breaks down as follows. The $\lg(64) = 6$ LSBs denote the offset within a line. The next $\lg(16) = 4$ bits denote the set index. The remaining $32 - 6 - 4 = 22$ bits denote the tag. The set index and tag combine to determine cache hits and misses, i.e. if the tag matches and the set index matches, a cache hit occurs. In practice, while there are often more lines and sets, this cache (or one extremely similar to it) is overwhelmingly what goes into modern commodity microprocessors.

3.1   Hardware Privilege Separation

Now consider the following hypothetical, simple data cache that is similar but supports privilege separation in hardware. What this means is the per-line metadata for the previous cache consisting of the tag gets extended to also include the privilege level for that line's contents. For simplicity's sake this paper considers only 1-bit privilege levels but the results are more generally applied. Figure 2 compares these two cache structures. One example of this 1-bit privilege level could be identifying ring 0 or ring 3 in the cache for x86 protection mode: a 0 (or 1) could denote the physical memory corresponding to that particular cache line belongs to ring 0 (or 3).

```
idx    tag   data          idx priv    tag   data
---  ------ ----           --- ----  ------ ----

  0 de30ec ????             0     1 de30ec ????
  1 096324 ????             1     0 096324 ????

  .      .    .             .     .      .    .

  .      .    .             .     .      .    .

  F 61eff8 ????             F     1 61eff8 ????
```

Fig. 2. Left: Example traditional cache without hardware privilege separation. Right: Example cache augmented with hardware privilege separation.

This paper assumes the cache replacement policy is oblivious to the semantics of this privilege level bit, i.e., it is simply another bit of the tag that only determines cache hits and misses. This means that privilege level 0 can evict privilege level 1 data and vice versa. If this were not the case, resource starvation would occur unless employing a more sophisticated cache structure (see e.g [10] for a discussion). Also a common argument for this behavior is better cache utilization, causing improved software performance that is a leading driver in industry.

3.2   Motivation

There are potentially many reasons to store the per-line privilege level with the cache metadata. Arguably the most appropriate use case is in debug scenarios. To debug the cache itself or programs where cache performance is critical, some architectures expose low level instructions that allow invasive access to the cache data and metadata. For example, this could be used by software engineers:

- To examine cache state and eliminate it as a potential source of bugs e.g. in hardware errata scenarios or coherency issues.
- To better understand their software's cache impact, and subsequently improve performance through analysis of said impact.

However, the cache cannot simply allow unchecked access to the lines and metadata. For example, privilege separation fails if privilege level 1 directly reads a cache line belonging to privilege level 0. So the cache needs to know the privilege level of each line's data for security reasons to enforce a sane access control policy, and having that information stored directly alongside the tag is arguably the most logical solution for the hardware itself to enforce said policy. For attempted accesses that would violate the access control policy, a reasonable response would be to issue a processor exception. This is similar to how e.g. a Memory Management Unit (MMU) handles accesses to unmapped virtual addresses, i.e. invalid page faults that usually result in segmentation faults.

3.3   A Covert Channel

Alice (privilege level 0) and Bob (privilege level 1) construct a storage covert channel out of the cache with privilege separation as follows. Assume wlog the cache structure in Fig. 2 and that Alice wants to send $\lg(16) = 4$ bits to Bob, denoted nibble b.

1. Bob loads from 16 memory locations that all have different index bits. This is the "prime" step and completely pollutes the cache, as well as populates all privilege level bits in the cache to 1, corresponding to Bob's privilege level.
2. Alice loads from a single memory location with index bits b. She gets a cache miss and evicts Bob's line from index b. Note that, after this step, Alice leaves the cache in the same state as Bob left it, other than index b: all lines have privilege level bit set to 1 except line with index b now set to 0.
3. Bob tries to read *directly* from all 16 lines in the cache: this is the "probe" step. When he reaches index b he triggers a processor exception because he is attempting to violate privilege separation, but nonetheless receives b from Alice, evidenced by the exception.

From the dishonest users' perspective, the main disadvantage of this covert channel is its detectability. Timing covert channels are difficult to detect since the only evidence of their presence is performance degradation. In this case, every time this particular processor exception occurs the system gets informed so there is an audit trail.

The main advantage of this covert channel is its signal-to-noise ratio. By nature, timing channels are heuristic – they are noisy and require tuning to a particular system and cache performance. This cache storage channel, however, goes unaffected by these variables that affect cache hit and miss latencies. The only thing the recipient needs to observe is the presence of the processor exception. This exception is deterministic, not heuristic.

3.4   A Side-Channel Attack

An access-driven cache-timing trace, as used in e.g. the attacks described in Sec. 2.2, is interpreted as a sequence of cache hits (H) and misses (M) on a per cache set (or line) basis. Note that the hits and misses are based on the memory access timings being above or below some threshold, so they are quite sensitive to a particular processor, cache, operating system, and system load – in practice they are rarely error-free but instead require some statistical analysis. Nevertheless, assume this timing trace is error-free. Attackers can "reconstruct" access-driven cache-timing traces with the cache storage channel described above with the following steps.

1. Read directly from a cache line. A processor exception indicates M, otherwise H.
2. If M go back to the first step. This requires another query because the processor exception most like wipes the cache state and/or triggers a reset.
3. If H continue with the next line.

For example, Consider the following timing trace.

`HMHHHMHHHHHHHMHHH`

The read from line 0 does not cause an exception, so the attacker logs H and continues. Line 1 causes an exception. The attacker logs M, queries the same plaintext again, reads from line 2, logs H and continues in this manner. Line 5 causes an exception. The attacker logs M, queries the same plaintext again, and continues in this manner. It takes the attacker four queries to reconstruct the trace: one for the initial query, and one for each processor exception ("cache miss").

Given the above analysis, cache storage attacks should exhibit the following characteristics when compared to cache-timing attacks.

- The number of queries theoretically increases because, compared to cache-timing attacks, each "cache miss" costs an additional query due to the processor exception.
- The traces themselves, however, are overwhelmingly more accurate because they are not heuristically based on timings.

This ease of reconstructing error-free cache-timing traces from error-free cache storage traces allows leveraging previous cache-timing results directly. For example, consider the attack by Neve and Seifert [7] summarized in Sec. 2.2. The key recovery algorithm is essentially the same, but the number of queries will increase. Figure 3 illustrates the implementation of the Neve and Seifert cache-timing attack using the cache storage attack techniques in this paper. In the cache-timing case, they state roughly 20 queries are needed to recover the last round key. Given that their analysis shows the average number of cache sets accessed is 10.3 and cache storage attacks need an initial query plus one query for each cache set accessed ("cache miss"), the expectation is $20 \cdot (10.3 + 1) = 226$ queries on average for the cache storage attack to succeed. The simulation results in Fig. 3 are consistent with this estimate.

3.5   Relevant Architectures

The running example in this paper has been privilege levels 0 and 1 corresponding to e.g. ring 0 and ring 3. To make these results more concrete, arguably the most relevant architecture for cache storage attacks is ARM with TrustZone extensions.

TrustZone technology provides hardware-assisted security mechanisms to software, in particular Trusted Execution Environments (TEE). TEEs are ubiquitous in the embedded space, e.g. mobile phones. In these cases, the mobile operating system such as Android runs in the normal world or untrusted world or insecure world or rich execution environment while the security-critical code runs in the secure world or trusted world or trusted execution environment.

At any given moment, ARM microprocessors that support TrustZone extensions operate in either secure or insecure mode. Insecure mode uses system calls

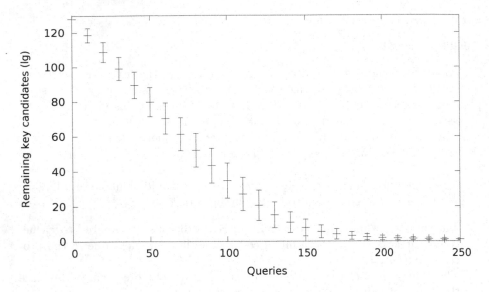

Fig. 3. AES cache storage attack simulation results. Average number of remaining key candidates (base-2 logarithm) as the number of encryption queries increases. Error bars are one standard deviation on each side.

(dedicated instructions in the ISA) to switch to secure mode, the transition handled by a piece of software ARM calls the monitor. From the system perspective, bus transactions originating from either the secure or non-secure world are tagged using the `AxPROT` bus attribute, essentially a binary value that tracks the privilege level of the transaction. Figure 4 illustrates this concept. Quoting the ARM documentation:

> In the caches, instruction and data, each line is tagged as Secure or Non-secure, so that Secure and Non-secure data can coexist in the cache. Each time a cache line fill is performed, the NS tag is updated appropriately.

Mapping this architecture to the previously described cache storage covert channel is simple: privilege level 0 corresponds to NS=0 and privilege level 1 to NS=1. This statement directly from ARM validates the previous assumptions in this paper with respect to the cache replacement policy – the data at different privilege levels coexists in the cache yet the replacement policy is oblivious to this distinction. Secure data can evict non-secure data and vice versa.

Further illustrating the applicability of cache storage attacks to ARM architecture with TrustZone extensions, the documentation continues, illustrated in Fig. 5:

> It is a desirable feature of any high performance design to support data of both security states in the caches. This removes the need for a cache flush when switching between worlds, and enables high performance software to communicate over the world boundary. To enable this the L1,

and where applicable level two and beyond, processor caches have been extended with an additional tag bit which records the security state of the transaction that accessed the memory.

The content of the caches, with regard to the security state, is dynamic. Any non-locked down cache line can be evicted to make space for new data, regardless of its security state. It is possible for a Secure line load to evict a Non-secure line, and for a Non-secure line load to evict a Secure line.

The cache attempts the [sic] match the PA and the NS-bit from the TLB with the tag of an existing cache line. If this succeeds it will return the data from that cache line, otherwise it will load the cache line from the external memory system.

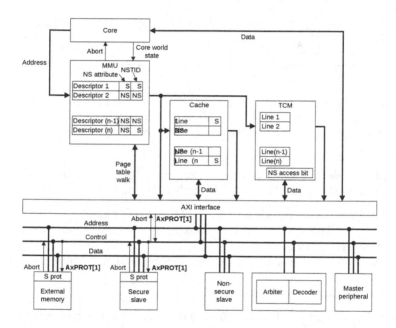

Fig. 4. ARM architecture with TrustZone extensions: propagation of the normal (NS=1) and secure (NS=0) signal (AxPROT) system-wide via bus transactions. Source: http://infocenter.arm.com/help/index.jsp?topic=/com.arm.doc. ddi0333h/Chdfjdgi.html

The last ingredient missing for realizing the cache storage covert channel is invasive access for direct cache line reads. These particular instructions will generally depends on the chip manufacturer, exposed through instruction-level CP15 ("coprocessor 15") commands. Such commands are generally used for e.g. performance monitoring, but these cache commands are encoded in an

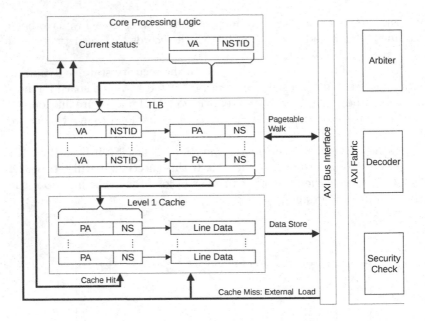

Fig. 5. ARM architecture with TrustZone extensions: cache logic with respect to the normal (NS=1) and secure (NS=0) worlds. Source: http://infocenter.arm.com/help/index.jsp?topic=/com.arm.doc.prd29-genc-009492c/ch03s03s02.html

implementation defined space (C15) so they are manufacturer dependent. Nevertheless, some examples follow, e.g. through CP15 and C15[2]:

The purpose of the data cache Tag RAM operation is to:
- read the data cache Tag RAM contents and write into the Data Cache Debug Register.
- write into the Data Cache Debug Register and write into the Data Tag RAM.

To read the Data Tag RAM, write CP15 with:

```
MCR p15, 3, <Rd>, c15, c2, 0  ;Data Tag RAM read operation
```

Transfer data to the Data Cache Debug Register to the core:

```
MRC p15, 3, <Rd>, c15, c0, 0 ;Read Data Cache Debug Register
```

While these particular commands are for reading tag data associated with a particular line, the effect for the purposes of this paper is the same. The documentation goes on to describe the register format to specify the set and way combination for the desired cache operation. Not specific to cache storage attacks but more generically for issuing instructions to CP15, MCR is for coprocessor to ARM transfers and MRC for ARM to coprocessor transfers.

---

[2] http://infocenter.arm.com/help/index.jsp?topic=/com.arm.doc.ddi0338g/Bgbedgaa.html

4   Conclusion

This paper introduces a new covert channel enabled by the data cache populating per-line privilege level bits and subsequently enforcing privilege separation on the lines. In contrast to previous covert timing channels that are inherently noisy, this covert storage channel is much easier to utilize because it does not rely on heuristic timings. While the use of this channel is easier to detect than covert timing channels since the attacker will trigger processor exceptions, it clearly fits the covert channel definition of Schaefer et al. [12] since the value of privilege level bits is certainly not intended to carry data.

Cache storage attacks are related to cache-timing attacks in the sense that the former can be used to construct an error-free side-channel trace for the latter, shown in Sec. 3.4. The resulting cache storage attack given on AES is otherwise a direct analog of the cache-timing attack, but requires more queries as shown by the experiment results. The outcome is the leaking of an AES key across privilege levels, clearly a violation of a system security policy.

Section 3.5 shows how cache storage attacks map nicely to ARM's TrustZone technology. It is worth noting that the instructions and commands needed to carry out the cache storage attack are almost certainly not available in NS=1 user space, so the attack would be from NS=1 kernel space (e.g. Android) to the NS=0 secure space (e.g. a TEE).

While ARM dictates the format used for cache line operations in the specification, the actual operations used for e.g. data cache line reads and writes are in the CP15 implementation defined C15 instruction space, left to the manufacturer. As such, the most logical countermeasure to cache storage attacks lies in these implementation defined instructions. Chip manufacturers should disallow these instructions while in NS=1 mode, or at a minimum default to disallow yet have the ability to issue these instructions from NS=1 be software configurable from NS=0.

References

1. Acıiçmez, O., Brumley, B.B., Grabher, P.: New results on instruction cache attacks. In: Mangard, S., Standaert, F.-X. (eds.) CHES 2010. LNCS, vol. 6225, pp. 110–124. Springer, Heidelberg (2010)
2. Bernstein, D.J.: Cache-timing attacks on AES (2005). http://cr.yp.to/antiforgery/cachetiming-20050414.pdf
3. Brumley, B.B., Hakala, R.M.: Cache-timing template attacks. In: Matsui, M. (ed.) ASIACRYPT 2009. LNCS, vol. 5912, pp. 667–684. Springer, Heidelberg (2009)
4. Hu, W.: Reducing timing channels with fuzzy time. In: IEEE Symposium on Security and Privacy, pp. 8–20 (1991)
5. Hu, W.: Lattice scheduling and covert channels. In: IEEE Symposium on Security and Privacy, pp. 52–61 (1992)
6. Karger, P.A., Wray, J.C.: Storage channels in disk arm optimization. In: IEEE Symposium on Security and Privacy, pp. 52–63 (1991)

7. Neve, M., Seifert, J.-P.: Advances on access-driven cache attacks on AES. In: Biham, E., Youssef, A.M. (eds.) SAC 2006. LNCS, vol. 4356, pp. 147–162. Springer, Heidelberg (2007)
8. Osvik, D.A., Shamir, A., Tromer, E.: Cache attacks and countermeasures: The case of AES. In: Pointcheval, D. (ed.) CT-RSA 2006. LNCS, vol. 3860, pp. 1–20. Springer, Heidelberg (2006)
9. Page, D.: Theoretical use of cache memory as a cryptanalytic side-channel. Cryptology ePrint Archive, Report 2002/169 (2002). https://eprint.iacr.org/2002/169
10. Page, D.: Partitioned cache architecture as a side-channel defence mechanism. Cryptology ePrint Archive, Report 2005/280 (2005). https://eprint.iacr.org/2005/280
11. Percival, C.: Cache missing for fun and profit. In: Proc. of BSDCan 2005 (2005). http://www.daemonology.net/papers/cachemissing.pdf
12. Schaefer, M., Gold, B., Linde, R., Scheid, J.: Program confinement in KVM/370. In: Proceedings of the 1977 Annual Conference, pp. 404–410. ACM (1977)
13. Wray, J.C.: An analysis of covert timing channels. In: IEEE Symposium on Security and Privacy, pp. 2–7 (1991)
14. Yarom, Y., Benger, N.: Recovering OpenSSL ECDSA nonces using the FLUSH+RELOAD cache side-channel attack. Cryptology ePrint Archive, Report 2014/140 (2014). https://eprint.iacr.org/2014/140

Design and Analysis of Block Ciphers

Analyzing Permutations for AES-like Ciphers: Understanding ShiftRows

Christof Beierle[1], Philipp Jovanovic[2], Martin M. Lauridsen[3][(✉)],
Gregor Leander[1], and Christian Rechberger[3]

[1] Horst Görtz Institute for IT Security, Ruhr-Universität Bochum,
Bochum, Germany
[2] Fakultät für Informatik und Mathematik, Universität Passau, Passau, Germany
[3] DTU Compute, Technical University of Denmark, Lyngby, Denmark
mmeh@dtu.dk

Abstract. Designing block ciphers and hash functions in a manner that resemble the AES in many aspects has been very popular since Rijndael was adopted as the Advanced Encryption Standard. However, in sharp contrast to the `MixColumns` operation, the security implications of the way the state is permuted by the operation resembling `ShiftRows` has never been studied in depth.

Here, we provide the first structured study of the influence of `ShiftRows`-like operations, or more generally, word-wise permutations, in AES-like ciphers with respect to diffusion properties and resistance towards differential- and linear attacks. After formalizing the concept of guaranteed trail weights, we show a range of equivalence results for permutation layers in this context. We prove that the trail weight analysis when using arbitrary word-wise permutations, with rotations as a special case, reduces to a consideration of a specific normal form. Using a mixed-integer linear programming approach, we obtain optimal parameters for a wide range of AES-like ciphers, and show improvements on parameters for Rijndael-192, Rijndael-256, PRIMATEs-80 and Prøst-128. As a separate result, we show for specific cases of the state geometry that a seemingly optimal bound on the trail weight can be obtained using cyclic rotations only for the permutation layer, i.e. in a very implementation friendly way.

Keywords: AES · AES-like · Differential cryptanalysis · Linear cryptanalysis · Diffusion · Optimization · Mixed-integer linear programming

1 Introduction

Since 2000 with the standardization of Rijndael [11] as the Advanced Encryption Standard (AES), an astonishing number of new primitives using components similar to the AES have seen the light of day. Examples of such include, but are

The work of Gregor Leander was funded by the BMBF UNIKOPS project.

K. Nyberg (ed.): CT-RSA 2015, LNCS 9048, pp. 37–58, 2015.
DOI: 10.1007/978-3-319-16715-2_3

not limited to, block ciphers 3D [19], ANUBIS [3], LED [16], mCrypton [21] and PRINCE [9], as well as hash functions like ECHO [5], Grøstl [14], LANE [18], PHOTON [15], Twister [13] and components of CAESAR candidates PAEQ [8], PRIMATEs [1], Prøst [20] and STRIBOB [25]. This can largely be attributed to the seminal wide-trail design strategy [12] which was introduced along with Rijndael and its predecessor SQUARE [10] for the first time.

The wide-trail strategy is an elegant way of ensuring good diffusion properties and at the same time allow designers to easily give bounds on the resistance towards differential- and linear cryptanalysis. Additionally, another advantage is that it decouples the choice of the non-linear layer and the linear layer to a large extent. In a nutshell, any good S-box combined with any good linear layer will result in a cipher resistant against linear- and differential attacks.

For AES-like ciphers, including all the above mentioned designs, the linear layer itself is composed of two parts: one resembles the AES `MixColumns` operation and the other resembles the AES `ShiftRows` operation. The `MixColumns`-like operation is a matrix multiplication of the columns of the state and the `ShiftRows`-like operation is a permutation of the words of the state.

For the former, the criteria are well understood. All that is required here is that this operation has a suitably high branch number. In short, the branch number corresponds to the minimal sum of the number of active S-boxes in an input/output column, provided an active input column (and the number of active S-boxes is the essential tool for bounding the success probability of linear- and differential attacks). In stark contrast, for the operation resembling `ShiftRows`, the situation is significantly less clear. Basically, the `ShiftRows`-like operation highly influences the number of active S-boxes when considering more than two rounds only. Understanding the bounds for more than two rounds is crucial for many good designs. With a well-chosen `ShiftRows`-like operation it is usually possible to derive much stronger bounds for more rounds than the trivial bound one gets by multiplying the two-round bound by half the number of rounds.

In the case of the AES (and others including [5,8,9]) one uses a so-called super-box argument to prove strong bounds on four rounds of the cipher. For others, the problem is modelled as a mixed-integer linear programs like in [1,20,24] which allows the computation of bounds for an (in principle) arbitrary number of rounds *for a given choice of the* `ShiftRows`-like operation. However, no structured approach for analyzing the influence of the `ShiftRows`-like operation on the security of the cipher has been undertaken previously. The results so far remain ad-hoc and specific to a given choice of parameters. Considering the large number of designs following this approach, this shortcoming is quite surprising and unsatisfactory from a scientific perspective. In particular, the choices made are often not optimal and not based on an adequate understanding of the implications.

Our Contribution. In this paper, we develop a structured approach to analyzing the permutation layer, i.e. the generalized `ShiftRows`-like operation, for AES-like ciphers with respect to diffusion and resistance towards differential- and linear cryptanalysis. For this, we start by defining a general framework for AES-like ciphers. Note that we do not restrict to the case where permutation is identical in all rounds but we allow for different choices of the permutation in different rounds. Moreover, we first consider arbitrary word-wise permutations and later restrict ourselves to word-wise rotations of the rows. The latter have the appeal of being efficiently implementable on many modern CPUs. Our following analysis consists of two parts.

First, and as a core contribution to a structured approach, we simplify the problem by introducing the notion of equivalent permutation parameters. It is intuitively clear that many choices of the permutation will lead to the same behavior of the cipher. One such example is changing the order of the rotation constants for the ShiftRows operation in the AES, i.e. rotate the first row by 3, the second by 2, and so on. We will make this intuition precise and, as will be shown below, discover more involved examples of the above.

The notion of equivalence will imply the same lower bound on the number of guaranteed active S-boxes. This is interesting theoretically, as it allows to simplify the problem. For example, we prove that a general permutation can never yield better results than a permutation that operates on the rows individually. Furthermore, using this notion of equivalence, we derive a normalized representation of any word-wise rotation of the rows. This allows to significantly reduce the problem domain and thus the search space for a computational approach.

In the second part of our analysis, we use this normalized representation in a combination with solving mixed-integer linear programs using the IBM ILOG CPLEX library [17]. The source code for this part is available as [4]. This results in optimal parameter suggestions for a wide range of AES-like ciphers. In particular, it allows us to suggest improved parameters for Rijndael-192, Rijndael-256, PRIMATEs-80 and Prøst-128 on this front, see Table 1 for details.

Finally, given our extensive experimental results, we conjecture an optimal lower bound on the number of active S-boxes possible for specific cases of the state geometry. Those parameters are such that they allow for an iterative version of the superbox argument mentioned above. We also provide a permutation which guarantees this conjectured optimal bound. In contrast to prior work, e.g. ECHO and PAEQ, this permutation layer is generic and, more importantly, realized with *cyclic row rotations only*. Thus, it allows for an easy and efficient implementation.

Outline. In Section 2 we give notation and define what we mean by AES-like ciphers. Then, in Section 3, we introduce, besides diffusion, the concept of guaranteed active S-boxes as a measure of the resistance against differential- and linear attacks. Section 4 provides reductions in order to identify equivalent permutation parameters for AES-like ciphers. We thereby also introduce the normal form of rotation matrices, considering only cyclic rotations of the state rows. Section 5 copes with modelling the problem using a mixed-integer linear programming approach in order to calculate optimal bounds for given state dimensions. In this context, some practical examples for rotation parameters are provided. Finally, Section 6 continues with a theoretic analysis of special cases of the state dimension and presents (conjectured) optimal solutions to the main criteria. We conclude the paper in Section 7.

2   Preliminaries

We use $\mathbb{F}_{q^r}$ to denote the finite field of size q^r with q prime. We use $\mathbb{Z}_n$ to interchangeably denote the group of integers modulo n and the set $\{0, 1, \ldots, n-1\}$. We refer to binary strings in $\mathbb{F}_2^m$ as *words*. We refer to $M \times N$ matrices with word entries as *states*. For a state X we use X_i to denote the ith row of X, and $X_{i,j}$ denotes word in the jth column of X_i. Let F be a function operating on states and let $\oplus$ be bitwise addition. For words x, x' we use the term *difference* to denote $x \oplus x'$, and let the notion extend to states where the differences are word-wise. For input states x, x' to F, we refer to $x \oplus x'$ and $F(x) \oplus F(x')$ as the *input difference* and *output difference*, respectively. For an $M \times N$ difference X, we use the symbol with a tilde on top, e.g. $\tilde{X}$, to denote the *activity pattern* of X, an $M \times N$ matrix over $\mathbb{F}_2$ where $\tilde{X}_{i,j} = 1$ if $X_{i,j} \neq 0$ and $\tilde{X}_{i,j} = 0$ otherwise. For $a, b \in \mathbb{F}_2^m$ we let $\langle a, b \rangle = \bigoplus_{i=0}^{m-1} a_i \cdot b_i$ denote the inner product of a and b, where subscript i denotes the ith bit. We extend this inner product to states, s.t. for $X, Y \in (\mathbb{F}_2^m)^{M \times N}$ we have $\langle X, Y \rangle = \bigoplus_{i \in \mathbb{Z}_M, j \in \mathbb{Z}_N} \langle X_{i,j}, Y_{i,j} \rangle$.

2.1   AES-like Ciphers

With the increasing popularity of the AES since its standardization, dozens of new ciphers that follow what we refer to as an *AES-like* design have seen the light of day. We describe formally our notion of AES-like ciphers in Definition 1.

Definition 1. *An AES-like cipher is a block cipher E_K which is parametrized by a fixed key K, the state dimension $M \times N$, the word size m, the number of rounds T and a permutation parameter $\pi = (\pi_0, \ldots, \pi_{T-1})$, where each π_t is a permutation on $\mathbb{Z}_M \times \mathbb{Z}_N$. It is composed of round functions $\mathcal{R}_i$, s.t. $E_K = \mathcal{R}_{T-1} \circ \cdots \circ \mathcal{R}_0$. Each round function is composed of the following bijective transformations on states, s.t. $\forall t \in \mathbb{Z}_T : \mathcal{R}_t = \texttt{AddRoundKey}_t \circ \texttt{Permute}_{\pi_t} \circ \texttt{MixColumns}_t \circ \texttt{SubBytes}:$*

1. *$\texttt{SubBytes}$ substitutes each word of the state according to one or several S-boxes $S : \mathbb{F}_2^m \to \mathbb{F}_2^m$.*
2. *$\texttt{MixColumns}_t$ applies, in round t, for all columns $j \in \mathbb{Z}_N$ left-multiplication by an $M \times M$ matrix $\mathtt{M}_j^t \in (\mathbb{F}_2^m)^{M \times M}$:*

$$\texttt{MixColumns}_t : (\mathbb{F}_2^m)^{M \times N} \to (\mathbb{F}_2^m)^{M \times N}$$
$$\forall j \in \mathbb{Z}_N : (X_{0,j}, \ldots, X_{M-1,j})^T \mapsto \mathtt{M}_j^t \cdot (X_{0,j}, \ldots, X_{M-1,j})^T,$$

where multiplication in $\mathbb{F}_2^m$ is defined by an arbitrary irreducible polynomial over $\mathbb{F}_2$ of degree m.

3. $\texttt{Permute}_{\pi_t}$ *permutes, in round t, the words within the state due to a given permutation π_t. We use the notation that for a position $(i,j) \in \mathbb{Z}_M \times \mathbb{Z}_N$ in the state, $\pi_t(i,j)$ gives the new position of that word under the permutation π_t:*

$$\texttt{Permute}_{\pi_t} : (\mathbb{F}_2^m)^{M \times N} \to (\mathbb{F}_2^m)^{M \times N}$$
$$\forall i \in \mathbb{Z}_M, \forall j \in \mathbb{Z}_N : X_{i,j} \mapsto X_{\pi_t(i,j)}.$$

4. $\texttt{AddRoundKey}_t$ *performs word-wise XOR to the state using the tth round key.*

Subsequently, we omit the $\texttt{AddRoundKey}_t$ operation of Definition 1 from consideration, as it does not affect diffusion properties nor resistance towards differential- and linear cryptanalysis of the AES-like cipher. Note also, that for generality we consider in Definition 1 an arbitrary word permutation $\texttt{Permute}_{\pi_t}$, while later we will, for efficiency reasons, resrict ourselves to row-wise rotations of the words as in the $\texttt{ShiftRows}$ operations of the AES.

3   Diffusion and Resistance to Differential/Linear Cryptanalysis

In this paper, we are concerned with two security aspects of an AES-like cipher, namely diffusion on the one hand and resistance against differential- and linear attacks on the other hand. We formally define our notations for both criteria in the following.

3.1   Diffusion

The first definition of diffusion is attributed to Shannon [26]. Informally, diffusion is about complicating the relationship between the ciphertext bits and plaintext bits. When designing a cipher, it is desirable to obtain what we call *full diffusion* after as few rounds as possible and indeed the number of rounds chosen for the cipher is often determined by exactly this number.

Definition 2 (Diffusion degree). *For a function $F : \mathbb{F}_2^\ell \to \mathbb{F}_2^n$, we define the diffusion degree $d(F)$ for F as the fraction of bits in the image under F that depend on each bit of the pre-image, i.e.*

$$d(F) = \frac{1}{n} \cdot \sharp \left\{ j \in \mathbb{Z}_n \mid \forall i \in \mathbb{Z}_\ell : \exists x \in \mathbb{F}_2^\ell : F(x^{(i)})_j \neq F(x)_j \right\},$$

where $F(x)_j$ denotes the jth bit of $F(x)$ and $x^{(i)}$ denotes the element x with the ith bit flipped. We say that F obtains full diffusion when $d(F) = 1$.

Definition 3 (Diffusion-optimality). *Fix the state dimensions $M \times N$. Consider a permutation sequence π for an AES-like cipher which obtains full diffusion after t rounds. We say that π is diffusion-optimal if there exists no $\pi' \neq \pi$ which obtains full diffusion after $t' < t$ rounds.*

3.2   Differential/Linear Cryptanalysis

Differential- and linear cryptanalysis were pioneered by Biham and Shamir [6, 7] and Matsui [23], respectively, to attack the DES. In a differential attack an attacker tries to predict the difference of the state after several rounds when plaintexts with a given difference are processed. In linear cryptanalysis, the attacker tries to find biased linear Boolean equations involving plaintext-, key- and ciphertext bits. Common to both attacks is that they are based on trails (or characteristics). The probability (resp. correlation) of those trails can be upper bounded by lower bounding the number of active S-boxes in any trail. Here, an S-box is active in a given trail if it has a non-zero input difference (resp. mask). In general, if p is the largest probability (resp. correlation) for the S-box to satisfy a differential- or linear property, and any trail has at least k active S-boxes, then the trail property holds with probability (resp. correlation) at most p^k. This way of ensuring resistance against linear and differential attacks is the basis of the wide-trail-strategy as introduced by Daemen and Rijmen in [12]. The second important merit of the wide-trail starategy is that it allows to treat the S-box and the linear-layer as black boxes as long as they fulfill certain conditions. In our work, we follow both aspects of this philosophy. The designer is interested in having the lightest trail as heavy as possible. Indeed, knowing this probability is essential when determining the number of rounds for the cipher in the design phase. We give definitions of trails and trail weights in the following.

Definition 4 (Trail and trail weight). *For an AES-like cipher E_K using m-bit words and state dimension $M \times N$, a T-round trail is a $(T+1)$-tuple $(X^0, \ldots, X^T) \in \left((\mathbb{F}_2^m)^{M \times N} \right)^{T+1}$ and the* weight *of the trail is defined as*

$$\sum_{t \in \mathbb{Z}_T} \sum_{i \in \mathbb{Z}_M} \sum_{j \in \mathbb{Z}_N} \tilde{X}_{i,j}^t.$$

A pair of inputs $x, x' \in (\mathbb{F}_2^m)^{M \times N}$ are said to follow *the differential trail $(X^0, \ldots, X^T)$ over T rounds if and only if $X^0 = x \oplus x'$ and*

$$\forall t \in \{1, \ldots, T\} : X^t = (\mathcal{R}_{t-1} \circ \cdots \circ \mathcal{R}_0)(x) \oplus (\mathcal{R}_{t-1} \circ \cdots \circ \mathcal{R}_0)(x').$$

If $(\alpha^0, \ldots, \alpha^T)$ is a T-round linear trail, then an input $x \in (\mathbb{F}_2^m)^{M \times N}$ is said to follow the linear trail $(\alpha^0, \ldots, \alpha^T)$ if and only if

$$\langle x, \alpha^0 \rangle = \langle \mathcal{R}_0(x), \alpha^1 \rangle = \cdots = \langle (\mathcal{R}_{T-1} \circ \cdots \circ \mathcal{R}_0)(x), \alpha^T \rangle.$$

We say that a trail is valid *for E_K if and only if there exists at least one input pair (respectively input, for linear trails), which follows the trail.*

Note from Definition 4 that the weight of a trail corresponds exactly to the number of active S-boxes over those T rounds. In the remainder of this work, we concentrate on the differential case. However, the results apply equally to linear trails as well.

Definition 5 (Branch number). *For a linear automorphism* $\theta : (\mathbb{F}_2^m)^M \rightarrow (\mathbb{F}_2^m)^M$, *the differential branch number* B_θ *is defined as*

$$B_\theta = \min_{\substack{x,x' \in (\mathbb{F}_2^m)^M \\ x \neq x'}} \left\{ \sum_{i \in \mathbb{Z}_M} \tilde{X}_i + \tilde{Y}_i \right\}, \qquad X = x \oplus x', Y = \theta(x) \oplus \theta(x').$$

In the context of an AES-like cipher E_K, *we say* E_K *has branch number* B_θ *if and only if it is the largest integer s.t. left multiplication by any of the* M_j^t *used in the* MixColumns$_t$ *operation has branch number at least* B_θ.

In order to calculate a useful lower bound on the number of active S-boxes in an efficient way, we focus on the Permute$_{\pi_t}$ part of the round function. The SubBytes operation will be considered as using an arbitrary S-box $S : \mathbb{F}_2^m \rightarrow \mathbb{F}_2^m$, and the analysis will be independent of the specifc instance of S. Each of the M_j^t matrices used in the MixColumns operation will be considered as black-box linear operations, under the requirement that the AES-like cipher has branch number B_θ. A formal definition of that idea is given in the following. For a T-round permutation parameter $\pi = (\pi_0, \ldots, \pi_{T-1})$, let $\widehat{\text{AES}}_{M,N}(\pi, B_\theta)$ denote the set of all $M \times N$ AES-like ciphers over T rounds with branch number B_θ using $\pi_0, \ldots, \pi_{T-2}$ in the first $T-1$ rounds. The reason for not including π_{T-1} is that our proofs in the following use the fact that for different permutation sequences we can re-model one AES-like cipher into another, up to the last round, and up to changing MixColumns operations (but maintaining the branch number).

Definition 6. *We   say   that   the   sequence   of   permutations* $\pi = (\pi_0, \ldots, \pi_{T-1})$ *tightly guarantees* k *active S-boxes for branch number* B_θ *if and only if there is a valid trail of weight* k *for some* $E_K \in \widehat{\text{AES}}_{M,N}(\pi, B_\theta)$ *and there is no valid trail of weight* $k' < k$, $k' > 0$, *for some* $E_K' \in \widehat{\text{AES}}_{M,N}(\pi, B_\theta)$. *We denote this property by* $\pi \xrightarrow{B_\theta} k$.

Definition 7 (Trail-optimality). *A sequence of permutations* $\pi = (\pi_0, \ldots, \pi_{T-1})$ *with* $\pi \xrightarrow{B_\theta} k$ *is said to be* trail-optimal *if there exists no* $\pi' = (\pi_0', \ldots, \pi_{T-1}')$ *s.t.* $\pi' \xrightarrow{B_\theta} k'$ *where* $k' > k$.

Appendix A provides a proof that the number of tightly guaranteed active S-boxes is really independent of the specific S-box instantiations. From Definition 6, it follows that the number of guaranteed active S-boxes is always a lower bound for the actual minimum number of active S-boxes in any concrete instantiation of an AES-like cipher.

4   Equivalent Permutations: Simplifying the Problem

In this section, we present a range of results which simplifies the problem of identifying good permutation parameters π for AES-like ciphers by showing when different permutation parameters are equivalent w.r.t. resistance towards differential- and linear attacks. Obviously, for a fixed branch number, many different π will tightly guarantee the same number of active S-boxes. Thus, identifying conditions under which two different permutation sequences $\pi \neq \pi'$ tightly guarantee the same bound is significant: for a theoretical understanding, this approach simplifies the problem while for a computer-aided search for a good π parameter, this significantly reduces the search space. In Definition 8, we specify what it means for two permutation sequences to be equivalent.

Definition 8 (Equivalence of permutation sequences). *Two permutation sequences π, π', for a T-round cipher, are said to be* equivalent*, denoted $\pi \sim \pi'$, if and only if for all possible branch numbers B_θ, the equality $\widehat{\mathrm{AES}}_{M,N}(\pi, B_\theta) = \widehat{\mathrm{AES}}_{M,N}(\pi', B_\theta)$ holds. Intuitively, this means that for all AES-like ciphers using π, there is an AES-like cipher using π' which it is functionally identical to, up until the last round.*

We remark that, using this notion of equivalence, one can transform each cipher E_K using π into a cipher E'_K using π' such that $E_K = \tau \circ E'_K$ for a permutation τ on the state words. Thus, equivalence will imply the same number of tightly guaranteed active S-boxes for all possible fixed branch numbers B_θ.

4.1   Equivalences for Permutation Sequences π

In order to prove the reduction to a normalized form on the round permutations, we show a range of observations in the following. Firstly, Lemma 9 is a combinatorial result on permutations on Cartesian products.

Lemma 9 (Representation of permutations on cartesian products). *Every permutation π_t on the words of an $M \times N$ state can be represented as $\pi_t = \gamma' \circ \phi \circ \gamma$ where γ, γ' are permuting the words within the columns and ϕ is permuting the words within the rows.*

Proof. Let $T_A, T_B, T_C, T_D \in (\mathbb{Z}_M \times \mathbb{Z}_N)^{M \times N}$ s.t. $T_{A_{i,j}} = (i, j)$ and let T_B, T_C and T_D be defined by the following diagram:

$$T_A \xrightarrow{\ \gamma\ } T_B \xrightarrow{\ \phi\ } T_C \xrightarrow{\ \gamma'\ } T_D.$$

To show the result, we let $T_D = \pi_t(T_A)$ and show how to construct the permutations such that $T_D = (\gamma' \circ \phi \circ \gamma)(T_A)$. We first observe the following two properties which must hold:

1. T_B must be a matrix where, within each column $j \in \mathbb{Z}_N$, it holds that i) the second coordinate of each point is equal to j, because γ only permutes within each column of T_A and ii) the set of first coordinates cover all of $\mathbb{Z}_M$, because T_B is a permutation of $\mathbb{Z}_M \times \mathbb{Z}_N$.
2. T_C must be a matrix where, for each column $j \in \mathbb{Z}_N$, the points in column j of T_C are the same as those in column j of T_D. This is required because otherwise going between T_C and T_D using a permutation operating in each column, is impossible.

If we can determine a matrix T_B with property (1) and a row permutation ϕ s.t. $T_C = \phi(T_B)$ has property (2), we are clearly done, because T_A and T_D can be obtained from T_B respectively T_C by applying a permutation on the columns.

For a matrix $A \in (\mathbb{Z}_M \times \mathbb{Z}_N)^{M \times N}$, let $Q(A)$ be an $N \times N$ matrix for which $Q(A)_{i,j}$ is the number of occurences of $j \in \mathbb{Z}_N$ in the second coordinate of the points in column $i \in \mathbb{Z}_N$ of A. As $Q(T_B)$ and $Q(T_C)$ are both magic squares of weight M, one can decompose $Q(T_C)$ into a sum of M permutation matrices by the Birkhoff-von Neumann Theorem (see e.g. [2, p. 164]), and thus

$$Q(T_C) = P_0 + \cdots + P_{M-1}.$$

Let ϕ be a permutation within each row, defined by applying P_i to row $i \in \mathbb{Z}_M$. Then $Q(\phi(T_B)) = Q(T_C)$.

What is left to show is that there exists a column permutation T_B of T_A s.t. the first coordinates in each column j of T_C is correct, given the fixed permutation ϕ. To see this, consider the case where T_C requires a point (a, b) to be in column j. Clearly, (a, b) is in column b of both T_A and T_B. Now, let P_i be such that it moves *some* point in position (a', b) of T_B from column b to column j of T_C. If $(a', b) = (a, b)$, then (a, b) does not need to be moved within column b from T_A to T_B by γ, but if $(a', b) \neq (a, b)$, one can use γ to move (a, b) to (a', b) so it ends up in column j of T_C. As each point (a, b) will only be present once in T_C, it can be moved once between T_A and T_B and never moved again. This procedure holds for all points (a, b), and as such the result follows.[1]   □

Lemma 10 (Equivalence under permutations within columns). *Let $\pi = (\pi_0, \ldots, \pi_{T-1})$ be a permutation sequence for an AES-like cipher E_K and let γ, γ' be arbitrary permutations on the words within the columns of a state. Then, $\forall t \in \mathbb{Z}_T$: $\pi \sim (\pi_0, \ldots, \gamma' \circ \pi_t \circ \gamma, \ldots, \pi_{T-1})$. In particular, the number of tightly guaranteed active S-boxes is invariant under inserting permutations, before and after any π_t, which act on the columns of the state separately.*

Proof. Fix the branch number B_θ and let $E_K \in \widetilde{\mathrm{AES}}_{M,N}(\pi, B_\theta)$. We consider any round $t \in \mathbb{Z}_T$.

We first show that $\pi \sim \pi' = (\pi_0, \ldots, \pi_t \circ \gamma, \ldots, \pi_{T-1})$. Let E'_K be like E_K but using permutation sequence π', with rounds denoted $\mathcal{R}'_t, t \in \mathbb{Z}_T$. Thus, $E'_K \in \widetilde{\mathrm{AES}}_{M,N}(\pi', B_\theta)$. It holds that

$$\mathcal{R}'_t = \mathtt{Permute}_{\pi_t} \circ \mathtt{Permute}_\gamma \circ \mathtt{MixColumns}_t \circ \mathtt{SubBytes}.$$

Since γ operates on the columns separately, one can define

$$\mathtt{MixColumns}'_t = \mathtt{Permute}_\gamma \circ \mathtt{MixColumns}_t,$$

which in turn is a linear layer for an AES-like cipher with the same branch number, and we have

$$\mathcal{R}'_t = \mathtt{Permute}_{\pi_t} \circ \mathtt{MixColumns}'_t \circ \mathtt{SubBytes}.$$

---

[1] Thanks to John Steinberger who had the idea for this proof.

Now, E'_K is a cipher which uses the permutation sequence π and thus $E'_K \in \widehat{\text{AES}}_{M,N}(\pi, B_\theta)$. The other inclusion follows the same way by applying γ^{-1}. For showing the case of $\pi' = (\pi_0, \ldots, \gamma' \circ \pi_t, \ldots, \pi_{T-1})$, the argument is parallel. By combining the two, the result follows. $\qquad\square$

As an easy result, one obtains Theorem 11, which we state without proof. Note that a permutation sequence is called ρ-*alternating*, written $\pi = (\pi_0, \ldots, \pi_{\rho-1})_T$, if it repeats the same ρ permutations alternatingly.

Theorem 11 (Reduction to permutations on the rows). *Let $\pi = (\pi_0, \ldots, \pi_{\rho-1})_T$ be a ρ-alternating permutation sequence. Then one can construct a $\pi' = (\pi'_0, \ldots, \pi'_{\rho-1})_T$ with $\pi \sim \pi'$, s.t. for each $t \in \mathbb{Z}_\rho$, it holds that π'_t permutes only the words in each row of the state.*

4.2 Equivalences for Rotation Matrices σ

While we have, until this point, focused on AES-like ciphers with arbitrary word-wise permutations $\texttt{Permute}_{\pi_t}$ as part of the round function, such general permutations are not suitable for designs of cryptographic primitives. To that end, we limit ourselves from this point on to AES-like ciphers where the permutation operation of the round function *cyclically rotates each row of the state from left-to-right* using a rotation matrix as specified in Definition 12.

Definition 12 (Rotation matrix). *Consider an AES-like cipher where the permutation operation in the round function consists of cyclic word-wise rotations of each state row. For such a cipher, we define a* rotation matrix *as a matrix $\sigma \in \mathbb{Z}_N^{\rho \times M}$, where ρ is a positive integer, such that*

1. *If $\rho = T$, then $\sigma_{t,i}$ denotes the rotation amount for row $i \in \mathbb{Z}_M$ in round t, and*
2. *If $\rho < T$, then we have the further requirement that the rotation constants alternate, such that $\sigma_{k,i}$ denotes the rotation amount for row $i \in \mathbb{Z}_M$ in rounds t where $t \equiv k \bmod \rho$,*

where, without loss of generality, we let the rotation direction be left-to-right.

As rotation matrices are a special case of arbitrary permutations, we remark that the notion of equivalence includes these as well. We simplify our notion of an AES-like cipher to only use row-wise rotations in the permutation part of each $\mathcal{R}_t$. In particular, we substitue the $\texttt{Permute}_{\pi_t}$ operation by

$$\texttt{ShiftRows}_{\sigma_t} : (\mathbb{F}_2^m)^{M \times N} \to (\mathbb{F}_2^m)^{M \times N}$$
$$\forall i \in \mathbb{Z}_M, \forall j \in \mathbb{Z}_N : X_{i,j} \mapsto X_{i,j+\sigma_{t \bmod \rho, i} \bmod N}.$$

Lemma 13 (Equivalence under re-ordering of row entries). *Let $\sigma \in \mathbb{Z}_N^{\rho \times M}$ be a rotation matrix and let $\vartheta_0, \ldots, \vartheta_{\rho-1}$ be arbitrary, independent permutations on the ρ rows of σ. Define σ' s.t. $\forall t \in \mathbb{Z}_\rho : \sigma'_t = \vartheta_t(\sigma_t)$. Then $\sigma \sim \sigma'$.*

Proof. This directly follows from Lemma 10, as using σ'_t is equivalent to using $\gamma' \circ \sigma_t \circ \gamma$ for appropriate permutations γ' and γ on the state columns. $\qquad\square$

Lemma 14 (Equivalence under row-wise constant addition). *Let* $\sigma \in \mathbb{Z}_N^{\rho \times M}$ *be a rotation matrix and let* $c_0, \ldots, c_{\rho-1} \in \mathbb{Z}_N$. *Define a rotation matrix* σ' *where* $\forall t \in \mathbb{Z}_\rho, \forall i \in \mathbb{Z}_M : \sigma'_{t,i} = \sigma_{t,i} + c_t \bmod N$. *Then* $\sigma \sim \sigma'$.

Proof. We split the proof into two cases: i) $T \leq \rho$ and ii) $T > \rho$. Consider first $T \leq \rho$. If $T < \rho$, one can add constants to $\sigma_T, \ldots, \sigma_{\rho-1}$, since these are never used anyway. Thus, let us consider $T = \rho$. We give a proof by induction that one can add independent constants $c_t, \ldots, c_{T-1}$ to $\sigma_t, \ldots, \sigma_{T-1}$ to obtain an equivalent rotation matrix σ', and proceed by induction on t. Clearly, one can add a constant to σ_{T-1} to obtain an equivalent σ', since the set $\widehat{\mathrm{AES}}_{M,N}(\sigma, B_\theta)$ does not cover the use of σ_{T-1}. Assuming the statement holds for $t, \ldots, T-1$, we now prove that it is possible to add a constant c_{t-1} to σ_{t-1} as well. Using the notation that $\mathrm{SR} = \mathrm{ShiftRows}$, $\mathrm{MC} = \mathrm{MixColumns}$, $\mathrm{SB} = \mathrm{SubBytes}$ and RS_k is a rotation of the whole state by k positions, we have

$$\mathcal{R}_t \circ \mathcal{R}_{t-1} = (\mathrm{SR}_{\sigma_t} \circ \mathrm{MC}_t \circ \mathrm{SB}) \circ (\mathrm{RS}_{-c_{t-1}} \circ \mathrm{RS}_{c_{t-1}}) \circ (\mathrm{SR}_{\sigma_{t-1}} \circ \mathrm{MC}_{t-1} \circ \mathrm{SB})$$

$$= \mathrm{SR}_{\sigma_t} \circ \mathrm{RS}_{-c_{t-1}} \circ \mathrm{RS}_{c_{t-1}} \circ \mathrm{MC}_t \circ \mathrm{RS}_{-c_{t-1}} \circ \mathrm{SB} \circ (\mathrm{RS}_{c_{t-1}} \circ \mathrm{SR}_{\sigma_{t-1}} \circ \mathrm{MC}_{t-1} \circ \mathrm{SB}),$$

since $\mathrm{RS}_{-c_{t-1}}$ commutes with SB. Now, since $\mathrm{RS}_{c_{t-1}} \circ \mathrm{MC}_t \circ \mathrm{RS}_{-c_{t-1}} =: \mathrm{MC}'_t$ defines a (just rotated) linear column mixing and since SR_{σ_t} commutes with $\mathrm{RS}_{-c_{t-1}}$, we have

$$\mathcal{R}_t \circ \mathcal{R}_{t-1} = (\mathrm{RS}_{-c_{t-1}} \circ \mathrm{SR}_{\sigma_t} \circ \mathrm{MC}'_t \circ \mathrm{SB}) \circ (\mathrm{RS}_{c_{t-1}} \circ \mathrm{SR}_{\sigma_{t-1}} \circ \mathrm{MC}_{t-1} \circ \mathrm{SB}),$$

and we see that by adding c_{t-1} to σ_{t-1} and $-c_{t-1}$ to σ_t we obtain an equivalent σ'. The result now follows by induction, since the addition of $-c_{t-1}$ to σ_t can be undone by the induction assumption.

For the case $T > \rho$, let H be a $T \times M$ matrix where $H_t = \sigma_k$ when $t \equiv k \bmod \rho$. For a T-round AES-like cipher E_K, H and σ are clearly equivalent rotation matrices. From the above, it follows we can add c_t to row t of H, $t \in \mathbb{Z}_T$, and obtain an equivalent H'. In particular, adding the same c_k to all rows t where $t \equiv k \bmod \rho$, we obtain H' which is equivalent to σ, and has the property that $H'_i = H'_j$ if $i \equiv j \bmod \rho$, and in particular the first ρ rows of H' equals σ' and the result follows. $\qquad\square$

Theorem 15 (Equivalence for rotation matrices). *Given a rotation matrix* $\sigma \in \mathbb{Z}_N^{\rho \times M}$, *one can obtain an equivalent matrix* $\sigma' \in \mathbb{Z}_N^{\rho \times M}$ *for which the following holds simultaneously*

1. *Each row* $\sigma'_t, t \in \mathbb{Z}_\rho$, *is lexicographically ordered,*
2. *For all* $t \in \mathbb{Z}_\rho$ *it holds that* $\sigma'_{t,0} = 0$ *and*
3. *For all* $t \in \mathbb{Z}_\rho$ *it holds that* $\sigma'_{t,1} \leq \frac{N}{2}$.

Proof. Points (1) and (2) follow directly from Lemma 13 and 14, respectively. For point (3), let us assume w.l.o.g that (1) and (2) hold and consider the case where $M \geq 2$ and consider the element $\sigma_{t,1}$ from some row σ_t. If $\sigma_{t,1} > \frac{N}{2}$, we add $-\sigma_{t,1} \bmod N$ and the result follows from Lemmas 13 and 14. $\qquad\square$

Besides Theorem 15, we heuristically suggest a search for optimal rotation matrices to restrict itself to matrices where all entries in a row are different, i.e. $\forall t \in \mathbb{Z}_\rho : \sigma_{t,j} = \sigma_{t,j'} \Leftrightarrow j = j'$, as equal entries in some σ_t are redundant w.r.t. the diffusion properties of the cipher. Moreover, when N is even, we require that σ contains at least one odd entry, because otherwise even-numbered columns never mix with odd-numbered columns. We refer to a rotation matrix which satisfies these properties, plus properties (1) – (3) of Theorem 15, as the *normal form* of its equivalence class of rotation matrices.

5   Mixed-Integer Linear Programming and Experimental Results

One advantage of modeling the S-boxes and linear layers as black boxes is that one easily can compute useful lower bounds on the number of guaranteed active S-boxes using a mixed-integer linear programming approach. We describe this approach next.

5.1   The Problem as a Mixed Integer Linear Program

In the following, we describe the mixed-integer linear program which models the problem of determining the tightly guaranteed trail weight under a given rotation matrix $\sigma \in \mathbb{Z}_N^{\rho \times M}$. We give the parameters, decision variables, the constraints and the target optimization as Model 1. This formulation is similar to that of Mouha et al. [24]. We note that Model 1 is specified for the case where each $\mathtt{M}_j^t$ used in the $\mathtt{MixColumns}_t$ operation is an MDS matrix, as this is usually what is applied in designs. If, on the other hand, non-MDS matrices are deployed, the model can be easily modified to cover these cases as well, at the cost of a slightly more complicated model. Theorem 16 formalizes how Model 1 provides us with the sought bound.

Theorem 16. *The solution of Model 1 is always a lower bound on the number of tightly guaranteed active S-boxes for an AES-like cipher with branch number B_θ and rotation matrix σ. If the branch number is optimal for the given dimensions and a linear mixing layer with this branch number exists (and the word length $m > \log_2(M + 2)$), this provides a tight bound.*

Proof. This follows from Corollary 27 in Appendix A.   □

Theorem 16 shows in particular that one can not hope to improve the bounds in a generic way for the case of AES-like ciphers using MDS matrices. That is to say that any argument to improve upon the bounds provided by the model will necessarily be a non-black box argument. Thus, in the spirit of the wide-trail strategy, one cannot improve upon those bounds.

Model 1: MILP model for determining the guaranteed trail weight using a fixed rotation matrix

Parameters

Name	Domain	Description
M	$\mathbb{Z}_+$	Number of rows in state
N	$\mathbb{Z}_+$	Number of columns in state
T	$\mathbb{Z}_+$	Number of rounds
ρ	$\mathbb{Z}_+$	Number of rows in rotation paramter σ
B_θ	$\mathbb{Z}_+$	Branch number of `MixColumns`
σ	$\mathbb{Z}_N^{\rho \times M}$	Rotation parameter

Decision variables

Name	Domain	Index domain	Description
$\tilde{X}_{i,j}^t$	$\mathbb{F}_2$	$i \in \mathbb{Z}_M, j \in \mathbb{Z}_N, t \in \mathbb{Z}_T \cup \{T\}$	$\tilde{X}_{i,j} = 1$ if and only if the word in position (i,j) is active before round $\mathcal{R}_t$
a_j^t	$\mathbb{F}_2$	$j \in \mathbb{Z}_N, t \in \mathbb{Z}_T$	Auxilliary variable; $a_j^t = 1$ if and only if column j has an active word before round $\mathcal{R}_t$

Minimize

$$\sum_{t \in \mathbb{Z}_T} \sum_{i \in \mathbb{Z}_M} \sum_{j \in \mathbb{Z}_N} \tilde{X}_{i,j}^t$$

subject to

$$\sum_{i \in \mathbb{Z}_M} \sum_{j \in \mathbb{Z}_N} \tilde{X}_{i,j}^0 \geq 1 \qquad (1)$$

$$\forall j \in \mathbb{Z}_N, \forall t \in \mathbb{Z}_T \quad : \quad \sum_{i \in \mathbb{Z}_M} \tilde{X}_{i,j}^t + \tilde{X}_{i,(j+\sigma_t \mod \rho, i) \mod N}^{t+1} \geq B_\theta \cdot a_j^t \qquad (2)$$

$$\forall i \in \mathbb{Z}_M, \forall j \in \mathbb{Z}_N, \forall t \in \mathbb{Z}_T : \qquad a_j^t \geq \tilde{X}_{i,j}^t \qquad (3)$$

5.2   Experimental Results

A part of our contribution is a wide range of optimal choices of rotation matrices for various state geometries $M \times N$, ρ and number of rounds T. For all our experiments, we concentrated on the case of MDS `MixColumns`$_t$ layers, i.e. AES-like ciphers with optimal branch number. Using the heuristic approach from Section 4.2, i.e. by brute-forcing the normal form of each equivalence class of rotation matrices, we provide optimal solutions for the analyzed cases as per Theorem 16. The full table of results is given in Appendix B.

We highlight in Table 1 results which suggest improvements for some existing AES-like primitives. We see that, in some cases, direct replacement of σ yields better bounds, while in other cases, one must increase ρ to obtain better bounds.

Among our findings are tight bounds which are not a multiple of the branch number for an even number of rounds. This implies that there exists some MDS linear mixing layers such that the lightest valid trail contains a two-round subtrail

Table 1. Improvements for existing AES-like primitives. An entry $(\rho_P, \mathcal{B}_P)/(\rho_M, \mathcal{B}_M)$ gives ρ and the number of tightly guaranteed S-boxes $\mathcal{B}$ in a T-round trail for the *primitive* (subscript P) and the *modified primitive* (subscript M), respectively. The † symbol indicates results where only diffusion-optimal σ were tested, which means actual obtainable bounds may be higher.

Primitive	$T = 5$	$T = 6$	$T = 7$	$T = 8$	$T = 10$	$T = 12$
Rijndael-192	–	$(1,42)/(1,45)$	$(1,46)/(1,48)$	$(1,50)/(1,57)$	–	$(1,87)/(1,90)$
Rijndael-256	–	$(1,50)/(2,55)$	–	–	$(1,85)/(2,90)$	$(1,105)/(2,111)$
PRIMATEs-80	$(1,54)/(2,56)$	–	–	–	–	–
Prøst-128	–	$(2,85)/(2,90)^\dagger$	$(2,96)/(2,111)^\dagger$	–	–	–

of weight more than B_θ. Thus, some optimal trails have non-optimal transitions locally.

6 Optimal Solutions

In this section we describe, for special cases of the state geometry, optimal solutions with respect to both our main criteria, i.e. with respect to diffusion properties on one hand and resistance towards differential/linear attacks on the other hand.

6.1 Diffusion-Optimal Rotation Matrices

Under the assumptions that each S-box $S : \mathbb{F}_2^m \to \mathbb{F}_2^m$ and each $\mathtt{M}_j^t$ matrix has the property that each output bit depends on each input bit, we describe in the following a way of tracking the diffusion properties for an AES-like cipher E_K. Let z be an arbitrary fixed bit of an input to E_K. When, in the beginning of a round, a single bit in a column depends on z, then each bit in the column will depend on z after applying $\mathtt{MixColumns} \circ \mathtt{SubBytes}$. Thus, with fixed parameters M, N and σ, determining how many rounds t are required to obtain full diffusion reduces to answering how many rounds are required to have at least one bit depending on z in each column: if this is obtained after t' rounds then full diffusion is obtained after $t = t' + 1$ rounds. This is formalized in the following.

Definition 17 (Sumset). *Let G be an additive group and let $A, B \subset G$. We define the* sumset *written $A + B$ as $A + B = \{a + b \mid a \in A, b \in B\}$, where the sum is over G. We write kA for the sumset $A + A + \cdots + A$ with k terms.*

Theorem 18. *Consider an AES-like cipher with fixed parameters M, N, ρ and σ. Let w.l.o.g. z denote a bit in the word $X_{0,0}$ for an input X. Let $\alpha(T) = (\alpha(T)_0, \ldots, \alpha(T)_{\rho-1})$ be a vector where α_i, $0 \leq i < \rho$, equals the number of times σ_i is used in a $\mathtt{ShiftRows}$ operation during T rounds of the cipher. Then, after T rounds, the indices of columns which contain bits depending on z are given by the sumset $\alpha(T)_0 \sigma_0 + \alpha(T)_1 \sigma_1 + \cdots + \alpha(T)_{\rho-1} \sigma_{\rho-1}$, where addition is over $\mathbb{Z}_N$.*

Proof. Let $S_{-1} = \{0\}$. We recursively define $S_t = \{v + s \mid s \in S_{t-1}, v \in \sigma_{t \bmod \rho}\}$ for $t \geq 0$, where addition is in $\mathbb{Z}_N$. Note that the set S_t corresponds exactly to the sumset $\alpha(t)_0\sigma_0 + \cdots + \alpha(t)_{\rho-1}\sigma_{\rho-1}$. Clearly, $S_0 = \{v \mid v \in \sigma_0\}$ is the set of indices of columns that contain words depending on z after round $\mathcal{R}_0$. Now, assume that S_t are the column indices which contain some word depending on z after $\mathcal{R}_t$. Then, after applying MixColumns$_{t+1}$, *all* words in columns $j \in S_t$ depend on z. Now, when we apply ShiftRows$_{\sigma_{t+1} \bmod \rho}$, the words depending on z are moved exactly to the indices given in S_{t+1}, and thus the result is obtained by induction.   □

Corollary 19. *Consider an AES-like cipher with fixed parameters M, N, ρ and σ. If t' is the smallest positive integer s.t. the sumset $\alpha(t')_0\sigma_0 + \cdots + \alpha(t')_{\rho-1}\sigma_{\rho-1}$ over $\mathbb{Z}_C$ generates all of $\mathbb{Z}_N$, then the cipher obtains full diffusion after $t = t' + 1$ rounds.*

Proof. The proof follows from Theorem 18. Note that we chose the input bit z from the word $X_{0,0}$. If it would be chosen from an arbitrary word $X_{i,j}$, the corresponding sumset would be just shifted by a constant c. However, these are the same sumsets for all possible c, since they generate all of $\mathbb{Z}_N$.   □

Theorem 20. *When $N = M^\rho$, a diffusion-optimal rotation matrix is $\sigma \in \mathbb{Z}_N^{\rho \times M}$ s.t. $\sigma_{t,i} = i \cdot M^t$ for $(t, i) \in \mathbb{Z}_\rho \times \mathbb{Z}_M$ or any σ' where the entries of σ are permuted. These obtain full diffusion after $\rho + 1$ rounds.*

Proof. The set of indices of columns containing a word depending on z after ρ rounds is given by the sumset $\sigma_0 + \cdots + \sigma_{\rho-1}$ over $\mathbb{Z}_N$. This sumset has $M^\rho = N$ sums, and thus equals $\mathbb{Z}_N$ if and only if no two sums in the sumset are equal. To see why this is the case, consider constructing M-adic numbers using the sums in the sumset. We pick exactly one element from each row of σ and add them. As the elements in row t are $\sigma_t = \begin{pmatrix} 0M^t & 1M^t & \cdots & (M-1)M^t \end{pmatrix}$, the choice for the sum from σ_t is the tth least significant digit in the M-adic representation of that number. In other words, the rows of σ form a base for the M-adic number system, and we can form any number up to $\sum_{t=0}^{\rho-1}(M-1)M^t = N - 1$ with it. Since M^ρ elements cannot be generated using less than ρ parameters in the sumset, the diffusion-optimaltiy of σ follows.   □

6.2   Trail-Optimal Solutions

In this section, we first state Theorem 21, which is of particular interest because of the large number of AES-like ciphers with square geometry. Considering its statement, square states can be understood quite well. We also give a conjecture on the optimality of guaranteed trail weights for $M \times M^n$ AES-like ciphers over 2^{n+1} rounds and give a construction which matches the conjectured bound.

Theorem 21 (Optimality for square geometries). *Let σ be a rotation matrix in normal form operating on a square state of dimension $M \times M$. Then the number of tightly guaranteed active S-boxes is invariant under increasing ρ. In particular, any σ has $\sigma \sim \begin{pmatrix} 0 & 1 & \cdots & M-1 \end{pmatrix}$. Furthermore, assuming the existence of at least one MDS linear layer and the word length $m > \log_2(M+2)$, we have $\sigma \xrightarrow{M+1} k(M+1)^2$ over $4k$ rounds for all $k \in \mathbb{N}$.*

Proof. As for any $\rho > 1$, each row σ_t of a rotation matrix σ in normal form will equal $(0 \ 1 \ \cdots \ M-1)$, or any permutation hereof, this is equivalent to having $\rho = 1$ by Lemma 13. In order to prove the second statement, we first apply the Four-Round Propagation Theorem [12, Theorem 3] of the AES in a repeated manner, which provides the stated $k(M+1)^2$ as a lower bound. It is left to argue that there is a valid $4k$-round trail of weight $k(M+1)^2$ for some E_K using the specific parameters. Therefore, we first define a four-round trail X of weight $(M+1)^2$ as

$$
X := \left(\begin{pmatrix} 1 & 0 & \cdots & 0 \\ 0 & 0 & \cdots & 0 \\ \vdots & \vdots & \ddots & \vdots \\ 0 & 0 & \cdots & 0 \end{pmatrix}, \begin{pmatrix} 1 & 0 & \cdots & 0 \\ 0 & 1 & \cdots & 0 \\ \vdots & \vdots & \ddots & \vdots \\ 0 & 0 & \cdots & 1 \end{pmatrix}, \begin{pmatrix} 1 & 1 & \cdots & 1 \\ 1 & 1 & \cdots & 1 \\ \vdots & \vdots & \ddots & \vdots \\ 1 & 1 & \cdots & 1 \end{pmatrix}, \begin{pmatrix} 1 & 0 & \cdots & 0 \\ 0 & 0 & \cdots & 1 \\ \vdots & \vdots & \ddots & \vdots \\ 0 & 1 & \cdots & 0 \end{pmatrix}, \begin{pmatrix} 1 & 0 & \cdots & 0 \\ 0 & 0 & \cdots & 0 \\ \vdots & \vdots & \ddots & \vdots \\ 0 & 0 & \cdots & 0 \end{pmatrix} \right).
$$

By repeating this structure k times, one can define a $4k$-round trail of weight $k(M+1)^2$. For the validity of this trail for some E_K, one can see that it is obtainable by only using the identity as the S-box and existing mixing steps, applying Corollary 27 in Appendix A.   □

Theorem 21 implies that a designer who wants to improve upon the bound for a square dimension necessarily has to choose a rotation parameter σ consisting of at least one σ_t which breaks the normal form structure. Intuitively, this would not only provide a worse bound but also worse diffusion properties. However, giving an argument for the trail-optimality considering all possible rotation matrices (resp. permutations) seems to be quite difficult.

For the special case of a hypercubed geometry, we give Conjecture 22.

Conjecture 22. Given the state dimension $M \times M^n$ for an AES-like cipher, then a trail-optimal choice of the permutation sequence π over 2^{n+1} rounds yields $\pi \xrightarrow{M+1} (M+1)^{n+1}$.

The Superbox Argument. The superbox argument is a commonly used proof technique to lower bound on the number of active S-boxes in an AES-like cipher over a certain number of rounds. It has been used for the AES but also for ECHO [5] and PAEQ [8].

One uses the fact that for a clever choice of the rotation matrix, the round operations can be commuted such that some part of the encryption first works locally, in parallel, on parts of the state which we call *superboxes*. Next the superboxes are combined using state-wide operations which effectively mix the superboxes together, only to split the state into superboxes again, working with the localized operations. Such a large structure is referred to as a *megabox*, and covers four rounds of the cipher.

One can show that if a superbox has active input, there are at least B_θ active S-boxes in the first two rounds inside this superbox. Now, with the right choice of rotation matrix, the operation that combines the superboxes again imply that for the next two rounds, the total number of active superboxes is at least B_θ. From this, one obtains a four-round lower bound of B_θ^2.

This concept, which is the idea behind the Four-Round Propagation Theorem [12, Theorem 3], can be easily generalized by iteration for appropriate dimensions of state in the AES-like cipher, and with an appropriately chosen rotation matrix. We stress, however, that choosing the rotation matrix correctly for the given state dimension is of paramount importance to assuring the argument that one has e.g. B_θ active superboxes in a megabox (or equivalently for higher dimensions).

As mentioned, in Theorem 23, we give a construction which achieves the bound given in the conjecture above. Note that (especially for a cubed state dimension) this approach is not new in itself. Our main point here is that, in clear distinction to prior work such as [8], we present an efficient way of implementing this idea by using cyclic rotations only. For a better visualization, Example 24 illustrates this construction for $M = 4$ and $n = 3$.

Theorem 23 (2^{n+1}-Round Propagation Theorem). *There exists a rotation matrix $\sigma \in \mathbb{Z}_{M^n}^{2^n \times M}$, such that every (non-zero) valid 2^{n+1}-round trail over all $E_K \in \widehat{\text{AES}}_{M,M^n}(\sigma, B_\theta)$ has a weight of at least B_θ^{n+1}. The rotations can be described as*

$$\forall j \in \mathbb{Z}_n \quad : \sigma_{2^{n-j}-2} = \sigma_{2^{n-j}-1} = \begin{pmatrix} 0 & M^j & 2M^j & \cdots & (M-1)M^j \end{pmatrix}$$
$$\forall j \in \mathbb{Z}_{n-1} : \forall i \in \mathbb{Z}_{2^{n-(j+1)}} \quad \sigma_i = \sigma_{2^{n-j}-3-i}.$$

Proof. For $n = 1$, the statement is precisely the Four-Round Propagation Theorem of the AES. Therefore, we first prove the theorem for the eight-round case, thus for $n = 2$. We need to show that

$$\sigma := \begin{pmatrix} 0 & M & 2M & \cdots & (M-1)M \\ 0 & M & 2M & \cdots & (M-1)M \\ 0 & 1 & 2 & \cdots & M-1 \\ 0 & 1 & 2 & \cdots & M-1 \end{pmatrix} \xrightarrow{B_\theta} \mathcal{B}$$

over eight rounds for a $\mathcal{B} \geq B_\theta^3$. For the proof, we rely on a straightforward generalization of the Four-Round Propagation Theorem to the dimension one higher than the standard AES, as described previously. In particular, if one can partition the $M \times M^2$ state into M sub-states of M columns each (i.e. consider them as $M \times M$ sub-states), such that in four consecutive rounds, the ShiftRows operating in the first and second rounds shifts each such sub-state as if using the vector $(0\ 1\ \cdots\ M-1)$, with respect to considering that particular $M \times M$ sub-state, then the number of guaranteed active S-boxes in each such sub-state over four rounds it at least B_θ^2 (assuming a non-zero input difference). Note that the rotations of the third and fourth round have no impact on the four-round trail weight.

Fig. 1. Positions of the 4 independent sets of columns in a 4×16 state

Using the σ specified, the first four rounds of E_K satisfies this property when the M sub-states of size $M \times M$ are taken to be every Mth column of the state, as indicated for a 4×16 state in Figure 1. The same thing holds when considering the last four rounds separately.

Now, due to the way the row shifting of the third round combines with the column mixing and row shifting of the fourth round, i.e. $\mathsf{SR}_{\sigma_3} \circ \mathsf{MC} \circ \mathsf{SB} \circ \mathsf{SR}_{\sigma_2}$, each $M \times M$ sub-state mixes completely with each of the $M \times M$ sub-states. As such, like in the Four-Round Propagation Theorem, the sum of active $M \times M$ sub-states from the third and fourth round is at least B_θ. Combining this observation with the generalized Four-Round Propagation Theorem, the result of $B_\theta \cdot B_\theta^2$ follows.

The general case is now obtained by induction. In order to do the iteration to $2^{(n+1)+1}$ rounds, one has to apply the 2^{n+1}-round propagation.   □

Example 24. Let $M = 4$, $n = 3$ and $B_\theta = 5$. Then the state has geometry 4×64. The guaranteed trail weight of 625 over 16 rounds can be realized using the rotation matrix

$$
\sigma = \begin{pmatrix}
0 & 16 & 32 & 48 \\
0 & 16 & 32 & 48 \\
0 & 4 & 8 & 12 \\
0 & 4 & 8 & 12 \\
0 & 16 & 32 & 48 \\
0 & 16 & 32 & 48 \\
0 & 1 & 2 & 3 \\
0 & 1 & 2 & 3
\end{pmatrix}.
$$

We remark that especially for higher dimensions, a rotation matrix following this construction is not of much practical interest as the diffusion properties are far from optimal. One open question is whether it is possible to obtain these bounds without using a rotation matrix which allows a proof using a superbox-like argument for general M. For the special case of $M = 2$ and $N = 4$, we found that

$$
\sigma = \begin{pmatrix} 0\,0\,0\,0\,0\,0\,0\,0 \\ 1\,1\,1\,1\,1\,2\,1\,1 \end{pmatrix}^T,
$$

which contains no superbox structure, yields $\sigma \xrightarrow{3} 27$ over eight rounds.

7   Conclusion

For AES-like ciphers, the linear mixing layer, often denoted `MixColumns`, is very well understood: one typically chooses mixing layers defined by MDS matrices to obtain optimal branch numbers. In sharp contrast to this, no systematic approach has been conducted to understand how the word-wise permutation layer in such ciphers affects the diffusion properties and resistance towards differential- and linear attacks. With this work, we close that gap.

Specifically, we consider arbitrary word-wise permutations, with special focus on rotations due to their elegant implementation characteristics. We formalized the concept of AES-like ciphers, guaranteed trail weights and equivalence of permutation parameters and, using these formalizations, proved a range of results which reduces the consideration to a special normalized form.

These results are employed in practice by connecting it with mixed-integer linear programming models for determining the guaranteed trail weights. To that end, we give a range of optimal word-wise rotations and improve on existing parameters for Rijndael-192, Rijndael-256, PRIMATEs-80 and Prøst-128.

Using superbox-like arguments we are able, as a separate result, to show for specific state geometries that a seemingly optimal bound on the trail weight can be obtained using cyclic rotations only for the permutation layer, i.e. in a very implementation friendly way. Also coming out of our analysis is the observation that square state geometries are, in some sense, ideal when it comes to solving the problem of determining the best word-wise rotations, as there is just one solution which is optimal.

A   Optimality of the Black-Box Model

One has to make sure that the definition of the tightly guaranteed active S-boxes is independent of the concrete S-box functions within the AES-like ciphers. This is shown in Lemma 25.

Lemma 25. *Let* $\theta : (\mathbb{F}_2^m)^M \to (\mathbb{F}_2^m)^M$ *be a linear automorphism with branch number* B_θ. *Let* $v = (v_1, \ldots, v_M) \in (\mathbb{F}_2^m)^M \setminus \{0\}$ *such that* $\theta(v) = w = (w_1, \ldots, w_M)$. *Then for all* $a_1, \ldots, a_{2M} \in \mathbb{F}_2^m \setminus \{0\}$, *one can construct a linear automorphism* θ' *with branch number* B_θ *such that* $\theta'(a_1 v_1, \ldots, a_M v_M) = (a_{M+1} w_1, \ldots, a_{2M} w_M)$.

Proof. Let $G = [I \mid A]$ be the generator matrix in standard form of the linear $[2M, M, B_\theta]_m$-code C corresponding to θ. Now one can construct an equivalent code C' with the same minimal distance by multiplying every column of G by non-zero scalars $a_1, \ldots, a_{2M}$ [27, p. 54-55]. In order to obtain a generator matrix $G' = [I \mid A']$ of C' in standard form, one scales the rows by the non-zero values $a_1^{-1}, \ldots, a_M^{-1}$. This does not change the generated code and defines the new mixing $\theta'(x) = A'x$.

$$
\begin{array}{c}
\phantom{a_1^{-1}} \quad\;\; a_1 \;\; \cdots \;\; a_M \;\; a_{M+1} \;\; \cdots \;\; a_{2M} \\
\begin{array}{c} a_1^{-1} \\ \vdots \\ a_M^{-1} \end{array}
\left(
\begin{array}{cccc}
1 & & & \\
 & \ddots & & \quad A' \\
 & & 1 &
\end{array}
\right)
\end{array}
$$

If the matrix A was invertible, then A' is invertible as well since A' is obtained from A by scaling the rows and the columns.   □

In order to prove Theorem 16, one will make use of the following two results.

Lemma 26. *Let* $\log_2(M + 2) < m$ *and let* C *be a linear* $[2M, M]_m$-*code which is MDS. For every subset* $S \subseteq \{1, \ldots, 2M\}$ *with* $M + 1 \le |S| \le 2M$, *there exists a vector* $v = (v_1, \ldots, v_{2M}) \in C$ *such that* $v_i \ne 0$ *if and only if* $i \in S$.

Proof. Define two subsets $S_1, S_2 \subseteq S$ such that $|S_1| = |S_2| = M + 1$ and $S_1 \cup S_2 = S$. This is possible since $|S| \ge M + 1$. From [22, Theorem 4] it follows that there exists two vectors $v^{(1)} = (v_1^{(1)}, \ldots, v_{2M}^{(1)})$ and $v^{(2)} = (v_1^{(2)}, \ldots, v_{2M}^{(2)})$ in C such that $v_i^{(j)} \neq 0$ if and only if $i \in S_j$. Now, one can construct v as a linear combination $v := v^{(1)} + cv^{(2)}$ with $c \in \mathbb{F}_2^m$ as follows. Choose $c \neq 0$ such that for all non-zero components $v_i^{(1)}$ in $v^{(1)}$ the identity

$$c \cdot v_i^{(2)} \neq -v_i^{(1)}$$

holds. This is possible because of the field property of $\mathbb{F}_2^m$ and since $2^m > M + 2$. □

Thus, given a concrete MDS transformation (which has a sufficiently large dimension), every activity pattern which fulfils the branch number property can be be realized. By applying Lemma 25, one obtains as a corollary:

Table 2. Results for $M = 2, 3, 4, 5$

T	M	N	B ($\rho=1$)	σ ($\rho=1$)	B ($\rho=2$)	σ ($\rho=2$)	B ($\rho=3$)	σ ($\rho=3$)	M	N	B ($\rho=1$)	σ ($\rho=1$)	B ($\rho=2$)	σ ($\rho=2$)	B ($\rho=3$)	σ ($\rho=3$)
2	2	2	3	(0,1)	3	(0,1),(0,1)	3	(0,1),(0,1),(0,1)	4	4	5	(0,1,2,3)	5	(0,1,2,3),(0,1,2,3)	5	(0,1,2,3),(0,1,2,3),(0,1,2,3)
3			5	(0,1)	5	(0,1),(0,1)	5	(0,1),(0,1),(0,1)			9	(0,1,2,3)	9	(0,1,2,3),(0,1,2,3)	9	(0,1,2,3),(0,1,2,3),(0,1,2,3)
4			9	(0,1)	9	(0,1),(0,1)	9	(0,1),(0,1),(0,1)			25	(0,1,2,3)	25	(0,1,2,3),(0,1,2,3)	25	(0,1,2,3),(0,1,2,3),(0,1,2,3)
5			10	(0,1)	10	(0,1),(0,1)	10	(0,1),(0,1),(0,1)			26	(0,1,2,3)	26	(0,1,2,3),(0,1,2,3)	26	(0,1,2,3),(0,1,2,3),(0,1,2,3)
6			12	(0,1)	12	(0,1),(0,1)	12	(0,1),(0,1),(0,1)			30	(0,1,2,3)	30	(0,1,2,3),(0,1,2,3)	30	(0,1,2,3),(0,1,2,3),(0,1,2,3)
7			14	(0,1)	14	(0,1),(0,1)	14	(0,1),(0,1),(0,1)			34	(0,1,2,3)	34	(0,1,2,3),(0,1,2,3)	34	(0,1,2,3),(0,1,2,3),(0,1,2,3)
8			18	(0,1)	18	(0,1),(0,1)	18	(0,1),(0,1),(0,1)			50	(0,1,2,3)	50	(0,1,2,3),(0,1,2,3)	50	(0,1,2,3),(0,1,2,3),(0,1,2,3)
10			21	(0,1)	21	(0,1),(0,1)	21	(0,1),(0,1),(0,1)			55	(0,1,2,3)	55	(0,1,2,3),(0,1,2,3)	55	(0,1,2,3),(0,1,2,3),(0,1,2,3)
12			27	(0,1)	27	(0,1),(0,1)	27	(0,1),(0,1),(0,1)			75	(0,1,2,3)	75	(0,1,2,3),(0,1,2,3)	75	(0,1,2,3),(0,1,2,3),(0,1,2,3)
2	2	4	3	(0,1)	3	(0,1),(0,1)	3	(0,1),(0,1),(0,1)	4	6	5	(0,1,2,3)	5	(0,1,2,3),(0,1,2,3)	5	(0,1,2,3),(0,1,2,3),(0,1,2,3)
3			5	(0,1)	5	(0,1),(0,1)	5	(0,1),(0,1),(0,1)			9	(0,1,2,3)	9	(0,1,2,3),(0,1,2,3)	9	(0,1,2,3),(0,1,2,3),(0,1,2,3)
4			9	(0,1)	9	(0,1),(0,1)	9	(0,1),(0,1),(0,1)			25	(0,1,2,3)	25	(0,1,2,3),(0,1,2,3)	25	(0,1,2,3),(0,1,2,3),(0,1,2,3)
5			13	(0,1)	13	(0,1),(0,1)	13	(0,1),(0,1),(0,1)			34	(0,1,2,3)	36	(0,1,2,4),(0,1,2,4)	37	(0,1,2,3),(0,1,2,4),(0,1,3,4)
6			18	(0,1)	18	(0,1),(0,1)	18	(0,1),(0,1),(0,1)			45	(0,1,3,4)	45	(0,1,3,4),(0,1,3,4)	45	(0,1,3,4),(0,1,3,4),(0,1,3,4)
7			21	(0,1)	22	(0,1),(0,1)	21	(0,1),(0,1),(0,1)			48	(0,1,3,4)	48	(0,1,3,4),(0,1,3,4)	48	(0,1,2,3),(0,1,2,3),(0,1,3,4)
8			24	(0,1)	24	(0,1),(0,1)	24	(0,1),(0,1),(0,1)			57	(0,1,3,4)	57	(0,1,3,4),(0,1,3,4)	57	(0,1,3,4),(0,1,3,4),(0,1,3,4)
10			30	(0,1)	30	(0,1),(0,1)	30	(0,1),(0,1),(0,1)			72	(0,1,3,4)	73	(0,1,2,3),(0,1,2,4)	74	(0,1,2,3),(0,1,2,3),(0,1,3,4)
12			36	(0,1)	36	(0,1),(0,1)	36	(0,1),(0,1),(0,1)			90	(0,1,3,4)	90	(0,1,3,4),(0,1,3,4)	90	(0,1,3,4),(0,1,3,4),(0,1,3,4)
2	2	6	3	(0,1)	3	(0,1),(0,1)	3	(0,1),(0,1),(0,1)	4	8	5	(0,1,2,3)	5	(0,1,2,3),(0,1,2,3)		
3			5	(0,1)	5	(0,1),(0,1)	5	(0,1),(0,1),(0,1)			9	(0,1,2,3)	9	(0,1,2,3),(0,1,2,3)		
4			9	(0,1)	9	(0,1),(0,1)	9	(0,1),(0,1),(0,1)			25	(0,1,2,3)	25	(0,1,2,3),(0,1,2,3)		
5			13	(0,1)	13	(0,1),(0,1)	13	(0,1),(0,1),(0,1)			41	(0,1,2,4)	41	(0,1,2,3),(0,1,3,4)		
6			18	(0,1)	21	(0,1),(0,2)	21	(0,1),(0,2),(0,2)			50	(0,1,2,4)	55	(0,1,2,3),(0,1,3,5)		
7			21	(0,1)	30	(0,3),(0,3)	36	(0,3),(0,3),(0,3)			65	(0,1,2,4)	65	(0,1,2,3),(0,1,4,7)		
8			24	(0,1)	36	(0,3),(0,3)	36	(0,3),(0,3),(0,3)			85	(0,1,2,4)	90	(0,1,2,3),(0,2,3,5)		
10			30	(0,1)	39	(0,1),(0,2)	42	(0,1),(0,1),(0,2)			105	(0,1,2,4)	111	(0,1,2,3),(0,2,3,5)		
12			36	(0,1)	45	(0,1),(0,2)	48	(0,1),(0,1),(0,3)			120	(0,1,2,4)				
14																
2	2	8	3	(0,1)	3	(0,1),(0,1)	3	(0,1),(0,1),(0,1)	4	10	5	(0,1,2,3)	5	(0,1,2,3),(0,1,2,3)		
3			5	(0,1)	5	(0,1),(0,1)	5	(0,1),(0,1),(0,1)			9	(0,1,2,3)	9	(0,1,2,3),(0,1,2,3)		
4			9	(0,1)	9	(0,1),(0,1)	9	(0,1),(0,1),(0,1)			25	(0,1,2,3)	25	(0,1,2,3),(0,1,2,3)		
5			13	(0,1)	13	(0,1),(0,1)	13	(0,1),(0,1),(0,1)			41	(0,1,2,4)	41	(0,1,2,3),(0,1,3,4)		
6			18	(0,1)	21	(0,1),(0,2)	21	(0,1),(0,2),(0,2)			60	(0,1,2,4)	65	(0,1,2,3),(0,1,4,7)		
7			21	(0,1)	31	(0,5),(0,1)	34	(0,2),(0,1),(0,3)			70	(0,1,3,4)	72	(0,1,2,3),(0,1,4,7)		
8			24	(0,1)	39	(0,1),(0,3)	42	(0,1),(0,2),(0,3)			80	(0,1,3,4)	82	(0,1,5,6),(0,2,5,7)		
10			30	(0,1)	51	(0,1),(0,3)	54	(0,1),(0,3),(0,2)								
12			36	(0,1)	56	(0,1),(0,3)	60	(0,1),(0,2),(0,3)								
2	3	3	4	(0,1,2)	4	(0,1,2),(0,1,2)	4	(0,1,2),(0,1,2),(0,1,2)	4	12	5	(0,1,2,3)	5	(0,1,2,3),(0,1,2,3)		
3			7	(0,1,2)	7	(0,1,2),(0,1,2)	7	(0,1,2),(0,1,2),(0,1,2)			9	(0,1,2,4)	9	(0,1,2,3),(0,1,2,4)		
4			16	(0,1,2)	16	(0,1,2),(0,1,2)	16	(0,1,2),(0,1,2),(0,1,2)			25	(0,1,2,4)				
5			17	(0,1,2)	17	(0,1,2),(0,1,2)	17	(0,1,2),(0,1,2),(0,1,2)			41	(0,1,2,4)				
6			20	(0,1,2)	20	(0,1,2),(0,1,2)	20	(0,1,2),(0,1,2),(0,1,2)			65	(0,1,4,5)				
7			23	(0,1,2)	23	(0,1,2),(0,1,2)	23	(0,1,2),(0,1,2),(0,1,2)			76	(0,1,4,5)				
8			32	(0,1,2)	32	(0,1,2),(0,1,2)	32	(0,1,2),(0,1,2),(0,1,2)			92	(0,1,4,5)				
10			36	(0,1,2)	36	(0,1,2),(0,1,2)	36	(0,1,2),(0,1,2),(0,1,2)								
12			48	(0,1,2)	48	(0,1,2),(0,1,2)	48	(0,1,2),(0,1,2),(0,1,2)								
2	3	6	4	(0,1,2)	4	(0,1,2),(0,1,2)	4	(0,1,2),(0,1,2),(0,1,2)	4	16	5	(0,1,2,3)	5	(0,1,2,3),(0,1,2,3)		
3			7	(0,1,2)	7	(0,1,2),(0,1,2)	7	(0,1,2),(0,1,2),(0,1,2)			9	(0,1,2,3)	9	(0,1,2,3),(0,1,2,3)		
4			16	(0,1,2)	16	(0,1,2),(0,1,2)	16	(0,1,2),(0,1,2),(0,1,2)			25	(0,1,2,3)	25†	(0,1,2,3),(0,1,2,3)		
5			20	(0,1,2)	25	(0,1,2),(0,1,3)	25	(0,1,2),(0,1,3),(0,1,3)			41	(0,1,2,4)	41†	(0,1,2,3),(0,1,2,3)		
6			24	(0,1,2)	36	(0,1,3),(0,1,3)	36	(0,1,3),(0,1,3),(0,2,3)			75	(0,1,4,6)	90†	(0,4,10,14),(0,2,11,13)		
7			28	(0,1,2)	38	(0,1,3),(0,2,3)	40	(0,1,3),(0,2,3),(0,1,2)			100	(0,1,4,5)	111†	(0,1,2,3),(0,3,7,11)		
8			32	(0,1,2)	41	(0,1,3),(0,1,3)	44	(0,1,2),(0,1,3),(0,2,3)			120	(0,1,4,6)				
10			40	(0,1,2)	56	(0,1,3),(0,1,3)	56	(0,1,3),(0,1,3),(0,2,3)								
12			48	(0,1,2)	72	(0,1,3),(0,1,3)	72	(0,1,2),(0,1,3),(0,2,3)								
2	3	9	4	(0,1,2)	4	(0,1,2),(0,1,2)	4	(0,1,2),(0,1,2),(0,1,2)	4	32	5	(0,1,2,3)	5†	(0,1,2,3),(0,1,2,3)		
3			7	(0,1,2)	7	(0,1,2),(0,1,2)	7	(0,1,2),(0,1,2),(0,1,2)			9	(0,1,2,3)	9†	(0,1,2,3),(0,1,2,3)		
4			16	(0,1,2)	16	(0,1,2),(0,1,2)	16	(0,1,2),(0,1,2),(0,1,2)			25	(0,1,2,3)	25†	(0,1,2,3),(0,1,2,3)		
5			25	(0,1,3)	25	(0,1,2),(0,1,3)	25	(0,1,2),(0,1,3),(0,1,3)			41	(0,1,2,4)				
6			36	(0,1,3)	44	(0,1,2),(0,2,5)	44	(0,1,2),(0,2,4),(0,3,6)			75	(0,1,4,6)				
7			42	(0,1,3)	53	(0,1,2),(0,2,5)	55	(0,1,2),(0,2,4),(0,3,6)								
8			48	(0,1,3)	60	(0,1,2),(0,1,4)	60	(0,1,2),(0,1,2),(0,2,5)								
10			60	(0,1,3)	69	(0,1,2),(0,1,4)	72	(0,1,2),(0,1,3),(0,3,6)								
12			72	(0,1,3)	92	(0,1,2),(0,2,5)	93	(0,1,2),(0,2,4),(0,3,6)								
2	2								5	8	6	(0,1,2,3,4)	6	(0,1,2,3,4),(0,1,2,3,4)		
3											11	(0,1,2,3,4)	11	(0,1,2,3,4),(0,1,2,3,4)		
4											36	(0,1,2,3,4)	36	(0,1,2,3,4),(0,1,2,3,4)		
5											54	(0,1,2,3,5)	56	(0,1,2,3,4),(0,1,3,5,6)		
6											62	(0,1,2,3,5)	62	(0,1,2,3,4),(0,1,2,3,5)		
7											67	(0,1,2,3,5)	67	(0,1,2,3,4),(0,1,2,3,5)		
8											72	(0,1,2,3,4)	72	(0,1,2,3,4),(0,1,2,3,4)		
9													95	(0,1,2,3,4),(0,1,2,3,4)		
10											108	(0,1,2,3,7)				

Corollary 27. *Let* $\log_2(M+2) < m$ *and let* A *be an existing MDS matrix,* $A \in (\mathbb{F}_2^m)^{M \times M}$. *Then for all* $v, w \in (\mathbb{F}_2^m)^M$ *with* $\text{weight}(v) + \text{weight}(w) \geq M + 1$, *there exists an MDS matrix* $A' \in (\mathbb{F}_2^m)^{M \times M}$ *such that* $w = A'v$.

B   Search Results

This appendix provides the results from our search for optimal rotation matrices. For $\rho \in \{1, 2, 3\}$ and a wide range of dimensions $M \times N$, number of rounds T and *some* trail-optimal choice of σ, we give the number of active S-boxes it tightly guarantees, denoted $\mathcal{B}$. Note that for $\rho = 2$ with the 4×16 and 4×32 geometries, entries marked with † are results restricted to diffusion-optimal σ due to the complexity of the model. As such, the optimal bound w.r.t. trail weights may be even higher.

References

1. Andreeva, E., Bilgin, B., Bogdanov, A., Luykx, A., Mendel, F., Mennink, B., Mouha, N., Wang, Q., Yasuda, K.: PRIMATEs. CAESAR Proposal (2014). http://competitions.cr.yp.to/round1/primatesv1.pdf
2. Asratian, A.S., Denley, T.M.J., Häggkvist, R.: Bipartite Graphs and Their Applications. Cambridge Tracts in Mathematics. Cambridge University Press (1998)
3. Barreto, P.S.L.M., Rijmen, V.: The ANUBIS Block Cipher. NESSIE submission (2000). http://www.larc.usp.br/pbarreto/AnubisPage.html
4. Beierle, C., Jovanovic, P., Lauridsen, M.M., Leander, G., Rechberger, C.: Source code for experimental results (2015). https://github.com/mmeh/understanding-shiftrows
5. Benadjila, R., Billet, O., Gilbert, H., Macario-Rat, G., Peyrin, T., Robshaw, M., Seurin, Y.: SHA-3 Proposal: ECHO (2010). http://crypto.rd.francetelecom.com/ECHO/
6. Biham, E., Shamir, A.: Differential cryptanalysis of DES-like cryptosystems. In: Menezes, A., Vanstone, S.A. (eds.) CRYPTO 1990. LNCS, vol. 537, pp. 2–21. Springer, Heidelberg (1991)
7. Biham, E., Shamir, A.: Differential Cryptanalysis of the Data Encryption Standard. Springer (1993)
8. Biryukov, A., Khovratovich, D.: PAEQ. CAESAR Proposal (2014). http://competitions.cr.yp.to/round1/paeqv1.pdf
9. Borghoff, J., Canteaut, A., Güneysu, T., Kavun, E.B., Knezevic, M., Knudsen, L.R., Leander, G., Nikov, V., Paar, C., Rechberger, C., Rombouts, P., Thomsen, S.S., Yalçın, T.: PRINCE – a low-latency block cipher for pervasive computing applications. In: Wang, X., Sako, K. (eds.) ASIACRYPT 2012. LNCS, vol. 7658, pp. 208–225. Springer, Heidelberg (2012)
10. Daemen, J., Knudsen, L.R., Rijmen, V.: The block cipher SQUARE. In: Biham, E. (ed.) FSE 1997. LNCS, vol. 1267, pp. 149–165. Springer, Heidelberg (1997)
11. Daemen, J., Rijmen, V.: AES Proposal: Rjindael (1998). http://csrc.nist.gov/archive/aes/rijndael/Rijndael-ammended.pdf
12. Daemen, J., Rijmen, V.: The wide trail design strategy. In: Honary, B. (ed.) Cryptography and Coding 2001. LNCS, vol. 2260, p. 222. Springer, Heidelberg (2001)

13. Fleischmann, E., Forler, C., Gorski, M., Lucks, S.: TWISTER – a framework for secure and fast hash functions. In: Bao, F., Li, H., Wang, G. (eds.) ISPEC 2009. LNCS, vol. 5451, pp. 257–273. Springer, Heidelberg (2009)

14. Gauravaram, P., Knudsen, L.R., Matusiewicz, K., Mendel, F., Rechberger, C., Schläffer, M., Thomsen, S.S.: Grøstl - a SHA-3 Candidate (2011). http://www. groestl.info/

15. Guo, J., Peyrin, T., Poschmann, A.: The PHOTON family of lightweight hash functions. In: Rogaway, P. (ed.) Advances in Cryptology – CRYPTO 2011. LNCS, vol. 6841, pp. 222–239. Springer, Heidelberg (2011)

16. Guo, J., Peyrin, T., Poschmann, A., Robshaw, M.: The LED block cipher. In: Preneel, B., Takagi, T. (eds.) CHES 2011. LNCS, vol. 6917, pp. 326–341. Springer, Heidelberg (2011)

17. IBM. ILOG CPLEX Optimizer, 1997–2014. http://www-01.ibm.com/software/commerce/optimization/cplex-optimizer/

18. Indesteege, S., Andreeva, E., De Cannière, C., Dunkelman, O., Käper, E., Nikova, S., Preneel, B., Tischhauser, E.: The LANE hash function. Submission to NIST (2008). http://www.cosic.esat.kuleuven.be/publications/article-1181.pdf

19. Nakahara Jr., J.: 3D: a three-dimensional block cipher. In: Franklin, M.K., Hui, L.C.K., Wong, D.S. (eds.) CANS 2008. LNCS, vol. 5339, pp. 252–267. Springer, Heidelberg (2008)

20. Kavun, E.B., Lauridsen, M.M., Leander, G., Rechberger, C., Schwabe, P., Yalçn, T.: Prøst. CAESAR Proposal (2014). http://proest.compute.dtu.dk

21. Lim, C.H., Korkishko, T.: mCrypton – a lightweight block cipher for security of low-cost RFID tags and sensors. In: Song, J.-S., Kwon, T., Yung, M. (eds.) WISA 2005. LNCS, vol. 3786, pp. 243–258. Springer, Heidelberg (2006)

22. MacWilliams, F.J., Sloane, N.J.A.: The Theory of Error-Correcting Codes. North-Holland Publishing Company, 2nd edn. (1978)

23. Matsui, M.: Linear cryptanalysis method for DES cipher. In: Helleseth, T. (ed.) EUROCRYPT 1993. LNCS, vol. 765, pp. 386–397. Springer, Heidelberg (1994)

24. Mouha, N., Wang, Q., Gu, D., Preneel, B.: Differential and linear cryptanalysis using mixed-integer linear programming. In: Wu, C.-K., Yung, M., Lin, D. (eds.) Inscrypt 2011. LNCS, vol. 7537, pp. 57–76. Springer, Heidelberg (2012)

25. Markku-Juhani, O.: Saarinen. STRIBOBr 1. CAESAR Proposal (2014). http://competitions.cr.yp.to/round1/stribobr1.pdf

26. Shannon, C.: Communication Theory of Secrecy Systems. Bell System Technical Journal **28**, 656–715 (1949)

27. Dominic, J.A.: Welsh. Codes and cryptography. Clarendon Press (1988)

Improved Attacks on Reduced-Round Camellia-128/192/256

Xiaoyang Dong[1], Leibo Li[1], Keting Jia[2], and Xiaoyun Wang[1,3(✉)]

[1] Key Laboratory of Cryptologic Technology and Information Security,
Ministry of Education, Shandong University, Jinan, China
xiaoyunwang@tsinghua.edu.cn,
{dongxiaoyang,lileibo}@mail.sdu.edu.cn
[2] Department of Computer Science and Technology, Tsinghua University,
Beijing, China
ktjia@mail.tsinghua.edu.cn
[3] Institute for Advanced Study, Tsinghua University, Beijing, China

Abstract. Camellia is a widely used block cipher, which has been selected as an international standard by ISO/IEC. In this paper, we consider a new family of differentials of round-reduced Camellia-128 depending on different key subsets. There are totally 224 key subsets corresponding to 224 types of 8-round differentials, which cover a fraction of $1 - 1/2^{15}$ of the keyspace. And each type of 8-round differential consists of 2^{43} differentials. Combining with the multiple differential attack techniques, we give the key-dependent multiple differential attack on 10-round Camellia-128 with data complexity 2^{91} and time complexity 2^{113}. Furthermore, we propose a 7-round property for Camellia-192 and an 8-round property for Camellia-256, and then mount the meet-in-the-middle attacks on 12-round Camellia-192 and 13-round Camellia-256, with complexity of 2^{180} encryptions and $2^{232.7}$ encryptions, respectively. All these attacks start from the first round in a single key setting.

Keywords: Camellia · Block cipher · Key-dependent attack · Multiple differential attack · Meet-in-the-middle attack

1 Introduction

The block cipher Camellia with 128-bit block size has variable key lengths of 128, 192, 256, named as Camellia-128, Camellia-192 and Camellia-256, respectively. It was proposed by NTT and Mitsubishi in 2000 [2]. Now Camellia has become a widely used block cipher as an e-government recommended cipher by CRYPTREC [9]. Besides, Camellia was selected as one of NESSIE block cipher portfolio [26] and international standard by ISO/IEC 18033-3 [14]. Therefore, Camellia has received a great deal of attention from cryptanalysts with various

© Springer International Publishing Switzerland 2015
K. Nyberg (ed.): CT-RSA 2015, LNCS 9048, pp. 59–83, 2015.
DOI: 10.1007/978-3-319-16715-2_4

attack methods, including higher order differential attack [13], linear and differential attack [26], truncated differential attacks [15,18,27], collision attack [30], square attacks [19,20], impossible differential attacks [21–23,25,31], meet-in-the-middle attacks [8,24] and zero correlation cryptanalysis [5] etc.

An important property of Camellia is FL/FL^{-1} layers inserted every 6 rounds. The FL/FL^{-1} functions are key-dependent functions which provide non-regularity across rounds to resist the differential cryptanalysis. Many previous papers presented attacks on simplified versions of Camellia without the FL/FL^{-1} layers and the whitening layers [18,20,22,25,26,30,31]. For the original Camellia, impossible differential attacks on 10/11/12-round Camellia-128/192/256 were given in [21], and recently improved by Boura et al. in [6]. The Meet-in-the-Middle (MITM) attack on Camellia was firstly proposed by Lu et al. in [24], which introduced attacks on 10-round Camellia-128, 11-round Camellia-192 and 12-round Camellia-256 utilizing 5-round and 6-round higher-order MITM properties of Camellia. However this attack does not start from the first round and excludes the whitening layers. Chen et al. [8] attacked 12-round Camellia from the first round by applying the attack model for AES in [10] to construct a 7-round MITM property of Camellia. Besides, zero-correlation cryptanalysis with FFT method(ZC FFT) was applied to 11-round Camellia-128 and 12-round Camellia-192 in [5], which was slightly better than exhaustive search with almost the full codebook.

In this paper, we analyze *the original versions of Camellia with FL/FL^{-1} layers and whitening key starting from the first round* by two methods: key-dependent multiple differential attack and meet-in-the-middle attack. Multiple differential attack [4,29] uses multiple differentials to accumulate the advantage of many differentials as a distinguisher. The key-dependent differential attack was proposed by Ben-Aroya and Biham [3] to analyze Lucifer, which covered a fraction of 55% of the keyspace. A similar idea was also used by Knudsen and Rijmen to analyze DFC in [16]. Later, Sun and Lai proposed the key-dependent attack to analyze IDEA [28] by distinguishing the non-random distribution of the intermediate values for different key subsets, which composed the full keyspace.

Our Contributions. In this paper, we first consider the key-dependent multiple differential attack (KDMDA) on Camellia-128, by studying the multiple differentials corresponding to different key subsets. There are 224 types of 8-round differentials corresponding to different key subsets for Camellia, and each includes 2^{43} differentials. Each key subset contains a fraction of $1/4$ of the keyspace. All the 224 subsets cover a fraction of $1 - 1/2^{15}$ of the keyspace. Using these differentials, we launch the multiple differential attack on 10-round Camellia-128, which needs 2^{91} chosen plaintexts and $2^{104.5}$ encryptions, and succeeds on a fraction of about 99.99% of the keyspace. It is easy to extend this attack to the full keyspace by exhaustive search on the remaining fraction of $1/2^{15}$ of the keyspace. This is the first differential attack on Camellia with FL/FL^{-1} layers.

The key-dependent multiple differential attack is also possible against Camellia-192/256. In order to get better analysis results, we explore the meet-in-the-middle attack on Camellia-192/256. Combined with the differential enumeration technique and multiset proposed by Dunkelman et al. [12], other improved techniques proposed by Derbez et al. [11] and the relations of intermediate variables and subkeys, we propose a new 7-round property for Camellia-192 and an 8-round property of Camellia-256 to reduce the number of elements in a multiset. Based on both properties, we attack the 12-round Camellia-192 and 13-round Camellia-256 which costs 2^{113} chosen plaintexts, 2^{180} encryptions and 2^{154} 128-bit memories for Camellia-192, 2^{113} chosen plaintexts, $2^{232.7}$ encryptions and 2^{227} 128-bit memories for Camellia-256, respectively. However, we can not construct a good property for Camellia-128 since the complexity of the precomputation phase are larger than 2^{128} and it should be further explored.

In this paper, we only discuss the attacks on *Camellia with FL/FL^{-1} layers and whitening key starting from the first round*. Table 1 summarizes our results along with the major previous results, where CP and CC refer to the number of chosen plaintexts and chosen ciphertexts, respectively.

Table 1. Summary of the Attacks on Reduced-Round Camellia

Rounds	Percentage of Key Space	Attack Type	Data	Time	Memory	Source
Camellia-128						
10	100%	Impossible Diff	$2^{113.8}$CP	2^{120}Enc	$2^{86.4}$Bytes	[21]
10	99.99%	KDMDA	2^{91}CP	$2^{104.5}$Enc	2^{96}Bytes	Section 4.4
10	100%	KDMDA	2^{91}CP	2^{113}Enc	2^{96}Bytes	Section 4.4
11	100%	ZC FFT	$2^{125.3}$KP	$2^{124.8}$Enc	$2^{112.0}$Bytes	[5]
Camellia-192						
11	100%	Impossible Diff	$2^{113.7}$CP	2^{184}Enc	$2^{143.7}$Bytes	[21]
12	100%	ZC FFT	$2^{125.7}$KP	$2^{188.8}$Enc	2^{112}Bytes	[5]
12	100%	MITM	2^{113}CP	2^{180}Enc	2^{158}Bytes	Section 5.2
Camellia-256						
12	100%	Impossible Diff	$2^{114.8}$CP/CC	2^{240}Enc	$2^{151.8}$Bytes	[21]
12	100%	MITM	2^{19}CP	$2^{231.2}$Enc	2^{229} Bytes	[8]
13	100%	MITM	2^{113}CC	$2^{232.7}$Enc	2^{231}Bytes	Section 5.3

The rest of this paper is organized as follows. Section 2 gives some notations and a brief description of Camellia. Section 3 describes some observations of Camellia used in our cryptanalysis. In Section 4, we give the 8-round multiple differentials of Camellia for different key subsets, and present key-dependent multiple differential attack on 10-round Camellia-128. Section 5 illustrates the meet-in-the-middle attacks on 12/13-round Camellia-192/256. Finally, we conclude the paper in Section 6.

2   Preliminaries

In this section we give the notations used throughout this paper, and then briefly describe the block cipher Camellia.

2.1   Notations

The following notations are used in this paper:

L_{r-1}, L'_{r-1}	the left 64-bit half of the r-th round input
R_{r-1}, R'_{r-1}	the right 64-bit half of the r-th round input
X_r	the state after the key addition layer of the r-th round
Y_r	the state after the substitution transformation layer of the r-th round
Z_r	the state after the diffusion layer of the r-th round
k_r	the subkey used in the r-th round
kw_i	the whitening key used in the beginning and an the end of Camellia, $i = 1, 2, 3, 4$
$X[i]$	the i-th byte of a bit string X ($1 \leq i \leq 8$), where the left most byte is the first byte
X_L (X_R)	the left (right) half of a bit string X,
$X\{i\}$	the i-th most significant bit of a bit string X ($1 \leq i \leq 128$), where the left-most bit is the most significant bit
ΔX	the difference of X and X'
$\text{ham}(X)$	the hamming weight of X, for example, $X = 00100010$, $\text{ham}(X)=2$
$\text{zero}(X)$	the number of X's zero bits, for example, $X = 00100010$, $\text{zero}(X)=6$
$\oplus, \wedge, \vee$	bitwise exclusive OR (XOR), AND, OR
$\neg x$	bitwise inversion of bit string x, e.g. $\neg 0x22 = 0xdd$
$\cup$	the union of sets
$|A|$	the size of the set A
$x \| y$	bit string concatenation of x and y
$\lll l$	bit rotation to the left by l bit

2.2   Brief Description of Camellia

Camellia [2] is a Feistel structure block cipher, and the number of rounds are 18/24/24 for Camellia-128/192/256, respectively. The encryption procedure (depicted in Appendix C) for 128-bit key is as follows.

Firstly, a 128-bit plaintext M is XORed with the whitening key ($kw_1 \| kw_2$) and separated into L_0 and R_0 of equal length. Then, for $r = 1$ to 18, except for $r = 6$ and 12, the following is carried out:

$$L_r = R_{r-1} \oplus F(L_{r-1}, k_r), \quad R_r = L_{r-1}.$$

For $r = 6$ and 12, do the following:

$$L_r^* = R_{r-1} \oplus F(L_{r-1}, k_r), \quad R_r^* = L_{r-1},$$
$$L_r = FL(L_r^*, kf_{r/3-1}), \quad R_r = FL^{-1}(R_r^*, kf_{r/3}),$$

Lastly, the 128-bit ciphertext C is computed as: $C = (R_{18} \| L_{18}) \oplus (kw_3 \| kw_4)$.

For 192- and 256-bit keys, the 128-bit plaintext M is XORed with the whitening key $(kw_1 \| kw_2)$ and separated into L_0 and R_0 of equal length. Then, for $r = 1$ to 24, except for $r = 6, 12$ and 18, the following is carried out:

$$L_r = R_{r-1} \oplus F(L_{r-1}, k_r), \quad R_r = L_{r-1}.$$

For $r = 6, 12$ and 18, do the following:

$$L_r^* = R_{r-1} \oplus F(L_{r-1}, k_r), \quad R_r^* = L_{r-1},$$
$$L_r = FL(L_r^*, kf_{r/3-1}), \quad R_r = FL^{-1}(R_r^*, kf_{r/3}),$$

Lastly, the 128-bit ciphertext C is computed as: $C = (R_{24} \| L_{24}) \oplus (kw_3 \| kw_4)$.

The round function F is composed of a key-addition layer, a substitution transformation layer S and a diffusion layer P. The key-addition layer is an XOR operation of the left half input of the round function and the round key, i.e. $X_r = L_{r-1} \oplus k_r$ for the r-th round. There are four types of 8×8 S-boxes s_1, s_2, s_3 and s_4 in the S transformation layer. Let the input of the substitution transformation S of the r-th round be $X_r = (x_1, x_2, x_3, x_4, x_5, x_6, x_7, x_8)$, the output Y_r is computed as follows:

$$Y_r = S(X_r) = \big(s_1(x_1), s_2(x_2), s_3(x_3), s_4(x_4), s_2(x_5), s_3(x_6), s_4(x_7), s_1(x_8)\big).$$

The linear transformation P is a diffusion operation based on the bytes. Let the input of the transformation P in round r be $Y_r = (y_1, y_2, y_3, y_4, y_5, y_6, y_7, y_8)$, the output be $Z_r = (z_1, z_2, z_3, z_4, z_5, z_6, z_7, z_8)$. $Z_r = P(Y_r)$ and its inverse P^{-1} are defined as follows:

$$
\begin{aligned}
z_1 &= y_1 \oplus y_3 \oplus y_4 \oplus y_6 \oplus y_7 \oplus y_8 & y_1 &= z_2 \oplus z_3 \oplus z_4 \oplus z_6 \oplus z_7 \oplus z_8 \\
z_2 &= y_1 \oplus y_2 \oplus y_4 \oplus y_5 \oplus y_7 \oplus y_8 & y_2 &= z_1 \oplus z_3 \oplus z_4 \oplus z_5 \oplus z_7 \oplus z_8 \\
z_3 &= y_1 \oplus y_2 \oplus y_3 \oplus y_5 \oplus y_6 \oplus y_8 & y_3 &= z_1 \oplus z_2 \oplus z_4 \oplus z_5 \oplus z_6 \oplus z_8 \\
z_4 &= y_2 \oplus y_3 \oplus y_4 \oplus y_5 \oplus y_6 \oplus y_7 & y_4 &= z_1 \oplus z_2 \oplus z_3 \oplus z_5 \oplus z_6 \oplus z_7 \\
z_5 &= y_1 \oplus y_2 \oplus y_6 \oplus y_7 \oplus y_8 & y_5 &= z_1 \oplus z_2 \oplus z_5 \oplus z_7 \oplus z_8 \\
z_6 &= y_2 \oplus y_3 \oplus y_5 \oplus y_7 \oplus y_8 & y_6 &= z_2 \oplus z_3 \oplus z_5 \oplus z_6 \oplus z_8 \\
z_7 &= y_3 \oplus y_4 \oplus y_5 \oplus y_6 \oplus y_8 & y_7 &= z_3 \oplus z_4 \oplus z_5 \oplus z_6 \oplus z_7 \\
z_8 &= y_1 \oplus y_4 \oplus y_5 \oplus y_6 \oplus y_7 & y_8 &= z_1 \oplus z_4 \oplus z_6 \oplus z_7 \oplus z_8
\end{aligned}
$$

The FL function is used every 6 rounds. FL is defined as $(a_L \| a_R, kf_L \| kf_R) \mapsto (b_L \| b_R)$, where $a_L, a_R, kf_L, kf_R, b_L$ and b_R are 32-bit words.

$$b_R = ((a_L \wedge kf_L) \lll 1) \oplus a_R, \quad b_L = (b_R \vee kf_R) \oplus a_L.$$

In accordance with the notations in [1], let the master key of Camellia be K. The subkeys K_L, K_R are simply generated from K. For Camellia-128, $K_L = K$, $K_R = 0$. For Camellia-192, K_L is the left 128-bit of K, i.e., $K_L = K\{1 - 128\}$, and the concatenation of the right 64-bit of K and its complement is used as K_R, i.e., $K_R = K\{129 - 192\} \| \neg K\{129 - 192\}$. For Camellia-256, $K_L = K\{1 - 128\}$, and $K_R = K\{129 - 256\}$. Two 128-bit keys K_A and K_B are derived from K_L and K_R by a non-linear transformation. Then the whitening keys kw_i $(i = 1, ..., 4)$, round subkeys k_r $(r = 1, ..., 24)$ and kf_j $(j = 1, ..., 6)$ are generated by rotating K_L, K_R, K_A or K_B. For more details of Camellia, we refer to [1].

3   Some Observations of Camellia

This section introduces some observations which help us analyze the reduced-round Camellia.

Observation 1. ([17]) Let X, X', K be l-bit values, and $\Delta X = X \oplus X'$, then the differential properties of AND and OR operations are:

$$(X \wedge K) \oplus (X' \wedge K) = \Delta X \wedge K,$$
$$(X \vee K) \oplus (X' \vee K) = \Delta X \oplus (\Delta X \wedge K).$$

Observation 2. Given the input difference of the i-th round $\Delta L_i = (\alpha, 0, 0, 0, 0, 0, 0, 0)$, $\Delta R_i = (0, 0, 0, 0, 0, 0, 0, 0)$, the output difference of $(i+3)$-th round ΔR_{i+3} and intermediate difference ΔY_{i+2} satisfy the following equations:

$P^{-1}(\Delta R_{i+3})[4] = \Delta L_i[1] = \alpha$, $P^{-1}(\Delta R_{i+3})[j] = 0$, $j = 6, 7$
$P^{-1}(\Delta R_{i+3})[1] = \Delta Y_{i+2}[1]$, $P^{-1}(\Delta R_{i+3})[j] = \Delta Y_{i+2}[j] \oplus P^{-1}(\Delta R_{i+3})[4]$, $j = 2, 3, 5, 8$.

Observation 3. Given the output difference of the $(i + 2)$-th round $\Delta L_{i+2} = (0, 0, 0, 0, 0, 0, 0, 0)$, $\Delta R_{i+2} = (\alpha, 0, 0, 0, 0, 0, 0, 0)$, the input difference of i-th round ΔR_i and the intermediate difference ΔY_{i+1} satisfy the following equations:

$P^{-1}(\Delta R_i)[4] = \Delta R_{i+2}[1] = \alpha$, $P^{-1}(\Delta R_i)[j] = 0$, $j = 6, 7$
$P^{-1}(\Delta R_i)[1] = \Delta Y_{i+1}[1]$, $P^{-1}(\Delta R_i)[j] = \Delta Y_{i+1}[j] \oplus P^{-1}(\Delta R_i)[4]$, $j = 2, 3, 5, 8$.

Observation 4. Let the input difference of FL^{-1} be $(\Delta a_L, 0)$. Then the output difference of FL^{-1} must be $(\Delta a_L, 0)$, when $\Delta a_L \wedge kf_{2L} = 0$.

4   Key-Dependent Multiple Differential Attack on Reduced-Round Camellia-128

In this section, we present truncated differential based on the diffusion layer P for different key subsets. Then, 224 different types of 8-round multiple differentials for different key subsets are constructed. Finally, we launch the key-dependent multiple differential attack on 10-round Camellia-128.

4.1   Some Truncated Differentials

Observation 5. *Let the input difference of P be $(y_1, y_2, 0, 0, 0, 0, 0, 0)$,*

- *if $y_1 \neq y_2$, the output difference of P is $(y_1, y_1 \oplus y_2, y_1 \oplus y_2, y_2, y_1 \oplus y_2, y_2, 0, y_1)$.*
- *if $y_1 = y_2$, the output difference of P is $(y_1, 0, 0, y_2, 0, y_2, 0, y_1)$.*

Observation 6. *([27]) If the input difference of P is $(y_1, y_2, y_3, y_4, y_5, y_6, 0, y_8)$, then the output difference of P is $(z_1, z_2, 0, 0, 0, 0, 0, 0)$ with probability 2^{-40}. And the following equations hold: $y_1 = y_6, y_2 = y_8, y_3 = y_4 = y_5 = y_1 \oplus y_2$.*

Proof. By computing the inversion of P, we get $y_8 = z_1, y_6 = z_2, y_5 = z_1 \oplus z_2, y_4 = z_1 \oplus z_2, y_3 = z_1 \oplus z_2, y_2 = z_1, y_1 = z_2$. Then, $y_1 = y_6, y_2 = y_8, y_3 = y_4 = y_5 = y_1 \oplus y_2$.   □

Using the above observations, we construct the following 4-round truncated differential with probability 2^{-56},

$$(00000000, * * 000000) \xrightarrow[Pr=1]{Round} (* * 000000, 00000000) \xrightarrow[Pr=1]{Round} (* * * * * * * 0*, * * 000000)$$
$$\xrightarrow[Pr=2^{-40}]{Round} (* * 000000, * * * * * * 0*) \xrightarrow[Pr=2^{-16}]{Round} (00000000, * * 000000)$$

Similarly, we get another three 4-round truncated differentials with probability 2^{-56} in the last three columns of Table 2.

Table 2. 4-Round Truncated Differentials

Active S-boxes: $0 \to 2 \to 7 \to 2$			
Case-1	Case-2	Case-3	Case-4
$(00000000, * * 000000)$	$(00000000, 0 * *00000)$	$(00000000, *00 * 0000)$	$(00000000, 00 * *0000)$
$(* * 000000, 00000000)$	$(0 * *00000, 00000000)$	$(*00 * 0000, 00000000)$	$(00 * *0000, 00000000)$
$(* * * * * * * 0*, * * 000000)$	$(* * * * * * 0, 0 * *00000)$	$(* * * * *0 * *, *00 * 0000)$	$(* * * *0 * **, 00 * *0000)$
$(* * 000000, * * * * * * 0*)$	$(0 * *00000, * * * * * * * 0)$	$(*00 * 0000, * * * * *0 * *)$	$(00 * *0000, * * * *0 * **)$
$(00000000, * * 000000)$	$(00000000, 0 * *00000)$	$(00000000, *00 * 0000)$	$(00000000, 00 * *0000)$

4.2   Key Subsets Corresponding to Truncated Differentials

In this section, we extend the 4-round truncated differentials in Table 2 by adding a FL/FL^{-1} layer at the bottom. As a result, we divide the full keyspace into different subsets corresponding to different differentials.

We denote the two nonzero input byte differences of FL^{-1} function as c_1, c_2. Then we get four types of input differences of the FL^{-1} function, which are $(c_1, c_2, 0, 0, 0, 0, 0, 0)$, $(0, c_1, c_2, 0, 0, 0, 0, 0)$, $(c_1, 0, 0, c_2, 0, 0, 0, 0)$, $(0, 0, c_1, c_2, 0, 0, 0, 0)$. To reduce the diffusion of the active S-boxes, we make the input and the output differences of the FL^{-1} function equal, which determines a key subset according to Observation 4. Therefore, a value of (c_1, c_2) corresponds to a key subset. Obviously, the lower the hamming weight of (c_1, c_2) is, the larger the size of the corresponding key subset will be. In order to reduce the complexity, we choose (c_1, c_2) to make the size of key subset as large as possible. According to Observation 5, in order to maintain the 4-round truncated differential, c_1 should be different from c_2. So we choose 56 values of (c_1, c_2) where $\mathrm{ham}(c_1) = 1$, $\mathrm{ham}(c_2) = 1$, and $c_1 \neq c_2$, see Table 3. Combining with 4 truncated differentials, we construct 224 key subsets, which are denoted as $KDset_i^j$, $j = 1, 2, 3, 4$ and $i = 1, 2 \cdots 56$.

$$KDset_i^1 = \{K | kf_{2L} = (\neg c_1^i \wedge *, \neg c_2^i \wedge *, *, *), * \in F_2^8\},$$
$$KDset_i^2 = \{K | kf_{2L} = (*, \neg c_1^i \wedge *, \neg c_2^i \wedge *, *), * \in F_2^8\},$$
$$KDset_i^3 = \{K | kf_{2L} = (\neg c_1^i \wedge *, *, *, \neg c_2^i \wedge *), * \in F_2^8\},$$
$$KDset_i^4 = \{K | kf_{2L} = (*, *, \neg c_1^i \wedge *, \neg c_2^i \wedge *), * \in F_2^8\}.$$

In each key subset, two bits of kf_{2L} are 0, and the other bits traverse all values. The size of a key subset is 2^{126} for Camellia-128. We denote the union of all $KDset_i^j$ as $PKSPACE$.

$$PKSPACE = \bigcup_{j=1}^{4} \bigcup_{i=1}^{56} KDset_i^j$$

Table 3. 56 Different Values of (c_1, c_2) in Hexadecimal

i	(c_1^i, c_2^i)	i	(c_1^i, c_2^i)	i	(c_1^i, c_2^i)	i	(c_1^i, c_2^i)	i	(c_1^i, c_2^i)	i	(c_1^i, c_2^i)	i	(c_1^i, c_2^i)	i	(c_1^i, c_2^i)
1	01, 02	8	02, 01	15	04, 01	22	08, 01	29	10, 01	36	20, 01	43	40, 01	50	80, 01
2	01, 04	9	02, 04	16	04, 02	23	08, 02	30	10, 02	37	20, 02	44	40, 02	51	80, 02
3	01, 08	10	02, 08	17	04, 08	24	08, 04	31	10, 04	38	20, 04	45	40, 04	52	80, 04
4	01, 10	11	02, 10	18	04, 10	25	08, 10	32	10, 08	39	20, 08	46	40, 08	53	80, 08
5	01, 20	12	02, 20	19	04, 20	26	08, 20	33	10, 20	40	20, 10	47	40, 10	54	80, 10
6	01, 40	13	02, 40	20	04, 40	27	08, 40	34	10, 40	41	20, 40	48	40, 20	55	80, 20
7	01, 80	14	02, 80	21	04, 80	28	08, 80	35	10, 80	42	20, 80	49	40, 80	56	80, 40

We collect the keys that do not belong to any one of the $KDset_i^j$ to form the remaining key set denoted as $RKset$, which is consisted of two classes:

Class 1 The pattern of kf_{2L} is $(*, \neg 0, *, \neg 0)$ or $(\neg 0, *, \neg 0, *)$, where '*' is a random byte. There are $2 \times (2^8)^2 - 1 = 2^{17} - 1$ possible kf_{2L}.

Class 2 The remaining keys are not included in Class 1.
- If $\mathrm{zero}(kf_{2L})=2$, the number of possible kf_{2L} is $8 \times 4 = 48$.
- If $\mathrm{zero}(kf_{2L})=3$, the number of possible kf_{2L} is $8C_4^3 = 32$.

– If zero(kf_{2L})=4, the number of possible kf_{2L} is $8C_4^4 = 8$.
Totally, there are $48 + 32 + 8 = 88$ possible kf_{2L}.

So the size of remaining key set is $2^{96} \times (88 + 2^{17} - 1) \approx 2^{113}$.

The $PKSPACE$ and remaining key set $RKset$ form the full keyspace $KSPACE$:

$$KSPACE = \left(\bigcup_{j=1}^{4} \bigcup_{i=1}^{56} KDset_i^j \right) \bigcup RKset.$$

Let the input difference of FL^{-1} function be $(c_1, c_2, 0, 0)$, which corresponds a key subset $KDset_i^1$. Therefore, for the key subset $KDset_i^1$, the probability for 4-round truncated differential of the case-1 appending a FL/FL^{-1} layer with output difference $(00000000, c_1c_2000000)$ is $2^{-56} \times 2^{-16} = 2^{-72}$.

4.3 Searching 8-Round Multiple Differentials for Every Key Subset

We use 4-round truncated differentials in Table 2 to construct 8-round differentials with FL/FL^{-1} functions. We extend the 4-round truncated differential by adding two rounds forward and appending a FL/FL^{-1} layer and two rounds at the bottom to obtain 8-round differentials. We get four types of 8-round differential patterns, named as type-1/-2/-3/-4 which are constructed by case-1/-2/-3/-4, respectively.

Property 1. For each $KDset_i^j$, $i = 1, 2, \cdots, 56$, $j = 1, 2, 3, 4$, we construct a family of 8-round multiple differentials.

1. There are 2^{31} input differences and 2^6 output differences which produce $2^{31+6} = 2^{37}$ 8-round differentials with the probability 2^{-125}.
2. 2^{38} input differences and 2^6 output differences produce $2^{38+6} = 2^{44}$ 8-round differentials with probability 2^{-126}.
3. 2^{45} input differences and 2^6 output differences produce $2^{45+6} = 2^{51}$ 8-round differentials with probability 2^{-127}.

Proof. We prove the Property 1 by type-1 differential pattern illustrated in Fig. 1.

For the top two rounds, we apply the following 2-round differential

$$(\Delta L_0, \Delta R_0) \xrightarrow[Pr_1]{Round} (a_1a_2000000, \ h00h0h0h) \xrightarrow[Pr=2^{-14}]{Round} (00000000, \ a_1a_2000000),$$

where $\Delta L_0 = (h, 0, 0, h, 0, h, 0, h), \Delta R_0 = P(h_1, 0, 0, h_4, 0, h_6, 0, h_8) \oplus (a_1, a_2, 0, 0, 0, 0, 0, 0)$.

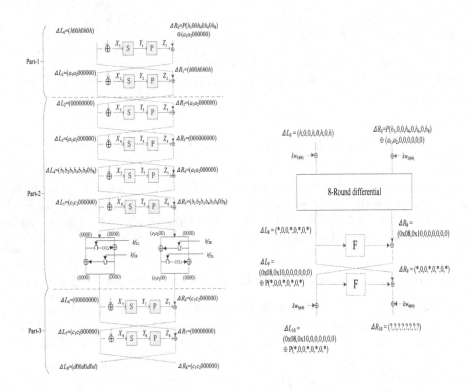

Fig. 1. Type-1: 8-Round Differential Pattern with FL/FL^{-1} Layer

Fig. 2. Multiple Differential Attack on 10-Round Camellia-128

By the 2-round differential, we know $\Delta Y_1 = (h_1, 0, 0, h_4, 0, h_6, 0, h_8)$, $\Delta Y_2 = (h, h, 0, 0, 0, 0, 0, 0)$. Obviously, there are $(2^8 - 1)$ ΔL_0. For each ΔL_0, there are $2^7 \times 2^7 = 2^{14}$ possible ΔL_1 with probability 2^{-14} as a result of two active S-boxes in round 2. Considering the 4 active S-boxes in the first round to compute Pr_1 and number of ΔY_1 values, there are $C_4^3 \cdot 2^7 = 2^9$ possible values of ΔY_1 with probability $2^{-6 \times 3} \times 2^{-7} = 2^{-25}$, $C_4^2 \cdot 2^{14} = 2^{16}$ possible values of ΔY_1 with probability $2^{-6 \times 2} \times 2^{-7 \times 2} = 2^{-26}$, $C_4^1 \cdot 2^{21} = 2^{23}$ possible values of ΔY_1 with probability $2^{-6} \times 2^{-7 \times 3} = 2^{-27}$, and 2^{28} possible values of ΔY_1 with probability 2^{-28}.

So, for the 2-round differential, there are $2^8 \times 2^9 \times 2^{14} = 2^{31}$ values of $(\Delta L_0, \Delta R_0)$ with probability $2^{-25} \times 2^{-14} = 2^{-39}$, $2^8 \times 2^{16} \times 2^{14} = 2^{38}$ values of $(\Delta L_0, \Delta R_0)$ with probability $2^{-26} \times 2^{-14} = 2^{-40}$, $2^8 \times 2^{23} \times 2^{14} = 2^{45}$ values of $(\Delta L_0, \Delta R_0)$ with probability $2^{-27} \times 2^{-14} = 2^{-41}$, and $2^8 \times 2^{28} \times 2^{14} = 2^{50}$ values of $(\Delta L_0, \Delta R_0)$ with probability $2^{-28} \times 2^{-14} = 2^{-42}$.

The last 2-round differential with the input difference $(00000000, c_1 c_2 000000)$ is

$$(00000000, \ c_1 c_2 000000) \xrightarrow[Pr=1]{Round} (c_1 c_2 000000, \ 00000000) \xrightarrow[Pr=2^{-14}]{Round} (d00d0d0d, \ c_1 c_2 000000).$$

There are about 2^6 ΔL_8. The probability of each $(\Delta L_7, \Delta R_7) \Rightarrow (\Delta L_8, \Delta R_8)$ is 2^{-13} or 2^{-14}.

Totally, there are 2^{31} input differences and 2^6 output differences which form $2^{31+6} = 2^{37}$ 8-round differentials, and the probability of each differential is $2^{-72-39-14} = 2^{-125}$; there are 2^{38} input differences and 2^6 output differences which form $2^{38+6} = 2^{44}$ 8-round differentials with probability $2^{-72-40-14} = 2^{-126}$; there are 2^{45} input differences and 2^6 output differences which form $2^{45+6} = 2^{51}$ 8-round differentials with probability $2^{-72-41-14} = 2^{-127}$.   □

Without loss of generality, we search type-1 differentials as an example to verify the correctness of Property 1 experimentally. The search procedure is as follows.

1. We exhaustively search differentials which match 4-round truncated differential with appending a FL/FL^{-1} layer depicted in Part-2 of Fig 1. Let $(00000000, a_1 a_2 000000)$ be input difference, and $(00000000, c_1 c_2 000000)$ be the input difference of the FL/FL^{-1} layer, where (c_1, c_2) is chosen in Table 3. Store the 4-round differential and its corresponding probability in a 56×2^{16} table, where "row" is indexed by (c_1, c_2), "column" is indexed by (a_1, a_2), and the elements are the corresponding probability Pr of the differential, which is calculated by the following equations. We denote $Y_4 = (a_1' a_2' 000000)$.

$$Pr_1 = Pr((a_1 a_2 000000) \xrightarrow{S} (a_1' a_2' 000000)), Pr_2 = Pr((c_1 c_2 000000) \xrightarrow{S} (a_1' a_2' 000000)),$$
$$Pr_3 = Pr(P(a_1', a_2', 0, 0, 0, 0, 0, 0) \xrightarrow{S} P^{-1}(a_1 \oplus c_1, a_2 \oplus c_2, 0, 0, 0, 0, 0, 0))$$
$$Pr = \sum_{a_1', a_2' \in F_2^8} Pr_1 \cdot Pr_2 \cdot Pr_3$$

2. For each row indexed by (c_1, c_2), calculate the output differences $(d_1 00 d_4 0 d_6 0 d_8, c_1 c_2 000000)$ of the 8-round differential, whose values form the output differences set, denoted as $\Delta OUTset$. And then for each column indexed by (a_1, a_2), collect the input differences of 8-round differential that could result in $(00000000, a_1 a_2 000000)$ differences after two rounds of encryption, to produce the input differences set, denoted as $\Delta INset$.

When $c_1 = 0x08$, $c_2 = 0x10$, we search type-1 differentials by PC, and obtain $|\Delta OUTset| = 57 \approx 2^6$. If the probability of each differential is larger than 2^{-125}, the $|\Delta INset|$ is $2^{31.1}$. If the probability of each differential is larger than 2^{-126}, the $|\Delta INset|$ is $2^{37.9}$. If the probability of each differential is larger than 2^{-127}, the $|\Delta INset|$ is $2^{44.8}$. Therefore, the experimental data reveals correctness of Property 1.

4.4 Key-Dependent Multiple Differential Attack on 10-Round Camellia-128

For every $KDset_i^j$, $i = 1, 2 \cdots 56$, $j = 1, 2, 3, 4$, we choose 2^{37} input differences from $\Delta INset$ where the probabilities are all larger than 2^{-126} and pick all the 2^6 output differences of $\Delta OUTset$. We launch multiple differential attack using these differentials. We repeat 224 times multiple differential attacks, if one of the attacks succeeds, the right key can be recovered. Otherwise the right key belongs to $RKset$. The following is one of the 224 attacks.

We choose type-1 differentials and $c_1 = 0x08$ $c_2 = 0x10$ to launch an attack, whose corresponding key subset is $KDset_{32}^1$. As the Fig. 2 shows, we add two rounds after the 8-round differentials distinguisher to analyse 10-round Camellia-128.

In [4], there is a strong condition that the set of input differences are "admissible". However, paper [29] proves the condition is not necessary when applying structure technique. Here, we take advantage of the structure attack model to implement multiple differential attack displayed as follows:

1. Choose 2^x structures of plaintexts, and each structure contains 2^{56} plaintexts with $L_0 = (\alpha_1, x_1, x_2, \alpha_1, x_3, \alpha_1, x_4, \alpha_1)$, $R_0 = P(\alpha_2, x_5, x_6, \alpha_3, x_7, \alpha_4, x_8, \alpha_5) \oplus (\alpha_6, \alpha_7, x_9, x_{10}, x_{11}, x_{12}, x_{13}, x_{14})$, where x_i are fixed values and α_j take all the possible values in each structure.
2. For each structure, ask for the encryptions of the plaintexts P and store the 2^{56} ciphertexts C, indexed by $P^{-1}(C_L)[1, 4, 6, 8]$. When choosing one ciphertext indexed by $P^{-1}(C_L)[1, 4, 6, 8]$ and another ciphertext indexed by $P^{-1}(C_L)[1, 4, 6, 8] \oplus P^{-1}(0x08, 0x10, 0, 0, 0, 0, 0, 0,)[1, 4, 6, 8]$, we get a pair whose difference matches ΔL_{10}. Totally, we get 2^{79+x} pairs.
3. For each pair, check whether the input difference is one of the 2^{37} input differences. There are about $2^{79+x} \times 2^{37} \times 2^{-56} = 2^{60+x}$ pairs left.
4. For each pair and each possible ΔR_9, where $|\Delta R_9| = |\Delta OUTset| = 2^6$, do the following substeps.
   (a) In the 10th round, we know the input difference and output difference of the F function, so we deduce 64-bit key $kw_3 \oplus k_{10}$ by the difference distribution table of S-boxes.
   (b) We calculate the output value of the F function in 10th round by the values of $kw_3 \oplus k_{10}$. In the 9th round, deduce 32-bit key $(kw_4 \oplus k_9)[1, 4, 6, 8]$ by the difference distribution table of S-boxes.
   (c) Increase the corresponding counter of 96-bit subkey $kw_3 \oplus k_{10}, (kw_4 \oplus k_9)[1, 4, 6, 8]$, and then we obtain 2^6 subkeys for every pair.
5. Check all counters and generate a list L of the l candidate subkeys whose counters are the highest l values.

We choose $x = 33$, then there are $2^{111+33} \times 2^{37-56} = 2^{125}$ pairs, and each matches one of the 2^{37} input differences. The counter expectation for right key is $2^{125} \times 2^6 \times 2^{-126} = 2^5$, and the expectation of the counter for wrong key is about $2^{125} \times 2^6 \times 2^{-128} = 2^3$. We use the Blondeau et al.'s method [4] to compute the success rate. We know the number of differentials is $|\Delta| = 2^{37} \times 2^6 = 2^{43}$, the sum of the probability of all differentials is $\sum_{i=1}^{|\Delta|} Pr_i = 2^{-83}$, the number of pairs is $N_s = 2^{125}$, the bit number of guessed subkey is $n_k = 96$, and $l = 2^{40}$, then the success probability is:

$$Ps \approx 1 - G_*[G^{-1}(1 - \frac{l-1}{2^{n_k} - 2}) - 1] = 99.9\%,$$

where the definitions of functions $G_*()$ and $G^{-1}()$ refer to Appendix B.

Key-Dependent Multiple Differential Attack on the $PKSPACE$. If the key belongs to the $PKSPACE$, obviously this happens with significantly high probability of $1 - \frac{1}{2^{15}} \approx 99.99\%$, then 224 multiple differential attacks can recover the key. For a particular j of $KDset_i^j, i = 1, 2, \cdots 56$, the 56 multiple differential attacks use the differentials which have the common input truncated difference, the structures can be shared in the 56 times multiple differential attacks. So the data complexity of the attack is about $2^{56+33} \times 4 = 2^{91}$ chosen plaintexts. The time complexity is $2^{93+6} \times \frac{2}{10} \times 224 = 2^{104.5}$ 10-round encryptions. The memory complexity is 2^{96} which is used to store the counters for each of the 224 multiple differential attacks.

Key-Dependent Multiple Differential Attack on the Full $KSPACE$. For each one of $KDset_i^j$, $i = 1, 2 \cdots, 56$, $j = 1, 2, 3, 4$, we launch the above multiple differential attack. If one of the attack succeeds, the right key will be recovered; if all fail, we exhaustively search all the subkeys in the $RKset$.

Success Rate. If the correct key belongs to the remaining keyspace, then we will definitely recover the key when traversing the remaining keyspace. If the correct key does not belong to the remaining keyspace, then one of the 224 multiple differential attacks recovers the correct key with the probability of Ps. So the success rate of the is the minimum of 224 Ps, which is about 99.9%.

Complexity Analysis. The data complexity of the attack is about $2^{56+33} \times 4 = 2^{91}$ chosen plaintexts. The whole attack procedure includes 224 multiple differential attacks and traversing the remaining key set. The time complexity is $2^{60+33+6} \times \frac{2}{10} \times 224 + 2^{113} = 2^{104.5} + 2^{113} \approx 2^{113}$. The memory complexity is 2^{96} which is used to store the counters for each of the 224 multiple differential attacks.

The key-dependent multiple differential attack is also available to 11-round Camellia-192 and 12-round Camellia-256. However, we find that it is more efficient for the meet-in-the-middle attack on Camellia-192/256.

5   MITM Attacks on Reduced-Round Camellia-192/256

In this section, we first present a brief description of meet-in-the-middle attack, and then give the meet-in-the-middle attack on reduced-round Camellia combining with multiset, the differential enumeration technique, the relations of intermediate variables and subkeys etc.

5.1 Description of Meet-in-the-Middle Attack

For the meet-in-the-middle attack, the encryption cipher E_K is divided into three parts $E_K = E_{K_2}^2 \circ E^m \circ E_{K_1}^1$, and there exists a specific property for the middle part E^m, which is used to construct a distinguisher and identify the correct key (K_1, K_2). The meet-in-the-middle methods we applied are similar to the MITM attaks on AES [11,12]. Therefore we introduce some definitions of $\delta-$set and multiset.

Definition 1. ($\delta-$set) *The $\delta-$set is a set of 256 intermediate states of Camellia that one byte traverses all values (the active byte) and the other bytes are constants (the inactive bytes).*

Definition 2. (Multiset of bytes [12]) *A multiset generalizes the set concept by allowing elements to appear more than once. Here, a multiset of 256 bytes can take as many as $\binom{511}{255} \approx 2^{506.7}$ different values.*

We explain the multiset with more details. Let a $\delta-$set $(X^0, \cdots, X^{255})$ be the inputs of E_m, where the j-th byte is a variable and the other bytes are kept constant. Let the i-th output byte of E_m be the output of the function. The outputs of function with the δ-set as inputs form a 2048-bit vector $E_K(X^0)[i] \| \cdots \| E_K(X^{255})[i]$ with ordered arrangement. However, if we don't consider the ordering of the output bytes, the 256-byte value will form a multiset $[E_K(X^0)[i] \oplus E_K(X^0)[i], E_K(X^0)[i] \oplus E_K(X^1)[i], \cdots, E_K(X^0)[i] \oplus E_K(X^{255})[i]]$. However, given two random functions $f, g: \mathbb{F}_{256} \to \mathbb{F}_{256}$, the multisets $(f(X^0), \cdots, f(X^{255}))$ and $(g(X^0), \cdots, g(X^{255}))$ are equal with a probability smaller than $2^{-467.6}$ (but not $2^{-506.17}$). For more details, we refer to [11].

The key part of the meet-in-the-middle attack on AES is to construct a function for the input active byte and one of the output bytes of E_m, and reduce the number of the function parameters by specific truncated differential, which decides the size of the multiset. Based on the subcipher E_m, a few rounds is extended at the top and bottom of E_m, i.e. the cipher $E_K = E_{K_2}^2 \circ E^m \circ E_{K_1}^1$. The attack procedure is described in Algorithm 1.

It is noticed that the number of values for a good multiset is much less than $2^{467.6}$. The precomputation phase is to compute all the values of multiset in a table.

5.2 MITM Attack on 12-Round Camellia-192

This section introduces a 7-round property starting from the third round and ending at the ninth round which is described in Property 2 outlined in Fig. 3.

Algorithm 1. The Main Procedure of Meet-in-the-Middle Attack

Precomputation phase: compute all values of the output sequence of the function constructed on E_m, and store them in a hash table.

Online phase:

1: Encrypt enough chosen plaintexts such that there exists a pair satisfying the specific differential.
2: Guess values of the subkeys K_1 and K_2 to find a pair satisfying the specific truncated differential.
3: Construct a δ-set based on the pair, and partially decrypt to get the corresponding 256 plaintexts.
4: Obtain the corresponding 256 plaintext-ciphertext pairs from the collected data. Then partially decrypt the ciphertexts to get the corresponding 256-byte value of the output sequence of E_m.
5: If a sequence value lies in the precomputation table, the guessed K_1 and K_2 may be right key.
6: Exhaustively search the remaining subkeys to obtain the right key.

The active byte of δ−set is defined at the first byte of the input of the third round $R_2[1]$.

Property 2. Encrypt 2^8 values of the δ−set through 7-round Camellia-192 starting from the third round, where $R_2[1]$ is the active byte, in the case that a pair of the δ−set conforms to the truncated differential outlined in Fig 3, then the corresponding multiset of bytes $(P^{-1}(\Delta L_8))[6]$ only takes about 2^{128} instead of $2^{467.6}$ values on average.

It is obvious that, the computation of the multiset of bytes $(P^{-1}(\Delta L_8))[6]$ associated with a δ−set is determined by a 36-byte intermediate variable

$$X_4[1]\|X_5[1,2,3,5,8]\|X_6\|kf_1\|kf_2\|X_7[2,3,5,7,8]\|X_8[6].$$

The main work is to prove that there are only 16 byte variables needed to compute the multiset.

Proof. If a pair of the δ-set conforms the truncated differential as in Fig. 3, the 18-byte variable $X_4[1]\|X_5[1,2,3,5,8]\|X_6\|X_7[2,3,5,8]$ is determined by the 9-byte difference $\Delta X_4[1]\|\Delta Y_4[1]\|\Delta Y_5[1,2,3,5,8]\|\Delta X_8[1]\|\Delta Y_8[1]$ and 128-bit sub-key $kf_1\|kf_2$. Here, the value $X_4[1]$ is deduced from the differences $\Delta X_4[1]$ and $\Delta Y_4[1]$. Similarly, the value $X_5[1,2,3,5,8]$ is obtained by the differences $\Delta Y_4[1], \Delta Y_5[1,2,3,5,8]$. In the backward direction, the difference ΔY_6 is computed by $\Delta Y_4[1], \Delta Y_8[1]$ and kf_1 since $\Delta L_4 = P(\Delta Y_4)$ and $\Delta L_6 = P(\Delta Y_8)$ in this case. The difference ΔX_6 is computed by $\Delta X_4[1], \Delta Y_5[1,2,3,5,8]$, which is used to deduce the value X_6. Similarly, the difference ΔY_7 is computed by

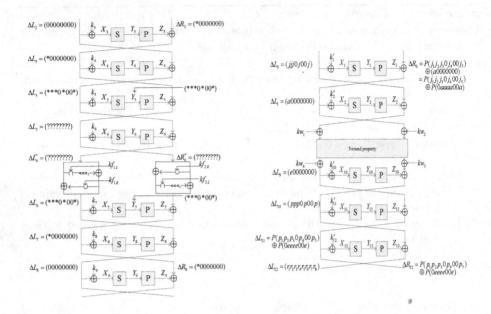

Fig. 3. The Truncated Differential of 7-round Camellia-192

Fig. 4. The MITM Attack on 12-round Camellia-192

the difference $\Delta X_4[1]$, $\Delta Y_5[1,2,3,5,8]$, $\Delta X_8[1]$ and kf_2, which helps us deduce $X_7[2,3,5,8]$ owing to $\Delta X_7 = P(\Delta Y_8)$.

Since $kf_1 \| kf_2$ has only 64-bit information by key schedule, the total 36-byte variable is computed by 19-byte variable $\Delta X_4[1] \| \Delta Y_4[1] \| \Delta Y_5[1,2,3,5,8] \| \Delta X_8[1] \| \Delta Y_8[1] \| X_7[7] \| X_8[6] \| kf_1$ in such case.

However, for every 19-byte variable, we find that the difference ΔY_7 equals to $P^{-1}(FL^{-1}(P(\Delta Y_5) \oplus \Delta L_3)) \oplus P^{-1}(\Delta L_7)$, where the probability that $\Delta Y_7[4,6,7]$ equals to 0 is 2^{-24}. So there are only about 2^{128} possible values for 36-byte intermediate variable, actually. $\square$

Based on the 7-round property, we extend two rounds on the top and three rounds on the bottom to attack the 12-round Camellia-192, see Fig.4. To reduce the computation complexity of the 12-round attack on Camellia-192, we retrieve the equivalent keys k'_1, k'_2, k'_{10}, k'_{11}, k'_{12}, and then deduce the master key. The equivalent keys are defined as $k'_1 = k_1 \oplus kw_1$, $k'_2 = k_2 \oplus kw_2$, $k'_{12} = k_{12} \oplus kw_4$, $k'_{11} = k_{11} \oplus kw_3$, and $k'_{10} = k_{10} \oplus kw_4$. Note that the master key could be deduced by the equivalent key using the method introduced in [7].

The key recovery is also composed of two phases: precomputation phase and online phase. In the precomputation phase, we get 2^{128} possible values of multiset as described in Property 2, and store them in a hash table $\mathcal{H}$. The attack procedure of the online phase is similar to Algorithm 1. However we take a balance of the time complexity of Step 2 and Step 3. We guess some related subkeys to find the possible pairs which may satisfy the truncated differential, and then construct the $\delta-$set to get their plaintexts.

The attack procedure of online phase is described as follows.

1. Choose 2^{57} structures of plaintexts, and each structure contains 2^{56} plaintexts that satisfy $L_0 = (\alpha, \alpha \oplus x_1, \alpha \oplus x_2, x_3, \alpha \oplus x_4, x_5, x_6, \alpha \oplus x_7)$, $R_0 = P(\beta_1, \beta_2, \beta_3, \beta_4, \beta_5, y_1, y_2, \beta_6)$, where $x_i(i = 1, ..., 7)$, y_1 and y_2 are constants, but α, β_j $(j = 1, ..., 6)$ take all possible values. Ask for corresponding ciphertexts for each structure, compute $P^{-1}(R_{12})$ and store the plaintext-ciphertext pairs $L_0 \| R_0 \| L_{12} \| R_{12}$ in a hash table indexed by 16-bit value $(P^{-1}(R_{12}))[6, 7]$. Hence, there are $2^{57} \times 2^{111} \times 2^{-16} = 2^{152}$ pairs whose differences satisfy $P^{-1}(\Delta R_{12})[6, 7] = 0$ on average.

2. For every pair, do the following substeps to find a pair with corresponding subkeys conforming the truncated differential.

   (a) For $l = 2, 3, 4, 5, 6, 7, 8$, guess the 8-bit value of $k'_{12}[l]$ one by one. Partially decrypt the ciphertext $R_{12}[l]$ and keep only the pairs which satisfy $\Delta Y_{12}[l] = P^{-1}(\Delta L_{12}[l])$. The expected number of pairs left is about $2^{152} \times 2^{7 \times (-8)} = 2^{96}$. After that guess $k'_{12}[1]$, partially decrypt the remaining pairs to get the value L_{10}.

   (b) For $l = 2, 3, 5, 8$, guess the 8-bit value of $k'_{11}[l]$. Compute the intermediate value $Y_{11}[l]$ and eliminate the pairs whose intermediate values do not satisfy $\Delta Y_{11}[l] = P^{-1}(\Delta R_{12})[l] \oplus P^{-1}(\Delta R_{12})[4]$(see Observation 2). Then guess $k'_{11}[1]$ and keep the pairs making $\Delta Y_{11}[1] = P^{-1}(\Delta R_{12})[1]$ hold. The expected number of remaining pairs is $2^{96} \times 2^{-40} = 2^{56}$.

   (c) Similarly, for $l = 1, 2, 3, 5, 8$, guess $k'_1[l]$ and discard the pairs which do not make the equations $\Delta Y_1[1] = P^{-1}(\Delta R_0)[1]$ and $\Delta Y_1[l] = P^{-1}(\Delta R_0)[l] \oplus P^{-1}(\Delta R_0)[4]$(see Observation 3) hold for $l = 2, 3, 5, 8$. Then the expected number of remaining pairs is $2^{56} \times 2^{-40} = 2^{16}$.

3. For the 2^{16} remaining pairs, if we want to find the pair in content with the 7-round truncated differential, we have to guess 64-bit equivalent key $k'_1[4, 6, 7] \| k'_2[1] \| k'_{11}[4, 6, 7] \| k'_{10}[1]$ under each 144-bit subkey guess. Obviously, it is infeasible, since the time complexity is greater than exhaustively searching in such case. However, there are about a pair satisfying the truncated differential, for the probability of the truncated differential occuring is about 2^{-16} for the remaining pairs. Therefore we construct the $\delta-$set for all 2^{16} pairs. If the guessed 144-bit key information is correct, then there should exist a pair to conform the truncated differential, and the corresponding value of the multiset should exist in the table $\mathcal{H}$. We construct a $\delta-$set for every remaining pair under 144-bit key guesses in the following.

(a) According to the differences $\Delta L_0[1]$ and $P^{-1}(\Delta R_0)[4]$, deduce the intermediate value $X_2[1]\|Y_2[1]$ of the pair by the difference distribution table of S-box s_1.

(b) For the pair $(L_0\|R_0, L_0'\|R_0')$ corresponding to $(X_2[1], X_2'[1])$, change the value $X_2'[1]$ to a different value $X_2''[1]$, compute $\Delta Y_2'[1] = s_1(X_2''[1]) \oplus s_1(X_2[1])$, and get the difference $\Delta L_0'[1, 2, 3, 5, 8]$. Then get the left half of the plaintext $L_0'' = L_0 \oplus \Delta L_0'$.

(c) Compute the difference $\Delta Y_1'[1, 2, 3, 5, 8]$ by the guessed subkey $k_1'[1, 2, 3, 5, 8]$. Then obtain the difference $\Delta R_0'$ and get the right half part $R_0'' = R_0 \oplus \Delta R_0'$. Here we get a new plaintext (L_0'', R_0'') of the $\delta-$set.

(d) Compute all left 253 values of $X_2[1]$ to obtain all plaintexts of the $\delta-$set, and identify the corresponding ciphertexts.

4. For each $\delta-$set under 144-bit key guesses, compute the intermediate value $Y_{11}[2, 3, 5, 8]$, $P^{-1}(L_{10})[6]$ for every plaintext-ciphertext pairs by above guessed subkey. Guess 8-bit key $k_{11}'[7]$ to compute the value $X_{10}[6]$.

5. Guess 8-bit key $k_{10}'[6]$ to compute the multiset of byte $(P^{-1}(\Delta L_8))[6] = \Delta Y_{10}[6] \oplus P^{-1}(\Delta L_{10})[6]$. Detect whether it belongs to $\mathcal{H}$. Here, we need to detect 2^{16} values of multiset for every 160-bit guessed key. Then find the correct subkey if one of 2^{16} values belongs to $\mathcal{H}$. Note that the probability that a wrong value of multiset could pass the check is about $2^{128} \times 2^{-467.6} = 2^{-339.6}$.

6. Compute the related part of the master key by the equivalent keys k_1', k_2', k_{10}', k_{11}', k_{12}', and search the unknown part.

Complexity Analysis. The precomputation phase needs about $2^{128} \times 2^8$ computations and 2^{130} 128-bit memories. Step 1 needs about 2^{113} encryptions. We also need 2^{113} 128-bit memories to store all plaintext-ciphertext pairs. The complexity of step 2 is dominated by substep 2.(c), which needs about 2^{168} computations. Step 3 needs about 2^{168} simple computations to construct 2^{16} δ-for every 144-bit key guess. Step 4 needs about $2^{160} \times 2^8 \times 2^8 \times 2^{-3} = 2^{173}$ 12-round encryptions. The time complexity of step 5 is equivalent to $2^{176} \times 2^8 \times 2^{-4} = 2^{180}$ 12-round encryptions. In total, the time complexity of the attack is about 2^{180} encryptions, the data complexity is about 2^{113} chosen plaintexts, the memory complexity is about 2^{130} 128-bit.

5.3   The Attack on 13-Round Camellia-256

This section introduces an 8-round property of Camellia-256, which starts from the fifth round and ends at the twelfth round introduced by Property 3. The truncated differential used in this section is outlined in Fig. 5 of Appendix A, the active byte of the $\delta-$set is located at $L_{12}'[5]$, and the corresponding byte of multiset is defined as $P^{-1}(\Delta L_4)[1]$.

Property 3. Decrypt 2^8 values of the δ-set through 8-round Camellia-256 starting from the 12-th round, where $L_{12}[5]$ is the active byte, in the case that a pair of the δ-set conforms to the 8-round truncated differential outlined in Fig 5 of Appendix A, then the corresponding multiset of bytes $(P^{-1}(\Delta L_4))[1]$ only takes about 2^{225} instead of $2^{467.6}$ values on average.

The sketch of Property 3 is similar to Property 2, we give the proof in Appendix A.

We mount a 13-round attack on Camellia-256 by adding four rounds in the forward and one round in the backward of the 8-round Camellia (see Fig. 6 in Appendix A). We also recover the equivalent keys k_1', k_2', k_3', k_4', k_{13}', and then deduce the master key, where the equivalent keys are defined as $k_1' = k_1 \oplus kw_1$, $k_2' = k_2 \oplus kw_2$, $k_3' = k_3 \oplus kw_1$, $k_4' = k_4 \oplus kw_2$, and $k_{13}' = k_{13} \oplus kw_4$. The attack is worked in the chosen-ciphertext model. In the precomputation phase, we compute all 2^{225} possible values of multiset, and store them in a hash table. The attack procedure of the online phase is described as follows.

1. Select 2^{81} structures of ciphertexts, and each structure contains 2^{32} ciphertexts

$$L_{13} = P(\alpha_1, x_1, x_2, x_3, \alpha_2, x_4, x_5, x_6), R_{13} = (\beta_1, y_1, y_2, y_3, \beta_2, y_4, y_5, y_6),.$$

   where x_i and y_i $(i = 1, ..., 6)$ are fixed values, and α_j, β_j $(j = 1, 2)$ take all the possible values. Decrypt and obtain the corresponding plaintexts. There are 2^{144} pairs totally.

2. Compute $P^{-1}(\Delta L_1)$ for every pair by guessing 64-bit subkey k_1', eliminate the pairs which do not satisfy $P^{-1}(\Delta L_1)[6, 7] = 0$. There are $2^{144-16} = 2^{128}$ pairs left on average.

3. For $l = 2, 3, 4, 5, 6, 7, 8$, guess the 8-bit value of $k_2'[l]$ one by one, compute the value $Y_2[l]$, and keep the pairs which make $\Delta Y_2[l] = P^{-1}(\Delta L_0[l])$ hold. Then guess $k_2'[1]$ to compute L_2. The number of pairs kept about $2^{128-7*8} = 2^{72}$.

4. For $l = 2, 3, 5, 8$, guess the 8-bit value of $k_3'[l]$. Compute $Y_3[l]$ and discard the pairs which do not conform $\Delta Y_3[l] = P^{-1}(\Delta L_1)[l] \oplus P^{-1}(\Delta L_1)[4]$(see Observation 3). Then guess $k_3'[1]$ and keep the pairs satisfying $\Delta Y_3[1] = P^{-1}(\Delta L_1)[1]$. There are 2^{32} pairs remain for every 168-bit guessed key after this step.

5. For $l = 1, 5$, guess the 8-bit value of $k_{13}'[l]$, and compute the value $\Delta Y_{13}[l]$. Delete the pairs which do not content $\Delta Y_{13}[l] = P^{-1}(\Delta L_{13}[l])$. Then guess $kf_{3R}[1]$, compute $\Delta L_{12}^*[1]$ by using Observation 1, and delete the pairs when $\Delta L_{12}^*[1] \neq 0$. Hereafter, the expected number of remaining pairs is about 2^8.

6. Compute the value L_3 by guessing 24-bit subkey $k_3'[4, 6, 7]$, and then deduce the value of subkey $k_4'[1]$ for every pair.

7. Construct the δ−set for every pair, and compute corresponding value of multiset. Detect whether it belongs to the precomputed table and find the possible correct key.

8. Compute the related part of the master key by the correct equivalent keys k_1', k_2', k_3', k_4', k_{13}', and search the unknown part.

Complexity Analysis. The time complexity of precomputation phase is about $2^{225} \times 2^8 \times 2^{-1} = 2^{232}$ 13-round encryptions. The memory complexity is about $2^{225} \times 2^2 = 2^{227}$ 128-bit. The time complexity of online phase is bounded to that of Step 6, which costs $2^{224} \times 2^8 \times 2^{-2} = 2^{230}$ 13-round encryptions, which also needs 2^{113} chosen ciphertexts to find the correct pairs. In total, the data, time and memory complexities of the attack, including the precomputation phase, are 2^{113} chosen ciphertexts, $2^{232.3}$ encryptions and 2^{227} 128-bit memories, respectively.

6   Conclusion

In this paper, we give the key-dependent multiple differential attack and meet-in-the-middle attacks on reduced-round Camellia-128/192/256. For key-dependent multiple differential attack, we divide the keyspace into 224+1 subsets to ensure the input and output difference of FL^{-1} function same, and then produce 224 types of corresponding 8-round differentials, and each type of differentials include 2^{43} differentials. Based on 8-round multiple differentials, we attack 10-round Camellia-128 for every key subsets, which works for about 99.99% of the keys, and exhaustively search for the remaining fraction of $1/2^{15}$ of the keyspace. This attack is more efficient than previous 10-round attack on Camellia-128.

Furthermore, we also discuss the security of reduced-round Camellia-192/256 against the meet-in-the-middle attack. Considering differential enumeration technique, multisets, intermediate variable relations and key relations etc, we mount the attacks on 12-round Camellia-192 and 13-round Camellia-256 with non-marginal complexities.

Acknowledgments. We would like to thank anonymous reviewers for their very helpful comments on the paper. This work is supported by the National Natural Science Foundation of China (No. 61133013) and 973 Program (No.2013CB834205), and the National Natural Science Foundation of China (No. 61402256 and 61272035).

A   The Proof of Property 3

By Property 3, the 8-round property starts from the fifth round and ends at the twelfth round. The active byte of δ−set is defined at the first bytes of the input of the third round $L_{12}[5]$, i.e., $L_{12}[5]$ is the active byte. Considering to decrypt 2^8 values of the δ−set through 8-round Camellia-256, in the case of that a pair of δ—set conforms to the 8-round truncated differential outlined in Fig. 5, we prove the corresponding multiset of bytes $P^{-1}(\Delta L_4)[1]$ has 2^{225} values.

Proof. If $\Delta L_{12}[5] \neq 0$ and there is no difference on the other bytes of the input (L_{12}, R_{12}), $(P^{-1}(\Delta L_4))[1]$ is determined by 321-bit intermediate variable

$$X_{11}[5]\|X_{10}[2,3,4,6,7,8]\|X_9\|X_8\|X_7\|kf_1\{9-33,42-64\}\|kf_{2L}[1]\|kf_{2R}[1]\|kf_{2L}\{9\}\|X_6[1].$$

However, if there exists a pair satisfying the truncated differential as described in Fig. 6, the 312-bit intermediate variable

$$X_{11}[5]\|X_{10}[2,3,4,6,7,8]\|X_9\|X_8\|X_7\|X_6[1]\|kf_1\{9-33,42-64\}\|kf_{2L}[1]$$

is determined by 216-bit variable

$$\Delta X_{11}[5]\|\Delta Y_{11}[5]\|\Delta Y_{10}[2,3,4,6,7,8]\|\Delta Y_9\|\Delta X_6[1]\|\Delta Y_6[1]\|kf_1\|kf_{2L}[1].$$

Besides, 9-bit value $kf_{2R}[1]\|kf_{2L}\{9\}$ are also necessary to compute $(P^{-1}(\Delta L_4))$ [1]. Hence the multiset of bytes $(P^{-1}(\Delta L_4))[1]$ could be computed by traversing all the 225-bit intermediate variable

$$\mathcal{V} = \Delta X_{11}[5]\|\Delta Y_{11}[5]\|\Delta Y_{10}[2,3,4,6,7,8]\|\Delta Y_9\|\Delta X_6[1]\|\Delta Y_6[1]\|kf_1\|kf_{2L}[1]\|kf_{2R}[1]\|kf_{2L}\{9\}.$$

That is to say there are about 2^{225} possible values of multiset totally.   □

B   Blondeau *et al.*'s Multiple Differential Cryptanalysis

Blondeau *et al.*'s propose multiple differential cryptanalysis in 2011. A precise analytical model as well as formulas to compute success rate has been given. The success rate of a multiple differential attack can be calculated as follows:

$$P_S \approx 1 - G_*[G^{-1}(1 - \frac{l-1}{2^{n_k} - 2}) - 1/N_s], \tag{1}$$

where n_k is the number of key candidates, l is the size of list to keep and N_s is the number of samples. The function G and G^* are defined as follows:

$$G_*(\tau) \overset{def}{=} G(\tau, p_*)$$
$$G(\tau) \overset{def}{=} G(\tau, p) \tag{2}$$

where $p_* = \Sigma_{i,j} p_*^{(}i,j)$ and $p = \frac{|\Delta|}{2^m|\Delta_0|}$. $\Sigma_{i,j}$ is the sum of probability of all differential characters and m is the block size. $|\Delta|$ denotes the number of input difference values while $|\Delta_0|$ is the number of differentials. $G^{(}-1)$ is defined by $G^{(}-1)(y) = \min x|G(x) > y$. $G(\tau, p_*)$ and $G(\tau, p)$ can be calculated as follows:

$$G(\tau, q) = \begin{cases} G_-(\tau, q) & if & \tau < q - 3\sqrt{q/N_s}, \\ 1 - G_+(\tau, q) & if & \tau > q + 3\sqrt{q/N_s}, \\ G_p(\tau, q) & otherwise, \end{cases} \tag{3}$$

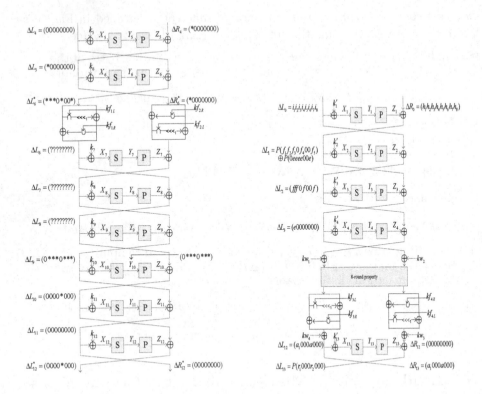

Fig. 5. The 8-round Truncated Differential of Camellia-256

Fig. 6. The Meet-in-the-Middle Attack on 13-round Camellia-256

where $G_p(\tau, q)$ is the cumulative distribution function of the Poisson distribution with parameter qN_s. $G_-(\tau, q)$ and $G_+(\tau, q)$ are defined as follows:

$$G_-(\tau, q) = e^{(-N_s D(\tau \| q))} \left[\frac{q\sqrt{1-\tau}}{(q-\tau)\sqrt{2\pi\tau N_s}} + \frac{1}{\sqrt{8\pi\tau N_s}} \right] \tag{4}$$

$$G_+(\tau, q) = e^{(-N_s D(\tau \| q))} \left[\frac{(1-q)\sqrt{\tau}}{(q-\tau)\sqrt{2\pi\tau N_s}} + \frac{1}{\sqrt{8\pi\tau N_s}} \right] \tag{5}$$

where $D(\tau \| q)$ is the Kullback-Leibler divergence defined by:

$$D(\tau \| q) = \tau ln(\frac{\tau}{q}) + (1 + \tau)ln(\frac{1-\tau}{1-q}) \tag{6}$$

C   Figure of the Camellia Algorithm

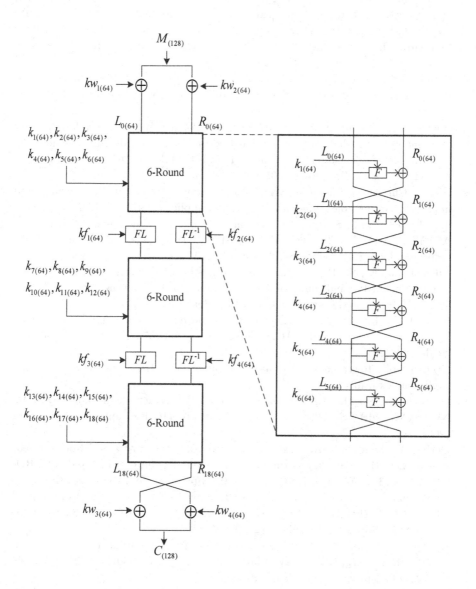

Fig. 7. : Encryption procedure of Camellia for 128-bit keys

References

1. Aoki, K., Ichikawa, T., Kanda, M., Matsui, M., Moriai, S., Nakajima, J., Tokita, T.: Specification of Camellia - a 128-bit Block Cipher. version 2.0 (2001)

2. Aoki, K., Ichikawa, T., Kanda, M., Matsui, M., Moriai, S., Nakajima, J., Tokita, T.: *Camellia*: a 128-bit block cipher suitable for multiple platforms - design and analysis. In: Stinson, D.R., Tavares, S. (eds.) SAC 2000. LNCS, vol. 2012, pp. 39–56. Springer, Heidelberg (2001)

3. Ben-Aroya, I., Biham, E.: Differential cryptanalysis of lucifer. In: Advances in CryptologyCRYPTO93, pp. 187–199. Springer (1994)

4. Blondeau, C., Gérard, B.: Multiple differential cryptanalysis: theory and practice. In: Joux, A. (ed.) FSE 2011. LNCS, vol. 6733, pp. 35–54. Springer, Heidelberg (2011)

5. Bogdanov, A., Geng, H., Wang, M., Wen, L., Collard, B.: Zero-correlation linear cryptanalysis with FFT and improved attacks on ISO standards camellia and CLEFIA. In: Lange, T., Lauter, K., Lisoněk, P. (eds.) SAC 2013. LNCS, vol. 8282, pp. 306–323. Springer, Heidelberg (2014)

6. Boura, Christina, Naya-Plasencia, María, Suder, Valentin: Scrutinizing and improving impossible differential attacks: applications to CLEFIA, camellia, LBlock and SIMON. In: Sarkar, Palash, Iwata, Tetsu (eds.) ASIACRYPT 2014. LNCS, vol. 8873, pp. 179–199. Springer, Heidelberg (2014). http://dx.doi.org/10.1007/978-3-662-45611-8_10

7. Chen, J., Jia, K., Yu, H., Wang, X.: New impossible differential attacks of reduced-round camellia-192 and camellia-256. In: Parampalli, U., Hawkes, P. (eds.) ACISP 2011. LNCS, vol. 6812, pp. 16–33. Springer, Heidelberg (2011)

8. Chen, J., Li, L.: Low data complexity attack on reduced camellia-256. In: Susilo, W., Mu, Y., Seberry, J. (eds.) ACISP 2012. LNCS, vol. 7372, pp. 101–114. Springer, Heidelberg (2012)

9. Cryptography Research and Evaluation Committees: http://www.cryptrec.go.jp/english/index.html

10. Demirci, H., Selçuk, A.A.: A meet-in-the-middle attack on 8-round AES. In: Nyberg, K. (ed.) FSE 2008. LNCS, vol. 5086, pp. 116–126. Springer, Heidelberg (2008)

11. Derbez, P., Fouque, P.-A., Jean, J.: Improved key recovery attacks on reduced-round AES in the single-key setting. In: Johansson, T., Nguyen, P.Q. (eds.) EUROCRYPT 2013. LNCS, vol. 7881, pp. 371–387. Springer, Heidelberg (2013)

12. Dunkelman, O., Keller, N., Shamir, A.: Improved single-key attacks on 8-round AES-192 and AES-256. In: Abe, M. (ed.) ASIACRYPT 2010. LNCS, vol. 6477, pp. 158–176. Springer, Heidelberg (2010)

13. Hatano, Y., Sekine, H., Kaneko, T.: Higher order differential attack of *Camellia* (II). In: Nyberg, Kaisa, Heys, Howard M. (eds.) SAC 2002. LNCS, vol. 2595, pp. 129–146. Springer, Heidelberg (2003)

14. International Organization for Standardization(ISO): International Standard-ISO/IEC 18033-3, Information technology-Security techniques-Encryption algorithms -Part 3: Block ciphers (2010)

15. Kanda, M., Matsumoto, T.: Security of camellia against truncated differential cryptanalysis. In: Matsui, M. (ed.) FSE 2001. LNCS, vol. 2355, pp. 286–299. Springer, Heidelberg (2002)

16. Knudsen, L.R., Rijmen, V.: On the decorrelated fast cipher (DFC) and its theory. In: Knudsen, L.R. (ed.) FSE 1999. LNCS, vol. 1636, pp. 81–94. Springer, Heidelberg (1999)

17. Kühn, U.: Improved cryptanalysis of MISTY1. In: Daemen, J., Rijmen, V. (eds.) FSE 2002. LNCS, vol. 2365, pp. 61–75. Springer, Heidelberg (2002)

18. Lee, S., Hong, S., Lee, S., Lim, J., Yoon, S.: Truncated differential cryptanalysis of camellia. In: Kim, K. (ed.) ICISC 2001. LNCS, vol. 2288, pp. 32–38. Springer, Heidelberg (2002)

19. Lei, D., Chao, L., Feng, K.: New observation on camellia. In: Preneel, B., Tavares, S. (eds.) SAC 2005. LNCS, vol. 3897, pp. 51–64. Springer, Heidelberg (2006)

20. Duo, L., Li, C., Feng, K.: Square like attack on camellia. In: Qing, S., Imai, H., Wang, G. (eds.) ICICS 2007. LNCS, vol. 4861, pp. 269–283. Springer, Heidelberg (2007)

21. Liu, Y., Li, L., Gu, D., Wang, X., Liu, Z., Chen, J., Li, W.: New observations on impossible differential cryptanalysis of reduced-round camellia. In: Canteaut, A. (ed.) FSE 2012. LNCS, vol. 7549, pp. 90–109. Springer, Heidelberg (2012)

22. Lu, J., Kim, J., Keller, N., Dunkelman, O.: Improving the efficiency of impossible differential cryptanalysis of reduced camellia and MISTY1. In: Malkin, T. (ed.) CT-RSA 2008. LNCS, vol. 4964, pp. 370–386. Springer, Heidelberg (2008)

23. Lu, J., Wei, Y., Fouque, P.A., Kim, J.: Cryptanalysis of reduced versions of the Camellia block cipher. IET Information Security 6(3), 228–238 (2012)

24. Lu, J., Wei, Y., Kim, J., Pasalic, E.: The higher-order meet-in-the-middle attack and its application to the camellia block cipher. In: Galbraith, S., Nandi, M. (eds.) INDOCRYPT 2012. LNCS, vol. 7668, pp. 244–264. Springer, Heidelberg (2012)

25. Mala, H., Shakiba, M., Dakhilalian, M., Bagherikaram, G.: New results on impossible differential cryptanalysis of reduced–round camellia–128. In: Jacobson Jr., M.J., Rijmen, V., Safavi-Naini, R. (eds.) SAC 2009. LNCS, vol. 5867, pp. 281–294. Springer, Heidelberg (2009)

26. Shirai, T.: Differential, linear, boomerang and rectangle cryptanalysis of reduced-round camellia. In: The Third NESSIE Workshop (2002)

27. Sugita, M., Kobara, K., Imai, H.: Security of reduced version of the block cipher camellia against truncated and impossible differential cryptanalysis. In: Boyd, C. (ed.) ASIACRYPT 2001. LNCS, vol. 2248, pp. 193–207. Springer, Heidelberg (2001)

28. Sun, X., Lai, X.: The key-dependent attack on block ciphers. In: Matsui, M. (ed.) ASIACRYPT 2009. LNCS, vol. 5912, pp. 19–36. Springer, Heidelberg (2009)

29. Wang, M., Sun, Y., Tischhauser, E., Preneel, B.: A model for structure attacks, with applications to PRESENT and serpent. In: Canteaut, A. (ed.) FSE 2012. LNCS, vol. 7549, pp. 49–68. Springer, Heidelberg (2012)

30. Wenling, W., Dengguo, F., Hua, C.: Collision attack and pseudorandomness of reduced-round camellia. In: Handschuh, H., Hasan, M.A. (eds.) SAC 2004. LNCS, vol. 3357, pp. 252–266. Springer, Heidelberg (2004)

31. Wu, W., Zhang, W., Feng, D.: Impossible Differential Cryptanalysis of Reduced-Round ARIA and Camellia. J. Comput. Sci. Technol. 22(3), 449–456 (2007)

Attribute and Identity Based Encryption

Duality in ABE: Converting Attribute Based Encryption for Dual Predicate and Dual Policy via Computational Encodings

Nuttapong Attrapadung[✉] and Shota Yamada

National Institute of Advanced Industrial Science and Technology (AIST),
Tsukuba, Japan
{n.attrapadung,yamada-shota}@aist.go.jp

Abstract. We show a generic conversion that converts an attribute based encryption (ABE) scheme for arbitrary predicate into an ABE scheme for its *dual predicate*. In particular, it can convert key-policy ABE (KP-ABE) into ciphertext-policy ABE (CP-ABE), and vice versa, for dually related predicates. It is generic in the sense that it can be applied to arbitrary predicates. On the other hand, it works only within the generic ABE framework recently proposed by Attrapadung (Eurocrypt'14), which provides a generic compiler that compiles a simple primitive called *pair encodings* into fully secure ABE. Inside this framework, Attrapadung proposed the first generic dual conversion that works only for subclass of encodings, namely, *perfectly secure encodings*. However, there are many predicates for which realizations of such encodings are not known, and hence the problems of constructing fully secure ABE for their dual predicates were left unsolved.

In this paper, we revisit the dual conversion of Attrapadung, and show that, somewhat surprisingly, the very same conversion indeed also works for broader classes of encodings, namely, *computationally secure encodings*. Consequently, we thus solve the above open problems as we obtain the first fully secure realizations of completely-unbounded CP-ABE and CP-ABE with short keys for Boolean formulae, via applying the conversion to previously proposed KP-ABE.

Moreover, we provide a generic conversion that converts ABE into its *dual-policy* variant. Dual-policy ABE (DP-ABE) conjunctively combines both KP-ABE and CP-ABE into one primitive, and hence can be useful in general-purpose applications. As for instantiations, we obtain the first realizations of fully secure DP-ABE for formulae, unbounded DP-ABE for formulae, and DP-ABE for regular languages. The latter two systems are the first to realize such functionalities, let alone are fully secure.

1 Introduction

Attribute-based encryption (ABE), introduced by Sahai and Waters [32], is a useful paradigm that generalizes traditional public key encryption. Instead of encrypting to a target recipient, a sender can specify in a more general way about who should be able to view the message. In ABE for *predicate R*, which

© Springer International Publishing Switzerland 2015
K. Nyberg (ed.): CT-RSA 2015, LNCS 9048, pp. 87–105, 2015.
DOI: 10.1007/978-3-319-16715-2_5

is a boolean function $R : \mathbb{X} \times \mathbb{Y} \to \{0, 1\}$, a private key, which is issued by an authority, is associated with an attribute $X \in \mathbb{X}$, while a ciphertext encrypting a message M is associated with an attribute $Y \in \mathbb{Y}$. A key for X can decrypt a ciphertext for Y if and only if $R(X, Y) = 1$. In a *key-policy* type of ABE (KP-ABE) [21], any $X \in \mathbb{X}$ is viewed as a *policy* function $X : \mathbb{Y} \to \{0, 1\}$ and the predicate evaluation is defined as $R(X, Y) = X(Y)$. On the other hand, in a *ciphertext-policy* type of ABE (CP-ABE) [7], any $Y \in \mathbb{Y}$ is viewed as a function $Y : \mathbb{X} \to \{0, 1\}$ where we define $R(X, Y) = Y(X)$. Perhaps, the most well-known ABE is for *Boolean formulae predicate*, considered by Goyal *et al.* [21], where policy functions are Boolean formulae over attributes and inputs to functions are Boolean assignments of attributes.

Duality in ABE. In this paper, we study the *duality* in ABE. For a predicate $R : \mathbb{X} \times \mathbb{Y} \to \{0, 1\}$, we define its *dual predicate* $\bar{R} : \mathbb{Y} \times \mathbb{X} \to \{0, 1\}$ as $\bar{R}(Y, X) = R(X, Y)$. Hence, key-policy and ciphertext-policy ABE are dual to each other in the sense that, when we view X as a function, ABE for R is of key-policy type, while its dual, ABE for $\bar{R}$, is of ciphertext-policy type.

Although any predicate and its dual are related by a very simple definition, ABE systems for both predicates are usually constructed separately and their security proofs are obtained using different techniques. In fact, until only recently, there was no known *generic* method that converts ABE into its dual. A first attempt for conversion was early done by Goyal *et al.* [22] but for only *specific* predicates, namely, they showed how to convert any KP-ABE into CP-ABE for bounded-size Boolean formulae. Only recently, Attrapadung [2] proposed the first *generic* dual conversion. It is generic in the sense that it can be applied to *arbitrary predicate*. More precisely, in [2], a generic framework for constructing fully-secure ABE was proposed, and inside the framework, a dual conversion was introduced. We first briefly describe the framework of [2].

Framework and Generic Dual Conversion of [2]. The framework of [2] provides an abstraction of the *dual system encryption* approaches, introduced by Waters [34] and extended by many works [25, 27–29, 36]. The framework of [2] decouples what seem to be an essential underlying primitive in the dual system approaches, called *pair encoding* schemes for predicates, and provides a generic construction that compiles any secure pair encoding for a predicate in consideration to a fully secure ABE for that predicate.[1] The security of encodings comes in two flavors: an *information-theoretical* notion, which captures the traditional dual system approach, and a *computational* notion, which generalizes the techniques in the ABE of Lewko and Waters [27]. Both notions imply fully secure ABE. However, it is the computational notion that empowers the framework of [2], since by using this notion, the first fully secure schemes are obtained in [2] for many ABE primitives of which only selectively secure constructions were known before, including KP-ABE for regular languages [35], KP-ABE for

---

[1] In our paper, we use "attribute based encryption" to refer to *public-index predicate encryption*, which is a sub-class of functional encryption categorized in [10]. In [2], the same class was referred as "functional encryption" (FE).

Boolean formulae with constant-size ciphertexts [6], and (completely) unbounded KP-ABE for Boolean formulae [26,31]. In fact, the latter two predicates are special cases of a new predicate called *key-policy over doubly spatial encryption* (KP-DSE), introduced and constructed in [2]. In addition, only the dual of the first ABE above, namely, CP-ABE for regular languages was also directly constructed in [2].

The first generic dual conversion was then given in [2]. It works by converting any pair encoding for R into a pair encoding for its dual, $\bar{R}$. A fully secure ABE scheme for $\bar{R}$ is then obtained via the generic construction. However, in [2], only the case for information-theoretical security of encodings was proved to be preserved via the conversion. Hence, it is not applicable to computationally secure encodings, which empower the framework of [2] in the first place. In particular, fully secure realizations of CP-ABE primitives that are the duals of KP-ABE for the predicates above, namely, unbounded CP-ABE for formulae and constant-size CP-ABE for formulae, and their generalization, ciphertext-policy over DSE (CP-DSE), have been left as open problems. To this end, our first goal is to provide a generic dual conversion that preserves computational security of encodings.

Dual-Policy ABE. Key-policy and ciphertext-policy types are useful in different applications. KP-ABE specifies policies over data attributes, and hence is useful for content-based access control. CP-ABE specifies policies over receiver attributes, and hence is useful for access control that directly specifies receiver policies. In order to make the most advantages of both types, a combined type called *dual-policy* ABE (DP-ABE) was proposed in [5]. DP-ABE conjunctively combines two predicates, namely, a predicate R and its dual predicate $\bar{R}$. The dual-policy predicate, denoted $[R \wedge \bar{R}] : (\mathbb{X} \times \mathbb{Y}) \times (\mathbb{Y} \times \mathbb{X}) \to \{0,1\}$, is defined by $[R \wedge \bar{R}]((X,Y'),(Y,X')) = R(X,Y) \wedge \bar{R}(Y',X')$. DP-ABE is already found useful in real-world applications due to its flexibility [1]. However, there was no known generic method to combine an ABE and its dual to obtain DP-ABE. It is our second goal to construct a generic conversion that converts ABE into its dual-policy variant.

Our Contributions. We revisit the generic dual conversion of [2] and prove that, somewhat surprisingly, the very same conversion indeed preserves the computational security of encodings. Hence, by applying it to the KP-DSE of [2], we immediately obtain the first fully secure CP-DSE. This implies the first fully secure realizations of completely unbounded CP-ABE for formulae and constant-size-*key* CP-ABE for formulae. We note that constant-size ciphertexts in KP-ABE (of [2]) becomes constant-size keys due to the duality.

We achieve the new theorem of the conversion by a very simple proof that relies on two ingredients. First, we restrict the syntax of pair encodings to the class we call *normal* pair encodings by posing a new simple requirement. Nevertheless, this restriction seems natural and does not affect any concrete pair encoding schemes proposed so far in [2]. Second, we *relax* the computational security but in such a way that the generic ABE construction still compiles encodings to fully secure ABE. Moreover, since we relax the security, all existing computationally secure encodings will satisfy the relaxed notion. The only draw-back is that the reduction cost for the resulting ABE will not have the same tightness as in the framework of [2], which achieve $O(q_1)$ reduction to the under-lying assumption. The converted ABE, however, achieves $O(q_{all})$ reduction cost, where q_1, q_{all} are the number of pre-challenge queries and all queries, respec-tively. To this end, we also directly construct a new CP-DSE scheme and prove its security with tightness $O(q_1)$.

We then propose a generic method to conjunctively combine any two pair encoding schemes. Hence, by combining with the generic dual conversion above, we obtain a generic conversion that converts any normal pair encoding scheme for R into a pair encoding for its *dual-policy*, namely, $[R \wedge \bar{R}]$. This implies the first realizations of fully secure DP-ABE for formulae, DP-DSE, unbounded DP-ABE for formulae, and DP-ABE for regular languages. The latter three systems are the first to realize such primitives, let alone are fully secure.

1.1   Our Approach

Recapturing the Framework of [2]. In the generic construction of ABE for R of [2], a ciphertext CT encrypting M, and a key SK take the forms of

$$\mathsf{CT} = (\boldsymbol{C}, C_0) = (g_1^{\boldsymbol{c}_Y(\boldsymbol{s},\boldsymbol{h})}, \ Me(g_1,g_1)^{\alpha s_0}), \qquad \mathsf{SK} = g_1^{\boldsymbol{k}_X(\alpha,\boldsymbol{r},\boldsymbol{h})}$$

where $\boldsymbol{c}_Y$ and $\boldsymbol{k}_X$ are *encodings* of attributes Y and X associated to a cipher-text and a key, respectively. Here, g_1 is a generator of subgroup of order p_1 of $\mathbb{G}$, which is a symmetric bilinear group of composite order $N = p_1 p_2 p_3$ with bilinear map $e : \mathbb{G} \times \mathbb{G} \to \mathbb{G}_T$. The bold fonts denote vectors. Intuitively, α plays the role of a master key, $\boldsymbol{h}$ represents common variables (or called parameters). These define a public key $\mathsf{PK} = (g_1^{\boldsymbol{h}}, e(g_1,g_1)^{\alpha})$. $\boldsymbol{s}, \boldsymbol{r}$ represents randomness in the ciphertext and the key, respectively, with s_0 being the first element in $\boldsymbol{s}$. The pair $(\boldsymbol{c}_Y, \boldsymbol{k}_X)$ form a *pair encoding* scheme for predicate R. It is exactly this primitive on which the framework of [2] studied and gave sufficient conditions for correctness (when $R(X,Y) = 1$) and security (when $R(X,Y) = 0$) so that, roughly speaking, the ABE scheme defined with CT, SK as above would be cor-rect and fully secure (see more detail in in §3). We refer the intuition for defining the computational security of encodings to [2], but informally recapture it here. The security requires that for $R(X,Y) = 0$, the following two distributions are computationally indistinguishable:

$$\left(g_2^{\boldsymbol{c}_Y(\boldsymbol{s},\boldsymbol{h})}, \ g_2^{\boldsymbol{k}_X(0,\boldsymbol{r},\boldsymbol{h})}\right) \qquad \text{and} \qquad \left(g_2^{\boldsymbol{c}_Y(\boldsymbol{s},\boldsymbol{h})}, \ g_2^{\boldsymbol{k}_X(\alpha,\boldsymbol{r},\boldsymbol{h})}\right),$$

where Y, X are chosen by the adversary. It has two sub-notions. For the notion where Y is queried before X, it is called *selective* master-key hiding. On the other hand, if X is queried before Y, we call *co-selective* master-key hiding. The naming mimics the (co-)selective security of ABE. These elements are defined over g_2, a generator of p_2-order subgroup of $\mathbb{G}$, and are only used in the proof.

The main idea for the generic dual conversion of [2] is natural: *simply using key encodings to define ciphertext encodings in the dual predicate, and vice versa.*

More precisely, from a pair encoding (c_Y, k_X) for R, a pair encoding $(\bar{c}_X, \bar{k}_Y)$ for $\bar{R}$ is constructed as

$$\bar{k}_Y(\bar{\alpha}, \bar{r}, \bar{h}) := \big(c_Y(s, h), \ \bar{\alpha} + \bar{\phi}s_0\big), \qquad \bar{c}_X(\bar{s}, \bar{h}) := \big(k_X(\bar{\phi}\bar{s}_0, r, h), \ \bar{s}_0\big),$$

where $\bar{h} := (h, \bar{\phi})$, $\bar{r} := s$, $\bar{s} := (\bar{s}_0, r)$. We leave the explanation to §4 and only motivate here for non-triviality of proving the preservability of the computational security through the conversion.

Difficulty and Our Idea. The security of original encodings only provides the indistinguishability of k for the case of $\alpha = 0$ and α is random. To establish the reduction, we need to use it to prove the indistinguishability of $\bar{k}$ for the case of $\bar{\alpha} = 0$ and $\bar{\alpha}$ is random. However, the non-triviality here stems from the fact that $\bar{k}$ is defined from c, where we do not have a sort of indistinguishability in the first place! We resolve this using a simple technique that establishes the "link" from k to $\bar{k}$ via simulation of the variable $\bar{\phi}$. Without going into details here, in order to do so, we only additionally require s_0 to be given out in $c_Y(s, h)$. But this restriction is natural and is satisfied by all the pair encodings proposed so far [2]. We thus call it the *normality* of pair encodings.

Our theorems state that if the original encoding is *selectively* master-key hiding, then the converted encoding for the dual is *co-selectively* master-key hiding, and vice versa. This follows intuitively from the fact that we swap key encodings with ciphertext encodings, and hence the order of queries from the adversary is also swapped. There is a caveat that while the original *selective* notion of [2] allows polynomially many key encoding queries, which results in tighter reduction for ABE, our conversion can deal with only one query. In other words, we relax the selective notion so that it will be preserved via the conversion. Nevertheless, this will affect only the reduction tightness of the resulting ABE, where the reduction will become $O(q_{\text{all}})$, instead of $O(q_1)$ as in [2].

Other Related Work. In this work, we allow only efficient tools, namely, bilinear groups. When basing on stronger (but much less efficient) tools, such as multi-linear maps [12,14], or cryptographic obfuscations [16], we can obtain ABE and FE for very general classes of predicates such as poly-size circuits [15,20], or Turing machines [18,19]. For these general classes, there were no known generic dual conversion. For the circuit predicate, KP-ABE can be converted into CP-ABE but for only *bounded-size circuits*, using universal circuits [16]. We remark that, until recently, all known ABE systems for these general classes are only selectively secure (or fully secure but with exponential reductions). Fully secure KP-ABE systems for circuits are recently proposed in [3,17]. The first (fully secure) CP-ABE for unbounded-size circuits was proposed also in [3].

2 Preliminaries

Predicate Family. We consider a predicate family $R = \{R_\kappa\}_{\kappa \in \mathbb{N}^c}$, for some constant $c \in \mathbb{N}$, where a relation $R_\kappa : \mathbb{X}_\kappa \times \mathbb{Y}_\kappa \to \{0, 1\}$ is a predicate function that maps a pair of key attribute in a space $\mathbb{X}_\kappa$ and ciphertext attribute in a space $\mathbb{Y}_\kappa$ to $\{0,1\}$. The family index $\kappa = (n_1, n_2, \ldots)$ specifies the description of a predicate from the family. We mandate the first entry n_1 in κ to specify the arithmetic domain, e.g., in composite-order setting, it is $\mathbb{Z}_N$ (i.e., $n_1 = N$).

Dual Predicate. For a predicate $R : \mathbb{X} \times \mathbb{Y} \to \{0,1\}$, its dual predicate is defined by $\bar{R} : \bar{\mathbb{X}} \times \bar{\mathbb{Y}} \to \{0,1\}$ where $\bar{\mathbb{X}} = \mathbb{Y}, \bar{\mathbb{Y}} = \mathbb{X}$ and $\bar{R}(X, Y) := R(Y, X)$.

ABE Syntax. An ABE scheme for predicate R consists of four algorithms:

- Setup$(1^\lambda, \kappa) \to (\mathsf{PK}, \mathsf{MSK})$: takes as input a security parameter 1^λ and a family index κ of predicate family R, and outputs a master public key PK and a master secret key MSK.
- Encrypt$(Y, M, \mathsf{PK}) \to \mathsf{CT}$: takes as input a ciphertext attribute $Y \in \mathbb{Y}_\kappa$, a message $M \in \mathcal{M}$, and public key PK. It outputs a ciphertext CT.
- KeyGen$(X, \mathsf{MSK}, \mathsf{PK}) \to \mathsf{SK}$: takes as input a key attribute $X \in \mathbb{X}_\kappa$ and the master key MSK. It outputs a secret key SK.
- Decrypt$(\mathsf{CT}, \mathsf{SK}) \to M$: given a ciphertext CT with its attribute Y and the decryption key SK with its attribute X, it outputs a message M or $\perp$.

We refer the (standard) definitions of correctness and security of ABE to [2].

Composite-Order Bilinear Groups. We use bilinear groups $(\mathbb{G}, \mathbb{G}_T)$ of composite order $N = p_1 p_2 p_3$, where p_1, p_2, p_3 are distinct primes, with an efficient bilinear map $e : \mathbb{G} \times \mathbb{G} \to \mathbb{G}_T$. A bilinear group generator $\mathcal{G}(\lambda)$ takes as input a security parameter λ and outputs $(\mathbb{G}, \mathbb{G}_T, e, N, p_1, p_2, p_3)$. Let $\mathbb{G}_{p_i}$ be the subgroup of order p_i of $\mathbb{G}$. We note that, nevertheless, we will not directly use properties of composite-order groups (such as orthogonality, subgroup decision assumptions) here. This is since the framework of [2] essentially decouples pair encoding schemes so that they need not incorporate such properties.

3   Pair Encoding Scheme

We recall the definition of pair encoding schemes as given in [2]. A pair encoding scheme for predicate family R consists of four deterministic algorithms given by $\mathsf{P} = (\mathsf{Param}, \mathsf{Enc1}, \mathsf{Enc2}, \mathsf{Pair})$:

- Param$(\kappa) \to n$. It takes as input an index κ and outputs n, which specifies the number of *common variables* in Enc1, Enc2. For default notation, let $\boldsymbol{h} = (h_1, \ldots, h_n)$ denote the common variables.
- Enc1$(X, N) \to \big(\boldsymbol{k} = (k_1, \ldots, k_{m_1}); m_2\big)$. It takes as inputs $X \in \mathbb{X}_\kappa$, $N \in \mathbb{N}$, and outputs a sequence of polynomials $\{k_i\}_{i \in [1, m_1]}$ with coefficients in $\mathbb{Z}_N$, and $m_2 \in \mathbb{N}$. We require that each polynomial k_i is a *linear combination of monomials* $\alpha, r_j, h_k r_j$, where $\alpha, r_1, \ldots, r_{m_2}, h_1, \ldots, h_n$ are variables.
- Enc2$(Y, N) \to \big(\boldsymbol{c} = (c_1, \ldots, c_{w_1}); w_2\big)$. It takes as inputs $Y \in \mathbb{Y}_\kappa$, $N \in \mathbb{N}$, and outputs a sequence of polynomials $\{c_i\}_{i \in [1, w_1]}$ with coefficients in $\mathbb{Z}_N$, and $w_2 \in \mathbb{N}$. We require that each polynomial c_i is a *linear combination of monomials* $s_j, h_k s_j$, where $s_0, s_1, \ldots, s_{w_2}, h_1, \ldots, h_n$ are variables.
- Pair$(X, Y, N) \to \boldsymbol{E}$. It takes as inputs X, Y, N, and output $\boldsymbol{E} \in \mathbb{Z}_N^{m_1 \times w_1}$.

Correctness. First, we require that for $(\boldsymbol{k}; m_2) \leftarrow \mathsf{Enc1}(X, N)$, $(\boldsymbol{c}; w_2) \leftarrow \mathsf{Enc2}(Y, N)$, $\boldsymbol{E} \leftarrow \mathsf{Pair}(X, Y, N)$, we have that if $R_N(X, Y) = 1$, then $\boldsymbol{k}\boldsymbol{E}\boldsymbol{c}^\top = \alpha s_0$. We note that since we can write $\boldsymbol{k}\boldsymbol{E}\boldsymbol{c}^\top = \sum_{i \in [1, m_1], j \in [1, w_1]} E_{i,j} k_i c_j$, this correctness amounts to check if there is a linear combination of $k_i c_j$ terms summed up to αs_0. Second, for $p | N$, if we let $\mathsf{Enc1}(X, N) \to (\boldsymbol{k}; m_2)$ and $\mathsf{Enc1}(X, p) \to (\boldsymbol{k}'; m_2)$, then $\boldsymbol{k} \bmod p = \boldsymbol{k}'$. The requirement for $\mathsf{Enc2}$ is similar.

Notation. In what follows, we denote $\boldsymbol{h} = (h_1, \ldots, h_n), \boldsymbol{r} = (r_1, \ldots, r_{m_2}), \boldsymbol{s} = (s_0, s_1, \ldots, s_{w_2})$. We will often use subscripts and write $\boldsymbol{k}_X$ and $\boldsymbol{c}_Y$ to emphasize the attributes X, Y.

Properties. As identified in [2], every pair encoding scheme straightforwardly satisfies the following two properties symbolically. *Parameter-vanishing* states the identity $\boldsymbol{k}(\alpha, \boldsymbol{0}, \boldsymbol{h}) = \boldsymbol{k}(\alpha, \boldsymbol{0}, \boldsymbol{0})$. *Linearity* states the identities: $\boldsymbol{k}(\alpha_1, \boldsymbol{r}_1, \boldsymbol{h}) + \boldsymbol{k}(\alpha_2, \boldsymbol{r}_2, \boldsymbol{h}) = \boldsymbol{k}(\alpha_1 + \alpha_2, \boldsymbol{r}_1 + \boldsymbol{r}_2, \boldsymbol{h})$ for $\boldsymbol{k}$, and $\boldsymbol{c}(\boldsymbol{s}_1, \boldsymbol{h}) + \boldsymbol{c}(\boldsymbol{s}_2, \boldsymbol{h}) = \boldsymbol{c}(\boldsymbol{s}_1 + \boldsymbol{s}_2, \boldsymbol{h})$ for $\boldsymbol{c}$. Combining the two identities for $\boldsymbol{k}$, we have that

$$\boldsymbol{k}(\alpha_1, \boldsymbol{0}, \boldsymbol{0}) + \boldsymbol{k}(\alpha_2, \boldsymbol{r}, \boldsymbol{h}) = \boldsymbol{k}(\alpha_1 + \alpha_2, \boldsymbol{r}, \boldsymbol{h}) \tag{1}$$

Normal Pair Encoding. Towards proving the security of our dual conversion, we require a new property for pair encoding. We formalize it as *normality*. This restriction is natural and all pair encoding schemes proposed so far [2,36] are not affected by this.

Definition 1 (Normal Pair Encoding). *We call a pair encoding scheme normal if s_0 is a polynomial in the sequence $\boldsymbol{c}(\boldsymbol{s}, \boldsymbol{h})$. Wlog, we denote $c_1 = s_0$ (the first polynomial in $\boldsymbol{c}$).*

3.1 Computational Security Definitions of Pair Encoding

We use the same computational security notion of pair encoding as defined in [2], albeit we re-formalize with additional refinement regarding the number of queries that can be asked by the adversary. The notion consists of two sub-notions: *selectively secure* and *co-selectively secure master-key hiding* (SMH, CMH) in a bilinear group generator $\mathcal{G}$. We first define the following game template, denoted as $\mathsf{Exp}_{\mathcal{G}, \mathsf{P}, \mathsf{G}, b, \mathcal{A}, t_1, t_2}(\lambda)$, for pair encoding P, a flavor $\mathsf{G} \in \{\mathsf{CMH}, \mathsf{SMH}\}$, $b \in \{0, 1\}$, and $t_1, t_2 \in \mathbb{N}$. It takes as input the security parameter λ and does the experiment with the adversary $\mathcal{A} = (\mathcal{A}_1, \mathcal{A}_2)$, and outputs b'. Denote by st a state information by $\mathcal{A}$. The game is defined as:

$$\mathsf{Exp}_{\mathcal{G}, \mathsf{P}, \mathsf{G}, b, \mathcal{A}, t_1, t_2}(\lambda) : (\mathbb{G}, \mathbb{G}_T, e, N, p_1, p_2, p_3) \leftarrow \mathcal{G}(\lambda), \ g_i \xleftarrow{\$} \mathbb{G}_{p_i} (\text{for } i = 1, 2, 3),$$

$$\alpha \xleftarrow{\$} \mathbb{Z}_N, \ n \leftarrow \mathsf{Param}(\kappa), \ \boldsymbol{h} \xleftarrow{\$} \mathbb{Z}_N^n,$$

$$\mathsf{st} \leftarrow \mathcal{A}_1^{\mathcal{O}^1_{\mathsf{G}, b, \alpha, \boldsymbol{h}}(\cdot)}(g_1, g_2, g_3), \ b' \leftarrow \mathcal{A}_2^{\mathcal{O}^2_{\mathsf{G}, b, \alpha, \boldsymbol{h}}(\cdot)}(\mathsf{st}),$$

where each oracle $\mathcal{O}^1, \mathcal{O}^2$ *can be queried at most t_1, t_2 times respectively*, and is defined as follows.

- **Selective Master-key Hiding Security.**
  - $\mathcal{O}^1_{\mathsf{SMH},b,\alpha,h}(Y)$: Run $(\boldsymbol{c}; w_2) \leftarrow \mathsf{Enc2}(Y, p_2)$; $s \xleftarrow{\$} \mathbb{Z}_{p_2}^{(w_2+1)}$; return $\boldsymbol{C} \leftarrow g_2^{\boldsymbol{c}(s,h)}$.
  - $\mathcal{O}^2_{\mathsf{SMH},b,\alpha,h}(X)$: If $R_{p_2}(X, Y) = 1$ for some Y queried to $\mathcal{O}^1$, then return $\perp$.

    Else, run $(\boldsymbol{k}; m_2) \leftarrow \mathsf{Enc1}(X, p_2)$; $r \xleftarrow{\$} \mathbb{Z}_{p_2}^{m_2}$; return $\boldsymbol{K} \leftarrow \begin{cases} g_2^{\boldsymbol{k}(0,r,h)} & \text{if } b = 0 \\ g_2^{\boldsymbol{k}(\alpha,r,h)} & \text{if } b = 1 \end{cases}$

- **Co-selective Master-key Hiding Security.**
  - $\mathcal{O}^1_{\mathsf{CMH},b,\alpha,h}(X)$: Run $(\boldsymbol{k}; m_2) \leftarrow \mathsf{Enc1}(X, p_2)$; $r \xleftarrow{\$} \mathbb{Z}_{p_2}^{m_2}$; return

$$\boldsymbol{K} \leftarrow \begin{cases} g_2^{\boldsymbol{k}(0,r,h)} & \text{if } b = 0 \\ g_2^{\boldsymbol{k}(\alpha,r,h)} & \text{if } b = 1 \end{cases}.$$

  - $\mathcal{O}^2_{\mathsf{CMH},b,\alpha,h}(Y)$: If $R_{p_2}(X, Y) = 1$ for some X queried to $\mathcal{O}^1$, then return $\perp$.

    Else, run $(\boldsymbol{c}; w_2) \leftarrow \mathsf{Enc2}(Y, p_2)$; $s \xleftarrow{\$} \mathbb{Z}_{p_2}^{(w_2+1)}$; return $\boldsymbol{C} \leftarrow g_2^{\boldsymbol{c}(s,h)}$.

We define the advantage of $\mathcal{A}$ against the pair encoding scheme P in the security game $\mathsf{G} \in \{\mathsf{SMH}, \mathsf{CMH}\}$ for bilinear group generator $\mathcal{G}$ with the bounded number of queries (t_1, t_2) as

$$\mathsf{Adv}_{\mathcal{A}}^{(t_1,t_2)\text{-}\mathsf{G}(\mathsf{P})}(\lambda) := \left| \Pr[\mathsf{Exp}_{\mathcal{G},\mathsf{P},\mathsf{G},0,\mathcal{A},t_1,t_2}(\lambda) = 1] - \Pr[\mathsf{Exp}_{\mathcal{G},\mathsf{P},\mathsf{G},1,\mathcal{A},t_1,t_2}(\lambda) = 1] \right|$$

We say that P is (t_1, t_2)-*selectively master-key hiding* in $\mathcal{G}$ if $\mathsf{Adv}_{\mathcal{A}}^{(t_1,t_2)\text{-}\mathsf{SMH}(\mathsf{P})}(\lambda)$ is negligible for all polynomial time attackers $\mathcal{A}$. Analogously, P is (t_1, t_2)-*co-selectively master-key hiding* in $\mathcal{G}$ if $\mathsf{Adv}_{\mathcal{A}}^{(t_1,t_2)\text{-}\mathsf{CMH}(\mathsf{P})}(\lambda)$ is negligible for all polynomial time attackers $\mathcal{A}$.

Poly-many Queries. We also consider the case where t_i is *not a-priori bounded* and hence the corresponding oracle can be queried polynomially many times. In such a case, we denote t_i as poly.

Remark 1 (Relation to Notions in [2]). The original notions considered in [2] are $(1, \mathsf{poly})$-SMH, $(1,1)$-CMH for selective and co-selective master-key hiding security, respectively. In this paper, our conversion will convert a $(1,1)$-SMH-secure pair encoding scheme into another scheme which is $(1,1)$-CMH-secure, and vice-versa. We note that $(1, \mathsf{poly})$-SMH trivially implies $(1,1)$-SMH.

We also refer the definition of *perfectly master-key hiding* to [2]. Informally, it requires α to be information-theoretically hidden from $\boldsymbol{c}_Y(s, h)$, $\boldsymbol{k}_X(\alpha, r, h)$ for any X, Y such that $R(X, Y) = 0$.

3.2 Implications to Fully Secure ABE

From a pair encoding scheme P for R, an ABE scheme for R, denoted $\mathsf{ABE}(\mathsf{P})$, can be achieved via the generic construction of [2], which we recall it here.

- $\mathsf{Setup}(1^\lambda, \kappa)$: Run $(\mathbb{G}, \mathbb{G}_T, e, N, p_1, p_2, p_3) \xleftarrow{\$} \mathcal{G}(\lambda)$. Pick generators $g_1 \xleftarrow{\$} \mathbb{G}_{p_1}$, $Z_3 \xleftarrow{\$} \mathbb{G}_{p_3}$. Obtain $n \leftarrow \mathsf{Param}(\kappa)$. Pick $\boldsymbol{h} \xleftarrow{\$} \mathbb{Z}_N^n$ and $\alpha \xleftarrow{\$} \mathbb{Z}_N$. The public key is $\mathsf{PK} = \left(g_1, e(g_1, g_1)^\alpha, g_1^{\boldsymbol{h}}, Z_3\right)$. The master secret key is $\mathsf{MSK} = \alpha$.

- Encrypt(Y, M, PK): Upon input $Y \in \mathbb{Y}_N$, run $(\boldsymbol{c}; w_2) \leftarrow \mathsf{Enc2}(Y, N)$. Pick $\boldsymbol{s} = (s_0, s_1, \ldots, s_{w_2}) \xleftarrow{\$} \mathbb{Z}_N^{w_2+1}$. Output a ciphertext $\mathsf{CT} = (\boldsymbol{C}, C_0)$ where $\boldsymbol{C} = g_1^{\boldsymbol{c}(\boldsymbol{s},\boldsymbol{h})} \in \mathbb{G}^{w_1}, C_0 = (e(g_1, g_1)^\alpha)^{s_0} M \in \mathbb{G}_T$. Note that $\boldsymbol{C}$ can be computed from $g_1^{\boldsymbol{h}}$ and $\boldsymbol{s}$ since $\boldsymbol{c}(\boldsymbol{s}, \boldsymbol{h})$ contains only linear combinations of monomials $s_i, s_h{}_j, s_i h_j$.
- KeyGen$(X, \mathsf{MSK}, \mathsf{PK})$: Upon input $X \in \mathbb{X}_N$, run $(\boldsymbol{k}; m_2) \leftarrow \mathsf{Enc1}(X, N)$. Parse $\mathsf{MSK} = \alpha$. Recall that $m_1 = |\boldsymbol{k}|$. Pick $\boldsymbol{r} \xleftarrow{\$} \mathbb{Z}_N^{m_2}, \boldsymbol{R}_3 \xleftarrow{\$} \mathbb{G}_{p_3}^{m_1}$. Output a secret key $\mathsf{SK} = g_1^{\boldsymbol{k}(\alpha, \boldsymbol{r}, \boldsymbol{h})} \cdot \boldsymbol{R}_3 \in \mathbb{G}^{m_1}$.
- Decrypt$(\mathsf{CT}, \mathsf{SK})$: Parse Y, X from CT, SK. Assume $R(X, Y) = 1$. Run $\boldsymbol{E} \leftarrow \mathsf{Pair}(X, Y)$. Compute $e(g_1, g_1)^{\alpha s_0} \leftarrow e(\boldsymbol{K}^{\boldsymbol{E}}, \boldsymbol{C})$, and $M \leftarrow C_0 / e(g_1, g_1)^{\alpha s_0}$.

Its correctness follows from that of the pair encoding, see [2]. Also in [2], it is proved that if P is $(1, \mathsf{poly})$-SMH and $(1, 1)$-CMH secure, then $\mathsf{ABE}(\mathsf{P})$ is fully secure with reduction $O(q_1)$. We recall this as follows. Let $\mathsf{Adv}_{\mathcal{A}}^{\mathsf{ABE}(\mathsf{P})}(\lambda)$ be the advantage of an adversary $\mathcal{A}$ against the full security of $\mathsf{ABE}(\mathsf{P})$.

Proposition 1 ([2]). *Suppose that a pair encoding P for predicate R is both $(1, 1)$-CMH and $(1, \mathsf{poly})$-SMH in $\mathcal{G}$. Suppose that the Subgroup Decision Assumption 1,2,3 (denoted as $\mathsf{SD1}, \mathsf{SD2}, \mathsf{SD3}$)[2] hold in $\mathcal{G}$. Suppose also that R is domain-transferable.[3] Then the ABE scheme $\mathsf{ABE}(\mathsf{P})$ in $\mathcal{G}$ for predicate R is fully secure. More precisely, for any PPT adversary $\mathcal{A}$, there exist PPT algorithms $\mathcal{B}_1, \mathcal{B}_2, \mathcal{B}_3, \mathcal{B}_4, \mathcal{B}_5$, whose running times are the same as $\mathcal{A}$ plus some polynomial times, such that for any λ,*

$$\mathsf{Adv}_{\mathcal{A}}^{\mathsf{ABE}(\mathsf{P})}(\lambda) \leq 2\mathsf{Adv}_{\mathcal{B}_1}^{\mathsf{SD1}}(\lambda) + (2q_1 + 3)\mathsf{Adv}_{\mathcal{B}_2}^{\mathsf{SD2}}(\lambda) + \mathsf{Adv}_{\mathcal{B}_3}^{\mathsf{SD3}}(\lambda)$$
$$+ q_1 \mathsf{Adv}_{\mathcal{B}_4}^{(1,1)\text{-}\mathsf{CMH}(\mathsf{P})}(\lambda) + \mathsf{Adv}_{\mathcal{B}_5}^{(1,\mathsf{poly})\text{-}\mathsf{SMH}(\mathsf{P})}(\lambda),$$

where q_1 is the number of queries in phase 1.

As a new corollary, we have that if P is $(1, 1)$-SMH and $(1, 1)$-CMH secure, then $\mathsf{ABE}(\mathsf{P})$ is fully secure with reduction $O(q_{\mathrm{all}})$. We state this as follows.

Corollary 1. *Suppose that a pair encoding scheme P for predicate R is both $(1, 1)$-CMH and $(1, 1)$-SMH in $\mathcal{G}$. Suppose that $\mathsf{SD1}, \mathsf{SD2}, \mathsf{SD3}$ hold in $\mathcal{G}$. Suppose also that R is domain-transferable. Then, $\mathsf{ABE}(\mathsf{P})$ in $\mathcal{G}$ for predicate R is fully secure. More precisely, for any PPT adversary $\mathcal{A}$, there exist PPT algorithms $\mathcal{B}_1, \mathcal{B}_2, \mathcal{B}_3, \mathcal{B}_4, \mathcal{B}_5$, whose running times are the same as $\mathcal{A}$ plus some poly times, such that for any λ,*

$$\mathsf{Adv}_{\mathcal{A}}^{\mathsf{ABE}(\mathsf{P})}(\lambda) \leq 2\mathsf{Adv}_{\mathcal{B}_1}^{\mathsf{SD1}}(\lambda) + (2q_{\mathrm{all}} + 1)\mathsf{Adv}_{\mathcal{B}_2}^{\mathsf{SD2}}(\lambda) + \mathsf{Adv}_{\mathcal{B}_3}^{\mathsf{SD3}}(\lambda)$$
$$+ q_1 \mathsf{Adv}_{\mathcal{B}_4}^{(1,1)\text{-}\mathsf{CMH}(\mathsf{P})}(\lambda) + q_2 \mathsf{Adv}_{\mathcal{B}_5}^{(1,1)\text{-}\mathsf{SMH}(\mathsf{P})}(\lambda),$$

where q_1 and q_2 denotes the number of queries in phase 1 and phase 2, respectively, and $q_{\mathrm{all}} = q_1 + q_2$.

---

[2] The $\mathsf{SD1}, \mathsf{SD2}, \mathsf{SD3}$ assumptions were introduced in [25]. We refer to [2, 25].
[3] Informally speaking, R is domain-transferable [2] if $R_N(X, Y) = R_p(X, Y)$ for any prime $p|N$ with high probability.

Proof (Proof of Corollary 1 (Sketch)). This corollary follows the proof of Proposition 1 in [2]. The only difference is that instead of switching all *post-challenge* keys *all at once* for the three games (normal to semi-functional type 1, to type 2, and to type 3), we switch each post-challenge key *one key per one game*, in just the same way as for each pre-challenge key (and as in the traditional dual system encryption proofs). This results in the cost q_2 for the reduction to the SMH security and the additional cost $2q_2 - 2$ for the reduction to SD2.

4 New Theorem for Generic Dual Conversion

In this section, we first recall the generic dual conversion of [2], where it was proved to hold for only the case of perfectly master-key hiding encoding. We restate this as Proposition 2. We then present our main results which are new theorems for the case of computationally secure encodings.

Dual Conversion of [2]. Given a pair encoding scheme P_R for predicate R, we construct a predicate encoding scheme $\mathcal{C}(\mathsf{P}_R)$ for $\bar{R}$ as follows. For Param $\rightarrow$ $(n, \boldsymbol{h})$, we set $\overline{\mathsf{Param}} = (n+1, \overline{\boldsymbol{h}})$ where $\overline{\boldsymbol{h}} = (\boldsymbol{h}, \bar{\phi})$, where $\bar{\phi}$ is a new variable. We then define

- $\overline{\mathsf{Enc1}}(X, N)$: Obtain $(\boldsymbol{c}_X(\boldsymbol{s}, \boldsymbol{h}); w_2) \leftarrow \mathsf{Enc2}(X, N)$ and parse $\boldsymbol{s} = (s_0, \ldots)$. Then, set

$$\bar{\boldsymbol{k}}_X(\bar{\alpha}, \bar{\boldsymbol{r}}, \bar{\boldsymbol{h}}) := \big(\boldsymbol{c}_X(\boldsymbol{s}, \boldsymbol{h}), \ \bar{\alpha} + \bar{\phi}s_0\big), \qquad\qquad \bar{\boldsymbol{r}} := \boldsymbol{s},$$

  and output $(\bar{\boldsymbol{k}}_X(\bar{\alpha}, \bar{\boldsymbol{r}}, \bar{\boldsymbol{h}}); w_2)$, where we treat $\bar{\alpha}$ as a new variable.
- $\overline{\mathsf{Enc2}}(Y, N)$: Obtain $(\boldsymbol{k}_Y(\alpha, \boldsymbol{r}, \boldsymbol{h}); m_2) \leftarrow \mathsf{Enc1}(Y, N)$. Then, set

$$\bar{\boldsymbol{c}}_Y(\bar{\boldsymbol{s}}, \bar{\boldsymbol{h}}) := \big(\boldsymbol{k}_Y(\bar{\phi}\bar{s}_0, \boldsymbol{r}, \boldsymbol{h}), \ \bar{s}_0\big), \qquad\qquad \bar{\boldsymbol{s}} := (\bar{s}_0, \boldsymbol{r}),$$

  and output $(\bar{\boldsymbol{c}}_Y(\bar{\boldsymbol{s}}, \bar{\boldsymbol{h}}); m_2)$, where we treat $\bar{s}_0$ as a new variable.

The correctness can be verified as follows. If $\bar{R}(X, Y) = 1$, then $R(Y, X) = 1$, hence from $\boldsymbol{c}(\boldsymbol{s}, \boldsymbol{h})$ and $\boldsymbol{k}(\bar{\phi}\bar{s}_0, \boldsymbol{r}, \boldsymbol{h})$, we can compute $(\bar{\phi}\bar{s}_0)s_0$, thanks to the correctness of P_R. From that, we obtain $(\alpha + \bar{\phi}s_0)(\bar{s}_0) - (\bar{\phi}\bar{s}_0)s_0 = \alpha\bar{s}_0$. We also note that $\mathcal{C}(\mathsf{P}_R)$ is normal by definition.

Proposition 2 ([2]). *If the pair encoding P_R for R is* perfectly *master-key hiding, then the pair encoding $\mathcal{C}(\mathsf{P}_R)$ for $\bar{R}$ is also* perfectly *master-key hiding.*

Theorem 1. *If the pair encoding P_R for R is normal and $(1, 1)$-co-selectively master-key hiding, then the pair encoding $\mathcal{C}(\mathsf{P}_R)$ for $\bar{R}$ is $(1, 1)$-selectively master-key hiding (with tight reduction).*

Theorem 2. *If the pair encoding P_R for R is normal and $(1, 1)$-selectively master-key hiding, then the pair encoding $\mathcal{C}(\mathsf{P}_R)$ for $\bar{R}$ is $(1, 1)$-co-selectively master-key hiding (with tight reduction).*

Proof (Proof of Theorem 1). Suppose that there is an adversary $\mathcal{A}$ against the $(1,1)$-SMH security of $\mathcal{C}(\mathsf{P}_R)$. We construct an algorithm $\mathcal{B}$ against the $(1,1)$-CMH security of P_R as follows. At the initialization, $\mathcal{B}$ first obtains g_1, g_2, g_3 from its challenger. $\mathcal{B}$ simply parses these to $\mathcal{A}$ for initialization.

(Simulating $\mathcal{O}^1$). In the $(1,1)$-SMH game, $\mathcal{A}$ first makes a ciphertext query for Y. $\mathcal{B}$ then makes a key query for Y to its challenger in its own $(1,1)$-CMH game and obtains $\boldsymbol{K} = g_2^{\boldsymbol{k}_Y(\alpha, \boldsymbol{r}, \boldsymbol{h})}$. The goal of $\mathcal{B}$ is to guess if $\alpha = 0$ or $\alpha \in_R \mathbb{Z}_N$. $\mathcal{B}$ samples $\bar{\phi}', \bar{s}_0 \xleftarrow{\$} \mathbb{Z}_N$ and *implicitly* defines $\bar{\phi} = \bar{\phi}' + \alpha/\bar{s}_0$. $\mathcal{B}$ then computes

$$\tilde{\boldsymbol{C}} = g_2^{\boldsymbol{k}_Y(\bar{\phi}'\bar{s}_0, 0, 0)} \cdot \boldsymbol{K} = g_2^{\boldsymbol{k}_Y(\bar{\phi}'\bar{s}_0 + \alpha, \boldsymbol{r}, \boldsymbol{h})} = g_2^{\boldsymbol{k}_Y(\bar{\phi}\bar{s}_0, \boldsymbol{r}, \boldsymbol{h})},$$

where the middle equation holds from the definition of $\boldsymbol{K}$ and thanks to the identity Eq. (1), while the last equation holds due to that $\bar{\phi}\bar{s}_0 = (\bar{\phi}' + \alpha/\bar{s}_0)\bar{s}_0 = \bar{\phi}'\bar{s}_0 + \alpha$. $\mathcal{B}$ then returns the ciphertext $\bar{\boldsymbol{C}} = (\tilde{\boldsymbol{C}}, g_2^{\bar{s}_0}) = g_2^{\bar{\boldsymbol{c}}_Y(\bar{\boldsymbol{s}}, \bar{\boldsymbol{h}})}$ to $\mathcal{A}$. This perfectly simulates the answer for the query Y to $\mathcal{O}^1$ for $\mathcal{A}$.

(Simulating $\mathcal{O}^2$). $\mathcal{A}$ makes a key query for X such that $\bar{R}(X, Y) = 0$. $\mathcal{B}$ then makes a ciphertext query for X to its challenger in its own $(1,1)$-CMH game, which can be done since $R(Y, X) = \bar{R}(X, Y) = 0$, and obtains $\boldsymbol{C} = g_2^{\boldsymbol{c}_X(\boldsymbol{s}, \boldsymbol{h})}$. $\mathcal{B}$ then *implicitly* defines $\bar{\alpha} = -\alpha s_0/\bar{s}_0$. This is distributed independently from other elements since the other place where α appears is in $\bar{\phi}$ but there, α is hidden by the random value $\bar{\phi}'$. $\mathcal{B}$ then computes

$$g_2^{\bar{\alpha} + \bar{\phi}s_0} = g_2^{(-\alpha s_0/\bar{s}_0) + (\bar{\phi}' + \alpha/\bar{s}_0)s_0} = g_2^{-\alpha s_0/\bar{s}_0 + \bar{\phi}'s_0 + \alpha s_0/\bar{s}_0} = g_2^{\bar{\phi}'s_0},$$

which can be computed since $g_2^{s_0}$ is available from $\boldsymbol{C}$ due to the *normality* of encoding. $\mathcal{B}$ returns $\bar{\boldsymbol{K}} = (\boldsymbol{C}, g_2^{\bar{\alpha}+\bar{\phi}s_0}) = g_2^{\bar{\boldsymbol{k}}_X(\bar{\alpha}, \bar{\boldsymbol{r}}, \bar{\boldsymbol{h}})}$ to $\mathcal{A}$. It perfectly simulates the answer for the query X to $\mathcal{O}^2$ for $\mathcal{A}$.

(Output). Finally, when $\mathcal{A}$ outputs b' as its guess, $\mathcal{B}$ also outputs the same value b'. Now since we have (implicitly) defined $\bar{\alpha} = -\alpha s_0/\bar{s}_0$, we have that if $\alpha = 0$, then $\bar{\alpha} = 0$, and if $\alpha \in_R \mathbb{Z}_N$, then $\bar{\alpha} \in_R \mathbb{Z}_N$. Therefore, the advantage of $\mathcal{B}$ is equal to that of $\mathcal{A}$. This concludes the proof.

Proof (Proof of Theorem 2). Suppose that there is an adversary $\mathcal{A}$ against the $(1,1)$-CMH security of $\mathcal{C}(\mathsf{P}_R)$. We claim that we can construct an efficient algorithm $\mathcal{B}$ against the $(1,1)$-SMH security of P_R that has the same advantage as $\mathcal{A}$, and hence conclude the proof. This can be done analogously to the previous proof. The only difference is the order of the key and ciphertext queries by $\mathcal{A}$. In the $(1,1)$-CMH game, $\mathcal{A}$ makes a key query for Y first, then a ciphertext query for X. But this is exactly the same order in the $(1,1)$-SMH game for $\mathcal{B}$, where $\mathcal{B}$ will ask a ciphertext query for Y first, then a key query for X. The detailed simulation is exactly the same as the previous proof.

The following corollary follows from the above two theorems and Corollary 1.

Corollary 2. *For any PPT adversary $\mathcal{A}$, there exist PPT algorithms $\mathcal{B}_1, \mathcal{B}_2, \mathcal{B}_3,$ $\mathcal{B}_4, \mathcal{B}_5$, whose running times are the same as $\mathcal{A}$ plus some polynomial times, such that for any λ,*

$$\mathsf{Adv}_{\mathcal{A}}^{\mathsf{ABE}(\mathcal{C}(\mathsf{P}))}(\lambda) \leq 2\mathsf{Adv}_{\mathcal{B}_1}^{\mathsf{SD1}}(\lambda) + (2q_{\mathrm{all}} + 1)\mathsf{Adv}_{\mathcal{B}_2}^{\mathsf{SD2}}(\lambda) + \mathsf{Adv}_{\mathcal{B}_3}^{\mathsf{SD3}}(\lambda)$$
$$+ q_1\mathsf{Adv}_{\mathcal{B}_4}^{(1,1)\text{-}\mathsf{SMH}(\mathsf{P})}(\lambda) + q_2\mathsf{Adv}_{\mathcal{B}_5}^{(1,1)\text{-}\mathsf{CMH}(\mathsf{P})}(\lambda),$$

where q_1 and q_2 denotes the number of queries in phase 1 and phase 2, respectively, and $q_{\mathrm{all}} = q_1 + q_2$.

5   Concrete Dual Schemes with Tighter Reduction

Our generic dual conversion in the previous section can convert $(1, 1)$-CMH-secure encoding into $(1, 1)$-SMH-secure encoding, and vice versa. This results in ABE with $O(q_{\mathrm{all}})$ reduction by Corollary 1. In this section, we provide a direct construction of pair encoding scheme of a certain dual predicate and show that it is $(1, 1)$-CMH-secure and $(1, \mathsf{poly})$-SMH-secure. Therefore, the resulting ABE enjoys tighter reduction of $O(q_1)$ by Proposition 1. We focus on the CP-DSE primitive, which is the dual of KP-DSE. Although we will obtain a specific scheme, we give a generic conversion that is extended from the previous conversion. This conversion has the same properties as in Theorem 1 and 2, that is, it converts $(1, 1)$-CMH-secure encoding into $(1, 1)$-SMH-secure encoding, and vice versa. The new result here is that we can prove the $(1, \mathsf{poly})$-SMH security of the encoding scheme for CP-DSE obtained by applying this new conversion to the encoding of KP-DSE in [2]. Intuitively, we use the *randomizer technique* from [2,27] for obtaining $(1, \mathsf{poly})$-SMH. To enable this, we require one more element each for a key and a ciphertext (elements related to $\bar{u}, \bar{\eta}$ below).

Extended Dual Conversion. Given a pair encoding scheme P_R for predicate R, we construct a predicate encoding scheme $\mathcal{EC}(\mathsf{P}_R)$ for $\bar{R}$ as follows. For $\mathsf{Param} \to (n, \boldsymbol{h})$, we set $\overline{\mathsf{Param}} = (n + 2, \overline{\boldsymbol{h}})$ where $\overline{\boldsymbol{h}} = (\boldsymbol{h}, \bar{\phi}, \bar{\eta})$, where $\bar{\phi}, \bar{\eta}$ are new variables. We then define

- $\overline{\mathsf{Enc1}}(X, N)$: Obtain $(\boldsymbol{c}_X(\boldsymbol{s}, \boldsymbol{h}); w_2) \leftarrow \mathsf{Enc2}(X, N)$ and parse $\boldsymbol{s} = (s_0, \dots)$. Then, set

$$\overline{\boldsymbol{k}}_X(\bar{\alpha}, \bar{\boldsymbol{r}}, \overline{\boldsymbol{h}}) := \big(\boldsymbol{c}_X(\boldsymbol{s}, \boldsymbol{h}), \ \bar{\alpha} + \bar{\phi}s_0 + \bar{u}\bar{\eta}, \ \bar{u}\big), \qquad \bar{\boldsymbol{r}} := (\boldsymbol{s}, \bar{u}),$$

and output $(\overline{\boldsymbol{k}}_X(\bar{\alpha}, \bar{\boldsymbol{r}}, \overline{\boldsymbol{h}}); w_2 + 1)$, where we treat $\bar{\alpha}, \bar{u}$ as new variables.
- $\overline{\mathsf{Enc2}}(Y, N)$: Obtain $(\boldsymbol{k}_Y(\alpha, \boldsymbol{r}, \boldsymbol{h}); m_2) \leftarrow \mathsf{Enc1}(Y, N)$. Then, set

$$\overline{\boldsymbol{c}}_Y(\bar{\boldsymbol{s}}, \overline{\boldsymbol{h}}) := \big(\boldsymbol{k}_Y(\bar{\phi}\bar{s}_0, \boldsymbol{r}, \boldsymbol{h}), \ \bar{s}_0, \ \bar{s}_0\bar{\eta}\big), \qquad \bar{\boldsymbol{s}} := (\bar{s}_0, \boldsymbol{r}),$$

and output $(\overline{\boldsymbol{c}}_Y(\bar{\boldsymbol{s}}, \overline{\boldsymbol{h}}); m_2)$, where we treat $\bar{s}_0$ as a new variable.

The correctness can be verified as follows. If $\bar{R}(X, Y) = 1$, then $R(Y, X) = 1$, hence from $\boldsymbol{c}(\boldsymbol{s}, \boldsymbol{h})$ and $\boldsymbol{k}(\bar{\phi}\bar{s}_0, \boldsymbol{r}, \boldsymbol{h})$, we can compute $(\bar{\phi}\bar{s}_0)s_0$, thanks to the correctness of P_R. We thus obtain $(\alpha + \bar{\phi}s_0 + \bar{u}\bar{\eta})(\bar{s}_0) - (\bar{\phi}\bar{s}_0)s_0 - \bar{u}(\bar{s}_0\bar{\eta}) = \alpha\bar{s}_0$.

Corollary 3. *If the pair encoding scheme* P_R *for* R *is* $(1,1)$-*CMH, then the pair encoding scheme* $\mathcal{EC}(\mathsf{P}_R)$ *for* $\bar{R}$ *is* $(1,1)$-*SMH. If the pair encoding scheme* P_R *for* R *is* $(1,1)$-*SMH, then the pair encoding scheme* $\mathcal{EC}(\mathsf{P}_R)$ *for* $\bar{R}$ *is* $(1,1)$-*CMH.*

Proof. The proof follows exactly in the same manner as Theorem 1, 2 except that the reduction $\mathcal{B}$ also randomly chooses $\bar{\eta}, \bar{u}$. The corresponding terms can be computed using $\bar{\eta}, \bar{u}$.

CP-DSE with Tighter Reduction. Due to the lack of space, we refer the definition of KP-DSE (and hence its dual, CP-DSE) to [2]. Let $\mathsf{P}_{\mathsf{KPDSE}}$ denote the pair encoding construction for KP-DSE of [2]. We obtain a new pair encoding for CP-DSE as $\mathcal{EC}(\mathsf{P}_{\mathsf{KPDSE}})$. We prove that it is $(1, \mathsf{poly})$-SMH-secure with tight reduction under a new assumption which is similar to the assumption use for proving the CMH security of $\mathsf{P}_{\mathsf{KPDSE}}$ of [2]. We defer the details to the full version.

6   Generic Conjunction and Conversion to Dual Policy

Let $R_1 : \mathbb{X}_1 \times \mathbb{Y}_1$, $R_2 : \mathbb{X}_2 \times \mathbb{Y}_2$ be two predicates. We define the *conjunctive predicate* of R_1, R_2 as $[R_1 \wedge R_2] : \tilde{\mathbb{X}} \times \tilde{\mathbb{Y}} \rightarrow \{0,1\}$ where $\tilde{\mathbb{X}} = \mathbb{X}_1 \times \mathbb{X}_2$, $\tilde{\mathbb{Y}} = \mathbb{Y}_1 \times \mathbb{Y}_2$ and $[R_1 \wedge R_2]((X_1, X_2), (Y_1, Y_2)) = 1$ iff $R_1(X_1, Y_1) = 1$ *and* $R_2(X_2, Y_2) = 1$. Next, let $R : \mathbb{X} \times \mathbb{Y}$ be a predicate. We define its *dual-policy predicate* (DP) as the conjunctive of itself and its dual predicate, $\bar{R}$. Hence, its notation is $[R \wedge \bar{R}]$.

Conjunctive Predicate Conversion. Given two pair encoding schemes: P_{R_1} for predicate R_1 and P_{R_2} for predicate R_2, we construct a predicate encoding scheme denoted $\mathcal{D}(\mathsf{P}_{R_1}, \mathsf{P}_{R_2})$ for predicate $[R_1 \wedge R_2]$ as follows. For $\mathsf{Param}_1 \rightarrow (n_1, \boldsymbol{h}_1)$, $\mathsf{Param}_2 \rightarrow (n_2, \boldsymbol{h}_2)$, we set $\widehat{\mathsf{Param}} = (n_1 + n_2, \hat{\boldsymbol{h}})$ where $\hat{\boldsymbol{h}} = (\boldsymbol{h}_1, \boldsymbol{h}_2)$. We then define

- $\widehat{\mathsf{Enc1}}((X_1, X_2), N)$: For $i = 1, 2$, obtain $(\boldsymbol{k}_{X_i}(\alpha_i, \boldsymbol{r}_i, \boldsymbol{h}_i); m_{2,i}) \leftarrow \mathsf{Enc1}_i(X_i, N)$. Then, set

$$\hat{\boldsymbol{k}}_{(X_1, X_2)}(\hat{\alpha}, \hat{\boldsymbol{r}}, \hat{\boldsymbol{h}}) := \big(\boldsymbol{k}_{X_1}(\hat{r}, \boldsymbol{r}_1, \boldsymbol{h}_1), \boldsymbol{k}_{X_2}(\hat{\alpha} - \hat{r}, \boldsymbol{r}_2, \boldsymbol{h}_2)\big), \quad \hat{\boldsymbol{r}} := (\boldsymbol{r}_1, \boldsymbol{r}_2, \hat{r}),$$

  and output $(\hat{\boldsymbol{k}}_X(\alpha, \hat{\boldsymbol{r}}, \hat{\boldsymbol{h}}); m_{2,1} + m_{2,2} + 1)$, where we treat $\hat{\alpha}, \hat{r}$ as new variables.
- $\widehat{\mathsf{Enc2}}(Y, N)$: For $i = 1, 2$, obtain $(\boldsymbol{c}_{Y_i}(\boldsymbol{s}_i, \boldsymbol{h}_i); w_{2,i}) \leftarrow \mathsf{Enc2}_i(Y_i, N)$. Parse $\boldsymbol{s}_i = (s_{0,i}, \boldsymbol{s}_i')$, and set

$$\hat{\boldsymbol{c}}_{(Y_1, Y_2)}(\hat{\boldsymbol{s}}, \hat{\boldsymbol{h}}) := \big(\boldsymbol{c}_{Y_1}((s_0, \boldsymbol{s}_1'), \boldsymbol{h}_1), \boldsymbol{c}_{Y_2}((s_0, \boldsymbol{s}_2'), \boldsymbol{h}_2)\big), \quad \hat{\boldsymbol{s}} := (s_0, \boldsymbol{s}_1', \boldsymbol{s}_2'),$$

  and output $(\hat{\boldsymbol{c}}_{(Y_1, Y_2)}(\hat{\boldsymbol{s}}, \hat{\boldsymbol{h}}); w_{2,1} + w_{2,2})$, where we treat s_0 as a new variable.

The correctness can be verified as follows. If $[R_1 \wedge R_2]((X_1, X_2), (Y_1, Y_2)) = 1$, then $R_1(X_1, Y_1) = 1$ *and* $R_2(X_2, Y_2) = 1$. Hence, from $\boldsymbol{k}_{X_1}(\hat{r}, \boldsymbol{r}_1, \boldsymbol{h}_1)$ and $\boldsymbol{c}_{Y_1}((s_0, \boldsymbol{s}_1'), \boldsymbol{h}_1)$, we obtain $\hat{r}s_0$, due to the correctness of P_{R_1}. Similarly, from $\boldsymbol{k}_{X_2}(\hat{\alpha} - \hat{r}, \boldsymbol{r}_2, \boldsymbol{h}_2)$ and $\boldsymbol{c}_{Y_2}((s_0, \boldsymbol{s}_2'), \boldsymbol{h}_2)$, we obtain $(\hat{\alpha} - \hat{r})s_0$, due to the correctness of P_{R_2}. From these, we obtain $\hat{r}s_0 + (\hat{\alpha} - \hat{r})s_0 = \hat{\alpha}s_0$.

Theorem 3. *If the pair encoding schemes P_{R_1} for R_1 and P_{R_2} for R_2 are perfectly master-key hiding, then the pair encoding scheme $\mathcal{D}(\mathsf{P}_{R_1}, \mathsf{P}_{R_2})$ for $[R_1 \wedge R_2]$ is also perfectly master-key hiding.*

Proof. Consider $(X_1, X_2), (Y_1, Y_2)$ such that $[R_1 \wedge R_2]((X_1, X_2), (Y_1, Y_2)) = 0$. If $R_1(X_1, Y_1) = 0$, from the perfect security of P_{R_1}, we have that $\hat{r}$ is hidden, hence $\hat{\alpha}$ is also hidden since it is masked with $\hat{r}$. If $R_2(X_2, Y_2) = 0$, from the perfect security of P_{R_2}, we have $\hat{\alpha} - \hat{r}$ is hidden and hence $\hat{\alpha}$ is also hidden. In both cases, we have that $\hat{\alpha}$ is hidden as required.

Theorem 4. *For the notion $\mathsf{X} \in \{(1,1)\text{-SMH}, (1,1)\text{-CMH}\}$, if the pair encoding schemes P_{R_1} for R_1 and P_{R_2} for R_2 are both normal and X-secure, then the pair encoding scheme $\mathcal{D}(\mathsf{P}_{R_1}, \mathsf{P}_{R_2})$ for $[R_1 \wedge R_2]$ is also X-secure. More precisely, for any PPT adversary $\mathcal{A}$, there exist a PPT algorithm $\mathcal{B}$, whose running time is the same as $\mathcal{A}$ plus some polynomial time, such that for any λ,*

$$\mathsf{Adv}_{\mathcal{A}}^{\mathsf{X}(\mathcal{D}(\mathsf{P}_{R_1}, \mathsf{P}_{R_2}))}(\lambda) \leq 2\mathsf{Adv}_{\mathcal{B}}^{\mathsf{X}(\mathsf{P}_{R_1})}(\lambda) + 2\mathsf{Adv}_{\mathcal{B}}^{\mathsf{X}(\mathsf{P}_{R_2})}(\lambda) \tag{2}$$

The following corollary is immediate from Theorem 1, 2, and 4.

Corollary 4. *If the pair encoding scheme P_R for R is normal, $(1,1)$-selectively, and $(1,1)$-co-selectively master-key hiding, then the pair encoding $\mathcal{D}(\mathsf{P}_R, \mathcal{C}(\mathsf{P}_R))$ for $[R \wedge \bar{R}]$ is also $(1,1)$-selectively and $(1,1)$-co-selectively master-key hiding.*

Proof (Proof of Theorem 4). We prove for the case of SMH. The case for CMH can be done in exactly the same manner except exchanging the order of oracles. Suppose that there is an adversary $\mathcal{A}$ against the $(1,1)$-SMH security of $\mathcal{D}(\mathsf{P}_{R_1}, \mathsf{P}_{R_2})$. We construct an algorithm $\mathcal{B}$ against the $(1,1)$-SMH security of either P_{R_1} or P_{R_2} as follows. Firstly, $\mathcal{B}$ flips a coin $b \xleftarrow{\$} \{1, 2\}$ for determining to break the $(1,1)$-SMH security of P_{R_b}. At the initialization, $\mathcal{B}$ first obtains g_1, g_2, g_3 from its challenger (of the $(1,1)$-SMH game for P_{R_b}). $\mathcal{B}$ simply parses these to $\mathcal{A}$ for initialization. Let $\tilde{b} = 1$ if $b = 2$, and $\tilde{b} = 2$ if $b = 1$. $\mathcal{B}$ will construct all parameters for $\mathsf{P}_{R_{\tilde{b}}}$ by itself by choosing $h_{\tilde{b}} \xleftarrow{\$} \mathbb{Z}_p^{n_{\tilde{b}}}$.

(Simulating $\mathcal{O}^1$). In the $(1,1)$-SMH game, $\mathcal{A}$ first makes a ciphertext query for (Y_1, Y_2). $\mathcal{B}$ then makes a key query for Y_b to its challenger (of the $(1,1)$-SMH game for P_{R_b}) and obtains $g_2^{c_{Y_b}(s_b, h_b)}$. Due to the normality, $\mathcal{B}$ can parse $g_2^{s_{0,b}}$ from this. We implicitly set $s_0 = s_{0,b}$. $\mathcal{B}$ chooses $\delta \xleftarrow{\$} \mathbb{Z}_p^{w_{2,\tilde{b}}}$ then computes $(g_2^{s_0})^{c_{Y_{\tilde{b}}}((1,\delta), h_{\tilde{b}})} = g_2^{c_{Y_{\tilde{b}}}((s_0, s_0\delta), h_{\tilde{b}})}$. This holds due to linearity. This implicitly sets $s'_{\tilde{b}} = s_0\delta$. $\mathcal{B}$ then returns $g_2^{c_{Y_b}(s_b, h_b)}$ and $g_2^{c_{Y_{\tilde{b}}}((s_0, s'_{\tilde{b}}), h_{\tilde{b}})}$ in the order according to b (*i.e.*, if $b = 1$, they are in this order, otherwise, we swap them).

(Simulating $\mathcal{O}^2$). The adversary $\mathcal{A}$ makes a key query for (X_1, X_2) such that $[R_1 \wedge R_2]((X_1, X_2), (Y_1, Y_2)) = 0$. There are two possible cases. If $R_b(X_b, Y_b) = 0$, then $\mathcal{B}$ makes a key query for X_b to its challenger (of the $(1,1)$-SMH game for P_{R_b}) and obtains $\boldsymbol{K}_b = g_2^{k_{X_b}(\alpha_b, r_b, h_b)}$. Otherwise, $R_b(X_b, Y_b) = 1$, $\mathcal{B}$ will ask some legitimate key query and simply outputs a random guess, while abort the game with $\mathcal{A}$. We now proceed with the former case, where it is further categorized into two cases:

- If $b = 1$, then $\mathcal{B}$ implicitly sets $\hat{\alpha} = \alpha_1$ and $\hat{r} = \alpha_1 + \hat{r}'$ where $\mathcal{B}$ chooses $\hat{r}' \xleftarrow{\$} \mathbb{Z}_p$. Hence, $\hat{\alpha} - \hat{r} = -\hat{r}'$. $\mathcal{B}$ computes $\hat{\boldsymbol{K}}_1 := g_2^{\boldsymbol{k}_{X_1}(\hat{r}',0,0)} \cdot \boldsymbol{K}_1 = g_2^{\boldsymbol{k}_{X_1}(\alpha_1+\hat{r}',\boldsymbol{r}_1,\boldsymbol{h}_1)} = g_2^{\boldsymbol{k}_{X_1}(\hat{r},\boldsymbol{r}_1,\boldsymbol{h}_1)}$, which holds from the identity Eq. (1). $\mathcal{B}$ then computes $\hat{\boldsymbol{K}}_2 := g_2^{\boldsymbol{k}_{X_2}(-\hat{r}',\boldsymbol{r}_2,\boldsymbol{h}_2)} = g_2^{\boldsymbol{k}_{X_2}(\hat{\alpha}-\hat{r},\boldsymbol{r}_2,\boldsymbol{h}_2)}$ by choosing $\boldsymbol{r}_2 \xleftarrow{\$} \mathbb{Z}_p^{m_{2,2}}$ (and recall that $\mathcal{B}$ possesses $\boldsymbol{h}_2$). $\mathcal{B}$ returns $(\hat{\boldsymbol{K}}_1, \hat{\boldsymbol{K}}_2)$ to $\mathcal{A}$.

- If $b = 2$, then $\mathcal{B}$ implicitly sets $\hat{\alpha} = \alpha_2$. $\mathcal{B}$ chooses $\hat{r} \xleftarrow{\$} \mathbb{Z}_p$. $\mathcal{B}$ computes $\hat{\boldsymbol{K}}_1 := g_2^{\boldsymbol{k}_{X_1}(\hat{r},\boldsymbol{r}_1,\boldsymbol{h}_1)}$ by choosing $\boldsymbol{r}_1 \xleftarrow{\$} \mathbb{Z}_p^{m_{2,1}}$ (and recall that $\mathcal{B}$ possesses $\boldsymbol{h}_1$). $\mathcal{B}$ then computes $\hat{\boldsymbol{K}}_2 := g_2^{\boldsymbol{k}_{X_2}(-\hat{r},0,0)} \cdot \boldsymbol{K}_2 = g^{\boldsymbol{k}_{X_2}(\hat{\alpha}-\hat{r},\boldsymbol{r}_2,\boldsymbol{h}_2)}$, which holds due to the identity Eq. (1). $\mathcal{B}$ returns $(\hat{\boldsymbol{K}}_1, \hat{\boldsymbol{K}}_2)$ to $\mathcal{A}$.

In both cases, we have $\hat{\alpha} = \alpha_b$. Hence $\mathcal{B}$ just outputs its guess (of whether $\alpha_b = 0$ or $\alpha_b \xleftarrow{\$} \mathbb{Z}_p$) to be exactly the same as the output of $\mathcal{A}$ (who guesses whether $\hat{\alpha} = 0$ or $\hat{\alpha} \xleftarrow{\$} \mathbb{Z}_p$). Since $\mathcal{B}$ aborts with probability $1/2$, we have the inequality (2).

7   Implied Instantiations

Policy over Doubly-Spatial Encryption. We obtain the first two (fully-secure) CP-DSE schemes. The first scheme is automatically obtained by applying the generic dual conversion to the KP-DSE of [2] (and use Theorem 1, 2). The resulting CP-DSE has reduction $O(q_{\text{all}})$, as shown in Corollary 2. The second scheme is directly constructed and has tighter reduction of $O(q_1)$ (see §5). We then obtain the first dual-policy over DSE (DP-DSE) by applying the generic conjunctive conversion to the KP-DSE of [2] and our first CP-DSE (and use Corollary 4).

ABE for Boolean Formulae (and Monotone Span Programs). We obtain various schemes:

- **Unbounded ABE.** We obtain the first fully-secure completely-unbounded CP-ABE schemes. Such schemes should pose no bounds such as the attribute set or policy size per ciphertext or key, the attribute universe size, and the number of attribute repetition (also called multi-use) in a policy. We use the fact that any pair encoding for CP-DSE implies an encoding for completely-unbounded CP-ABE as a special case. This is shown for the key-policy case in [2], but is also straightforward for the ciphertext-policy case by just exchanging key and ciphertext encodings. Hence, we have two completely-unbounded CP-ABE schemes, one with $O(q_{\text{all}})$ and one with $O(q_1)$ reduction. We then obtain the first completely-unbounded DP-ABE by applying the generic conjunctive conversion to the unbounded KP-ABE of [2] and our first unbounded CP-ABE (and use Corollary 4), or equivalently, we can view unbounded DP-ABE as a special case of DP-DSE.

Table 1. Previous schemes and our new instantiations, positioned by predicates and properties, where we recall that KP, CP, DP stands for key-policy, ciphertext-policy, and dual-policy, respectively

Predicate	Properties			KP	CP	DP
	Security	Universe	Multi-use			
Policy over DSE	full	-	-	A14 [2]	**Ours**	**Ours**
Unbounded ABE	selective	large	unbound	LW11 [26], RW13 [31]	RW13 [31]	none none
	full	small	unbound	LW12 [27]	LW12 [27]	none
	full	large	bound	OT12 [30]	OT12 [30]	none
	full	large	unbound	A14 [2]	**Ours**	**Ours**
Short-Cipher ABE	selective	large	unbound	ALP11 [6]	open[‡]	open
	full	large	unbound	A14 [2]	open[‡]	open
Short-Key ABE	selective	large	unbound	BGG+14 [8]	none	open
	full	large	unbound	open	**Ours**	open
(Bounded) ABE	selective	large	unbound	GPSW06 [21]	W11 [34]	AI09 [5]
	full	small	bound	LOS+10 [28]	LOS+10 [28]	**Ours**
	full	large	bound	OT10 [29], A14 [2]	OT10 [29], A14 [2]	**Ours**
Regular Languages	selective	small	-	W12 [35]	none	none
	full	large	-	A14 [2]	A14 [2]	**Ours**

[†] 'none' means that there was no previous work and it is subsumed by another system with stronger properties (*e.g.,* fully-secure). 'open' means that it remains an open problem. '-' means no defined property.

[‡] Short-cipher CP-ABE were given in [4,11,13,24] but only for subclasses of span programs (AND, threshold).

- **ABE with Short Keys.** Any pair encoding for CP-DSE implies an encoding for CP-ABE with constant-size keys as a special case. This is analogous to the implication of KP-ABE with short ciphertexts from KP-DSE shown in [2]. We use the same implication but swap key and ciphertext encodings, hence short ciphertexts become short keys. From this, we obtain the first fully-secure CP-ABE with short keys. Note that it requires bounded-size attribute set per key.

- **(Bounded) ABE.** By applying the generic conjunctive conversion to the bounded KP-ABE and CP-ABE of [28] (and use Theorem 3), we obtain a fully-secure bounded DP-ABE for small-universe. Similarly, we obtain a large-universe variant from other KP-ABE and CP-ABE in [2] (namely, Scheme 12,13 in [2]). These systems require the bounds on the size of attribute sets for each ciphertext (in KP-ABE) or each key (in CP-ABE). Nevertheless, the underlying security of these encodings are perfectly master-key hiding, which is for free (no assumption needed for it), hence these systems use only subgroup decision assumptions required for the framework of [2].

ABE for Regular Languages (ABE-RL). In KP-ABE for regular languages, we have a key associated to the description of a deterministic finite automata (DFA) M, while a ciphertext is associated to a string w, and $R(M, w) = 1$ if the automata M accepts the string w. We refer to [2, 35] for detailed definitions. By applying the generic conjunctive conversion and Theorem 4 to the KP-ABE-RL and CP-ABE-RL in [2], we obtain the first (fully-secure) DP-ABE-RL.

References

1. Akinyele, J., Lehmann, C., Green, M., Pagano, M., Peterson, Z., Rubin, A.: Self-Protecting Electronic Medical Records Using Attribute-Based Encryption. Cryptology ePrint Archive, Report 2010/565
2. Attrapadung, N.: Dual system encryption via doubly selective security: framework, fully secure functional encryption for regular languages, and more. In: Nguyen, P.Q., Oswald, E. (eds.) EUROCRYPT 2014. LNCS, vol. 8441, pp. 557–577. Springer, Heidelberg (2014)
3. Attrapadung, N.: Fully Secure and Succinct Attribute Based Encryption for Circuits from Multi-linear Maps. Cryptology ePrint Archive: Report 2014/772
4. Attrapadung, N., Herranz, J., Laguillaumie, F., Libert, B., Panafieu, E., Rafols, C.: Attribute-based encryption schemes with constant-size ciphertexts. Theoretical Computer Science **422**, 15–38 (2012)
5. Attrapadung, N., Imai, H.: Dual-policy attribute based encryption. In: Abdalla, M., Pointcheval, D., Fouque, P.-A., Vergnaud, D. (eds.) ACNS 2009. LNCS, vol. 5536, pp. 168–185. Springer, Heidelberg (2009)
6. Attrapadung, N., Libert, B., de Panafieu, E.: Expressive key-policy attribute-based encryption with constant-size ciphertexts. In: Catalano, D., Fazio, N., Gennaro, R., Nicolosi, A. (eds.) PKC 2011. LNCS, vol. 6571, pp. 90–108. Springer, Heidelberg (2011)
7. Bethencourt, J., Sahai, A., Waters, B.: Ciphertext-policy attribute-based encryption. In: IEEE Symposium on Security and Privacy, pp. 321–334 (2007)
8. Boneh, D., Gentry, C., Gorbunov, S., Halevi, S., Nikolaenko, V., Segev, G., Vaikuntanathan, V., Vinayagamurthy, D.: Fully key-homomorphic encryption, arithmetic circuit ABE and compact garbled circuits. In: Nguyen, P.Q., Oswald, E. (eds.) EUROCRYPT 2014. LNCS, vol. 8441, pp. 533–556. Springer, Heidelberg (2014)
9. Boneh, D., Hamburg, M.: Generalized identity based and broadcast encryption schemes. In: Pieprzyk, J. (ed.) ASIACRYPT 2008. LNCS, vol. 5350, pp. 455–470. Springer, Heidelberg (2008)
10. Boneh, D., Sahai, A., Waters, B.: Functional encryption: definitions and challenges. In: Ishai, Y. (ed.) TCC 2011. LNCS, vol. 6597, pp. 253–273. Springer, Heidelberg (2011)
11. Chen, C., Chen, J., Lim, H.W., Zhang, Z., Feng, D., Ling, S., Wang, H.: Fully secure attribute-based systems with short ciphertexts/signatures and threshold access structures. In: Dawson, E. (ed.) CT-RSA 2013. LNCS, vol. 7779, pp. 50–67. Springer, Heidelberg (2013)
12. Coron, J.-S., Lepoint, T., Tibouchi, M.: Practical multilinear maps over the integers. In: Canetti, R., Garay, J.A. (eds.) CRYPTO 2013, Part I. LNCS, vol. 8042, pp. 476–493. Springer, Heidelberg (2013)

13. Emura, K., Miyaji, A., Nomura, A., Omote, K., Soshi, M.: A ciphertext-policy attribute-based encryption scheme with constant ciphertext length. In: Bao, F., Li, H., Wang, G. (eds.) ISPEC 2009. LNCS, vol. 5451, pp. 13–23. Springer, Heidelberg (2009)
14. Garg, S., Gentry, C., Halevi, S.: Candidate multilinear maps from ideal lattices. In: Johansson, T., Nguyen, P.Q. (eds.) EUROCRYPT 2013. LNCS, vol. 7881, pp. 1–17. Springer, Heidelberg (2013)
15. Garg, S., Gentry, C., Halevi, S., Sahai, A., Waters, B.: Attribute-based encryption for circuits from multilinear maps. In: Canetti, R., Garay, J.A. (eds.) CRYPTO 2013, Part II. LNCS, vol. 8043, pp. 479–499. Springer, Heidelberg (2013)
16. Garg, S., Gentry, C., Halevi, S., Raykova, M., Sahai, A., Waters, B.: Candidate indistinguishability obfuscation and functional encryption for all circuits. In: FOCS 2013, pp. 40–49 (2013)
17. Garg, S., Gentry, C., Halevi, S., Zhandry, M.: Fully Secure Attribute Based Encryption from Multilinear Maps. Cryptology ePrint Archive: Report 2014/622
18. Goldwasser, S., Kalai, Y., Popa, R.A., Vaikuntanathan, V., Zeldovich, N.: Reusable garbled circuits and succinct functional encryption. In: STOC 2013, pp. 555–564 (2013)
19. Goldwasser, S., Kalai, Y.T., Popa, R.A., Vaikuntanathan, V., Zeldovich, N.: How to run turing machines on encrypted data. In: Canetti, R., Garay, J.A. (eds.) CRYPTO 2013, Part II. LNCS, vol. 8043, pp. 536–553. Springer, Heidelberg (2013)
20. Gorbunov, S., Vaikuntanathan, V., Wee, H.: Attribute-based encryption for circuits. In: STOC 2013, pp. 545–554 (2013)
21. Goyal, V., Pandey, O., Sahai, A., Waters, B.: Attribute-based encryption for fine-grained access control of encrypted data. In: ACM CCS 2006, pp. 89–98 (2006)
22. Goyal, V., Jain, A., Pandey, O., Sahai, A.: Bounded ciphertext policy attribute based encryption. In: Aceto, L., Damgård, I., Goldberg, L.A., Halldórsson, M.M., Ingólfsdóttir, A., Walukiewicz, I. (eds.) ICALP 2008, Part II. LNCS, vol. 5126, pp. 579–591. Springer, Heidelberg (2008)
23. Hamburg, M.: Spatial Encryption (Ph.D. Thesis). Cryptology ePrint Archive: Report 2011/389
24. Herranz, J., Laguillaumie, F., Ràfols, C.: Constant size ciphertexts in threshold attribute-based encryption. In: Nguyen, P.Q., Pointcheval, D. (eds.) PKC 2010. LNCS, vol. 6056, pp. 19–34. Springer, Heidelberg (2010)
25. Lewko, A., Waters, B.: New techniques for dual system encryption and fully secure HIBE with short ciphertexts. In: Micciancio, D. (ed.) TCC 2010. LNCS, vol. 5978, pp. 455–479. Springer, Heidelberg (2010)
26. Lewko, A., Waters, B.: Unbounded HIBE and attribute-based encryption. In: Paterson, K.G. (ed.) EUROCRYPT 2011. LNCS, vol. 6632, pp. 547–567. Springer, Heidelberg (2011)
27. Lewko, A., Waters, B.: New proof methods for attribute-based encryption: achieving full security through selective techniques. In: Safavi-Naini, R., Canetti, R. (eds.) CRYPTO 2012. LNCS, vol. 7417, pp. 180–198. Springer, Heidelberg (2012)
28. Lewko, A., Okamoto, T., Sahai, A., Takashima, K., Waters, B.: Fully secure functional encryption: attribute-based encryption and (Hierarchical) inner product encryption. In: Gilbert, H. (ed.) EUROCRYPT 2010. LNCS, vol. 6110, pp. 62–91. Springer, Heidelberg (2010)
29. Okamoto, T., Takashima, K.: Fully secure functional encryption with general relations from the decisional linear assumption. In: Rabin, T. (ed.) CRYPTO 2010. LNCS, vol. 6223, pp. 191–208. Springer, Heidelberg (2010)

30. Okamoto, T., Takashima, K.: Fully secure unbounded inner-product and attribute-based encryption. In: Wang, X., Sako, K. (eds.) ASIACRYPT 2012. LNCS, vol. 7658, pp. 349–366. Springer, Heidelberg (2012)
31. Rouselakis, Y., Waters, B.: Practical constructions and new proof methods for large universe attribute-based encryption. In: ACM CCS 2013, pp. 463–474 (2013)
32. Sahai, A., Waters, B.: Fuzzy identity-based encryption. In: Cramer, R. (ed.) EUROCRYPT 2005. LNCS, vol. 3494, pp. 457–473. Springer, Heidelberg (2005)
33. Waters, B.: Ciphertext-policy attribute-based encryption: an expressive, efficient, and provably secure realization. In: Catalano, D., Fazio, N., Gennaro, R., Nicolosi, A. (eds.) PKC 2011. LNCS, vol. 6571, pp. 53–70. Springer, Heidelberg (2011)
34. Waters, B.: Dual system encryption: realizing fully secure IBE and HIBE under simple assumptions. In: Halevi, S. (ed.) CRYPTO 2009. LNCS, vol. 5677, pp. 619–636. Springer, Heidelberg (2009)
35. Waters, B.: Functional encryption for regular languages. In: Safavi-Naini, R., Canetti, R. (eds.) CRYPTO 2012. LNCS, vol. 7417, pp. 218–235. Springer, Heidelberg (2012)
36. Wee, H.: Dual system encryption via predicate encodings. In: Lindell, Y. (ed.) TCC 2014. LNCS, vol. 8349, pp. 616–637. Springer, Heidelberg (2014)

Revocable Hierarchical Identity-Based Encryption: History-Free Update, Security Against Insiders, and Short Ciphertexts

Jae Hong Seo[1]([⊠]) and Keita Emura[2]

[1] Department of Mathematics, Myongji University, Yongin, Korea
`jaehongseo@mju.ac.kr`
[2] Security Fundamentals Lab, NSRI, NICT, Tokyo, Japan
`k-emura@nict.go.jp`

Abstract. In the context of Identity-Based Encryption (IBE), both revocation and delegation of key generation are important functionalities. Although a number of IBE schemes with *either* efficient revocation *or* efficient delegation of key generation functionality have been proposed, an important open problem is efficiently delegating both the key generation and revocation functionalities in IBE systems. Seo and Emura (CT-RSA 2013) proposed the first realization of Revocable Hierarchical IBE (RHIBE), a sole IBE scheme that achieves both functionalities simultaneously. However, their approach implements history-preserving updates, wherein a low-level user must know the history of key updates performed by ancestors in the current time period, and it renders the scheme very complex.

In this paper, we present a new method to construct RHIBE that implements history-free updates. Our history-free approach renders the scheme simple and efficient. As a second contribution, we redefine the security model for RHIBE to ensure security against *insiders*, where adversaries are allowed to obtain all internal system information, e,g., state information. In addition, we also consider the decryption key exposure attack, which was considered by Seo and Emura (PKC 2013).

Further, we propose two RHIBE schemes with shorter secret keys and constant size ciphertexts that implement the aforementioned history-free updates approach and security model. For revocation, our constructions use the Complete Subtree (CS) method and the Subset Difference (SD) method. Both schemes are selectively secure in the standard model under the q-weak Bilinear Diffie-Hellman Inversion (q-wBDHI) assumption.

1 Introduction

Several systems are built upon unreliable public networks; therefore, it is necessary to secure communications among computers in such systems. To this end, most systems use key management systems based on *Public Key Infrastructure (PKI)*. However, it is at times challenging to handle a large number of public key certificates in conventional PKI key management schemes, and therefore, such

© Springer International Publishing Switzerland 2015
K. Nyberg (ed.): CT-RSA 2015, LNCS 9048, pp. 106–123, 2015.
DOI: 10.1007/978-3-319-16715-2_6

schemes are rendered impractical, particularly in the case of large distributed systems. To resolve this problem, Shamir [26] introduced Identity-Based Encryption (IBE), which allows the use of an arbitrary bit string , such as an email address, as a public key. In IBE systems, the Key Generation Center (KGC) plays an important role in that it generates all the secret keys of users and establishes secure channels to transmit each user's secret key. However, a large number for users results in considerable workload for a single KGC to handle, and mitigating the same is an important issue. Horwitz and Lynn [11] introduced the concept of Hierarchical IBE (HIBE) which enables the KGC to delegate key generation functionality to a low-level KGC. Apart from improved efficiency, which is a prominent advantage of HIBE, there are several applications of HIBE, e.g., forward secure encryption [7], public key broadcast encryption [9], etc.

Boneh and Franklin proposed the first IBE construction, in [5], that explained a trivial way to revoke users; encryptors use the current time as a part of the recipient's identity, and for each time period, the KGC issues new secret keys for non-revoked users. However, this trivial revocation method that updates individual non-revoked users' secret keys imposes an excessive workload on the KGC. Boldyreva, Goyal, and Kumar [1] proposed a Revocable IBE (RIBE) scheme that drastically reduces the workload of the KGC, from linear complexity to logarithmic complexity in the number of users. The first fully secure RIBE construction has been proposed by Libert and Vergnaud [15]. Their RIBE construction is based on a variant [16] of Waters IBE [28]. Moreover, Seo and Emura [22,24] refined the security model of Boldyreva-Goyal-Kumar's RIBE scheme by considering a new realistic threat, called *decryption key exposure*. Note that all aforementioned schemes with revocation functionality, except for Boneh-Franklin's non-scalable one, use Complete Subtree (CS) revocation method due to Naor, Naor, and Lotspiech [17]. There is another revocation methodology of Naor-Naor-Lotspiech, called Subset Difference (SD), which has better performance than CS in the transmission complexity but larger secret key size. Very recently, Lee, Lee, and Park [13] proposed the first RIBE with the subset difference revocation method. RIBE from lattice also has been proposed in [8] though it does not consider decryption key exposure attack. Moreover, RIBE with rejoin funcionality has been considered in [25] where the same identity can be used after a secret key is revoked.

Previous Approach for Revocable HIBE. In the design of Revocable HIBE (RHIBE), it must be noted that a low-level user may remain in the system only if the corresponding parent user remains in the system for a given time period; that is, low-level secret keys can remain activated only till the parent secret key remains activated. In particular, as pointed out by Seo and Emura [21], a trivial combination of RIBE and HIBE will result in an impractical scheme with an exponential number of secret keys, as each secret key in all known scalable RIBE schemes consist of several partial keys, and only one of them is used to generate a decryption key according to the current key update.[1] More specifically, if we

---

[1] There is another RHIBE construction proposed by Tsai, Tseng, and Wu [27]. However, we do not consider that scheme because it is not scalable.

Table 1. Revocable Hierarchical Identity-Based Encryption schemes

	SK size	CT size	KU size	Model	Sec. ag. insiders	DKE resist.	Assum.
Trivial	$\omega(2^\ell)$						
SE [21]	$O(\ell^2 \log N)$	$O(\ell)$	$O(r \log \frac{N}{r})$	Std., Sel.	✗	✗	static
CS const.	$O(\ell \log N)$	$O(1)$	$O(\ell r \log \frac{N}{r})$	Std., Sel.	✓	✓	q-type
SD const.	$O(\ell(\log N)^2)$	$O(1)$	$O(\ell r)$	Std., Sel., SRL	✓	✓	q-type

Std.: standard model, Sel.: selective security, SRL: selective revocation list [1,13]
ℓ: maximum hierarchical level, N: maximum number of users in the system,
r: number of revoked users.

consider a RIBE scheme wherein each secret key consists of n partial keys, where n is defined according to the revocation methodology, and we naturally extend this RIBE to RHIBE, then a second level user will have n^2 partial keys because for each partial key of the parent the second level user will have to prepare n partial keys, and therefore the second level user can survive irrespective of which partial key of he parent is activated for the current time period. This approach yields $O(n^\ell)$ secret key size, which is exponential in the hierarchical level ℓ.

In the above trivial combination of RIBE and HIBE, each low-level user has all possible, exponential in number, partial keys. However, Seo and Emura [21] pointed out that all of such partial keys are not used in practice, and to address this issue, proposed the first RHIBE scheme with polynomial size secret keys, which afforded an asymmetric trade-off between computational cost and secret key size (See [23], which is the full version of [21]). In the Seo-Emura scheme, for each time period, each user first generates an appropriate secret key by multiplying some of the partial keys, which depends on the partial keys used by ancestors. This process enables users to generate an exponential number of different keys, however only some of them are generated in practice. The resulting scheme achieves a selective security notion and polynomial size parameters; in particular, linear ciphertext size in the hierarchical level of the recipient. Note that the Seo-Emura scheme implemented *history-preserving* key updates. In their scheme, for each time period, each user chose one partial key contained in their secret key. Then, for selecting or generating a partial key, every descendant had to know which partial key of the ancestor was used in each time period; that is, such information is also announced in the key updates. Consequently, the history-preserving approach rendered the scheme very complex as it inherently generated many correlations among the secret keys (and therefore key updates) of different level users. In fact, although Seo and Emura endeavored to simplify their scheme and security proof through ensuring independent distribution of each part of the scheme, their scheme emerged very complicated owing to recursively defined secret keys and key updates.

Our Contribution. We revisit both the security model and design methodology for RHIBE, and accordingly, aim to design practical RHIBE schemes that are secure against as many realistic threats as possible. Our contributions are summarized below.

- New design approach implementing *history-free* updates
- New security model that safeguards against *insiders* and the decryption key exposure attack
- Two constructions: Shorter secret keys and ciphertexts

We present a comparison in Table 1. First, we present a new methodology for constructing RHIBE, that features a *history-free* approach wherein a low-level user does not need to know the history of the key updates of ancestors. Through our proposed approach, we can construct RHIBE schemes that have several advantages over that proposed by Seo and Emura [21]. Our schemes are advantageous in that, their construction is *simple-and-intuitive* in comparison with [21] because there are no undesirable correlations and recursive functions. Furthermore, the resulting schemes have better performance; for example, the secret key size of the Seo-Emura RHIBE scheme increases quadratically in the hierarchy of the user owing to their history-preserving approach, but in our approach, the increase is linear.

Second, we redefine the security model for RHIBE. In particular, we point out that the Seo-Emura adversarial model [21] accounts for only *outsiders*, i.e., only adversaries that do not have access to state information used by internal users of the RHIBE system. The state information of each user contains important information; for example, in [21] a user in the system uses a Binary Tree BT to apply a tree-based broadcast encryption technique for revoking children users, and each node in the BT has a corresponding value used to bridge between the children's secret key and the key update information generated by the parent user. This information constitutes a part of the state information maintained by a user and is crucial to the revocation methodology.[2] It should be noted that in the security model of RIBE, we do not need to account for state information leakage because the latter is maintained only by the KGC and it is usually assumed that the KGC is not compromised. Unlike RIBE, each user in RHIBE is also a low-level KGC; therefore users of the RHIBE system always have access to state information or at least their own state information. Therefore, to account for compromised *insiders*, we have to assume that an adversary has access to state information (at least their own). Therefore, we introduce a new security model that covers more threats than those considered by the Seo-Emura model. One may think that securing against insiders simply involves altering the security model through the introduction of an additional oracle for state information. However, the related security proof involves certain obstacles. For example, the security proof in [21] does not support a direct modification to account for security against insiders because the simulated distribution of state information in [21] is different from the ideal ones, so that it cannot be given to the adversary for the new security model. Therefore, we need a different approach to prove security against insiders. In addition to insider security, the proposed security model also covers the recently introduced *decryption key exposure* [22,24].

---

[2] This approach is first proposed by Boldyreva et al. [1] and followed by the almost all scalable R(H)IBEs, including the Seo-Emura RHIBE scheme [21].

Finally, we propose two RHIBE schemes with shorter secret keys and constant size ciphertexts. Our first construction uses the Complete Subtree (CS) for revocation, while the second uses the Subset Difference (SD) revocation method [17]. Both the proposed schemes are proved to be selectively secure in the standard model under the decisional q-weak Bilinear Diffie-Hellman Inversion (q-wBDHI) assumption introduced by Boneh, Boyen, and Goh (BBG) [3,4]. The key update size of our schemes have ℓ terms and the security is based on non-static assumption. It should be noted that this difference is owing to the property of the underlying BBG HIBE scheme [3,4]. More precisely, the delegation of key generation method in BBG HIBE inherently requires the secret key to contain all delegation keys such that the key updates in the proposed schemes must also have delegation parts. We expect that if RHIBE is built on the basis of Boneh-Boyen's (BB) HIBE [2], which is publicly delegatable, through our design methodology, then we can remove ℓ terms from the key update size. Then, the resulting RHIBE based on BB HIBE will have a $O(\ell)$ ciphertext size. Note that we only consider selective security of our RHIBE constructions. Although it is considered that adaptive security is the strongest and selective security is slightly weaker than adaptive security, no adaptively secure RHIBE scheme has been proposed yet and we believe that selective security is adequately effective. A selectively secure scheme may serve as a good steppingstone for an adaptively secure scheme, and also the former could also be a reasonable tradeoff with regard to performance in certain circumstances, as pointed out by Rouselakis and Waters [19].

IBE is one of the simplest version of attribute-based encryption [10,20], inner product encryption [12,18], and more generally functional encryption [6]. Key delegation and revocation are two important functionalities not only in the context of IBE but also in the context of functional encryption. We expect our methodology to help in the practical design of functional encryption that include both delegation of key generation and revocation functionalities.

Our Methodology. The most important requirement that RHIBE has to satisfy is that the system has to restrict a low-level user from generating key updates only if they are not revoked. To this end, in the *history-preserving* approach of Seo and Emura's RHIBE scheme [21], a parent user's secret key is used to generate a corresponding children's secret key and a parent user's key update is used to generate a corresponding children's key update.

To achieve a *history-free* construction, we begin with the simple observation that the following two situations are equivalent; (1) a user ID is not revoked at time T, and (2) the user can generate the decryption key $dk_{ID,T}$. Based on this observation, we define the key update algorithm and the secret key generation algorithm as follows (here, we omit certain detail, e.g., what θ means, however we explain it in Section 4). The key update algorithm takes $dk_{ID,T}$ as input and the key update on T is computed by multiplying a random P_θ^{-1} to $dk_{ID,T}$. Then, a child of ID, say ID′, can create of multiplied $dk_{ID',T}$ by P_θ^{-1}, according to the delegation property of dk. On the other hand, the secret key generation algorithm runs similar to the secret key generation algorithm of the underlying HIBE; however it uses P_θ instead of the master key of the underlying ordinary

HIBE scheme. That is, the secret key generation algorithm does not require any secret information from the ancestors. Then, the product of the secret key for ID' and the key update yields a valid decryption key $\mathsf{dk}_{\mathsf{ID}',T}$. Even if the secret key does not contain any secret information, in particular, the master secret key, it is necessary to recover dk. Here, P_θ is the state information of the user ID and it plays the role of a delegation key in our constructions. Our proposed construction is a simple one; in fact, the explanation provided herein is a simplified version that does not discuss about the specific revocation method employed, such as the CS method, but contains our key observations for a simple-and-intuitive RHIBE construction.

The above approach is well harmonized with the CS revocation method. Roughly speaking, P_θ's are mutually independent and random when the CS method is used, so that the secret key generation algorithm can be defined irrespective of the master secret key. However, in this regard, the SD revocation method is slightly more complicated. Again roughly speaking, in the Lee-Lee-Park RHIBE scheme using the SD method [13], P_θ's must have correlations so that the master secret key information can be contained. In other words, our history-free approach cannot be applied directly, and another technique is required to circumvent this obstacle. To resolve this problem, we introduce a *false* master key into each of the secret keys so that each secret key is completely independent from those of the ancestors, and in particular, the master secret key. Furthermore, each false master key serves as a bridge between a children user's secret key and the key update generated by their parent user.

Organization. The next section gives preliminaries for the remaining sections. In Section 3, we redefine the syntax and the security model for RHIBE by considering our new approach (history-free updates) and more threats. We present our two constructions via history-free approach in Section 4 and 5. Finally, we state a short conclusion and open problems in the related area.

2   Preliminaries

Notation. We use a complete binary tree BT for revocation. For a leaf node θ in BT, $\mathsf{Path}(\theta)$ means a set of all nodes lying on the path between the root node and θ. Sometimes, we assign a node to an identity ID. If it is not confusing, we also use $\mathsf{Path}(\mathsf{ID})$ to denote the path from the corresponding node of ID to the root note.

2.1   Subset-Cover Revocation Framework

The subset-cover revocation framework is a general methodology for revocation schemes due to Naor, Naor, Lotspiech [17]. The CS and SD are instances of the subset-cover revocation framework. Both CS and SD have subset assignment algorithms that take a binary tree BT, a revocation list RL, and the current time T, and then output a set of subsets covering only non-revoked users, where each user is assigned in a unique leaf node in BT. In this subsection, we review subset assignment algorithms for both the CS method and the SD method.

We first define notation. If v is a non-leaf node, then v_l denotes the left child of v. Similarly, v_r is the right child of v. We assume that each user is assigned to a unique leaf node. If a user, which is assigned to v, is revoked on time T, then (v, T) is added into RL.

The CS Method. The subset assignment algorithm for the CS method, denoted by KUNode, is defined as follows.

KUNode(BT, RL, T) :   X, Y ← ∅;

For $\forall (v_i, T_i) \in RL$,   if $T_i \leq T$, then add Path(v_i) to X;

For $\forall v \in X$,   if $v_l \notin X$, then add v_l to Y;

if $v_r \notin X$, then add v_r to Y;

If $|RL| = 0$, then add root to Y;

Return Y;

In fact, KUNode outputs a set of nodes. Then, each node v uniquely defines a subtree rooted at v.

The SD Method. We describe the subset assignment algorithm for the SD method, denoted by SD.KUNode. Unlike the KUNode algorithm, SD.KUNode outputs a set of pairs of nodes (v_i, v_j), where v_i is an ancestor of v_j. Each (v_i, v_j) uniquely defines a subset $S_{i,j}$ such that a leaf node $u \in S_{i,j}$ iff it is in the subtree rooted at v_i but not in the subtree rooted at v_j. We denote by $ST(RL)$ the (directed) Steiner Tree induced by the set RL of vertices and the root; that is, the minimal subtree of the complete binary tree BT that connects all the leaves in RL so that $ST(RL)$ is unique. The detail of SD.KUNode is given below.

SD.KUNode(BT, RL, T) :   T ← $ST(RL)$;

Until T consists of just a single node,

1. Find two leaves v_i and v_j in T such that the least-common-ancestor v of v_i and v_j does not contain any other leaf of T in its subtree. Let v_l and v_k be the two children of v such that v_i is a descendant of v_l and v_j is a descendant of v_k. (If there is only one leaf left, make $v_i = v_j$ to the leaf, v to be the root of T and $v_l = v_k = v$.)
2. If $v_l \neq v_i$ then add the subset $S_{l,i}$ to the collection; likewise, if $v_k \neq v_j$ add the subset $S_{k,j}$ to the collection.
3. Remove from T all the descendants of v and make it a leaf.

The algorithm KUNode often denotes its resulting subsets. Similarly, SD.KUNode also denotes its resulting set.

Bilinear Groups and Complexity Assumption. We assume that there exists a group generator algorithm $\mathcal{G}(1^\lambda)$ that outputs $(p, \mathbb{G}, \mathbb{G}_t, e)$, where $\mathbb{G}$ and $\mathbb{G}_t$ are groups of prime order $p = \Theta(2^\lambda)$ and $e : \mathbb{G} \times \mathbb{G} \to \mathbb{G}_t$ is an efficiently computable non-degenerate bilinear map.

Definition 1 ([4]). *We say that the decisional ℓ-wBDHI assumption holds on $\mathcal{G}$ if given $g, h, g^\alpha, g^{\alpha^2}, \ldots, g^{\alpha^\ell} \in \mathbb{G}$, there is no polynomial time adversary distinguishing $e(g, h)^{\alpha^{\ell+1}}$ from a random element in $\mathbb{G}_t$ with non-negligible advantage, where $\mathcal{G}(1^\lambda) \to (p, \mathbb{G}, \mathbb{G}_t, e)$, $g, h \xleftarrow{\$} \mathbb{G}$, and $\alpha \xleftarrow{\$} \mathbb{Z}_p$.*

3   Revocable Hierarchical Identity-Based Encryption

We provide a new definition of RHIBE via *history-free approach* and its security model. First, we consider the history-free approach as follows; the key update generation algorithm KeyUp takes a decryption key dk as input and the secret key generation algorithm SKGen does not take a secret key given from the parent. The secret key is used only for generating the decryption key dk. Therefore, we do not need to worry about undesirable correlations relating the secret key; e.g., in the definition of [21], the secret key is used as inputs of SKGen and KeyUp.

Although inputs of algorithms in Definition 2 are slightly different from those in [21], we note that inputs in our algorithms can be computed from inputs in the corresponding algorithms in [21] so that RHIBE satisfying our definition can be adapted to satisfy the definition in [21]. For example, our KeyUp algorithm takes $dk_{ID|_{k-1}, T}$ as input instead of $sk_{ID|_{k-1}}$, $ku_{ID|_{k-2}, T}$, and T, but $dk_{ID|_{k-1}, T}$ can be generated by the DKGen algorithm taking $sk_{ID|_{k-1}}$, $ku_{ID|_{k-2}, T}$, and T as input.

Algorithms. We first define notations used in algorithms' description. We sometimes use the notation $ID|_{k-1}$ to emphasize the identity ID's level $(k-1)$. In the case $k = 1$, $ID|_{k-1}$ means the KGC. $st_{ID|_{k-1}}$, $ku_{ID|_{k-1}, T}$, and $RL_{ID|_{k-1}}$ are state information kept by the user $ID|_{k-1}$, the key update published by the user $ID|_{k-1}$ on time T, and the revocation list managed by $ID|_{k-1}$, respectively. For the case $k = 1$, we use st_0, $ku_{0, T}$, and RL_0, respectively.

Definition 2. *RHIBE consists of seven algorithms* Setup, SKGen, KeyUp, DKGen, Enc, Dec, *and* Revoke *defined as follows.*

Setup($1^\lambda, N, \ell$): *Given the security parameter 1^λ, maximum number of users in each level N, and maximum hierarchical length ℓ , it outputs the public system parameter* mpk, *the master secret key* msk, *initial state information* st_0, *and empty revocation list* RL. *We assume that* mpk *contains description of message space $\mathcal{M}$, identity space $\mathcal{I}$, and time space $\mathcal{T}$. For simplicity, we often omit* mpk *in the input of other algorithms.*

SKGen($st_{ID|_{k-1}}, ID|_k$): *It takes state information $st_{ID|_{k-1}}$ and an identity $ID|_k$ as inputs, and then outputs the secret key $sk_{ID|_k}$ and updates $st_{ID|_{k-1}}$.*[3]

---

[3] State information takes a role of the delegation key.

KeyUp($\mathsf{dk}_{\mathsf{ID}|_{k-1},T}, \mathsf{st}_{\mathsf{ID}|_{k-1}}, RL_{\mathsf{ID}|_{k-1}}, T$): *It takes the revocation list* $RL_{\mathsf{ID}|_{k-1}}$, *state information* $\mathsf{st}_{\mathsf{ID}|_{k-1}}$, *the decryption key* $\mathsf{dk}_{\mathsf{ID}|_{k-1},T}$, *and a time period* T *as inputs. For* $k = 1$, *we set* $\mathsf{dk}_{\mathsf{ID}|_{k-1},T}$ *to be* msk *disregarding* T. *Then, it outputs the key update* $\mathsf{ku}_{\mathsf{ID}|_{k-1},T}$.

DKGen($\mathsf{sk}_{\mathsf{ID}|_k}, \mathsf{ku}_{\mathsf{ID}|_{k-1},T}$): *Given the secret key* $\mathsf{sk}_{\mathsf{ID}|_k}$ *of* $\mathsf{ID}|_k$ *and the key update* $\mathsf{ku}_{\mathsf{ID}|_{k-1},T}$, *it outputs the decryption key* $\mathsf{dk}_{\mathsf{ID}|_k,T}$ *of* $\mathsf{ID}|_k$ *on time* T *if* $\mathsf{ID}|_k$ *is not revoked on time* T *by the parent.*

Enc(M, ID, T): *It takes a message* M, *a recipient identity* ID *and the current time* T *as inputs and outputs the ciphertext* CT.

Dec($\mathsf{CT}, \mathsf{dk}_{\mathsf{ID},T}$): *This algorithm takes as inputs a ciphertext* CT *and the decryption key* $\mathsf{dk}_{\mathsf{ID},T}$, *and then outputs the message.*

Revoke($\mathsf{ID}|_k, T, RL_{\mathsf{ID}|_{k-1}}$): *Given an identity* $\mathsf{ID}|_k$ *and a time* T, *the revocation list* $RL_{\mathsf{ID}|_{k-1}}$ *managed by* $\mathsf{ID}|_{k-1}$, *who is the parent user of* $\mathsf{ID}|_k$, *is updated by adding* (ID, T).

Correctness. We require the following correctness condition to be satisfied: For any output Setup $\rightarrow$ (mpk, msk), any message $M \in \mathcal{M}$, any identity $\mathsf{ID}|_k \in \mathcal{I}$ where $k \in [1, \ell]$, any time $T \in \mathcal{T}$, all possible states $\{\mathsf{st}_{\mathsf{ID}|_i}\}_{i \in [1,k-1]}$, and all possible revocation lists $\{RL_{\mathsf{ID}|_i}\}_{i \in [1,k-1]}$, if $\mathsf{ID}|_k$ is not revoked on time T, the following probability should be 1; i is initialized by 1. While $i \in [1, k]$, repeatedly run

$$\left(\begin{array}{l} \mathsf{SKGen}(\mathsf{st}_{\mathsf{ID}|_{i-1}}, \mathsf{ID}|_i) \rightarrow \mathsf{sk}_{\mathsf{ID}|_i}; \\ \mathsf{KeyUp}(\mathsf{dk}_{\mathsf{ID}|_{i-1},T}, \mathsf{st}_{\mathsf{ID}|_{i-1}}, RL_{\mathsf{ID}|_{i-1}}) \rightarrow \mathsf{ku}_{\mathsf{ID}|_{i-1}}; \\ \mathsf{DKGen}(\mathsf{sk}_{\mathsf{ID}|_i}, \mathsf{ku}_{\mathsf{ID}|_{i-1},T}) \rightarrow \mathsf{dk}_{\mathsf{ID}|_i,T}; \\ i \leftarrow i + 1; \end{array} \right)$$

Finally, compute Enc($M, \mathsf{ID}|_k, T$) $\rightarrow$ CT and Dec($\mathsf{CT}, \mathsf{dk}_{\mathsf{ID}|_k,T}$) $\rightarrow M'$. The perfect correctness requires that the probability that $M = M'$ to be 1, where the probability is taken over the randomness used in all algorithms.[4]

Security Model. Next, we define the security model for RHIBE. In our proposed construction, we consider security against a stronger adversary than that considered in [21]. In contrast to the previous model [21], our security model accounts for an adversary that can obtain not only secret keys but also state information of a chosen identity. Furthermore, we also account for the decryption key exposure attack [22,24] by considering an adversary that has access to the decryption key oracle with reasonable restriction. Therefore, our security model is a natural extension of the security model for the RIBE scheme in [22,24], while accounting for more realistic adversaries than [21].

First, we define oracles SKGen($\cdot$), DKGen($\cdot, \cdot$), KeyUp($\cdot, \cdot$) and Revoke($\cdot, \cdot$) that $\mathcal{A}$ is allowed to access. We assume that all oracles have a shared storage containing state information and revocation lists.

SKGen($\cdot$): Given an identity ID, it outputs the corresponding secret key $\mathsf{sk}_{\mathsf{ID}}$ and state information $\mathsf{st}_{\mathsf{ID}}$.

---

[4] Again, we note that for brevity, in the definition of RHIBE we set $\mathsf{dk}_{\mathsf{ID}|_{i-1},T}$ to be msk when $i = 1$, and we omit mpk in all algorithms' input.

DKGen$(\cdot,\cdot)$: It takes an identity ID and a time T, and then outputs the corresponding decryption key $\mathsf{dk}_{\mathsf{ID},T}$.

KeyUp$(\cdot,\cdot)$: If $\mathcal{A}$ sends $\mathsf{ID}|_{k-1}$ and T, then the oracle returns the corresponding key update $\mathsf{ku}_{\mathsf{ID}|_{k-1},T}$. If $k = 1$, it means that $\mathcal{A}$ asks the key updates for the first level users generated by the KGC.

Revoke$(\cdot,\cdot)$: Given an identity $\mathsf{ID}|_k$ and a time period T, it adds a pair $(\mathsf{ID}|_k, T)$ into the revocation list $RL_{\mathsf{ID}|_{k-1}}$, where $\mathsf{ID}|_{k-1}$ is the parent of $\mathsf{ID}|_k$.

Given a RHIBE scheme $\mathcal{RHIBE}$ = (Setup, SKGen, DKGen, KeyUp, Enc, Dec, Revoke) and an adversary $\mathcal{A} = \{\mathcal{A}_0, \mathcal{A}_1, \mathcal{A}_2\}$, we define an experiment $\mathbf{Exp}_{\mathcal{RHIBE},\mathcal{A}}^{\mathrm{IND\text{-}sRID\text{-}CPA}}(1^\lambda, N, \ell; \rho)$, where ρ is a random tape for all randomness used in the experiment. In the following, $\mathcal{O}$ is a set of oracles (SKGen$(\cdot)$, DKGen$(\cdot,\cdot)$, KeyUp$(\cdot,\cdot)$, Revoke$(\cdot,\cdot)$).

$\boxed{\mathbf{Exp}_{\mathcal{RHIBE},\mathcal{A}}^{\mathrm{IND\text{-}sRID\text{-}CPA}}(1^\lambda, N, \ell; \rho)}$

$(\mathsf{ID}|_{k^*}^*, T^*, state_0) \leftarrow \mathcal{A}_0; (\mathsf{mpk}, \mathsf{msk}) \leftarrow \mathsf{Setup}(1^\lambda, N, \ell);$

$(M_0^*, M_1^*, state_1) \leftarrow \mathcal{A}_1^{\mathcal{O}}(\mathsf{mpk}, state_0); b \xleftarrow{\$} \{0,1\}; \mathsf{CT}^* \leftarrow \mathsf{Enc}(M_b^*, \mathsf{ID}|_{k^*}^*, T^*);$

$b' \leftarrow \mathcal{A}_2^{\mathcal{O}}(\mathsf{mpk}, \mathsf{CT}^*, state_1); \text{Return} \begin{cases} 1 \text{ if } b = b' \text{ and the Conditions are satisfied} \\ 0 \text{ otherwise} \end{cases}$

Conditions:

1. M_0^* and M_1^* have the same length.
2. $\mathcal{A}$ has to query to KeyUp$(\cdot,\cdot)$ and Revoke$(\cdot,\cdot)$ in increasing order of time.
3. $\mathcal{A}$ cannot query to Revoke$(\cdot,\cdot)$ on time T if it already queried to KeyUp$(\cdot,\cdot)$ on time T.
4. If $\mathsf{ID}|_{k'}^*$ is queried to SKGen$(\cdot)$ on time T', where $k' \leq k^*$ and $T' \leq T$, then $\mathcal{A}$ must query to revoke the challenge identity $\mathsf{ID}|_{k^*}^*$ or one of its ancestors on time $T' \leq T'' \leq T$.
5. $\mathcal{A}$ cannot query decryption keys $\mathsf{dk}_{\mathsf{ID}|_{k'}^*, T^*}$ of the challenge identity or its ancestors on the challenge time T^*, where $k' \leq k^*$.

The advantage of $\mathcal{A}$, denoted by $\mathbf{Adv}_{\mathcal{RHIBE},\mathcal{A}}^{\mathrm{IND\text{-}sRID\text{-}CPA}}(1^\lambda, N, \ell)$, in the experiment $\mathbf{Exp}_{\mathcal{RHIBE},\mathcal{A}}^{\mathrm{IND\text{-}sRID\text{-}CPA}}$ is defined as $\left| \Pr_\rho[\mathbf{Exp}_{\mathcal{RHIBE},\mathcal{A}}^{\mathrm{IND\text{-}sRID\text{-}CPA}}(1^\lambda, N, \ell; \rho) \rightarrow 1] - \frac{1}{2} \right|$.

Definition 3 (IND-sRID-CPA). *For a RHIBE scheme $\mathcal{RHIBE}$, we say that $\mathcal{RHIBE}$ is IND-sRID-CPA secure if for any polynomials N and ℓ and probabilistic polynomial time algorithm $\mathcal{A}$, the function $\mathbf{Adv}_{\mathcal{RHIBE},\mathcal{A}}^{\mathrm{IND\text{-}sRID\text{-}CPA}}(1^\lambda, N, \ell)$ is a negligible function in the security parameter 1^λ.*

4 RHIBE via Complete Subtree

4.1 Our Construction

In this section, we present our first RHIBE construction, which is based on the BBG HIBE scheme [3] and the CS method [17], via history-free approach.

For the convenience of explanation, we assume that $\mathsf{sk}_{\mathsf{ID}|_{k-1}}$, $\mathsf{BT}_{\mathsf{ID}|_{k-1}}$, and $\mathsf{ku}_{\mathsf{ID}|_{k-1}}$ mean msk, BT_0, and ku_0, respectively if $k = 1$. The KeyUp algorithm takes a decryption key, except for the KGC's case. Therefore, we separately explain the KeyUp algorithm between using the msk and using a decryption key.

$\mathsf{Setup}(1^\lambda, N, \ell)$: Run $\mathcal{G}(1^\lambda) \rightarrow (p, \mathbb{G}, \mathbb{G}_t, e)$. Choose $g, h, g_2, u_1, \ldots, u_\ell, u', h' \xleftarrow{\$} \mathbb{G}$ and $\alpha \xleftarrow{\$} \mathbb{Z}_p$ and set $g_1 = g^\alpha$. Publish $\mathsf{mpk} = \{N, g, h, u_1, \ldots, u_\ell, g_1, g_2, u', h'\}$ and keep $\mathsf{msk} = \{g_2^\alpha\}$ in a secure storage.

$\mathsf{SKGen}(\mathsf{st}_{\mathsf{ID}|_{k-1}}, \mathsf{ID}|_k)$: $\mathsf{st}_{\mathsf{ID}|_{k-1}}$, which is kept by $\mathsf{ID}|_{k-1}$, contains the binary tree $\mathsf{BT}_{\mathsf{ID}|_{k-1}}$. For $\mathsf{ID}|_k := (\mathsf{I}_1, \ldots, \mathsf{I}_k)$, assign a random leaf node of $\mathsf{BT}_{\mathsf{ID}|_{k-1}}$ to $\mathsf{ID}|_k$. For each node θ in $\mathsf{Path}(\mathsf{ID}|_k) \subset \mathsf{BT}_{\mathsf{ID}|_{k-1}}$, recall P_θ if it is stored. Otherwise, choose $P_\theta \xleftarrow{\$} \mathbb{G}$, assign and store it in the corresponding node. We call P_θ msk-*shade* at θ. For each $\theta \in \mathsf{Path}(\mathsf{ID}|_k)$, choose $r_\theta \xleftarrow{\$} \mathbb{Z}_p$ and compute $\mathsf{sk}_{\mathsf{ID}|_k} = \left\{ P_\theta (u_1^{\mathsf{I}_1} \cdots u_k^{\mathsf{I}_k} h)^{r_\theta}, \ g^{r_\theta}, \ u_{k+1}^{r_\theta}, \ldots, u_\ell^{r_\theta} \right\}_{\theta \in \mathsf{Path}(\mathsf{ID}|_k)}$.

$\mathsf{KeyUp}(\mathsf{msk}, \mathsf{st}_0, RL_0, T)$: State information st_0 contains the binary tree BT_0. Compute a set $\mathsf{KUNode}(\mathsf{BT}_0, RL_0, T)$. For each $\theta \in \mathsf{KUNode}(\mathsf{BT}_0, RL_0, T)$ recall msk-shade at θ if it is defined. Otherwise, choose a new msk-shade at θ and store it to the corresponding node. Finally, the key update $\mathsf{ku}_{0,T}$ is generated as follows: Choose $t_\theta \xleftarrow{\$} \mathbb{Z}_p$ for each $\theta \in \mathsf{KUNode}(\mathsf{BT}_0, RL_0, T)$ and compute $\mathsf{ku}_{0,T} = \left\{ P_\theta^{-1} g_2^\alpha (u'^T h')^{t_\theta}, \ g^{t_\theta} \right\}_{\theta \in \mathsf{KUNode}(\mathsf{BT}_0, RL_0, T)}$.
P_θ is a part of state information, but t_θ is a temporary integer used in this key update only.

$\mathsf{DKGen}(\mathsf{sk}_{\mathsf{ID}|_k}, \mathsf{ku}_{\mathsf{ID}|_{k-1}, T})$: Let $\mathsf{ID}|_k = (\mathsf{I}_1, \ldots, \mathsf{I}_k)$. Parse $\mathsf{ku}_{\mathsf{ID}|_{k-1}, T} = \left\{ \tilde{a}_{0,\theta}, \tilde{a}_{1,\theta}, \tilde{a}_{2,\theta}, \tilde{b}_{k,\theta}, \ldots, \tilde{b}_{\ell,\theta} \right\}_{\theta \in \mathsf{S}}$; for simplicity, if $k = 1$, we set $\tilde{a}_{1,\theta} = \tilde{b}_{k,\theta} = \cdots = \tilde{b}_{\ell,\theta} = 1_\mathbb{G}$, where $1_\mathbb{G}$ is the identity in $\mathbb{G}$. If $(\mathsf{ID}|_k, \cdot) \notin RL_{\mathsf{ID}|_{k-1}}$, then there should be at least one node in $\mathsf{Path}(\mathsf{ID}|_k) \cap \mathsf{S}$, say θ. For such θ, let the secret key be $(a_0, a_1, b_{k+1}, \ldots, b_\ell)$. Compute $(A_0, A_1, A_2, B_{k+1}, \ldots, B_\ell)$ as

$$(a_0 \tilde{a}_{0,\theta} \tilde{b}_{k,\theta}^{\mathsf{I}_k}, \ a_1 \tilde{a}_{1,\theta}, \ \tilde{a}_{2,\theta}, \ b_{k+1} \tilde{b}_{k+1,\theta}, \ldots, b_\ell \tilde{b}_{\ell,\theta}).$$

Finally, re-randomize the result and output it as $\mathsf{dk}_{\mathsf{ID}|_k, T}$. We explain how to re-randomize it later.

$\mathsf{KeyUp}(\mathsf{dk}_{\mathsf{ID}|_{k-1}, T}, \mathsf{st}_{\mathsf{ID}|_{k-1}}, RL_{\mathsf{ID}|_{k-1}}, T)$: For $\theta \in \mathsf{KUNode}(\mathsf{BT}_{\mathsf{ID}|_{k-1}}, RL_{\mathsf{ID}|_{k-1}}, T)$, recall P_θ if it is stored. Otherwise, choose $P_\theta \xleftarrow{\$} \mathbb{G}$ at random and store it in the corresponding node. Let $\mathsf{dk}_{\mathsf{ID}|_{k-1}, T}$ be $(a_0, a_1, a_2, b_k, \ldots, b_\ell)$. For each node θ in $\mathsf{KUNode}(\mathsf{BT}_{\mathsf{ID}|_{k-1}}, RL_{\mathsf{ID}|_{k-1}}, T)$, re-randomize the decryption key with fresh randomness so that obtain $(a_{0,\theta}, a_{1,\theta}, a_{2,\theta}, b_{k,\theta}, \ldots, b_{\ell,\theta})$. Finally, the key update $\mathsf{ku}_{\mathsf{ID}|_{k-1}, T}$ is generated by as follows:

$$\left\{ P_\theta^{-1} \cdot a_{0,\theta}, \ a_{1,\theta}, \ a_{2,\theta}, \ b_{k,\theta}, \ldots, b_{\ell,\theta} \right\}_{\theta \in \mathsf{KUNode}(\mathsf{BT}_{\mathsf{ID}|_{k-1}}, RL_{\mathsf{ID}|_{k-1}}, T)}$$

$\mathsf{Enc}(M, \mathsf{ID}|_k, T)$: Let $\mathsf{ID}|_k = (\mathsf{I}_1, \ldots, \mathsf{I}_k)$. Choose an integer $s \xleftarrow{\$} \mathbb{Z}_p$ at random and compute $\mathsf{CT} = (M \cdot e(g_1, g_2)^s, g^s, (u_1^{\mathsf{I}_1} \cdots u_k^{\mathsf{I}_k} h)^s, (u'^T h')^s)$.

$\mathsf{Dec}(\mathsf{CT}, \mathsf{dk}_{\mathsf{ID}|_k, T})$: Let $\mathsf{ID}|_k = (\mathsf{l}_1, \dots, \mathsf{l}_k)$ and parse $\mathsf{CT} = (C', C_0, C_1, C_2)$ and $\mathsf{dk}_{\mathsf{ID}|_k, T} = (a_0, a_1, a_2, , b_{k+1}, \dots, b_\ell)$. Compute and output

$$C' \cdot \frac{e(a_1, C_1) \cdot e(a_2, C_2)}{e(a_0, C_0)}.$$

$\mathsf{Revoke}(\mathsf{ID}|_k, T, RL_{\mathsf{ID}|_{k-1}}, \mathsf{st}_{\mathsf{ID}|_{k-1}})$: Update $RL_{\mathsf{ID}|_{k-1}}$ by adding a pair $(\mathsf{ID}|_k, T)$.

Correctness. Here, we check the correctness of the scheme. From the shape of the ciphertext for $\mathsf{ID}|_k$ and T, we can easily see that if $\mathsf{dk}_{\mathsf{ID}|_k, T}$ is of the form $(g_2^\alpha (u_1^{\mathsf{l}_1} \cdots u_k^{\mathsf{l}_k} h)^r (u'^T h')^t, g^r, g^t, b_{k+1}, \dots, b_\ell)$, then the decryption algorithm correctly outputs the plaintext with probability 1. Using mathematical induction, we can show that $\mathsf{dk}_{\mathsf{ID}|_i, T}$, which is obtained by i times repeatedly performing SKGen, KeyUp and DKGen, is of the desired form $(g_2^\alpha (u_1^{\mathsf{l}_1} \cdots u_i^{\mathsf{l}_i} h)^r (u'^T h')^t, g^r, g^t, u_{i+1}^r, \dots, u_\ell^r)$ for some r and t.

Decryption/Secret Key Re-randomization. The decryption key for $\mathsf{ID} = (\mathsf{l}_1, \dots, \mathsf{l}_i)$ on time T has is of the form $(g_2^\alpha (u_1^{\mathsf{l}_1} \cdots u_i^{\mathsf{l}_i} h)^r (u'^T h')^t, g^r, g^t, u_{i+1}^r, \dots, u_\ell^r)$. Since u_i's, h, and g are publicly available, anyone can re-randomize given decryption key $\mathsf{dk}_{\mathsf{ID}, T} = (a_0, a_1, a_2, b_{i+1}, \dots, b_k)$ by computing

$$\left(a_0 (u_1^{\mathsf{l}_1} \cdots u_i^{\mathsf{l}_i} h)^{r'} (u'^T h')^{t'}, a_1 g^{r'}, a_2 g^{t'}, b_{i+1} u_{i+1}^{r'}, \dots, b_\ell u_\ell^{r'} \right)$$

with fresh random integers r' and t'. Similarly, secret key can be also re-randomized.

4.2 Security Analysis

Theorem 1. *The proposed RHIBE scheme defined over the bilinear group $(\mathbb{G}, \mathbb{G}_t, e)$ is IND-sRID-CPA secure under the decisional ℓ-wBDHI assumption on $\mathcal{G}$, where $(\mathbb{G}, \mathbb{G}_t, e)$ is generated by $\mathcal{G}$ and ℓ is the maximum hierarchy.*

The proof of the theorem directly comes with the following lemmas.

Lemma 1 ([3]). *The BBG HIBE scheme defined over the bilinear group $(\mathbb{G}, \mathbb{G}_t, e)$ is IND-sID-CPA secure under the ℓ-wBDHI assumption on $\mathcal{G}$, where $(\mathbb{G}, \mathbb{G}_t, e)$ is generated by $\mathcal{G}$.*

Lemma 2. *The proposed RHIBE scheme is IND-sRID-CPA secure if BBG HIBE is IND-sID-CPA secure.*

Due to space constraint, we relegate the proof of Lemma 2 to the full version.

5 RHIBE via Subset Difference

In this section, we present our second RHIBE scheme, which is based on the BBG HIBE scheme [3] and the SD revocation method [17], and which implements the proposed history-free approach. For RIBE, Lee, Lee, and Park (LLP) [13] demonstrated how to combine the Boneh-Boyen (BB) IBE [2] scheme and the SD revocation method. Because the BBG HIBE scheme has a similar structure as the BB IBE scheme, one may assume that the same approach that was used in the previous section can be applied to the LLP RIBE scheme [13]. However, there are some important differences between our RHIBE scheme with the CS method and the LLP RIBE scheme with the SD method. In our construction, P_θ's are mutually independent random elements. However, the SD revocation method requires more complicated handling. For instance, in the LLP RIBE scheme [13], there are correlations among P_θ so that the master secret key information should be contained. Therefore, another technique is required to overcome this problem.

To resolve this problem, we introduce a *false* master key into each of the secret keys so that each secret key is completely independent from those of the ancestors, and in particular, the master secret key. Furthermore, each false master key serves as a bridge between a children user's secret key and the key update generated by their parent user.

Without loss of generality, we assume that the maximum number of users in the system is a power of 2, that is, $N = 2^n$. We define two functions between a set of nodes and their levels, where the root node is level-0 and a leaf node is level-n. Let Leaves be a set of leaf nodes.

$$
\begin{aligned}
\mathsf{NtL_{BT}} : \qquad &\mathsf{BT} &\rightarrow& \qquad \{0,\ldots,n\} \\
&\text{node} &\mapsto& \qquad \text{its level} \\
\mathsf{LtN_u} : \mathsf{Leaves} \times &\{0,\ldots,n\} &\rightarrow& \qquad \mathsf{Path(u)} \\
&(\mathsf{u},i) &\mapsto& \quad i\text{-th level node in } \mathsf{Path(u)}
\end{aligned}
$$

If subscripts of NtL and LtN are clear in the context, we often omit them. Instead, we say that NtL is BT-*dependent* and LtN is u-*dependent*. From the above definitions, we can easily check that $\mathsf{NtL_{BT}}(\cdot)$ is surjective but not injective for full binary tree BT with 2^n leaves, and $\mathsf{LtN_u}(\mathsf{u},\cdot)$ is bijective for a leaf node u. In particular, $\mathsf{NtL_{BT}} \circ \mathsf{LtN_u}(\mathsf{u},\cdot)$ is the identity map defined over $\{0,\ldots,n\}$ and $\mathsf{LtN_u}(\mathsf{u}, \mathsf{NtL_{BT}}(\mathsf{v})) = \mathsf{v}$ if and only if $\mathsf{v} \in \mathsf{Path(u)} \subset \mathsf{BT}$.

Additionally, we define a function $F(\mathrm{k},y,x,\beta)$ as follows.

$$
\begin{aligned}
F(\mathrm{k},y,x,\beta) : \mathcal{K} \times \{0,1\}^* \times \mathbb{Z}_p \times \mathbb{Z}_p &\rightarrow& \mathbb{Z}_p \\
(\mathrm{k},y,x,\beta) &\mapsto& \mathsf{PRF_k}(y)x + \beta,
\end{aligned}
$$

where PRF is a pseudorandom function. If k and β are fixed and clear from the context, we shortly denote F by $f_y(x)$. That is, $f_y(x)$ is a linear function such that the leading coefficient is chosen uniformly and y-*dependently* and the constant is fixed as β.

We assume that each node in binary tree has unique name so that we can easily identify it. In this paper, we use a sufficiently large p such that $\mathbb{Z}_p$ has exponentially many elements. If it is not confusing, we sometimes consider (the label of) each node in binary trees as an element in $\mathbb{Z}_p$. If needed, we can use collision-resistant hashes from a unique node name to $\mathbb{Z}_p$.

5.1 Our Construction

In Figure 1, we provide a pictorial description of our RHIBE construction, in particular, it focuses on a binary tree for delegation and key updates that each user (except the lowest user) in the hierarchy of IBE has. Note that the description in Figure 1 is almost the same as the non-hierarchical RIBE due to [13], except the false master key β, and this *small-but-important* difference enables us to apply our methodology for history-free

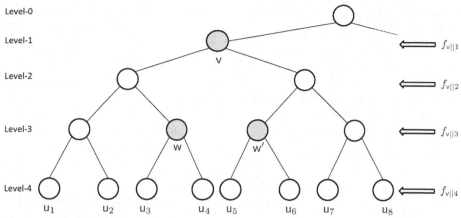

Assume that $(v, w') \in$ SD.KUNode. Then u_1, u_2, u_3, u_4, u_7, and u_8 are not revoked, and u_5 and u_6 are revoked.

The key update contains information about a point $f_{v\|3}(w')$. u_3's secret key contains information about a point $f_{v\|3}(w)$. Using interpolation u_3 can recover a constant term of the linear polynomial $f_{v\|3}(x)$, which is the false master key. On the other hand, the revoked users u_5 and u_6 cannot, since they have only one point $f_{v\|3}(w')$ of the linear polynomial $f_{v\|3}(x)$.

Fig. 1. A pictorial description of RHIBE via the SD method

RHIBE construction. Let $\Delta_{i,S}(x)$ be a Lagrange coefficient defined as $\prod_{j \in S, j \neq i} \frac{x-j}{i-j}$ for $i \in \mathbb{Z}_p$ and $S \subset \mathbb{Z}_p$.

Setup$(1^\lambda, 2^n, \ell)$: Run $\mathcal{G}(1^\lambda) \to (p, \mathbb{G}, \mathbb{G}_t, e)$. Choose $g, h, g_2, u_1, \ldots, u_\ell, u', h' \xleftarrow{\$} \mathbb{G}$ and $\alpha \xleftarrow{\$} \mathbb{Z}_p$ and set $g_1 = g^\alpha$. Publish mpk $= \{g, h, u_1, \ldots, u_\ell, g_1, g_2, u', h'\}$ and keep msk $= \{g_2^\alpha\}$ in a secure storage.

SKGen$(\mathsf{st}_{\mathsf{ID}|_{k-1}}, \mathsf{ID}|_k)$: State information $\mathsf{st}_{\mathsf{ID}|_{k-1}}$, which is kept by $\mathsf{ID}|_{k-1}$, contains the binary tree $\mathsf{BT}_{\mathsf{ID}|_{k-1}}$, a key k for PRF, and a *false* master secret key β, where at the very first time k and β are chosen at random. (For each identity, k and β are randomly chosen and fixed so that we use the notation $f_y(x)$ instead of $F(\mathsf{k}, y, x, \beta)$.) For $\mathsf{ID}|_k = (\mathsf{l}_1, \ldots, \mathsf{l}_k)$, assign a random leaf node, say u, in $\mathsf{BT}_{\mathsf{ID}|_{k-1}}$. For every $i, j \in \{0, \ldots, n\}$ such that $i \leq j$, choose $r_{i,j} \xleftarrow{\$} \mathbb{Z}_p$ and compute $\mathsf{sk}_{\mathsf{ID}|_k}^{(i,j)} = \left(g_2^{f_{\mathsf{LtN}(u,i)\|j}(\mathsf{LtN}(u,j))}(u_1^{\mathsf{l}_1} \cdots u_k^{\mathsf{l}_k} h)^{r_{i,j}}, \; g^{r_{i,j}}, u_{k+1}^{r_{i,j}}, \ldots, u_\ell^{r_{i,j}} \right)$, where LtN is u-dependent. Then, $\mathsf{sk}_{\mathsf{ID}|_k} = \left\{ \mathsf{sk}_{\mathsf{ID}|_k}^{(i,j)} \right\}_{i \leq j \in \{0, \ldots, n\}}$.

KeyUp$(\mathsf{msk}, \mathsf{st}_0, RL_0)$: st_0 contains the binary tree BT_0, a key k for PRF, and a false master secret key β. Compute a set SD.KUNode(BT_0, RL_0, T). $\mathsf{ku}_{0,T}$ is generated as follows. For each $(v, w) \in$ SD.KUNode(BT_0, RL_0, T), choose $t_{v,w} \xleftarrow{\$} \mathbb{Z}_p$ and compute $\mathsf{ku}_{0,T}^{(v,w)} = \left(g_2^{f_{v\|\mathsf{NtL}(w)}(w)}(u'^T h')^{t_{v,w}}, \; g^{t_{v,w}} \right)$, where NtL is BT_0-dependent. Then, $\mathsf{ku}_{0,T}$ is

$$\left\{ (g_2^{\alpha - \beta}(u'^T h')^t, g^t) \right\} \bigcup \left\{ \mathsf{ku}_{0,T}^{(v,w)} \right\}_{(v,w) \in \mathsf{SD.KUNode}(\mathsf{BT}_0, RL_0, T)}, \quad \text{where } t \xleftarrow{\$} \mathbb{Z}_p.$$

$\mathsf{DKGen}(\mathsf{sk}_{\mathsf{ID}|_k}, \mathsf{ku}_{\mathsf{ID}|_{k-1}, T})$: Let $\mathsf{ID}|_k = (\mathsf{l}_1, \ldots, \mathsf{l}_k)$ and u be the node associating $\mathsf{ID}|_k$ in $\mathsf{BT}_{\mathsf{ID}|_{k-1}}$. Parse $\mathsf{ku}_{\mathsf{ID}|_{k-1}, T}$ is the union of $\left\{ (U_0, U_1, U_2, V_k, \ldots, V_\ell) \right\}$ and $\left\{ U_0^{(\mathsf{v},\mathsf{w})}, \right.$ $U_1^{(\mathsf{v},\mathsf{w})}, \quad U_2^{(\mathsf{v},\mathsf{w})}, \quad V_k^{(\mathsf{v},\mathsf{w})}, \ldots, V_\ell^{(\mathsf{v},\mathsf{w})} \left. \right\}_{(\mathsf{v},\mathsf{w}) \in \mathsf{S}}$. If $k = 1$, we can set $U_1^{(\mathsf{v},\mathsf{w})} = V_k^{(\mathsf{v},\mathsf{w})} = \cdots = V_\ell^{(\mathsf{v},\mathsf{w})} = 1_{\mathbb{G}}$, where $1_{\mathbb{G}}$ is the identity in $\mathbb{G}$. If $(\mathsf{ID}|_k, \cdot) \notin RL_{\mathsf{ID}|_{k-1}}$, then there should exist at least one pair $(\mathsf{v}, \mathsf{w}) \in \mathsf{S}$ such that $\mathsf{v} \in \mathsf{Path}(\mathsf{u})$ and $\mathsf{w} \notin \mathsf{Path}(\mathsf{u})$. (The SD-method guarantees it.) For such the pair (v, w), consider $\mathsf{sk}_{\mathsf{ID}|_k}^{(\mathsf{NtL}(\mathsf{v}), \mathsf{NtL}(\mathsf{w}))} = (K_0, K_1, L_{k+1}, \ldots, L_\ell)$, where NtL is $\mathsf{BT}_{\mathsf{ID}|_{k-1}}$-dependent. Define $\overrightarrow{U}$, $\overrightarrow{U}^{(\mathsf{v},\mathsf{w})}$, and $\overrightarrow{K}^{(\mathsf{v},\mathsf{w})}$ by $(U_0 (V_k)^{\mathsf{l}_k}, U_1, U_2, V_{k+1}, \ldots, V_\ell), (U_0^{(\mathsf{v},\mathsf{w})} (V_k^{(\mathsf{v},\mathsf{w})})^{\mathsf{l}_k}, U_1^{(\mathsf{v},\mathsf{w})}, U_2^{(\mathsf{v},\mathsf{w})}, V_{k+1}^{(\mathsf{v},\mathsf{w})}, \ldots, V_\ell^{(\mathsf{v},\mathsf{w})})$, and $(K_0, K_1, K_2, L_{k+1}, \ldots, L_\ell)$, respectively, where K_2 is $1_{\mathbb{G}}$. Let $S = \{\mathsf{LtN}_\mathsf{u}(\mathsf{u}, \mathsf{NtL}(\mathsf{w})), \mathsf{w}\}$. $\mathsf{dk}_{\mathsf{ID}|_k, T}$ is computed by $\overrightarrow{U} \cdot (\overrightarrow{U}^{(\mathsf{v},\mathsf{w})})^{\Delta_{\mathsf{w}, S}(0)} \cdot (\overrightarrow{K}^{(\mathsf{v},\mathsf{w})})^{\Delta_{\mathsf{LtN}_\mathsf{u}(\mathsf{NtL}(\mathsf{w})), \S}(0)}$, where a vector to an exponent means a component-wise exponentiation. The algorithm outputs $\mathsf{dk}_{\mathsf{ID}|_k, T}$ after re-randomization.

$\mathsf{KeyUp}(\mathsf{dk}_{\mathsf{ID}|_{k-1}, T}, \mathsf{st}_{\mathsf{ID}|_{k-1}}, RL_{\mathsf{ID}|_{k-1}})$: $\mathsf{st}_{\mathsf{ID}|_{k-1}}$ contains $\mathsf{BT}_{\mathsf{ID}|_{k-1}}$, a key k for PRF, and a false master secret key β.
Let $\mathsf{dk}_{\mathsf{ID}|_{k-1}, T}$ be $(a_0, a_1, a_2, b_k, \ldots, b_\ell)$. Re-randomize the decryption key. The key update $\mathsf{ku}_{\mathsf{ID}|_{k-1}, T}$ is generated as follows. For each $(\mathsf{v}, \mathsf{w}) \in \mathsf{SD.KUNode}$ $(\mathsf{BT}_{\mathsf{ID}|_{k-1}}, RL_{\mathsf{ID}|_{k-1}}, T)$, choose $t_{\mathsf{v},\mathsf{w}}, r_{\mathsf{v},\mathsf{w}} \xleftarrow{\$} \mathbb{Z}_p$ and compute $\mathsf{ku}_{\mathsf{ID}|_{k-1}, T}^{(\mathsf{v},\mathsf{w})}$ by $\left(g_2^{f_{\mathsf{v} \| \mathsf{NtL}(\mathsf{w})}(\mathsf{w})} (u_1^{\mathsf{l}_1} \cdots u_{k-1}^{\mathsf{l}_k} h)^{r_{\mathsf{v},\mathsf{w}}} (u'^T h')^{t_{\mathsf{v},\mathsf{w}}}, \ g^{t_{\mathsf{v},\mathsf{w}}}, \ u_k^{r_{\mathsf{v},\mathsf{w}}}, \ldots, u_\ell^{r_{\mathsf{v},\mathsf{w}}} \right)$, where NtL is $\mathsf{BT}_{\mathsf{ID}|_{k-1}}$-dependent. Then, $\mathsf{ku}_{\mathsf{ID}|_{k-1}, T}$ is

$$\left\{ (a_0 \cdot g^{-\beta}, a_1, a_2, b_k, \ldots, b_\ell) \right\} \bigcup \left\{ \mathsf{ku}_{\mathsf{ID}|_{k-1}, T}^{(\mathsf{v},\mathsf{w})} \right\}_{(\mathsf{v},\mathsf{w}) \in \mathsf{SD.KUNode}(\mathsf{BT}_{\mathsf{ID}|_{k-1}}, RL_{\mathsf{ID}|_{k-1}}, T)}.$$

$\mathsf{Enc}(M, \mathsf{ID}|_k, T)$, $\mathsf{Dec}(\mathsf{CT}, \mathsf{dk}_{\mathsf{ID}|_k, T})$, and $\mathsf{Revoke}(\mathsf{ID}|_k, T, RL_{\mathsf{ID}|_{k-1}}, \mathsf{st}_{\mathsf{ID}|_{k-1}})$ are the same as those of the CS-construction.

Note that the decryption key is publicly re-randomizable like our RHIBE via the CS method. We can check the correctness of the above scheme by showing that the decryption key generated by the DKGen algorithm has the same form as that in the RHIBE scheme with complete subtree. We omit the details.

5.2   Security Analysis

In contrast to the CS-based RHIBE scheme, the SD-based RHIBE scheme is secure for a *selective revocation model*, wherein the adversary needs to issue the revocation list in the challenge time T^* before the adversary receives the public parameters.[5]

Let us provide a short intuition for security of the SD-based RHIBE scheme in the selective revocation list model. In general, our RHIBE construction using the SD method is equivalent to our RHIBE construction using the CS method, except in their revocation methodology. In particular, the handling of binary trees is different. Owing to the similarity (in particular, in mpk and decryption keys) in the two constructions, we

---

[5] Note that selectively secure Lee-Lee-Park RIBE via the SD method is also proven in the selective revocation list model [13].

can apply almost the same strategy from the proof of Lemma 2; e.g., the decryption key oracle can be constructed identically. State information to which an internal adversary will have access to is normally generated. Only key update and secret key queries related to state information that an adversary will not have access to should be carefully simulated. The biggest difference between the two constructions in terms of the security proof is that msk-shades in a binary tree are mutually independent, but points of $f_y(x)$ have correlations. To correctly deal with these correlations in T^* correctly, the simulator will need to know the revocation list in T^* before generating mpk.

6 Concluding Remarks

The delegation of key generation capabilities is important in not only IBEs, but also functional encryption. In addition, revoking keys is necessary in public key encryption, in particular, dynamic systems. We revisited both the security issue and the methodology to combine both functionalities in the context of IBE. As a result, we presented *simple-and-intuitive* constructions in the newly proposed security model covering more realistic adversaries.

There are many interesting open problems. Attaining both revocation and delegation functionalities in functional encryption such as attribute-based encryption and inner-product encryption is an important open problem. It is also interesting to construct a fully secure RHIBE scheme; In the security proof, we reduce new constructions to the underlying selectively secure BBG HIBE scheme. Our proof technique essentially uses the selectively security notion, like the Seo-Emura history-preserving construction [21], so that it cannot directly apply to fully secure RHIBE scheme. Removing the restriction in maximum hierarchy of RHIBE scheme like Lewko-Waters' unbounded HIBE [14] is also an interesting open problem.

Acknowledgments. We gratefully acknowledge Hyung Tae Lee for helpful collaboration at an early stage of this study.

References

1. Boldyreva, A., Goyal, V., Kumar, V.: Identity-based encryption with efficient revocation. In: Ning, P., Syverson, P.F., Jha, S. (eds.) ACM CCS 2008, pp. 417–426 (2008)
2. Boneh, D., Boyen, X.: Efficient selective-ID secure identity-based encryption without random oracles. In: Cachin, C., Camenisch, J.L. (eds.) EUROCRYPT 2004. LNCS, vol. 3027, pp. 223–238. Springer, Heidelberg (2004)
3. Boneh, D., Boyen, X., Goh, E.-J.: Hierarchical identity based encryption with constant size ciphertext. In: Cramer, R. (ed.) EUROCRYPT 2005. LNCS, vol. 3494, pp. 440–456. Springer, Heidelberg (2005)
4. Boneh, D., Boyen, X., Goh, E.: Hierarchical identity based encryption with constant size ciphertexts (2005). http://eprint.iacr.org/2005/015 (full version of [3])
5. Boneh, D., Franklin, M.K.: Identity-based encryption from the weil pairing. SIAM J. Comput. **32**(3), 586–615 (2003)
6. Boneh, D., Sahai, A., Waters, B.: Functional encryption: definitions and challenges. In: Ishai, Y. (ed.) TCC 2011. LNCS, vol. 6597, pp. 253–273. Springer, Heidelberg (2011)

7. Canetti, R., Halevi, S., Katz, J.: A forward-secure public-key encryption scheme. In: Biham, E. (ed.) EUROCRYPT 2003. LNCS, vol. 2656, pp. 255–271. Springer, Heidelberg (2003)
8. Chen, J., Lim, H.W., Ling, S., Wang, H., Nguyen, K.: Revocable identity-based encryption from lattices. In: Susilo, W., Mu, Y., Seberry, J. (eds.) ACISP 2012. LNCS, vol. 7372, pp. 390–403. Springer, Heidelberg (2012)
9. Dodis, Y., Fazio, N.: Public key broadcast encryption for stateless receivers. In: Feigenbaum, J. (ed.) DRM 2002. LNCS, vol. 2696, pp. 61–80. Springer, Heidelberg (2003)
10. Goyal, V., Pandey, O., Sahai, A., Waters, B.: Attribute-based encryption for fine-grained access control of encrypted data. In: ACM CCS 2006, pp. 89–98. ACM (2006)
11. Horwitz, J., Lynn, B.: Toward hierarchical identity-based encryption. In: Knudsen, L.R. (ed.) EUROCRYPT 2002. LNCS, vol. 2332, pp. 466–481. Springer, Heidelberg (2002)
12. Katz, J., Sahai, A., Waters, B.: Predicate encryption supporting disjunctions, polynomial equations, and inner products. In: Smart, N.P. (ed.) EUROCRYPT 2008. LNCS, vol. 4965, pp. 146–162. Springer, Heidelberg (2008)
13. Lee, K., Lee, D.H., Park, J.H.: Efficient revocable identity-based encryption via subset difference methods. eprint.iacr.org/2014/132 (2014)
14. Lewko, A., Waters, B.: Unbounded HIBE and attribute-based encryption. In: Paterson, K.G. (ed.) EUROCRYPT 2011. LNCS, vol. 6632, pp. 547–567. Springer, Heidelberg (2011)
15. Libert, B., Vergnaud, D.: Adaptive-ID secure revocable identity-based encryption. In: Fischlin, M. (ed.) CT-RSA 2009. LNCS, vol. 5473, pp. 1–15. Springer, Heidelberg (2009)
16. Libert, B., Vergnaud, D.: Towards black-box accountable authority IBE with short ciphertexts and private keys. In: Jarecki, S., Tsudik, G. (eds.) PKC 2009. LNCS, vol. 5443, pp. 235–255. Springer, Heidelberg (2009)
17. Naor, D., Naor, M., Lotspiech, J.: Revocation and tracing schemes for stateless receivers. In: Kilian, J. (ed.) CRYPTO 2001. LNCS, vol. 2139, pp. 41–62. Springer, Heidelberg (2001)
18. Okamoto, T., Takashima, K.: Hierarchical predicate encryption for inner-products. In: Matsui, M. (ed.) ASIACRYPT 2009. LNCS, vol. 5912, pp. 214–231. Springer, Heidelberg (2009)
19. Rouselakis, Y., Waters, B.: Practical constructions and new proof methods for large universe attribute-based encryption. In: Sadeghi, A., Gligor, V.D., Yung, M. (eds.) ACM CCS 2013, pp. 463–474. ACM (2013)
20. Sahai, A., Waters, B.: Fuzzy identity-based encryption. In: Cramer, R. (ed.) EUROCRYPT 2005. LNCS, vol. 3494, pp. 457–473. Springer, Heidelberg (2005)
21. Seo, J.H., Emura, K.: Efficient delegation of key generation and revocation functionalities in identity-based encryption. In: Dawson, E. (ed.) CT-RSA 2013. LNCS, vol. 7779, pp. 343–358. Springer, Heidelberg (2013)
22. Seo, J.H., Emura, K.: Revocable identity-based encryption revisited: security model and construction. In: Kurosawa, K., Hanaoka, G. (eds.) PKC 2013. LNCS, vol. 7778, pp. 216–234. Springer, Heidelberg (2013)
23. Seo, J.H., Emura, K.: Revocable hierarchical identity-based encryption. Theor. Comput. Sci. **542**, 44–62 (2014)
24. Seo, J.H., Emura, K.: Revocable identity-based cryptosystem revisited: Security models and constructions. IEEE Transactions on Information Forensics and Security **9**(7), 1193–1205 (2014)

25. Seo, J.H., Emura, K.: Revocable identity-based encryption with rejoin functionality. IEICE Transactions **97–A**(8), 1806–1809 (2014)
26. Shamir, A.: Identity-based cryptosystems and signature schemes. In: Blakely, G.R., Chaum, D. (eds.) CRYPTO 1984. LNCS, vol. 196, pp. 47–53. Springer, Heidelberg (1985)
27. Tsai, T., Tseng, Y., Wu, T.: RHIBE: constructing revocable hierarchical ID-based encryption from HIBE. Informatica, Lith. Acad. Sci. **25**(2), 299–326 (2014)
28. Waters, B.: Efficient identity-based encryption without random oracles. In: Cramer, R. (ed.) EUROCRYPT 2005. LNCS, vol. 3494, pp. 114–127. Springer, Heidelberg (2005)

Membership

Revisiting Cryptographic Accumulators, Additional Properties and Relations to Other Primitives

David Derler[(✉)], Christian Hanser, and Daniel Slamanig

Institute for Applied Information Processing and Communications (IAIK),
Graz University of Technology (TUG), Inffeldgasse 16a, 8010 Graz, Austria
{david.derler,christian.hanser,daniel.slamanig}@tugraz.at

Abstract. Cryptographic accumulators allow to accumulate a finite set of values into a single succinct accumulator. For every accumulated value, one can efficiently compute a witness, which certifies its membership in the accumulator. However, it is computationally infeasible to find a witness for any non-accumulated value. Since their introduction, various accumulator schemes for numerous practical applications and with different features have been proposed. Unfortunately, to date there is no unifying model capturing all existing features. Such a model can turn out to be valuable as it allows to use accumulators in a black-box fashion.

To this end, we propose a unified formal model for (randomized) cryptographic accumulators which covers static and dynamic accumulators, their universal features and includes the notions of undeniability and indistinguishability. Additionally, we provide an exhaustive classification of all existing schemes. In doing so, it turns out that most accumulators are distinguishable. Fortunately, a simple, light-weight generic transformation allows to make many existing dynamic accumulator schemes indistinguishable. As this transformation, however, comes at the cost of reduced collision freeness, we additionally propose the first indistinguishable scheme that does not suffer from this shortcoming. Finally, we employ our unified model for presenting a black-box construction of commitments from indistinguishable accumulators as well as a black-box construction of indistinguishable, undeniable universal accumulators from zero-knowledge sets. Latter yields the first universal accumulator construction that provides indistinguishability.

1 Introduction

A (static) cryptographic accumulator scheme allows to accumulate a finite set $\mathcal{X} = \{x_1, \ldots, x_n\}$ into a succinct value $\mathsf{acc}_{\mathcal{X}}$, the so called accumulator. For every element $x_i \in \mathcal{X}$, one can efficiently compute a so called witness wit_{x_i} to certify

The authors have been supported by the European Commission through project FP7-FutureID, grant agreement number 318424. An extended version of this paper is available in the IACR Cryptology ePrint Archive.

© Springer International Publishing Switzerland 2015
K. Nyberg (ed.): CT-RSA 2015, LNCS 9048, pp. 127–144, 2015.
DOI: 10.1007/978-3-319-16715-2_7

the membership of x_i in $\mathrm{acc}_\mathcal{X}$. However, it should be computationally infeasible to find a witness for any non-accumulated value $y \notin \mathcal{X}$ (*collision freeness*). Dynamic accumulators are an extension that allows to dynamically add/delete values to/from a given accumulator and to update existing witnesses accordingly (without the need to fully recompute these values on each change of the accumulated set). Besides providing membership witnesses, universal accumulators also support non-membership witnesses for values $y \notin \mathcal{X}$. Here, collision freeness also covers that it is computationally infeasible to create non-membership witnesses for values $x_i \in \mathcal{X}$. Over time, further security properties, that is, *undeniability* and *indistinguishability* have been proposed. Undeniability is specific to universal accumulators and says that it should be computationally infeasible to compute two contradicting witnesses for $z \in \mathcal{X}$ and $z \notin \mathcal{X}$. Indistinguishability says that neither the accumulator nor the witnesses leak information about the accumulated set $\mathcal{X}$ and, thus, requires randomized accumulator schemes.

Applications: Accumulators were originally proposed for timestamping purposes [5], i.e., to record the existence of a value at a particular point in time. Over time, other applications such as membership testing, distributed signatures, accountable certificate management [7] and authenticated dictionaries [22] have been proposed. Accumulators are also used as building block in redactable [33,34], sanitizable [13], P-homomorphic signatures [2], anonymous credentials [38], group signatures [39], privacy-preserving data outsourcing [37] as well as for authenticated data structures [21]. Moreover, accumulator schemes that allow to prove the knowledge of a (non-membership) witness for an unrevealed value in zero-knowledge (introduced for off-line e-cash in [36]) are now widely used for revocation of group signatures and anonymous credentials [12]. Quite recently, accumulators were also used in Zerocoin [28], an anonymity extension to the Bitcoin cryptocurrency.

Since their introduction, numerous accumulator schemes with somewhat different features have been proposed. Basically, the major lines of work are schemes in hidden order groups (RSA), known order groups (DL) and hash-based constructions (which may use, but typically do not require number theoretic assumptions).

Hidden Order Groups: The original RSA-based scheme of Benaloh and de Mare [5] has been refined by Baric and Pfitzmann [4], who strengthen the original security notion to *collision freeness*. In [35], Sander proposed to use RSA moduli with unknown factorization to construct trapdoor-free accumulators. Camenisch and Lysyanskaya [12] extended the scheme in [4] with capabilities to dynamically add/delete values to/from the accumulator, which constituted the first *dynamic accumulator* scheme. Their scheme also supports *public updates* of existing witnesses, that is, updates without the knowledge of any trapdoor. Later, Li et al. [24] added support for non-membership witnesses to [12] and, therefore, obtained *universal dynamic accumulators*. They also proposed an optimization for more efficient updates of non-membership witnesses, for which, however, weaknesses have been identified later [26,32]. Lipmaa [25] generalized RSA accumulators to modules over Euclidean rings. In all aforementioned schemes, the accumulation domain is restricted to primes in order to guarantee collision freeness. In [39], Tsudik and Xu proposed a variation of [12], which allows to accumulate semiprimes. This yields a collision-free accumulator under the assumption that the used semiprimes are hard to factor and their factorization is not publicly known. Moreover, in [40] an accumulator scheme that allows to accumulate arbitrary integers and supports batch updates of witnesses has been proposed. Yet, this scheme was broken in [9].

Known Order Groups: In [29], Nguyen proposed a dynamic accumulator scheme which works in pairing-friendly groups of prime order p. It is secure under the t-SDH assumption and allows to accumulate up to t values from the domain $\mathbb{Z}_p$. Later, Damgård and Triandopoulos [16] as well as Au et al. [3] extended Nguyen's scheme with universal features. Quite recently, Acar and Nguyen [1] eliminated the upper bound t on the number of accumulated elements of the t-SDH accumulator. To this end, they use a set of accumulators, each containing a subset of the whole set to be accumulated. An alternative accumulator scheme for pairing friendly groups of prime order has been introduced by Camenisch et al. [11]. It supports public updates of witnesses and the accumulator and its security relies on the t-DHE assumption.

Hash-Based Constructions: Buldas et al. [7,8] presented the very first universal dynamic accumulator that satisfies *undeniability* (termed as undeniable attester and formalized in context of accumulators in [25]). Their construction is based on collision-resistant hashing and the use of hash-trees. Another hash-tree based construction of a universal accumulator that satisfies a notion similar to undeniability has been proposed in [10] (the scheme is called a strong universal accumulator). Quite recently, another accumulator based on hash-trees, which uses commitments based on bivariate polynomials modulo RSA composites as a collision-resistant hash function, has been introduced in [6]. For the sake of completeness, we also mention the construction of static accumulators in the random oracle model based on Bloom filters, proposed by Nyberg [30,31].

Contribution: The contributions of this paper are as follows:

– While some papers [3–5,12,29] do not explicitly formalize accumulator schemes, formal definitions are given in [1,10,11,14,20,24,25,40]. However, these models are typically tailored to the functionalities of the respective scheme. While they widely match for the basic notion of (static) accumulators (with the exception of considering randomized accumulators), they differ when it comes to dynamic and universal accumulators. To overcome this issue, we propose a unified formal model for accumulators, which is especially valuable when treating accumulators in a black-box fashion. We, thereby, also include the notion of undeniability [7,8,25] and a strengthened version of the recent indistinguishability notion [17]. Besides, we also confirm the intuition and show that undeniability is a strictly stronger notion than collision freeness.

- We provide an exhaustive classification of existing accumulator schemes and show that most existing accumulator schemes are distinguishable in our model. To resolve this issue, we propose a simple, light-weight generic transformation that allows to add indistinguishability to existing dynamic accumulators and prove the security of the so-obtained schemes. As this transformation, however, comes at the cost of reduced collision freeness, we additionally propose the first indistinguishable scheme that does not suffer from this shortcoming. Note that due to the lack of space, the indistinguishable accumulator scheme is provided in the extended version of this paper.
- Since accumulators are somehow related to commitments to sets [19,23], commitments to vectors [14] and to zero-knowledge sets [27], it is interesting to study their relationship. Interestingly, we can formally show that indistinguishable accumulators imply non-interactive commitment schemes. Furthermore, we formally show that zero-knowledge sets imply indistinguishable, undeniable universal accumulators, yielding the first construction of such accumulators.

2   Preliminaries

By acc we denote an accumulator and if we want to make the accumulated set $\mathcal{X} = \{x_1, \ldots, x_n\}$ explicit, we write $\mathsf{acc}_\mathcal{X}$. Given an accumulator $\mathsf{acc}_\mathcal{X}$, a membership witness for an element $x_i \in \mathcal{X}$ is denoted by wit_{x_i}, whereas a non-membership witness for an element $y_j \notin \mathcal{X}$ is denoted by $\underline{\mathsf{wit}}_{y_j}$. The accumulator secret key (trapdoor) is denoted by $\mathsf{sk}_{\mathsf{acc}}$, while the public key is denoted by $\mathsf{pk}_{\mathsf{acc}}$. By $a \xleftarrow{R} A$, we denote that a is chosen uniformly at random from the set A.

A function $\epsilon : \mathbb{N} \to \mathbb{R}^+$ is called *negligible* if for all $c > 0$ there is a k_0 such that $\epsilon(k) < 1/k^c$ for all $k > k_0$. In the remainder of this paper, we use ϵ to denote such a negligible function.

3   A Unified Model for Cryptographic Accumulators

In the original sense, accumulator schemes were defined by the following properties (see, e.g., [12,24]). Thereby, $\mathcal{Z}_I$ represents the domain of values to be accumulated and $\mathcal{Z}_A$ the accumulator domain.

Efficient generation: There is an efficient probabilistic algorithm that, on input of a security parameter κ, defines a functionality $f : \mathcal{Z}_A \times \mathcal{Z}_I \to \mathcal{Z}_A$, i.e., generates the accumulator specific key pair ($\mathsf{sk}_{\mathsf{acc}}$, $\mathsf{pk}_{\mathsf{acc}}$) (where $\mathsf{sk}_{\mathsf{acc}}$ is a trapdoor for f).

Efficient evaluation: There is an efficient algorithm that computes $f(\mathsf{acc}, x)$.

Quasi-commutativity: It holds that $f(f(\mathsf{acc}, x_1), x_2) = f(f(\mathsf{acc}, x_2), x_1)$ $\forall x_1, x_2 \in \mathcal{Z}_I, \mathsf{acc} \in \mathcal{Z}_A$.

Assuming that it is computationally infeasible to invert f without knowing $\mathsf{sk_{acc}}$, the quasi-commutativity directly yields a way to define witnesses. For instance, $f(\mathsf{acc}, x_1)$ can serve as witness for the accumulation of x_2. Nonetheless, it is more meaningful to provide a more abstract algorithmic definition of accumulators as done subsequently, since there are several constructions that do not fit into this characterization (for instance, hash-tree constructions do not require the quasi-commutativity property).

Trusted vs. Non-Trusted Setup: Known accumulators that rely on number theoretic assumptions require a trusted setup, i.e., a TTP runs the setup algorithm Gen and discards the trapdoor $\mathsf{sk_{acc}}$ afterwards. Here, access to $\mathsf{sk_{acc}}$ allows to break collision freeness (and its stronger form: undeniability). Consequently, correctness of the accumulator scheme also needs to hold if $\mathsf{sk_{acc}}$ is omitted in all algorithms, which is the case for all existing schemes. In contrast, in constructions relying on collision-resistant hash functions (not based on number theoretic assumptions) there is no trapdoor at all and, therefore, no trusted setup is required. In order to study number theoretic accumulators without trusted setup, Lipmaa [25] proposed a modified model which divides the Gen algorithm into a Setup and a Gen algorithm. In this model, the adversary can control the randomness used inside Setup and, thus, knows the trapdoor. Nevertheless, it can neither access nor influence the randomness of the Gen algorithm. This model, however, still requires a partially trusted setup and also does not fit to the known order group setting, which makes it not generally applicable.[1] Consequently, when considering the state of the art it seems most reasonable to define a security model with respect to a trusted setup as we will do subsequently. We emphasize that this model is compatible with all existing constructions. Nevertheless, it remains a challenging open issue to design accumulators based on standard assumptions which are secure without any trusted setup.

3.1   Definitions

In the following, we provide a definition for (static) accumulators, which we adapt from [20,40]. In contrast to previous models, we explicitly consider randomized accumulator schemes. Then, we extend this model in order to formalize dynamic accumulators. It is similar to [11,14], but avoids shortcomings such as missing private updates. Based on this, we define universal and universal dynamic accumulators and propose a suitable security model. Furthermore, we discuss undeniable and indistinguishable accumulators, give formalizations for these properties, and, investigate relationships between security properties.

---

[1] This model is tailored to the hidden order group setting, where Setup produces a composite modulus N. Gen chooses a random generator g of a large subgroup of $\mathbb{Z}_N^*$. Then, the adversary knows the factorization of N but does not control the choice of g. RSA accumulators are obviously insecure in this setting, but Lipmaa provides secure solutions based on modules over an Euclidean ring, which, however, rely on rather unstudied assumptions.

We call accumulators that have an upper bound t on the number of accumulated values t-*bounded accumulators* and *unbounded* otherwise. In order to model this, our Gen algorithm takes an additional parameter t, where $t = \infty$ is used to indicate that the accumulator is unbounded. For the sake of completeness, we model the algorithms such that they support an optional input of the trapdoor (denoted as $\mathsf{sk}_{\mathsf{acc}}^{\sim}$) since this often allows to make the algorithms more efficient. However, we stress that we consider the trusted setup model and, hence, adversaries are not given access to the trapdoor $\mathsf{sk}_{\mathsf{acc}}^{\sim}$. Consequently, if $\mathsf{sk}_{\mathsf{acc}}^{\sim}$ is set, the party running the algorithm needs to be fully trusted.

Definition 1 (Static Accumulator). *A static accumulator is a tuple of efficient algorithms* (Gen, Eval, WitCreate, Verify) *which are defined as follows:*

Gen($1^\kappa, t$): *This algorithm takes a security parameter κ and a parameter t. If $t \neq \infty$, then t is an upper bound on the number of elements to be accumulated. It returns a key pair* ($\mathsf{sk}_{\mathsf{acc}}, \mathsf{pk}_{\mathsf{acc}}$), *where* $\mathsf{sk}_{\mathsf{acc}} = \emptyset$ *if no trapdoor exists.*

Eval(($\mathsf{sk}_{\mathsf{acc}}^{\sim}, \mathsf{pk}_{\mathsf{acc}}$), $\mathcal{X}$): *This (probabilistic)[2] algorithm takes a key pair* ($\mathsf{sk}_{\mathsf{acc}}^{\sim}$, $\mathsf{pk}_{\mathsf{acc}}$) *and a set $\mathcal{X}$ to be accumulated and returns an accumulator* $\mathsf{acc}_{\mathcal{X}}$ *together with some auxiliary information* aux.

WitCreate(($\mathsf{sk}_{\mathsf{acc}}^{\sim}, \mathsf{pk}_{\mathsf{acc}}$), $\mathsf{acc}_{\mathcal{X}}$, aux, x_i): *This algorithm takes a key pair* ($\mathsf{sk}_{\mathsf{acc}}^{\sim}$, $\mathsf{pk}_{\mathsf{acc}}$), *an accumulator* $\mathsf{acc}_{\mathcal{X}}$, *auxiliary information* aux *and a value x_i. It returns $\bot$, if $x_i \notin \mathcal{X}$, and a witness* wit_{x_i} *for x_i otherwise.*

Verify($\mathsf{pk}_{\mathsf{acc}}$, $\mathsf{acc}_{\mathcal{X}}$, wit_{x_i}, x_i): *This algorithm takes a public key* $\mathsf{pk}_{\mathsf{acc}}$, *an accumulator* $\mathsf{acc}_{\mathcal{X}}$, *a witness* wit_{x_i} *and a value x_i. It returns true if wit_{x_i} is a witness for $x_i \in \mathcal{X}$ and false otherwise.*

Henceforth, we call an accumulator *randomized* if the Eval algorithm is probabilistic. Based on Definition 1, we can now formalize *dynamic accumulators*. We widely align our definitions with [20,40], but, in addition, we need to consider that the various dynamic accumulator schemes proposed so far differ regarding the *public updatability* of witnesses and the accumulator.

Definition 2 (Dynamic   Accumulator).   *A   dynamic   accumulator is   a   static   accumulator   that   additionally   provides   efficient   algorithms* (Add, Delete, WitUpdate) *which are defined as follows:*

Add(($\mathsf{sk}_{\mathsf{acc}}^{\sim}, \mathsf{pk}_{\mathsf{acc}}$), $\mathsf{acc}_{\mathcal{X}}$, aux, x_i): *This algorithm takes a key pair* ($\mathsf{sk}_{\mathsf{acc}}^{\sim}, \mathsf{pk}_{\mathsf{acc}}$), *an accumulator* $\mathsf{acc}_{\mathcal{X}}$, *auxiliary information* aux, *as well as a value x_i to be added. If $x_i \in \mathcal{X}$, it returns $\bot$. Otherwise, it returns the updated accumulator* $\mathsf{acc}_{\mathcal{X}'}$ *with $\mathcal{X}' \leftarrow \mathcal{X} \cup \{x_i\}$ and updated auxiliary information* aux'.

Delete(($\mathsf{sk}_{\mathsf{acc}}^{\sim}, \mathsf{pk}_{\mathsf{acc}}$), $\mathsf{acc}_{\mathcal{X}}$, aux, x_i): *This algorithm takes a key pair* ($\mathsf{sk}_{\mathsf{acc}}^{\sim}$, $\mathsf{pk}_{\mathsf{acc}}$), *an accumulator* $\mathsf{acc}_{\mathcal{X}}$, *auxiliary information* aux, *as well as a value x_i to be removed. If $x_i \notin \mathcal{X}$, it returns $\bot$. Otherwise, it returns the updated accumulator* $\mathsf{acc}_{\mathcal{X}'}$ *with $\mathcal{X}' \leftarrow \mathcal{X} \setminus \{x_i\}$ and auxiliary information* aux'.

---

[2] If Eval is probabilistic, the internally used randomness is denoted as r. If we want to make the randomness used by the Eval algorithm explicit, we will write Eval$_r$.

WitUpdate$((\mathsf{sk}_{\mathsf{acc}}^{\sim}, \mathsf{pk}_{\mathsf{acc}}), \mathsf{wit}_{x_i}, \mathsf{aux}, x_j)$: *This algorithm takes a key pair* $(\mathsf{sk}_{\mathsf{acc}}^{\sim}, \mathsf{pk}_{\mathsf{acc}})$, *a witness* wit_{x_i} *to be updated, auxiliary information* aux *and a value* x_j *which was added/deleted to/from the accumulator, where* aux *indicates addition or deletion. It returns an updated witness* wit'_{x_i} *on success and* $\perp$ *otherwise.*

Below, we define *universal accumulators* and emphasize that features provided by universal accumulators can be seen as supplementary features to both *static* and *dynamic* accumulators.

Definition 3 (Universal Accumulator). *A universal accumulator is a static or a dynamic accumulator with the following properties. For static accumulator schemes the algorithms* WitCreate *and* Verify *take an additional boolean parameter* type, *indicating whether the given witness is a membership* (type $= 0$) *or non-membership* (type $= 1$) *witness. For dynamic accumulator schemes this additionally applies to* WitUpdate.

3.2 Security Model

Now, we introduce a security model for accumulators, which we adapt from [24] and further extend by undeniability and indistinguishability.

Classic Notion: A secure accumulator scheme is required to be *correct* and *collision-free*. Correctness says that for all honestly generated keys, all honestly computed accumulators and witnesses, the Verify algorithm will always return true. We stress that correctness also needs to hold when all algorithms are executed without $\mathsf{sk}_{\mathsf{acc}}$. Since the correctness property is straightforward, we omit its formal definition. Collision freeness informally states that it is neither feasible to find a witness for a non-accumulated value nor feasible to find a non-membership witness for an accumulated value. More formally:

Definition 4 (Collision Freeness). *A cryptographic accumulator of type* $\mathsf{t} \in \{\mathsf{static}, \mathsf{dynamic}\}$ *and* $\mathsf{u} \in \{\mathsf{universal}, \mathsf{non\text{-}universal}\}$ *is collision-free, if for all PPT adversaries* $\mathcal{A}$ *there is a negligible function* $\epsilon(\cdot)$ *such that:*

$$\Pr\left[\begin{array}{c} (\mathsf{sk}_{\mathsf{acc}}, \mathsf{pk}_{\mathsf{acc}}) \leftarrow \mathsf{Gen}(1^{\kappa}, \mathsf{t}), \ \mathcal{O} \leftarrow \{\mathcal{O}^{\mathsf{t}}, \mathcal{O}^{\mathsf{u}}\}, \\ (\mathsf{wit}_{x_i}^* / \underline{\mathsf{wit}}_{x_i}^*, x_i^*, \mathcal{X}^*, r^*) \leftarrow \mathcal{A}^{\mathcal{O}}(\mathsf{pk}_{\mathsf{acc}}) : \\ (\mathsf{Verify}(\mathsf{pk}_{\mathsf{acc}}, \mathsf{acc}^*, \mathsf{wit}_{x_i}^*, x_i^*, 0) = \mathtt{true} \ \wedge \ x_i^* \notin \mathcal{X}^*) \ \vee \\ (\mathsf{Verify}(\mathsf{pk}_{\mathsf{acc}}, \mathsf{acc}^*, \underline{\mathsf{wit}}_{x_i}^*, x_i^*, 1) = \mathtt{true} \ \wedge \ x_i^* \in \mathcal{X}^*) \end{array} \right] \le \epsilon(\kappa),$$

where $\mathsf{acc}^* \leftarrow \mathsf{Eval}_{r^*}((\mathsf{sk}_{\mathsf{acc}}, \mathsf{pk}_{\mathsf{acc}}), \mathcal{X}^*)$ *and* $\mathcal{A}$ *has oracle access to* $\mathcal{O}^{\mathsf{t}}$ *and* $\mathcal{O}^{\mathsf{u}}$ *which are defined as follows:*

$$\mathcal{O}^{\mathsf{t}} := \begin{cases} \{\mathcal{O}^{\mathsf{E}(\cdot,\cdot,\cdot)}\} & \textit{if } \mathsf{t} = \mathsf{static}, \\ \{\mathcal{O}^{\mathsf{E}(\cdot,\cdot,\cdot)}, \mathcal{O}^{\mathsf{A}(\cdot,\cdot,\cdot,\cdot)}, \mathcal{O}^{\mathsf{D}(\cdot,\cdot,\cdot,\cdot)}\} & \textit{otherwise.} \end{cases}$$

$$\mathcal{O}^{\mathsf{u}} := \begin{cases} \{\mathcal{O}^{\mathsf{W}(\cdot,\cdot,\cdot,\cdot)}, \mathcal{O}^{\underline{\mathsf{W}}(\cdot,\cdot,\cdot,\cdot)}\} & \textit{if } \mathsf{u} = \mathsf{universal}, \\ \{\mathcal{O}^{\mathsf{W}(\cdot,\cdot,\cdot,\cdot)}\} & \textit{otherwise.} \end{cases}$$

Thereby, $\mathcal{O}^\mathsf{E}, \mathcal{O}^\mathsf{A}$ and $\mathcal{O}^\mathsf{D}$ represent the oracles for the algorithms Eval, Add, and Delete, respectively. An adversary is allowed to query them an arbitrary number of times. In case of randomized accumulators the adversary outputs randomness r^*, whereas r^* is omitted for deterministic accumulators. Likewise, the adversary can control the randomness r used by $\mathcal{O}^\mathsf{E}$ for randomized accumulators. Therefore, $\mathcal{O}^\mathsf{E}$ takes an additional parameter for r (which is missing for deterministic accumulators). The oracles $\mathcal{O}^\mathsf{W}$ and $\mathcal{O}^{\underline{\mathsf{W}}}$ allow the adversary to obtain membership witnesses for members and non-membership witnesses for non-members, respectively. Thereby, the environment keeps track of all oracle queries (and answers) and lets the respective oracle return $\perp$ if calls to it are not consistent with respect to previous queries. Furthermore, we assume that the adversary outputs either a membership witness $\mathsf{wit}^*_{x_i}$ or a non-membership witness $\underline{\mathsf{wit}}^*_{x_i}$ (denoted by $\mathsf{wit}^*_{x_i}/\underline{\mathsf{wit}}^*_{x_i}$). If the accumulator is non-universal, one simply omits the non-membership related parts.

One distinction to previous models is that we model (non-)membership witness generation via oracles. This way, we can ensure that security proofs take the simulation of (non-)membership witnesses into account, which is vital and could be overseen otherwise.

Definition 5 (Secure Accumulator). *A cryptographic accumulator is* secure *if it is correct and collision-free.*

Undeniable accumulators: In [25], Lipmaa formalized undeniability for accumulators. A universal accumulator is *undeniable* if it is computationally infeasible to find a membership as well as a non-membership witness for the same value – independently of whether it is contained in an accumulator or not. More formally undeniability is defined as:

Definition 6 (Undeniability). *A universal cryptographic accumulator of type* $\mathsf{t} \in \{\mathsf{static}, \mathsf{dynamic}\}$ *is* undeniable, *if for all PPT adversaries $\mathcal{A}$ there is a negligible function $\epsilon(\cdot)$ such that:*

$$\Pr\left[\begin{array}{c} (\mathsf{sk}_{\mathsf{acc}}, \mathsf{pk}_{\mathsf{acc}}) \leftarrow \mathsf{Gen}(1^\kappa, \mathsf{t}), (\mathsf{wit}^*_{x_i}, \underline{\mathsf{wit}}^*_{x_i}, x^*_i, \mathsf{acc}^*) \leftarrow \mathcal{A}^{\mathcal{O}^\mathsf{t}}(\mathsf{pk}_{\mathsf{acc}}) : \\ \mathsf{Verify}(\mathsf{pk}_{\mathsf{acc}}, \mathsf{acc}^*, \mathsf{wit}^*_{x_i}, x^*_i, 0) = \mathtt{true} \ \wedge \\ \mathsf{Verify}(\mathsf{pk}_{\mathsf{acc}}, \mathsf{acc}^*, \underline{\mathsf{wit}}^*_{x_i}, x^*_i, 1) = \mathtt{true} \end{array}\right] \le \epsilon(\kappa),$$

where, $\mathcal{A}$ has oracle access to $\mathcal{O}^\mathsf{t}$ which is defined as follows:

$$\mathcal{O}^\mathsf{t} := \begin{cases} \{\mathcal{O}^{\mathsf{E}(\cdot,\cdot,\cdot)}, \mathcal{O}^{\mathsf{W}(\cdot,\cdot,\cdot,\cdot)}, \mathcal{O}^{\underline{\mathsf{W}}(\cdot,\cdot,\cdot,\cdot)}\} & \textit{if } \mathsf{t} = \mathsf{static}, \\ \{\mathcal{O}^{\mathsf{E}(\cdot,\cdot,\cdot)}, \mathcal{O}^{\mathsf{A}(\cdot,\cdot,\cdot,\cdot)}, \mathcal{O}^{\mathsf{D}(\cdot,\cdot,\cdot,\cdot)}, \mathcal{O}^{\mathsf{W}(\cdot,\cdot,\cdot,\cdot)}, \mathcal{O}^{\underline{\mathsf{W}}(\cdot,\cdot,\cdot,\cdot)}\} & \textit{otherwise.} \end{cases}$$

Notice that the definition of the oracles is as in the definition of collision freeness for universal accumulators.

Definition 7. *A universal accumulator is* undeniable *if it is a secure accumulator satisfying the undeniability property.*

Indistinguishable Accumulators: Li et al. [24] pointed out informally (without giving any formalizations) that the accumulation of an additional random value from the accumulation domain renders guessing the accumulated set infeasible. Later, de Meer et al. [17] tried to formalize this intuition via an additional *indistinguishability* property. Unfortunately, there are some issues with their notion. Firstly, it only covers static accumulators and, secondly, indistinguishability in the vein of [24] weakens collision resistance. Basically, one can easily generate a membership witness for the random value. Secondly, the security game in [17] allows to prove indistinguishability of deterministic accumulators, which are clearly not indistinguishable. In particular, the random value is chosen and accumulated within the security game. However, this non-determinism is not required to be part of the accumulator construction itself. Consequently, a deterministic accumulator can satisfy this notion while being trivially distinguishable. From this, we conclude that the non-determinism must be intrinsic to the Eval algorithm.[3]

There are several ways to turn a deterministic scheme into a randomized one. As already discussed, indistinguishability can be achieved by adding a random value from the accumulation domain. Aside from this, it can also be obtained by randomizing the Eval algorithm without modifying the set $\mathcal{X}$ (as, for instance, done in the extended version of this paper). Apparently, the latter option depends on the specific accumulator scheme, whereas the shortcomings in [17] can be addressed by introducing a generic transformation for the former approach (cf. Transformation 1).

Definition 8 (Indistinguishability). *A cryptographic accumulator of type* $t \in$ *{static, dynamic} and* $u \in$ *{universal, non-universal} is indistinguishable, if for all PPT adversaries* $\mathcal{A}$ *there is a negligible function* $\epsilon(\cdot)$ *such that:*

$$\Pr\left[\begin{array}{c} (\mathsf{sk_{acc}}, \mathsf{pk_{acc}}) \leftarrow \mathsf{Gen}(1^\kappa, t),\ b \xleftarrow{R} \{0,1\}, \\ (\mathcal{X}_0, \mathcal{X}_1, \mathsf{state}) \leftarrow \mathcal{A}(\mathsf{pk_{acc}}), (\mathsf{acc}_{\mathcal{X}_b}, \mathsf{aux}) \leftarrow \mathsf{Eval}((\mathsf{sk}_{\widetilde{acc}}, \mathsf{pk_{acc}}), \\ \mathcal{X}_b), \mathcal{O} \leftarrow \{\mathcal{O}^t, \mathcal{O}^u\},\ b^* \leftarrow \mathcal{A}^{\mathcal{O}}(\mathsf{pk_{acc}}, \mathsf{acc}_{\mathcal{X}_b}, \mathsf{state}) : b = b^* \end{array}\right] \leq \frac{1}{2} + \epsilon(\kappa),$$

where $\mathcal{X}_0$ *and* $\mathcal{X}_1$ *are two distinct subsets of the accumulation domain and* $\mathcal{O}^t$ *as well as* $\mathcal{O}^u$ *are defined as follows:*

$$\mathcal{O}^t := \begin{cases} \{\mathcal{O}^{\mathsf{E}(\cdot,\cdot,\cdot)}\} & \textit{if } t = \mathsf{static}, \\ \{\mathcal{O}^{\mathsf{E}(\cdot,\cdot,\cdot)}, \mathcal{O}^{\mathsf{A}_\cup(\cdot,\cdot,\mathsf{aux},\cdot)}, \mathcal{O}^{\mathsf{D}_\cap(\cdot,\cdot,\mathsf{aux},\cdot)}\} & \textit{otherwise.} \end{cases}$$

$$\mathcal{O}^u := \begin{cases} \{\mathcal{O}^{\mathsf{W}(\cdot,\cdot,\mathsf{aux},\cdot)}, \mathcal{O}^{\underline{\mathsf{W}}(\cdot,\cdot,\mathsf{aux},\cdot)}\} & \textit{if } u = \mathsf{universal}, \\ \{\mathcal{O}^{\mathsf{W}(\cdot,\cdot,\mathsf{aux},\cdot)}\} & \textit{otherwise.} \end{cases}$$

If the probability above is exactly $1/2$ *we have* unconditional *indistinguishability, whereas we have computational indistinguishability if the probability is negligibly different from* $1/2$.

---

[3] Independently from our work, this observation was quite recently also made in [18] by the authors of [17]: The insertion of the random value has been removed from the game and the Eval algorithm is now required to be non-deterministic.

Here, $\mathcal{O}^{\mathsf{E}}$ is defined as before and all other oracles can only be called for the challenge accumulator. We require that the input parameter aux for the oracles is kept up to date and is provided by the environment, since the knowledge of aux would allow the adversary to trivially win the game. Furthermore, note that this game does not allow the adversary to control the randomness used for the evaluation of $\mathsf{acc}_{\mathcal{X}_b}$ (while it can be controlled when calling $\mathcal{O}^{\mathsf{E}}$). For the definitions of the remaining oracles, we use $\mathcal{X}_{\cup} := \mathcal{X}_0 \cup \mathcal{X}_1$ and $\mathcal{X}_{\cap} := \mathcal{X}_0 \cap \mathcal{X}_1$ to restrict the adversary from oracle queries which would trivially allow to win the game. $\mathcal{O}^{\mathsf{A}_\cup}$ as well as $\mathcal{O}^{\mathsf{D}_\cap}$ allow the adversary to execute the Add and Delete algorithms. Thereby, $\mathcal{O}^{\mathsf{A}_\cup}$ allows only queries for values $x_i \notin \mathcal{X}_{\cup}$, whereas $\mathcal{O}^{\mathsf{D}_\cap}$ allows only queries for values $x_i \in \mathcal{X}_{\cap}$. Furthermore, upon every Add and Delete the sets $\mathcal{X}_{\cup}$ and $\mathcal{X}_{\cap}$ are updated consistently. Oracles $\mathcal{O}^{\mathsf{W}}$ and $\mathcal{O}^{\underline{\mathsf{W}}}$ are as above, with the difference that $\mathcal{O}^{\mathsf{W}}$ allows only queries for values $x_i \in \mathcal{X}_{\cap}$, while $\mathcal{O}^{\underline{\mathsf{W}}}$ allows only queries for values $y_j \notin \mathcal{X}_{\cup}$.

Transformation 1. *On input a set $\mathcal{X}$, the Eval algorithm samples an element $x_r \notin \mathcal{X}$ uniformly at random from the accumulation domain. Next, it computes and returns $(\mathsf{acc}_{\mathcal{X}'}, \mathsf{aux}')$ for $\mathcal{X}' \leftarrow \mathcal{X} \cup \{x_r\}$ and $\mathsf{aux}' \leftarrow (\mathsf{aux}, x_r)$.*

Note that aux needs to be kept consistent for all other algorithms that require this input parameter. As already noted above, collision freeness no longer holds for $\mathcal{X}$ but with respect to $\mathcal{X} \cup \{x_r\}$. To draw a line between inherently randomized constructions and such relying on Transformation 1, we differentiate between indistinguishability and collision-freeness-weakening (cfw) indistinguishability:

Definition 9 (Indistinguishability). *Let $\mathcal{X}$ be the set in $\mathsf{acc}_{\mathcal{X}_b}$. A cryptographic accumulator is called* indistinguishable *if it is a secure, indistinguishable accumulator and $\mathcal{X} = \mathcal{X}_b$.*

Definition 10 (cfw-Indistinguishability). *Let $\mathcal{X}$ be the set in $\mathsf{acc}_{\mathcal{X}_b}$. A cryptographic accumulator is called* collision-freeness-weakening (cfw) indistinguishable *if it is a secure, indistinguishable accumulator and $\mathcal{X} \neq \mathcal{X}_b$.*

3.3   Relation Between Security Properties

Intuitively, undeniability seems to be a strictly stronger security requirement than collision freeness. We confirm this intuition below:

Lemma 1. *Every undeniable universal accumulator is collision-free.*

We prove the lemma above in the extended version of this paper.

As mentioned in [25], a black-box reduction in the other direction is impossible. [8] provides a collision-free universal accumulator that is not undeniable. Therefore, this proves the following lemma by counterexample:

Lemma 2. *Not every collision-free universal accumulator is undeniable.*

4   Categorizing Cryptographic Accumulators

Now, we give a comprehensive overview of existing accumulator schemes in Table 1. We categorize them regarding their static or dynamic nature and universal features and provide a characterization of their public updating capabilities (of witnesses and of accumulators, respectively). In particular, we tag an accumulator as dynamic, if witness and accumulator value updates can be performed in constant time, i.e., independent of the size of $\mathcal{X}$. If the same is possible without having access to the accumulator trapdoor, then we tag the accumulator as *publicly updatable*. Furthermore, the properties undeniability and indistinguishability have not been considered for most existing accumulator schemes so far. Therefore, we provide a classification regarding their indistinguishability (when using Transformation 1) and provide the respective proofs in the extended version. Likewise, we prove the undeniability of [3,16] in the extended version. For the sake of completeness, our comparison also includes static accumulator schemes [4,5,30,31].

5   Commitments from Indistinguishable Accumulators

In [14], it has been shown that universal dynamic accumulators can be black-box constructed from vector commitments. The question arises whether it is also possible to provide black-box constructions for certain types of commitments from indistinguishable accumulators. It is apparent that it is not possible to build vector commitments solely from accumulators in a black-box fashion, since their position binding would at least require some additional encoding. Nevertheless, we will show how to construct non-interactive commitments from indistinguishable 1-bounded accumulators. In the extended version, we show that such accumulators actually exist, i.e., we build the first indistinguishable t-bounded dynamic accumulator by modifying [29].

5.1   Black-Box Construction of Non-Interactive Commitments

Before we can start, we present a standard formal definition of non-interactive commitment schemes.

Definition 11 (Non-Interactive Commitment Scheme). *A non-interactive commitment scheme is a triple of efficient algorithms* (Gen, Commit, Open), *which are defined as follows:*

Gen(1^κ): *This (probabilistic) algorithm takes input a security parameter κ and outputs the public parameters* pp.

Commit(pp, m): *This (probabilistic) algorithm takes input* pp *and a message m and outputs a commitment C together with a corresponding opening information O.*

Open(pp, C, O): *This deterministic algorithm takes input* pp, *a commitment C with corresponding opening information O and outputs $\perp$ if C is not a valid commitment to any message and message m otherwise.*

Table 1. Overview of features of existing accumulator schemes. *Legend: D...dynamic, U...universal, Pub. Updates...constant cost for public updates of witnesses and accumulators, a...add, d...delete, ZK...zero-knowledge (non-)membership proofs, B...bounded, $|pk_{acc}|$...public parameter size, $|wit|$...membership witness size, $|\underline{wit}|$...non-membership witness size, Und...undeniability, Ind...(cfw) indistinguishability, ✓...yes, ✗...no, -...not available, ?...left open, ‡...proven in the extended version of this paper.*

		Type		Pub. Updates									
						acc							
	Scheme	D	U	wit	$\underline{wit}$	a	d	ZK	B	$\lvert pk_{acc}\rvert$	$\lvert wit\rvert$	$\lvert\underline{wit}\rvert$	Und.	Ind.
s-RSA	BDM [5]	-	-	-	-	-	-	-				-	-	cfw‡
	BP [4]	-	-	-	-	-	-	-	-	$\mathcal{O}(1)$	$\mathcal{O}(1)$	-		cfw[17]
	CL [12]	✓	-	✓	-	✓	-	✓	-					cfw‡
q-SDH	LLX [24]	✓	✓	✓	✓	✓	-	✓	-			$\mathcal{O}(1)$	?	✗‡
	NY [29]	✓	✓	✓	-	-	-	-	-	$\mathcal{O}(t)$	$\mathcal{O}(1)$	-	-	cfw‡
	DT [16], ATSM [3]	✓	✓	✓	✓	-	-	✓	✓		$\mathcal{O}(1)$	$\mathcal{O}(1)$	✓‡	✗‡
	This paper (extended version)	✓	-	✓	✓	-	✓	✓	-	$\mathcal{O}(1)$	-	-	-	✓‡
t-DHE	CKS [11]	✓	-	✓	-	-	✓	✓	✓	$\mathcal{O}(t)$	$\mathcal{O}(1)$	$\mathcal{O}(1)$	-	✗‡
VC	CF (RSA∓, CDH†) [14]	✓	-	✓	✓	✓	✓	-	✓	$\mathcal{O}(t)^{\mp}$, $\mathcal{O}(t^2)^{\dagger}$	$\mathcal{O}(1)$	$\mathcal{O}(1)$	?	✗‡
ZKS	This paper (Sec. 6)	-	✓	-	-	-	-	-	-	instantiation-dependent			✓‡	✓‡
CRH	BLL [7,8]	-	✓	-	-	-	-	-	-				✓	✗‡
	CHKO [10]	-	✓	-	-	-	-	-	-	$\mathcal{O}(1)$	$\mathcal{O}(\log t)$	$\mathcal{O}(\log t)$	?	✗‡
	BC [6]	-	-	-	-	-	-	✓	-				-	✗‡[17], ✗
ROM	NB [30,31]	-	-	-	-	-	-	-	✓	$\mathcal{O}(1)$	-	-	-	-

For security, a non-interactive commitment scheme is required to provide *correctness*, *binding* and *hiding*. We omit a formal definition of correctness as it is straightforward. The remaining properties are defined as follows.

Definition 12 (Binding). *A non-interactive commitment scheme is* binding, *if for all PPT adversaries $\mathcal{A}$ there is a negligible function $\epsilon(\cdot)$ such that*

$$\Pr\left[\begin{array}{l} \mathsf{pp} \leftarrow \mathsf{Gen}(1^\kappa), (C^*, O^*, O'^*) \leftarrow \mathcal{A}(\mathsf{pp}), m \leftarrow \mathsf{Open}(\mathsf{pp}, C^*, O^*), \\ m' \leftarrow \mathsf{Open}(\mathsf{pp}, C^*, O'^*) : m \neq m' \;\wedge\; m \neq \bot \;\wedge\; m' \neq \bot \end{array}\right] \leq \epsilon(\kappa).$$

Definition 13 (Hiding). *A non-interactive commitment scheme is* hiding, *if for all PPT adversaries $\mathcal{A}$ there is a negligible function $\epsilon(\cdot)$ such that*

$$\Pr\left[\begin{array}{c} \mathsf{pp} \leftarrow \mathsf{Gen}(1^\kappa), (m_0, m_1, \mathsf{state}) \leftarrow \mathcal{A}(\mathsf{pp}), b \xleftarrow{R} \{0,1\}, \\ (C, O) \leftarrow \mathsf{Commit}(\mathsf{pp}, m_b), b^* \leftarrow \mathcal{A}(\mathsf{pp}, C, \mathsf{state}) : \\ b = b^* \end{array}\right] \leq \frac{1}{2} + \epsilon(\kappa).$$

In Scheme 1, we present a black-box construction of commitments from indistinguishable accumulators and prove the so obtained construction secure (Theorem 1). Before we continue, we want to recall that in the trusted setup model all algorithms can be correctly executed without $\mathsf{sk_{acc}}$.

$\mathsf{Gen}(1^\kappa)$: This algorithm runs $(\mathsf{sk}_{\widetilde{\mathsf{acc}}}, \mathsf{pk_{acc}}) \leftarrow \mathsf{Acc.Gen}(1^\kappa, 1)$, discards $\mathsf{sk_{acc}}$ and returns $\mathsf{pp} \leftarrow \mathsf{pk_{acc}}$.

$\mathsf{Commit}(\mathsf{pp}, m)$: This algorithm chooses randomness r, runs $(C, \mathsf{aux}) \leftarrow \mathsf{Eval}_r((\emptyset, \mathsf{pk_{acc}}), m)$, computes $\mathsf{wit}_m \leftarrow \mathsf{WitCreate}((\emptyset, \mathsf{pk_{acc}}), C, \mathsf{aux}, m)$, sets $O \leftarrow (r, m, \mathsf{wit}_m, \mathsf{aux})$ and returns (C, O).

$\mathsf{Open}(\mathsf{pp}, C, O)$: This algorithm checks whether $\mathsf{Eval}_r((\emptyset, \mathsf{pk_{acc}}), m) \stackrel{?}{=} C$ and whether $\mathsf{Verify}(\mathsf{pk_{acc}}, C, \mathsf{wit}_m, m) \stackrel{?}{=} \mathsf{true}$ and returns m on success and $\bot$ otherwise.

Scheme 1: Commitment Scheme from Indistinguishable Accumulators

Theorem 1. *If indistinguishable 1-bounded accumulators exist, then non-interactive commitments exist as well.*

We prove Theorem 1 in the extended version of this paper.

The black-box construction from Scheme 1 can easily be extended to support commitments to sets (where the opening is always with respect to the entire set) by setting the bound t of the bounded accumulator to the desired set size. Furthermore, using $\mathsf{sk_{acc}}$ as trapdoor, one can also construct trapdoor commitments.

We finally note that cfw-indistinguishable accumulators (and hence also Transformation 1) are not useful for constructing commitments. The reason for this is that the accumulation of the additional random value immediately breaks the binding property.

6 Zero-Knowledge Sets Imply Indistinguishable Undeniable Accumulators

Zero-knowledge sets (ZK-sets) [27] allow to commit to a set $\mathcal{X}$ and then prove predicates of the form $x_i \in \mathcal{X}$ or $x_i \notin \mathcal{X}$ without revealing anything else about the set. We observe that ZK-sets can be used to model indistinguishable, unbounded, undeniable accumulators. Unfortunately, there is no formal security definition for zero-knowledge sets (in [23] only the algorithms are formalized, while security is stated informally). However, zero-knowledge sets are a special instance of zero-knowledge elementary databases (ZK-EDB) [27]. ZK-EDBs store key-value pairs and when querying the database with a key, the respective value is returned (or $\bot$ if the given key is not contained in the EDB). Thereby, no further information about the remaining EDB leaks. Therefore, ZK-sets are ZK-EDBs where the values for all contained keys are set to 1 (or the values are omitted at all). We can, thus, define the security on the basis of the models in [15,27] as follows.

Definition 14 (ZK-set). *A ZK-set is a tuple of efficient algorithms* (Gen, Commit, Query, Verify), *which are defined as follows:*

Gen(1^κ): *This (probabilistic) algorithm takes input a security parameter κ and outputs a public key* pk.

Commit(pk, $\mathcal{X}$): *This algorithm takes input the public key* pk *and a set $\mathcal{X}$ and outputs a commitment C to $\mathcal{X}$.*

Query(pk, $\mathcal{X}, C, x$): *This algorithm takes input the public key* pk, *a set $\mathcal{X}$, a corresponding commitment C and and value x. It outputs a proof π_x if $x \in \mathcal{X}$ and a proof $\underline{\pi}_x$ if $x \notin \mathcal{X}$.*

Verify(pk, $C, x, \pi_x/\underline{\pi}_x$): *This algorithm takes input the public key* pk, *a commitment C and a value x. Furthermore, it either takes a membership proof π_x or a non-membership proof $\underline{\pi}_x$ (denoted by $\pi_x/\underline{\pi}_x$). It outputs* true *if the proof can be correctly verified and* false *otherwise.*

For security, ZK-sets require *perfect completeness*, *soundness* and *zero-knowledge*. Perfect completeness requires that for every honestly generated key, every honestly computed commitment C, value x and corresponding proof $\pi_x/\underline{\pi}_x$, the Verify algorithm always returns true. Since this property is straightforward, we do not formally state it here. We formally define the remaining properties:

Definition 15 (Soundness). *A ZK-set is sound, if for all PPT adversaries $\mathcal{A}$ there is a negligible function $\epsilon(\cdot)$ such that*

$$\Pr\left[\begin{array}{c} \mathsf{pk} \leftarrow \mathsf{Gen}(1^\kappa), (C^*, x^*, \pi_x^*, \underline{\pi}_x^*) \leftarrow \mathcal{A}(\mathsf{pk}) : \\ \mathsf{Verify}(\mathsf{pk}, C^*, \pi_x^*, x^*) = \texttt{true} \ \wedge \ \mathsf{Verify}(\mathsf{pk}, C^*, \underline{\pi}_x^*, x^*) = \texttt{true} \end{array}\right] \leq \epsilon(\kappa)$$

Definition 16 (Zero Knowledge). *A ZK-set is* zero-knowledge, *if for all PPT adversaries $\mathcal{A}$ there is a negligible function $\epsilon(\cdot)$ such that*

$$\left| \Pr \left[\begin{array}{c} \mathsf{pk} \leftarrow \mathsf{Gen}(1^\kappa), \\ (\mathcal{X}, \mathsf{state}_\mathcal{A}) \leftarrow \mathcal{A}(\mathsf{pk}), \\ C \leftarrow \mathsf{Commit}(\mathsf{pk}, \mathcal{X}), \\ \mathcal{A}^{\mathcal{O}^\mathsf{Q}(\cdot, \mathcal{X}, \cdot, \cdot)}(\mathsf{state}_\mathcal{A}, \\ \mathsf{pk}, C) = \mathtt{true} \end{array} \right] - \Pr \left[\begin{array}{c} (\mathsf{pk}, \mathsf{state}_\mathcal{S}) \leftarrow \mathcal{S}^\mathsf{G}(1^\kappa), \\ (\mathcal{X}, \mathsf{state}_\mathcal{A}) \leftarrow \mathcal{A}(\mathsf{pk}), \\ (C, \mathsf{state}'_\mathcal{S}) \leftarrow \mathcal{S}^\mathsf{E}(\mathsf{pk}, \mathsf{state}_\mathcal{S}), \\ \mathcal{A}^{\mathcal{S}^\mathsf{Q}(\mathsf{state}'_\mathcal{S}, \cdot, \mathcal{X}, \cdot, \cdot)}(\mathsf{state}_\mathcal{A}, \\ \mathsf{pk}, C) = \mathtt{true} \end{array} \right] \right| \leq \epsilon(\kappa)$$

Here, $\mathcal{O}^\mathsf{Q}$ allows the adversary to execute the Query algorithm, whereas $\mathcal{S} = (\mathcal{S}^\mathsf{G}, \mathcal{S}^\mathsf{E}, \mathcal{S}^\mathsf{Q})$ denotes a PPT simulator, which allows to execute the simulated Gen, Eval and Query algorithms, respectively. We note that the definition above is tailored to cover computational zero-knowledge. It could, however, easily be modified to also cover statistical or perfect zero knowledge.

In Scheme 2 we present a black-box construction of indistinguishable unbounded undeniable accumulators from ZK-sets.

Gen(1^κ): This algorithm runs $\mathsf{pk} \leftarrow$ ZKS.Gen(1^κ) and returns $(\mathsf{sk}_\mathsf{acc}, \mathsf{pk}_\mathsf{acc}) \leftarrow (\emptyset, \mathsf{pk})$.

Eval($(\emptyset, \mathsf{pk}_\mathsf{acc}), \mathcal{X}$): This algorithm runs $\mathsf{acc}_\mathcal{X} \leftarrow$ ZKS.Commit($\mathsf{pk}_\mathsf{acc}, \mathcal{X}$) and returns $\mathsf{acc}_\mathcal{X}$ together with $\mathsf{aux} \leftarrow \mathcal{X}$.

WitCreate($(\emptyset, \mathsf{pk}_\mathsf{acc}), \mathsf{acc}_\mathcal{X}, \mathsf{aux}, x_i, \mathsf{type}$): This algorithm obtains $\mathcal{X}$ from aux and runs $\pi_{x_i}/\overline{\pi}_{x_i} \leftarrow$ ZKS.Query($\mathsf{pk}, \mathcal{X}, \mathsf{acc}_\mathcal{X}, x_i$). If $\pi_{x_i}/\overline{\pi}_{x_i}$ conflicts with the requested witness type, it returns $\bot$. Otherwise it returns $\mathsf{wit}_{x_i} \leftarrow \pi_{x_i}$ or $\underline{\mathsf{wit}}_{x_i} \leftarrow \underline{\pi}_{x_i}$, respectively.

Verify($\mathsf{pk}_\mathsf{acc}, \mathsf{acc}, \mathsf{wit}_{x_i}, x_i, \mathsf{type}$): This algorithm checks whether type conflicts with the type of the supplied witness and returns $\bot$ if so. Otherwise it returns the result of ZKS.Verify($\mathsf{pk}, \mathsf{acc}, x_i, \mathsf{wit}_{x_i}$).

Scheme 2: Indistinguishable Unbounded Undeniable Accumulator from ZK-Sets

Theorem 2. *If ZK-sets exist, then indistinguishable, unbounded, undeniable accumulators exist as well.*

We prove Theorem 2 in the extended version of this paper.

The above black-box construction yields the first construction of indistinguishable undeniable accumulators. We note that it is, however, questionable whether the two notions of ZK-sets and indistinguishable undeniable accumulators are equivalent (as the simulation based model of zero-knowledge appears to be stronger than the game based indistinguishability model).

In [23], Kate et al. introduced nearly ZK-sets. The difference to ordinary ZK-sets is that nearly ZK-sets have a public upper bound on the cardinality of set $\mathcal{X}$. It is apparent that these constructions imply indistinguishable t-bounded undeniable accumulators. In further consequence, this means that nearly ZK-sets can also be used to construct commitments (cf. Section 5).

References

1. Acar, T., Nguyen, L.: Revocation for delegatable anonymous credentials. In: Catalano, D., Fazio, N., Gennaro, R., Nicolosi, A. (eds.) PKC 2011. LNCS, vol. 6571, pp. 423–440. Springer, Heidelberg (2011)
2. Ahn, J.H., Boneh, D., Camenisch, J., Hohenberger, S., Shelat, A., Waters, B.: Computing on authenticated data. In: Cramer, R. (ed.) TCC 2012. LNCS, vol. 7194, pp. 1–20. Springer, Heidelberg (2012)
3. Au, M.H., Tsang, P.P., Susilo, W., Mu, Y.: Dynamic universal accumulators for DDH groups and their application to attribute-based anonymous credential systems. In: Fischlin, M. (ed.) CT-RSA 2009. LNCS, vol. 5473, pp. 295–308. Springer, Heidelberg (2009)
4. Barić, N., Pfitzmann, B.: Collision-free accumulators and fail-stop signature schemes without trees. In: Fumy, W. (ed.) EUROCRYPT 1997. LNCS, vol. 1233, pp. 480–494. Springer, Heidelberg (1997)
5. Benaloh, J., de Mare, M.: One-way accumulators: a decentralized alternative to digital signatures. In: Helleseth, T. (ed.) EUROCRYPT 1993. LNCS, vol. 765, pp. 274–285. Springer, Heidelberg (1994)
6. Boneh, D., Corrigan-Gibbs, H.: Bivariate polynomials modulo composites and their applications. In: Sarkar, P., Iwata, T. (eds.) ASIACRYPT 2014. LNCS, vol. 8873, pp. 42–62. Springer, Heidelberg (2014). http://eprint.iacr.org/2014/719
7. Buldas, A., Laud, P., Lipmaa, H.: Accountable certificate management using undeniable attestations. In: ACM CCS, pp. 9–17. ACM (2000)
8. Buldas, A., Laud, P., Lipmaa, H.: Eliminating Counterevidence with Applications to Accountable Certificate Management. Journal of Computer Security 10 (2002)
9. Camacho, P., Hevia, A.: On the impossibility of batch update for cryptographic accumulators. In: Abdalla, M., Barreto, P.S.L.M. (eds.) LATINCRYPT 2010. LNCS, vol. 6212, pp. 178–188. Springer, Heidelberg (2010)
10. Camacho, P., Hevia, A., Kiwi, M., Opazo, R.: Strong accumulators from collision-resistant hashing. In: Wu, T.-C., Lei, C.-L., Rijmen, V., Lee, D.-T. (eds.) ISC 2008. LNCS, vol. 5222, pp. 471–486. Springer, Heidelberg (2008)
11. Camenisch, J., Kohlweiss, M., Soriente, C.: An accumulator based on bilinear maps and efficient revocation for anonymous credentials. In: Jarecki, S., Tsudik, G. (eds.) PKC 2009. LNCS, vol. 5443, pp. 481–500. Springer, Heidelberg (2009)
12. Camenisch, J.L., Lysyanskaya, A.: Dynamic accumulators and application to efficient revocation of anonymous credentials. In: Yung, M. (ed.) CRYPTO 2002. LNCS, vol. 2442, pp. 61–76. Springer, Heidelberg (2002)
13. Canard, S., Jambert, A.: On extended sanitizable signature schemes. In: Pieprzyk, J. (ed.) CT-RSA 2010. LNCS, vol. 5985, pp. 179–194. Springer, Heidelberg (2010)
14. Catalano, D., Fiore, D.: Vector commitments and their applications. In: Kurosawa, K., Hanaoka, G. (eds.) PKC 2013. LNCS, vol. 7778, pp. 55–72. Springer, Heidelberg (2013)
15. Chase, M., Healy, A., Lysyanskaya, A., Malkin, T., Reyzin, L.: Mercurial Commitments with Applications to Zero-Knowledge Sets. Journal of Cryptology 26(2), 251–279 (2013)
16. Damgård, I., Triandopoulos, N.: Supporting Non-membership Proofs with Bilinear-map Accumulators. Cryptology ePrint Archive, Report 2008/538 (2008). http://eprint.iacr.org/2008/538
17. de Meer, H., Liedel, M., Pöhls, H.C., Posegga, J.: Indistinguishability of One-Way Accumulators. Technical Report MIP-1210, Faculty of Computer Science and Mathematics (FIM), University of Passau (2012)

18. de Meer, H., Pöhls, H.C., Posegga, J., Samelin, K.: Redactable signature schemes for trees with signer-controlled non-leaf-redactions. In: Obaidat, M.S., Filipe, J. (eds.) ICETE 2012. CCIS, vol. 455, pp. 155–171. Springer, Heidelberg (2014)
19. Fauzi, P., Lipmaa, H., Zhang, B.: Efficient non-interactive zero knowledge arguments for set operations. In: Christin, N., Safavi-Naini, R. (eds.) FC 2014. LNCS, vol. 8437, pp. 214–231. Springer, Heidelberg (2014). http://eprint.iacr.org/2014/006
20. Fazio, N., Nicolisi, A.: Cryptographic Accumulators: Definitions. Constructions and Applications, Technical report (2002)
21. Ghosh, E., Ohrimenko, O., Tamassia, R.: Verifiable Member and Order Queries on a List in Zero-Knowledge. Cryptology ePrint Archive, Report 2014/632 (2014). http://eprint.iacr.org/2014/632
22. Goodrich, M.T., Tamassia, R., Hasic, J.: An efficient dynamic and distributed cryptographic accumulator. In: Chan, A.H., Gligor, V.D. (eds.) ISC 2002. LNCS, vol. 2433, pp. 372–388. Springer, Heidelberg (2002)
23. Kate, A., Zaverucha, G.M., Goldberg, I.: Constant-size commitments to polynomials and their applications. In: Abe, M. (ed.) ASIACRYPT 2010. LNCS, vol. 6477, pp. 177–194. Springer, Heidelberg (2010)
24. Li, J., Li, N., Xue, R.: Universal accumulators with efficient nonmembership proofs. In: Katz, J., Yung, M. (eds.) ACNS 2007. LNCS, vol. 4521, pp. 253–269. Springer, Heidelberg (2007)
25. Lipmaa, H.: Secure accumulators from euclidean rings without trusted setup. In: Bao, F., Samarati, P., Zhou, J. (eds.) ACNS 2012. LNCS, vol. 7341, pp. 224–240. Springer, Heidelberg (2012)
26. Mashatan, A., Vaudenay, S.: A Fully Dynamic Universal Accumulator. Proceedings of the Romanian Academy 14, 269–285 (2013)
27. Micali, S., Rabin, M.O., Kilian, J.: Zero-knowledge sets. In: FOCS, pp. 80–91 (2003)
28. Miers, I., Garman, C., Green, M., Rubin, A.D.: Zerocoin: anonymous distributed E-cash from bitcoin. In: IEEE Symposium on Security and Privacy, pp. 397–411. IEEE (2013)
29. Nguyen, L.: Accumulators from bilinear pairings and applications. In: Menezes, A. (ed.) CT-RSA 2005. LNCS, vol. 3376, pp. 275–292. Springer, Heidelberg (2005)
30. Nyberg, K.: Commutativity in cryptography. In: 1st International Trier Conference in Functional Analysis. Walter Gruyter & Co (1996)
31. Nyberg, K.: Fast accumulated hashing. In: Gollmann, D. (ed.) FSE 1996. LNCS, vol. 1039, pp. 83–87. Springer, Heidelberg (1996)
32. Peng, K., Bao, F.: Vulnerability of a non-membership proof scheme. In: SECRYPT, pp. 1–4, July 2010
33. Pöhls, H.C., Peters, S., Samelin, K., Posegga, J., de Meer, H.: Malleable signatures for resource constrained platforms. In: Cavallaro, L., Gollmann, D. (eds.) WISTP 2013. LNCS, vol. 7886, pp. 18–33. Springer, Heidelberg (2013)
34. Pöhls, H.C., Samelin, K.: On updatable redactable signatures. In: Boureanu, I., Owesarski, P., Vaudenay, S. (eds.) ACNS 2014. LNCS, vol. 8479, pp. 457–475. Springer, Heidelberg (2014)
35. Sander, T.: Efficient accumulators without trapdoor extended abstract. In: Varadharajan, V., Mu, Y. (eds.) ICICS 1999. LNCS, vol. 1726, pp. 252–262. Springer, Heidelberg (1999)
36. Sander, T., Ta-Shma, A., Yung, M.: Blind, auditable membership proofs. In: Frankel, Y. (ed.) FC 2000. LNCS, vol. 1962, pp. 53–71. Springer, Heidelberg (2001)

37. Slamanig, D.: Dynamic accumulator based discretionary access control for out-sourced storage with unlinkable access. In: Keromytis, A.D. (ed.) FC 2012. LNCS, vol. 7397, pp. 215–222. Springer, Heidelberg (2012)
38. Sudarsono, A., Nakanishi, T., Funabiki, N.: Efficient proofs of attributes in pairing-based anonymous credential system. In: Fischer-Hübner, S., Hopper, N. (eds.) PETS 2011. LNCS, vol. 6794, pp. 246–263. Springer, Heidelberg (2011)
39. Tsudik, G., Xu, S.: Accumulating composites and improved group signing. In: Laih, C.-S. (ed.) ASIACRYPT 2003. LNCS, vol. 2894, pp. 269–286. Springer, Heidelberg (2003)
40. Wang, P., Wang, H., Pieprzyk, J.: A new dynamic accumulator for batch updates. In: Qing, S., Imai, H., Wang, G. (eds.) ICICS 2007. LNCS, vol. 4861, pp. 98–112. Springer, Heidelberg (2007)

Non-Interactive Zero-Knowledge Proofs of Non-Membership

Olivier Blazy[1](✉), Céline Chevalier[2], and Damien Vergnaud[3]

[1] XLim, Université de Limoges, Limoges, France
olivier.blazy@unilim.fr
[2] Université Paris II, Paris, France
[3] ENS, Paris, France

Abstract. Often, in privacy-sensitive cryptographic protocols, a party commits to a secret message m and later needs to prove that m belongs to a language $\mathcal{L}$ or that m does *not* belong to $\mathcal{L}$ (but does not want to reveal any further information). We present a method to prove in a non-interactive way that a committed value does not belong to a given language $\mathcal{L}$. Our construction is generic and relies on the corresponding proof of membership to $\mathcal{L}$. We present an efficient realization of our proof system by combining smooth projective hash functions and Groth-Sahai proof system.

In 2009, Kiayias and Zhou introduced zero-knowledge proofs with witness elimination which enable to prove that a committed message m belongs to a set $\mathcal{L}$ in such a way that the verifier accepts the interaction only if m does not belong to a set determined by a public relation Q and some *private* input m' of the verifier. We show that the protocol they proposed is flawed and that a dishonest prover can actually make a verifier accept a proof for any message $m \in L$ even if $(m, m') \in Q$. Using our non-interactive proof of non-membership of committed values, we are able to fix their protocol and improve its efficiency.

Our approach finds also efficient applications in other settings, e.g. in anonymous credential systems and privacy-preserving authenticated identification and key exchange protocols.

Keywords: Zero knowledge · Witness elimination · Smooth projective hash function · Groth-Sahai proof system

1   Introduction

In cryptography, when designing privacy-sensitive applications, the use of commitments and corresponding zero-knowledge proofs is often indispensable. They allow a prover to convince a verifier that a digitally committed value is a member of a given language (without revealing any further information beyond this

---

This is an extended abstract. The full paper [BCV15] is available at the Cryptology Eprint Archive, http://eprint.iacr.org.

CNRS – UMR 8548 and INRIA – EPI Cascade.

K. Nyberg (ed.): CT-RSA 2015, LNCS 9048, pp. 145–164, 2015.
DOI: 10.1007/978-3-319-16715-2_8

membership). An important instance of this problem consists in showing that the committed value lies in a given finite set (*e.g.* in e-auctions or e-voting protocols, a bidder or voter has to prove that his secret bid or vote is chosen from a list of candidates, see [CCs08] and references therein). However one usually wants to demonstrate more complex properties about committed values. For instance in anonymous credentials systems and privacy-preserving authenticated identification or key exchange protocols, a user must usually prove the possession of a credential issued by an authority (without revealing it).

For the latter primitives, it is often necessary to prove combination of simple statements about several credentials issued by the authority (OR, AND, and NOT connectives) [CG08,ILV11]. For instance, a crucial requirement is that credentials issued can be later revoked. In principle, revocation lists can be used for anonymous credentials by having the user to prove in zero-knowledge that his credential is *not* contained in the list. However, this is usually inefficient since the computational and communication costs grow with the number of entries in the list. Recently, Bayer and Groth [BG13] proposed an efficient interactive solution for blacklisting anonymous users (with logarithmic growth) but their elegant technique does not generalize readily to prove the non-membership to arbitrary languages.

In these scenarios, it is usually desired that the zero-knowledge proofs are non-interactive. For example, in the e-voting scenario, the membership proof is a part of the vote validity proof that is verified by various parties without any active participation of the voter. In this paper, we present a generic method to prove in a non-interactive way that a committed value does not belong to a given language. Our approach finds efficient applications in various settings, e.g. in zero-knowledge with witness elimination [KZ09] or language authenticated key exchange [BBC+13a].

1.1   Related Work

A commitment scheme allows a user to commit to a message m by publishing a commitment C, and this commitment can be opened at a later point in time. It can be seen as the digital analogue of a "sealed envelope": the security properties required are called the *hiding* property (one cannot learn anything about the message m from the commitment C) and *binding* property (one cannot open the commitment C to a different message $m' \neq m$). Zero-knowledge proofs of knowledge are two party protocols, which allow a prover to convince a verifier that he knows some secret piece of information, without the verifier being able to learn anything about the secret value (except for what is revealed by the claim itself). Often in cryptographic protocols, a party chooses a message m and then commits to it. He keeps the message secret and publishes the commitment. He later needs to prove that m belongs to a finite set $\mathcal{L}$ or that m does *not* belong to $\mathcal{L}$, but cannot reveal anything about m.

For a finite set $\mathcal{L}$ with no additional structure, the most efficient combination of commitment and zero-knowledge proof was recently proposed by Bayer and Groth [BG13]. The interactive proof system is quite efficient: it has $O(\log(\#\mathcal{L}))$

communication and computational complexity and significantly improves the previous proposals with $O(\sqrt{\#\mathcal{L}})$ complexity [Pen11]. It can be made non-interactive in the random oracle model by using the Fiat-Shamir heuristic.

There also exist efficient membership proofs for families of very large sets $\mathcal{L}$ equipped with an "algebraic structure" (e.g. the set of valid message/digital signatures pairs for a given public key whose cardinal is exponential in the security parameter). Most of them also admit efficient non-membership proof systems. However, up to now there is no generic construction and these zero-knowledge proofs of non-membership of committed values require specific security analysis.

1.2   Contributions of the Paper

The first contribution of the paper is to present an efficient non-interactive technique to prove (in zero-knowledge) that a committed message does not belong to a set $\mathcal{L}$. The proof is generic and relies on a proof of membership to $\mathcal{L}$ with specific mild properties. In particular, it is independent of the size of $\mathcal{L}$ and if there exists an efficient proof of membership for committed values, one gets readily an efficient proof of non-membership. Instantiated with a combination of *smooth projective hash functions* and Groth-Sahai proof system, we obtain very efficient realization for non-interactive proof of non-membership of committed values.

In 2009, Kiayias and Zhou [KZ09] introduced *zero-knowledge proofs with witness elimination*. This primitive enables to prove that a committed message m belongs to a set $\mathcal{L}$ (with a witness w) in such a way that the verifier accepts the interaction only if w does not belong to a set determined by a public relation Q and some *private* input w' of the verifier. The verifier does not learn anything about w (except that $m \in \mathcal{L}$ and $(w, w') \notin Q$) and the prover does not learn anything about w'. The primitive can obviously be used to handle revocation lists. It was motivated in [KZ09] by privacy-preserving identification schemes when a user wishes to authenticate himself to a verifier while preserving his anonymity and the verifier makes sure the prover does not match the identity of a suspect user that is tracked by the authorities (without leaking any information about the suspect identity).

We show that the original proposal of zero-knowledge proofs with witness elimination from [KZ09] is flawed and that a dishonest prover can actually make a verifier accept a proof for any message $m \in L$ even if $(w, w') \in Q$. In particular, in the suspect tracking scenario, a dishonest prover can identify himself even if he is on the suspect list. Therefore, their protocol does not achieve the claimed security. However we explain how to apply our proof of non-membership to fix it. We obtain a proof system that achieves the security goal and is more efficient than the original (insecure) solution.

Finally, we briefly present applications of our proof of non-membership to other settings such as anonymous credentials and privacy-preserving authenticated key exchange.

2   Preliminaries

In this section we recall various classical definitions, tools used throughout this paper. We use classical definitions and notations and the familiar reader may skip this section.

2.1   Definitions

Encryption An encryption scheme $\mathcal{E}$ is described through four algorithms (Setup, KeyGen, Encrypt, Decrypt):

- Setup($1^{\mathfrak{K}}$), where $\mathfrak{K}$ is the security parameter, generates the global parameters param of the scheme;
- KeyGen(param) outputs a pair of keys, a (public) encryption key ek and a (private) decryption key dk;
- Encrypt(ek, $M; \rho$) outputs a ciphertext $\mathcal{C}$, on the message M, under the encryption key ek, with randomness ρ;
- Decrypt(dk, $\mathcal{C}$) outputs the plaintext M, encrypted in the ciphertext $\mathcal{C}$ or $\perp$.

Such encryption scheme is required to have the classical properties, *Correctness* and *Indistinguishability under Chosen Plaintext Attack* (see [BCV15, GM84] for formal definitions).

Zero-Knowledge Proofs Classical definitions and notations for *non-interactive* zero-knowledge proof systems are given in the full version [BCV15].

2.2   Classical Hypotheses

A bilinear group is a tuple $(p, \mathbb{G}_1, \mathbb{G}_2, \mathbb{G}_T, e, g_1, g_2)$ where $\mathbb{G}_1, \mathbb{G}_2$ and $\mathbb{G}_T$ are cyclic groups of prime order p, generated respectively by g_1, g_2 and $e(g_1, g_2)$ and $e : \mathbb{G}_1 \times \mathbb{G}_2 \to \mathbb{G}_T$ is a non-degenerated bilinear form, *i.e.*:

$$\forall X \in \mathbb{G}_1, \forall Y \in \mathbb{G}_2, \forall \lambda, \mu \in \mathbb{Z}_p : e(X^\lambda, Y^\mu) = e(X, Y)^{\lambda\mu}$$

and $e(g_1, g_2)$ does indeed generate the prime order group $\mathbb{G}_T$. In the following we will suppose there exists a polynomial time algorithm which outputs such bilinear groups.

In this paper, we will present concrete instantiation based on standard problems on groups:

Decisional Diffie Hellman (DDH) [Bon98]: The Decisional Diffie-Hellman hypothesis states that in a group $(p, \mathbb{G}, g)$ (written in multiplicative notation), given (g^μ, g^ν, g^ψ) for unknown $\mu, \nu \xleftarrow{\$} \mathbb{Z}_p$, it is hard to decide whether $\psi = \mu\nu$.

Symmetric External Diffie Hellman (SXDH) [ACHdM05]: this variant used in bilinear groups $(p, \mathbb{G}_1, \mathbb{G}_2, \mathbb{G}_T, e, g_1, g_2)$, states that DDH is hard in both $\mathbb{G}_1$ and $\mathbb{G}_2$.

2.3   Classical Tools

Smooth Projective Hash Functions [CS02] Smooth projective hash functions (SPHF) were introduced by Cramer and Shoup [CS02]. A projective hashing family is a family of hash functions that can be evaluated in two ways: using the (secret) hashing key, one can compute the function on every point in its domain, whereas using the (public) *projected* key one can only compute the function on a special subset of its domain. Such a family is deemed *smooth* if the value of the hash function on any point outside the special subset is independent of the projected key.

Smooth Projective Hashing System: A Smooth Projective Hash Function over a language $\mathfrak{L} \subset X$, onto a set $\mathbb{G}$, is defined by five algorithms (Setup, HashKG, ProjKG, Hash, ProjHash):

- Setup($1^{\mathfrak{K}}$) where $\mathfrak{K}$ is the security parameter, generates the global parameters param of the scheme, and the description of an $\mathcal{NP}$ language $\mathfrak{L}$;
- HashKG($\mathfrak{L}$, param), outputs a hashing key hk for the language $\mathfrak{L}$;
- ProjKG(hk, ($\mathfrak{L}$, param), W), derives the projection key hp, possibly depending on the word W [GL03, ACP09] thanks to the hashing key hk.
- Hash(hk, ($\mathfrak{L}$, param), W), outputs a hash value $v \in \mathbb{G}$, thanks to the hashing key hk, and W
- ProjHash(hp, ($\mathfrak{L}$, param), W, w), outputs the hash value $v' \in \mathbb{G}$, thanks to the projection key hp and the witness w that $W \in \mathfrak{L}$.

In the following, we consider $\mathfrak{L}$ as a hard-partitioned subset of X, *i.e.* it is computationally hard to distinguish a random element in $\mathfrak{L}$ from a random element in $X \setminus \mathfrak{L}$.

A Smooth Projective Hash Function SPHF should satisfy the following properties:

- *Correctness*: Let $W \in \mathfrak{L}$ and w a witness of this membership. Then, for all hashing keys hk and associated projection keys hp we have Hash(hk, ($\mathfrak{L}$, param), W) = ProjHash(hp, ($\mathfrak{L}$, param), W, w).
- *Smoothness*: For all $W \in X \setminus \mathfrak{L}$ the following distributions are statistically indistinguishable:

$$\left\{ (\mathfrak{L}, \text{param}, W, \text{hp}, v) \;\middle|\; \begin{array}{l} \text{param} = \text{Setup}(1^{\mathfrak{K}}), \\ \text{hk} = \text{HashKG}(\mathfrak{L}, \text{param}), \\ \text{hp} = \text{ProjKG}(\text{hk}, (\mathfrak{L}, \text{param}), W), \\ v = \text{Hash}(\text{hk}, (\mathfrak{L}, \text{param}), W) \end{array} \right\}$$

$$\simeq \left\{ (\mathfrak{L}, \text{param}, W, \text{hp}, v) \;\middle|\; \begin{array}{l} \text{param} = \text{Setup}(1^{\mathfrak{K}}), \\ \text{hk} = \text{HashKG}(\mathfrak{L}, \text{param}), \\ \text{hp} = \text{ProjKG}(\text{hk}, (\mathfrak{L}, \text{param}), W), \\ v \xleftarrow{\$} \mathbb{G} \end{array} \right\}.$$

- *Pseudo-Randomness*: If $W \in \mathfrak{L}$, then without a witness of membership the two previous distributions should remain computationally indistinguishable.

The article [BBC+13b] introduced a new notation for SPHF: For a language $\mathfrak{L}$, we assume there exist a function Γ and a family of functions Θ, such that $u \in \mathfrak{L}$, if and only if, $\Theta(u)$ is a linear combination of the rows of $\Gamma(u)$. We furthermore require that a user, who knows a witness w of the membership $u \in \mathfrak{L}$, can efficiently compute the linear combination λ.

With the above notations, the hashing key is a vector $\mathsf{hk} = \alpha$, while the projection key is, for a word u, $\mathsf{hp} = \gamma(u) = \Gamma(u) \odot \alpha$ (where $\odot$ denotes the Hadamard product, i.e. the entry-wise product). Then, the hash value is: $\mathsf{Hash}(\mathsf{hk}, u) \stackrel{\text{def}}{=} \Theta(u) \odot \alpha = \lambda \odot \gamma(u) \stackrel{\text{def}}{=} \mathsf{ProjHash}(\mathsf{hp}, u, w)$.

Groth-Sahai Proof System. Groth and Sahai [GS08] proposed non-interactive zero-knowledge proofs of satisfiability of certain equations over bilinear groups, called *pairing product equations*. To prove satisfiability of an equation (which is the statement of the proof), a Groth-Sahai proof uses commitments and shows that the committed values satisfy the equation. The proof consists again of group elements and is verified by a pairing equation derived from the statement.

We refer to [GS08] for details of the Groth-Sahai proof system.

3 Proof of No-Statement

3.1 Generic Technique

In this section, we are going to present a way to prove exclusion statement, following a Commit and Prove approach ([CLOS02]).

The underlying idea is that, we are going to try to build a proof of validity for the statement (which is supposed to not be verified), and prove that we are failing to do so while being completely honest. Hence once we prove that the proof is correctly generated, the fact that the verification fails means that the initial statement did not hold (under the completeness of the proof).

Let us consider a language $\mathcal{L}$. We assume that it is easy to test whether a word w belongs to $\mathcal{L}$ (in probabilistic polynomial time).

Let $\mathcal{E} = (\mathsf{Setup}, \mathsf{KeyGen}, \mathsf{Encrypt}, \mathsf{Decrypt})$ be an encryption scheme and let $(\mathsf{ek}, \mathsf{dk})$ be a pair of keys output by $\mathsf{KeyGen}(\mathsf{param})$ (where param are global parameters output by $\mathsf{Setup}(1^{\mathfrak{K}})$). We assume that the encryption scheme is *without redundancy* [PP03]: *i.e.* all ciphertexts are valid (which means here "reachable"), the encryption function is not only a probabilistic injection, but also a surjection. A prover possesses a word w not in a language $\mathcal{L}$ which is encrypted in C using some randomness r, $C = \mathsf{Encrypt}(\mathsf{ek}, w; r)$. The prover wants to prove that C encrypts a word that does *not* belong to $\mathcal{L}$ in zero-knowledge. To construct our proof system, we are going to follow a generic approach by combining two different proof systems (in our following instantiations the first proof will be a SPHF, while the second one will be a Groth Sahai NIZK).

Formally, we assume there is a sound and correct non-interactive (NI) proof system Π_a for the language defined by the binary relation $\mathcal{R} = \{(\mathcal{C}, (w, r)), C = \mathsf{Encrypt}(\mathsf{ek}, w; r) \wedge w \in \mathcal{L}\}$ and we will construct a NIZK proof system for the language defined by the binary relation $\hat{\mathcal{R}} = \{(\mathcal{C}, (w, r)), C = \mathsf{Encrypt}(\mathsf{ek}, w; r) \wedge w \notin \mathcal{L}\}$.

We assume that Π_a satisfies the following properties:

- there exists a randomization algorithm that takes a proof π_a output by $\Pi_a.\mathsf{Prove}(\mathcal{C}, (w, r))$ and some randomness r', ρ' and outputs a properly distributed proof π_a' on the same word w encrypted in the ciphertext $\mathcal{C}'$ using randomness r'^1.

- Π_a verifies the *indistinguishability of proofs* property: given a pair $(\mathcal{C}, (w, r)) \in \hat{R}$ where $\mathcal{C}$ is an encryption of a word $w \notin \mathcal{L}$ using randomness r, it should be hard to distinguish an invalid proof generating *honestly* as $\Pi_a.\mathsf{Prove}(\mathcal{C}, (w, r))$ from a random value.[2]

- there exists a NI zero-knowledge proof system Π_b where given an output π_a proves that it is indeed the correct result from $\Pi_a.\mathsf{Prove}(\mathcal{C}, (w, r); \rho)$ even if $w \notin \mathcal{L}$. We also require the extra property, that either Π_b has perfect soundness or possesses a trapdoor allowing to recover ρ.

Assuming these three properties, our NI zero-knowledge proof system for the language defined by the binary relation $\hat{\mathcal{R}}$, $\Pi = (\mathsf{no.Setup}, \mathsf{no.TSetup}, \mathsf{no.Prove}, \mathsf{no.Verify}, \mathsf{no.Simulate})$, is defined as follows:

$\mathsf{no.Setup}(1^\mathfrak{K})$: runs $\mathcal{E}.\mathsf{Setup}(1^\mathfrak{K})$ to compute the global parameters param and also
$\mathsf{KeyGen}(\mathsf{param})$ to obtain a key pair $(\mathsf{ek}, \mathsf{dk})$. It also runs $\Pi_a.\mathsf{Setup}(1^\mathfrak{K})$ to obtain crs_a and $\Pi_b.\mathsf{Setup}(1^\mathfrak{K})$ to obtain crs_b. It outputs the common reference string $\mathsf{crs} = (\mathsf{crs}_a, \mathsf{crs}_b, \mathsf{param}, \mathsf{ek})$.
$\mathsf{no.TSetup}(1^\mathfrak{K})$: runs $\mathcal{E}.\mathsf{Setup}(1^\mathfrak{K})$ to compute the global parameters param and also $\mathsf{KeyGen}(\mathsf{param})$ to obtain a key pair $(\mathsf{ek}, \mathsf{dk})$. It also runs $\Pi_a.\mathsf{Setup}(1^\mathfrak{K})$ to obtain crs_a and $\Pi_b.\mathsf{TSetup}(1^\mathfrak{K})$ to obtain (crs_b, τ_b). It outputs the common reference string $\mathsf{crs} = (\mathsf{crs}_a, \mathsf{crs}_b, \mathsf{param}, \mathsf{ek})$ and the trapdoor $\tau = (\mathsf{dk}, \tau_b)$.
$\mathsf{no.Prove}(\mathcal{C}, w, s, \mathsf{crs}; \rho)$: Computes $\pi_a := \Pi_a.\mathsf{Prove}(\mathcal{C}, (w, r); \rho)$, and a proof $\pi_b := \Pi_b.\mathsf{Prove}(\pi_a, \mathcal{C}, (w, r), \rho; \rho')$, and outputs (π_a, π_b)
$\mathsf{no.Verify}(\mathcal{C}, \pi_a, \pi_b)$: returns 1 if and only if π_a is invalid for Π_a and π_b is valid for Π_b ((*i.e.* $\Pi_a.\mathsf{Verify}(\mathcal{C}, \pi_a) = 0$ and $\Pi_b.\mathsf{Verify}(\pi_b, \pi_a, \mathcal{C}) = 1$).
$\mathsf{no.Simulate}(\mathcal{C}, \tau)$: picks uniformly at random π_a and uses the trapdoor τ_b to run $\Pi_b.\mathsf{Simulate}(\tau_b, \pi_a, \mathcal{C})$ to get π_b. It outputs (π_a, π_b).

The correctness follows immediately from the correctness of the two proofs. Indeed if (π_a, π_b) is output by $\mathsf{no.Prove}(\mathcal{C}, w, s, \mathsf{crs}; \rho)$, π_a output should not verify (*i.e.* $\Pi_a.\mathsf{Verify}(\mathcal{C}, \pi_a) = 0$) as the input $(C, (w, s)) \notin \mathcal{R}$.

---

[1] The idea is that there is no "weak" randomness, and so if the adversary breaks the completeness of the proof for a pair w, ρ, any pair w, ρ' leads to invalid proofs even in w is in $\mathcal{L}$. This property is easy to achieve with homomorphic proof system, Groth Sahai and SPHF are good candidates for example.

[2] This property does not hold for Groth Sahai proofs, given a correctly computed invalid proof for an equation like $\mathcal{X} = \mathcal{A}$, when in fact $\mathcal{X} = \mathcal{B}$, one can simply rely on the homomorphic properties of the verification to check if $GS.\mathsf{Verify}(\pi, \mathcal{C}, \mathcal{B})$ holds, hence distinguishing π from a random value.

Theorem 1. *The proof system Π is sound if Π_a is correct and Π_b is sound.*

Proof. We assume there exists an adversary against the soundness of our proof system, we will show there exists an adversary $\mathcal{B}$ that can use this adversary to break the soundness of Π_b. An adversary against the soundness of our scheme outputs $(\mathcal{C}, \pi_a, \pi_b)$ such that while no.Verify$(\mathcal{C}, \pi_a, \pi_b)$ holds, the plaintext in $\mathcal{C}$ does indeed belong to $\mathcal{L}$.

We will distinguish two kind of adversaries, those who compute π_a honestly, and those who does not. This means that either π_a is invalid for a valid word w and some randomness ρ, or that the adversary gives an incorrect output π_a and managed to build a proof π_b stating that it is computed correctly.

The adversary $\mathcal{B}$ now decrypts the ciphertext $\mathcal{C}$ to recover the word w, picks some fresh r' and encrypts it into a $\mathcal{C}'$ (this is a randomization of the first ciphertext) and tries to compute Π_a.Prove$(\mathcal{C}', w, r'; \rho')$. Either with advantage greater than $\varepsilon/2$ this proof does not hold, and so $\mathcal{B}$ managed to break the correctness of the proof system Π_a. Either with advantage greater than $\varepsilon/2$ this proof holds, this means that the π_a output by the adversary was not correctly computed, hence this lead to breaking the soundness of Π_b. (As the second proof given by the adversary is valid while proving an incorrect statement). $\qquad\square$

Theorem 2. *The proof system Π is zero-knowledge assuming the zero-knowledge property of Π_b and the indistinguishability of proofs of Π_a.*

Proof. It is easy to see that the output of no.TSetup and no.Setup are indistinguishable (by the zero-knowledge property of Π_b). We assume there exists an adversary against the Zero-Knowledge property of our scheme with advantage ε, we are going to follow a sequence of games to give an upper bound on this value. We have to prove that the distributions $\{\mathsf{Prove}(\mathsf{crs}, \mathcal{C}, (w, r))\}$ and $\{\mathsf{Simulate}(\mathsf{crs}, \mathcal{C})\}$ are indistinguishable for a ciphertext $\mathcal{C} = \mathsf{Encrypt}(\mathsf{ek}, w; r)$ with $w \notin \mathcal{L}$ generated by the adversary.

$\mathcal{G}_0$ We start from the real game (*i.e.* $\pi \xleftarrow{\$} \mathsf{Prove}(\mathsf{crs}, \mathcal{C}, (w, r))$).

$\mathcal{G}_1$ In this game, the simulator uses the Zero-Knowledge trapdoor τ_b from Π_b to simulate the proofs on the valid statement π_a (*i.e.* it outputs $\pi_a := \Pi_a$.Prove$(\mathcal{C}, (w, r); \rho)$ and $\pi_b := \Pi_b$.Simulate$(\pi_a, \mathcal{C}, (w, r); \rho')$).
Here the adversary has advantage $\varepsilon_1 \leq \varepsilon + \mathsf{Adv}_{\mathsf{ZK}}$,

$\mathcal{G}_2$ In this game, the simulator outputs a random value instead of π_a and simulates π_b. Under the indistinguishability of the proofs on π_a, this game is similar to the previous one.
Here the adversary has advantage $\varepsilon_2 \leq \varepsilon_1 + \mathsf{Adv}_{\mathsf{ind}_\pi}$,

In this last game, one obtains the algorithm no.Simulate$(\mathcal{C}, \tau)$ and we get $\varepsilon \leq \mathsf{Adv}_{\mathsf{ZK}} + \mathsf{Adv}_{\mathsf{ind}}$. $\qquad\square$

Prover		Verifier
$V, \boldsymbol{v}, w_v$		$\mathfrak{L}_p, \mathfrak{L}_u$

$(\mathsf{hp}_v, \mathsf{hk}_v) := (\Gamma_v(\mathfrak{L}_p) \odot \boldsymbol{\alpha}_v, \boldsymbol{\alpha}_v)$

$H_v := \Theta_v(V, \mathfrak{L}_p) \odot \boldsymbol{\alpha}_v \quad \xrightarrow{\;\mathfrak{V} = (\mathsf{hp}_v, H_v, \boldsymbol{v})\;} \quad H_v' := \mathfrak{L}_u \odot \mathsf{hp}_v \overset{?}{\neq} H_v$

$\xleftarrow{\qquad \mathsf{hp}_u \qquad} \quad (\mathsf{hp}_u, \mathsf{hk}_u) := (\Gamma_u(\mathfrak{V}) \odot \boldsymbol{\alpha}_u, \boldsymbol{\alpha}_u)$

$H_u' := (w_v, \mathsf{hk}_v) \odot \mathsf{hp}_u \quad \xrightarrow{\qquad H_u' \qquad} \quad H_u' \overset{?}{=} \Theta_u(\mathfrak{V}) \odot \mathsf{hk}_u.$

Fig. 1. Generic SPHF-based proof of exclusion

3.2 Concrete Examples

In order to instantiate the previous proposition, we need some techniques to prove that a statement is invalid. To do so, we propose the approach consisting in generating a proof as if the statement was valid, and show that while this proof does not hold it was honestly generated.

As we show in our application to zero-knowledge with witness elimination in Section 4, Kiayias and Zhou aimed to do so in [KZ09], but incompletely. Additionally, they did it using an external proof system, that adds several rounds of interaction. (*i.e.* they use a sigma protocol to prove the (partial-)validity of a proof based on smooth projective hash functions.)

In the following we propose new techniques to do so via classical proof systems, first by proving the validity of a SPHF-proof via another SPHF, and then by mixing Groth-Sahai methodology with SPHF. Our generic approach from Section 3.1, requires the second proof to be zero-knowledge, and the first one to be homomorphicly randomizable and to achieve the indistinguishability on the proof. Groth Sahai provides the zero-knowledge while smooth projective hashing provides the indistinguishability via its pseudo-randomness.

We are going to work on SPHF-friendly languages. Recent works have drastically increased the range of languages manageable with SPHF (*e.g.* [BBC+13a, BBC+13b]), to every kind of pairing product equations over graded rings, so this will not really limit applications of theses techniques in concrete protocols.

We assume that languages $\mathfrak{L}$ have additional parameters $\mathfrak{L}_p, \mathfrak{L}_u$, the first part is a public description of a specificity of the language needed to build a smooth projective hash function on it, while the other one is private and is needed for verification purpose. (In case of a revocation language $\mathfrak{L}$, $\mathfrak{L}_p$ is a commitment to the revocation list, while $\mathfrak{L}_u$ is the randomness from the commitment.)

Non-Zero-Knowledge Proofs, Using Smooth Projective Hash Functions. To show that a word committed into $\boldsymbol{v}$ is not in a language described by $\mathfrak{L}_p$, one ends up doing the following (cf Figure 1):

Where the first SPHF is on the language described by $\mathfrak{L}_p$ while the other one is based on the language of a correct computation between a hash value, a projection key and a ciphertext (as there is a dependency between those two terms it seems improbable to be able to do better in this case).

A more concrete example. In order to explain the previous formalism, let us now give a more concrete example, with a language described by an ElGamal encryption of a word U. The prover possesses a word V, the verifier the word U and publishes an ElGamal ciphertext of U: $\mathfrak{L}_p = (h^s U, g^s)$. The prover encrypts his word V using ElGamal encryption scheme and proves to the verifier that V is not the plaintext encrypted in $\mathfrak{L}_p$. Following the previous technique we can achieve a 3-round proof as described on Figure 2. The second SPHF is smooth

Prover		Verifier
$V, h^r V, g^r, r$		$\mathfrak{L}_p = (h^s U, g^s), U, s$

$(\mathsf{hp}_v, \mathsf{hk}_v) := (h^\lambda g^\mu, (\lambda, \mu)) \xrightarrow{\mathfrak{V}' = (\mathsf{hp}_v, h^r V, g^r)}\quad H'_v := \mathsf{hp}_v^s$

$\xleftarrow{\mathsf{hp}_u, \mathfrak{L}_p}\quad \mathsf{hp}_u := (h^\delta (h^s U/(h^r V))^\beta, g^\delta (g^s/g^r)^\beta,$
$\mathsf{hp}_v^\beta g^\gamma),$
$\mathsf{hk}_u := (\delta, \beta, \gamma)$

$H'_u := \mathsf{hp}_{u,1}^\lambda \mathsf{hp}_{u,2}^\mu \mathsf{hp}_{u,3}^r \xrightarrow{H'_u, H_v}\quad H'_v \overset{?}{\neq} H_v \wedge H'_u \overset{?}{=} \mathsf{hp}_v^\delta H_v^\beta (g^r)^\gamma.$
$H_v := (h^s U/V)^\lambda (g^s)^\mu$

Fig. 2. Tweaked ElGamal based SPHF proof of inequality

if and only if $V = U$, this means that technically an adversary can break the soundness of the verification of the valid computation of hp_v, H_v when the word V is different from U. However in this case, the protocol should already return yes so he cannot gain anything from doing so. The proof requires overall 10 group elements: 2 for the initial commit of U, 2 for the one of V, 2 overall for hp_v, H_v and 4 for hp_u, H'_u.

We stress that, this construction differs from the generic approach in the sense that $\mathfrak{L}_p$ instead of being known before the protocol like in the generic construction from Figure 1, can be set on the fly and postpone to the second flow. While this proof is not zero-knowledge in any way, it will find some use in our LAKE (*Language-Authenticated Key Exchange*) application in the full version.

Zero-Knowledge Proofs, Using Groth-Sahai Non-Interactive Proof Technique. We now want to supersede the last proof with a zero-knowledge proof. So once again we do a smooth projective hash function for the first language, and then prove using a Groth Sahai proof that we indeed know the associated hash key, such that the hash value and the projection key are consistent, that way we can reduce the protocol interactivity to one flow as explained in Figure 3.

A more concrete example. If we consider our former example with a Groth Sahai proof instead of the second SPHF we end up with a one-round protocol. Overall

Prover	Verifier
V, v, w_v	$\mathfrak{L}_p, \mathfrak{L}_u$

$$(\mathsf{hp}_v, \mathsf{hk}_v) := (\Gamma_v(\mathfrak{L}_p) \odot \alpha_v, \alpha_v)$$
$$H_v := \Theta_v(V, \mathfrak{L}_p) \odot \alpha_v$$

$$\pi = GS.\mathsf{Prove}(H_v \wedge \mathsf{hp}_v; \mathsf{hk}_w) \quad \xrightarrow{\mathfrak{V}' = \mathsf{hp}_v, v, \pi, H_v} \quad H_v' := \mathfrak{L}_u \odot \mathsf{hp}_v$$
$$H_v \overset{?}{\neq} H_v' \wedge \mathsf{Verify}(\pi).$$

Fig. 3. Generic SPHF + NIZK proof of inequality

this would require 4 elements in $\mathbb{G}_1$ for the hash proof, 6 other in $\mathbb{G}_1$ for the additional commitments, 4 in each group for the quadratic proof, 1 in $\mathbb{G}_1$ for one of the multi scalar exponentiation equation and 2 scalars for the other. Overall, the protocol is very efficient and only requires the transmission of 15 elements in $\mathbb{G}_1$, 4 elements in $\mathbb{G}_2$ and 2 scalars in $\mathbb{Z}_p$.

3.3   Transformation from a NIZK to a SS-NIZK

In one of the following applications, we will need our proof of exclusion to be simulation-sound ([Sah99]). There is a generic transformation from Groth Sahai based NIZK proofs to Simulation-Sound.

To construct a Simulation-Sound proof that some word w does not belong to a language $\mathfrak{L}$, one uses the following roadmap, assuming the common reference string crs contains a common reference string for the Groth-Sahai proof system crs_{GS}, a verification key pk for a Structure-Preserving Signature scheme [AFG+10], and the prover already possesses a pair of primary keys (psk, ppk) for a one-time two-tier signature scheme [BS07][3]:

1. generates a secondary signing/verification key pair (ssk, spk) for the one-time two-tier signature.
2. commits to a random tuple of elements R corresponding to a signature.
3. generates, using Groth Sahai and our exclusion proof, a proof π that either w does not belong to $\mathfrak{L}$, or that R is a valid signature of the verification key spk of the one-time signature, under the public key pk contained in the CRS crs.
4. sends this proof π, the verification key of the one-time signature, and the corresponding one-time signature of everything under (psk, ssk).

Referring to [HJ12], it can be shown that this scheme is Zero-Knowledge under the Indistinguishability of the two types of Groth-Sahai common reference strings, and that both the simulation-soundness and the soundness come from the unforgeability of the two involved signatures.

---

[3] This can easily be achieved by applying a Chameleon Hash on itself for example.

4 Application to Zero-Knowledge with Witness Elimination

In [KZ09], Kiayias and Zhou introduced the notion of zero-knowledge proofs with witness elimination. They described it through a universally composable ideal functionality, directly giving strong guideline as how to achieve a generic construction.

Ideal Functionality for Zero-Knowledge with Witness Elimination. In the universal composability (UC) framework, once a protocol is proved secure, it can be used in arbitrary contexts retaining its security properties (*i.e.* when composed with other instances of the same or other protocols). The security in this framework is defined in the sense of protocol emulation (*i.e.* a protocol P emulates some protocol P', if P does not affect the security of anything else than P' would have). To prove security in the UC framework, we define an ideal functionality $\mathcal{F}$ which can be thought of as an incorruptible trusted party that takes inputs from all parties and hands back outputs to the parties. The functionality $\mathcal{F}$ is a formal specification of a cryptographic task and is secure by definition. Hence, if a protocol P emulates $\mathcal{F}$, one can infer that it securely realizes the given task in arbitrary contexts.

The ideal functionality for Zero-Knowledge with Witness Elimination $\mathcal{F}_{ZKWE}^{\mathcal{R},\mathcal{Q}}$ proposed by Kiayias and Zhou builds upon that of Zero-Knowledge (proposed in 2001 by Canetti [Can01]) , with the extra requirement that the prover shows that it did not use some eliminated witnesses to prove the statement. We recall it on Figure 4.

It is parametrized by two binary relations $\mathcal{R}$ and $\mathcal{Q}$. The prover $\mathcal{P}$ is given an input $\langle x, w \rangle$ (Prove query) and the verifier $\mathcal{V}$ is given an input w' (Verify query). The verifier should only accept if $\mathcal{R}(x, w)$ and $\neg\mathcal{Q}(w, w')$ hold. Furthermore, it should not learn anything from the protocol except the value x and the existence of such a witness w. Following the authors of [KZ09], we do not deal here with adaptive corruptions. The functionality proceeds in three steps:

- Upon receiving a (Prove, sid, $\langle x, w \rangle$) query from the prover $\mathcal{P}$: While blocking the secret inputs from the adversary, it leaks a bit through the (LeakProve, sid, $\langle x, \varphi \rangle$, $\mathcal{P}$) answer to tell the adversary whether $\mathcal{R}(x, w)$ holds. As explained in [KZ09], this does not affect the security properties of the protocol as long as the elimination relation $\mathcal{Q}$ is such that the $\mathcal{F}_{ZKWE}^{\mathcal{R},\mathcal{Q}}$ functionality emulates the $\mathcal{F}_{ZK}^{\mathcal{R}}$ functionality (the prover can easily learn whether the witness is valid or not). The requirement on $\mathcal{Q}$ is that given a witness w, one can sample a witness w' such that $\mathcal{Q}(w, w')$ happens with negligible probability. This is in particular the case for the substring equality considered in their article and for the more general membership to the languages considered here (see Section 5).
- Upon receiving a (Verify, sid, w') query from party $\mathcal{V}$: While blocking the secret inputs from the adversary, it leaks the information that $\mathcal{V}$ sent his witness through the (LeakVerify, sid, $\mathcal{V}$) answer.

- Upon receiving a (InflVerify, sid) query from the adversary: it leaks a last bit through the (RetVerify, sid, b) answer to tell the adversary whether $Q(w, w')$ holds. The query InflVerify can be asked only once, capturing a similar property to the resistance to offline dictionary attacks in the case of password-based protocols.

$\mathcal{F}_{ZKWE}^{\mathcal{R}, \mathcal{Q}}$ is parametrized with the ZK relation $\mathcal{R}$ and the elimination relation $\mathcal{Q}$.

- Upon receiving (Prove, sid, $\langle x, w \rangle$) from party $\mathcal{P}$ where sid $= (\mathcal{P}, \mathcal{V}, \text{sid}')$, record $\langle \mathcal{P}, x, w \rangle$, send (LeakProve, sid, $\langle x, \varphi \rangle, \mathcal{P}$) to the adversary, where $\varphi = 1$ if $\mathcal{R}(x, w)$ holds, and $\varphi = 0$ otherwise. Ignore future (Prove, ...) inputs.
- Upon receiving (Verify, sid, w') from party $\mathcal{V}$ where sid $= (\mathcal{P}, \mathcal{V}, \text{sid}')$, record $\langle T, w' \rangle$, send (LeakVerify, sid, $\mathcal{V}$) to the adversary. Ignore future (Verify, ...) inputs.
- Upon receiving (InflVerify, sid) from the adversary, if $\mathcal{R}(x, w)$ and $\neg Q(w, w')$ hold, then send (RetVerify, sid, 1) to party $\mathcal{V}$. Else if $\neg\mathcal{R}(x, w)$ holds or $Q(w, w')$ holds, then send (RetVerify, sid, 0) to party $\mathcal{V}$.

Fig. 4. Functionality $\mathcal{F}_{ZKWE}^{\mathcal{R}, \mathcal{Q}}$

Generic Approach. After receiving the witness w' eliminated by the verifier, the construction of a zero-knowledge proof with witness elimination as presented by Kiayias and Zhou in [KZ09] requires two main parts by the prover. First, in a regular zero-knowledge proof, he starts by proving that the statement $\mathcal{R}(x, w)$ is indeed fulfilled, and then, in another part a little bit trickier, he has to prove that the witness he used does not belong to the elimination list, which is $\neg Q(w, w')$. We recall on Figure 5 their original generic construction. In a nutshell, they proceed in three steps:

- In a first step, the verifier sends an encryption C' of the eliminated witness w' to the prover.
- In a second step, the prover computes an encryption C of his witness w, generates a hash key hk = HashKG, computes a projection key hp = ProjKG(hk) and computes the hash value $\kappa = \text{Hash}(C', (C, w), \text{hk})$. He sends hp and κ to the verifier. The aim of this smooth projective hash function is to ensure that $w \neq w'$.
- In a last step, both players engage in a zero-knowledge proof of membership (ZKPM) subprotocol to show that $\mathcal{R}(x, w)$ holds.

A Flaw in the Original Approach. In the protocol presented in [KZ09] that we recalled in the previous section, Kiayias and Zhou propose to prove that

---

Common reference string: crs = (pk, ρ), where pk is a public key of an encryption scheme $\mathcal{E}$, and ρ is a reference string of a Zero-Knowledge Proof of Membership (ZKPM) scheme.

Protocol steps: Upon receiving (Verify, sid, w') from the environment, party $\mathcal{V}$ selects $r' \xleftarrow{\$} U$ and computes $\mathcal{C}' = \mathsf{Encrypt}(\mathsf{pk}, w'; r')$, and sends (move$_1$, $\mathcal{C}'$) to party $\mathcal{P}$.

Upon receiving (Prove, sid, x, w) from the environment, party $\mathcal{P}$ first checks if $(x, w) \in \mathcal{R}$ and waits for a move$_1$ message from party $\mathcal{V}$. After receiving move$_1$ message:

- if $\neg \mathcal{R}(x, w)$ holds, then party $\mathcal{P}$ sends party $\mathcal{V}$ a message (move$_2$, "no valid proof"),
- else if $\mathcal{R}(x, w)$ holds, then party $\mathcal{P}$ computes $\mathcal{C} = \mathsf{Encrypt}(\mathsf{pk}, w; r)$, and then party $\mathcal{P}$ sends party $\mathcal{V}$ a message (move$_2$, hp, κ), where hk = HashKG, hp = ProjKG(hk), $\kappa = \mathsf{Hash}(\mathcal{C}', (\mathcal{C}, w), \mathsf{hk})$. Now, parties $\mathcal{P}$ and $\mathcal{V}$ play the roles of prover and verifier respectively to run a ZKPM subprotocol, to show that $x, \mathcal{C}', \kappa$ is consistent:

$$\exists (w, r), (x, w) \in R \wedge \mathcal{C} = \mathsf{Encrypt}(\mathsf{pk}, w; r) \wedge \kappa = \mathsf{Hash}(\mathcal{C}', (\mathcal{C}, w), \mathsf{hk}).$$

Upon receiving (move$_2$, "no valid proof") from party $\mathcal{P}$, party $\mathcal{V}$ returns (RetVerify, sid, 0) to the environment. Else if receiving (move$_2$, hp, κ), party $\mathcal{V}$ computes $\kappa' = \mathsf{ProjHash}(\mathcal{C}, (\mathcal{C}', w', r'), \mathsf{hp})$ and if $\kappa \neq \kappa'$ party and $\mathcal{V}$ accepts the ZKPM proof in the subprotocol above, then party $\mathcal{V}$ returns (RetVerify, sid, 1) to the environment; otherwise returns (RetVerify, sid, 0) to the environment.

Fig. 5. Initial Generic construction of the protocol for Zero-Knowledge Proofs with Witness Elimination

---

$\neg \mathcal{Q}(w, w')$ by doing an implicit proof of equality (*i.e.* $\mathcal{Q}(w, w')$) using a smooth projective hash function. They make the prover send the hash value κ, and ask the verifier to check whether it is equal to the projected hash value κ'. If those values are different, then the relation $\mathcal{Q}(w, w')$ does not stand, which proves that the witness is not eliminated.

However, this requires the prover to be honest in this process, as if he sends a inconsistent projection key to the verifier, then it will lead to an inequality between the hash and the projected hash values, meaning that the proof of membership to the elimination list (*i.e.* $\mathcal{Q}(w, w')$) will not hold, and finally that he will be able to convince the verifier with an invalid statement with overwhelming probability.

This issue comes from the fact that the validity of the projection key hp is nowhere verified in the generic description. Intuitively, this verification should be part of the following ZKPM subprotocol. In their description, the latter does not involve the computation of hp in any way, so that there is the possibility for the prover to send a bogus one in order to avoid collision for words in the elimination list. This way, the prover is able to get its ZKPM proof for $\mathcal{R}(x, w)$ accepted while using a witness of the elimination list, without being caught by the verifier.

5   A Generic Fix and Several Concrete Instantiations

Improvement. Before fixing Kiayias and Zhou's protocol, we start by giving some other improvements. First, the authors only considered equalities or substring equalities for the relation $\mathcal{Q}$. We improve this by allowing $\mathcal{Q}$ to be a more general relation of membership to a language specified by w': $\mathcal{Q}(w, w') \Leftrightarrow w \in \mathcal{L}_{w'}$. More precisely, following 3.1, we assume that the description of the language is public, meaning that given w', one learns $\mathcal{L}_{w'}$ automatically. We also assume that given w, one can easily and publicly check whether $w \in \mathcal{L}_{w'}$ or $w \notin \mathcal{L}_{w'}$.

Furthermore, in order to be able to satisfy $\mathcal{F}^{\mathcal{R},\mathcal{Q}}_{ZKWE}$, we assume that given $\mathcal{L}_{w'}$, the simulator will be able to generate $w_1 \in \mathcal{L}_{w'}$ and $w_2 \notin \mathcal{L}_{w'}$. This is a natural assumption and can be achieved in different ways: either, this is publicly achievable by anybody; Or the language $\mathcal{L}_{w'}$ is randomizable and w' includes a witness included in $\mathcal{L}_{w'}$ from which it is possible to generate $w \in \mathcal{L}_{w'}$; Or we assume that $\mathcal{S}$ possesses a trapdoor (stored into the CRS). In most applications, we will be in the second case, where the language $\mathcal{L}_{w'}$ is randomizable.

Our second improvement is to replace most of the interactive proofs by possibly *non-interactive* proofs of knowledge, using the proofs of non-membership given in Section 3. More details follow in the next section.

A Generic Fix. As already explained in Section 4, the problem of the initial generic protocol given by the authors of [KZ09] lies in the Sigma protocol, which does not involve the computation of hp in any way. To avoid this issue, we now include in the Zero-Knowledge proof a new proof that the projection key hp was correctly generated.

Our new generic protocol is presented on Figure 6. From a high point of view, the proof π_1 is the same as in [KZ09] and proves the validity of the statement x under the witness w, namely that $\mathcal{R}(x, w)$ holds.

The non-interactive proof π_2 replaces their interactive ZKPM subprotocol, and ensures that $\mathcal{Q}(w, w')$ does not hold (*i.e.* w is not in the exclusion language). As explained in Section 3, this proof consists in the combination of a ciphertext $\mathcal{C}$ of w and a proof π_2 of non-membership. This latter proof is divided into a proof π_a of membership of w in the language defined by w' (which should not hold), and a second proof π_b showing that, while the proof π_a does not hold, it has been honestly generated, so there exists some randomness used to prove π_1, and some extra randomness, such that the expected proof of equality is indeed π_a. By completeness of the proof, this proves that w is indeed not included in the language defined by w'.

Common Reference String: crs = (pk, ρ_1, ρ_2), where pk is a public key of an encryption scheme $\mathcal{E}$ (both Encrypt and no.Encrypt use $\mathcal{E}$), ρ_1 is a reference string of a zero-knowledge proof of membership (for the relation $\mathcal{R}$), and ρ_2 is a reference string of a zero-knowledge proof of non-membership (for the relation $\mathcal{Q}$).

Protocol steps: Upon receiving (Verify, sid, w') from the environment, party $\mathcal{V}$ selects a random r' and computes $\mathcal{C}' = \mathsf{Encrypt}(\mathsf{pk}, w'; r')$, and sends (move$_1$, $\mathcal{C}'$) to party $\mathcal{P}$.

Upon receiving (Prove, sid, x, w) from the environment, party $\mathcal{P}$ first checks if $\mathcal{R}(x, w)$ holds and waits for a move$_1$ message from party $\mathcal{V}$. After receiving move$_1$ message:

- if $\neg\mathcal{R}(x, w)$ holds, then party $\mathcal{P}$ sends party $\mathcal{V}$ a message (move$_2$, "no valid proof"),
- else if $\mathcal{R}(x, w)$ holds, then party $\mathcal{P}$ selects three random values r, $\mathbf{r_1}$ and $\mathbf{r_2}$ and sends party $\mathcal{V}$ a message (move$_2$, π_1, ($\mathcal{C}, \pi_2$)), where $\pi_1 = \mathsf{ZK.Prove}(x, w, \mathcal{R}; \mathbf{r_1})$ and $(\mathcal{C}, \pi_2) = \mathsf{SS.no.Prove}(w, w', \mathcal{Q}, \mathbf{r_1}; \mathbf{r_2})$, meaning in particular that $\mathcal{C} = \mathsf{Encrypt}(\mathsf{pk}, w; r)$.

Upon receiving (move$_2$, "no valid proof") from party $\mathcal{P}$, party $\mathcal{V}$ returns (RetVerify, sid, 0) to the environment. Else if receiving (move$_2$, π_1, ($\mathcal{C}, \pi_2$)), party $\mathcal{V}$ checks both proofs and returns (RetVerify, sid, 1) to the environment if they are correct, and (RetVerify, sid, 0) otherwise.

Fig. 6. Generic Construction of Zero Knowledge proof with Witness Elimination

Theorem 3. *This generic construction fulfils the Zero-Knowledge with Witness-Elimination Functionality $\mathcal{F}_{ZKWE}^{\mathcal{R},\mathcal{Q}}$ under the assumption that π_1 is a zero-knowledge proof of membership for the relation $\mathcal{R}$, and π_2 is a zero-knowledge proof of non-membership for the relation $\mathcal{Q}$, as defined in section 3.*

Due to lack of space, the proof of Theorem 3 is provided in the full version.

Concrete Instantiation of the Fixed and Improved Protocol. In their original article [KZ09], Kiayias and Zhou present a concrete instantiation of the protocol, where a user proves being in a possession of a valid pair (m, σ) of a Boneh Boyen [BB04] signature σ, on a message m. To show the potency of our approach, we propose to instantiate their original scheme more efficiently, in a round-optimal way, without the initial flaw described in Section 4. In order to have an easy message recovery, we are going to do a naive bit per bit commitment. While this is not necessarily the most efficient approach in practice, asymptotically this is already more efficient than their use of Paillier encryption (a quadratic cost instead of a cubic one using Paillier encryption).

The scheme is described on Figure 7. The proof consists of a commitment to $\sigma, \lambda, \mu, \theta$ (*i.e.* 12 group elements), and a proof of two linear multi-scalar exponentiation equations (2 elements each), one of a quadratic (9 group elements), and ℓ quadratic scalar equations. Overall, $31 + 9\ell$ group elements are exchanged [4] in two flows. For a concrete security parameter, the initial (flawed) scheme was more efficient but required 2 additional rounds. However, as many elements live in a RSA modulus space, asymptotically our scheme has a better efficiency, both in number of rounds and communication size.

Prover		Verifier
(m, σ)		σ'

$$r', s' \xleftarrow{\$} \mathbb{Z}_p$$

$$
\begin{array}{l}
C_v := \mathsf{Encrypt}(\sigma; t, z) \\
\mathsf{hp}_v := (u^\lambda g^\mu, v^\theta g^\mu) \\
\mathsf{hk}_v := (\lambda, \theta, \mu) \\
H_v := (c_3'/\sigma)^\mu (c_1')^\lambda (c_2')^\theta
\end{array}
\xleftarrow{\quad c' \quad}
c' := \mathsf{Encrypt}(\sigma'; r', s')
$$

$$
\begin{array}{l}
\pi = GS.\mathsf{Prove}(\mathsf{hp}_v, H_v; \mathsf{hk}_v, C_v; \\
\qquad\qquad \sigma, t, z, \mathsf{hk}_v)
\end{array}
\xrightarrow{\quad (\mathsf{hp}_v, C_v, \pi) \quad}
\begin{array}{l}
H_v' := \mathsf{hp}_v^{(r', s')} = (u^\lambda g^\mu)^{r'}(v^\theta g^\mu)^{s'} \\
H_v' \overset{?}{\neq} H_v \wedge \mathsf{Verify}(\pi).
\end{array}
$$

The proof π considers the language:

$$
\exists t, z, m, \lambda, \theta, \mu, \sigma, \left\{
\begin{array}{l}
C_v = \mathsf{Encrypt}(\sigma; t, z) \\
\mathsf{hp}_v = (u^\lambda g^\mu, v^\theta g^\mu) \\
H_s = (c_3'/\sigma)^\mu (c_1')^\lambda (c_2')^\theta \\
e(\sigma, \mathsf{vkg}^m) = 1_T
\end{array}
\right.
$$

Fig. 7. Concrete Construction of zero-knowledge with witness elimination

6 Other Applications

6.1 Anonymous Credentials not Verifying a Property

Anonymous Credentials were introduced by Chaum in [Cha85], and were widely used ever since as a means for users to authenticate themselves while protecting their privacy.

Most constructions consist in a first interaction, where a user obtains a signature on some message which corresponds to "his credentials". When this user wants to authenticate, he then proves that he knows a signature on a message he does not want to leak but that fulfils some property.

Camenisch and Groß[CG08] proposed a way to build anonymous credentials with efficient attributes, and more recently Izabachène et al. proposed in [ILV11] a nearly non-interactive instantiation of this protocol. Their protocol requires an

---

[4] This estimation is very rough, and optimization like running a KDF on the hash value could further improve the efficiency, but that is beyond the point of this construction.

interaction to prove the AND of several credentials. Interestingly, their technique for proving the NAND of credentials is non-interactive, so combining this technique with our proof of No-Statement we can non-interactively prove the AND of several credentials by doing a NOT(NAND). Similarly, we can transform their non-interactive NOR into the non-interactive OR they were lacking, rendering their protocol completely non-interactive.

6.2 Language Authenticated Key Exchange

In [BBC+13a], the authors introduced the notion of Language Authenticated Key Exchange which allows two users to agree on a shared session key if and only if they each possess a word in a language chosen secretly by the other.

Interestingly, the construction requires their languages to be "randomizable" which fits well with our description. In [BBC+13a], they handle AND connectives of languages (*i.e.* intersection of languages) and limited form of OR connectives (*i.e.* union of languages). However, there was no known way to handle exclusion languages, but our technique allows to solve this and so extend the range of advanced languages manageable by those LAKE. We can also remove the limitation on the union of languages by using the connective NOT(AND(NOT)).

In their LAKE constructions, the SPHF is of course not zero-knowledge, and no simulation is required on this part (as everything is managed by the UC commitment) so one can use our proofs without requiring the "simulation sound" part. An interesting trade-off can also be achieved if the proof of validity of the SPHF computation is managed with a SPHF instead of a Groth Sahai proof, at the cost of (at most) one extra round in the protocol which would allow to avoid the use of pairings.

In the inner part of a LAKE protocol, those proofs can be run simultaneously on both sides, making it 4 flows instead of 2 in the original paper, but it allows to handle previous languages as well as their complements.

Acknowledgements.. This work was supported in part by the French ANR-12-INSE-0014 SIMPATIC Project.

References

[ACHdM05] Ateniese, G., Camenisch, J., Hohenberger, S., de Medeiros, B.: Practical group signatures without random oracles. Cryptology ePrint Archive, Report 2005/385 (2005)

[ACP09] Abdalla, M., Chevalier, C., Pointcheval, D.: Smooth projective hashing for conditionally extractable commitments. In: Halevi, S. (ed.) CRYPTO 2009. LNCS, vol. 5677, pp. 671–689. Springer, Heidelberg (2009)

[AFG+10] Abe, M., Fuchsbauer, G., Groth, J., Haralambiev, K., Ohkubo, M.: Structure-preserving signatures and commitments to group elements. In: Rabin, T. (ed.) CRYPTO 2010. LNCS, vol. 6223, pp. 209–236. Springer, Heidelberg (2010)

[BB04]   Boneh, D., Boyen, X.: Short signatures without random oracles. In: Cachin, C., Camenisch, J.L. (eds.) EUROCRYPT 2004. LNCS, vol. 3027, pp. 56–73. Springer, Heidelberg (2004)

[BBC+13a]   Ben Hamouda, F., Blazy, O., Chevalier, C., Pointcheval, D., Vergnaud, D.: Efficient UC-secure authenticated key-exchange for algebraic languages. In: Kurosawa, K., Hanaoka, G. (eds.) PKC 2013. LNCS, vol. 7778, pp. 272–291. Springer, Heidelberg (2013)

[BBC+13b]   Benhamouda, F., Blazy, O., Chevalier, C., Pointcheval, D., Vergnaud, D.: New techniques for SPHFs and efficient one-round PAKE protocols. In: Canetti, R., Garay, J.A. (eds.) CRYPTO 2013, Part I. LNCS, vol. 8042, pp. 449–475. Springer, Heidelberg (2013)

[BCV15]   Blazy, O., Chevalier, C., Vergnaud, D.: Non-interactive zero-knowledge proofs of non-membership. Cryptology ePrint Archive (2015); Full version of the present paper

[BG13]   Bayer, S., Groth, J.: Zero-knowledge argument for polynomial evaluation with application to blacklists. In: Johansson, T., Nguyen, P.Q. (eds.) EUROCRYPT 2013. LNCS, vol. 7881, pp. 646–663. Springer, Heidelberg (2013)

[Bon98]   Boneh, D.: The decision diffie-hellman problem. In: Buhler, J.P. (ed.) ANTS 1998. LNCS, vol. 1423, pp. 48–63. Springer, Heidelberg (1998)

[BS07]   Bellare, M., Shoup, S.: Two-tier signatures, strongly unforgeable signatures, and fiat-shamir without random oracles. In: Okamoto, T., Wang, X. (eds.) PKC 2007. LNCS, vol. 4450, pp. 201–216. Springer, Heidelberg (2007)

[Can01]   Canetti, R.: Universally composable security: A new paradigm for cryptographic protocols. In: 42nd Annual Symposium on Foundations of Computer Science, pp. 136–145. IEEE Computer Society Press (October 2001)

[CCs08]   Camenisch, J.L., Chaabouni, R., Shelat, A.: Efficient protocols for set membership and range proofs. In: Pieprzyk, J. (ed.) ASIACRYPT 2008. LNCS, vol. 5350, pp. 234–252. Springer, Heidelberg (2008)

[CG08]   Camenisch, J., Groß, T.: Efficient attributes for anonymous credentials. In: ACM CCS 2008: 15th Conference on Computer and Communications Security, pp. 345–356. ACM Press (October 2008)

[Cha85]   Chaum, D.: Security without identification: Transaction systems to make big brother obsolete. Commun. ACM 28(10), 1030–1044 (1985)

[CLOS02]   Canetti, R., Lindell, Y., Ostrovsky, R., Sahai, A.: Universally composable two-party and multi-party secure computation. In: 34th Annual ACM Symposium on Theory of Computing, pp. 494–503. ACM Press (May 2002)

[CS02]   Cramer, R., Shoup, V.: Universal hash proofs and a paradigm for adaptive chosen ciphertext secure public-key encryption. In: Knudsen, L.R. (ed.) EUROCRYPT 2002. LNCS, vol. 2332, pp. 45–64. Springer, Heidelberg (2002)

[GL03]   Gennaro, R., Lindell, Y.: A framework for password-based authenticated key exchange. In: Biham, E. (ed.) Advances in Cryptology - EUROCRYPT 2003. LNCS, vol. 2656, pp. 524–543. Springer, Heidelberg (2003)

[GM84]   Goldwasser, S., Micali, S.: Probabilistic encryption. Journal of Computer and System Sciences 28(2), 270–299 (1984)

[GS08]   Groth, J., Sahai, A.: Efficient non-interactive proof systems for bilinear groups. In: Smart, N.P. (ed.) EUROCRYPT 2008. LNCS, vol. 4965, pp. 415–432. Springer, Heidelberg (2008)

[HJ12] Hofheinz, D., Jager, T.: Tightly secure signatures and public-key encryption. In: Safavi-Naini, R., Canetti, R. (eds.) CRYPTO 2012. LNCS, vol. 7417, pp. 590–607. Springer, Heidelberg (2012)

[ILV11] Izabachène, M., Libert, B., Vergnaud, D.: Block-wise P-signatures and non-interactive anonymous credentials with efficient attributes. In: Chen, L. (ed.) IMACC 2011. LNCS, vol. 7089, pp. 431–450. Springer, Heidelberg (2011)

[KZ09] Kiayias, A., Zhou, H.-S.: Zero-knowledge proofs with witness elimination. In: Jarecki, S., Tsudik, G. (eds.) PKC 2009. LNCS, vol. 5443, pp. 124–138. Springer, Heidelberg (2009)

[Pen11] Peng, K.: A general, flexible and efficient proof of inclusion and exclusion. In: Kiayias, A. (ed.) CT-RSA 2011. LNCS, vol. 6558, pp. 33–48. Springer, Heidelberg (2011)

[PP03] Phan, D.H., Pointcheval, D.: Chosen-ciphertext security without redundancy. In: Laih, C.-S. (ed.) ASIACRYPT 2003. LNCS, vol. 2894, pp. 1–18. Springer, Heidelberg (2003)

[Sah99] Sahai, A.: Non-malleable non-interactive zero knowledge and adaptive chosen-ciphertext security. In: 40th Annual Symposium on Foundations of Computer Science, pp. 543–553. IEEE Computer Society Press (October 1999)

Secure and Efficient Implementation of AES Based Cryptosystems

Implementing GCM on ARMv8

Conrado P.L. Gouvêa[1]($\boxtimes$) and Julio López[2]

[1] KRYPTUS Information Security Solutions, Campinas, Brazil
conradoplg@kryptus.com
[2] University of Campinas (Unicamp), Campinas, Brazil
jlopez@ic.unicamp.br

Abstract. The Galois/Counter Mode is an authenticated encryption scheme which is included in protocols such as TLS and IPSec. Its implementation requires multiplication over a binary finite field, an operation which is costly to implement in software. Recent processors have included instructions aimed to speed up binary polynomial multiplication, an operation which can be used to implement binary field multiplication. Some processors of the ARM architecture, which was reported in 2014 to be present in 95 % of smartphones, include such instructions. In particular, recent devices such as the iPhone 5s and Galaxy Note 4 have ARMv8 processors, which provide instructions able to multiply two 64-bit binary polynomials and to encrypt using the AES cipher. In this work we present an optimized and timing-resistant implementation of GCM over AES-128 using these instructions. We have obtained timings of 1.71 cycles per byte for GCM authenticated encryption (9 times faster than the timing on ARMv7), 0.51 cycles per byte for GCM authentication only (11 times faster) and 1.21 cycles per byte for AES-128 encryption (8 times faster).

Keywords: GCM · Authenticated encryption · ARM · Efficient implementation

1 Introduction

Authenticated encryption (AE) schemes provide both confidentiality and authentication in a single algorithm, preventing common errors when combining separate encryption and authentication schemes. The Galois/Counter Mode (GCM) [6] is an authenticated encryption scheme included the TLS and IPSec protocols and in the NIST standard SP 800-38D. It uses an underlying block cipher which is usually AES.

ARM is a RISC processor architecture which ubiquitous in mobile devices due to its relatively low power consumption. The eighth version of the ARM architecture (ARMv8) is the first supporting 64-bit processing and it has become commercially available with the release of the iPhone 5s, a smartphone featuring

---

The second author was partially supported by a research productivity scholarship from CNPq Brazil.

© Springer International Publishing Switzerland 2015
K. Nyberg (ed.): CT-RSA 2015, LNCS 9048, pp. 167–180, 2015.
DOI: 10.1007/978-3-319-16715-2_9

an ARMv8 processor named Apple A7. Other devices with ARMv8 processors include the iPhone 6 and 6 Plus (Apple A8 processor), the iPad Air 2 (Apple A8X processor), the Galaxy Note 4 (Cortex A53/A57 processor) and the Nexus 9 (Nvidia Denver processor).

ARMv8 introduced many changes in the architecture, but one specific addition is a 64-bit multiplier capable of multiplying polynomials over $\mathbb{F}_2$, also known as binary polynomials. The GCM employs multiplications over the finite field $\mathbb{F}_{2^{128}}$ which in turn can be computed with the help of binary multiplication, raising the question of how the ARMv8 performs when running GCM. ARMv8 also supports instructions which are able to carry out AES encryption and decryption.

In this work, we present an efficient and timing-resistant implementation of GCM over AES-128 using the new ARMv8 multiplier and AES instructions along with the ARM vector instruction set (named NEON). We compare it to an optimized and timing-resistant implementation for the ARMv7 architecture based on previous works in the literature. We provide benchmarks of our three implementations (ARMv7, ARMv8 on 32-bit mode and ARMv8 on 64-bit mode) for six different processors: the ARMv7-based Cortex A9 and Cortex A15, along with the ARMv8-based Apple A7, Apple A8X and Cortex A53/A57. Our implementation is available online[1] to allow the reproduction of our results.

Related Work. An efficient implementation of GCM for ARMv7 using the `VMULL.P8` NEON instruction, which computes eight 8×8-bit polynomial multiplications, is described in [1]. When encrypting and authenticating large messages they have achieved 38.6, 41.9 and 31.1 cycles per byte (cpb), for the Cortex A8, A9 and A15 processors respectively, using a non timing-resistant AES implementation. When using GCM for authentication only their results are 13.7, 13.6 and 9.2 cpb respectively.

Polyakov [7], working for the OpenSSL project, has improved on the [1] implementation by unrolling code, improving modular reduction and reordering instructions, obtaining 8.45 cpb on the Cortex A8, 10.2 cpb on the Cortex A9 and 9.33 cpb on the Snapdragon S4 for GCM authentication.

Recent Intel processors have added the `PCLMULQDQ` instruction, which is able to multiply 64-bit binary polynomials, akin to what is now supported by ARMv8. Gueron and Kounavis [4] describe how to implement GCM with this instruction, also taking advantage of the Intel AES-NI instructions which support AES. Gueron reports [3] 1.79, 1.79 and 0.4 cpb for authenticated encryption on the Sandy Bridge, Ivy Bridge and Haswell processors respectively.

Paper Structure. Section 2 describes the ARM architecture, while Section 3 describes the GCM algorithm. Our software implementation is described in Section 4 and results are reported in 5. Concluding remarks are given in Section 6. Appendix A lists the pseudo-assembly code for algorithms described in this work.

---

[1] https://github.com/conradoplg/authenc

2   ARM Architecture

ARM is a well known family of RISC processor architectures introduced in 1985 which now holds 95% of the smartphone segment [8]. Up to version 7, ARM was a 32-bit architecture. Its most recent version, ARMv8, supports both 32-bit and 64-bit processing. The 32-bit ARMv8 architecture is known as AArch32, while the 64-bit is known as AArch64. An ARMv8 processor can support both, allowing the execution of 32-bit and 64-bit applications. ARM processors may also support a single-instruction multiple-data (SIMD) module called the "NEON engine".

Each architecture is implemented by different core designs, and each core design can be implemented by different chips. For example, Cortex A9 and Apple A6 are two core designs following the ARMv7 architecture, while OMAP 4660 and Exynos 4 are chips implementing the same Cortex A9 core design.

ARMv7 and AArch32 feature sixteen 32-bit registers (R0–R15) and sixteen 128-bit NEON registers (Q0–Q15). The NEON registers can also be viewed as pairs of 64-bit registers (D0–D32) such that, for example, D0 is the lower part of Q0 and D1 is its higher part.

AArch64 features thirty two 64-bit registers (X0–X31) and thirty two 128-bit NEON registers (V0–V31). The NEON registers can no longer be viewed as pairs of 64-bit registers, though the lower part of each register can be referenced as D0–D15.

2.1   Binary Polynomial Multiplication Support

When restricted to ARMv7, the instruction VMULL.P8 is critical for the efficient implementation of GCM, as shown in [1]. Its inputs are two 64-bit NEON registers, each interpreted as eight 8-bit binary polynomials, and its output is a single 128-bit NEON register interpreted as eight 16-bit binary polynomials containing the eight results of pairwise binary multiplications, as illustrated in Figure 1. In [1] it is shown how to compute a full 64×64-bit multiplication with eight VMULL.P8 instructions and some additional data processing.

AArch32 provides a new VMULL.P64 instruction. Its inputs are two 64-bit NEON registers, each interpreted as a single 64-bit binary polynomial, and its output is a single 128-bit NEON register containing the result of the binary multiplication of both operands. Therefore, a single instruction can carry out a 64×64-bit multiplication. It is also shown in Figure 1.

AArch64 provides two instructions, PMULL and PMULL2, both of which carry out a single 64×64-bit multiplication. In both cases, the inputs are 128-bit registers; their difference is that in PMULL the lower 64-bit parts of the inputs are used as operands, while in PMULL2 the higher 64-bit parts are used. Both are also shown in Figure 1.

2.2   AES Support

ARMv7 does not have any specific AES support, while ARMv8 supports AES in both AArch32 and AArch64 with the AESE, AESD, AESMC and AESIMC NEON

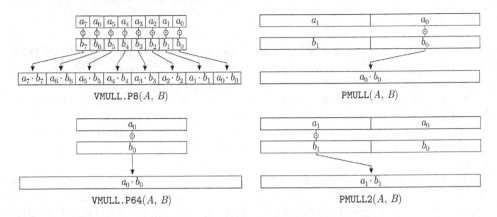

Fig. 1. Binary polynomial multiplication NEON instructions: `VMULL.P8` (ARMv7), `VMULL.P64` (ARMv8 AArch32) and `PMULL/PMULL2` (ARMv8 AArch64)

instructions. `AESE` performs the AddRoundKey, SubBytes and ShiftRows AES steps, while `AESMC` performs MixColumns. The last AddRoundKey step can be carried out with a regular NEON XOR instruction (`VEOR` in AArch32, `EOR` in AArch64).

Instruction support is summarized in Table 1.

Table 1. Instruction support across devices. Assumes NEON support (not every chip supports it).

	ARMv7	ARMv8	
		AArch32	AArch64
VMULL.P8	Yes	Yes	No
VMULL.P64	No	Yes	No
PMULL/PMULL2	No	No	Yes
AES instructions	No	Yes	Yes

3   GCM

The Galois/Counter Mode (GCM) [6] is an authenticated encryption scheme which is built upon a block cipher, usually AES. Its inputs are: a key; a nonce; the plaintext which will be encrypted and authenticated; and additional data which will only be authenticated. It outputs the ciphertext and an 128-bit authentication tag.

The GCM encryption is based on the underlying block cipher in CTR mode, while its authentication is based on a function named GHASH, described in Algorithm 1. The GHASH inputs are: the ciphertext; an initial 128-bit value; and a 128-bit constant H derived from the key. It outputs a 128-bit value used to compute the authentication tag. The timing consuming operation in GHASH is the multiplication over the binary field $\mathbb{F}_{2^{128}}$; the fact that one of the operands is always the same (H) can lead into some optimizations.

Algorithm 1. GHASH function

Input: Input X with n 128-bit blocks, 128-bit initial value Y, 128-bit constant H
Output: Updated Y
  1: **function** GHASH(X, Y, H)
  2:      $X_1, \ldots, X_n \leftarrow X$
  3:      **for** $i \leftarrow 1$ **to** n **do**
  4:          $Y \leftarrow (X_i \oplus Y) \otimes H$ $\triangleright$ Multiplication in $\mathbb{F}_{2^{128}}$
  5:      **return** Y

An often confusing aspect of GCM is its bit order. When interpreting a byte vector as a binary field element, two choices must be made: which byte is the least significant in the vector, and which bit is the least significant in each byte. GCM chooses a little-endian approach for the byte order, but a big-endian approach for the bit order. For example, the polynomial $a(z) = 1$ is represented as the 16-byte string 80 00 00 00 00 00 00 00 00 00 00 00 00 00 00 00. However, this means that is not possible to speed up the computation using anything larger than bytes (i.e. words), since left and right shifts will not respect the byte/bit order of GCM. This can be solved by either of two approaches: the first is to reverse the bits inside each byte in the GHASH input before carrying out any computations, and reversing them again when computing the authentication tag. The second approach, proposed by [4], is to reverse the bytes in the vector instead. This leads to a reversed binary field element, which can be correctly multiplied by reversing the modular reduction algorithm in the binary field multiplication. The advantage of the second approach is that in most cases it is simpler to reverse the bytes in a vector than reversing the bits in each byte.

4   Software Implementation

Efficiency is important, but security is even more. A secure implementation offers some degree of protection against side channel attacks. Our aim is to protect against timing attacks by avoiding loops, branches and table lookups which are dependent on secret data.

Given an irreducible m-degree polynomial $f(z)$, the binary field $\mathbb{F}_{2^{128}}$ can be defined as the set of polynomials with degree at most $m - 1$ over $\mathbb{F}_2$. In software, each field element can be stored in a vector of W-bit words, where each word contains W coefficients of the polynomial. Field addition is simply the xor of the operands. Field multiplication consists of the polynomial multiplication of the operands, followed by a reduction modulo an irreducible polynomial. GCM uses multiplication in the binary field $\mathbb{F}_{2^{128}}$ with the irreducible polynomial $f(z) = z^{128} + z^7 + z^2 + z + 1$.

4.1   Binary Polynomial Multiplication

The polynomial multiplication used to be carried out with the help of precomputed tables, shifts and xors [5]. However, this has changed with the advent of instructions supporting binary polynomial multiplication. In ARMv7, we simply followed the approach described in [1], which builds a 64×64-bit multiplier using eight invocations of the VMULL.P8 instruction. This multiplier is then used three times (with the Karatsuba algorithm) to build the full 128×128-bit multiplier.

In AArch32, the whole 64×64-bit multiplication is available in the VMULL.P64 instruction. Again, we use Karatsuba to build the full 128×128-bit multiplier, which is listed in Algorithm 2, using three VMULL.P64 calls. In AArch64, however, our approach is a little different. While the PMULL and PMULL2 instructions offer the same operation of VMULL.P64, in AArch64 is no longer possible to reference the upper part of a 128-bit register as a separate 64-bit register. In order to get the upper part we use the EXT instruction with a register zeroed beforehand. To reduce the use of EXT we abandon Karatsuba and call PMULL(2) four times. Our AArch64 multiplier is listed in Algorithm 3.

Algorithm 2. 128×128-bit binary polynomial multiplier for ARMv8 AArch32 (VMULL.P64)

Input: 128-bit registers aq (ah|al) (first operand), bq (bh|bl) (second operand).
Output: 128-bit registers r0q (r0h|r0l) (lower 128 bits of the result), r1q (r1h|r1l) (higher 128 bits of the result).
　　　Uses temporary 128-bit register tq (th|tl).
1: vmull.p64 r0q, al, bl
2: vmull.p64 r1q, ah, bh
3: veor th, bl, bh
4: veor tl, al, ah
5: vmull.p64 tq, th, tl
6: veor tq, r0q
7: veor tq, r1q
8: veor r0h, tl
9: veor r1l, th

Algorithm 3. 128×128-bit binary polynomial multiplier for ARMv8 AArch64 (PMULL)

Input: 128-bit registers a (first operand), b (second operand), z (zeroed register).
Output: 128-bit registers r0 (lower 128 bits of the result), r1 (higher 128 bits of the result).
　　　Uses temporary 128-bit registers t0, t1.
1: pmull r0.1q, a.1d, b.1d
2: pmull2 r1.1q, a.2d, b.2d
3: ext.16b t0, b, b, #8
4: pmull t1.1q, a.1d, t0.1d
5: pmull2 t0.1q, a.2d, t0.2d
6: eor.16b t0, t0, t1
7: ext.16b t1, z, t0, #8
8: eor.16b r0, r0, t1
9: ext.16b t1, t0, z, #8
10: eor.16b r1, r1, t1

Algorithm 4. 256-bit to 128-bit GCM reflected polynomial reduction for ARMv8 AArch32 using VMULL.P64

Input: 128-bit registers r0q (r0h|r0l) (lower 128 bits of the operand), r1q (r1h|r1l) (higher 128 bits of the operand), 64-bit register pd (holding constant 0xc200000000000000)
Output: 128-bit register aq (ah|al).
   Uses temporary 128-bit register t0 (t0h|t0l). Clobbers inputs.
 1: vmull.p64 t0q, r0l, pd
 2: veor r0h, t0l
 3: veor r1l, t0h
 4: vmull.p64 t0q, r0h, pd
 5: veor r1q, t0q
 6: veor aq, r0q, r1q

4.2   GCM Reflection

In ARMv7 there is no straightforward procedure to reflect the bits of each byte in a byte vector using NEON instructions. For this reason, in order to avoid the costly lookup tables required for the reflection, we used the reflection trick described in [4] which requires inverting the bytes of 16-byte vectors. This is carried out in NEON using the VREV64.8 instruction, which can reverse the bytes inside a pair of 64-bit registers. These registers can then be swapped using the VSWP instruction to finish the procedure. In ARMv8 AArch32 the same approach is used. ARMv8 AArch64, however, supports the RBIT instruction which reverses the bits of each byte in a byte vector (including 16-byte vectors). This is exactly what is required by GCM and in this case the reflection trick is no longer necessary.

4.3   Modular Reduction

Modular reduction is slightly more complex. Write the GCM modulus as $f(z) = z^{128} + r(z)$, where $r(z) = z^7 + z^2 + z + 1$. The well known approach is to consider that $z^{128} \equiv r(z) \pmod{z^{128} + r(z)}$, allowing us to write the 256-bit operand to be reduced as $a(z) = h(z)z^{128} + \ell(z) \equiv h(z)r(z) + \ell(z)$. That is, we simply multiply the higher part of the operand by $r(z)$ and add it to $\ell(z)$. If the result is still larger than 128 bits, we reduce again.

   The old approach to compute the multiplication by $r(z)$ is to use shift and xors. However, it is now possible to simply compute it with the binary multiplication instructions, using the constant $r(z)$ as one of the operands; this is the approach we used on both ARMv8 AArch32 and AArch64 with VMULL.P64 and PMULL. Nevertheless, on ARMv7, the shift and xors approach is slightly faster due to the non straightforward use of the VMULL.P8 multiplier required to carry out the reduction. Our reduction algorithms are listed in Algorithms 4 and 5. The ARMv7 reduction is from [7] and is listed for reference in Algorithm 8 in the Appendix.

Algorithm 5. 256-bit to 128-bit GCM polynomial reduction for ARMv8 AArch64 using PMULL

Input: 128-bit registers r0 (lower 128 bits of the operand), r1 (higher 128 bits of the operand), p (holding constant 0x00000000000000870000000000000087), z (zeroed)
Output: 128-bit register a.
    Uses temporary 128-bit registers t0, t1. Clobbers inputs.
1: pmull2 t0.1q, r1.2d, p.2d
2: ext t1.16b, t0.16b, z.16b, #8
3: eor.16b r1, r1, t1
4: ext t1.16b, z.16b, t0.16b, #8
5: eor.16b r0, r0, t1
6: pmull t0.1q, a1.1d, p.1d
7: eor.16b a, r0, t0

Lazy reduction. On ARMv8 the polynomial multiplication is very fast due to the instruction support for 64-bit polynomial multiplication. For this reason, the modular reduction becomes comparatively more expensive and starts to dominate the running time of the field multiplication. Thus we have employed the technique known as "lazy reduction", described in the GCM context in [4]. It requires the unrolling of the GHASH function, as follows. GHASH can be written recursively as $Y_i = (X_i \oplus Y_{i-1}) \otimes H$ which, by decoupling the field multiplication, becomes $Y_i = (X_i \oplus Y_{i-1}) \cdot H \bmod f(z)$. This can be unrolled, for example, as $Y_i = [(X_i \cdot H) \oplus (X_{i-1} \cdot H^2) \oplus (X_{i-2} \cdot H^3) \oplus (X_{i-3} \cdot H^4)] \bmod f(z)$ which requires a single modular reduction for every four polynomial multiplications. This requires 256-bit polynomial addition, which is simple, and the precomputation of powers of the H value, which can be precomputed in advance since H only depends on the key. In our implementation we use a eightfold unrolling of GHASH; the powers of H are entirely kept in NEON registers during the GHASH computation.

4.4   AES

ARMv7 does not have any AES instructions. For this reason, we have used a bitsliced, timing-resistant NEON-based implementation from Bernstein and Schwabe available in SUPERCOP[2].

ARMv8 does support AES with special instructions, as mentioned. The 128-bit key AES with its 10 rounds requires ten AESE instructions, nine AESMC and one xor, totaling twenty instructions. Since these instructions operate on the same 128-bit value they present a great deal of dependency between then, slowing their execution. For this reason, we interleave two AES block encryptions in order to reduce these dependencies (this is possible since GCM uses the counter mode for encryption). For efficiency, we keep the entire AES expanded key in NEON registers throughout the encryption. Algorithm 9 in the Appendix illustrates the use of AES instructions in the encryption of a single block in AES-CTR.

---

[2] http://bench.cr.yp.to/supercop.html

Contrasting with the Intel AES instructions, ARMv8 does not offer instructions for computing the AES key schedule, which therefore must be implemented. The key schedule requires S-box lookups, which are usually implemented with precomputed tables. However, this approach is subject to timing attacks since the indexes are secret. (This may seem to be a non-issue since the key schedule is usually run only once for each. key, which makes side channel attacks very difficult. However, we believe it is best to not rely on assumptions on the cipher usage — for example, a simplified API could run the key schedule for every encryption.) In order to offer timing resistance and good performance, we have implemented the key schedule with the help of a function which is able to lookup four bytes in the S-box. It is possible to write this function based on AES instructions, as described for the Intel processor in [2], but we need to adapt the code to the ARM/NEON architecture. We implemented it with the AESE instruction by observing that, when used with a zeroed round key, the instruction simply lookups sixteen bytes in the S-box and shuffles them with MixColumns. By unshuffling the bytes it is possible to build our lookup function with AESE in a timing-resistant manner. While it could be possible to lookup sixteen bytes with a single instruction, we use only four, since the AES key schedule works in groups of four bytes.

Our four-byte S-box lookup algorithm works by filling a 16-byte register with the constant 0x52 in each byte, then writing the four bytes to look up in the lower four bytes. AESE is called with a zero round key, leading to a shuffled 16-byte substituted result. Each 0x52 in the input is substituted by zeroes with AESE, and the four substituted bytes we are interested in are now in different columns due to MixColumns. We now simply add the columns (recall that AES works in column-major order) in order to get a four-byte result. Our code is listed in Algorithms 6 and 7.

Algorithm 6. Four-byte AES S-box lookup for ARMv8 AArch32 using AESE

Input: 32-bit register r0 (four bytes to lookup in the S-box).
Output: 32-bit register r0 (values after lookup).
    Uses temporary 128-bit registers q0 (d1|d0, s3|s2|s1|s0), q1.
 1: vmov.i8 q0, #0x52
 2: vmov.i8 q1, #0
 3: vmov s0, r0
 4: aese q0, q1
 5: veor d0, d1
 6: vpadd.i32 d0, d0, d1
 7: vmov r0, s0

4.5   GCM

With the binary multiplier and the AES encryption, the rest of the GCM implementation is straightforward. There are two approaches: encryption can be interleaved with GHASH, or the encryption is completely carried out and

---

Algorithm 7. Four-byte AES S-box lookup for ARMv8 AArch64 using AESE

Input: 32-bit register w0 (four bytes to lookup in the S-box).
Output: 32-bit register w0 (values after lookup).
    Uses temporary 128-bit registers v0, v1.

```
1: movi.16b v0, #0x52
2: movi.16b v1, #0
3: mov v0.S[0], w0
4: aese.16b v0, v1
5: addv s0, v0.4s
6: mov w0, v0.S[0]
```

---

then GHASH is executed. We have followed the latter approach, since it allows to keep the all AES round keys in NEON registers throughout the encryption. The former approach has the advantage that each block of ciphertext is written once and is never read again by GCM (since GHASH can read it directly from a NEON register after the encryption); we have not tried this approach but we believe it would be slower. The first approach does imply that is not possible to use a streaming API that encrypts or decrypts an arbitrary amount of data, since the entire message must be encrypted and the ciphertext must be read from the start in order to compute its GHASH. However, we think this is not a problem since streaming APIs can be dangerous: they release plaintext to the user before authenticating it, burdening the user with the task of destroying any plaintext stored if it is found to be not authentic. It is still possible to build a streaming API by dividing the plaintext in packets and encrypting and authenticating them separately.

5   Performance Results

Timings were obtained by measuring the time taken by the encryption of a 10,000-byte message inside a loop with 256 iterations. We did not use the popular SUPERCOP benchmark tool since it does not support the iOS and Android operating systems which were required for our experiments. The performance was measured on a PandaBoard board with a 1 GHz ARMv7 Cortex-A9 processor, an Arndale board with a 1.7 GHz ARMv7 Cortex-A15 processor, a Galaxy Note 4 SM-N910C with a hybrid 8-core processor (four 1.3 GHz ARMv8 Cortex-A53 cores and four 1.9 GHz ARMv8 Cortex-A57 cores — all of them supporting only the AArch32 mode), an iPhone 5s with a 1.3 GHz ARMv8 Apple A7 processor and an iPad Air 2 with a 1.5 GHz ARMv8 Apple A8X processor. On the Note 4 and Cortex boards time was measured with the clock_gettime function, while on the iPhone and iPad we used the mach_absolute_time function. Timings were converted to cycles assuming the clocks listed. On the Note 4 we forced our program to run on a specific core using the sched_setaffinity function. Our results are reported in Table 2. Algorithm timings do not include the time required for key setup, which is listed separately.

Table 2. Results in cycles per byte (except key setup, given in cycles)

Cortex	A9 ARMv7 .P8[a]	A15 ARMv7 .P8[a]	A53 ARMv8 AArch32 .P8[a]	.P64[b]	A57 ARMv8 AArch32 .P8[a]	.P64[b]
AES-128-CTR	22.0	15.6	22.3	1.88	15.6	1.84
AES-128 setup	3358	2437	3244	690	2386	647
GCM auth only	10.7	8.3	9.6	1.21	8.1	0.95
GCM encryption	32.8	23.9	32.5	3.08	23.4	2.78
GCM setup	6450	4651	6337	1423	4582	1216

Apple	A7 ARMv8 AArch32 .P8[a]	.P64[b]	AArch64 PMULL[c]	A8X ARMv8 AArch32 .P8[a]	.P64[b]	AArch64 PMULL[c]
AES-128-CTR	9.8	1.21	1.21	9.8	1.19	1.19
AES-128 setup	1420	901	739	1419	875	749
GCM auth only	6.0	0.51	0.50	5.9	0.48	0.51
GCM encryption	15.9	1.71	1.71	15.7	1.68	1.70
GCM setup	2771	1298	1075	2706	1323	1062

[a] Bitsliced software AES; VMULL.P8-based binary multiplier
[b] AES instructions; VMULL.P64-based binary multiplier
[c] AES instructions; PMULL-based binary multiplier

First, note that simply changing from the Cortex A15 to the Apple A7 processor, using the same implementation, leads to a 33% speedup in GCM. This can be attributed in advancements in the processor design, with a larger number of instructions being issued on the same cycle. However, changing from the Cortex A15 to the Cortex A57 leads to small timing differences, which probably means that the design of these processors are mostly the same, apart from the ARMv8 AArch32 support of the latter. We also found no significant difference between the results for the Apple A7 and A8X processors. The Cortex A53 is slower than the A57 by up to 10% (.P64) and 40% (.P8) as expected, since it's supposed to be a simpler core which consumes less energy.

Comparing the VMULL.P8 and VMULL.P64 implementations on the Apple A7, it can be seen that GCM authentication is 11.76 times faster using the new VMULL.P64 instruction; AES-128-CTR encryption is 8.1 faster using the new AES instructions. Combined, these results lead to GCM authenticated encryption being 9.3 faster. The A8X processor shows similar results. On the Cortex A53 these speedups are 7.9, 11.9 and 10.6 while on the A57 they are 8.5, 8.5 and 8.4 respectively.

The VMULL.P64 and PMULL implementations offer practically the same performance. This is not surprising since the implementations do not differ greatly.

The 64-bit architecture does not make much difference since our code is mostly NEON and practically does not uses regular ARM registers for data processing.

Finally, when comparing the Apple A7 and Cortex A57 processors, we observe that the first is 46% faster for VMULL.P64 GCM authentication and 34% faster for AES-128-CTR with AES instructions, leading to a 38% faster GCM authenticated encryption.

6   Conclusions and Future Work

The GCM mode is known for the hardness in implementing it in an efficient and secure manner. However, the ARMv8 binary polynomial multiplication and AES instructions can make GCM up to 10 times faster compared to an efficient timing-resistant ARMv7 implementation, making the scheme an ideal choice for protecting communications in smartphones. These instructions enable a natural resistance against timing attacks, since no branches nor table lookups are required.

Finally, our techniques for binary multiplication in $\mathbb{F}_{2^{128}}$ can be extended for larger binary fields which can be used for a fast and secure software implementation of binary elliptic curves.

A   Additional Algorithms

Algorithm 8. 256-bit to 128-bit GCM reflected polynomial reduction for ARMv7 from [7]

Input: 128-bit registers r0q (r0h|r0l) (lower 128 bits of the operand), r1q (r1h|r1l) (higher 128 bits of the operand).

Output: 128-bit register aq (ah|al).

Uses temporary 128-bit registers t0 (t0h|t0l), t1 (t1h|t1l). Clobbers inputs.

```
 1: vshl.i64 t0q, r0q, #57
 2: vshl.i64 t1q, r0q, #62
 3: veor t1q, t1q, t0q
 4: vshl.i64 t0q, r0q, #63
 5: veor t1q, t1q, t0q
 6: veor r0h, r0h, t1l
 7: veor r1l, r1l, t1h
 8: vshr.u64 t1q, r0q, #1
 9: veor r1q, r1q, r0q
10: veor r0q, r0q, t1q
11: vshr.u64 t1q, t1q, #6
12: vshr.u64 r0q, r0q, #1
13: veor r0q, r0q, r1q
14: veor aq, r0q, t1q
```

Algorithm 9. AES-128-CTR encryption of a single block with AES instructions

Input: 128-bit registers k0–k10 (AES round keys), `ctr` (counter); regular ARM registers in (pointer to 128-bit input block), out (pointer to 128-bit output block)

Output: Encrypted counter xored with input written to memory pointed by `out`.
Uses temporary 128-bit registers t0, t1.

```
 1: mov.16b t0, ctr
 2: aese.16b t0, k00
 3: aesmc.16b t0, t0
 4: aese.16b t0, k01
 5: aesmc.16b t0, t0
 6: aese.16b t0, k02
 7: aesmc.16b t0, t0
 8: aese.16b t0, k03
 9: aesmc.16b t0, t0
10: aese.16b t0, k04
11: aesmc.16b t0, t0
12: aese.16b t0, k05
13: aesmc.16b t0, t0
14: aese.16b t0, k06
15: aesmc.16b t0, t0
16: aese.16b t0, k07
17: aesmc.16b t0, t0
18: aese.16b t0, k08
19: aesmc.16b t0, t0
20: aese.16b t0, k09
21: eor.16b t0, t0, k10
22: ld1.16b {t1}, [in], #16
23: eor.16b t1, t1, t0
24: st1.16b {t1}, [out], #16
```

References

1. Câmara, D., Gouvêa, C.P.L., López, J., Dahab, R.: Fast software polynomial multiplication on ARM processors using the NEON engine. In: Cuzzocrea, A., Kittl, C., Simos, D.E., Weippl, E., Xu, L. (eds.) CD-ARES 2013 Workshops. LNCS, vol. 8128, pp. 137–154. Springer, Heidelberg (2013)

2. Gueron, S.: Intel's new AES instructions for enhanced performance and security. In: Dunkelman, O. (ed.) FSE 2009. LNCS, vol. 5665, pp. 51–66. Springer, Heidelberg (2009)

3. Gueron, S.: AES-GCM software performance on the current high end CPUs as a performance baseline for CAESAR competition. Presented in DIAC 2013: Directions in Authenticated Ciphers (2014). http://2013.diac.cr.yp.to/slides/gueron.pdf

4. Gueron, S., Kounavis, M.E.: Intel carry-less multiplication instruction and its usage for computing the GCM mode. White Paper (2010)

5. López, J., Dahab, R.: High-speed software multiplication in $\mathbb{F}_{2^m}$. In: Roy, B., Okamoto, E. (eds.) INDOCRYPT 2000. LNCS, vol. 1977, pp. 203–212. Springer, Heidelberg (2000)

6. McGrew, D.A., Viega, J.: The security and performance of the galois/counter mode (GCM) of operation. In: Canteaut, A., Viswanathan, K. (eds.) INDOCRYPT 2004. LNCS, vol. 3348, pp. 343–355. Springer, Heidelberg (2004)
7. Polyakov, A.: The OpenSSL project. OpenSSL Git repository (2014). http://git.openssl.org/gitweb/?p=openssl.git;a=commitdiff; h=f8cee9d08181f9e966ef01d3b69ba78b6cb7c8a8
8. Ranger, S.: Internet of things and wearables drive growth for ARM. ZDNet, April 2014. http://www.zdnet.com/internet-of-things-and-wearables-drive-growth-for-arm-7000028684/

Higher-Order Masking in Practice: A Vector Implementation of Masked AES for ARM NEON

Junwei Wang[1,2], Praveen Kumar Vadnala[2], Johann Großschädl[2],
and Qiuliang Xu[1]([✉])

[1] School of Computer Science and Technology, Shandong University, Jinan 250100,
Shandong, China
i.junwei.wang@gmail.com, xql@sdu.edu.cn
[2] Laboratory of Algorithmics, Cryptology and Security, University of Luxembourg,
Walferdange, Luxembourg
{praveen.vadnala,johann.groszschaed}@uni.lu

Abstract. Real-world software implementations of cryptographic algorithms need to be able to resist various kinds of side-channel attacks, in particular Differential Power Analysis (DPA). Masking is a widely-used countermeasure to protect block ciphers like the Advanced Encryption Standard (AES) against DPA attacks. The basic principle is to split all sensitive intermediate variables manipulated by the algorithm into two shares and process these shares separately. However, this approach still succumbs to higher-order DPA attacks, which exploit the joint leakage of a number of intermediate variables. A viable solution is to generalize masking such that at least $d + 1$ shares are used to protect against d-th order attacks. Unfortunately, all current higher-order masking schemes introduce a significant computational overhead compared to unmasked implementations. To facilitate the deployment of higher-order masking for the AES in practice, we developed a vector implementation of Coron et al's masking scheme (FSE 2012) for ARM NEON processors. After a comprehensive complexity analysis, we found that Coron et al's scheme with n shares for each sensitive variable needs $\mathcal{O}(n^2)$ multiplications in the field $\mathrm{GF}(2^8)$ and $\mathcal{O}(n^2)$ random-number generations. Both of these performance-critical operations are executed with only 15 instructions in our software, which is possible thanks to the rich functionality of the NEON instruction set. Our experimental results demonstrate that the performance penalty caused by the integration of higher-order masking is significantly lower than in generally assumed and reported in previous papers. For example, our second-order DPA-protected AES (with three shares for each sensitive variable) is merely eight times slower than an unmasked baseline implementation that resists cache-timing attacks.

1 Introduction

Differential Power Analysis (DPA) [4] is a cryptanalytic technique that exploits variations in the power consumption of a cryptographic device (e.g. smart card) to obtain the secret key. DPA attacks first appeared in the literature in the late

© Springer International Publishing Switzerland 2015
K. Nyberg (ed.): CT-RSA 2015, LNCS 9048, pp. 181–198, 2015.
DOI: 10.1007/978-3-319-16715-2_10

1990s [17] and have since then received much attention from the cryptographic research community. Basically, a DPA attack consists of two phases, namely an acquisition phase and an analysis phase. In the former phase, the attacker has to acquire a set of power consumption traces of the target device while it executes a cryptographic algorithm with different inputs (i.e. different plaintexts or ciphertexts). Then, in the analysis phase, he applies sophisticated statistical techniques to determine the correlation between the measured power traces and certain intermediate values of the cryptographic algorithm based on the known inputs and a predicted (i.e. guessed) part of the secret key. More precisely, the attacker uses the computed intermediate values to partition the power traces into several categories and determines the correlation (e.g. the difference in the averages of the categories) between the measured traces and the intermediate values. Normally, the highest correlation is obtained with a partitioning where the guessed key is the actual secret key processed by the device [18].

Masking is a widely-used method to protect symmetric ciphers, such as the AES [9], against DPA attacks by randomizing all sensitive intermediate values [18]. The basic idea is to split the intermediate values into multiple shares, and then process all operations on each share separately throughout the execution of the algorithm. Of course, at the end of the computation, the shares have to be recombined to get the correct result. For example, a sensitive value x can be split into two shares x_1 and x_2, whereby x_1 is a newly generated random value (the so-called mask) and x_2 is computed as $x_2 = x \otimes x_1$ for a certain operation $\otimes$ that depends on the algorithm. Based on the nature of this operation, we can distinguish between arithmetic masking, Boolean masking, and multiplicative masking[1]. In any case, the power consumption does not depend on the sensitive value any more, i.e. information leaked from the mask x_1 alone or the masked value x_2 alone is not sufficient to reveal x.

DPA attacks involving only a single independent variable are referred to as first-order DPA attacks. In contrast, higher-order DPA attacks exploit the joint leakage of several variables manipulated by a (masked) implementation of an algorithm. Here, the term *order* denotes the number of intermediate variables exposed to the attacker. An implementation made first-order DPA resistant via masking is still vulnerable to second-order DPA attacks [6,7,19,23], which aim to exploit the combined leakage from two intermediate variables at the expense of increased effort (i.e. more power samples are required and the analysis phase is computationally more costly). For example, if two points in the power traces are correlated to intermediate values x and y, where the secret $z = x \oplus y$, then the combination of leakage information of these two intermediate values can be used to predict the secret z. In general, an n-th order masking scheme can be defeated by an $(n + 1)$-th order DPA attack [5].

No single countermeasure is able to fully protect a cryptosystem against all higher-order DPA attacks. However, the effort to successfully mount a higher-order DPA attack grows exponentially as the order increases. Thus, taking into account the attacker's ability, it suffices in practice when an implementation is

---

[1] In this paper, we focus on the AES and, hence, $\otimes$ is in our case $\oplus$ (logical XOR).

made resistant against DPA attacks up to a certain order [18]. In general, in a
d-th order masking scheme, every sensitive value is split into $n = d + 1$ shares
such that $x = x_1 \oplus \cdots \oplus x_n$, whereby $x_1, \cdots, x_{n-1}$ are independently generated
random masks, and $x_n = x \oplus x_1 \oplus \cdots \oplus x_{n-1}$ is the masked data. When a d-th
order masking scheme is executed, each share x_i gets processed separately so as
to ensure that the combination of any d shares is independent of the sensitive
variable, i.e. the combination of d leakages does not leak information about the
sensitive variable. As a consequence, a d-th order DPA attack exploiting up to
d joint leakages can not reveal the secret key anymore.

The AES consists of several rounds, each performing linear transformations
and one non-linear transformation called SubBytes [9]. The linear parts can be
trivially masked by applying the transformations on each share separately since
$f(x) = f(x_1) \oplus \cdots \oplus f(x_n)$, where $f(\cdot)$ denotes a linear function and x is given
as $x = x_1 \oplus \cdots \oplus x_n$. However, the actual difficulty is the secure masking of the
SubBytes transformation, especially the secure masking of the S-box. At CHES
2010, Rivain and Prouff [20] introduced a generic masking scheme for the AES
to make it secure against d-th order attacks. Very recently, Coron et al showed
that said scheme is not resistant to d-th order attacks as claimed and provided
a fix [8]. A comprehensive treatment of various higher-order masking schemes
proposed in the literature can be found in [12,13]. The main problem with all
current proposals is the massive computational overhead they introduce; in the
most extreme case, the performance penalty exceeds three orders of magnitude
[7]. As a consequence, it is widely presumed that higher-order masking of the
AES is not suitable for adoption in real-world applications.

In this paper we show that high-order masking for the AES, if implemented
efficiently, incurs significantly less overhead than widely assumed and reported
in related literature. To this end, we developed a masked AES implementation
for ARM NEON processors (e.g. Cortex-A8) [1] that combines algorithmic improvements with a vector-parallel execution of the underlying operations. The
algorithmic improvements we describe in the following sections include the use
of a composite-field representation along with Barrett reduction for performing
multiplications in the binary finite field $GF(2^8)$ [10]. We first present a baseline
AES implementation that is resistant against so-called cache attacks (but does
not include DPA countermeasures) using NEON instructions. When compared
with Brian Gladman's lookup-table-based implementation for 32-bit processors
[11], it turns out that our baseline software is roughly 50% slower, but able to
withstand any form of cache attack. Therefore, it is suited to serve as reference
for performance comparisons. We then present the first vector implementation
of a high-order DPA countermeasure for the AES using the NEON instruction
set. Our masked AES is based on Coron et al's corrected version of the Rivain-
Prouff countermeasure. After a thorough complexity analysis, we found that the
most performance-critical parts are the field multiplications and pseudorandom
number generations. Thanks to the rich functionality of the NEON instruction
set, these two operations can be executed with only 15 instructions.

Algorithm 1. SecMult: Masked multiplication in $GF(2^8)$ with n shares [7]

Input: Shares x_i satisfying $x_1 \oplus \cdots \oplus x_n = x$, shares y_i satisfying $y_1 \oplus \cdots \oplus y_n = y$

Output: Shares z_i satisfying $z_1 \oplus \cdots \oplus z_n = xy$

1: **for** $i = 1$ to n **do**
2:     $z_i \leftarrow x_i \cdot y_i$
3: **end for**
4: **for** $i = 1$ to n **do**
5:     **for** $j = i + 1$ to n **do**
6:         $r_0 \leftarrow GF(2^8)$
7:         $r_1 \leftarrow (r_0 \oplus x_i \cdot y_j) \oplus x_j \cdot y_i$
8:         $z_i \leftarrow z_i \oplus r_0$
9:         $z_j \leftarrow z_j \oplus r_1$
10:     **end for**
11: **end for**
12: **return** $z_1, \ldots, z_n$

---

2   Previous Work

This section covers existing algorithms for secure higher-order masking of the AES. We first review the higher-order masking scheme proposed by Rivain and Prouff [20]. Then, we describe the flaw in the original algorithm and its fix due to Coron et al [8].

2.1   Provably Secure Higher-Order Masking of the AES

The first technique to protect the AES against higher-order DPA attacks was presented by Rivain and Prouff at CHES 2010 [20]. Their approach is based on the higher-order masking scheme proposed by Ishai, Sahai and Wagner (ISW) to protect any circuit against a d-limited adversary who can tap any d wires in the circuit at a given time [15]. The major idea behind the ISW framework is to represent a circuit performing a cryptographic operation as a combination of Boolean AND and NOT gates (which is possible since NAND is a universal gate), and to protect these gates independently. Securing a NOT gate is trivial because $NOT(x_1 \oplus x_2 \oplus \cdots \oplus x_n) = NOT(x_1) \oplus x_2 \oplus \cdots \oplus x_n$. To protect an AND gate, they introduced an elegant technique that requires each of the two input bits to be split up into $2d + 1$ shares. Rivain and Prouff showed that this method can be extended from AND, i.e. multiplication in $GF(2)$, to multiplication in any field of characteristic 2, including $GF(2^8)$. We recall their solution in Algorithm 1. They also reduced the number of shares for a d-th order secure masking scheme from $2d + 1$ (as required for the ISW method) to $d + 1$.

As mentioned before, masking a linear function $f(\cdot)$ is easy because

$$f(x) = f(x_1) \oplus f(x_2) \oplus \cdots \oplus f(x_n) \tag{1}$$

The only non-linear operation of the AES S-box is inversion in the finite field $GF(2^8)$. Since the inverse x^{-1} of $x \in GF(2^8)$ equals x^{254}, the authors perform the secure computation of inversion via secure exponentiation, which comprises several secure multiplications and squarings in $GF(2^8)$. To securely mask the field multiplications, the authors extended the technique for masking a logical AND (i.e. a multiplication in $GF(2)$) proposed in [15], which can be applied to securely mask a multiplication in any field of characteristic 2. Furthermore, to protect the power function $x \rightarrow x^{254}$, Rivain and Prouff proposed an algorithm that requires only four field multiplications (see Appendix A). Later, Kim et al improved the efficiency of this algorithm via composite-field arithmetic [16].

2.2   Higher-Order Side-Channel Security and Mask Refreshing

Algorithm 5 (included in Appendix A) executes a RefreshMasks function before SecMult to ensure that the inputs are independent[2]. RefreshMasks modifies the shares using freshly-generated (pseudo-)random numbers. When we denote the new random numbers with $(r_i)_{1 \le i \le d}$, then a call of RefreshMasks$((x_i)_{1 \le i \le d+1})$ performs the following operation:

$$x_0 = x_0 \oplus \bigoplus_{1 \le i \le d} r_i \tag{2}$$

$$(x_i)_{1 \le i \le d} = x_i \oplus r_i \tag{3}$$

Even though the functions RefreshMasks and SecMult are "individually" secure against d-th order attacks, Coron et al discovered in [8] that a flaw arises when they are used together for computations of the form $x \cdot g(x)$, where $g(\cdot)$ is a linear function. As demonstrated in [8], a joint leakage of $\lfloor n/2 \rfloor + 1$ intermediate variables can be exploited due to the involvement of the RefreshMasks function in certain cases. Therefore, the claim that the Rivain-Prouff masking scheme is secure against d-th order attacks (where $d = n - 1$) is not valid anymore. To eventually eliminate this flaw, Coron et al presented a new d-th order masked multiplication of the form $x \cdot g(x)$. In detail, suppose

$$f(x, y) = (x \cdot g(y)) \oplus (g(x) \cdot y) \tag{4}$$

where $x, y \in GF(2^8)$ and $g(\cdot)$ is a linear function over $GF(2^8)$. Then,

$$f(x, y) = f(x, r) \oplus f(x, y \oplus r) \tag{5}$$

due to the bilinearity of $f(\cdot)$ [8]. Hence, the flaw is fixed by recalculating r_1 in line 7 of Algorithm 1 as follows

$$r_1 = r_0 \oplus f(x_i, x_j)$$
$$= (r_0 \oplus f(x_i, r_0')) \oplus f(x_i, x_j \oplus r_0') \tag{6}$$

---

[2] As explained in the full version of [20], SecMult is only secure when the inputs are d-independent of each other. Namely, every $2d$-tuple containing d elements from the input x (i.e. $(x_i)_{1 \le i \le d+1}$) and d elements from the input y (i.e. $(y_i)_{1 \le i \le d+1}$) should be uniformly distributed and independent of x and y.

Algorithm 2. SecH: Masked multiplication $h(x) = x \cdot g(x)$ over $GF(2^8)$ with n shares, where $g(\cdot)$ is a linear function [8]

Input: Shares x_i satisfying $x_1 \oplus \cdots \oplus x_n = x$, and $g(x_i)$ for each x_i
Output: Shares y_i, satisfying $y_1 \oplus \cdots \oplus y_n = y = x \cdot g(x)$
  1: **for** $i = 1$ to n **do**
  2:     $y_i \leftarrow x_i \cdot g(x_i)$
  3: **end for**
  4: **for** $i = 1$ to n **do**
  5:     **for** $j = i + 1$ to n **do**
  6:         $r_0 \leftarrow GF(2^8)$
  7:         $r_0' \leftarrow GF(2^8)$
  8:         $r_1 \leftarrow r_0 \oplus (x_i \cdot g(r_0')) \oplus (r_0' \cdot g(x_i)) \oplus (x_i \cdot g(x_j \oplus r_0')) \oplus ((x_j \oplus r_0') \cdot g(x_i))$
  9:         $y_i \leftarrow y_i \oplus r_0$
10:         $y_j \leftarrow y_j \oplus r_1$
11:     **end for**
12: **end for**
13: **return** $y_1, \ldots, y_n$

---

where r_0' is a freshly-generated random element of the field $GF(2^8)$. Algorithm 2 shows a variant of this technique for secure computation of $h = x \cdot g(x)$ with linear memory complexity. For each pair of shares x_i, x_j, this algorithm has to generate an extra random number to split up the computation of $f(x_i, x_j)$ as specified by Equation (6). The computation of r_1 in line 8 of Algorithm 2 also requires four extra additions and two more multiplications in $GF(2^8)$ compared to line 7 of Algorithm 1. Nonetheless, by using look-up tables for the function $h(x) = x \cdot g(x)$, Coron et al managed to reduce the execution time of a masked S-box operation by between 24% (for $d = 1$) and 35% (for $d = 3$) in relation to the Rivain-Prouff method. Therefore, they concluded in [8] that their masking scheme is not only secure, but also faster than the original one.

3   Our Implementation

In this section, we describe our implementation of the higher-order secure AES from [8] for ARM NEON processors (e.g. Cortex-A8, A15). We first introduce our approach for performing multiplication in $GF(2^8)$, which is, according to our analysis, the most costly operation of a masked AES, and then describe a method to secure the full cipher.

3.1   Vector Implementation of Multiplication in $GF(2^8)$

Barrett Reduction for Integers. In order to optimize the modular reduction operation $r = a \bmod n$, where a, n are integers and $a < n^2$, Barrett came up with an algorithm that requires a pre-computed constant depending only on the modulus n [2]. This so-called Barrett reduction is designed to replace the trial division with multiplications, which yields much better performance.

The general idea of Barrett reduction is based on the following equation

$$a \bmod n = a - \left\lfloor \frac{a}{n} \right\rfloor n. \tag{7}$$

One can precompute $m = 1/n$, in which case the modular reduction operation is transformed into two multiplications and one subtraction. However, since the quotient $m = 1/n$ can only be represented as a floating point number and Barrett's algorithm is supposed to work with integers, it adopts a trick to avoid calculating on floating numbers. Suppose k is the minimal integer such that $2^k > n$, which means we can precompute $m = \lfloor 2^{2k}/n \rfloor$. Let $q = \lfloor ma/4^k \rfloor$, $r = a - qn$ then $\lfloor a/n \rfloor - 1 < q \leq \lfloor a/n \rfloor$ and

$$a \bmod n = \begin{cases} r & \text{if } r < n, \\ r - n & \text{otherwise.} \end{cases} \tag{8}$$

The entire algorithm requires two multiplications, one shift operation[3] and at most two subtractions.

Modular Reduction in $\mathbb{F}_q[x]$. In order to perform modular reduction over $\mathbb{F}_q[x]$, Dhem generalized Barrett's modular reduction over integers to work with polynomials [10]. Theorem 1 indicates that Barrett modular reduction can be adapted to extension fields with polynomial presentation.

Theorem 1 (Quotient Evaluation in $\mathbb{F}_q[x]$, adpated from [10]). *Suppose* $U(x)$, $N(x)$, $Z(x)$ *and* $Q(x)$ *are polynomials over* $\mathbb{F}_q$, *and* $U(x) = Q(x)N(x) + Z(x)$ *(i.e., $Z(x) = U(x) \bmod N(x)$), then*

$$Q(x) = \left\lfloor \frac{U(x)}{N(x)} \right\rfloor = \left\lfloor \frac{\left\lfloor \frac{U(x)}{x^p} \right\rfloor \left\lfloor \frac{x^{p+\beta}}{N(x)} \right\rfloor}{x^\beta} \right\rfloor = \left\lfloor \frac{T(x)R(x)}{x^\beta} \right\rfloor, \tag{9}$$

where $p = deg(N(x))$[4], $\beta \geq deg(U(x)/x^p)$ and $\lfloor A(x)/B(x) \rfloor$ stands for the quotient of polynomial division $A(x)/B(x)$, ignoring the reminder.

According to Theorem 1, we can perform the modular reduction operation $U(x) = Z(x) \bmod N(x)$ over $\mathbb{F}_q[x]$ in three steps as follows.

Step 1. Evaluate the quotient $Q(x) = \lfloor U(x)/N(x) \rfloor$ according to Theorem 1.
Step 2. Calculate the product $V(x) = Q(x)N(x)$.
Step 3. Obtain the reminder $Z(x) = U(x) - V(x)$.

In most applications, $N(x)$ is fixed, e.g., $N(x) = x^8 + x^4 + x^3 + x + 1$ in the case of AES. Therefore, we can accelerate the computation of $Q(x)$ by pre-computing $R(x) = \lfloor x^{p+\beta}/N(x) \rfloor$. Although Theorem 1 holds when $\beta \geq deg(U(x)/x^p)$, there is no need to choose $\beta > deg(U(x)/x^p)$, because the bigger β, the bigger $R(x)$ and the more computation is required. In general, we can choose $\beta = \alpha - p$, where

---

[3] A division by 4^k is nothing else than a simple right-shift operation by $2k$ bits.
[4] $deg(A(x))$ stands for the degree of polynomial $A(x)$.

$deg(U(x))$ is bounded by some constant value α. Thus, the evaluation of $Q(x)$ is simplified to one multiplication and two shift operations (i.e., division by x^p and x^β, similar to the case of integers [3]). Overall, a Barrett modular reduction for polynomials over $\mathbb{F}_q[x]$ consists of two multiplications, two shift operations and one subtraction.

Field Multiplication in $\mathbb{F}_{2^8}$ (i.e., GF(2^8)). A complete field multiplication in $\mathbb{F}_{2^8} = \mathbb{F}_2[x]/q(x)$, where $q(x) = x^8 + x^4 + x^3 + x + 1$, consists of two steps: multiplying two polynomials $a(x)$ and $b(x)$ of degree ≤ 7 and modular reduction of the product $p(x)$ with respect to $q(x)$. Since we have `vmull.p8` instruction in NEON, a polynomial multiplication can be easily carried out in parallel. Hence, the only operation we have to pay attention to is the modular reduction.

Polynomial operations over $\mathbb{F}_2[x]$ have some special characteristics (given below), which can be used to speed up the modular reduction operation. [5]

1. A polynomial of degree $m - 1$ can be represented by an array of m bits.
2. The subtraction of two polynomials is same as addition.
3. The product of a polynomial of degree $m - 1$ and a polynomial of degree $n - 1$ is a polynomial of degree $m + n - 2$, which can be represented by $(m + n - 1)$ bits. In the case of GF(2^8), we have $m, n \leq 7$, and therefore $m + n - 2 \leq 12$. However, for two integers consisting of m and n bits, the product has a length of $(m + n)$ bits.
4. The addition of two polynomials of degree m is a polynomial of degree m. In case of two integers of m-bit length, the addition may have a length of $(m + 1)$ bits.
5. The reminder of division of two polynomials is one degree smaller than the divisor (modulus). In the case of GF(2^8), the degree of the irreducible polynomial $q(x)$ is 8. However, in the case of integers, the reminder might have the same length as the divisor (in binary representation).

Using the observations above, we designed Algorithm 3, which realizes field multiplications in GF(2^8).

In the pre-computations stage, we know that the degree of the product of two polynomials of degree $\leq p - 1$ cannot exceed $\alpha = 2 * (p - 1)$. Here, $p = deg(N(x)) = 8$ and hence $\beta \geq \alpha - p = 6$. In order to optimize the computation, we can choose an $R(x)$ that can be stored in a single byte, which means $R(x)$ should have a degree of ≤ 7. Since $R(x) = \lfloor x^{p+\beta}/N(x) \rfloor$, we can for example pick $\beta = 6$ and $R(x) = x^6 + x^2 + x$. Alternatively, we can pick $\beta = 7$ and $R(x) = x^7 + x^3 + x^2 + 1$. However, for $\beta \geq 8$, $R(x)$ has a degree ≥ 8, which is not desirable.

In total, one field multiplication requires three polynomial multiplications, two shift operations and one addition. Moreover, the execution sequence of this technique for field multiplication is independent of the processed operands and, hence, it is resistant against timing attacks.

---

[5] Some of the characteristics are also valid in $\mathbb{F}_q[x]$, where $q > 2$.

Algorithm 3. Multiplication in $GF(2^8)$ using Barrett reduction

---

Input: Polynomials $A(x), B(x) \in GF(2^8)$
Output: Polynomial $Z(x) = A(x) \cdot B(x) \bmod N(x)$, where $N(x) = x^8 + x^4 + x^3 + x + 1$
Pre-computation:

1: $p \leftarrow \deg(N(x))$ $\triangleright\ p = 8$
2: $\alpha \leftarrow 2(p-1)$ $\triangleright\ \alpha = 14$
3: $\beta \geq \alpha - p$ $\triangleright\ \beta \geq 6$
4: $R(x) \leftarrow \lfloor x^{p+\beta}/N(x) \rfloor$ $\triangleright\ R(x) = x^6 + x^2 + x$ if $\beta = 6$

Polynomial multiplication and Barrett modular reduction (Theorem 1):

1: $U(x) \leftarrow A(x) \cdot B(x)$ $\triangleright\ \deg(U(x)) \leq 14$
2: $T(x) \leftarrow \lfloor U(x)/x^p \rfloor$ $\triangleright\ \deg(T(x)) \leq 6$
3: $S(x) \leftarrow T(x) \cdot R(x)$ $\triangleright\ \deg(S(x)) \leq \beta + 6$
4: $Q(x) \leftarrow \lfloor S(x)/x^\beta \rfloor$ $\triangleright\ \deg(Q(x)) \leq 6$
5: $V(x) \leftarrow Q(x) \cdot N(x)$ $\triangleright\ \deg(V(x)) \leq 14$
6: $Z(x) \leftarrow U(x) + V(x)$
7: **return** $Z(x)$

Vector Implementation of Field Multiplication in $GF(2^8)$. Since the AES state consists of 16 bytes, we aim at vectorizing the transformations on all the 16 bytes. In order to perform 16 field multiplications in parallel, we define a function named `fmult` as follows:

```
uint8x16_t fmult(uint8x16_t a, uint8x16_t b);
```

The `fmult` function takes two arguments of type `uint8x16_t`[6] (i.e. a vector of 16 bytes) and returns a vector of 16 bytes. The most and least significant eight bytes of the vector $U(x) = A(x) \cdot B(x)$ can be calculated in parallel using `vmull.p8` instruction. To compute $T(x) = \lfloor \frac{U(x)}{x^8} \rfloor$, we right shift every element in $U(x)$ by 8 bits with help of the `vshrn.i16` instruction. The vectors $S(x) = T(x) \cdot R(x)$ and $Q(x) = \lfloor \frac{S(x)}{x^6} \rfloor$ can similarly be calculated using `vmull.p8` and `vshrn.i16` respectively. Since the most significant byte of each element in $V(x)$ and $U(x)$ are the same so that they cancel out each other in the last step (namely, $V(x) + U(x)$), we only need to calculate the least significant byte of each element of $V(x)$. Since $V(x) = Q(x) \cdot N(x)$, where $N(x) = x^8 + x^4 + x^3 + x + 1$ is 100011011 in binary presentation (0x11B in hexadecimal format), we have

$$V(x) \bmod x^8 = (Q(x) \bmod x^8) \cdot (N(x) \bmod x^8).$$

Since $deg(Q(x)) \leq 7$ and $N(x) \bmod x^8 = x^4 + x^3 + x + 1$, the least significant byte of $V(x)$, i.e., $V(x) \bmod x^8$, is calculated in the following way,

$$V(x) \bmod x^8 = (Q(x) \bmod x^8) \cdot (x^4 + x^3 + x + 1).$$

---

[6] In NEON jargon, `uint8x16_t` is a quadword vector of 16 unsigned 8-bit integers.

Finally, the `veor` instruction conducts the XOR operation (addition) of the least significant byte of each element in $U(x)$ and $V(x)$. Consequently, only 15 instructions are used in our vector implementation of the field multiplication in $GF(2^8)$, which is less than one instruction per byte.

3.2   Vector Implementation of Round Operations

We now describe our implementation of all the round operations of AES. [7] It is easy to mask a linear function $f(\cdot)$, since

$$f(x) = f(x_1) \oplus \cdots \oplus f(x_n), \tag{10}$$

where $x = x_1 \oplus \cdots \oplus x_n$. The operations *AddRoundKey*, *ShiftRows* and *MixColumns* are linear and can be implemented in a straightforward way. The non-linear part of the cipher i.e., S-Box consists of an inversion in $GF(2^8)$ and an affine transformation. Masking the affine transformation is similar to masking a linear function. Masking the inversion involves several subroutines: masking the field squaring, masking the field multiplication and masking $h(x) = x \cdot g(x)$, where $g(\cdot)$ is a linear function. We will discuss these subroutines separately below.

AddRoundKey. *AddRoundKey* is a linear function, because it is simply an XOR operation. Due to the convenient vector XOR instruction `veor`, we only need one instruction to implement this operation.

ShiftRows. *ShiftRows* left-rotates bytes in the n-th row of the state matrix by $(n-1)$ positions.

$$ShiftRows: \begin{bmatrix} x_{00} & x_{01} & x_{02} & x_{03} \\ x_{10} & x_{11} & x_{12} & x_{13} \\ x_{20} & x_{21} & x_{22} & x_{23} \\ x_{30} & x_{31} & x_{32} & x_{33} \end{bmatrix} \mapsto \begin{bmatrix} x_{00} & x_{01} & x_{02} & x_{03} \\ x_{11} & x_{12} & x_{13} & x_{10} \\ x_{22} & x_{23} & x_{20} & x_{21} \\ x_{33} & x_{30} & x_{31} & x_{32} \end{bmatrix} \tag{11}$$

As it only rearranges the order of bytes in an AES state, it is also a linear transformation. We use a lookup table based on the number of shifts required for each byte and store it in a static array. We then reorder the state bytes according to the look-up table by using the vector table look-up instruction `vtbl.8`. [8] We require four instructions to implement *ShiftRows* operation, two each for loading the table and reordering the state bytes.

---

[7] We do not describe the implementation of key expansion as it can be obtained in a similar way.

[8] Note that the table look-up here is not based on the secret key, hence is not vulnerable to cache-timing attacks.

MixColumns. *MixColumns* can be performed by left-multiplying each column with a constant byte matrix $\mathcal{M}$ with four rows and four columns, where the multiplication is applied on $GF(2^8)$.

$$
MixColumns : \begin{bmatrix} x_0 \\ x_1 \\ x_2 \\ x_3 \end{bmatrix} \mapsto \begin{bmatrix} 2 & 3 & 1 & 1 \\ 1 & 2 & 3 & 1 \\ 1 & 1 & 2 & 3 \\ 3 & 1 & 1 & 2 \end{bmatrix} \begin{bmatrix} x_0 \\ x_1 \\ x_2 \\ x_3 \end{bmatrix} \tag{12}
$$

The multiply by 2 can be realized via a single left-shift and a XOR operation; the multiply by 3 is realized via combination of a multiply by 2 and an XOR operation. The parallel implementation of *MixColumns* resistant against timing attacks (i.e., without conditional branches) can be obtained with only 13 instructions.

Field Squaring. Squaring is a linear operation in $\mathbb{F}_2^n$ and hence can be masked by squaring the shares independently.

Field Multiplication. The vector implementation of the field multiplication can be carried out in a straightforward way using **SecMult** (Algorithm 1) and `fmult` function.

Masking $h(x) = x \cdot g(x)$. Table lookups are a common way to improve the execution time of this operation. To mask $h(x) = x \cdot g(x)$, we can also store a look-up table for $h(x)$. However, we cannot perform vector-parallel look-ups into a table of more than 32 elements with NEON instructions. Hence, in our implementation, we manually compute the values (as in Line 8 of Algorithm 3).

Affine Transformation. Suppose the byte $x = [x_0 x_1 \cdots x_7]$, where $x_0, \cdots, x_7$ are bits, is one of the shares of the multiplicative inverse calculated in the last step. After the affine transformation, x should be modified as follows:

$$
\begin{bmatrix} x_7 \\ x_6 \\ x_5 \\ x_4 \\ x_3 \\ x_2 \\ x_1 \\ x_0 \end{bmatrix} = \begin{bmatrix} x_7 \oplus x_6 \oplus x_5 \oplus x_4 \oplus x_3 \\ x_6 \oplus x_5 \oplus x_4 \oplus x_3 \oplus x_2 \\ x_5 \oplus x_4 \oplus x_3 \oplus x_2 \oplus x_1 \\ x_4 \oplus x_3 \oplus x_2 \oplus x_1 \oplus x_0 \\ x_7 \quad\quad \oplus x_3 \oplus x_2 \oplus x_1 \oplus x_0 \\ x_7 \oplus x_6 \quad\quad\quad\quad x_2 \oplus x_1 \oplus x_0 \\ x_7 \oplus x_6 \oplus x_5 \quad\quad\quad\quad \oplus x_1 \oplus x_0 \\ x_7 \oplus x_6 \oplus x_5 \oplus x_4 \quad\quad\quad\quad\quad \oplus x_0 \end{bmatrix} \oplus \begin{bmatrix} 0 \\ 1 \\ 1 \\ 0 \\ 0 \\ 0 \\ 1 \\ 1 \end{bmatrix} \tag{13}
$$

Hence, five steps have to be carried out to implement the affine transformation.

Step 1. Cyclic left shift of x by one bit: $y = [x_7 x_0 x_1 x_2 x_3 x_4 x_5 x_6]$.
Step 2. Cyclic left shift of x by two bits: $z = [x_6 x_7 x_0 x_1 x_2 x_3 x_4 x_5]$.
Step 3. Cyclic left shift of x by three bits: $v = [x_5 x_6 x_7 x_0 x_1 x_2 x_3 x_4]$.
Step 4. Cyclic left shift of x by four bits: $w = [x_4 x_5 x_6 x_7 x_0 x_1 x_2 x_3]$.
Step 5. Finally, $x = x \oplus y \oplus z \oplus v \oplus w \oplus 0x63$.

4   Improved Implementation of Secure Inversion over Composite Field

The most costly operation in the implementation of the AES S-box is computing the multiplicative inverse over finite field $GF(2^8)$. In order to accelerate the evaluation of inversion operation, several composite field methods were proposed [21,22]. Kim *et al.*, [16] used this idea to fasten the secure high-order masking of AES S-box proposed by Rivian-Prouff [20]. However, as it also uses **RefreshMaks** procedure, the attack from [8] is also valid here. In this section, we describe a method to overcome the attack.

Composite Field. In a typical composite field method, one first maps an element over $GF(2^8)$ into an element over composite field using an isomorphism function δ. Then, the inversion is computed over the composite field. In the end, the result is transformed back to an element over $GF(2^8)$ by the inverse mapping function δ^{-1}. More precisely, for any element $A = a_h\gamma + a_l$ in composite field $GF((2^4)^2)$, where $a_h, a_l \in GF((2^4)^2)$, the multiplicative inverse of A can be carried out as $A^{-1} = (A^{17})^{-1} \cdot A^{16}$, according to the equation in [14]. Here, A^{16} can be computed by four bitwise XOR operations, since $A^{16} = a_h\gamma + (a_h + a_l)$. The value A^{17} can be obtained by multiplying A and A^{16} over $GF((2^4)^2)$, i.e., $A^{17} = \lambda a_h^2 + (a_h + a_l)a_l$ (since $\gamma^2 + \gamma = \lambda$). Hence, the inversion of $x \in GF(2^8)$ can be completed by performing the following steps:

Step 1. Apply the isomorphism function δ, such that $A = a_h\gamma + a_l = \delta(x) \in GF((2^4)^2)$, where $a_l, a_h \in GF(2^4)$.

Step 2. Compute A^{17} as $d = \lambda a_h^2 + (a_h + a_l)a_l \in GF(2^4)$.

Step 3. Evaluate the inversion of A^{17}, namely, $d' = d^{-1}$.

Step 4. Compute the inversion $A^{-1} = (A^{17})^{-1} \cdot A^{16} = a_h'\lambda + a_l'$ where $a_h' = d'a_h \in GF(2^4)$ and $a_l' = d(a_h + a_l) \in GF(2^4)$.

Step 5. Compute the inversion of x by applying the inverse mapping function δ', i.e., $x^{-1} = \delta'(a_h'\gamma + a_l')$.

Secure Inversion over Composite Field. Instead of securely raising an element to 254, [16] performs secure inversion by using composite field method, i.e., they securely mask the aforementioned five steps.

As previously mentioned, the linear functions δ and δ' can be masked by simply applying the function on each share separately. The field multiplication in $GF(2^4)$ can be masked in the same way as shown in Algorithm 1. The multiplicative inversion in $GF(2^4)$, i.e., raising the operand to 14, can be implemented as a combination of two linear operations (namely, squaring and raising to power 4) and one secure field multiplication, which is constructed as follows,

$$x \xrightarrow{x^2} x^2 \xrightarrow[\textbf{RefreshMasks}]{x^2x} x^3 \xrightarrow{(x^3)^4} x^{12} \xrightarrow{x^{12}x^2} x^{14}. \tag{14}$$

All these operations can be directly masked using the techniques proposed in [20]. To implement their solutions on embedded systems, the authors suggest to precompute several tables of 16 elements or 256 elements, such as field multiplication table, squaring table and isomorphism function table, which can significantly improve the overall performance. The running times can be further reduced by combining the inverse isomorphism function and affine function.

Our Improved Implementation of Secure Inversion over Composite Field. Due to the involvement of **RefreshMasks** procedure, the secure inversion in [16] is also vulnerable to the attack mentioned in [8]. In order to avoid this attack, we propose a new secure inversion algorithm as shown in Algorithm 4, where **SecH** is a variant of Algorithm 2 over $GF(2^4)$. The security of Algorithm 2 directly follows from the proof given in Section 4 of [8]. To optimize the performance, we store a pre-computed table for the function h in our corrected implementation.

Algorithm 4. SecInv4: Masked exponentiation by 14 over $\mathbb{F}_{2^4}$ with n shares

---

Input: Shares x_i satisfying $x_1 \oplus \cdots \oplus x_n = x$
Output: Shares y_i satisfying $y_1 \oplus \cdots \oplus y_n = x^{254}$
1: **for** $i = 1$ to n **do**
2:     $w_i \leftarrow x_i^2$ $\triangleright \bigoplus_i w_i = x^2$
3: **end for**
4: $(z_1, \cdots, z_n) \leftarrow \mathbf{SecH}((x_1, \cdots, x_n), (w_1, \cdots, w_n))$ $\triangleright \bigoplus_i z_i = x^3$
5: **for** $i = 1$ to n **do**
6:     $z_i \leftarrow z_i^4$ $\triangleright \bigoplus_i z_i = x^{12}$
7: **end for**
8: $(y_1, \cdots, y_n) \leftarrow \mathbf{SecMult}((z_1, \cdots, z_n), (w_1, \cdots, w_n))$ $\triangleright \bigoplus_i y_i = x^{14}$

The vector table look-up instruction `vtbl.8` can do a parallelized look-up in a table of at most 32 elements, and hence is not suitable for tables of 256 elements such as the field multiplication table over $GF(2^4)$, the isomorphism and inverse isomorphism tables. For the field multiplication over $GF(2^4)$, we again utilize the Barrett's reduction technique. Compared to Algorithm 3, the algorithm to perform field multiplication over $GF(2^4)$ is simpler. More preciously, we can ignore Step 3 and Step 4 in Algorithm 3, since in the case of $GF(2^4)$, if we choose $\beta = 2$, the polynomial $R(x) = x^\beta = x^2$ and these two steps actually cancel each other and do nothing but set $Q(x) = T(x)$. Besides, all temporary values in the algorithm can be stored in a single byte. Consequently, only 6 instructions are used in our vector implementation of the field multiplication in $GF(2^4)$, which is much faster than table look-up. We present our algorithm to perform field multiplication over $GF(2^4)$ in Appendix B.

5   Implementation Results

5.1   Baseline Implementation

For performance comparison, we need a baseline implementation that is resistant against timing attacks, i.e., we need an implementation that does not use look-up tables. Hence, we developed a baseline implementation using the ARM NEON instruction set from scratch, which performs the inversion in $GF(2^8)$ by using composite field method. In fact, the baseline implementation is exactly the implementation that we mentioned in Section 4 where only one share (i.e., without any freshly generated random masks) is involved. To achieve better performance, we optimized the baseline implementation with pure NEON assembly language and unrolled all the loops, i.e., we eliminated all avoidable loss of efficiency.

Usually, Gladman's AES implementation [11] is used as a starting point for comparison. However, his implementation [11] uses look-up tables, and is vulnerable to cache-timing attacks. Hence, it is not suitable as baseline implementation for comparison, even though it achieves very good execution time. Nevertheless, we do a comparison between Gladman's implementation and our baseline implementation and it shows that both the key expansion and the encryption process of our baseline implementation is only marginally (1.5 times) slower than Gladman's implementation.

5.2   Comparison

Our Implementation. In Table 1, we present the speedup factor of our improved implementation (in Section 4) where the secure inversion in $GF(2^8)$ is computed over composite field, compared with our implementation of [8](given in Section 3) where we compute the secure inversion through exponentiation. Table 1 also shows the penalty factor due to the integration of high-order DPA countermeasures into our implementation (in Section 4) compared to the baseline implementation (given in Section 5.1).   In the case of first-, second- and

Table 1. Speedup factor of our improved implementation in Section 4 compared to Section 3, and penalty factor of our improved implementation compared to the baseline implementation

order	unmasked	1	2	3	4	5	6	7
Section 3	2,281	10,050	21,277	36,808	69,022	97,578	131,164	169,806
Section 4	*1,141*	4,869	9,127	14,855	34,875	47,640	61,915	77,820
Speedup Factor	2.0	2.1	2.3	2.5	2.0	2.0	2.1	2.2
Penalty Factor	-	4.3	8.0	13.0	30.6	41.8	54.3	68.2

third-order, we use the highly-optimized "pure" NEON assembly implementation, which is approximately $(order + 1)^2$ times slower than the baseline implementation. In all other cases, we use the mixed C and NEON assembly (i.e. the generic) implementation, which is a little more than $(order + 1)^2$ times slower than the baseline implementation.

A Note on Random Numbers. We used a Pseudorandom Number Generator (PRNG) based on Linear Feedback Shift Register (LFSR). However most of the LFSR based PRNG are not cryptographically secure. To avoid this, one can replace the PRNG used with a stream cipher such as Salsa20.[9] The vectorized implementation of Salsa20 requires only 5.6 cycles/byte [3] and hence do not significantly impact our results.

Related Work. Here, we compare our implementation results with different countermeasures from CHES 2010 [20], CHES 2011 [16] and Eurocrypt 2014 [7]. However, in the original papers, the implementations were evaluated on platforms that are completely different from ARM NEON, which means these comparisons have to be taken with a pinch of salt. For example, the implementation reported in [16] was written in C and evaluated on an 8-bit ATmega128 processor, while Coron's [7] implementation was in C on a MacBook Air with a 64-bit Intel processor clocked at 1.86 GHz. Therefore, it makes only sense to compare the penalty factor of the different implementations for a given orders (see Table 2), but not the absolute execution times. Table 2 shows that our results are significantly better than that of the others. With our proposed implementation, the second and third order secure AES is only 8 and 13 times slower than the unmasked implementation. Moreover, our results achieve a speedup factor of three compared with the fastest solutions available.

Table 2. Penalty factor of different masking implementations

Implementation	Platform	1st-order	2nd-order	3rd-order	4th-order
Rivain-Prouff [20]	8-bit 8051	65	132	235	–
Kim et al [16]	8-bit AVR	–	22	39	–
Coron [7]	64-bit Intel	439	1205	2411	4003
Our work (Sect. 3)	32-bit ARM	9	19	32	60
Our work (Sect. 4)	32-bit ARM	4	8	13	31

6   Conclusions

We addressed the efficiency problem of masking schemes for the AES, which is particularly pronounced if one aims to achieve higher-order DPA resistance. In fact, all higher-order masking schemes described in the open literature perform very badly in software and are, therefore, little attractive for use in real-world applications. We found that the performance-critical operations of the Rivain-Prouff scheme (and its corrected version) are the multiplication in $GF(2^8)$ and the generation of random numbers. By combining algorithmic improvements in the low-level arithmetic (e.g. composite-field representation, Barrett reduction) with an efficient implementation that exploits the vector-level parallelism of the NEON engine, we managed to reduce the computational overhead to a degree that is (more) acceptable in practice. For example, our vector implementation of the AES with integrated second-order countermeasures (using three shares

---

[9] For further improving the security of random numbers, one could also use True Random Number Generator (TRNG) to seed the PRNG.

per sensitive variable) is only eight times slower than a baseline implementation without DPA countermeasures. A third-order DPA protected implementation is about 13 times slower than our baseline variant. In summary, our work shows that higher-order masking of the AES, when implemented efficiently, is not prohibitively expensive in terms of execution time. Besides the AES, also various AES-based authenticated encryption schemes, which are currently evaluated in the CAESAR competition, can take advantage of the masking implementation described in this paper.

Acknowledgments. This work was partially supported by the National Natural Science Foundation of China under grant No. 61173139. The full source code of the implementation described in this paper is available under MIT license on GitHub at https:// github.com/junwei-wang/AES-ARM-NEON.

A   Algorithm for Secure Exponentiation in $GF(2^8)$

Algorithm 5. SecExp254: Masked exponentiation by 254 in $GF(2^8)$ with n shares [20]

Input: Shares x_i satisfying $x_1 \oplus \cdots \oplus x_n = x$
Output: Shares y_i satisfying $y_1 \oplus \cdots \oplus y_n = y = x^{254}$

1: **for** $i = 1$ to n **do**
2:     $z_i \leftarrow x_i^2$ $\triangleright \bigoplus_i z_i = x^2$
3: **end for**
4: RefreshMasks$(z_1, \cdots, z_n)$
5: $(y_1, \cdots, y_n) \leftarrow$ SecMult$((z_1, \cdots, z_n), (x_1, \cdots, x_n))$ $\triangleright \bigoplus_i y_i = x^3$
6: **for** $i = 1$ to n **do**
7:     $w_i \leftarrow y_i^4$ $\triangleright \bigoplus_i w_i = x^{12}$
8: **end for**
9: RefreshMasks$(w_1, \cdots, w_n)$
10: $(y_1, \cdots, y_n) \leftarrow$ SecMult$((y_1, \cdots, y_n), (w_1, \cdots, w_n))$ $\triangleright \bigoplus_i y_i = x^{15}$
11: **for** $i = 1$ to n **do**
12:     $y_i \leftarrow y_i^{16}$ $\triangleright \bigoplus_i y_i = x^{240}$
13: **end for**
14: $(y_1, \cdots, y_n) \leftarrow$ SecMult$((y_1, \cdots, y_n), (w_1, \cdots, w_n))$ $\triangleright \bigoplus_i y_i = x^{252}$
15: $(y_1, \cdots, y_n) \leftarrow$ SecMult$((y_1, \cdots, y_n), (z_1, \cdots, z_n))$ $\triangleright \bigoplus_i y_i = x^{254}$
16: **return** $y_1, \cdots, y_n$

B   Algorithm for Field Multiplication in $GF(2^4)$

Algorithm 6. Field multiplication in $GF(2^4)$

Input: Polynomials $A(x)$ and $B(x)$ in $GF(2^4)$
Output: Polynomial $Z(x) = A(x) \cdot B(x) \bmod N(x)$, where $N(x) = x^4 + x + 1$.

Pre-computation:

1: $p \leftarrow deg(N(x))$ $\triangleright\ p = 4$
2: $\alpha \leftarrow 2 * (p - 1)$ $\triangleright\ \alpha = 6$
3: $\beta \geq \alpha - p$ $\triangleright\ \beta \geq 2$
4: $R(x) \leftarrow \lfloor \frac{x^{p+\beta}}{N(x)} \rfloor$ $\triangleright\ R(x) = x^2$ if $\beta = 2$

Multiplication with Barrett modular reduction(Theorem 1):

1: $U(x) \leftarrow A(x) \cdot B(x)$ $\triangleright\ deg(U(x)) \leq 14$
2: $T(x) \leftarrow \lfloor \frac{U(x)}{x^p} \rfloor$ $\triangleright\ deg(T(x)) \leq 6$ and $Q(x) = T(x)$
3: $V(x) \leftarrow Q(x) \cdot N(x)$ $\triangleright\ deg(V(x)) \leq 14$
4: $Z(x) \leftarrow U(x) + V(x)$

References

1. ARM Holdings plc. NEON Programmer's Guide, Version 1.0. (2013). http://infocenter.arm.com/help/index.jsp?topic=/com.arm.doc.den0018a/index.html
2. Barrett, P.: Implementing the rivest shamir and adleman public key encryption algorithm on a standard digital signal processor. In: Odlyzko, A.M. (ed.) CRYPTO 1986. LNCS, vol. 263, pp. 311–323. Springer, Heidelberg (1987)
3. Bernstein, D.J., Schwabe, P.: NEON crypto. In: Prouff, E., Schaumont, P. (eds.) CHES 2012. LNCS, vol. 7428, pp. 320–339. Springer, Heidelberg (2012)
4. Caddy, T.: Differential power analysis. In: van Tilborg, H.C., Jajodia, S. (eds.) Encyclopedia of Cryptography and Security, pp. 336–338. Springer (2011)
5. Chari, S., Jutla, C., Rao, J.R., Rohatgi, P.: A cautionary note regarding evaluation of aes candidates on smart-cards. In: Second Advanced Encryption Standard Candidate Conference, pp. 133–147 (1999)
6. Chari, S., Jutla, C.S., Rao, J.R., Rohatgi, P.: Towards sound approaches to counteract power-analysis attacks. In: Wiener, M. (ed.) CRYPTO 1999. LNCS, vol. 1666, pp. 398–412. Springer, Heidelberg (1999)
7. Coron, J.-S.: Higher order masking of look-up tables. In: Nguyen, P.Q., Oswald, E. (eds.) EUROCRYPT 2014. LNCS, vol. 8441, pp. 441–458. Springer, Heidelberg (2014)
8. Coron, J.-S., Prouff, E., Rivain, M., Roche, T.: Higher-order side channel security and mask refreshing. In: Moriai, S. (ed.) FSE 2013. LNCS, vol. 8424, pp. 410–424. Springer, Heidelberg (2014)
9. Daemen, J., Rijmen, V.: The Design of Rijndael: AES - The Advanced Encryption Standard. Springer (2002)
10. Dhem, J.-F.: Efficient modular reduction algorithm in $\mathbb{F}_q[x]$ and its application to "left to right" modular multiplication in $\mathbb{F}_2[x]$. In: Walter, C.D., Koç, Ç.K., Paar, C. (eds.) CHES 2003. LNCS, vol. 2779, pp. 203–213. Springer, Heidelberg (2003)

11. Gladman, B.R.: AES and combined encryption/authentication modes, June 2006. http://gladman.plushost.co.uk/oldsite/AES/index.php
12. Grosso, V., Standaert, F.-X., Faust, S.: Masking vs. multiparty computation: how large is the gap for AES? In: Bertoni, G., Coron, J.-S. (eds.) CHES 2013. LNCS, vol. 8086, pp. 400–416. Springer, Heidelberg (2013)
13. Grosso, V., Standaert, F., Faust, S.: Masking vs. multiparty computation: how large is the gap for AES? J. Cryptographic Engineering **4**(1), 47–57 (2014)
14. Guajardo, J., Paar, C.: Efficient algorithms for elliptic curve cryptosystems. In: Kaliski Jr., B.S. (ed.) CRYPTO 1997. LNCS, vol. 1294, pp. 342–356. Springer, Heidelberg (1997)
15. Ishai, Y., Sahai, A., Wagner, D.: Private circuits: securing hardware against probing attacks. In: Boneh, D. (ed.) CRYPTO 2003. LNCS, vol. 2729, pp. 463–481. Springer, Heidelberg (2003)
16. Kim, H.S., Hong, S., Lim, J.: A fast and provably secure higher-order masking of AES S-box. In: Preneel, B., Takagi, T. (eds.) CHES 2011. LNCS, vol. 6917, pp. 95–107. Springer, Heidelberg (2011)
17. Kocher, P., Jaffe, J., Jun, B.: Differential power analysis. In: Wiener, M. (ed.) CRYPTO 1999. LNCS, vol. 1666, pp. 388–397. Springer, Heidelberg (1999)
18. Mangard, S., Oswald, E., Popp, T.: Power Analysis Attacks: Revealing the Secrets of Smart Cards, vol. 31. Springer (2008)
19. Messerges, T.S.: Using second-order power analysis to attack DPA resistant software. In: Koç, Ç.K., Paar, C. (eds.) CHES 2000. LNCS, vol. 1965, pp. 238–251. Springer, Heidelberg (2000)
20. Rivain, M., Prouff, E.: Provably secure higher-order masking of AES. In: Mangard, S., Standaert, F.-X. (eds.) CHES 2010. LNCS, vol. 6225, pp. 413–427. Springer, Heidelberg (2010). http://eprint.iacr.org/2010/441
21. Rudra, A., Dubey, P.K., Jutla, C.S., Kumar, V., Rao, J.R., Rohatgi, P.: Efficient rijndael encryption implementation with composite field arithmetic. In: Koç, Ç.K., Naccache, D., Paar, C. (eds.) CHES 2001. LNCS, vol. 2162, pp. 171–184. Springer, Heidelberg (2001)
22. Satoh, A., Morioka, S., Takano, K., Munetoh, S.: A Compact rijndael hardware architecture with S-box optimization. In: Boyd, C. (ed.) ASIACRYPT 2001. LNCS, vol. 2248, pp. 239–254. Springer, Heidelberg (2001)
23. Waddle, J., Wagner, D.: Towards efficient second-order power analysis. In: Joye, M., Quisquater, J.-J. (eds.) CHES 2004. LNCS, vol. 3156, pp. 1–15. Springer, Heidelberg (2004)

Chosen Ciphertext Attacks
in Theory and Practice

Completeness of Single-Bit Projection-KDM Security for Public Key Encryption

Fuyuki Kitagawa[1,2]([⊠]), Takahiro Matsuda[2],
Goichiro Hanaoka[2], and Keisuke Tanaka[1]

[1] Tokyo Institute of Technology, Meguro, Tokyo, Japan
{kitagaw1,keisuke}@is.titech.ac.jp
[2] National Institute of Advanced Industrial Science and Technology (AIST),
Tsukuba, Ibaraki, Japan
{t-matsuda,hanaoka-goichiro}@aist.go.jp

Abstract. Applebaum (EUROCRYPT 2011, J. Cryptology 2014) showed that it is possible to convert a public key encryption (PKE) scheme which is key dependent message (KDM) secure with respect to projection functions (also called *projection-KDM secure*) into a PKE scheme which is KDM secure with respect to any function family that can be computed in fixed polynomial time, without using any other assumption. This result holds in both of the chosen plaintext attack (CPA) and the chosen ciphertext attack (CCA) settings. In the CPA setting, he furthermore showed that even a projection-KDM secure 1-bit PKE scheme is sufficient to construct a KDM secure PKE scheme with respect to polynomial time computable functions. The existence of the latter trivially implies that of the former, and in this sense, he mentioned that single-bit projection-KDM security in the CPA setting and (multi-bit) projection-KDM security in the CCA setting are *complete*.

In this paper, we show that *single-bit* projection-KDM security is *complete* also in the CCA setting. More specifically, as our main technical result, we show how to construct a projection-KDM-CCA secure multibit PKE scheme from a projection-KDM-CCA secure 1-bit PKE scheme, without using any other assumption. The combination of our result and Applebaum's result shows that one can construct a PKE scheme which is KDM-CCA secure with respect to any polynomial time computable functions from a projection-KDM-CCA secure 1-bit PKE scheme, without using additional assumptions.

Keywords: Public key encryption · KDM security · Chosen ciphertext security · Projection function

1 Introduction

1.1 Background and Motivation

Key dependent message (KDM) security, introduced by Black, Rogaway, and Shrimpton [11], and independently by Camenisch and Lysyanskaya [16], guarantees confidentiality of communication even if an adversary can get a ciphertext

© Springer International Publishing Switzerland 2015
K. Nyberg (ed.): CT-RSA 2015, LNCS 9048, pp. 201–219, 2015.
DOI: 10.1007/978-3-319-16715-2_11

of secret keys. KDM security is useful for many practical applications including anonymous credential systems [16] and hard disk encryption systems (e.g., Bit-Locker [11]). In addition, KDM security is also theoretically important because it can be used to show that computational security and axiomatic security are equivalent [1,2]. KDM security is defined in both the chosen plaintext attack (CPA) and chosen ciphertext attack (CCA) settings. In order to take active adversaries into consideration, we need CCA security for many applications. Moreover, CCA security implies non-malleability [9,18], and thus it is also considered as a desirable security notion for public key encryption (PKE) schemes used in practice. In this paper, we focus on PKE schemes that satisfy KDM security under CCA, namely *KDM-CCA* security.

KDM security is defined with respect to a function family $\mathcal{F}$. Let ℓ denote the number of keys and $\mathbf{sk} = (sk_1, \cdots, sk_\ell)$ be secret keys. Informally, a PKE scheme [1] is said to be $\mathcal{F}$-KDM secure if confidentiality of messages is protected even when an adversary can see a ciphertext of $f(\mathbf{sk})$ under j-th public key for any $f \in \mathcal{F}$ and $j \in \{1, \cdots, \ell\}$. In order to take various situations into consideration, it is desirable to construct a PKE scheme which is KDM secure with respect to a rich function family.

Today, it has been widely studied how to construct a KDM secure PKE scheme with respect to a rich function family based on a KDM secure PKE scheme with respect to a simpler function family [7,10,14]. Applebaum [3] called such a procedure KDM amplification, and he achieved a large KDM amplification gap. Specifically, he showed how to construct a PKE scheme which is KDM secure with respect to functions that can be computed in a-priori fixed polynomial time of the input and output length (also called *length-dependent KDM secure* [7]) using a PKE scheme which is KDM secure with respect to projection functions (*projeciton-KDM secuce*, for short). A projeciton function is a function each of whose output bit depends on at most one bit of an input. The projection function family is one of the simplest function families, and it is known that length-dependent KDM security is strong enough for various applications (e.g., axiomatic security applications [1,2,7]). We note that his result on KDM amplification works also in the CCA setting. Moreover, in the CPA setting, he showed that even a projection-KDM secure 1-bit PKE scheme is sufficient to construct a length-dependent secure PKE scheme. The existence of the latter trivially implies that of the former, and in this sense, he mentioned that single-bit projection-KDM security is *complete* in the CPA setting.

On the other hand, to the best of our knowledge, we need a non-interactive zero-knowledge (NIZK) proof system for NP languages to construct a length-dependent KDM-CCA secure scheme from a projection-KDM-CCA secure "1-bit" scheme. (For symmetric key encryption schemes, it is known that single-bit projection-KDM security is complete in the CCA setting [3,6].) This is because we need to use Camenisch, Chandran and Shoup's [15] transformation from a $\mathcal{F}$-KDM-CPA secure scheme to a $\mathcal{F}$-KDM-CCA secure scheme, where $\mathcal{F}$ is

---

[1] Unless stated otherwise, we assume that the message space of a PKE scheme is $\{0,1\}^*$.

a function family. In addition, it is still unknown whether we can construct a NIZK proof system from a KDM-CCA secure PKE scheme. Therefore, that we need to use a NIZK proof system to amplify KDM-CCA security means that we need to use an additional assumption, and thus, the "completeness" of single-bit projection-KDM security has not been shown in the CCA setting. In cryptography, it is very important to clarify the minimum assumption to realize various primitives. Furthermore, NIZK proofs are usually quite impractical, and the known efficient NIZK proofs (such as the Groth-Sahai proofs [19]) can only be used for languages related to bilinear groups, and thus their applicability is not so wide. Therefore, it is both theoretically and practically meaningful to clarify whether we can show the completeness of single-bit projection-KDM security in the CCA setting. Hence, in this paper, we tackle the following question: *Is single-bit projection-KDM security complete in the CCA setting?*

1.2   Our Results

Based on the above motivation, we tackle the above question and show the positive result. Namely we prove that single-bit projection-KDM-CCA security is complete in the sense of the following theorem.

Theorem 1 (Informal). *If there exists a projection-KDM-CCA secure 1-bit PKE scheme, then there also exists a length-dependent KDM-CCA secure PKE scheme.*

More specifically, as our main technical result, we show how to construct a projection-KDM-CCA secure multi-bit PKE scheme using a projection-KDM-DCCA secure 1-bit PKE scheme and a (non-KDM-)CCA secure PKE scheme. DCCA security is a security notion defined by Hohenberger, Lewko and Waters [21], and it is weaker than CCA security. We note that KDM-CCA security implies KDM-DCCA security, and we can construct a (non-KDM-)CCA secure scheme from a projection-KDM-CCA secure 1-bit scheme [21,24]. Therefore, we do not use any additional assumption, and we obtain Theorem 1 based on the combination of our result and the result by Applebaum [3]. We describe an overview of the results on KDM secure PKE in Fig 1.

As mentioned in Section 1.1, to the best of our knowledge, when we construct a length-dependent KDM-CCA secure PKE scheme using existing results, we need to use a NIZK proof system. Since a NIZK proof system is quite inefficient, it is an important problem to construct a length-dependent KDM-CCA secure PKE scheme without using a NIZK proof system. From our result, in order to solve this problem, we only have to construct a PKE scheme which satisfies single-bit projection-KDM-DCCA security that is much weaker and simpler, and thus potentially easier to achieve, than length-dependent KDM-CCA security.

1.3   Overview of Our Techniques

In this paper, as our main technical result, we show how to expand the message space of a projection-KDM-CCA secure PKE scheme. Our construction consists of two steps. In this section, we provide an overview of each step.

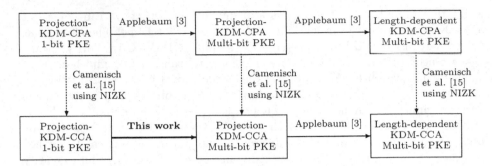

Fig. 1. Overview of the results on KDM secure PKE. An arrow from box X to box Y indicates that X can be used to construct Y. The dashed arrows indicate that NIZK proofs are additionally required.

First step: First, we explain why, in the CCA setting, we cannot use the same construction as Applebaum [3] used in the CPA setting to expand the message space of a projection-KDM secure PKE scheme. Specifically, he constructed the following bit-by-bit PKE scheme using a 1-bit PKE scheme. When the scheme encrypts arbitrary length message $m = m_1 \cdots m_n$, the scheme first encrypts $m_1, \cdots, m_n$ into $c_1, \cdots, c_n$ using the building block 1-bit scheme, and then outputs $c_1 \| \cdots \| c_n$ as a resulting ciphertext. Here, we note that a projection function is a function each of whose output bit depends on at most one bit of an input, and thus we can decompose a projection function f into n single-bit projection functions $f_1(\cdot), \cdots, f_n(\cdot)$ such that $f(\cdot) = f_1(\cdot) \| \cdots \| f_n(\cdot)$, where n is the output length of f. Due to this property, the bit-by-bit scheme can be shown to be projection-KDM-CPA secure, if so is the building block scheme.

However, we cannot use this bit-by-bit construction to expand the message space of (both KDM- and non-KDM-)CCA secure PKE scheme. This is because, in the security game, an adversary can make a decryption query which contains a part of the challenge ciphertext, and get a partial decryption result of it. However, we notice that the bit-by-bit scheme is not in general CCA secure, but is secure in the sense of *DCCA security* defined by Hohenberger, Lewko, and Waters [21]. (Also, DCCA security can be seen as a generalization of Unquoted CCA security defined by Myers and Shelat [24].)

A DCCA secure PKE scheme has a *detecting function* F in addition to the ordinary key generation, encryption and decryption algorithms. The detecting function F is a boolean function which, given two ciphertexts c^* and c, checks whether the decryption result of c is useful to distinguish c^*. (If a ciphertext c is useful, then F outputs 1.) Then DCCA security guarantees confidentiality as long as an adversary does not get the decryption result of a ciphertext c which satisfies $F(c^*, c) = 1$, where c^* is the challenge ciphertext. Also, a DCCA secure PKE scheme is required to satisfy a security notion called *unpredictability*. Unpredictability guarantees that without seeing a target ciphertext c^*, an adversary cannot generate a ciphertext c which satisfies $F(c^*, c) = 1$. In this paper, we extend DCCA security to the KDM setting, and define KDM security for a detectable PKE scheme. We call it KDM-DCCA security. In addition, the bit-by-bit scheme can be shown to be projection-KDM-DCCA secure, if the building block 1-bit PKE scheme is projection-KDM-CCA secure. (Actually, we show that a projection-KDM-"D"CCA secure 1-bit scheme is sufficient as a building block.)

Second step: In the second step, we show how to construct a projection-KDM-CCA secure PKE scheme using a projection-KDM-DCCA secure PKE scheme and a (non-KDM-)CCA secure PKE scheme as building blocks. Specifically, we construct a "double-layered" encryption scheme whose inner layer scheme is a projeciton-KDM-DCCA secure scheme Π_{in} and whose outer layer scheme is a CCA secure PKE scheme Π_{out}. Myers and Shelat [24], and Hohenberger et al. [21] also used the double-layered construction to construct a CCA secure multi-bit PKE scheme, but there is a big difference between theirs and ours. Both of the constructions [21,24] encrypt the outer scheme's random coin by the inner scheme. When decrypting a ciphertext, both constructions check the validity of the ciphertext by re-encrypting the inner ciphertext using the random coin that is recovered by decrypting the inner ciphertext, and checking if it equals the received ciphertext (which is a ciphertext of the outer scheme). This validity check by re-encryption is necessary in the constructions of [21,24] for achieving CCA security. However, interestingly, we will show that *neither "embedding of randomness into the inner scheme" nor "the validity check by re-encryption" is needed in our construction*. This is because in our construction, we use a CCA secure PKE scheme as the outer scheme, which is strong enough to enable us to avoid complicated arguments required in the security proofs of the constructions in [21,24]. We note that the goal of [21,24] was to achieve CCA security, and thus using a CCA secure scheme as one of the building blocks does not make sense in their works. On the other hand, our goal is to achieve a projection-KDM-CCA secure scheme, something stronger than ordinary CCA security, and thus using a CCA secure scheme makes sense in our case. Furthermore, due to the results of [21,24], we can construct a CCA secure multi-bit PKE scheme based only on a projection-KDM-CCA secure 1-bit PKE scheme, and thus using a CCA secure scheme is not an additional assumption.

Security of our double-layered PKE scheme. Finally, we provide an intuitive explanation that our double-layered PKE scheme Π is projection-KDM-CCA secure. In our construction, a message is first encrypted into c_{in} by the inner scheme Π_{in}, which is in turn encrypted into c_{out} by the outer scheme Π_{out}, and this c_{out} is a ciphertext of our construction Π. In the security game of projection-KDM security, an adversary can make a KDM query which is composed of an index of a key j and a projection function f. For this KDM query, according to the challenge bit, a challenger returns a ciphertext of $f(\mathbf{sk})$ or $0^{|f(\mathbf{sk})|}$ under j-th public key, where $\mathbf{sk} = (sk^1, \cdots, sk^\ell)$ and ℓ is the number of keys. For simplicity of the explanation here, suppose an adversary makes only one KDM query, in which case the result c^*_{out} of the query can be considered as the challenge ciphertext of the adversary. Suppose c^*_{out} is an encryption of the inner ciphertext c^*_{in}. Intuitively, it may seem that since the outer scheme Π_{out} is CCA secure, the adversary is not able to gain any information about c_{in}^* from c_{out}^*, and also since the inner scheme Π_{in} satisfies unpredictability, the adversary cannot make a decryption query c_{out} whose inner ciphertext c_{in} satisfies $F(c_{in}^*, c_{in}) = 1$ in the security game. (We call such a decryption query a *bad decryption query*.) Therefore, it also may seem that we can easily reduce the KDM security of our construction Π to the KDM security of the inner scheme Π_{in}. However, there is one problem. A secret key sk of our construction Π consists of two parts (sk_{in}, sk_{out}), where sk_{in} and sk_{out} are a secret key of the inner scheme Π_{in} and that of Π_{out}, respectively, and thus a KDM query for Π is a function of $sk = (sk_{in}, sk_{out})$, while the KDM query for the inner scheme Π_{in} is a function of only sk_{in}. Therefore, in order to reduce the KDM security of Π to the KDM security of Π_{in}, the reduction algorithm has to convert a KDM query for Π to a KDM query for Π_{in}. Namely, let $\mathbf{sk}_{in} = (sk_{in}^1, \cdots, sk_{in}^\ell)$ and $\mathbf{sk}_{out} = (sk_{out}^1, \cdots, sk_{out}^\ell)$, then we have to convert a projection function f to a projection function $\tilde{f}$ such that $f(\mathbf{sk}_{in}, \mathbf{sk}_{out}) = \tilde{f}(\mathbf{sk}_{in})$. It is not clear whether we can conduct such a conversion between KDM queries for general function classes. However, we show that we can conduct such a conversion for the projection function family due to the property that each output bit of a projection function depends on at most one bit of an input. Therefore, we can solve the above problem and prove the security of our scheme.

1.4   Related Work

Circular security, defined by Camenisch and Lysyanskaya [16], guarantees confidentiality of communication even when there is a key cycle encryption in the system. Key cycle encryption means encrypting sk_i under $pk_{(i \bmod \ell)+1}$ when there are ℓ pairs of keys in the system. KDM security is a generalization of circular security.

Boneh, Halevi, Hamburg, and Ostrovsky [12] constructed the first KDM secure PKE scheme in the standard model based on the decisional Diffie-Hellman (DDH) assumption. Their scheme is KDM secure with respect to the family of affine functions (*affine-KDM* secure, for short) which is a relatively simple function family. Today, we know constructions of affine-KDM secure PKE schemes based on the learning with errors (LWE) [4], quadratic residuosity (QR) [13], decisional composite residuosity (DCR) [13,23] and learning parity with noise (LPN) [4] assumptions. Also, Hofheinz [20] showed the first construction of a circular-CCA secure scheme whose security can be directly proved from number-theoretic assumptions.

Barak, Haitner, Hofheinz, and Ishai [7] and Brakerski, Goldwasser, and Kalai [14] showed KDM amplification results. Both of the results achieve a large amplification gap, while require some additional properties on the building blocks (other than that the building blocks are KDM secure). In addition, unlike Applebaum's KDM amplification method, it is unclear whether these KDM amplification results [7,14] work in the CCA setting. Bellare, Hoang, and Rogaway [10] showed a KDM amplification method that works only in the CPA setting but is more efficient than Applebaum's. Recently, Kitagawa, Matsuda, Hanaoka, and Tanaka [22] showed a similar result that works in the CCA setting.

Unruh et al. [5] defined a security notion called *adKDM* security. adKDM security takes adaptive corruptions and arbitrary active attacks into consideration, and thus it is a stronger security notion than ordinary KDM security. In addition, they showed that the OAEP encryption scheme satisfies adKDM security in the random oracle model. Recently, Davies and Stam [17] studied KDM security of hybrid encryption in the random oracle model.

2 Preliminaries

In this section we define some notations and cryptographic primitives.

2.1 Notations

In this paper, $x \xleftarrow{r} X$ denotes selecting an element from a finite set X uniformly at random, and $y \leftarrow \mathsf{A}(x)$ denotes assigning to y the output of an algorithm A on an input x. For strings x and y, $x \| y$ denotes the concatenation of x and y. λ denotes a security parameter. A function $f(\lambda)$ is a negligible function if $f(\lambda)$ tends to 0 faster than $\frac{1}{\lambda^c}$ for every constant $c > 0$. We write $f(\lambda) = \mathsf{negl}(\lambda)$ to denote $f(\lambda)$ being a negligible function. PPT stands for probabilistic polynomial time. $[\ell]$ denotes the set of integers $\{1, \cdots, \ell\}$. ϕ denotes an empty set.

2.2 Public Key Encryption

In this section we define public key encryption (PKE).

Definition 1 (Public key encryption). *A PKE scheme Π is a three tuple* $(\mathsf{KG}, \mathsf{Enc}, \mathsf{Dec})$ *of PPT algorithms.*

- *The key generation algorithm KG, given a security parameter 1^λ, outputs a public key pk and a secret key sk.*
- *The encryption algorithm Enc, given a public key pk and a message $m \in \mathcal{M}$, outputs a ciphertext c, where $\mathcal{M}$ is the plaintext space of Π.*
- *The decryption algorithm Dec, given a secret key sk and a ciphertext c, outputs a message $\tilde{m} \in \{\bot\} \cup \mathcal{M}$.*

Correctness. *We require $\mathsf{Dec}(sk, \mathsf{Enc}(pk, m)) = m$ for every $m \in \mathcal{M}$ and $(pk, sk) \leftarrow \mathsf{KG}(1^\lambda)$.*

Next, we define KDM-CCA security for PKE schemes.

Definition 2 (KDM-CCA security). *Let Π be a PKE scheme, $\mathcal{F}$ be a function family, and ℓ be the number of keys. We define the $\mathcal{F}$-KDM-CCA game between a challenger and an adversary $\mathcal{A}$ as follows.* $\mathbf{sk}$ *denotes* $(sk^1, \cdots, sk^\ell)$.

Initialization. *First the challenger selects a challenge bit* $b \xleftarrow{r} \{0, 1\}$. *Next the challenger generates ℓ key pairs* $(pk^j, sk^j) \leftarrow \mathsf{KG}(1^\lambda)(j = 1, \cdots, \ell)$ *and sends* $(pk^1, \cdots, pk^\ell)$ *to* $\mathcal{A}$. *Finally, the challenger prepares the KDM query list* L_{kdm} *into which pairs of the form* (j, c) *will be stored, where* $j \in [\ell]$ *is an index and c is a ciphertext, and which is initially empty.*

$\mathcal{A}$ may adaptively make palynomially many queries of the following two types.

KDM queries. (j^*, f), *where* $j^* \in [\ell]$ *and* $f \in \mathcal{F}$. *If* $b = 1$ *then the challenger returns* $c^* \leftarrow \mathsf{Enc}(pk^{j^*}, f(\mathbf{sk}))$; *If* $b = 0$ *then the challenger returns* $c^* \leftarrow \mathsf{Enc}(pk^{j^*}, 0^{|f(\mathbf{sk})|})$. *Finally, the challenger adds* (j^*, c^*) *to* L_{kdm}.

Decryption queries. (j, c), *where* $j \in [\ell]$ *and c is a ciphertext. The challenger returns* $\perp$ *if* $(j, c) \in L_{kdm}$; *Otherwise, the challenger returns* $m \leftarrow \mathsf{Dec}(sk^j, c)$.

Final phase. *$\mathcal{A}$ outputs* $b' \in \{0, 1\}$.

We say that the PKE scheme Π is $\mathcal{F}$-KDM-CCA secure if for any PPT adversary $\mathcal{A}$, we have $\mathsf{Adv}_{\Pi, \mathcal{A}}^{\mathcal{F}\text{-}kdmcca}(\lambda) := |\Pr[b = b'] - \frac{1}{2}| = \mathsf{negl}(\lambda)$.

As we can see, KDM security is defined with respect to function families. In this paper, we focus on KDM-CCA security with respect to the following function families.

Projection functions. A projection function is a function in which each output bit depends on at most a single bit of an input. Let f be a function and $y = y_1 \cdots y_m$ be the output of the function f on an input $x = x_1 \cdots x_n$, that is $f(x) = y$. We say that f is a projection function if it satisfies the following property.

$$\forall j \in [m], \exists i \in [n] : y_j \in \{0, 1, x_i, 1 - x_i\}$$

Let $\mathcal{P}_{u,v}^\ell = \{f | f : (\{0, 1\}^u)^\ell \to \{0, 1\}^v$ is a projection function.$\}$ and $\mathcal{P}_u^\ell = \{f | f : (\{0, 1\}^u)^\ell \to \{0, 1\}^*$ is a projection function.$\}$.

Constant functions. A constant function always outputs the same value regardless of an input. Let the function family $\mathcal{C}$ be $\{f : \{0, 1\}^* \to \{0, 1\}^*$ is a constant function.$\}$. Then we notice that $\mathcal{C}$-KDM-CCA security is equivalent to CCA security. More precisely, $\mathcal{C}$-KDM-CCA security is equivalent to CCA security in the multi-user setting formalized by Bellare et al. [8]. In addition, Bellare et al. show that multi-user CCA security is equivalent to (single-user) CCA security. Therefore we see that $\mathcal{C}$-KDM-CCA security is equivalent to CCA security. Also, a constant function is a special case of a projection function, and thus $\mathcal{C}$ is a subset of the family of projection functions.

Polynomial time computable functions. A polynomial time computable function is a function which can be computed in polynomial time of the input and output length. KDM security with respect to any polynomial time computable function is the strongest notion of KDM security, which is called *full-KDM security*. Then there is a slightly weaker notion called *length-dependent KDM security* [7]. Specifically, let p be a polynomial and the function family $\mathcal{L}_u^{\ell,p}$ be $\{f : (\{0, 1\}^u)^\ell \to \{0, 1\}^*$ is a function which can be computed in fixed polynomial p of the input and output length.}, then we say that a PKE scheme is *p-length-dependent KDM secure* if the scheme is $\mathcal{L}_u^{\ell,p}$-KDM secure for every polynomial ℓ. It is known that length-dependent KDM security is strong enough for various applications (e.g., axiomatic security applications [1,2,7]).

Applebaum [3] showed that single-bit projection-KDM security in the CPA setting and projection-KDM security in the CCA setting are complete. Here, we only review the result in the CCA setting.

Theorem 2 (Completeness of projection-KDM-CCA security [3]). *Let Π' be a PKE scheme which is $\mathcal{P}_u^\ell$-KDM-CCA secure for every polynomial ℓ. Then, for every polynomial p, we can construct a p-length-dependent KDM-CCA secure PKE scheme Π using Π' as a building block, without using any other assumption.*

2.3 Detectable Public Key Encryption

Hohenberger et al. [21] define detectable PKE. In this section, we review the definition.

Definition 3 (Detectable public key encryption). *A detectable PKE scheme Π is a four tuple $(\mathsf{KG}, \mathsf{Enc}, \mathsf{Dec}, \mathsf{F})$ of PPT algorithms.*

- *KG, Enc and Dec are defined in exactly the same way as those of a PKE scheme.*
- *The detecting function F, given a public key pk and two ciphertexts c^* and c, outputs $b \in \{0,1\}$. If $b = 1$, then we say that c^* and c are related.*

The correctness of a detectable PKE scheme is defined in the same way as that of a PKE scheme.

Moreover, we require the following *unpredictability* for a detectable PKE scheme.

Definition 4 (Unpredictability). *Let Π be a detectable PKE scheme. We define the unpredictability game between a challenger and an adversary $\mathcal{A}$ as follows.*

Initialization. *The challenger generates $(pk, sk) \leftarrow \mathsf{KG}(1^\lambda)$ and sends pk to $\mathcal{A}$. $\mathcal{A}$ may make polynomially many decryption queries.*
Decryption queries. *c which is a ciphertext. The challenger returns $m \leftarrow \mathsf{Dec}(sk, c)$.*
Final phase. *The adversary sends a message $m^* \in \mathcal{M}$ and a ciphertext c to the challenger, and the challenger computes $c^* \leftarrow \mathsf{Enc}(pk, m^*)$.*

We say that the detectable PKE scheme Π satisfies unpredictability if for any PPT adversary $\mathcal{A}$, we have $\mathsf{Adv}_{\Pi,\mathcal{A}}^{unp}(\lambda) := \Pr[\mathsf{F}(pk, c^*, c) = 1] = \mathsf{negl}(\lambda)$.

Hohenberger et al. consider a security notion for a detectable PKE scheme, which is called *DCCA security* (which stands for detectable CCA security). Here, we extend it to the KDM setting, and define KDM security for a detectable PKE scheme. We call it KDM-DCCA security.

Definition 5 (KDM-DCCA security). *Let Π be a detectable PKE scheme, $\mathcal{F}$ be a function family, and ℓ be the number of keys. We define the $\mathcal{F}$-KDM-DCCA game between a challenger and an adversary $\mathcal{A}$ in the same way as the $\mathcal{F}$-KDM-CCA game except that the way the challenger responds to decryption queries is changed as follows.*

Decryption queries. *(j, c), where $j \in [\ell]$ and c is a ciphertext. The challenger returns $\perp$ if there is an entry $(j^*, c^*) \in L_{kdm}$ which satisfies $j^* = j$ and $\mathsf{F}(pk^j, c^*, c) = 1$; Otherwise, the challenger returns $m \leftarrow \mathsf{Dec}(sk^j, c)$.*

We say that the detectable PKE scheme Π is $\mathcal{F}$-KDM-DCCA secure if for any PPT adversary $\mathcal{A}$, we have $\mathsf{Adv}_{\Pi,\mathcal{A}}^{\mathcal{F}\text{-}kdmdcca}(\lambda) := |\Pr[b = b'] - \frac{1}{2}| = \mathsf{negl}(\lambda)$.

3   From Single-bit Projection-KDM-DCCA Security to Multi-bit Projection-KDM-CCA Security

In this section, we show our main technical result: how to construct a multi-bit projection-KDM-CCA secure PKE scheme from a single-bit projection-KDM-DCCA secure detectable PKE scheme. More specifically, we construct a PKE scheme which is $\mathcal{P}_{s+t}^{\ell}$-KDM-CCA secure for every polynomial ℓ using a detectable PKE scheme which is $\mathcal{P}_{s,1}^{\ell}$-KDM-DCCA secure for every polynomial ℓ as a building block, where s is the secret key length of the building block scheme, and t is some polynomial (to be specified later).

There are two steps in our construction. In the first step (Section 3.1), we construct a $\mathcal{P}_s^{\ell}$-KDM-DCCA secure detectable PKE scheme from a $\mathcal{P}_{s,1}^{\ell}$-KDM-DCCA secure detectable PKE scheme, and in the second step (Section 3.2), we construct a $\mathcal{P}_{s+t}^{\ell}$-KDM-CCA secure PKE scheme using a $\mathcal{P}_s^{\ell}$-KDM-DCCA secure detectable PKE scheme and a CCA secure PKE scheme as building blocks, where t is the secret key length of the building block CCA secure scheme.

3.1   Single-bit to Multi-bit Amplification of Projection-KDM-DCCA Security

In this section, we show how to construct a multi-bit detectable PKE scheme which satisfies projection-KDM-DCCA security and unpredictability, using a 1-bit detectable PKE scheme which satisfies the same security notions. The construction is as follows. Let $\Pi' = (\mathsf{KG}', \mathsf{Enc}', \mathsf{Dec}', \mathsf{F}')$ be a 1-bit detectable PKE scheme. Then, using Π' as the building block, we construct a multi-bit detectable PKE scheme $\Pi = (\mathsf{KG}, \mathsf{Enc}, \mathsf{Dec}, \mathsf{F})$ as described in Fig. 2. We note

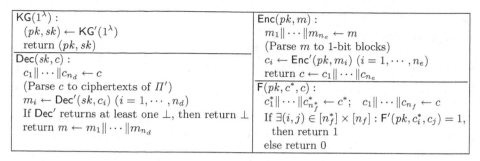

KG(1^λ) :	Enc(pk, m) :
$(pk, sk) \leftarrow$ KG$'(1^\lambda)$	$m_1\| \cdots \|m_{n_e} \leftarrow m$
return (pk, sk)	(Parse m to 1-bit blocks)
Dec(sk, c) :	$c_i \leftarrow$ Enc$'(pk, m_i)$ $(i = 1, \cdots, n_e)$
$c_1\| \cdots \|c_{n_d} \leftarrow c$	return $c \leftarrow c_1\| \cdots \|c_{n_e}$
(Parse c to ciphertexts of Π')	F(pk, c^*, c) :
$m_i \leftarrow$ Dec$'(sk, c_i)$ $(i = 1, \cdots, n_d)$	$c_1^*\| \cdots \|c_{n_f^*}^* \leftarrow c^*$; $c_1\| \cdots \|c_{n_f} \leftarrow c$
If Dec$'$ returns at least one $\perp$, then return $\perp$	If $\exists (i, j) \in [n_f^*] \times [n_f]$: F$'(pk, c_i^*, c_j) = 1$,
return $m \leftarrow m_1\| \cdots \|m_{n_d}$	then return 1
	else return 0

Fig. 2. The "bit-by-bit" construction of a projection-KDM-DCCA secure multi-bit detectable PKE scheme Π from a projection-KDM-DCCA 1-bit detectable PKE scheme Π'.

that the message space of Π is $\{0, 1\}^*$. Hereafter, let s be the length of a secret key of Π'.

Hohenberger et al. [21] show that this bit-by-bit scheme is DCCA secure if the building block 1-bit detectable PKE scheme is DCCA secure. Particularly, they show that if the building block satisfies unpredictability, then so does the resulting scheme. Formally, the following theorem holds.

Theorem 3. *[21] Let Π' be a detectable PKE scheme which satisfies unpredictability. Then Π is also a detectable PKE scheme which satisfies unpredictability.*

We prove that if the 1-bit detectable PKE scheme Π' is $\mathcal{P}_{s,1}^\ell$-KDM-DCCA secure for every polynomial ℓ which denotes the number of keys, then the multi-bit detectable PKE scheme Π is $\mathcal{P}_s^\ell$-KDM-DCCA secure for every polynomial ℓ. Formally, the following theorem holds.

Theorem 4. *Let Π' be a detectable PKE scheme which is $\mathcal{P}_{s,1}^\ell$-KDM-DCCA secure for every polynomial ℓ. Then Π is a detectable PKE scheme which is $\mathcal{P}_s^\ell$-KDM-DCCA secure for every polynomial ℓ.*

Proof. Let ℓ be a polynomial. Using an adversary $\mathcal{A}$ that attacks the $\mathcal{P}_s^\ell$-KDM-DCCA security of Π, we construct the following adversary $\mathcal{B}$ that attacks the $\mathcal{P}_{s,1}^\ell$-KDM-DCCA security of Π'.

Initialization. On input ℓ public keys $(pk^1, \cdots, pk^\ell)$ of Π', $\mathcal{B}$ sends these ℓ public keys to $\mathcal{A}$.

KDM queries. For a KDM query $(j^*, f) \in [\ell] \times \mathcal{P}_s^\ell$ from $\mathcal{A}$, $\mathcal{B}$ first computes a projection functions $f_1, \cdots, f_{n_e} \in \mathcal{P}_{s,1}^\ell$ such that $f(\cdot) = f_1(\cdot)\| \cdots \|f_{n_e}(\cdot)$, where n_e is the output length of f. (We note that since f is projection function, $f_1, \cdots, f_{n_e}$ are also projection functions.) Then $\mathcal{B}$ makes KDM queries $(j^*, f_1), \cdots, (j^*, f_{n_e})$ to the challenger to get the answers $c_1, \cdots, c_{n_e}$, and returns $c \leftarrow c_1\| \cdots \|c_{n_e}$ to $\mathcal{A}$.

Decryption queries. For a decryption query (j, c) from $\mathcal{A}$, $\mathcal{B}$ returns $\perp$ to $\mathcal{A}$ if F$(pk^j, c^*, c) = 1$ holds for an answer c^* of a previous KDM query whose

KG(1^λ) :	Enc(PK, m) :	Dec(SK, c_{out}) :
$(pk_{in}, sk_{in}) \leftarrow \mathsf{KG_{in}}(1^\lambda)$	$(pk_{in}, pk_{out}) \leftarrow PK$	$(sk_{in}, sk_{out}) \leftarrow SK$
$(pk_{out}, sk_{out}) \leftarrow \mathsf{KG_{out}}(1^\lambda)$	$c_{in} \leftarrow \mathsf{Enc_{in}}(pk_{in}, m)$	$c_{in} \leftarrow \mathsf{Dec_{out}}(sk_{out}, c_{out})$
$PK \leftarrow (pk_{in}, pk_{out})$	$c_{out} \leftarrow \mathsf{Enc_{out}}(pk_{out}, c_{in})$	If $c_{in} = \bot$ then return $\bot$
$SK \leftarrow (sk_{in}, sk_{out})$	return c_{out}	$m \leftarrow \mathsf{Dec_{in}}(sk_{in}, c_{in})$
return (PK, SK)		return m

Fig. 3. The "double-layered" construction of a projection-KDM-CCA secure scheme Π from a projectoin-KDM-DCCA secure multi-bit detectable PKE scheme Π_{in} and a (non-KDM-)CCA secure PKE scheme Π_{out}.

index of the key is j. Otherwise $\mathcal{B}$ parses c as $c_1, \cdots, c_{n_d}$ and queries these n_d ciphertexts as decryption queries to the challenger to get the answers $m_1, \cdots, m_{n_d}$. If the challenger returns at least one $\bot$, then $\mathcal{B}$ returns $\bot$ to $\mathcal{A}$. Otherwise, $\mathcal{B}$ returns $m \leftarrow m_1 \| \cdots \| m_{n_d}$ to $\mathcal{A}$.

Final phase. When $\mathcal{A}$ terminates with output $b' \in \{0, 1\}$, $\mathcal{B}$ outputs $\beta' = b'$.

We note that, for $\mathcal{A}$, $\mathcal{B}$ perfectly simulates the $\mathcal{P}_s^\ell$-KDM-DCCA game in which the challenge bit is the same as that of $\mathcal{P}_{s,1}^\ell$-KDM-DCCA game between the challenger and $\mathcal{B}$, and $\mathcal{B}$ just outputs $\mathcal{A}$'s output. Therefore, we have $\mathsf{Adv}_{\Pi', \mathcal{B}}^{\mathcal{P}_{s,1}^\ell\text{-}kdmdcca}(\lambda) = \mathsf{Adv}_{\Pi, \mathcal{A}}^{\mathcal{P}_s^\ell\text{-}kdmdcca}(\lambda)$. Since Π' is $\mathcal{P}_{s,1}^\ell$-KDM-DCCA secure, we see that $\mathsf{Adv}_{\Pi, \mathcal{A}}^{\mathcal{P}_s^\ell\text{-}kdmdcca}(\lambda) = \mathsf{negl}(\lambda)$. Since the choice of ℓ is arbitrary, Π is $\mathcal{P}_s^\ell$-KDM-DCCA secure for every polynomial ℓ.   □ **(Theorem 4)**

3.2   From Projection-KDM-DCCA Security to Projection-KDM-CCA Security

In this section, using a projection-KDM-DCCA secure PKE scheme as a building block, we construct a projection-KDM-CCA secure PKE scheme. The construction is as follows. Let $\Pi_{in} = (\mathsf{KG_{in}}, \mathsf{Enc_{in}}, \mathsf{Dec_{in}}, \mathsf{F})$ be a detectable PKE scheme and $\Pi_{out} = (\mathsf{KG_{out}}, \mathsf{Enc_{out}}, \mathsf{Dec_{out}})$ be a PKE scheme. (For convenience, we call Π_{in} the *inner* scheme and Π_{out} the *outer* scheme.) We require that the message space of Π_{in} and that of Π_{out} are $\{0, 1\}^*$. Then, we construct a PKE scheme Π as described in Fig. 3. We note that the message space of Π is also $\{0, 1\}^*$. Hereafter, we assume that the length of a secret key of Π_{in} and that of Π_{out} are s and t, respectively, and thus that of Π is $s + t$. Then we show the following theorem.

Theorem 5. *Let Π_{in} be a detectable PKE scheme which is unpredictable and $\mathcal{P}_s^\ell$-KDM-DCCA secure for every polynomial ℓ, and let Π_{out} be a CCA secure PKE scheme. Then Π is a PKE scheme which is $\mathcal{P}_{s+t}^\ell$-KDM-CCA secure for every polynomial ℓ.*

Proof. We prove this theorem via a sequence of games. Let ℓ be a polynomial, and let $\mathcal{A}$ be an adversary that attacks the $\mathcal{P}_{s+t}^\ell$-KDM-CCA security of our scheme Π, and makes at most Q_{kdm} KDM queries and Q_{dec} decryption queries.

In the proof, $\mathbf{SK}$, $\mathbf{sk}_{\text{in}}$, and $\mathbf{sk}_{\text{out}}$ denote $(SK^1, \cdots, SK^\ell)$, $(sk_{\text{in}}^1, \cdots, sk_{\text{in}}^\ell)$, and $(sk_{\text{out}}^1, \cdots, sk_{\text{out}}^\ell)$, respectively. In the original KDM-CCA game of Definition 2, each entry of L_{kdm} is of the form (j, c_{out}), where j is the index of the key and c_{out} is the resulting ciphertext of a KDM query. For convenience, we assume that L_{kdm} also stores the information of the inner ciphertext c_{in} in addition to (j, c_{out}), that is the challenger adds the index of the key j^*, the resulting ciphertext c_{out}^*, and Π_{in}'s ciphertext c_{in}^* to L_{kdm} after responding to a KDM query. This change does not affect $\mathcal{A}$'s view since $\mathcal{A}$ cannot see L_{kdm}. Now, consider the following sequence of games.

Game 0. This is the $\mathcal{P}_{s+t}^\ell$-KDM-CCA game regarding our PKE scheme Π.

Here, we define a *bad decryption query* as follows.

Bad decryption query: A decryption query (j, c_{out}) which satisfies both of the following conditions: (a) $(j, c_{\text{out}}, *) \notin L_{kdm}$; $\mathsf{Dec}_{\text{out}}(sk_{\text{out}}^j, c_{\text{out}}) = c_{\text{in}} \neq \perp$, and (b) there is an entry $(j^*, c_{\text{out}}^*, c_{\text{in}}^*) \in L_{kdm}$ which satisfies $j^* = j$ and $\mathsf{F}(pk_{\text{in}}^j, c_{\text{in}}^*, c_{\text{in}}) = 1$. Furthermore, in addition to (b), if $(j^*, c_{\text{out}}^*, c_{\text{in}}^*)$ is the entry which the challenger added when responding to i^*-th KDM query, then we say that such a decryption query is a *bad decryption query for i^*-th KDM query*.

Game 1. Same as Game 0 except that if $\mathcal{A}$ makes a bad decryption query, then the challenger returns $\perp$.

Game 2. Same as Game 1 except that if $\mathcal{A}$ makes a KDM query (j^*, f), then c_{in}^* is always computed by $c_{\text{in}}^* \leftarrow \mathsf{Enc}_{\text{in}}(pk_{\text{in}}^{j^*}, 0^{|f(\mathbf{SK})|})$.

Game 3. Same as Game 2 except that if $\mathcal{A}$ makes a KDM query (j^*, f), then c_{out}^* is computed by $c_{\text{out}}^* \leftarrow \mathsf{Enc}_{\text{out}}(pk_{\text{out}}^{j^*}, 0^{|c_{\text{in}}^*|})$.

For $i = 0, ..., 3$, we define the following events in Game i:

S_i: $\mathcal{A}$ succeeds in guessing the challenge bit, that is $b = b'$ occurs.
B_i: $\mathcal{A}$ makes at least one bad decryption query.

Then, we can estimate $\mathsf{Adv}_{\Pi, \mathcal{A}}^{\mathcal{P}_{s+t}^\ell\text{-}kdmcca}(\lambda)$ as follows:

$$\mathsf{Adv}_{\Pi, \mathcal{A}}^{\mathcal{P}_{s+t}^\ell\text{-}kdmcca}(\lambda) = |\Pr[S_0] - \frac{1}{2}|$$

$$\leq |\Pr[S_0] - \Pr[S_1]| + |\Pr[S_1] - \frac{1}{2}|$$

$$\overset{(*)}{\leq} |\Pr[S_1] - \frac{1}{2}| + \Pr[B_1]$$

$$\leq |\Pr[S_1] - \frac{1}{2}| + \sum_{i \in [2]} |\Pr[B_i] - \Pr[B_{i+1}]| + \Pr[B_3] \quad (1)$$

We notice that Game 0 and Game 1 are identical unless the event B_0 (resp. B_1) occurs in Game 0 (reap. Game 1). Therefore, we see that $|\Pr[S_0] - \Pr[S_1]| \leq \Pr[B_0] = \Pr[B_1]$, and thus we get the inequality $(*)$. Below, we show that each term of the right side of the inequality (1) is negligible.

Lemma 1. *Let Π_{in} be $\mathcal{P}_s^\ell$-KDM-DCCA secure. Then $|\Pr[S_1] - \frac{1}{2}| = \text{negl}(\lambda)$.*

Proof. Using the adversary $\mathcal{A}$ that attacks Π, we construct an adversary $\mathcal{B}$ that attacks the $\mathcal{P}_s^\ell$-KDM-DCCA security of Π_{in}. In order to simulate Game 1 for $\mathcal{A}$, for a KDM query $(j^*, f) \in [\ell] \times \mathcal{P}_{s+t}^\ell$ from $\mathcal{A}$, $\mathcal{B}$ has to return a ciphertext of $f(\mathbf{SK})$ or $0^{|f(\mathbf{SK})|}$ according to the challenge bit. However, $\mathcal{B}$ does not have $\mathbf{sk}_{\text{in}}$ which are secret keys of Π_{in}. Therefore, $\mathcal{B}$ has to compute $\tilde{f} \in \mathcal{P}_s^\ell$ such that $f(\mathbf{SK}) = \tilde{f}(\mathbf{sk}_{\text{in}})$ using $\mathbf{sk}_{\text{out}}$, and make a KDM query $(j^*, \tilde{f})$ to the challenger.

We first describe such a conversion of a projection function. Let $f \in \mathcal{P}_{s+t}^\ell$, and $\mathbf{z} = (z^1, \cdots, z^\ell) = (x^1\|y^1, \cdots, x^\ell\|y^\ell)$ be a variable of f, where $x^u \in \{0,1\}^s$ and $y^u \in \{0,1\}^t (u = 1, \cdots, \ell)$. Let $\mathbf{x} = (x^1, \cdots, x^\ell)$ and $\mathbf{y} = (y^1, \cdots, y^\ell)$. In the following, we describe the conversion algorithm conv which, given a projection function $f \in \mathcal{P}_{s+t}^\ell$ and a vector $\mathbf{y}_* \in (\{0,1\}^t)^\ell$ (which is considered as constants), outputs a projection function $\tilde{f} \in \mathcal{P}_s^\ell$ such that $f(\mathbf{z}) = \tilde{f}(\mathbf{x})$. (Note that the variable of $\tilde{f}$ is $\mathbf{x}$.) In the description of conv, $x^{u,v}$ (resp. $y^{u,v}$) denotes the v-th bit of x^u (resp. y^u), and f^w (resp. $\tilde{f}^w$) denotes the function which computes the w-th bit of the output of f (resp. $\tilde{f}$) for every input. [2]

$\mathsf{conv}(f, \boldsymbol{y}_*)$:
    $n \leftarrow$ the output length of f
    $f^1\|\cdots\|f^n \leftarrow f$
    for ($w = 1$ to n)
        If $f^w(\mathbf{z}) = y^{u,v}$ for some $(u,v) \in [\ell] \times [t]$, then define $\tilde{f}^w(\mathbf{x}) := y_*^{u,v}(\text{const.})$
        If $f^w(\mathbf{z}) = 1 - y^{u,v}$ for some $(u,v) \in [\ell] \times [t]$, then define
            $\tilde{f}^w(\mathbf{x}) := 1 - y_*^{u,v}(\text{const.})$
        If $f^w(\mathbf{z}) = x^{u,v}$ for some $(u,v) \in [\ell] \times [s]$, then define $\tilde{f}^w(\mathbf{x}) := x^{u,v}$
        If $f^w(\mathbf{z}) = 1 - x^{u,v}$ for some $(u,v) \in [\ell] \times [s]$, then define $\tilde{f}^w(\mathbf{x}) := 1 - x^{u,v}$
        If $f^w(\mathbf{z}) = d \in \{0,1\}$(i.e. f^w is a constant function), then define
            $\tilde{f}^w(\mathbf{x}) := d(\text{const.})$
    define $\tilde{f}(\mathbf{x}) := \tilde{f}^1(\mathbf{x})\|\cdots\|\tilde{f}^n(\mathbf{x})$
    return $\tilde{f}$

We can see that $\tilde{f} \in \mathcal{P}_s^\ell$, and it holds that $f(\mathbf{z}) = \tilde{f}(\mathbf{x})$ for every fixed $\mathbf{y}$. We notice that conv is computable in polynomial time. Then, we describe the adversary $\mathcal{B}$ as follows.

Initialization. On input ℓ public keys $(pk_{\text{in}}^1, \cdots, pk_{\text{in}}^\ell)$ of Π_{in}, $\mathcal{B}$ first generates ℓ pairs of Π_{out}'s keys $(pk_{\text{out}}^j, sk_{\text{out}}^j) \leftarrow \mathsf{KG}_{\text{out}}(1^\lambda)(j = 1, \cdots, \ell)$. Then $\mathcal{B}$ sets $PK^j \leftarrow (pk_{\text{in}}^j, pk_{\text{out}}^j)(j = 1, \cdots, \ell)$ and $\mathbf{sk}_{\text{out}} \leftarrow (sk_{\text{out}}^1, \cdots, sk_{\text{out}}^\ell)$, and sends $(PK^1, \cdots, PK^\ell)$ to $\mathcal{A}$. Finally $\mathcal{B}$ sets $L_{kdm} \leftarrow \phi$.

KDM queries. For a KDM query $(j^*, f) \in [\ell] \times \mathcal{P}_{s+t}^\ell$ from $\mathcal{A}$, $\mathcal{B}$ first computes $\tilde{f} \leftarrow \mathsf{conv}(f, \mathbf{sk}_{\text{out}})$. Then $\mathcal{B}$ makes a KDM query $(j^*, \tilde{f})$ to the challenger to get the answer c_{in}^*, and computes $c_{\text{out}}^* \leftarrow \mathsf{Enc}_{\text{out}}(pk_{\text{out}}^{j^*}, c_{\text{in}}^*)$. Finally, $\mathcal{B}$ returns c_{out}^* to $\mathcal{A}$ and adds $(j^*, c_{\text{out}}^*, c_{\text{in}}^*)$ to L_{kdm}.

---

[2] Note that since f is a projection function, each $f^w(\mathbf{z})$ is one of the following forms:$\{0$ or 1 (const.), $x^{u,v}$ or $1 - x^{u,v}$ for some $(u,v) \in [\ell] \times [s]$, $y^{u,v}$ or $1 - y^{u,v}$ for some $(u,v) \in [\ell] \times [t]\}$.

Decryption queries. For a decryption query (j, c_{out}) from $\mathcal{A}$, $\mathcal{B}$ returns $\bot$ to $\mathcal{A}$ if $(j, c_{out}, *) \in L_{kdm}$. Otherwise $\mathcal{B}$ computes $c_{in} \leftarrow \mathsf{Dec}_{out}(sk_{out}^j, c_{out})$ and returns $\bot$ to $\mathcal{A}$ if $c_{in} = \bot$ or there is an entry $(j^*, c_{out}^*, c_{in}^*) \in L_{kdm}$ which satisfies $j^* = j$ and $\mathsf{F}(pk_{in}^j, c_{in}^*, c_{in}) = 1$. Otherwise $\mathcal{B}$ makes a decryption query (j, c_{in}) to the challenger to get the answer m, and returns m to $\mathcal{A}$.

Final phase. When $\mathcal{A}$ terminates with output $b' \in \{0, 1\}$, $\mathcal{B}$ outputs $\beta' = b'$.

We note that, for $\mathcal{A}$, $\mathcal{B}$ perfectly simulates Game 1 in which the challenge bit for $\mathcal{A}$ is the same as that in the game between the challenger and $\mathcal{B}$. Moreover, $\mathcal{B}$ just outputs $\mathcal{A}$'s output. Therefore, we have $|\Pr[S_1] - \frac{1}{2}| = \mathsf{Adv}_{\Pi_{in}, \mathcal{B}}^{\mathcal{P}_s^\ell\text{-}kdmdcca}(\lambda)$. Since Π_{in} is $\mathcal{P}_s^\ell$-KDM-DCCA secure, we see that $|\Pr[S_1] - \frac{1}{2}| = \mathsf{negl}(\lambda)$.

$\square$ **(Lemma 1)**

Lemma 2. *Let Π_{in} be $\mathcal{P}_s^\ell$-KDM-DCCA secure. Then $|\Pr[B_1] - \Pr[B_2]| = \mathsf{negl}(\lambda)$.*

Proof. Using the adversary $\mathcal{A}$ that attacks Π, we construct the following adversary $\mathcal{B}$ that attacks the $\mathcal{P}_s^\ell$-KDM-DCCA security of Π_{in}.

Initialization. On input ℓ public keys $(pk_{in}^1, \cdots, pk_{in}^\ell)$ of Π_{in}, $\mathcal{B}$ first selects $b \xleftarrow{r} \{0, 1\}$ and generates ℓ pairs of Π_{out}'s keys $(pk_{out}^j, sk_{out}^j) \leftarrow \mathsf{KG}_{out}(1^\lambda)(j = 1, \cdots, \ell)$. Then $\mathcal{B}$ sets $PK^j \leftarrow (pk_{in}^j, pk_{out}^j)(j = 1, \cdots, \ell)$ and $\mathbf{sk}_{out} \leftarrow (sk_{out}^1, \cdots, sk_{out}^\ell)$, and sends $(PK^1, \cdots, PK^\ell)$ to $\mathcal{A}$. Finally, $\mathcal{B}$ sets $L_{kdm} = \phi$.

KDM queries. For a KDM query $(j^*, f) \in [\ell] \times \mathcal{P}_{s+t}^\ell$ from $\mathcal{A}$, $\mathcal{B}$ first computes the following two functions: a projection function $f_1 \leftarrow \mathsf{conv}(f, \mathbf{sk}_{out})$ and a constant function f_0 such that $f_0(\cdot) = 0^{|f(\cdot)|}$, where conv is the conversion algorithm between projection functions that we described in the proof of Lemma 1. Then $\mathcal{B}$ makes a KDM query (j^*, f_b) to the challenger to get the answer c_{in}^*, and computes $c_{out}^* \leftarrow \mathsf{Enc}_{out}(pk_{out}^{j^*}, c_{in}^*)$. Finally, $\mathcal{B}$ returns c_{out}^* to $\mathcal{A}$ and adds $(j^*, c_{out}^*, c_{in}^*)$ to L_{kdm}.

Decryption queries. For a decryption query from $\mathcal{A}$, $\mathcal{B}$ responds in the same manner as $\mathcal{B}$ in the proof of Lemma 1.

Final phase. When $\mathcal{A}$ terminates, $\mathcal{B}$ checks whether $\mathcal{A}$ made at least one bad decryption query. If this is the case, then $\mathcal{B}$ outputs $\beta' = 1$; Otherwise, $\mathcal{B}$ outputs $\beta' = 0$.

Let β be a challenge bit in the game between the challenger and $\mathcal{B}$. When $\beta = 0$, for a KDM query (j^*, f) from $\mathcal{A}$, c_{in}^* is always a ciphertext of $0^{|f(\mathbf{SK})|}$. Therefore, $\mathcal{B}$ perfectly simulates Game 2 for $\mathcal{A}$ if $\beta = 0$. On the other hand, when $\beta = 1$, $\mathcal{B}$ perfectly simulates Game 1 in which the challenge bit for $\mathcal{A}$ is b. This is because, when $\beta = 1$, whether c_{in}^* is a ciphertext of $f(\mathbf{SK})$ or $0^{|f(\mathbf{SK})|}$ is determined according to the bit b chosen randomly by $\mathcal{B}$. Moreover, regardless of the choice of β, $\mathcal{B}$ outputs 1 only if $\mathcal{A}$ makes at least one bad decryption query. Therefore, we have

$$\mathsf{Adv}_{\Pi_{in}, \mathcal{B}}^{\mathcal{P}_s^\ell\text{-}kdmdcca}(\lambda) = \frac{1}{2}|\Pr[\beta' = 1|\beta = 1] - \Pr[\beta' = 1|\beta = 0]|$$

$$= \frac{1}{2}|\Pr[B_1] - \Pr[B_2]|.$$

Since Π_{in} is $\mathcal{P}_s^\ell$-KDM-DCCA secure, we see that $|\Pr[B_1] - \Pr[B_2]| = \text{negl}(\lambda)$.

$\square$ (**Lemma 2**)

Lemma 3. *Let Π_{out} be CCA secure. Then $|\Pr[B_2] - \Pr[B_3]| = \text{negl}(\lambda)$.*

Proof. Let $\mathcal{C} = \{f : \{0,1\}^* \to \{0,1\}^*$ is a constant function.$\}$. As mentioned in Section 2.2, CCA security is equivalent to $\mathcal{C}$-KDM-CCA security. In this proof, using the adversary $\mathcal{A}$ that attacks Π, we construct the following adversary $\mathcal{B}$ that attacks the $\mathcal{C}$-KDM-CCA security of Π_{out}.

Initialization. On input ℓ public keys $(pk_{\text{out}}^1, \cdots, pk_{\text{out}}^\ell)$ of Π_{out}, $\mathcal{B}$ first generates ℓ pairs of Π_{in}'s keys $(pk_{\text{in}}^j, sk_{\text{in}}^j) \leftarrow \text{KG}_{\text{in}}(1^\lambda)(j = 1, \cdots, \ell)$. Then $\mathcal{B}$ sets $PK^j \leftarrow (pk_{\text{in}}^j, pk_{\text{out}}^j)(j = 1, \cdots, \ell)$ and sends $(PK^1, \cdots, PK^\ell)$ to $\mathcal{A}$. Finally, $\mathcal{B}$ sets $L_{kdm} = \phi$.

KDM queries. For a KDM query $(j^*, f) \in [\ell] \times \mathcal{P}_{s+t}^\ell$ from $\mathcal{A}$, $\mathcal{B}$ computes $c_{\text{in}}^* \leftarrow \text{Enc}_{\text{in}}(pk_{\text{in}}^{j^*}, 0^{|f(\mathbf{SK})|})$ and a constant function $f_c \in \mathcal{C}$ such that $f_c(\cdot) = c_{\text{in}}^*$. Then $\mathcal{B}$ makes a KDM query (j^*, f_c) to the challenger to get the answer c_{out}^*. Finally, $\mathcal{B}$ returns c_{out}^* to $\mathcal{A}$ and adds $(j^*, c_{\text{out}}^*, c_{\text{in}}^*)$ to L_{kdm}.

Decryption queries. For a decryption query (j, c_{out}) from $\mathcal{A}$, $\mathcal{B}$ returns $\bot$ to $\mathcal{A}$ if $(j, c_{\text{out}}, *) \in L_{kdm}$. Otherwise $\mathcal{B}$ makes a decryption query (j, c_{out}) to the challenger and gets the answer c_{in}. If $c_{\text{in}} = \bot$ or there is an entry $(j^*, c_{\text{out}}^*, c_{\text{in}}^*) \in L_{kdm}$ which satisfies $j^* = j$ and $\text{F}(pk_{\text{in}}^j, c_{\text{in}}^*, c_{\text{in}}) = 1$, then $\mathcal{B}$ returns $\bot$ to $\mathcal{A}$; Otherwise $\mathcal{B}$ computes $m \leftarrow \text{Dec}_{\text{in}}(sk_{\text{in}}^j, c_{\text{in}})$ and returns m to $\mathcal{A}$.

Final phase. When $\mathcal{A}$ terminates, $\mathcal{B}$ checks whether $\mathcal{A}$ made at least one bad decryption query. If this is the case, then $\mathcal{B}$ outputs $\beta' = 1$; Otherwise, $\mathcal{B}$ outputs $\beta' = 0$.

Let β be a challenge bit in the game between the challenger and $\mathcal{B}$. When $\beta = 1$, for a KDM query (j^*, f), c_{out}^* is a ciphertext of c_{in}^* (and c_{in}^* is in turn a ciphertext of $0^{|f(\mathbf{SK})|}$). Therefore, $\mathcal{B}$ perfectly simulates Game 2 for $\mathcal{A}$ if $\beta = 1$. On the other hand, when $\beta = 0$, c_{out}^* is a ciphertext of $0^{|c_{\text{in}}^*|}$, hence $\mathcal{B}$ perfectly simulates Game 3 for $\mathcal{A}$ if $\beta = 0$. Moreover, in both cases, $\mathcal{B}$ outputs 1 only if $\mathcal{A}$ makes at least one bad decryption query. Therefore, we have

$$\text{Adv}_{\Pi_{\text{out}}, \mathcal{B}}^{\mathcal{C}\text{-}kdmcca}(\lambda) = \frac{1}{2}|\Pr[\beta' = 1|\beta = 1] - \Pr[\beta' = 1|\beta = 0]| = \frac{1}{2}|\Pr[B_2] - \Pr[B_3]|.$$

Since Π_{out} is CCA secure, and hence $\mathcal{C}$-KDM-CCA secure, we have $\text{Adv}_{\Pi_{\text{out}}, \mathcal{B}}^{\mathcal{C}\text{-}kdmcca}(\lambda) = \text{negl}(\lambda)$. Therefore, we see that $|\Pr[B_2] - \Pr[B_3]| = \text{negl}(\lambda)$.

$\square$ (**Lemma 3**)

Lemma 4. *Let Π_{in} be unpredictable. Then $\Pr[B_3] = \text{negl}(\lambda)$.*

Proof. Using the adversary $\mathcal{A}$ that attacks Π, we construct the following adversary $\mathcal{B}$ that attacks the unpredictability of Π_{in}.

Initialization. On input a public key pk_{in}^* of Π_{in}, $\mathcal{B}$ first selects $r_0 \xleftarrow{r} [\ell]$ and sets $pk_{\text{in}}^{r_0} \leftarrow pk_{\text{in}}^*$. Then $\mathcal{B}$ generates $\ell - 1$ pairs of Π_{in}'s keys $(pk_{\text{in}}^j, sk_{\text{in}}^j) \leftarrow \mathsf{KG}_{\text{in}}(1^\lambda)(j = 1, \cdots, r_0 - 1, r_0 + 1, \cdots, \ell)$ and ℓ pairs of Π_{out}'s keys $(pk_{\text{out}}^j, sk_{\text{out}}^j) \leftarrow \mathsf{KG}_{\text{out}}(1^\lambda)(j = 1, \cdots, \ell)$. Next, $\mathcal{B}$ sets $PK^j \leftarrow (pk_{\text{in}}^j, pk_{\text{out}}^j)(j = 1, \cdots, \ell)$ and sends $(PK^1, \cdots, PK^\ell)$ to $\mathcal{A}$. Finally, $\mathcal{B}$ sets $L_{kdm} = \phi$.

KDM queries. For a KDM query $(j^*, f) \in [\ell] \times \mathcal{P}_{s+t}^\ell$ from $\mathcal{A}$, $\mathcal{B}$ computes $c_{\text{in}}^* \leftarrow \mathsf{Enc}_{\text{in}}(pk_{\text{in}}^{j^*}, 0^{|f(\mathbf{SK})|})$ and $c_{\text{out}}^* \leftarrow \mathsf{Enc}_{\text{out}}(pk_{\text{out}}^{j^*}, 0^{|c_{\text{in}}^*|})$, and returns c_{out}^* to $\mathcal{A}$. Finally, $\mathcal{B}$ adds $(j^*, c_{\text{out}}^*, c_{\text{in}}^*)$ to L_{kdm}.

Decryption queries. For a decryption query (j, c_{out}) from $\mathcal{A}$, $\mathcal{B}$ returns $\bot$ to $\mathcal{A}$ if $(j, c_{\text{out}}, *) \in L_{kdm}$. Otherwise $\mathcal{B}$ computes $c_{\text{in}} \leftarrow \mathsf{Dec}_{\text{out}}(sk_{\text{out}}^j, c_{\text{out}})$ and returns $\bot$ to $\mathcal{A}$ if $c_{\text{in}} = \bot$ or there is an entry $(j^*, c_{\text{out}}^*, c_{\text{in}}^*) \in L_{kdm}$ which satisfies $j^* = j$ and $\mathsf{F}(pk_{\text{in}}^j, c_{\text{in}}^*, c_{\text{in}}) = 1$. Otherwise if $j = r_0$, then $\mathcal{B}$ makes a decryption query c_{in} to the challenger to get the answer m, and returns m to $\mathcal{A}$; if $j \neq r_0$, then $\mathcal{B}$ computes $m \leftarrow \mathsf{Dec}_{\text{in}}(sk_{\text{in}}^j, c_{\text{in}})$ and returns m to $\mathcal{A}$.

Final phase. When $\mathcal{A}$ terminates, $\mathcal{B}$ first selects $r_1 \xleftarrow{r} [Q_{kdm}]$ and $r_2 \xleftarrow{r} [Q_{dec}]$. Let (j^{r_1}, f^{r_1}) be the r_1-th KDM query and let $(j^{r_2}, c_{\text{out}}^{r_2})$ be the r_2-th decryption query made by $\mathcal{A}$. $\mathcal{B}$ aborts if it holds that $(j^{r_2}, c_{\text{out}}^{r_2}, *) \in L_{kdm}$ or $j^{r_1} \neq j^{r_2}$ or $j^{r_2} \neq r_0$ or $\mathsf{Dec}_{\text{out}}(sk_{\text{out}}^{j^{r_2}}, c_{\text{out}}^{r_2}) = c_{\text{in}}^{r_2} = \bot$. Otherwise, $\mathcal{B}$ outputs $(c_{\text{in}}^{r_2}, 0^{|f^{r_1}(\mathbf{SK})|})$.

We see that $\mathcal{B}$ perfectly simulates Game 3 for $\mathcal{A}$. In Game 3, an answer c_{out}^* for a KDM query does not contain any information about c_{in}^*. In addition, the distribution of each c_{in}^* generated in Game 3 is identical to that of the ciphertext which $\mathcal{B}$'s challenger generates in the unpredictability game. Therefore, we see that $\mathcal{B}$ succeeds in attacking the unpredictability of Π_{in} with the probability that r_0, r_1 and r_2 are chosen randomly, r_2-th decryption query from $\mathcal{A}$ is a bad decryption query for r_1-th KDM query and the index of the key is r_0. We define the following event $B_3^{i_1, i_2}$ for every $i_1 \in [Q_{kdm}]$ and $i_2 \in [Q_{dec}]$.

$B_3^{i_1, i_2}$: In Game 3, the i_2-th decryption query made by $\mathcal{A}$ is a bad decryption query for the i_1-th KDM query made by $\mathcal{A}$.

Then we have $\Pr[B_3] \leq \sum_{i_1 \in [Q_{kdm}]} \sum_{i_2 \in [Q_{dec}]} \Pr[B_3^{i_1, i_2}]$. The choices of r_0, r_1, and r_2 are uniformly random and independent of $\mathcal{A}$, and thus does not affect the behavior of $\mathcal{A}$. Therefore we see that

$$\mathsf{Adv}_{\Pi_{\text{in}}, \mathcal{B}}^{unp}(\lambda) = \sum_{i_1 \in [Q_{kdm}]} \sum_{i_2 \in [Q_{dec}]} \Pr[B_3^{i_1, i_2} \wedge r_1 = i_1 \wedge r_2 = i_2 \wedge j^{r_1} = r_0]$$

$$= \sum_{i_1 \in [Q_{kdm}]} \sum_{i_2 \in [Q_{dec}]} \Pr[B_3^{i_1, i_2}] \cdot \Pr[r_1 = i_1] \cdot \Pr[r_2 = i_2] \cdot \Pr[j^{r_1} = r_0]$$

$$= \frac{1}{Q_{kdm} Q_{dec} \ell} \sum_{i_1 \in [Q_{kdm}]} \sum_{i_2 \in [Q_{dec}]} \Pr[B_3^{i_1, i_2}]$$

From the above, we have $\Pr[B_3] \leq Q_{kdm} Q_{dec} \ell \cdot \mathsf{Adv}_{\Pi_{\text{in}}, \mathcal{B}}^{unp}(\lambda)$. Since Π_{in} is unpredictable, and Q_{kdm}, Q_{dec}, and ℓ are polynomials, we see that $\Pr[B_3] = \mathsf{negl}(\lambda)$.

$\square$ **(Lemma 4)**

From the inequality (1) and Lemmas 1 to 4, we have $\mathsf{Adv}_{\Pi,\mathcal{A}}^{\mathcal{P}_{s+t}^{\ell}\text{-}kdmcca}(\lambda) = $ negl(λ). Since the choice of ℓ is arbitrary, we see that Π is $\mathcal{P}_{s+t}^{\ell}$-KDM-CCA secure for every polynomial ℓ. $\square$ **(Theorem 5)**

4   Conclusion

From Theorems 3, 4 and 5, we showed that it is possible to construct a projection-KDM-CCA secure multi-bit PKE scheme using only a projection-KDM-DCCA secure 1-bit PKE scheme. Due to our result and Theorem 2 (which is shown by Applebaum [3]), we can conclude that we can obtain a length-dependent KDM-CCA secure PKE scheme from a projection-KDM-DCCA secure 1-bit PKE scheme, without using any other assumption. Formally, the following theorem holds.

Theorem 6 (Completeness of single-bit projection-KDM-DCCA security). *Let Π' be a detectable PKE scheme whose secret key length is s and which is unpredictable and $\mathcal{P}_{s,1}^{\ell}$-KDM-DCCA secure for every polynomial ℓ. Then, for every polynomial p, we can construct a p-length-dependent KDM-CCA secure PKE scheme Π using Π' as a building block, without using any other assumption.*

As mentioned earlier, it is still unknown how to construct a length-dependent KDM-CCA secure PKE scheme without using a NIZK proof system, and thus it is an important open problem. From our result, in order to solve this problem, we can concentrate on the construction of a 1-bit detectable PKE scheme which satisfies unpredictability and projection-KDM-DCCA security.

References

1. Abadi, M., Rogaway, P.: Reconciling two views of cryptography (the computational soundness of formal encryption). J. Cryptology **20**(3), 395 (2007)
2. Adão, P., Bana, G., Herzog, J., Scedrov, A.: Soundness and completeness of formal encryption: The cases of key cycles and partial information leakage. Journal of Computer Security **17**(5), 737–797 (2009)
3. Applebaum, B.: Key-dependent message security: Generic amplification and completeness. J. Cryptology **27**(3), 429–451 (2014). (The proceedings version appears in EUROCRYPT 2011)
4. Applebaum, B., Cash, D., Peikert, C., Sahai, A.: Fast cryptographic primitives and circular-secure encryption based on hard learning problems. In: Halevi, S. (ed.) CRYPTO 2009. LNCS, vol. 5677, pp. 595–618. Springer, Heidelberg (2009)
5. Backes, M., Dürmuth, M., Unruh, D.: OAEP is secure under key-dependent messages. In: Pieprzyk, J. (ed.) ASIACRYPT 2008. LNCS, vol. 5350, pp. 506–523. Springer, Heidelberg (2008)
6. Backes, M., Pfitzmann, B., Scedrov, A.: Key-dependent message security under active attacks - brsim/uc-soundness of symbolic encryption with key cycles. In: CSF 2007, pp. 112–124 (2007)

7. Barak, B., Haitner, I., Hofheinz, D., Ishai, Y.: Bounded key-dependent message security. In: Gilbert, H. (ed.) EUROCRYPT 2010. LNCS, vol. 6110, pp. 423–444. Springer, Heidelberg (2010)

8. Bellare, M., Boldyreva, A., Micali, S.: Public-key encryption in a multi-user setting: security proofs and improvements. In: Preneel, B. (ed.) EUROCRYPT 2000. LNCS, vol. 1807, pp. 259–274. Springer, Heidelberg (2000)

9. Bellare, M., Desai, A., Pointcheval, D., Rogaway, P.: Relations among notions of security for public-key encryption schemes. In: Krawczyk, H. (ed.) CRYPTO 1998. LNCS, vol. 1462, pp. 26–45. Springer, Heidelberg (1998)

10. Bellare, M., Hoang, V., Rogaway, P.: Garbling schemes. IACR Cryptology ePrint Archive, 2012:265 (2012) (The proceedings version appears in ACMCCS 2012)

11. Black, J., Rogaway, P., Shrimpton, T.: Encryption-scheme security in the presence of key-dependent messages. In: Nyberg, K., Heys, H. (eds.) SAC 2002. LNCS, vol. 2595, pp. 62–75. Springer, Heidelberg (2003)

12. Boneh, D., Halevi, S., Hamburg, M., Ostrovsky, R.: Circular-secure encryption from decision diffie-hellman. In: Wagner, D. (ed.) CRYPTO 2008. LNCS, vol. 5157, pp. 108–125. Springer, Heidelberg (2008)

13. Brakerski, Z., Goldwasser, S.: Circular and leakage resilient public-key encryption under subgroup indistinguishability - (or: quadratic residuosity strikes back). In: Rabin, T. (ed.) CRYPTO 2010. LNCS, vol. 6223, pp. 1–20. Springer, Heidelberg (2010)

14. Brakerski, Z., Goldwasser, S., Kalai, Y.T.: Black-box circular-secure encryption beyond affine functions. In: Ishai, Y. (ed.) TCC 2011. LNCS, vol. 6597, pp. 201–218. Springer, Heidelberg (2011)

15. Camenisch, J., Chandran, N., Shoup, V.: A public key encryption scheme secure against key dependent chosen plaintext and adaptive chosen ciphertext attacks. In: Joux, A. (ed.) EUROCRYPT 2009. LNCS, vol. 5479, pp. 351–368. Springer, Heidelberg (2009)

16. Camenisch, J., Lysyanskaya, A.: An efficient system for non-transferable anonymous credentials with optional anonymity revocation. In: Pfitzmann, B. (ed.) EUROCRYPT 2001. LNCS, vol. 2045, pp. 93–118. Springer, Heidelberg (2001)

17. Davies, G.T., Stam, M.: KDM security in the hybrid framework. In: Benaloh, J. (ed.) CT-RSA 2014. LNCS, vol. 8366, pp. 461–480. Springer, Heidelberg (2014)

18. Dolev, D., Dwork, C., Naor, M.: Non-malleable cryptography (extended abstract). In: STOC 1991, pp. 542–552 (1991)

19. Groth, J., Sahai, A.: Efficient noninteractive proof systems for bilinear groups. SIAM J. Comput. 41(5), 1193–1232 (2012)

20. Hofheinz, D.: Circular chosen-ciphertext security with compact ciphertexts. In: Johansson, T., Nguyen, P.Q. (eds.) EUROCRYPT 2013. LNCS, vol. 7881, pp. 520–536. Springer, Heidelberg (2013)

21. Hohenberger, S., Lewko, A., Waters, B.: Detecting dangerous queries: a new approach for chosen ciphertext security. In: Pointcheval, D., Johansson, T. (eds.) EUROCRYPT 2012. LNCS, vol. 7237, pp. 663–681. Springer, Heidelberg (2012)

22. Kitagawa, F., Matsuda, T., Hanaoka, G., Tanaka, K.: Efficient key dependent message security amplification against chosen ciphertext attacks. In: Lee, J., Kim, J. (eds.): ICISC 2014. LNCS, vol. 8949, pp. 1–17. Springer, Heidelberg (2015)

23. Malkin, T., Teranishi, I., Yung, M.: Efficient circuit-size independent public key encryption with KDM security. In: Paterson, K.G. (ed.) EUROCRYPT 2011. LNCS, vol. 6632, pp. 507–526. Springer, Heidelberg (2011)

24. Myers, S., Shelat, A.: Bit encryption is complete. In: FOCS 2009, pp. 607–616 (2009)

Format Oracles on OpenPGP

Florian Maury, Jean-René Reinhard[(✉)], Olivier Levillain, and Henri Gilbert

ANSSI, Paris, France
{florian.maury,jean-rene.reinhard,olivier.levillain,
henri.gilbert}@ssi.gouv.fr

Abstract. The principle of padding oracle attacks has been known in the cryptography research community since 1998. It has been generalized to exploit any property of decrypted ciphertexts, either stemming from the encryption scheme, or the application data format. However, this attack principle is being leveraged time and again against proposed standards and real-world applications. This may be attributed to several factors, e.g., the backward compatibility with standards selecting oracle-prone mechanisms, the difficulty of safely implementing decryption operations, and the misuse of libraries by non cryptography-savvy developers. In this article, we present several format oracles discovered in applications and libraries implementing the OpenPGP message format, among which the popular GnuPG application. We show that, if the oracles they implement are made available to an adversary, e.g., by a frontend application, he can, by querying repeatedly these oracles, decrypt all OpenPGP symmetrically encrypted packets. The corresponding asymptotic query complexities range from 2 to 2^8 oracle requests per plaintext byte to recover.

Keywords: GnuPG · Authenticated encryption · Chosen ciphertext attacks · Padding oracle · Format oracle · Implementation

1 Introduction

As defined in [4], a padding oracle attack is a particular type of side-channel attack where the attacker is assumed to have access to an oracle which returns True only when a chosen ciphertext corresponds to a correctly padded plaintext under a given scheme. Bleichenbacher [5] first applied this kind of attack to the PKCS#1 version v1.5 asymmetric encryption scheme. Vaudenay [15] showed that the same principle can be applied in the case of symmetric encryption when structured padding schemes are used. The "padding" terminology was introduced because the first attacks of this kind applied to specific padding schemes. They can be generalized to any format constraint on the plaintext providing redundancy, either imposed by the cryptographic scheme, or by the application using encryption, as illustrated by Klíma and Rosa on the PKCS#7

This work was partially supported by the French National Research Agency through the BLOC project (contract ANR-11-INS-011).

© Springer International Publishing Switzerland 2015
K. Nyberg (ed.): CT-RSA 2015, LNCS 9048, pp. 220–236, 2015.
DOI: 10.1007/978-3-319-16715-2_12

format [10] and Mitchell [12]. We call this generalized form of oracle attacks *format oracle attacks*.

This type of attacks initially stems from the misconception that encryption mechanisms can provide a weak form of integrity through the following procedure: a format containing redundancy, e.g., fixed byte values, or linear relations, is applied to the plaintext before encryption. After decryption, it is checked whether the result satisfies the redundancy. Due to the malleability of some encryption schemes, and use of format properties that are satisfied with relatively high probability by random messages, this opens the way to chosen-ciphertext plaintext recovery attacks. Indeed, a format oracle leaks some information on the decryption of the submitted request. If all submitted requests are related to the same target ciphertext, its decryption may be obtained by aggregating the corresponding information leakage.

Format oracle answers come in different flavours. They all rely on a variation of the behaviour of the decryption procedure related to some property of the decrypted value: specific byte values expected at some positions or high-level consistency constraints for example. The most explicit forms of information leakage are characteristic error messages. Format oracles can also be obtained by exploring logged information. Finally, more implicit oracles, relying on timing leaks, memory caching strategies, and other side-channels, are also possible. Even though the principle of padding, and format, oracles has been known for over 15 years, numerous publications [1,2,4,7,13,14] attest that they are quite pervasive, and may continue to be instantiated in modern applications.

A general countermeasure against these attacks consists in checking the integrity of ciphertexts before performing any decryption, thus eliminating any chosen-ciphertext attack possibility by construction. Unfortunately, due to backward compatibility issues, many standards still do not support proper authenticated encryption. Moreover, this may require a two-pass authenticated decryption that may be impractical when large streams of data are processed. As a consequence, a less satisfying fallback solution has been adopted in several contexts: ensuring implementations do not instantiate format oracles in order to avoid the exploitation of these attacks. This sometimes leads to convoluted implementations, since one has to ensure that no side-channel leaks information. Another concern is the misuse of cryptographic toolkits and libraries. Such software is developed by programmers proficient in cryptography. They strive to make their implementation resistant against state-of-the-art attacks, by selecting robust cryptography, and by avoiding side-channel leakage. Yet, most programmers using cryptographic libraries are not expert cryptographic security evaluators. They can legitimately expect them to behave as secure modules, unless explicetely advised otherwise. Therefore, if sufficient warnings are not made, they may incorrectly perceive some of their outputs, e.g., sensitive error messages, as innocuous.

OpenPGP [9] is a message format used to preserve privacy by providing encryption. It is notably implemented in the popular GnuPG toolkit. Recently, two JavaScript libraries, OpenPGP.js and Google-backed End-to-End, have been released.

Previous attacks against OpenPGP implementations leveraged the malleability of the encryption mode used in OpenPGP to recover plaintexts. A first attack [8], by Jallad, Katz and Schneier, achieves complete decryption of ciphertexts but requires access to a decryption oracle, that may be implemented by an inadvertent user transmitting random-looking decryption results to the adversary. A second attack [11], by Mister and Zuccherato, takes advantage of a less powerful oracle related to the CFB-mode variation used by OpenPGP to detect the use of an erroneous decryption key and enables to recover two bytes from every ciphertext block. This second attack is an example of a padding oracle attack. Some mitigation measures have been adopted against these attacks, like removing the CFB-mode oracle when decryption relies on asymmetric cryptography, or introducing encryption with integrity. However some implementations still leak in certain use cases the information exploited by these attacks: the security ultimately relies on the careful use of the application.

The main contribution of this article is the identification of several new format oracles in OpenPGP implementations. We show that many OpenPGP applications and libraries, e.g., GnuPG, OpenPGP.js, and End-to-End, actually leak sensitive information in error messages raised during the decryption of OpenPGP encrypted messages. If these error messages are mishandled, e.g., by a front-end application, the identified oracles can be leveraged to fully decrypt any encrypted message, thus demonstrating that the error messages are not innocuous with regards to confidentiality. This leads us to believe that the handling of errors, e.g., decryption errors, is a part of the API of cryptographic libraries that should receive more attention. To minimize the risk of implementation errors, cryptographic library providers should prevent any unnecessary leakage of information, and clearly identify the elements of the API that are sensitive.

Similarly to previously published padding oracle attacks, these attacks are chosen-ciphertext attacks requiring interactions with a legitimate recipient of the target message. The complexity of these format oracle attacks ranges from 2 to 2^8 queries to the format oracle per byte to decrypt, according to the leveraged oracle. We implemented these attacks against GnuPG and experimentally confirmed their complexity.

We reported our findings to the developers of the mentioned OpenPGP implementations. They took them into account by patching their implementations to remove some possible oracles (cf Section 5 for details).

In Section 2.1, we give an overview of the OpenPGP message format and its (authenticated) encryption mechanism. Section 3 presents format oracles, which are implemented by GnuPG, OpenPGP.js, and End-to-End, when they are viewed as libraries, and Section 4 how these format oracles can be leveraged to decrypt ciphertexts. In Section 5, we discuss countermeasures to thwart them.

Notations. We denote E a block cipher and n its blocksize expressed in bytes. E_K denotes encryption under key K.

Let $||$ denote the concatenation. Let P be a non-empty message $P \in (\{0,1\}^8)^*$. Let $|P|$ be its byte length. It can be decomposed into a sequence of blocks $P_1||P_2||\ldots||P_m$, where P_i is an n-byte block for $i < m$, and P_m is a non-empty, possibly incomplete, block.[1] Let $\|P\| = m$ denote the number of blocks of P in this decomposition. Furthermore, for $j \in [1, |P|]$, let $P[j]$ be the j-th byte of message P. $P_i[j]$ is the j-th byte of the i-th block of P. For $j \in [1, |P|]$, $P[-j]$ is the j-th byte from the end: $P[-j] = P[|P| + 1 - j]$. Let $\overline{P} = P[-2] \| P[-1]$ be the concatenation of the last two bytes of P.

Explicit byte values are given in hexadecimal form, e.g., 0xD3. 0x00$_u$ denotes the concatenation of u zero bytes.

2   OpenPGP Format Description

2.1   Packet Structure of OpenPGP Message Format

Overview. All values (data, keys, etc.) considered by OpenPGP are structured and processed in *packets*. Well-formed OpenPGP messages follow a grammar described in [9, section 11.3], which specifies a recursive composition of packets and OpenPGP messages: an OpenPGP message is a concatenation of packets, some of which may contain a processed form of an OpenPGP message. Each packet is a sequence of bytes, with a (tag, length, value) structure.[2] The first byte, called the *tag*, encodes the type of information that the packet contains. The length field encodes the length of the value field. The value contains the payload of the packet, and its structure depends on the considered packet type.

Data Packet Structures. All user data is found either in literal, compressed, or encrypted packets. Encrypted packets come in two flavours, one providing only confidentiality, another providing both confidentiality and integrity protection.

Literal Packets. We denote T_ℓ the one-byte tag value of literal packets. The literal packet LitPacket(D) stores data D in an unprocessed way, preceded by a header containing some metadata, e.g., a file name or a date.

Compressed Packets. We denote T_c the one-byte tag value of compressed packets. The compressed packet CompPacket$^{T_a}(Z)$ stores the value Z resulting from the compression under algorithm T_a of an OpenPGP message. The payload of compressed packets contains a byte T_a, encoding the compression algorithm, followed by the compressed value Z.

Encrypted Packets. Let T_e be the one-byte tag value of encrypted data packets. The encrypted packet EncPacket$_K^E(C)$ without integrity protection stores the ciphertext resulting from an encryption. The payload is simply the ciphertext C resulting from the encryption of an OpenPGP message using block cipher E with key K. The encryption procedure is detailed in Section 2.2.

---

[1] We abusively also refer to this part of the decomposition as a block.

[2] This is an approximation, since the new length format introduced in the specification [9] supports partial length values, but this does not affect our attacks.

Encrypted Integrity Protected Packets. We denote T_E the one-byte tag value of encrypted integrity protected data packets. The encrypted integrity protected packet `EncIntPacket`$_K^E(C)$ stores data after integrity protection and encryption steps, detailed in Section 2.2. The payload of the packet contains a version byte, set to 1, followed by the ciphertext C resulting from the encryption of an OpenPGP message using block cipher E with key K.

Key Packets. The generation/decryption of the ciphertext contained in an encrypted packet, with or without integrity protection, involves a secret key K that is securely stored in a key packet `KeyPacket`$_A(K, E)$, that is transmitted along with the encrypted packet. This key packet also encodes the block cipher primitive E selected by the sender. Only recipient A can extract the key from the key packet, because he either shares a passphrase with the sender, or he owns a given private key. The latter is the general use case, and is a form of hybrid encryption, where asymmetric encryption protects a message key used to symmetrically encrypt data. In the following, we assume that the legitimate recipient unlocks the message key, and focus on the symmetric encryption mechanism.

2.2 Encryption Procedures

Encryption with integrity protection uses a block cipher in CFB mode with an all-zero IV. Initial encryption randomization is obtained by prepending to the plaintext packet(s) a block R of n random bytes. The last two bytes of the random block $\overline{R} = R[-2]||R[-1]$ are repeated as the first two bytes of the second block. This redundancy provides an early way to detect the use of a wrong key derived for example from an erroneous passphrase. This test was used in [11] to recover 16 bits of plaintext per block.

A suffix starting with two fixed byte values, `0xD3`||`0x14` is appended. These represent the header (tag and length) of an OpenPGP Modification Detection Code (MDC) packet. Then, a SHA-1 digest is computed over the concatenation of the prefix, the plaintext packet(s), and the header of the MDC packet. The resulting 20 bytes are the payload of the MDC packet, which are further appended in order to obtain the input P of the encryption. A graphical representation of the encoding of P can be found in Figure 1. The CFB chaining equation is given by the following formula[3]:

$$C_i = E_K(C_{i-1}) \oplus P_i \tag{1}$$

We comment briefly on the security of encryption with integrity protection in OpenPGP in Appendix A.

Encryption without integrity protection presents only slight variations. First, no suffix is appended after the plaintext. Second, the state of the CFB encryption function is resynchronized after the encryption of the prefix. That is to say, the first $n + 2$ bytes are encrypted using CFB mode, then the CFB state is set to

---

[3] By convention C_0 is the all-zero IV, and is not transmitted. Note also that in case the last P_i is shorter than a block, the value of $E_K(C_{i-1})$ is truncated accordingly.

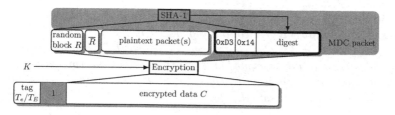

Fig. 1. Encrypted packets format and encryption procedures. The elements on gray background only appear in encrypted integrity protected packets.

the last n bytes of the current ciphertext, i.e., starting from the third byte, and the encryption of the plaintext in CFB mode resumes from this point.

3   Format Oracles

A format oracle describes a side-channel leaking information on the decrypted values corresponding to given ciphertexts. Format oracles generalize padding oracles in two directions. Firstly, the test performed by the oracle is not restricted to the padding of the plaintext, but can also take into account any constraint of the (application-related) format of the plaintext. Secondly, the format oracles may leak plaintext information faster than classical padding oracles. We say a format oracle is *boolean* when its output is simply the result of some format verification on the decrypted ciphertext, and *leaky* if it provides additional information.

As we shall see in the rest of this section, OpenPGP libraries leak through their error messages partial information on the decrypted values corresponding to submitted ciphertexts. For example, GnuPG generally emits non-fatal errors on the standard error stream `stderr` if the result of decryption presents format inconsistencies. Among these messages, it is worthwhile to distinguish so-called *status messages*, that are specifically intended to provide information to applications using GnuPG as a backend. Thus, any leakage through status messages is particularly worrisome.

Should the mentioned error messages be made available to an adversary by an inadvertent application, a format oracle would be instantiated. In particular, JavaScript libraries are expected to run in possibly hostile environment, where exceptions and error messages should be sanitized.

It is difficult to formalize completely the oracle definitions, because they rely on the format of OpenPGP messages. We shall see in the Section 4 that for specially crafted ciphertexts, most of these oracles enable to test whether a decrypted ciphertext byte takes a value in a specific set, possibly a singleton.

The *Invalid Identifier* Oracles. An OpenPGP packet contains several constrained values. For example, the RFC specifies that the packet tag is a one-byte value with its most significant bit (MSB) set to 1. Such constrained identifiers are pervasive in the OpenPGP specification: packet tags, compression methods, encryption algorithms, etc.

Definition 1. *An invalid identifier* oracle *is a leaky oracle taking as input a key packet* $\mathtt{KeyPacket}_A(K, E)$ *containing a key* K *for an algorithm* E, *and a symmetrically encrypted packet containing a ciphertext* C. *It tests whether, when parsing the packets in the decrypted ciphertext, all bytes interpreted as some type of identifiers respect the associated constraints. Furthermore, it leaks the values of the bytes that do not satisfy this format.*

The GnuPG error messages `invalid packet (ctb=XX)`, where `XX` is an offending packet tag, with MSB equal to 0, provide an *invalid tag* oracle. The OpenPGP.js exception messages `Compression algorithm XX not implemented` provide an *invalid compression method* oracle leaking the offending compression method `XX`. For End-to-End, the `Unsupported id: XX` exception messages provide an *invalid algorithm identifier* oracle.

The *Double Literal* Oracle. The OpenPGP specification [9] states that only a single literal data packet may be found in any OpenPGP message. OpenPGP implementations may check that only one such packet exists in a message or otherwise emit a specific error message. This leads us to consider the following format oracle:

Definition 2. *The* double literal *oracle is a boolean format oracle that takes the same input as the* invalid identifier *oracle. It tests whether the tags of any two consecutive OpenPGP packets in the decrypted ciphertext are both literal packet tags.*

The GnuPG `WARNING: multiple plaintexts seen` error messages and the `proc_pkt.plaintext 89_BAD_DATA` status messages[4] provide a *double literal* oracle. OpenPGP.js provides this oracle as well.

The *MDC Packet Header* Oracle. A potential format oracle can be found in the encryption with integrity protection mechanism of OpenPGP. As described in Section 2.1, the input of the encryption function during the encryption with integrity protection process is infused with some format so that the plaintext is the concatenation of an OpenPGP message followed by an MDC packet. Furthermore, OpenPGP mandates the use of SHA-1 as the hash function for MDC packets during encryption, and defines the header of these packets (tag and length). Thus, for the decryption of a legitimate ciphertext, the 22nd and 21st bytes counting from the end after decryption have prescribed values. This leads us to consider the following format oracle:

Definition 3. *The* MDC packet header *oracle is a boolean format oracle that takes as input a key packet* $\mathtt{KeyPacket}_A(K, E)$ *containing a key* K *for an algorithm* E, *and* $\mathtt{EncIntPacket}_K^E(C)$, *a symmetrically encrypted integrity protected packet. Denoting* P *the decrypted ciphertext, the oracle tests whether* $P[-22] = \mathtt{0xD3}$ *and* $P[-21] = \mathtt{0x14}$.

---

[4] These status message are emitted unless they are explicitly inhibited by the caller, through setting the flag `--allow-multiple-messages`.

GnuPG `mdc_packet with invalid encoding` error messages provide an MDC packet header oracle, as well as its `DECRYPTION FAILED` status messages combined with the absence of a `BAD MDC` status messages. `Modification Detection Code not properly formatted` error messages, that can be returned by a low-level function of the End-to-End library, provide the same oracle.

The definition of the MDC packet header oracle is a slight simplification of the behaviour that can be found in OpenPGP libraries. More details are given in Appendix B.

4 Plaintext Recovery Attacks

4.1 Overview of Format Oracle Attacks Against OpenPGP

In the following, we consider an encrypted packet whose payload contains the target ciphertext value C^*, and a corresponding key packet $\text{KeyPacket}_A(K, E)$. Note that the attacker does not have access to the key K that protects the target encrypted packet. Only user A can recover K from the key packet, using a passphrase or a private key. The objective of the attacker is to recover the decryption P^* of C^* by leveraging a format oracle implemented by user A. The attacker performs several requests to the oracle, with specially crafted, format oracle specific, ciphertexts $C = C(B, u, a)$, were B is the target block, u is the target position in the block, and a is the tested value. The oracle answers leak information allowing to decrypt ciphertext C^* step by step.

OpenPGP symmetric encryption relies on variants of the CFB mode of operation. Let us notice that in order to decrypt a CFB encrypted message, it is sufficient to be able to recover the encrypted value of any block. Applying this recovery procedure on block C_i^*, we get $E_K(C_i^*)$ which can be used to decrypt C_{i+1}^* through Equation 1: $P_{i+1}^* = C_{i+1}^* \oplus E_K(C_i^*)$.

The attacks presented enables to attack any type of encrypted data, be it encrypted packets with/without integrity protection, or symmetrically encrypted session key packets. More details are given in Appendix C.

A general attack overview is given in Algorithm 1. The attack complexities are expressed in the maximal number of queries to the format oracle. The corresponding average complexity is half the maximal complexity. We now describe, for the format oracles described in Section 3 the structure of the submitted ciphertexts $C(B, u, a)$. The presented query ciphertexts only contain the payload specific to the studied oracle. If the decryption function enforces other constraints, e.g., checks the initial redundancy of OpenPGP plaintexts, the query ciphertexts can be tweaked, as described in Appendix B.

4.2 Plaintext Recovery Using Tag Oracles

First we describe how to leverage an invalid tag oracle, that is a specific case of an invalid identifier oracle, or a double literal oracle. The same principle can be

---

Algorithm 1. Transforming a format oracle into an attack: overview

> **for all** ciphertext blocks C_i^* **do**
> > **for all** (byte) positions $1 \leq u \leq n$ in the ciphertext block **do**
> > > **for all** possible (byte) values a **do**
> > > > Submit ciphertext $C(C_i^*, u, a)$ to the oracle
> > > > **if** oracle returns **True then**
> > > > > deduce the value of $E_K(C_i^*)$ at position u from a

---

applied to leverage any invalid identifier oracle. In order to recover $E_K(B)[u]$, we consider ciphertexts with the following format:

$$C(B, u, a) = T_\ell \oplus \alpha || U \oplus \beta || \texttt{0x00}_{n-2} || B || \texttt{0x00}_{u-1} || a,$$

where U is the byte whose value is $2n + u - 3$, and α and β are the bytes used to decrypt the first two bytes of ciphertext. We can assume that these two bytes can be predicted by an attacker from C^* (cf Appendix B).

These ciphertexts are built so that the corresponding plaintexts contain a first literal packet of length $U = 2n + u - 3$. The zero paddings ensure that B starts at a block boundary, and that the tag of the second packet is located at position u of the block following B. For the double literal oracle (resp. for the invalid packet tag oracle), we let a (resp. the MSB of a) take all possible values. After decryption, this lets the tag (resp. the MSB of the tag) of the second packet take all possible values. The format oracle returns **True** if $E_K(B)[u] \oplus a$ is a valid tag (resp. it leaks $E_K(B)[u] \oplus a$ if its MSB is 0). We give a graphical representation of this procedure in Figure 2. The maximal number of requests to recover this byte is approximatively 2^6 (resp. 2). Only about 2^6 requests are needed instead of 2^8, because there are 5 possible tag values (cf [9]).

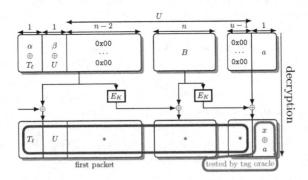

Fig. 2. Recovery procedure of $x = E_K(B)[u]$, using a tag oracle

4.3   Plaintext Recovery using the MDC Packet Header Oracle

Basic Recovery of the Encrypted Value of a Block. To recover $E_K(B)$, we consider the ciphertexts with the following format:

$$C(B, u, (a, b)) = B||0x00_{u-1}||a||b||0x00_{20}.$$

B is block aligned, $1 \leq u \leq n - 2$ pads the ciphertext so that the target bytes are located at position u and $u + 1$ of the following block, and the final 20 zeros ensures that a and b are considered as the MDC header.

Recovering $E_K(B)[u]$ and $E_K(B)[u + 1]$. In order to recover two consecutive bytes of $E_K(B)$, we let a and b take all possible 2^{16} values. This lets the bytes located at the MDC packet header position after decryption take all 2^{16} possible values. Thus the format oracle returns True for a unique pair a', b', and we have, through Equation 1: $E_K(B)[u] = 0xD3 \oplus a', E_K(B)[u + 1] = 0x14 \oplus b'$. We give a graphical representation of a special case of this procedure in Figure 3. The maximal number of requests to recover these bytes is 2^{16}.

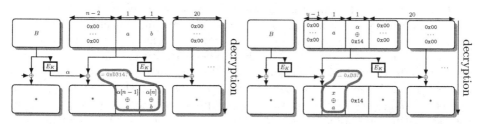

Fig. 3. Recovery of the last two bytes of $E_K(B)$

Fig. 4. Recovery of $x = E_K(B)[u]$, knowing $\alpha = E_K(B)[u + 1]$

Recovering $E_K(B)[u]$ knowing $E_K(B)[u + 1]$. We can use the knowledge of $E_K(B)[u + 1]$ to speed up the recovery of $E_K(B)[u]$. We fix $b = E_K(B)[u + 1] \oplus 0x14$ and let byte a take all possible values. This fixes the second byte of the MDC packet header after decryption to the $0x14$ value and lets the first byte of the header take all possible 2^8 values. Thus the format oracle returns True for a unique value a', and we have through Equation 1: $E_K(B)[u] = 0xD3 \oplus a'$. We give a graphical representation of this procedure in Figure 4. The number of requests to recover this byte is 2^8. It is straightforward to adapt this procedure to recover $E_K(B)[u + 1]$ using the knowledge of $E_K(B)[u], 1 \leq u \leq n - 1$, for a cost of 2^8 requests. By incrementally applying these procedures after initially recovering two consecutive bytes of the encrypted value of the block, we can recover $E_K(B)$ with $2^{16} + (n - 2)2^8$ requests. Overall, we can decrypt the whole ciphertext with $||C^*||(2^{16} + (n - 2)2^8)$ requests.

Improved Recovery Procedure. It is possible to lower further the complexity of these attacks to 2^8 requests per byte to decrypt for long messages. These optimisations are detailed in Appendix D.

5   Security Analysis

Mitigation. A basic way of preventing the attacks presented in section 4 would be to remove all leakage through error messages produced by the application during decryption. Adopting this measure for cryptographic libraries and applications that may be used as backend for other applications ensures that the leakage is not mishandled by calling applications. It can be seen as a misuse-resistance property.

However this may not remove more implicit forms of format oracles. A sound way to prevent format oracle attacks would be to thwart chosen-ciphertext attacks by systematically using authenticated encryption and implementing a thorough "Verify-then-Decrypt" paradigm during decryption, so that no check is performed on the decryption result before the integrity of the ciphertext is cryptographically verified. Such a paradigm cannot be implemented in the case of OpenPGP, since the ciphertext needs to be decrypted before the integrity can be verified. However, it is still possible to obtain a safe implementation by adopting a "Verify-then-Release" paradigm, i.e., the decryption result is buffered, and any processing of the decryption result is deferred until the integrity has been verified. Note that for this solution to be effective, serious compatibility issues can be raised. Indeed, in the case of OpenPGP, this solution would require to deprecate the decryption of messages encrypted without integrity protection. Indeed, if this operation leaks information, it can be used to attack packets encrypted with integrity protection through a downgrade attack, as detailed in Appendix C.

Note also that this cannot be reduced to the choice of the authenticated encryption mode: the implementation of the decryption procedure is crucial to the security of authenticated encryption. In the case of GnuPG implementation of OpenPGP encryption with integrity protection, decryption and MAC computations are performed in parallel, and the decryption result is interpreted on the fly before MAC verification. This behaviour is at odds with the security models under which authenticated encryption modes are evaluated. Even an implementation of the "Encrypt-then-MAC" paradigm, mode that is perceived to be generally safe, can be implemented in this way, and may thus be vulnerable to oracle attacks.

When relying on authenticated encryption to prevent format oracles is not an option, cryptographic toolkits/libraries have to settle for establishing a safe API, that is resistant against misuse by a non cryptography-savvy developer. This can be done by eliminating as much as possible potential leakage of information, by providing a high-level API free of such leakage, and/or explicitly advertising the sensitive information leaked by the API. Errors raised by the exported functions are part of the API and should be considered when studying the leakage channels.

Future Perspective: State-of-the-Art Authenticated Encryption. The international competition CAESAR, which aims at identifying good authenticated encryption schemes, has seen the formalisation of security properties related to the security of the decryption procedure, e.g., the definition of the *Release of Unverified Plaintext* setting [3]. Some of the CAESAR candidates may turn out to provide a solution suitable in the context of OpenPGP, and resistance against chosen-ciphertexts attacks even if the decrypted value is processed on-the-fly. Another interesting venue of research that can be followed is to consider the decryption errors into the security model used to study the authenticated encryption mode, following [6]. In both cases however, it is not easily achievable for existing applications to adopt an authenticated encryption mode satisfying stronger security notions. In the case of OpenPGP, it would require an update of the OpenPGP specifications and may entail interoperability issues.

Disclosure. We reported our findings to the developers of three OpenPGP applications/libraries: GnuPG, End-to-End and OpenPGP.js.

GnuPG developers acknowledged that unattended usages of their library leaked information via the standard error stream. However, they consider that GnuPG is not at fault, and that it is the responsibility of the users and integrators not to mishandle the leaked warnings and error messages. A patch partially removing the MDC packet header oracle has been integrated in GnuPG 1.4.17 and GnuPG 2.0.23. The inclusion in GnuPG documentation of a security disclaimer warning against padding/format oracles was also discussed.

Google End-to-End developers stated that "the API contract [they] should try to follow is that users of [the high-level API of the library] should be safe to print to an untrusted adversary the errors it throws" and that information leaks conveying useful information should be considered as security bugs. As a result, they tracked every unhandled exceptions in End-to-End. They also removed the MDC packet header leak. OpenPGP.js developers followed a similar approach.

6 Conclusion

We highlighted potential format oracles in the OpenPGP message format. If the error messages of the three OpenPGP applications/libraries we studied, GnuPG, OpenPGP.js, and End-to-End, are mishandled, the format oracles are implemented, and they can be used to decrypt data encrypted using OpenPGP.

Modern cryptographic standards should provide strong integrity guarantees, by using only authenticated encryption. Cryptographic application and library providers should be aware of the presented attacks, and develop their products with the following idea in mind: while decrypting a message, *no* information should be leaked about the plaintext until the integrity has been checked. In particular, this includes format constraint checks and timing info leaks. The safest way to meet this requirement is to forbid *any* processing of the plaintext until the integrity has been checked. Library developers should at least strive to specify high-level API free of format oracles, and document the outputs of their libraries that are susceptible to leak sensitive information.

A   Discussion on OpenPGP Authenticated Encryption Scheme

OpenPGP provides encryption with integrity protection, claiming to use the Hash-then-Encrypt paradigm ([9, section 5.13], "An MDC is intentionally not a MAC"). This paradigm is known not to satisfy state-of-the-art integrity requirements. However, the first random block R that is prepended to the plaintext before encryption and hash computation acts as a MAC session key, for a MAC of the form $H(K\|M)$.[5] Thus, OpenPGP actually seems to implement a form of the MAC-then-Encrypt paradigm. The complete security analysis of this mode is not the object of this paper and is left as an open question.

B   Adapting Crafted Ciphertexts to the Format Oracle

The access to the MDC packet header format oracle may be subject to some conditions on the decrypted ciphertext. We found that it was easy to tweak the submitted ciphertext to accommodate the conditions we encountered.

Guessing $C_2^*[3]$ and $C_2^*[4]$. The first real plaintext bytes, $C_2^*[3]$ and $C_2^*[4]$, are part of the tag header. In practice, two cases may arise, depending on the preferences included in the recipient's key:

- the data is compressed, which corresponds to a T_c tag, followed by the compression algorithm T_a, thus $C_2^*[3] = T_c$ and $C_2^*[4] = T_a$;
- the data is simply a litteral, which leads to a $C_2^*[3] = T_\ell$, with the following bytes encoding the litteral length. This length (and therefore $C_2^*[4]$) can be deduced from the overall encrypted packet size.

Random Prefix Redundancy. As seen in section 2.1, prior encryption, a random prefix with basic redundancy is prepended to the payload. The check on the redundancy at the beginning of decryption is meant to get an early detection method that a wrong key is used to decrypt. In case the key is derived from a passphrase, this enables to detect erroneous passphrase inputs. [11] used this check to instantiate a format oracle that led to the ability to decrypt the first 16 bit of any ciphertext block. This redundancy check may still be present and a failure may suppress the "MDC packet header" oracle. In order to ensure that the random prefix redundancy check is always satisfied, it is sufficient to prefix any ciphertext considered in our attacks with the first two blocks of the target ciphertext: instead of submitting C, the attacker submits $C_1^*\|C_2^*\|C$. In the case of tag format oracles, only the first two bytes of C_2^* are used, with the payload ciphertext immediately following.

---

[5] This MAC is known to be vulnerable to classical extension attacks, but they seem to be irrelevant in the OpenPGP context, since the MAC value is encrypted.

Compression. Some implementations, as GnuPG, process in parallel decryption and decompression, and abort decryption if a decompression error is detected. In order to ensure no compression error occurs, the attacker can tweak the submitted ciphertext to trick the implementation into considering the content as a literal packet. This is relatively easy, since it only depends on the third byte of the second block of the encryption input. If the target ciphertext corresponds to a compressed packet, we have $C_2^*[3] \oplus E_K(C_1^*)[3] = T_c$. If we consider the block $C^\# = C_2^* \oplus (\mathtt{0x00}_2 || T_\ell \oplus T_c || \mathtt{0x00}_{n-3})$, the decryption of ciphertexts of the form $C_1^* || C^\# || C$ verifies the redundancy of the prefix and the plaintext first packet will be considered a literal packet.

C   Attacking Any Encrypted Packet Types

We show in this section that the malleability of packet tags allows for masquerading a given packet as a packet of a different type. In particular, it allows us to use the MDC packet header oracle to decrypt any symmetrically encrypted packet. The same conclusion holds for the other format oracles: it is thus possible to use a format oracle present in the encryption-only part of a library to attack an encrypted packet with integrity protection.

Encrypted Packets without Integrity Protection. It is worthwhile to note that encrypted packets without integrity protection can also be decrypted by using the MDC packet header oracle. Indeed, the target key packet can be used indifferently for encryption with or without integrity protection. Furthermore, the encryption procedure of encrypted packets without integrity protection is also based on CFB mode, with an all-zero IV and a random prefix composed of a random block of n bytes followed by the repetition of the last two bytes of the random block. The variation introduced by the CFB state resynchronization does not modify the attack principle, it only introduces a slight shift in the splitting of the ciphertext into blocks. In order to decrypt $\mathtt{EncPacket}_K^E(C^*)$, an encrypted data packet without integrity protection, containing ciphertext C^*, it is enough to recover the encryption of the blocks of the truncated ciphertext obtained by removing the first two bytes of C^*. The random prefix redundancy constraints and compression constraints can be satisfied in the same manner as for encrypted integrity protected packets.

Note that, considering only the MDC packet header oracle, this leads to the non-intuitive result that the implementation of an authenticated encryption scheme weakens the security of the encryption scheme without integrity.

Symmetrically Encrypted Session Key Packets. We give additional details on symmetrically encrypted key packets. The protection of the key stored by these packets relies on a passphrase. The key packet contains the information necessary to derive a key K_p from the passphrase. If the key packet contains an encrypted key, it can be decrypted into K using K_p with the appropriate block cipher in CFB mode, with an all zero IV. Otherwise, K_p is used directly to process data, $K = K_p$.

The attacks can also be applied to the decryption of symmetrically encrypted session key packets, when they contain an encrypted key. Indeed, the same encryption algorithm, CFB with an all-zero IV is used. Furthermore, by removing the encrypted session key from the target encrypted session key packet, one gets a session key packet for the key derived from the passphrase, that can be used to mount the attack. Contrary to the cases of encrypted data packets, no ciphertext blocks corresponding to a plaintext satisfying the random prefix redundancy are available. However, by performing 2^{16} requests, with an identical first block, and all possible values for the first two bytes of the second block, such a pair of ciphertext block can be found, if necessary. Attacking session key packets may be preferable to attacking the data packets they protect, since they are usually shorter, and thus their decryption requires less requests.

By the way, the fact that truncating a session key packet gives a valid key packet that can be used to attack the confidentiality of the initial packet is an undesirable property of the symmetrically encrypted session key packet format. It would have been better to build the format of these packets around a key wrap mechanism, providing both confidentiality and integrity of the session key and its metadata.

D   Details of the Improved Recovery Procedure Using the MDC Packet Header Oracle

The cost of the basic recovery procedure described in the previous section can be decomposed, for each block, into an expensive first step that recovers initial knowledge on an encrypted block, followed by several cheaper steps that recover the rest of the encrypted block. Starting from the information leaked by the target ciphertext C^*, it would be tempting to apply only the cheaper steps, for a cost of 2^8 requests per byte to decrypt. But a direct approach fails because of the behaviour of decryption at block boundaries. We describe two procedures enabling to recover initial knowledge on $E_K(B)$ for about 2^8 requests. We then discuss the cost of decrypting C^* as a function of its length.

Type I procedure. This procedure enables to test whether $E_K(B)[n] = a \oplus \text{0xD3}$ for one request, provided a test block T satisfying $T[n] = a$ and $E_K(T)[1]$ is known. The format of the request ciphertext is $B||T||(E_K(T)[1] \oplus \text{0x14})||\text{0x00}_{20}$. A graphical representation is given in Figure 5.

Type II procedure. This procedure enables to recover $E_K(B)[1]$ for 2^8 requests, provided $B[n] = a$ and a test block T satisfying $E_K(T)[n] = a \oplus \text{0xD3}$. The format of the request ciphertexts is $T||B||b||\text{0x00}_{20}$, with b a byte taking all possible values. A graphical representation is given in Figure 5.

Decryption Strategy. Note that each of the previous procedures can be applied to any block to recover a first byte of its encrypted value for a cost of 2^8 once a collection of 2^8 test blocks, presenting all variations of a, has been obtained.

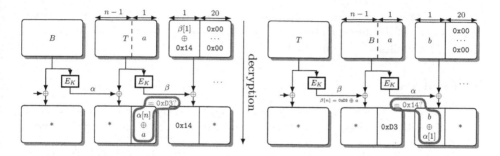

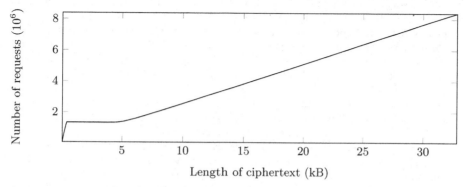

Fig. 5. Type I (left) and type II (right) byte recovery procedures

Fig. 6. Number of requests to decrypt a ciphertext as a function of its byte length, assuming 128-bit blocks. When ciphertexts are long enough, the complexity is linear, equal to 2^8 requests per byte.

In order to decrypt the target ciphertext C^*, one starts by recovering the block corresponding to the position of the MDC header. Every time a block is recovered, it may provide a new test block that may help to start recovering the remaining ones. Type II and type I procedures are applied as much as possible to start recovering blocks, and the incremental basic procedure is used to finish the encrypted block recovery. If type I and type II procedures cannot be applied, we either apply directly the basic block recovery procedure, or apply type I and type II procedures to extra (pseudo-)ciphertext blocks.

Decryption Complexity. We performed simulations to identify the best strategy, with regards to the ciphertext length. If the number of ciphertext block is small, $\|C\| \leq 25$, it is best to apply the basic recovery procedure when the type I and type II procedures cannot be applied. If the number of block is medium $26 \leq \|C\| \leq 267$, the best strategy is to artificially add random ciphertext blocks to have 267 blocks. The message is longer, but it is cheaper to decrypt because the type I and II procedures are applied more often. For long messages, $\|C\| > 267$, it is not necessary to add random blocks, since the cost of decrypting additional block exceeds the cost benefit. In the rare cases were type I and II procedures are not sufficient, one resorts to the basic procedure. Furthermore, for very long messages, the decryption cost is effectively 2^8 requests per byte. Assuming a 128-bit block cipher, 25 (resp. 267) blocks translate into 400B (resp. 4KB). The results are summarized in Figure 6.

References

1. Albrecht, M.R., Paterson, K.G., Watson, G.J.: Plaintext Recovery Attacks against SSH. In: IEEE Symposium on Security and Privacy, pp. 16–26. IEEE Computer Society (2009)
2. AlFardan, N.J., Paterson, K.G.: Lucky Thirteen: Breaking the TLS and DTLS Record Protocols. In: IEEE Symposium on Security and Privacy, pp. 526–540. IEEE Computer Society (2013)
3. Andreeva, E., Bogdanov, A., Luykx, A., Mennink, B., Mouha, N., Yasuda, K.: How to Securely Release Unverified Plaintext in Authenticated Encryption. Cryptology ePrint Archive, Report 2014/144 (2014). http://eprint.iacr.org/
4. Bardou, R., Focardi, R., Kawamoto, Y., Simionato, L., Steel, G., Tsay, J.-K.: Efficient Padding Oracle Attacks on Cryptographic Hardware. In: Safavi-Naini, R., Canetti, R. (eds.) CRYPTO 2012. LNCS, vol. 7417, pp. 608–625. Springer, Heidelberg (2012)
5. Bleichenbacher, D.: Chosen Ciphertext Attacks against Protocols Based on the RSA Encryption Standard PKCS #1. In: Krawczyk, H. (ed.) CRYPTO 1998. LNCS, vol. 1462, pp. 1–12. Springer, Heidelberg (1998)
6. Boldyreva, A., Degabriele, J.P., Paterson, K.G., Stam, M.: On Symmetric Encryption with Distinguishable Decryption Failures. In: Moriai, S. (ed.) FSE 2013. LNCS, vol. 8424, pp. 367–390. Springer, Heidelberg (2014)
7. Jager, T., Somorovsky, J.: How to break XML encryption. In: Chen, Y., Danezis, G., Shmatikov, V. (eds.) ACM Conference on Computer and Communications Security, pp. 413–422. ACM (2011)
8. Jallad, K., Katz, J., Schneier, B.: Implementation of Chosen-Ciphertext Attacks against PGP and GnuPG. In: Chan, A.H., Gligor, V.D. (eds.) ISC 2002. LNCS, vol. 2433, pp. 90–101. Springer, Heidelberg (2002)
9. Callas, J., Donnerhacke, L., Finney, H., Shaw, D., Thayer, R.: OpenPGP Message Format. RFC 4880 (Proposed Standard) (November 2007)
10. Klíma, V., Rosa, T.: Side Channel Attacks on CBC Encrypted Messages in the PKCS#7 Format. Cryptology ePrint Archive, Report 2003/098 (2003). http://eprint.iacr.org/
11. Mister, S., Zuccherato, R.J.: An Attack on CFB Mode Encryption as Used by OpenPGP. In: Preneel, B., Tavares, S. (eds.) SAC 2005. LNCS, vol. 3897, pp. 82–94. Springer, Heidelberg (2006)
12. Mitchell, C.J.: Error Oracle Attacks on CBC Mode: Is There a Future for CBC Mode Encryption? In: Zhou, J., López, J., Deng, R.H., Bao, F. (eds.) ISC 2005. LNCS, vol. 3650, pp. 244–258. Springer, Heidelberg (2005)
13. Möller, B., Duong, T., Kotowicz, K.: Google Security Advisory: This POODLE Bites: Exploiting The SSL 3.0 Fallback (2014). https://www.openssl.org/bodo/ssl-poodle.pdf
14. Paterson, K.G., AlFardan, N.J.: Plaintext-Recovery Attacks Against Datagram TLS. In: NDSS. The Internet Society (2012)
15. Vaudenay, S.: Security Flaws Induced by CBC Padding - Applications to SSL, IPSEC, WTLS. In: Knudsen, L.R. (ed.) EUROCRYPT 2002. LNCS, vol. 2332, pp. 534–546. Springer, Heidelberg (2002)

Algorithms for Solving Hard Problems

Finding Shortest Lattice Vectors in the Presence of Gaps

Wei Wei[1,2], Mingjie Liu[3], and Xiaoyun Wang[2,4(✉)]

[1] State Key Laboratory of Information Security, Institute of Information Engineering, Chinese Academy of Sciences, Beijing, China
weiwei1@iie.ac.cn
[2] Institute for Advanced Study, Tsinghua University, Beijing, China
[3] Beijing Research Institute of Telemetry, Beijing, China
liumj9705@pku.edu.cn
[4] Key Lab of Cryptologic Technology and Information Security, Ministry of Education, Shandong University, Jinan, China
xiaoyunwang@mail.tsinghua.edu.cn

Abstract. The λ_i-gap λ_i/λ_1 among the successive minima of a lattice especially its λ_2-gap often provides useful information for analyzing the security of lattice-based cryptographic schemes. In this paper, we mainly study the efficiency of shortest vector problem (SVP) algorithms for lattices with λ_i-gap. First, we prove new upper bounds for the packing density of this type of lattices. Based on these results, we discuss the efficiency of the ListSieve-Birthday algorithm proposed by Pujol and Stehlé for SVP, and obtain the conclusion that the complexity will decrease obviously as the λ_i-gap increases. Particularly, ListSieve-Birthday becomes faster than the current best deterministic (Voronoi cell-based) algorithm for SVP, as long as λ_2-gap is larger than 1.78. When λ_2-gap is up to 28, the time complexity is $2^{0.9992n+o(n)}$, and the coefficient factor of n is approximately to 0.802 if λ_2-gap is large enough. Moreover, we provide an SVP approximation algorithm modified by the ListSieve-Birthday algorithm. This algorithm terminates sieve process earlier and relaxes the birthday search, and hence decreases the time complexity significantly.

Keywords: Lattice · Successive minima · Shortest vector problem · Gap · Sieve

1 Introduction

A lattice is a discrete subgroup of $\mathbb{R}^m$ whose elements are integer linear combinations of n ($n \leq m$) linearly independent vectors. Shortest vector problem (SVP) and closest vector problem (CVP) are hard problems in complexity theory. The intractability of two problems guarantees the security of lattice-based cryptographic schemes. Therefore, the study of fast algorithms for SVP, CVP, as well as their approximate variants, is of cryptographic importance.

© Springer International Publishing Switzerland 2015
K. Nyberg (ed.): CT-RSA 2015, LNCS 9048, pp. 239–257, 2015.
DOI: 10.1007/978-3-319-16715-2_13

Successive minima in a lattice are a sequence $\{\lambda_i\}_{1\leq i\leq n}$, where λ_i is the radius of the smallest ball centered in the origin containing i linearly independent lattice vectors. We call λ_i/λ_1 the λ_i-gap. Gaps, especially the λ_2-gap, are found in some well-known lattice-based cryptosystems. For example, the first provable lattice cryptosystem proposed by Ajtai [1] is based on the hardness of solving the uSVP$_\gamma$ problem (i.e., finding the shortest vector for lattices with $\lambda_2/\lambda_1 > \gamma$) with $\gamma = n^c$ for some positive constant c. As to the security of cryptographic schemes based on uSVP, Lyubashevsky and Micciancio [17] established reductions from a decision variant of approximate SVP and bounded distance decoding problem (a special case of closest vector problem) to uSVP$_\gamma$.

However, some cryptographic schemes face serious security problems because of the gap between λ_2 and λ_1 in their corresponding lattices(see [6]). For example, general knapsack cryptosystems [4,18] are vulnerable to low density attacks because of the λ_2-gap in the lattices on which they are based; the λ_2-gap in the embedded lattice of GGH [7,23] makes it easier to search the shortest vector. For the public-key cryptosystem NTRU, Coppersmith and Shamir [5] constructed a cryptographic lattice with dimension $2N$ to analyze its security. A heuristic analysis reported in [12] indicates that NTRU lattice has λ_{N+1}-gap. Hence it is obvious that fast search algorithms for SVP of lattices with gaps are practically important in lattice-based cryptanalysis.

Solving SVP has been a problem of lasting interest. Many deterministic enumeration algorithms are found in the literature (e.g., [13,26,32]), with computational time ranging from $2^{O(n^2)}$ to $2^{O(n\log n)}$ and with polynomial (in dimension n) space. In 2010, Micciancio and Voulgaris [21] provided a deterministic algorithm for SVP which is based on the Voronoi cell computation with computational time $2^{2n+o(n)}$ and space $2^{n+o(n)}$. Another type of algorithms for SVP is the random sieve which was first proposed by Ajtai et al. [2] in 2001. This algorithm, known as AKS sieve, is the first single exponential time complexity $(2^{O(n)})$ algorithm for solving SVP with $2^{O(n)}$ space. In 2010, Micciancio and Voulgaris [22] presented another random sieve algorithm named ListSieve, which solves SVP in time $2^{3.199n+o(n)}$ and space $2^{1.325n+o(n)}$. The time complexity was further improved to $2^{2.465n+o(n)}$ by Pujol and Stehlé [27] using the birthday attack, and this improved algorithm named ListSieve-Birthday is the best theoretically provable sieving algorithm for SVP up until now. Also, under some random assumptions, there are heuristic versions of AKS sieve algorithm [24,33,34], which are more efficient in practice.

This paper primarily concerns shortest vectors for lattices with gaps. Our main purpose is to study the efficiency of the ListSieve-Birthday algorithm for SVP on lattices with λ_i-gap. Firstly, we estimate the packing density of lattices possessing λ_2-gap, then analyze the efficiency of the ListSieve-Birthday algorithm for SVP in this type of lattices. Particularly, we indicate that this algorithm becomes more and more efficient as the λ_2-gap increases. The time and space complexity will be less than $2^{1.999n+o(n)}$ and $2^{0.999n+o(n)}$ respectively when λ_2-gap is larger than 1.78. The coefficient factor of n in the time complexity decreases to 0.9992 if λ_2-gap is up to 28, and approximately to 0.802 when

λ_2-gap is large enough. Secondly, we generalize the above results to λ_i-gap. The analysis shows that the reduction of complexity of ListSieve-Birthday not only depends on the value of λ_i-gap, but also the position of λ_i ($2 \leq i \leq n$). Finally, we give a modified version of the ListSieve-Birthday algorithm [27] focusing on approximate SVP algorithm. This modification produces shorter lattice vectors with much less time compared to that in [27] by stopping the sieve early and relaxing the birthday search.

This paper is organized as follows: Section 2 is the preliminaries where some notations and useful lemmas are included. In section 3, we revisit the ListSieve-Birthday algorithm combining with our new estimation of the packing density in lattices with λ_2-gap. Section 4 shows the efficiency of ListSieve-Birthday on lattices possessing λ_i-gap ($2 \leq i \leq n$). In section 5, we present an approximate SVP algorithm modified by ListSieve-Birthday. Section 6 concludes the paper.

2 Preliminaries

2.1 Notations and Background

Let $B = \{\mathbf{b_1}, \ldots, \mathbf{b_n}\} \subseteq \mathbb{R}^m$ consist of n linearly independent vectors. The lattice generated by the basis B is defined as

$$\mathcal{L}(B) = \left\{ \sum_{i=1}^{n} x_i \mathbf{b_i} : x_i \in \mathbb{Z} \right\}.$$

The integers n and m are called its rank and dimension. If $m = n$, we say that the lattice is full-rank. Without loss of generality, we only consider the shortest vector problem in the full-rank lattices, since other cases can be converted to full-rank lattices with dimension n.

The fundamental parallelepiped $\mathcal{P}(B)$ is defined to be $\{\Sigma_i x_i \mathbf{b_i} : 0 \leq x_i < 1\}$. For any $\mathbf{x} \in \mathbb{R}^n$, there exists a unique vector $\mathbf{y} \in \mathcal{P}(B)$ such that $\mathbf{y} - \mathbf{x} \in \mathcal{L}(B)$. This vector is denoted as $\mathbf{y} = \mathbf{x} \mod \mathcal{P}(B)$, and it can be computed in polynomial time given B and $\mathbf{x}$.

In this paper, we use $\|\mathbf{x}\|$ to denote the Euclidean norm of a vector $\mathbf{x} = (x_1, x_2, \ldots, x_n) \in \mathbb{R}^n$, i.e., $\|\mathbf{x}\| = \sqrt{x_1^2 + x_2^2 + \cdots + x_n^2}$. The n-dimensional ball centered at $\mathbf{x}$ with radius r is denoted by $\mathcal{B}_n(\mathbf{x}, r)$; $\mathbf{x}$ is omitted when it is the origin. For any finite set C, denote $|C|$ as its number of elements.

Next, we give some computational complexity problems and some results in lattice theory that are of relevance to our discussion.

- **Shortest Vector Problem (SVP)**: Given a basis of a lattice $\mathcal{L}$, find a nonzero lattice vector $\mathbf{v}$ such that $\|\mathbf{v}\| \leq \|\mathbf{u}\|$ for any nonzero vector $\mathbf{u} \in \mathcal{L}$.
- **γ-Approximate Shortest Vector Problem (SVP$_\gamma$)**: Given a basis of a lattice $\mathcal{L}$, find a nonzero lattice vector $\mathbf{v}$ such that $\|\mathbf{v}\| \leq \gamma\|\mathbf{u}\|$, for any nonzero vector $\mathbf{u} \in \mathcal{L}$.
- **γ-Unique Shortest Vector Problem (uSVP$_\gamma$)**: Given a basis of a lattice $\mathcal{L}$ such that $\lambda_2(\mathcal{L}) > \gamma \cdot \lambda_1(\mathcal{L})$, find a shortest nonzero vector in $\mathcal{L}$.

- γ-**Bounded Distance Decoding (BDD$_\gamma$):** Given a basis of a lattice $\mathcal{L}$ and a target vector $\mathbf{t} \in \mathbb{R}^n$ such that $\mathrm{dist}(\mathbf{t}, \mathcal{L}) < \gamma \lambda_1(\mathcal{L})$, find a lattice vector $\mathbf{v}$ closest to $\mathbf{t}$, i.e., $\mathrm{dist}(\mathbf{v}, \mathbf{t}) \leq \mathrm{dist}(\mathbf{u}, \mathbf{t})$ for any vector $\mathbf{u} \in \mathcal{L}$.

Given a basis of an n-dimensional lattice, the LLL algorithm [16] produces another basis of the lattice which consists of shorter vectors and is referred as an LLL-reduced basis. The size of the reduced basis can be bounded as follows.

Lemma 1. *[16] Let $\mathbf{b}_1, \mathbf{b}_2, \ldots, \mathbf{b}_n$ be an LLL-reduced basis, then $\|\mathbf{b}_j\|$* $\leq \left((1 + \varepsilon) \sqrt{\frac{4}{3}} \right)^{n-1} \lambda_j.$

According to the above property of LLL-reduced basis, for a fixed i ($1 \leq i \leq n$), we can guess a μ_i such that $\lambda_i \leq \mu_i \leq (1 + \frac{1}{n}) \lambda_i$ by polynomially many trials of μ_i. This approximation is essential in ListSieve-Birthday and our approximate SVP algorithm in Section 5. When $i = 1$, we simply write μ_1 as μ.

Finally in this subsection, we recall the conceptual modification τ which was first presented by Regev [30]. Here, we introduce the version from the reference [27]. Let $\mathbf{s}$ be a shortest lattice vector and $I_{\mathbf{s}} = \{\mathbf{x} \in \mathcal{B}_n(\xi\mu) : \mathbf{x} + \mathbf{s} \in \mathcal{B}_n(\xi\mu)\}$, where μ is an approximate value of λ_1 and ξ is a fixed positive parameter (see Fig. 1). Let $\tau : \mathcal{B}_n(\xi\mu) \longrightarrow \mathcal{B}_n(\xi\mu)$ be a map such that $\tau(\mathbf{x}) = \mathbf{x} + \mathbf{s}$, if $\mathbf{x} \in I_{\mathbf{s}}$; $\tau(\mathbf{x}) = -\mathbf{x}$, if $\mathbf{x} \notin I_{\mathbf{s}}$. This transformation τ preserves the uniform distribution on $\mathcal{B}_n(\xi\mu)$. Usually, τ is applied to prove the success probability in sieve algorithms for SVP.

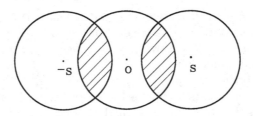

Fig. 1. τ Transformation

2.2   The ListSieve-Birthday Algorithm

We recall the ListSieve-Birthday algorithm whose efficiency is the main concern in this paper. We also need some technical lemmas from the reference [27] for proving the new upper bound for the complexity of ListSieve-Birthday with the occurrence of gaps among λ_i for $1 \leq i \leq n$.

Briefly, the ListSieve-Birthday algorithm contains a main body and two routines, i.e., Sample Algorithm and Reduction Algorithm. It is clear that the main body algorithm has two loops. The first loop constructs a list T by reducing each randomly generated vector with vectors previously added to the list. The second loop produces another list U whose elements are reduced in terms of the list T.

Sample Algorithm

Input: An LLL-reduced basis of a lattice $\mathcal{L}$, perturbation radius $\xi\mu$, where $\xi > \frac{1}{2}$

Output: A lattice vector $\mathbf{u}$ and a perturbed vector $\mathbf{u}'$

1: Choose $\mathbf{x}$ uniformly in $\mathcal{B}_n(\xi\mu)$
2: $\mathbf{u}' \longleftarrow (-\mathbf{x}) \mod \mathcal{P}(B)$
3: $\mathbf{u} \longleftarrow \mathbf{u}' + \mathbf{x}$
4: Return $(\mathbf{u}, \mathbf{u}')$

Reduction Algorithm

Input: A pair $(\mathbf{u}, \mathbf{u}')$ returned from Sample Algorithm, where $\mathbf{u}$ is a lattice vector and $\mathbf{u}'$ is a perturbed vector, a List $T \subseteq \mathcal{L}$ and reduced factor $\delta < 1$

Output: A reduced pair $(\mathbf{u}, \mathbf{u}')$

1: While $(\exists \mathbf{w} \in T) : \|\mathbf{u}' - \mathbf{w}\| \leq \delta \|\mathbf{u}'\|$
2:     $(\mathbf{u}, \mathbf{u}') \longleftarrow (\mathbf{u} - \mathbf{w}, \mathbf{u}' - \mathbf{w})$
3: end while
4: Return $(\mathbf{u}, \mathbf{u}')$

Algorithm 1. The ListSieve-Birthday Algorithm

Input: An LLL reduced basis $\mathbf{B}$, $N_1, N_2, \gamma > 1$, reduced factor $\delta < 1, \frac{\gamma}{2} > \xi > \frac{1}{2}, \mu \simeq \lambda_1$

Output: A shortest non-zero lattice vector

1: $T \longleftarrow \emptyset, U \longleftarrow \emptyset$
2: for $i = 1$ to N_1 do
3:     $(\mathbf{t}_i, \mathbf{t}'_i) \longleftarrow$ Reduction(Sample($\mathbf{B}, \xi\mu$),T,δ)
4:     If $\|\mathbf{t}_i\| > \gamma\mu$ then
5:         $T \longleftarrow T \cup \{\mathbf{t}_i\}$
6:     end if
7: end for
8: for $i = 1$ to N_2 do
9:     $(\mathbf{u}_i, \mathbf{u}'_i) \longleftarrow$ Reduction(Sample($\mathbf{B}, \xi\mu$),T,δ)
10:    $U \longleftarrow U \cup \{\mathbf{u}_i\}$
11: end for
12: find closest distinct points $(\mathbf{u}_i, \mathbf{u}_j)$ in U
13: Return $\mathbf{u}_i - \mathbf{u}_j$

This implies that the vectors in U are not only short (with high probability) but also independent and identically distributed.

It is proved in the reference [27] that with suitable choices of the parameters N_1, N_2, γ, δ, ξ and μ, the ListSieve-Birthday algorithm can be used to solve SVP with probability $1 - 2^{-\Omega(n)}$[1] in time $2^{2.465n + o(n)}$. We will use the same parameters in our discussions in this paper. The precise choices of these parameters are given in the following lemmas.

Lemma 2. *[27] Let $c_l = -\frac{1}{2} \log_2(1 - \frac{2\xi}{\gamma}) + 0.401$. The List T in the algorithm contains at most $N_L(n) = 2^{c_l n + o(n)}$ vectors.*

---

[1] One writes $f(n) = \Omega(g(n))$, if there exist two positive constants c and n_0, for all $n \geq n_0$, $0 \leq cg(n) \leq f(n)$.

Lemma 3. *[24] Let $c_g = -\frac{1}{2}\log_2(1 - \frac{1}{4\xi^2})$, and $\mathbf{s}$ be a shortest non-zero vector of $\mathcal{L}(\mathbf{B})$. Denote $I_{\mathbf{s}} = \{\mathbf{x} \in \mathcal{B}_n(\xi\mu) : \mathbf{x} + \mathbf{s} \in \mathcal{B}_n(\xi\mu)\}$. If $\mathbf{x}$ is chosen uniformly in $\mathcal{B}_n(\xi\mu)$, then $Pr(\mathbf{x} \in I_{\mathbf{s}}) \geq \frac{1}{N_G}$, where $N_G = 2^{c_g n + o(n)}$.*

The parameter N_1 is related to the number $N_1^{max} = 4\lceil N_L N_G \rceil$. The following lemma is from Lemma 6 of reference [27].

Lemma 4. *Consider the ListSieve-Birthday algorithm with N_1 chosen uniformly in the set $\{0, 1, 2,$*
$\ldots, N_1^{max} - 1\}$. Let E_i be the event $\|\mathbf{u}_i\| \leq \gamma\mu$ for $i \leq N_2$, and $p = Pr(E_i | \mathbf{x}_i \in I_{\mathbf{s}})$. Then $p > \frac{1}{2}$ holds with probability higher than $\frac{1}{2}$.

3 Revisiting the ListSieve-Birthday Algorithm on Lattices with λ_2-gap

The gap between λ_1 and λ_2 leads to certain sparse distribution of lattice points, which will certainly help us find the shortest lattice vector in this case. In this section, we estimate a new upper bound on the number of lattice points in a sphere. Combining with the new bound, we analyze the effect of λ_2-gap on the complexity of the ListSieve-Birthday algorithm. Furthermore, we give some discussions on the complexity of solving SVP in cryptographic instances with λ_2-gaps.

3.1 Packing Density of Lattices with λ_2-gap

In this subsection, we prove the new upper bound for packing density of lattices with λ_2-gap, which results in reducing the complexity of ListSieve-Birthday. The following lemma, which was proven in [14], is a main tool to our proof.

Lemma 5. *[14] Let $E \in \mathbb{R}^n \setminus \{\mathbf{0}\}$. If there exists $\phi_0 > 0$ such that for any $\mathbf{u}, \mathbf{v} \in E$, we have $\phi_{\mathbf{u},\mathbf{v}} > \phi_0$ where $\phi_{\mathbf{u},\mathbf{v}}$ denotes the angle between $\mathbf{u}$ and $\mathbf{v}$, then $|E| \leq 2^{cn + o(n)}$ with $c = -\frac{1}{2}\log_2[1 - \cos(\min(\phi_0, 62.99°))] - 0.099$.*

In the following, we prove the upper bound of packing density by counting the number of lattice points in a sphere.

Theorem 1. *For an n-dimensional lattice L, if $\lambda_2(L) > \alpha\lambda_1(L)$, then $|\mathcal{B}_n(\gamma\mu) \cap L| \leq N_B(n) = 2^{c_b n + o(n)}$, where $c_b = \log_2 \gamma - \log_2 \alpha + 0.401$, and $1 \leq \alpha < \gamma \leq c\alpha \leq \text{poly}(n)$ with a numerical constant $c > 1$.*

Proof. Let $\beta = 1 + \frac{1}{n}$. The ball $\mathcal{B}_n(\alpha\lambda_1)$ contains exactly $1 + 2\lfloor\alpha\rfloor$ lattice points. We partition $\mathcal{B}_n(\gamma\mu) \setminus \mathcal{B}_n(\alpha\lambda_1)$ into coronas $T_r = \mathcal{B}_n(\beta r) \setminus \mathcal{B}_n(r)$ for $r = \alpha\lambda_1, \alpha\lambda_1\beta, \cdots, \alpha\lambda_1\beta^k$ with $k \leq n\log_2 \frac{\gamma}{\alpha} = \tilde{O}(n)$. It is sufficient to show that any corona contains at most $2^{c_b n + o(n)}$ lattice points.

Lattice points contained in T_r can be divided into two sets according to the following rule.

1. Initialize A and B to be two null sets.
2. Randomly select a lattice point $\mathbf{x}$ from T_r. Put $\mathbf{x}$ into A.
3. For each point $\mathbf{z} \in L \cap T_r$,
   if there exists a lattice point $\mathbf{y} \in A$ such that $\|\mathbf{z} - \mathbf{y}\| < \alpha\lambda_1$,
     then store $\mathbf{z}$ into B,
   else store $\mathbf{z}$ into A.

This rule partitions $T_r \cap L$ into two sets A and B. It is clear that any distinct points $\mathbf{u}, \mathbf{v} \in A$ satisfy $\|\mathbf{u}-\mathbf{v}\| \geq \alpha\lambda_1$. Notice that the construction of A depends on the initial point selected into it. Accordingly, there are many selections of A. Whereas we just need one of them to support our proof. The definition of B apparently relies on A. From the above process, we define $B = \{\mathbf{w} \in (T_r \cap L) \backslash A : \exists \mathbf{v} \in A, \text{such that } \|\mathbf{w} - \mathbf{v}\| < \alpha\lambda_1\}$. Next we estimate the size of A and B separately.

From the definition of B, it is clear that each point of B is located in a sphere centered at some point of A with radius $\alpha\lambda_1$. Considering the fact that $\mathcal{B}_n(\alpha\lambda_1)$ contains $1 + 2\lfloor\alpha\rfloor$ lattice points, we obtain

$$|B| \leq (1 + 2\lfloor\alpha\rfloor)|A|.$$

Next, the only work is to determine the size of A. Since any points $\mathbf{u}, \mathbf{v} \in A$ satisfy $\|\mathbf{u} - \mathbf{v}\| \geq \alpha\lambda_1$, it is easy to know that,

$$\langle \mathbf{u}, \mathbf{v} \rangle \leq \frac{1}{2}\left(\|\mathbf{u}\|^2 + \|\mathbf{v}\|^2 - \alpha^2\lambda_1^2\right).$$

This implies that,

$$\cos \phi_{\mathbf{u},\mathbf{v}} = \frac{\langle \mathbf{u}, \mathbf{v} \rangle}{\|\mathbf{u}\| \cdot \|\mathbf{v}\|}$$

$$\leq \frac{1}{2}\left(\frac{\|\mathbf{u}\|}{\|\mathbf{v}\|} + \frac{\|\mathbf{v}\|}{\|\mathbf{u}\|} - \frac{\alpha^2\lambda_1^2}{\|\mathbf{u}\| \cdot \|\mathbf{v}\|}\right)$$

$$\leq 1 + \frac{1}{n} - \frac{\alpha^2\lambda_1^2}{2\gamma^2\mu^2}$$

$$\leq 1 + \frac{1}{n} - \frac{\alpha^2}{2(1 + \frac{1}{n})^2\gamma^2}.$$

Since $\gamma > \alpha$, for any sufficiently large n we have

$$\lim_{n \to \infty}\left(1 + \frac{1}{n} - \frac{\alpha^2}{2(1 + \frac{1}{n})^2\gamma^2}\right) = 1 - \frac{\alpha^2}{2\gamma^2} > \frac{1}{2}.$$

So $\arccos(1 - \frac{\alpha^2}{2\gamma^2}) < 60°$. Because $1 + \frac{1}{n} - \frac{\alpha^2}{2(1+\frac{1}{n})^2\gamma^2}$ is decreasing as the growth of n, $1 + \frac{1}{n} - \frac{\alpha^2}{2(1+\frac{1}{n})^2\gamma^2} \leq 1 - \frac{\alpha^2}{2\gamma^2} + \epsilon$ holds for sufficiently large n and any $\epsilon \leq \frac{\alpha^2}{2\gamma^2}$. Denote $\phi_0 = \arccos(1 - \frac{\alpha^2}{2\gamma^2} + \epsilon)$, then $\phi_0 \leq \arccos(1 - \frac{\alpha^2}{2\gamma^2}) < 60°$. By $\phi_{\mathbf{u},\mathbf{v}} \geq \arccos \phi_0$ and Lemma 5, we get

$$|A| \leq 2^{c_b n + o(n)},$$

where $c_b = \log_2 \gamma - \log_2 \alpha + 0.401 - \log_2(\sqrt{1 - \frac{2\gamma^2\epsilon}{\alpha^2}})$. The last item of c_b is essentially $o(1)$ due to the choice of ϵ. So we get $|A| \le 2^{c_b n + o(n)}$, where $c_b = \log_2 \gamma - \log_2 \alpha + 0.401$.

Therefore, we obtain an estimation of the number of lattice points in T_r as follows,

$$|A| + |B| = (2 + 2\lfloor\alpha\rfloor)|A| \le \text{poly}(n)2^{c_b n + o(n)} = 2^{c_b n + o(n)},$$

where $c_b = \log_2 \gamma - \log_2 \alpha + 0.401$.

Since the number of T_r is polynomial, we finally get

$$|\mathcal{B}_n(\gamma\mu) \cap L| \le N_B(n) = 2^{c_b n + o(n)},$$

where $c_b = \log_2 \gamma - \log_2 \alpha + 0.401$.   □

3.2   The Complexity of ListSieve-Birthday on Lattices with λ_2-gap

Utilizing the result of Theorem 1, we analyze the efficiency of the ListSieve-Birthday on lattices with λ_2-gap. As mentioned above, the most efficient deterministic algorithm [21] can solve SVP in time $2^{2n+o(n)}$ and space $2^{n+o(n)}$. Our computation reveals that, ListSieve-Birthday algorithm is faster than the deterministic algorithm so long as the λ_2-gap of the lattice is larger than 1.78. The complexity will decrease further as the λ_2-gap increases.

Theorem 2. *For sufficiently large n, ListSieve-Birthday returns a shortest nonzero lattice vector with probability $\ge 1/8$.*

The proof is the same as Lemma 7 in the reference[27] since the gap does not influence the correctness of the algorithm. For the sake of completeness, we provide it in Appendix A.

We renew the upper bound for the complexity of ListSieve-Birthday on lattices with λ_2-gap in the following theorem.

Theorem 3. *For an n-dimensional lattice L with $\lambda_2(L) > \alpha\lambda_1(L)$, the ListSieve-Birthday algorithm returns a shortest nonzero lattice vector with probability higher than $1/8$ in time $2^{c_{time}n+o(n)}$ and space $2^{c_{space}n+o(n)}$, where $c_{time} = \max(c_g + 2c_l, 2c_g + c_b)$, $c_{space} = \max(c_l, c_g + c_b/2)$, $c_l = -\frac{1}{2}\log_2(1 - \frac{2\xi}{\gamma}) + 0.401$, $c_g = -\frac{1}{2}\log_2(1 - \frac{1}{4\xi^2})$, $c_b = \log_2 \gamma - \log_2 \alpha + 0.401$. Particularly, if $\alpha \ge 1.78$, we can get $c_{time} \le 1.999$ and $c_{space} \le 0.999$ by optimizing ξ and γ.*

Proof. The time complexity of the first loop is $|T|N_1 \le 2^{(c_g+2c_l)n+o(n)}$ and that of the second loop is $|T| \cdot |U| \le 2^{(c_l+c_g+c_b/2)n+o(n)}$. The time to find the closest pair in U is $|U|^2 \le 2^{(2c_g+c_b)n+o(n)}$. Among these three parts, the cost of the second loop is small enough to be negligible. So the total time complexity is $2^{c_{time}n+o(n)}$ with $c_{time} = \max(c_g + 2c_l, 2c_g + c_b)$. It is clear that the space complexity is $|T| + |U| = 2^{c_{space}n+o(n)}$, where $|T| \le 2^{c_l n+o(n)}$ and $|U| \le 2^{(c_g+c_b/2)n+o(n)}$. So $c_{space} = \max(c_l, c_g + c_b/2)$.

Table 1. c_{time}s corresponding to different values of λ_2-gap

α	ξ	γ	c_{time}
1.78	1.0020	4.0409	1.9969
2	1.0163	4.3316	1.9158
3	1.0759	5.6593	1.6677
5	1.1768	8.3301	1.4246
8	1.2992	12.3483	1.2585
12	1.4308	17.7075	1.1502
28	1.7952	39.0991	0.9992
100	2.6293	134.8910	0.8859
500	4.4019	664.7420	0.8306

To minimize the time complexity, let $2c_l = c_g + c_b$. This implies that,

$$\gamma = 2\xi + 2^{\log_2 \alpha + 0.401} \sqrt{1 - \frac{1}{4\xi^2}}.$$

When the λ_2-gap $\alpha = 1.7723$, by selecting $\xi = 1.0015$ and $\gamma = 4.0308$, we get $c_{time} \leq 1.999$ and $c_{space} \leq 0.999$. $\qquad\qquad\qquad\qquad\qquad\qquad\qquad\qquad\qquad$ □

In order to illustrate the efficiency of ListSieve-Birthday on lattices with gaps, we calculate some instances of the coefficient factor c_{time} in the time complexity corresponding to different values of λ_2-gap α in Table 1. It can be found that the time complexity drops off obviously with respect to the growth of λ_2-gap.

3.3   Discussions on SVP Search for Some Lattice-Based Cryptosystems

In practice, most cryptographic lattices possess λ_2-gap, which may lead to serious security problems. Based on the analysis in subsection 3.1 and 3.2, we will discuss the time complexity of solving the SVP on some cryptosystems with λ_2-gap.

In 2005, Regev proposed a cryptosystem [31] based on the LWE (Learning with Errors) problem[31]. After that, various LWE-based cryptosystems have been designed and some of them provided new functionalities, such as fully-homomorphic encryption, noisy multilinear maps, and indistinguishability obfuscation[9, 10, 15, 28, 31]. The input of LWE problem is a pair $(\mathbf{A}, \mathbf{v} = \mathbf{A}\mathbf{s} + \mathbf{e})$, where $\mathbf{A} \in \mathbb{Z}_q^{m \times n}$ and $\mathbf{s} \in \mathbb{Z}_q^n$ are chosen uniformly, and $\mathbf{e} \in \mathbb{Z}_q^m$ is chosen according to some distribution χ. The search version of LWE is to recover $\mathbf{s}$ and the decision one is to distinguish $\mathbf{v}$ from a uniformly distributed vector in $\mathbb{Z}_q^m$. The hardness of LWE problem was studied in[31] and it is proved that for the discrete Gaussian distribution $D_{\mathbb{Z}^m, \alpha q}$ with $\alpha q \geq 2\sqrt{n}$, the search-LWE is at least as hard as quantumly approximating a worst-case (the decision variant of) SVP of n-dimensional lattice within an approximation factor $\tilde{O}(n/\alpha)$. In [25], Peikert presented a classical reduction for (the decision variant of) SVP at the cost of increasing q. Several years later, at STOC 2013, Brakerski et. al. gave a real classical reduction [3].

The search LWE problem is to find a closest lattice vector from the target $\mathbf{v}$ in the q-ary lattice $\Lambda_q(\mathbf{A}^T) = \{\mathbf{y} \in \mathbb{Z}^m : \mathbf{y} = \mathbf{As} \bmod q \text{ for } \mathbf{s} \in \mathbb{Z}_q^n\}$, so it can be regarded as an instance of BDD problem. Based on the embedding technique, a lower bound of the λ_2-gap in an embedded lattice to solve LWE problem was computed in the reference[19]. Because the expression of lower bound of λ_2-gap is complicated, the authors get a simple expression by analyzing the identity-based encryption system based on LWE proposed by Gentry et. al. [11]. In this system, the set of parameters are selected as $m = 6n \log_2 q$, where q is a prime in $[n^2/2, n^2]$, and the error samples from the Gaussian distribution $D_{\mathbb{Z}^m, \delta q}$ where $\delta = \frac{1}{\sqrt{m} \log_2^2 m}$. It is concluded that the corresponding embedded lattice of this LWE problem has a λ_2-gap larger than $7.3 \log_2^2 m$[19]. The technique is based on the fact that the hardness of the LWE problem cannot be increased by enlarging the dimension m, which is similar to the discussion on SIS problem in the reference [20].

By our analysis of ListSieve-Birthday on lattices with λ_2-gap, we give a further assessment to this scheme as follows.

Corollary 1. *ListSieve-Birthday can find the unique shortest vector of the LWE embedded lattice in the identity-based encryption system[11] with time and space complexity about $2^{0.802m+o(m)}$ and $2^{0.401m+o(m)}$ respectively.*

Proof. Let $c_g + 2c_l = 2c_g + c_b$ to minimize the time complexity as in the proof of Theorem 3, where $c_l = -\frac{1}{2} \log_2(1 - \frac{2\xi}{\gamma}) + 0.401$, $c_g = -\frac{1}{2} \log_2(1 - \frac{1}{4\xi^2})$, $c_b = \log_2 \gamma - \log_2 \alpha + 0.401$, and $\alpha = 7.3 \log_2^2 m$ is the λ_2-gap. Then we have

$$\gamma = 2\xi + 2^{\log_2 \alpha + 0.401} \sqrt{1 - \frac{1}{4\xi^2}}.$$

Together with $\alpha = 7.3 \log_2^2 m$, we get the time complexity $2^{c_{time}n+o(n)}$ with

$$c_{time} = c_g + 2c_l$$
$$= 0.802 + \log_2\left(\frac{1}{\sqrt{1 - \frac{1}{4\xi^2}}} + \frac{2\xi}{\alpha \cdot 2^{0.401}(1 - \frac{1}{4\xi^2})}\right).$$

If the parameter n is selected to be larger than 128, then the λ_2-gap of the embedded lattice could be estimated as 1288 at least. The time and space complexity are $2^{0.8172m+o(m)}$ and $2^{0.4086m+o(m)}$ by selecting $\xi = 6.0033$ and $\gamma = 1706.8020$. The coefficient factor of c_{time} in the time complexity becomes smaller when m is larger, and it is approximately to 0.802 when m is large enough by chosing the parameter $\xi = o(\alpha)$.   □

The Ajtai-Dwork cryptosystem was the first cryptosystem based on the worst-case hardness of uSVP$_{O(n^8)}$, and the approximation factor was subsequently improved to $O(n^2)$[8]. Another cryptosystem based on the hardness of uSVP$_{O(n^{1.5})}$ was proposed by Regev [29]. Since the gap of uSVP lattices may cause security threats, cryptosystems based on the hardness of standard problems on general lattices aroused new interest, such as cryptosystems based on the hardness of GapSVP proposed by Regev [31] and Peikert[25]. Considering the reduction from uSVP$_\gamma$ to GapSVP$_\gamma$ [17], the cryptosystem [25] could be equivalently based on the hardness of uSVP$_{\tilde{O}(n^2)}$. For lattices possessing polynomial λ_2-gap, similarly as the analysis in Corollary 1, the factor c_{time} in the time complexity of ListSieve-Birthday is approximately to 0.802 if n is large enough.

Another type of cryptography instances are the BDD-based cryptosystems. Among them, the Goldreich-Goldwasser-Halevi (GGH) cryptosystem [7] is a typical one. We make a brief description of the GGH cryptosystem. The private key is a short basis $\mathbf{R}$. Transform $\mathbf{R}$ to a non-reduced basis $\mathbf{B}$, which is the public key. Define L to be the lattice generated by $\mathbf{R}$. A message $\mathbf{m} \in \mathbb{Z}^n$ is encrypted to $\mathbf{c} = \mathbf{mB} + \mathbf{e}$ where the error vector $\mathbf{e}$ is uniformly chosen from $\{-\delta, \delta\}^n$ and δ is a parameter usually selected as 3. The ciphertext can be decrypted as $\mathbf{m} = \lfloor \mathbf{cR}^{-1} \rceil \mathbf{RB}^{-1}$. In the reference [23], Nguyen gave some approximations of the embedded lattice gap corresponding to instances of GGH challenges. Among the five challenges, the expected λ_2-gap is larger than 9.4. By Theorem 3, the factor c_{time} in the time complexity of ListSieve-Birthday is 1.2120 by selecting $\xi = 1.3485$ and $\gamma = 14.2243$.

4   Complexity of ListSieve-Birthday on Lattices with λ_{i+1}-gap

An n-dimensional lattice L possessing a λ_{i+1}-gap α means that, there exists a $\alpha > 1$ such that $\lambda_{i+1}(L) > \alpha\lambda_1(L)$. In this section, we prove the upper bound for packing density of lattices with λ_{i+1}-gap. Based on the upper bound, we compute the new complexity of ListSieve-Birthday on this type of lattices, which is related to the size and location of gaps.

4.1   Packing Density of Lattices with λ_{i+1}-gap

The upper bound for packing density of lattices with λ_{i+1}-gap is given in the following theorem. The sketch of this proof is similar to that of Theorem 1.

Theorem 4. *For an n-dimensional lattice L, if $\lambda_{i+1}(L) > \alpha\lambda_1(L)$, then $|\mathcal{B}_n(\gamma\mu)$ $\cap L| \leq N_B(n) = 2^{(\log_2 \gamma - \log_2 \alpha + 0.401)n + (\log_2 \alpha + 0.401)i + o(n)}$, where $1 \leq \alpha < \gamma \leq c\alpha \leq \text{poly}(n)$ with a numerical constant $c > 1$.*

Proof. Similar to the proof of Theorem 1, let $\beta = 1 + \frac{1}{n}$ and partition $\mathcal{B}_n(\gamma\mu)$ $\backslash\mathcal{B}_n(\alpha\lambda_1)$ into coronas $T_r = \mathcal{B}_n(\beta r)\backslash\mathcal{B}_n(r)$ for $r = \alpha\lambda_1, \alpha\lambda_1\beta, \cdots, \alpha\lambda_1\beta^k$ with $k = \tilde{O}(n)$. Divide $L \cap T_r$ into two sets (A, B) by the same rule in Theorem 1.

According to the analysis in Theorem 1, an upper bound $2^{(\log_2 \gamma - \log_2 \alpha + 0.401)}$ $n+o(n)$ for the size of A can be obtained immediately. Since any point of B lies in a sphere centered in some point of A with radius $\alpha\lambda_1$, we can get

$$|B| \leq |L \cap \mathcal{B}_n(\alpha\lambda_1)| \cdot |A|.$$

Next, we give an upper bound for the number of lattice points in $\mathcal{B}_n(\alpha\lambda_1)$.

Because $\lambda_{i+1}(L) > \alpha\lambda_1(L)$, there are at most i linearly independent lattice vectors in $\mathcal{B}_n(\alpha\lambda_1)$. Suppose $\{\mathbf{b}_1, \ldots, \mathbf{b}_i\}$ be a set of linearly independent vectors in $L \cap \mathcal{B}_n(\alpha\lambda_1)$. Then $L \cap \mathcal{B}_n(\alpha\lambda_1) \subset L \cap \mathrm{span}(\mathbf{b}_1, \ldots, \mathbf{b}_i)$, which implies that $L \cap \mathcal{B}_n(\alpha\lambda_1) = L \cap (\mathcal{B}_n(\alpha\lambda_1) \cap \mathrm{span}(\mathbf{b}_1, \ldots, \mathbf{b}_i))$. Thus the rank of $L \cap \mathcal{B}_n(\alpha\lambda_1)$ is i and $L \cap \mathcal{B}_n(\alpha\lambda_1)$ consists of lattice vectors lie in $\mathcal{B}_n(\alpha\lambda_1) \cap \mathrm{span}(\mathbf{b}_1, \ldots, \mathbf{b}_i)$. By some transformation of coordinates, $L \cap \mathcal{B}_n(\alpha\lambda_1)$ can be regarded as the lattice points in the new coordinates, which lie in the i-dimensional sphere with radius $\alpha\lambda_1$. By Lemma 5, this can be bounded by $2^{(\log_2 \alpha + 0.401)i + o(i)}$. Then, we get

$$|B| \leq |A| \cdot 2^{(\log_2 \alpha + 0.401)i + o(i)}.$$

Therefore, the number of lattice points in T_r is at most

$$|A| + |B| \leq (1 + 2^{(\log_2 \alpha + 0.401)i + o(i)})|A| \leq 2^{(\log_2 \gamma - \log_2 \alpha + 0.401)n + (\log_2 \alpha + 0.401)i + o(n)}.$$

Finally, we get

$$|\mathcal{B}_n(\gamma\mu) \cap L| \leq \mathrm{poly}(n) \cdot (|A| + |B|) \leq 2^{(\log_2 \gamma - \log_2 \alpha + 0.401)n + (\log_2 \alpha + 0.401)i + o(n)}.$$

$\square$

The location of gap happened among the successive minima will significantly influence the density of lattice points distribution. We care about the range of i, which makes ListSieve-Birthday algorithm faster than all the existing random SVP algorithms except the heuristic ones. From $2^{(\log_2 \gamma - \log_2 \alpha + 0.401)n + (\log_2 \alpha + 0.401)i + o(n)} \leq 2^{(\log_2 \gamma + 0.401)n + o(n)}$ where the right of the inequality is the packing density bound for general lattices[27], it can be derived that $i \leq \frac{\log_2 \alpha}{\log_2 \alpha + 0.401} n$. This gives the upper bound for i. We list the ranges of i corresponding to some instances of α in Table 2.

Table 2. i'bounds corresponding to different instances of α

α k	1.78	2	3	5	8	12	28	100	500
$i(\leq)$	$0.6747n$	$0.7138n$	$0.7981n$	$0.8527n$	$0.8821n$	$0.8994n$	$0.9230n$	$0.9431n$	$0.9572n$

4.2   Complexity of ListSieve-Birthday on Lattices with λ_{i+1}-gap

The complexity of the ListSieve-Birthday algorithm on lattices with λ_{i+1}-gap can be obtained in the same way with Theorem 3, so the proof is omitted.

Theorem 5. *For an n-dimensional lattice L with $\lambda_{i+1}(L) > \alpha\lambda_1(L)$, the ListSieve-Birthday algorithm returns a shortest nonzero lattice vector with probability higher than $1/8$ in time $2^{c_{time}n + o(n)}$ and space $2^{c_{space}n + o(n)}$, where $c_{time} = \max(c_g + 2c_l, 2c_g + c_d)$, $c_{space} = \max(c_l, c_g + c_d/2)$. Here, $c_l = -\frac{1}{2}\log_2(1 - \frac{2\xi}{\gamma}) + 0.401$, $c_g = -\frac{1}{2}\log_2(1 - \frac{1}{4\xi^2})$, $c_d = \log_2 \gamma - \log_2 \alpha + 0.401 + (\log_2 \alpha + 0.401)\frac{i}{n}$.*

To minimize the time complexity, let $2c_l = c_g + c_d$, which implies

$$\gamma = 2\xi + 2^{(\log_2 \alpha + 0.401)(1 - \frac{i}{n})} \sqrt{1 - \frac{1}{4\xi^2}}.$$

Then

$$c_{time} = 0.802 + \log_2 \left(\frac{1}{\sqrt{1 - \frac{1}{4\xi^2}}} + \frac{2\xi}{(\gamma - 2\xi)\sqrt{1 - \frac{1}{4\xi^2}}} \right)$$

$$= 0.802 + \log_2 \left(\frac{1}{\sqrt{1 - \frac{1}{4\xi^2}}} + \frac{2\xi}{(\alpha \cdot 2^{0.401})^{(1 - \frac{i}{n})}\sqrt{1 - \frac{1}{4\xi^2}}} \right).$$

We compute some values of c_{time} corresponding to different α and i in the following Table 3. It illustrates that the time complexity not only depends on the value of α, but also the location of λ_i-gap.

Table 3. c_{time} corresponding to different α and i

α \ i	1.78	2	3	5	8	12	28	100	500
$\frac{n}{16}$	1.9225	1.8539	1.6417	1.4282	1.2767	1.1744	1.0244	0.9035	0.8393
$\frac{n}{8}$	1.9574	1.8916	1.6862	1.4757	1.3231	1.2180	1.0597	0.9261	0.8508
$\frac{n}{4}$	2.0297	1.9703	1.7814	1.5805	1.4287	1.3200	1.1473	0.9875	0.8857
$\frac{n}{2}$	2.1848	2.1411	1.9972	1.8337	1.7000	1.5968	1.4145	1.2116	1.0455
$\frac{3n}{4}$	2.3541	2.3302	2.2490	2.1513	2.0658	1.9956	1.8587	1.6777	1.4876

Among various lattice-based cryptographic schemes, the NTRU encryption cryptosystem is very practical, and it was adopted to the standard of IEEE Std 1363.1 in 2008. To analyze its security, Coppersmith and Shamir[5] constructed a cryptographic lattice with dimension $2N$. A heuristic analysis reported in[12] indicates that NTRU lattice has λ_{N+1}-gap, which is approximately $\sqrt{\frac{Nq}{4\pi e (d_f \cdot d_g)^{1/2}}}$, where N, q, d_f, d_g is a series of parameters. In the intial version [12], a group of recommended parameters is $N = 503$, $q = 256$, $d_f = 216$, and $d_g = 72$. Substituting these values into the evaluation of the λ_{N+1}-gap yields 5.4980. By numerical computation, the time to solve this SVP of NTRU lattice is $2^{1.8054n + o(n)}$, where $n = 2N$ is the dimension of the NTRU lattice.

5   The Approximate SVP Algorithm

In this section, we propose an SVP approximation algorithm modified from the ListSieve-Birthday algorithm [27], which is used to obtain sufficiently many γ-approximate shortest vectors. Compared with ListSieve-Birthday, our Algorithm 2 terminates sieve process earlier and relaxes the birthday search. The number N_2 of sieved vectors is much smaller than that of the ListSieve-Birthday algorithm, which decreases the time complexity significantly.

Algorithm 2. The Approximate SVP Algorithm

Input: An LLL reduced basis $\mathbf{B}$, $N_1, N_2, \gamma > 1$, $d \geq 1$, dimension n, reduced factor $\delta < 1$, $\frac{\gamma}{1+1/\delta} > \xi > \frac{1}{2}$, $\mu \simeq \lambda_1$

Output: A shortest non-zero lattice vector or a pair of sets $(U, \overline{U})$ with U the set of sieved lattice vectors, $\overline{U} = \{\mathbf{u} \in U : \|\mathbf{u}\| \leq \gamma\mu\}$ and $|\overline{U}| \geq d$

1: $T \longleftarrow \emptyset, U \longleftarrow \emptyset, \overline{U} \longleftarrow \emptyset$
2: for $i = 1$ to N_1 do
3:     $(\mathbf{t}_i, \mathbf{t}_i') \longleftarrow$ Reduction(Sample($\mathbf{B}, \xi\mu$), T, δ)
4:     If $\|\mathbf{t}_i\| > \gamma\mu$ then
5:         $T \longleftarrow T \cup \{\mathbf{t}_i\}$
6:     end if
7: end for
8: for $i = 1$ to N_2 do
9:     $(\mathbf{u}_i, \mathbf{u}_i') \longleftarrow$ Reduction(Sample($\mathbf{B}, \xi\mu$), T, δ)
10:     $U \longleftarrow U \cup \{\mathbf{u}_i\}$
11:     if $\|\mathbf{u}_i\| \leq \gamma\mu$ then
12:         $\overline{U} \longleftarrow \overline{U} \cup \{\mathbf{u}_i\}$
13:     end if
14: end for
15: find closest distinct points $(\mathbf{u}_i, \mathbf{u}_j)$ in U
16: if $\|\mathbf{u}_i - \mathbf{u}_j\| \leq \mu$
17:     Return $\mathbf{u}_i - \mathbf{u}_j$
18:else
19:     Return $(U, \overline{U})$

The sieve steps in Algorithm 2 and ListSieve-Birthday are the same except that we store an additional set $\overline{U}$ which is a subset of U satisfying $\overline{U} = \{\mathbf{u} \in U : \|\mathbf{u}\| \leq \gamma\mu\}$. The approximation factor γ is exactly the same as the sieving parameter in ListSieve-Birthday. So, the previous analysis from Lemma 2, Lemma 3 and Lemma 4 applies to our Algorithm 2 as well.

In the description of Algorithm 2, we use the same notations as in Lemma 2, Lemma 3 and Lemma 4. The algorithm succeeds if a shortest non-zero lattice vector is returned or $\overline{U}$ contains at least d distinct lattice vectors whose perturbation $\mathbf{x}$ is in $I_\mathbf{s}$. Some parameters are given as follows: N_1 is chosen uniformly from the set $\{0, 1, 2, \ldots, N_1^{max} - 1\}$, $N_2 = 8dN_G$, $\delta = 1 - \frac{1}{n}$. Other parameters will be determined later.

The following lemma proves the correctness of Algorithm 2. Its proof is similar to that of Lemma 7 in the reference [27]. One can refer to Appendix B for the details.

Lemma 6. *Let $N_2 = 8dN_G$, and assume that n is sufficiently large. Then with probability higher than $1/8$, Algorithm 2 succeeds.*

Now, we are able to estimate the complexity of Algorithm 2.

Theorem 6. *Let $c_{time} = \max\{2c_l + c_g, 2c_g\}$ and $c_{space} = \max\{c_l, c_g\}$. Let $d = 2^{o(c_g n)}$. Then with probability $1 - 2^{-\Omega(n)}$, Algorithm 2 succeeds with time $2^{c_{time}n + o(n)}$ and space $2^{c_{space}n + o(n)}$.*

Proof. The time complexity of the first loop in steps 2-7 is $N_1 N_L$, and that of the second loop of steps 8-14 is $N_2 N_L$. The complexity of steps 15-19 is N_2^2. So the total time complexity is $2^{c_{time}n + o(n)}$, where $c_{time} = \max\{2c_l + c_g, 2c_g\}$. It is obvious that space complexity is $|T| + |U| = 2^{c_{space}n + o(n)}$, where $c_{space} = max\{c_l, c_g\}$.

Calling the algorithm n times ensures that it succeeds with probability exponentially close to 1. □

We remark that the expression of the time complexity bound in Theorem 6 reaches its optimal value when $\xi = \frac{\sqrt[3]{\gamma}}{2}$. In this case we see that $c_{time} = 0.802 - 1.5\log_2(1 - \gamma^{-\frac{2}{3}})$, and the corresponding c_{space} is $0.401 - 0.5\log_2(1 - \gamma^{-\frac{2}{3}})$.

We compare the complexity bounds for Algorithm 2 and Algorithm 1 (ListSieve-Birthday) for uSVP$_\gamma$ in Table 4. The SVP$_\gamma$ algorithm can be trivially applied to find the unique shortest lattice vector with λ_2-gap$\geq \gamma$. But from Table 4, it is easy to see that ListSieve-Birthday based on our new analysis appears more efficient than the direct application of SVP$_\gamma$ algorithm.

Table 4. Comparision of complexity bounds for algorithm 2 and ListSieve-Birthday for uSVP$_\gamma$

		Algorithm 2		ListSieve-Birthday for uSVP$_\gamma$
γ	ξ	c_{time}	ξ	c_{time}
2.71	0.6971	2.3655	1.0594	1.7250
3.61	0.7670	1.9993	1.1089	1.5712
8	1	1.4246	1.2992	1.2585
15	1.2331	1.1907	1.5143	1.1019

6   Conclusion

In this paper, we prove new upper bounds for the packing density of lattices with λ_i-gap and renew the complexity of the ListSieve-Birthday algorithm. We show that, the complexity will drop off obviously as the growth of λ_i-gap. Specifically, the time complexity of ListSieve-Birthday is less than $2^{1.999n + o(n)}$ if λ_2-gap is larger than 1.78. The coefficient factor of n in the time complexity is approximately to 0.802 when λ_2-gap is large enough. Moreover, we modify ListSieve-Birthday to obtain an SVP approximation algorithm, which decreases the time complexity obviously.

Acknowledgments. The authors would like to thank the anonymous referees for their helpful comments which have improved the quality of this manuscript. This work is supported by China's 973 Program (Grant No. 2013CB834205) and the National Natural Science Foundation of China (Grant No. 61133013).

Appendix

A. Let $\mathbf{s}$ be a shortest vector of lattice L whose norm is approximately μ, and recall that $I_{\mathbf{s}} = \{\mathbf{x} \in \mathcal{B}_n(\xi u) : \mathbf{x} + \mathbf{s} \in \mathcal{B}_n(\xi u)\}$. Let $N_2 = \lceil 8N_G \rceil \lceil \sqrt{N_B} \rceil$. According to Lemma 4, with probability higher than $1/2$, $Pr(\|\mathbf{u}_i\| \leq \gamma\mu | \mathbf{y}_i \in I_{\mathbf{s}}) \geq \frac{1}{2}$ holds for any $i \leq N_2$. Thus

$$\Pr\left((\|\mathbf{u}_i\| < \gamma\mu) \cap (\mathbf{y}_i \in I_{\mathbf{s}})\right) = \Pr\left(\|\mathbf{u}_i\| < \gamma\mu | \mathbf{y}_i \in I_{\mathbf{s}}\right)\Pr(\mathbf{y}_i \in I_{\mathbf{s}}) \geq \frac{1}{2N_G}.$$

Let $Y = |\{i \leq N_2 : \|\mathbf{u}_i\| \leq \gamma\mu, \mathbf{y}_i \in I_{\mathbf{s}}\}|$. Based on the analysis above, the random variable Y obeys a binomial distribution of parameter $p \geq \frac{1}{2N_G}$. Since the expectation and variance are $\mathbb{E}(Y) = pN_2 \geq 4\lceil \sqrt{N_B} \rceil$ and $\text{Var}(Y) = p(1-p)N_2 \leq \mathbb{E}(Y)$ respectively, by Chebyshev's inequality we have

$$
\begin{aligned}
\Pr(Y > 2\lceil \sqrt{N_B} \rceil) &= 1 - \Pr(Y \leq 2\lceil \sqrt{N_B} \rceil) \\
&\geq 1 - \Pr(|Y - \mathbb{E}(Y)| \geq \mathbb{E}(Y) - 2\lceil \sqrt{N_B} \rceil) \\
&\geq 1 - \frac{\text{Var}(Y)}{(\mathbb{E}(Y) - 2\lceil \sqrt{N_B} \rceil)^2} \\
&\geq 1 - \frac{\mathbb{E}(Y)}{(\mathbb{E}(Y) - 2\lceil \sqrt{N_B} \rceil)^2} \\
&\geq 1 - \frac{1}{\lceil \sqrt{N_B} \rceil} \\
&\geq \frac{4}{5},
\end{aligned}
$$

when $N_B \geq 25$.

This implies that there are at least $2\lceil \sqrt{N_B} \rceil$ independent and identically distributed lattice points with probability higher than $4/5$ which could be sampled into the ball with radius $\gamma\mu$. Let $S = \mathcal{B}_n(\gamma\mu) \cap L$, the probability of a collision occurs (which means there exist two distinct indices $i, j \leq N_2$ such that $\mathbf{u}_i = \mathbf{u}_j$ and $\mathbf{y}_i, \mathbf{y}_j \in I_{\mathbf{s}}$) is greater than

$$\frac{1}{2} \times \frac{4}{5} \times \left(1 - \prod_{i \leq 2\lceil \sqrt{N_B} \rceil} \left(1 - \frac{i}{|S|}\right)\right) \geq \frac{2}{5}\left(1 - \exp\left(-\frac{2\lceil \sqrt{N_B} \rceil(2\lceil \sqrt{N_B} \rceil - 1)}{2N_B}\right)\right)$$

$$\geq \frac{2}{5}\left(1 - \frac{1}{e}\right) \geq \frac{1}{4}.$$

Since the perturbations $\mathbf{y}_i$ are chosen randomly in $\mathcal{B}_n(\gamma\mu)$, the probability of $\mathbf{y}_i \in I_{\mathbf{s}}$ be sampled is the same with $\mathbf{y}_i + \mathbf{s} \in I_{\mathbf{s}} + \mathbf{s}$. So, the two perturbations corresponding to the collision could be $\mathbf{y}_i + \mathbf{s}$ and $\mathbf{y}_j$ with probability $1/4$. Because the corresponding pair of $\mathbf{y}_i$ and $\mathbf{y}_i + \mathbf{s}$ are $(\mathbf{u}'_i, \mathbf{u}_i)$ and $(\mathbf{u}'_i, \mathbf{u}_i + \mathbf{s})$

respectively, and the actions of the reduction only depend on the perturbed vectors, the collision occurs with corresponding lattice points $\mathbf{u}_i + \mathbf{s}$ and $\mathbf{u}_j(= \mathbf{u}_i)$. Similarly, the two perturbations corresponding to the collision could be $\mathbf{y}_i$ and $\mathbf{y}_j + \mathbf{s}$ with probability $1/4$. Thus, the there exist two lattice points in the list U at a distance of μ with probability $1/2$. Hence, ListSieve-Birthday can return a shortest nonzero lattice vector with probability higher than $1/8$.

B. Let $\mathbf{s}$ be a shortest vector of the lattice whose norm is approximately μ. According to Lemma 4, with probability higher than $\frac{1}{2}$, $Pr(\|\mathbf{u}_i\| \leq \gamma\mu|\mathbf{x}_i \in I_\mathbf{s}) \geq \frac{1}{2}$ holds. Since the vectors in the list U are independent and identically distributed and the relation $\mathbf{u}_i - \mathbf{u}_i' = \mathbf{x}_i$ is preserved during the sieve process, we see that

$$Pr((\|\mathbf{u}_i\| \leq \gamma\mu) \cap (\mathbf{x}_i \in I_\mathbf{s})) = Pr(\|\mathbf{u}_i\| \leq \gamma\mu|\mathbf{x}_i \in I_\mathbf{s})Pr(\mathbf{x}_i \in I_\mathbf{s}) \geq \frac{1}{2N_G}.$$

Let $X = \{i \leq N_2 : \|\mathbf{u}_i\| \leq \gamma\mu, \mathbf{x}_i \in I_\mathbf{s}\}$. Based on the analysis above, the random variable $|X|$ obeys a binomial distribution of parameter $p \geq \frac{1}{2N_G}$. Since the expectation and variance are $\mathbb{E}(|X|) = pN_2$ and $\mathbb{D}(|X|) = p(1-p)N_2$ respectively, by Chebyshev's inequality we have

$$Pr(|X| \leq d) \leq Pr(||X| - \mathbb{E}(|X|)| \geq \mathbb{E}(|X|) - d) \leq \frac{\mathbb{D}(|X|)}{(\mathbb{E}(|X|) - d)^2} \leq \frac{4}{9d} \leq \frac{1}{2}$$

when $d \geq 1$.

That means we have $|X| > d$ with probability higher than $\frac{1}{2}$. The following discussion will be divided into two cases.

Case 1. If there are distinct $i, j \in X$ such that $\mathbf{u}_i = \mathbf{u}_j$, we claim that a shortest vector can be found by pairwise subtracting the elements in U with high probability.

We modify the Sample Algorithm in the second loop by applying τ with probability $1/2$ on every perturbation $\mathbf{x}$. τ maintains the uniform distribution on $\mathcal{B}_n(\xi\mu)$, and the output distribution of the modified algorithm should be exactly the same as that of the original algorithm. Furthermore, we have

$$\mathbf{u}_x' = -\mathbf{x} \mod \mathcal{P}(B) \quad = \quad \tau(-\mathbf{x}) \mod \mathcal{P}(B) \quad = \quad \mathbf{u}_{\tau(-x)}'.$$

This means that for $\mathbf{x} \in I_\mathbf{s}$, if the original Sample Algorithm returns $(\mathbf{u}, \mathbf{u}')$, then its modification (i.e., after τ transformation) outputs $(\mathbf{u} + \mathbf{s}, \mathbf{u}')$. Since in the Reduction Algorithm, the sieve makes its decision based on $\mathbf{u}'$ instead of $\mathbf{u}$, the τ transformation has no effect on the Reduction Algorithm.

Since $\mathbf{u}_i = \mathbf{u}_j$, with probability $1/2$, $\mathbf{u}_i$ is changed to $\mathbf{u}_i + \mathbf{s}$, or $\mathbf{u}_j$ is changed to $\mathbf{u}_j + \mathbf{s}$, but not both, after using τ to the second loop. This means that the shortest vector $\mathbf{s}$ is in $\{\mathbf{w}_1 - \mathbf{w}_2 : \mathbf{w}_1, \mathbf{w}_2 \in U\}$. Since the modified algorithm does not change the the distribution in U, Algorithm 2 returns the shortest vector in this step as well.

Case 2. If for any distinct $i, j \in X$, $\mathbf{u}_i \neq \mathbf{u}_j$, then at least d distinct vectors whose perturbation $\mathbf{x}$ is in $I_\mathbf{s}$ are in $\overline{U}$.

Multiplying the three probabilities together, the success probability of Algorithm 2 is higher than $\frac{1}{8}$.

References

1. Ajtai, M., Dwork, C.: A public-key cryptosystem with worst-case/average-case equivalence. In: STOC 1997, pp. 284–293. El Paso, Texas, USA (1997)
2. Ajtai, M., Kumar, R., Sivakumar, D.: A sieve algorithm for the shortest lattice vector problem. In: STOC 2001, Heraklion, Crete, Greece, pp. 266–275. ACM, New York (2001)
3. Brakerski, Z., Langlois, A., Peikert, C., et al.: Classical hardness of learning with errors. In: Boneh, D., Roughgarden, T., Feigenbaum, J. (eds.) STOC, pp. 575–584. ACM (2013)
4. Coster, M.J., Joux, A., Macchia, B.A., Odlyzko, A.M., Schnorr, C.P., Stern, J.: An improved low-density subset sum algorithm. Computational Complexity **2**, 97–186 (1992)
5. Coppersmith, D., Shamir, A.: Lattice attacks on NTRU. In: Fumy, W. (ed.) EUROCRYPT 1997. LNCS, vol. 1233, pp. 52–61. Springer, Heidelberg (1997)
6. Gama, N., Nguyen, P.Q.: Predicting lattice reduction. In: Smart, N.P. (ed.) EUROCRYPT 2008. LNCS, vol. 4965, pp. 31–51. Springer, Heidelberg (2008)
7. Goldreich, O., Goldwasser, S., Halevi, S.: Public-key cryptosystems from lattice reduction problems. In: Kaliski Jr., B.S. (ed.) CRYPTO 1997. LNCS, vol. 1294, pp. 112–131. Springer, Heidelberg (1997)
8. Goldreich, O., Goldwasser, S., Halevi, S.: Eliminating Decryption Errors in the Ajtai-Dwork Cryptosystem. In: Kaliski Jr., B.S. (ed.) CRYPTO 1997. LNCS, vol. 1294, pp. 105–111. Springer, Heidelberg (1997)
9. Garg, S., Gentry, C., Halevi, S.: Candidate multilinear maps from ideal lattices. In: Johansson, T., Nguyen, P.Q. (eds.) EUROCRYPT 2013. LNCS, vol. 7881, pp. 1–17. Springer, Heidelberg (2013)
10. Garg, S., Gentry, C., Halevi, S., Raykova, M., Sahai, A., Waters, B.: Candidate indistinguishability obfuscation and functional encryption for all circuits. FOCS, pp. 40–49 (2013)
11. Gentry, C., Peikert, C., Vaikuntanathan, V.: Trapdoors for hard lattices and new cryptographic constructions. In: STOC 2008, pp. 197–206, Victoria, British Columbia, Canada (2008)
12. Hoffstein, J., Pipher, J., Silverman, J.H.: NTRU: a ring-based public key cryptosystem. In: Buhler, J.P. (ed.) ANTS 1998. LNCS, vol. 1423, pp. 267–288. Springer, Heidelberg (1998)
13. Kannan, R.: Improved algorithms for integer programming and related lattice problems. In: STOC 1983, pp. 193–206. Boston, Massachusts, USA (1983)
14. Kabatiansky, G., Levenshtein, V.: Bounds for packings on a sphere and in space. Problemy Peredachi Informatsii **14**(1), 3–25 (1978)
15. Kawachi, A., Tanaka, K., Xagawa, K.: Multi-bit cryptosystems based on lattice problems. Proceedings of Public Key CryptographyCPKC 2007, pp. 315C329. Springer (2007)
16. Lenstra, A.K., Lenstra Jr., H.W., Lovász, L.: Factoring polynomials with rational coefficients. Mathematische Annalen **261**, 513–534 (1982)
17. Lyubashevsky, V., Micciancio, D.: On bounded distance decoding, unique shortest vectors, and the minimum distance problem. In: Halevi, S. (ed.) CRYPTO 2009. LNCS, vol. 5677, pp. 577–594. Springer, Heidelberg (2009)

18. Lagarias, J.C., Odlyzko, A.M.: Solving low-density subset sum problems. Jounal of the Association for Computing Machinery **32**(1), 229–246 (1985)
19. Liu, M.J., Wang, X.Y., Xu, G.W., Zheng, X.X.: Shortest lattice vectors in the presence of gaps. IACR Cryptology ePrint Archive **2011**, 139 (2011)
20. Micciancio, D., Regev, O.: Lattice-based cryptography. Post-Quantum Cryptography, Springer, pp. 147C191 (2009)
21. D. Micciancio, P.Voulgaris, A deterministic single exponential time algorithm for most lattice problems based on Voronoi cell computations. In: STOC 2010, pp. 351–358. Cambridge, Massachusts, USA (2010)
22. Micciancio, D., Voulgaris, P.: Faster exponential time algorithms for the shortest vector problem. In: SODA 2010, pp. 1468–1480. Austin, Texas, USA (2010)
23. Nguyên, P.Q.: Cryptanalysis of the Goldreich-Goldwasser-Halevi cryptosystem from Crypto1997. In: Wiener, M. (ed.) CRYPTO 1999. LNCS, vol. 1666, p. 288. Springer, Heidelberg (1999)
24. Nguyen, P.Q., Vidick, T.: Sieve algorithms for the shortest vector problem are practical. J. of Mathematical Cryptology **2**(2), 181–207 (2008)
25. Peikert, C.: Public-key cryptosystems from the worst-case shortest vector problem. In: STOC 2009, pp. 333–342, Bethesda, MD, USA (2009)
26. Pohst, M.: On the computation of lattice vectors of minimal length, successive minima and reduced bases with applications. ACM SIGSAM Bulletin **15**(1), 37–44 (1981)
27. Pujol, X., Stehlé, D.: Solving the shortest lattice vector problem in time $2^{2.465n}$. Cryptology ePrint Archive, Report 2009/605(2009) http://eprint.iacr.org/2009/605
28. Peikert, C., Vaikuntanathan, V., Waters, B.: A framework for efficient and composable oblivious transfer. In: Proceedings of Advances in CryptologyCCRYPTO 2008, p. 554C571. Springer (2008)
29. Regev, O.: New lattice-based cryptographic constructions. J. ACM **51**(6), 899–942 (2004)
30. Regev, O.: Lecture notes on lattices in computer science (2004). http://www.cs.tau.ac.il/odedr/teaching/latticesfall2004/index.html
31. Regev, O.: On lattices, learing with errors, random linear codes, and cryptography. J. ACM **56**(6), 1–40 (2009)
32. Schnorr, C.P., Euchner, M.: Lattice basis reduction: improved practical algorithms and solving subset sum problems. Mathematics of Programming **66**, 181–199 (1994)
33. Wang, X.Y., Liu, M.J.,Tian, C.L., Bi, J.G.: Improved Nguyen-Vidick heuristic sieve algorithm for shortest vector problem. In: ASIACCS 2011, pp. 1–9, Hongkong, China (2011)
34. Zhang, F., Pan, Y.B., Hu, G.R.: A three-level sieve algorithm for the shortest vector problem. Selected Areas in Cryptography, pp. 29–47 (2013)

A Simple and Improved Algorithm for Integer Factorization with Implicit Hints

Koji Nuida[1,2]($\boxtimes$), Naoto Itakura[3], and Kaoru Kurosawa[3]

[1] National Institute of Advanced Industrial Science and Technology (AIST),
Tsukuba, Ibaraki 305-8568, Japan
k.nuida@aist.go.jp
[2] Japan Science and Technology Agency (JST) PRESTO Researcher,
Tsukuba, Japan
[3] Ibaraki University, Hitachi, Ibaraki 316-8511, Japan
naotoitakura@gmail.com, kurosawa@mx.ibaraki.ac.jp

Abstract. Given two integers $N_1 = p_1q_1$ and $N_2 = p_2q_2$ with α-bit primes q_1, q_2, suppose that the t least significant bits of p_1 and p_2 are equal. May and Ritzenhofen (PKC 2009) developed a factoring algorithm for N_1, N_2 when $t \geq 2\alpha+3$; Kurosawa and Ueda (IWSEC 2013) improved the bound to $t \geq 2\alpha + 1$. In this paper, we propose a polynomial-time algorithm in a parameter κ, with an improved bound $t = 2\alpha - O(\log \kappa)$; it is the first non-constant improvement of the bound. Both the construction and the proof of our algorithm are very simple; the worst-case complexity of our algorithm is evaluated by an easy argument. We also give some computer experimental results showing the efficiency of our algorithm for concrete parameters, and discuss potential applications of our result to security evaluations of existing factoring-based primitives.

Keywords: Integer factorization with implicit hint · Gaussian reduction

1 Introduction

For a large number of computationally secure cryptographic schemes in the literature, including the RSA cryptosystem [12], the (expected) computational hardness of integer factorization is a necessary (and sometimes sufficient) condition for their security. Consequently, the actual hardness of integer factorization has been intensively studied so far, e.g., [5,6,11].

Among these work, there exists a direction of studies on integer factorization with *hints*. One of the most famous results was given by Coppersmith [2]; the factorization of a composite integer $N = pq$ with primes p, q becomes efficient when a half of the most significant bits of p are revealed. In the setting, a hint for the factorization is given *explicitly*.

On the other hand, there are also previous results where some *implicit* hints are supposed. May and Ritzenhofen [8] considered the following setting: Given two RSA moduli $N_1 = p_1q_1$ and $N_2 = p_2q_2$, it is supposed that the t least

© Springer International Publishing Switzerland 2015
K. Nyberg (ed.): CT-RSA 2015, LNCS 9048, pp. 258–269, 2015.
DOI: 10.1007/978-3-319-16715-2_14

significant bits of p_1 and of p_2 are equal. Here the precise values of their t common bits are *not* given; i.e., the hint is only implicit. They showed that, if q_1 and q_2 are α-bit primes and $t \geq 2\alpha + 3$, then N_1 and N_2 can be factorized efficiently. Recently, Kurosawa and Ueda [4] gave an improved algorithm providing a better bound $t \geq 2\alpha + 1$; they also slightly generalized the situation in such a way that $p_1 \equiv p_2 \pmod{T}$ for some parameter $T > q_1{}^2 + q_2{}^2$ (the original case corresponds to $T = 2^t$). In this paper, we improve these results further, yielding a better bound for T.

1.1   Our Contributions

In this paper, we study the integer factorization of composite integers $N_1 = p_1 q_1$ and $N_2 = p_2 q_2$ with implicit hint $p_1 \equiv p_2 \pmod{T}$. We aim at developing a polynomial-time algorithm with respect to a certain parameter κ; for example, in potential applications of the result to security evaluations of the Okamoto–Uchiyama cryptosystem [10] and Takagi's variant of the RSA cryptosystem [14] (discussed in Sect. 5), κ is the security parameter for each scheme. Then we propose an algorithm to factorize N_1 or N_2 with probability one in polynomial time with respect to the parameter κ under the condition[1]

$$\log T = 2 \log Q - O(\log \kappa) \tag{1}$$

where Q is an upper bound for q_1, q_2. When $Q = 2^\alpha$ and $T = 2^t$ for integer parameters α and t, our condition above is equivalent to

$$2\alpha - t = O(\log \kappa)$$

which is significantly better than the best existing bound $2\alpha - t \leq -1$ in [4].[2] We emphasize that our result is the first result achieving *non-constant* improvement of the bound (which is independent of the size of the other factors p_1 and p_2).

The essence of our remarkable improvement from the previous results [4,8] can be explained as follows. In the previous results, a two-dimensional lattice L associated to the given composite integers N_1, N_2 is defined, and it is shown that its *shortest vector*, calculated by Gaussian reduction algorithm, coincides with the vector (q_1, q_2) of the target factors under their condition for T and Q (or t and α, when $T = 2^t$ and $Q = 2^\alpha$). Now we point out that, the Gaussian reduction algorithm outputs not only the shortest vector, but also the *second shortest vector* of the lattice L. Our main idea is to utilize the second shortest vector (together with the shortest vector) which was not previously used; this new ingredient enables us to improve the algorithm.

Another noteworthy characteristic of our result is its simplicity; it relies solely on the basic fact that the vector $\boldsymbol{q} = (q_1, q_2)$, which lies in the lattice L, can be

---

[1] In fact, some easy-to-satisfy conditions are also required for the sake of completeness.

[2] It was shown in [4] that their algorithm fails (rather than being inefficient) when the bound is not satisfied; hence our result is indeed an improvement of the previous work.

expressed by using the shortest vector v and the second shortest vector u of L as $q = av + bu$ for some integers a, b. Our algorithm finds the correct coefficients a, b by exhaustive search; now our improved condition (1) guarantees that there are only polynomially many (with respect to κ) candidates of (a, b). Our proof is also very simple and elementary; it does not use any typical facts for lattices such as Minkowski bound and Hadamard's inequality (which were used in the previous work [4,8]).

We performed some computer experiments, which show that our proposed algorithm indeed works efficiently (e.g., the average running time on an ordinary PC was approximately 221 sec. $\approx$ 4 min. for $\alpha = 250$ and $t = 475$). We also discuss potential applications of our proposed algorithm to some existing schemes such as the Okamoto–Uchiyama cryptosystem [10] and Takagi's variant of the RSA cryptosystem [14]. We emphasize that our algorithm does *not* require the implicitly correlated factors p_1, p_2 to be primes; this property is necessary for applications to the security evaluations of these two schemes.

1.2   Related Work

As mentioned above, for the case of the factorization of two integers, our result improves the previous results by May and Ritzenhofen [8] and Kurosawa and Ueda [4]. On the other hand, May and Ritzenhofen also studied the factorization of three or more integers which are implicitly correlated in a similar manner. Such an extension of our result is left as a future research topic.

Sarkar and Maitra [13] analyzed the more general cases by using the technique of Coppersmith [2] in which (i) some least significant bits (LSBs) of p_1 and p_2 are the same, (ii) some most significant bits (MSBs) of them are the same and (iii) some LSBs and some MSBs are the same.[3] We note that (ii) and (iii) are out of the scope of this paper.

In their method, however, it is assumed that p_1 and p_2 are primes of same size. On the other hand, in our method, p_1 and p_2 can be of different sizes, and they do not need to be primes.

Finally, the proposed algorithm would play a significant role in its potential applications to security evaluations of factoring-based schemes where the hard-to-factorize composite integers are highly unbalanced. Such schemes include recent variants of the (batch) fully homomorphic encryption over integers based on the error-free approximate GCD assumptions [1,9]. We emphasize that, the above-mentioned advantage of our proposed algorithm, i.e., it has no restrictions for the properties of p_1 and p_2, is indispensable in these applications.

1.3   Organization of the Paper

In Sect. 2, we summarize basic notations and terminology, as well as some properties of Gaussian reduction algorithm for two-dimensional lattice. In Sect. 3, we clarify our problem setting, describe our proposed factorization algorithm,

---

[3] In a recent preprint [7], Lu et al. announced that they improved these results.

and then show its correctness and computational complexity. In Sect. 4, we give the results of our computer experiments to show the efficiency of our proposed algorithm. Finally, in Sect. 5, we discuss potential applications to security evaluations of some existing cryptographic schemes.

2 Preliminaries

For two-dimensional vectors $v = (v_1, v_2), u = (u_1, u_2) \in \mathbb{R}^2$, let $||v|| = \sqrt{v_1{}^2 + v_2{}^2}$ and $(v, u) = v_1 u_1 + v_2 u_2$ denote the Euclidean norm and the standard inner product. For a two-dimensional lattice $L \subset \mathbb{Z}^2$, let $\lambda_1 = \lambda_1(L)$ and $\lambda_2 = \lambda_2(L)$ denote the *successive minima* of L; i.e., λ_i is the minimal radius of a ball containing i linearly independent vectors of L.

We recall that, in a two-dimensional lattice L, a basis (v_1, v_2) of L satisfying $||v_1|| = \lambda_1$ and $||v_2|| = \lambda_2$ can be efficiently obtained by Gaussian reduction algorithm. Here we describe the algorithm:

Definition 1 (Gaussian reduction algorithm). *Given any basis (b_1, b_2) of a lattice L, Gaussian reduction algorithm performs as follows:*

1. *First, order the vectors b_1, b_2 and rename those as v_1, v_2, in such a way that $||v_1|| \leq ||v_2||$.*
2. *Set $\mu := \lfloor (v_1, v_2)/||v_1||^2 \rceil$, i.e., the integer closest to $(v_1, v_2)/||v_1||^2$ (if two integers have equal smallest distance from the value, then choose the one with smaller absolute value).*
3. *Repeat the following, until μ becomes 0:*
   (a) Update v_2 by $v_2 \leftarrow v_2 - \mu v_1$.
   (b) If $||v_2|| < ||v_1||$, then swap v_1 and v_2.
   (c) Set $\mu := \lfloor (v_1, v_2)/||v_1||^2 \rceil$.
4. *Output the pair (v_1, v_2).*

The following property is well-known; see e.g., [3]:

Proposition 1. *The Gaussian reduction algorithm outputs a basis (v_1, v_2) of the lattice L satisfying $||v_1|| = \lambda_1$ and $||v_2|| = \lambda_2$. Moreover, the computational complexity of the algorithm is $O(\log^2 \max\{||b_1||, ||b_2||\})$.*

We also use the following property of Gaussian reduction algorithm:

Lemma 1. *For any input (b_1, b_2) and the corresponding output (v_1, v_2) of Gaussian reduction algorithm, we have $|\det(b_1, b_2)| = |\det(v_1, v_2)|$, where we write $\det((x_1, x_2), (y_1, y_2)) := \det \begin{pmatrix} x_1 & x_2 \\ y_1 & y_2 \end{pmatrix} = x_1 y_2 - x_2 y_1$.*

Proof. The transformations for (v_1, v_2) performed at each step of Gaussian reduction algorithm are one of the followings:

- Subtract a scalar multiple of v_1 from v_2; it preserves the value $\det(v_1, v_2)$.
- Swap v_1 and v_2; it changes the value $\det(v_1, v_2)$ to $-\det(v_1, v_2)$.

Hence, the absolute value of $\det(v_1, v_2)$ is not changed, as desired.

3 Our Proposed Algorithm

3.1 Problem Setting

Let $N_1 = p_1 q_1$ and $N_2 = p_2 q_2$ be given composite numbers. Let $T \geq 2$ be an integer parameter (for example, a power of two as in [8]) with $T < N_1$ and $T < N_2$. In this paper, we consider the following situation:

- We have $p_1 \equiv p_2 \equiv p \pmod{T}$ for some *unknown* integer p.
- Any two of N_1, N_2 and T are coprime to each other.

When $T = 2^t$ for an integer t, the first condition means that the t least significant bits of p_1 and p_2 are equal (the precise t bits are not known). We emphasize that *we do NOT assume that each of p_1, p_2, q_1 and q_2 is a prime*; this fact plays an indispensable role in the potential applications of our result discussed in Sect. 5. The second condition implies that any two of q_1, q_2 and T are coprime to each other, and p is coprime to T (indeed, if p and T have a common divisor $a > 1$, then p_1 and p_2, hence N_1 and N_2, are multiples of a, a contradiction).

3.2 The Algorithm

In order to describe our proposed algorithm, first we define, for given composite numbers N_1 and N_2, the following two-dimensional lattice L:

$$L := \{(x_1, x_2) \in \mathbb{Z}^2 \mid N_2 x_1 - N_1 x_2 \equiv 0 \pmod{T}\} .$$

We have a basis of L consisting of two vectors $(1, N_2/N_1 \bmod T)$ and $(0, T)$, where $N_2/N_1 \bmod T$ signifies the unique integer ν in $[0, T-1]$ with $N_1 \nu \equiv N_2 \pmod{T}$. It is indeed a basis of L, since N_1 and T are coprime; if $(0, x_2) \in L$, then we have $N_1 x_2 \equiv 0 \pmod{T}$, therefore x_2 must be a multiple of T.

We now describe our proposed algorithm to find a non-trivial factor of at least one of the given composite numbers N_1 and N_2:

1. Compute, by Gaussian reduction algorithm with initial basis consisting of $(1, N_2/N_1 \bmod T)$ and $(0, T)$, a basis $(\boldsymbol{v} = (v_1, v_2), \boldsymbol{u} = (u_1, u_2))$ of the lattice L above with $\|\boldsymbol{v}\| = \lambda_1 = \lambda_1(L)$ and $\|\boldsymbol{u}\| = \lambda_2 = \lambda_2(L)$.
2. Compute $\gcd(v_1, N_1)$, $\gcd(v_2, N_2)$, $\gcd(u_1, N_1)$ and $\gcd(u_2, N_2)$, and if at least one of those is different from 1, then output it and stop.
3. If $v_1 u_2 - v_2 u_1 < 0$, then replace $\boldsymbol{u}$ with $-\boldsymbol{u}$.
4. For $A = 2, 3, \ldots$, execute the following:
   (a) For integers $a, b \neq 0$ satisfying $|a| + |b| = A$, execute the following: If $|a u_1 - b v_1|$ is a non-trivial factor of N_1, then output it and stop.

3.3 Analysis of Our Algorithm

We analyze the correctness and the efficiency of our proposed algorithm. First, note that (since $T \geq 2$)

$$\|(1, N_2/N_1 \bmod T)\| \leq \sqrt{1^2 + (T-1)^2} < T = \|(0, T)\| , \tag{2}$$

therefore by Proposition 1, the complexity of Step 1 of our algorithm (consisting of Gaussian reduction algorithm) is $O(\log^2 T)$. Secondly, the lattice L contains the vector $\boldsymbol{q} := (q_1, q_2)$; indeed, we have

$$N_2 q_1 - N_1 q_2 = p_2 q_2 q_1 - p_1 q_1 q_2 \equiv p q_2 q_1 - p q_1 q_2 = 0 \pmod{T} \ .$$

Now we show the following property for Step 2 of our algorithm:

Lemma 2. *If our algorithm stops in Step 2, then the output of the algorithm is correctly a non-trivial factor of either N_1 or N_2. Moreover, if $\|\boldsymbol{q}\| < \lambda_2$, then our algorithm always stops in Step 2.*

Proof. We have $\lambda_2 \leq T$ by (2), therefore $\lambda_2 < N_1$ and $\lambda_2 < N_2$ by the condition in Sect. 3.1. This implies that all of $|v_1|$, $|v_2|$, $|u_1|$ and $|u_2|$ are smaller than N_1 and N_2. Hence, $\gcd(v_1, N_1)$ will be a non-trivial factor of N_1 if $\gcd(v_1, N_1) \neq 1$, and the same holds for $\gcd(v_2, N_2)$, $\gcd(u_1, N_1)$ and $\gcd(u_2, N_2)$. This implies the first part of the claim.

For the second part, if $\|\boldsymbol{q}\| < \lambda_2$, then $\boldsymbol{q}$ and $\boldsymbol{v}$ are linearly dependent by the definition of $\lambda_2 = \lambda_2(L)$; $c\boldsymbol{v} = c'\boldsymbol{q}$ for some coprime integers $c, c' \neq 0$. Since q_1 and q_2 are coprime, we have $|c| = 1$ and $\boldsymbol{v} = \pm c'\boldsymbol{q}$. Moreover, since $\|\boldsymbol{q}\| \geq \|\boldsymbol{v}\|$ by the choice of $\boldsymbol{v}$, we have $|c'| = 1$. Therefore, we have $|v_1| = q_1$ and $\gcd(v_1, N_1) = q_1 \neq 1$. This completes the proof of Lemma 2.

Note that the computation of gcd in Step 2 can be done in polynomial time with respect to $\max\{\log N_1, \log N_2\}$. By virtue of Lemma 2, to see the correctness of our algorithm, we may focus on the case where the algorithm does not stop at Step 2. Now we have $\lambda_2 \leq \|\boldsymbol{q}\|$ by Lemma 2.

Since $\boldsymbol{u}$ and $\boldsymbol{v}$ form a basis of L and $\boldsymbol{q} \in L$, there are integers $a_0, b_0 \in \mathbb{Z}$ satisfying

$$\boldsymbol{q} = a_0 \boldsymbol{u} + b_0 \boldsymbol{v} \ , \tag{3}$$

or equivalently

$$\begin{pmatrix} q_1 \\ q_2 \end{pmatrix} = \begin{pmatrix} a_0 u_1 + b_0 v_1 \\ a_0 u_2 + b_0 v_2 \end{pmatrix} = \begin{pmatrix} u_1 & v_1 \\ u_2 & v_2 \end{pmatrix} \begin{pmatrix} a_0 \\ b_0 \end{pmatrix} \ . \tag{4}$$

Consequently, if the pair (a, b) in Step 4a of our algorithm becomes $(a_0, -b_0)$, then our algorithm stops with output q_1, which is indeed a non-trivial factor of N_1. Now we have $a_0 \neq 0$ by (3), since q_1 is coprime to v_1 (note that v_1 is coprime to $N_1 = p_1 q_1$, since our algorithm does not stop at Step 2 by the current assumption). Similarly, we have $b_0 \neq 0$. This completes the proof of the property that our algorithm stops within a finite computational time and its output is always a non-trivial factor of either N_1 or N_2 (we note that $|a_0| + |b_0| \geq 2$, since $a_0, b_0 \neq 0$).

From now, we evaluate the number of iterations in Step 4, by evaluating the sizes of a_0 and b_0 above. Now Lemma 1 implies that

$$\det \begin{pmatrix} u_1 & v_1 \\ u_2 & v_2 \end{pmatrix} = \det \begin{pmatrix} u_1 & u_2 \\ v_1 & v_2 \end{pmatrix} = \pm \det \begin{pmatrix} 1 & N_2/N_1 \bmod T \\ 0 & T \end{pmatrix} = \pm T \ ,$$

while $\det\begin{pmatrix} u_1 & v_1 \\ u_2 & v_2 \end{pmatrix} = u_1v_2 - u_2v_1 < 0$ by virtue of Step 3 of our algorithm,

therefore we have $\det\begin{pmatrix} u_1 & v_1 \\ u_2 & v_2 \end{pmatrix} = -T$. Hence the system of equations (4) can be inverted as

$$\begin{pmatrix} a_0 \\ b_0 \end{pmatrix} = \begin{pmatrix} u_1 & v_1 \\ u_2 & v_2 \end{pmatrix}^{-1} \begin{pmatrix} q_1 \\ q_2 \end{pmatrix} = \frac{1}{-T} \begin{pmatrix} v_2 & -v_1 \\ -u_2 & u_1 \end{pmatrix} \begin{pmatrix} q_1 \\ q_2 \end{pmatrix} ,$$

namely

$$a_0 = \frac{q_1v_2 - q_2v_1}{-T} , \ b_0 = \frac{-q_1u_2 + q_2u_1}{-T} . \tag{5}$$

Now we introduce the following additional assumption, where Q is an integer parameter:

 – We have $q_1, q_2 \leq Q$ for any given N_1, N_2.

We emphasize that the parameter Q is used in the analysis of the algorithm only, and is not needed by our algorithm itself. By Lemma 2, we may focus on the case $\lambda_2 \leq ||q||$; otherwise, our algorithm stops at Step 2. Note that $||q|| = \sqrt{q_1^2 + q_2^2} \leq \sqrt{2} \cdot Q$, therefore $\lambda_2 \leq \sqrt{2} \cdot Q$. Now by (5), we have

$$|a_0| = \left| \frac{q_1v_2 - q_2v_1}{-T} \right| \leq \frac{|q_1v_2| + |q_2v_1|}{T} \leq \frac{Q}{T}(|v_1| + |v_2|) \leq \frac{Q}{T}\sqrt{2} \cdot ||v||$$

and similarly $|b_0| \leq (Q/T)\sqrt{2} \cdot ||u||$. Since $||v|| \leq ||u|| = \lambda_2$ by the choice of v and u, it follows that

$$|a_0|, |b_0| \leq \frac{Q}{T}\sqrt{2} \cdot \lambda_2 \leq \frac{2Q^2}{T} ,$$

therefore $|a_0| + |b_0| \leq 4Q^2/T$. Hence, the index A in Step 4 of our algorithm does not exceed $A_0 := \lfloor 4Q^2/T \rfloor$ during the execution. Since Step 4a of our algorithm is repeated at most $4A$ times for each choice of A, the total number of executions of Step 4a is at most $\sum_{A=2}^{A_0} 4A = 2A_0(A_0+1)-4$. Moreover, for each $1 \leq A \leq A_0$, Step 4a for each choice of (a, b) can be done in polynomial time with respect to $\log A_0$, $\log Q$ and $\log N_1$ (note that $|a|, |b| \leq A_0$ and $|v_1|, |u_1| \leq \lambda_2 \leq \sqrt{2} \cdot Q$).

Summarizing the argument, our algorithm runs in polynomial time with respect to the maximum among $\log T$, $\log N_1$, $\log N_2$, $\log(4Q^2/T)$, $\log Q$ and $4Q^2/T$. Here, the values $\log(4Q^2/T) (\leq 4Q^2/T)$ and $\log T (\leq \log N_1$, since $T < N_1, N_2)$ are redundant. Moreover, we have $\max\{4Q^2/T, \log N_1\} \geq \log Q$; indeed, if $4Q^2/T < \log Q$, then we have $4Q^2/N_1 < \log Q$ (since $T < N_1$), $N_1 > 4Q^2/\log Q > 4Q$, and $\log N_1 > \log Q$. Therefore, the value $\log Q$ above is also redundant. Hence, we have the following result:

Theorem 1. *In the setting of Sect. 3.1, suppose that $q_1, q_2 \leq Q$. Then our proposed algorithm in Sect. 3.2 always outputs a non-trivial factor of either N_1 or N_2, and its computational complexity is polynomially bounded with respect to $\max\{\log N_1, \log N_2, Q^2/T\}$.*

By Theorem 1, if κ is another parameter (e.g., when the factorization problem we are discussing is the base of security of some cryptographic scheme, κ can be chosen as the security parameter for the scheme) and all of $\log N_1$, $\log N_2$ and Q^2/T are of polynomial order with respect to κ, then our proposed algorithm runs in polynomial time with respect to κ. For example, we can set $\kappa = \max\{\log N_1, \log N_2, Q^2/T\}$. If $\max\{\log N_1, \log N_2, Q^2/T\} = Q^2/T$, then $\kappa = Q^2/T$. In this case, we have $\log_2 \kappa = 2\alpha - t$ where $\alpha = \log_2 Q$ and $t = \log_2 T$ (see Theorem 2 below).

A typical situation for Theorem 1 (studied also in the previous work [4,8]) is that, q_1 and q_2 are α-bit integers and the t least significant bits of p_1 and p_2 coincide with each other. In this case, Theorem 1 implies the following result:

Theorem 2. *Let κ be a parameter as mentioned above. Suppose that the bit lengths of N_1 and N_2 are polynomial in κ, and let $Q = 2^\alpha$ and $T = 2^t$. Then our proposed algorithm runs in polynomial time with respect to κ if*

$$t = 2\alpha - O(\log \kappa) \ .$$

More intuitively, if $t = 2\alpha - \lambda$, then the proposed algorithm runs in time $O(2^\lambda) \cdot$ poly$(\log N_1, \log N_2)$. This sufficient condition for t is significantly improved from the conditions $t \geq 2\alpha + 3$ in [8] and $t \geq 2\alpha + 1$ in [4]. In particular, this is the first result achieving that the difference $2\alpha - t$ can be beyond of constant order.

4   Computer Experiments

We performed a computer experiment to evaluate the running time of our proposed algorithm; see Figure 1. Here we set $Q = 2^\alpha$, $\alpha = 250$ (i.e., q_1 and q_2 are 250-bit primes), $T = 2^t$, and the bit length t of implicit hints is chosen as $t = 501, 500, \ldots, 475$. The other factors p_1 and p_2 have 750-bit lengths. We used an ordinary machine environment, namely our algorithm is written in C++ with NTL for large-integer arithmetic, on CentOS 6.5 with 2.4GHz CPU and 32GB RAM. For each t, we calculated the average running time of our algorithm for 100 experiments (N_1 and N_2 are correctly factorized at every experiment). Our experimental result shows that our algorithm can successfully factorize the integers efficiently, even for a significantly better parameter $t = 475$ than the best bound $t \geq 2\alpha + 1 = 501$ in the previous results (now the average running time is approximately 221 sec. $\approx$ 4 min.). We emphasize that, in the previous paper by Kurosawa and Ueda [4], their computer experiments showed that, for the same choice of $\alpha = 250$, their algorithm succeeded in only 40% of the experiments when $t = 500$, and it did not succeed at all when $t \leq 499$ (see Table 1 of [4]). This means that our algorithm is indeed an improvement of the previous results.

We also evaluated the sufficient number A of iterations for the main loop of our proposed algorithm by computer experiments. We used the same parameters and machine environment as above. For each t, we calculated the maximum, average, and minimum of the numbers of iterations for 100 experiments; see Figure 2 (the factorization succeeded at every experiment again). We note that the upper bound

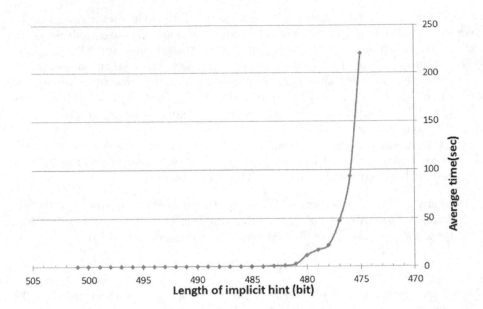

Fig. 1. Running time of our proposed algorithm (here the bit lengths of q_1 and q_2 are $\alpha = 250$ bits, $T = 2^t$, and the range of t is $\{501, 500, \dots, 475\}$)

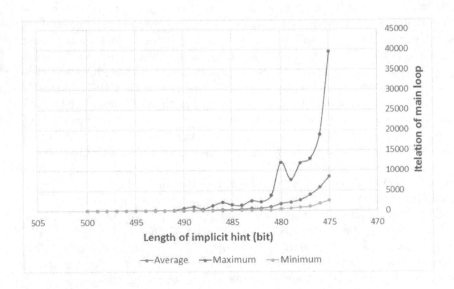

Fig. 2. Number A of iterations for the main loop (here the bit lengths of q_1 and q_2 are $\alpha = 250$ bits, $T = 2^t$, and the range of t is $\{500, 499, \dots, 475\}$)

of A given in our theoretical analysis in Sect. 3.3 is $\lfloor 4Q^2/T \rfloor = 2^{502-t}$; it is, for example, $2^{27} \approx 1.34 \times 10^8$ for $t = 475$. Our experimental result suggests that this theoretical bound of A would still be far from the precise value; further analyses to improve the bound of A are left as a future research topic.

5 Potential Applications

It is noteworthy that the implicitly correlated factors p_1, p_2 need not be primes in our proposed algorithm; see Sect. 3.1. This widens the potential applications of our method to security evaluations of existing schemes. In this section, we consider the cases of the Okamoto–Uchiyama cryptosystem [10] (Sect. 5.1) and Takagi's variant of the RSA cryptosystem [14] (Sect. 5.2).

5.1 Okamoto–Uchiyama Cryptosystem

In the Okamoto–Uchiyama cryptosystem [10], the public key involves a composite number of the form $n = (p')^2 \cdot q'$, where p' and q' are different large primes of the same bit length. Here p' and q' should be secret against the adversary; a necessary condition for the security of the scheme is the hardness of factorizing the integer n. Now we regard the integers $(p')^2$ and q' as p_i and q_i in our algorithm, respectively; we emphasize again that the factor p_i in our method is not necessarily a prime.

More precisely, given two public keys $n_1 = p_1'^2 \cdot q_1'$ and $n_2 = p_2'^2 \cdot q_2'$ of the Okamoto–Uchiyama cryptosystem, we consider the following situation: $p_1'^2 \equiv p_2'^2 \pmod{T}$ and $q_1', q_2' \leq Q$, where T and Q are parameters. To simplify the argument, we set $Q := 2^\alpha$ where α is the common bit length of p_i' and q_i'. Then our proposed algorithm factorizes at least one of n_1 and n_2 in polynomial time with respect to the security parameter κ, if Q^2/T is of polynomial order in κ, or equivalently, if $2\alpha - \log_2 T = O(\log \kappa)$.

From now, we discuss the frequency of the condition $p_1'^2 \equiv p_2'^2 \pmod{T}$ being satisfied, in the situation of the previous work [4,8] and our situation. First, in the situation of [4,8], T and Q should satisfy $\log_2 T \geq 2\alpha + 1$, therefore $T \geq 2p_1'^2$ and $T \geq 2p_2'^2$. Now the condition $p_1'^2 \equiv p_2'^2 \pmod{T}$ implies that $p_1'^2 = p_2'^2$ as integers, i.e., $p_1' = p_2'$, which is a trivial case. This means that the algorithms in [4,8] cannot be applied to the present case.

In contrast, in our method, the parameter $\log_2 T$ may be smaller than 2α, hence there *is* a (non-trivial) possibility of the case $p_1'^2 \equiv p_2'^2 \pmod{T}$. Going into detail, $p_1'^2 \equiv p_2'^2 \pmod{T}$ is equivalent to $p_1' - p_2' \equiv 0 \pmod{T_1}$ and $p_1' + p_2' \equiv 0 \pmod{T_2}$ for some factorization $T = T_1 T_2$ of T. Hence, to increase the possibility of the case $p_1'^2 \equiv p_2'^2 \pmod{T}$, it would be better to use the parameter T with many possibilities of appropriate factorizations $T = T_1 T_2$. Now if T_1 and T_2 have an odd common divisor $d > 1$, then $2p_1'$ and $2p_2'$, hence p_1' and p_2', are multiples of d. This is not desirable, since p_1' and p_2' are primes. By the observation, it seems better to use a smooth and square-free T; then the number of possible factorizations $T = T_1 T_2$ with *coprime* factors T_1, T_2 is increased. For example, we may let T be the product of all primes smaller than a certain threshold. For such parameters T, further evaluations of how frequently given two composite numbers n_1, n_2 satisfy the condition above are left as a future research topic.

5.2   Takagi's Variant of RSA

A similar argument is also applicable to Takagi's variant of the RSA cryptosystem [14]. In the scheme, the public key involves a composite number of the form $N = (p')^r \cdot q'$, where p' and q' are different large primes of the same bit length and $r \geq 2$. We regard the integers $(p')^r$ and q' as p_i and q_i in our algorithm, respectively. Since the case $r = 2$ is essentially the same as the case of the Okamoto–Uchiyama cryptosystem (Sect. 5.1), here we focus on the other case $r \geq 3$. In the case, the bit length of the factor $(p')^r$ becomes much larger than that of the other factor q', which would make the condition $p_1'^r \equiv p_2'^r \pmod{T}$ easier to satisfy under the requirement $\log_2 T = 2 \log_2 Q - O(\log \kappa)$ for our proposed algorithm. On the other hand, when $r \geq 3$, the analysis of the condition $p_1'^r \equiv p_2'^r \pmod{T}$ would be more difficult than the condition $p_1'^2 \equiv p_2'^2 \pmod{T}$ in the case of the Okamoto–Uchiyama cryptosystem. A detailed analysis of our method in relation to Takagi's RSA is left as a future reserach topic.

Acknowledgments. The authors thank the members of Shin-Akarui-Angou-Benkyo-Kai, especially Atsushi Takayasu, for several discussions on this work. The authors also thank the anonymous reviewers for their precious comments.

References

1. Cheon, J.H., Coron, J.-S., Kim, J., Lee, M.S., Lepoint, T., Tibouchi, M., Yun, A.: Batch fully homomorphic encryption over the integers. In: Johansson, T., Nguyen, P.Q. (eds.) EUROCRYPT 2013. LNCS, vol. 7881, pp. 315–335. Springer, Heidelberg (2013)
2. Coppersmith, D.: Finding a small root of a bivariate integer equation; factoring with high bits known. In: Maurer, U.M. (ed.) EUROCRYPT 1996. LNCS, vol. 1070, pp. 178–189. Springer, Heidelberg (1996)
3. Galbraith, S.D.: Mathematics of Public Key Cryptography. Cambridge University Press (2012)
4. Kurosawa, K., Ueda, T.: How to Factor N_1 and N_2 When $p_1 = p_2 \bmod 2^t$. In: Sakiyama, K., Terada, M. (eds.) IWSEC 2013. LNCS, vol. 8231, pp. 217–225. Springer, Heidelberg (2013)
5. Lenstra Jr, H.W.: Factoring Integers with Elliptic Curves. Ann. Math. **126**, 649–673 (1987)
6. Lenstra, A.K., Lenstra Jr, H.W.: The Development of the Number Field Sieve. Springer, Heidelberg (1993)
7. Lu, Y., Peng, L., Zhang, R., Lin, D.: Towards Optimal Bounds for Implicit Factorization Problem, IACR Cryptology ePrint Archive 2014/825 (2014)
8. May, A., Ritzenhofen, M.: Implicit factoring: on polynomial time factoring given only an implicit hint. In: Jarecki, S., Tsudik, G. (eds.) PKC 2009. LNCS, vol. 5443, pp. 1–14. Springer, Heidelberg (2009)

9. Nuida, K., Kurosawa, K.: (Batch) Fully Homomorphic Encryption over Integers for Non-Binary Message Spaces. In: EUROCRYPT 2015 (2015, to appear). IACR Cryptology ePrint Archive 2014/777 (2014)
10. Okamoto, T., Uchiyama, S.: A New Public-Key Cryptosystem as Secure as Factoring. In: Nyberg, K. (ed.) EUROCRYPT 1998. LNCS, vol. 1403, pp. 308–318. Springer, Heidelberg (1998)
11. Pomerance, C.: The quadratic sieve factoring algorithm. In: Beth, T., Cot, N., Ingemarsson, I. (eds.) EUROCRYPT 1984. LNCS, vol. 209, pp. 169–182. Springer, Heidelberg (1985)
12. Rivest, R.L., Shamir, A., Adleman, L.M.: A Method for Obtaining Digital Signatures and Public-Key Cryptosystems. Commun. ACM **21**(2), 120–126 (1978)
13. Sarkar, S., Maitra, S.: Approximate Integer Common Divisor Problem Relates to Implicit Factorization. IEEE Transactions on Information Theory **57**(6), 4002–4013 (2011)
14. Takagi, T.: Fast RSA-type Cryptosystem Modulo $p^k q$. In: Krawczyk, H. (ed.) CRYPTO 1998. LNCS, vol. 1462, p. 318. Springer, Heidelberg (1998)

Constructions of Hash Functions
and Message Authentication Codes

Hash Functions from Defective Ideal Ciphers

Jonathan Katz[1] , Stefan Lucks[2], and Aishwarya Thiruvengadam[1]([✉])

[1] Department of Computer Science, University of Maryland, College Park, USA
{jkatz,aish}@cs.umd.edu
[2] Bauhaus-Universität Weimar, Weimar, Germany
stefan.lucks@uni-weimar.de

Abstract. Cryptographic constructions are often designed and analyzed in idealized frameworks such as the random-oracle or ideal-cipher models. When the underlying primitives are instantiated in the real world, however, they may be far from ideal. Constructions should therefore be *robust* to known or potential defects in the lower-level primitives.

With this in mind, we study the construction of collision-resistant hash functions from "defective" ideal ciphers. We introduce a model for ideal ciphers that are vulnerable to differential *related-key attacks*, and explore the security of the classical PGV constructions from such weakened ciphers. We find that although *none* of the PGV compression functions are collision-resistant in our model, it is possible to prove collision resistance up to the birthday bound for iterated (Merkle-Damgård) versions of four of the PGV constructions. These four resulting hash functions are also optimally preimage-resistant.

Keywords: Ideal ciphers · Related key attacks · Hash functions

1 Introduction

Cryptographic constructions based on some lower-level primitive are often designed and analyzed by modeling the primitive as an ideal object, e.g., a random oracle [2], a random permutation [14], or an ideal cipher [30]. When the underlying primitive is instantiated, however, it may turn out to have "defects" and be far from ideal. An important goal is thus to design constructions that are *robust* to known or potential defects in the primitive(s) that will be used when the constructions are implemented in the real world.

We stress here that our concerns go beyond the well-known results showing that these idealized models cannot, in general, be instantiated [8,11]. Indeed, the known counterexamples are contrived, and it is reasonable to conjecture that "natural" constructions proven secure in these idealized models will remain secure when instantiated with "sufficiently good" real-world hash functions and

Research supported in part by NSF award #1223623.

K. Nyberg (ed.): CT-RSA 2015, LNCS 9048, pp. 273–290, 2015.
DOI: 10.1007/978-3-319-16715-2_15

block ciphers. The question we are concerned with is: what happens if the underlying primitive turns out not to be as good as originally thought?

For example, consider a construction analyzed in the ideal-cipher model which is instantiated with some real-world block cipher. Block ciphers are primarily designed and evaluated as (strong) pseudorandom permutations [15,25]; other properties (e.g., the presence of "weak keys"), though examined to some extent, receive comparatively less attention. We can ask:

> *How* **robust** *is the given construction when instantiated with a block cipher that may be a good pseudorandom permutation, but is blatantly "defective" as an ideal cipher?*

Variants of this question have been investigated previously; see our discussion of related work below.

Here, we focus on one aspect of the above question: we examine constructions of *collision-resistant hash functions* when instantiated with block ciphers that are vulnerable to *related-key attacks* [3,21]. (In a related-key attack, roughly speaking, there is some predictable relationship between the behavior of the cipher when using keys that are related in some particular way. A formal definition is given later.) We choose this aspect for its practical relevance:

- Many prominent hash functions—including SHA-2 as well as some of the SHA-3 finalists—are based on an underlying (tweakable) block cipher, and it is important to analyze and understand the security of these constructions. Moreover, from a theoretical perspective it is known that treating the block cipher as a pseudorandom permutation is insufficient for proving collision resistance [31]. Beginning with the work of Black, Rogaway, and Shrimpton [9,10], researchers have analyzed hash-function designs in the ideal-cipher model.
- Related-key attacks have been demonstrated against several real-world block ciphers [4,5,12,13,19,20,28], including DES (cf. the well-known complementation property), GOST, TEA, KASUMI, and AES-192/256 [6,7]. Related-key attacks on an underlying cipher have also been used specifically to attack other primitives such as hash functions [5,12] (most famously in a collision attack on the hash function used in the Microsoft XBox system) as well as message authentication codes (e.g., an attack on RMAC [22]).

1.1   Our Results

In this work, we focus on differential related-key attacks in which the keys as well as the plaintexts are chosen with specific differences. The first such attack we are aware of is due to Kelsey, Schneier, and Wagner [19]. Several other works [4–7,12,13,20,28] have made use of differential related-key attacks.

Let E denote a block cipher. We consider linear related-key attacks in which there are fixed constants $\triangle k, \triangle x, \triangle y$ (with $\triangle k$ nonzero[1]) such that $E(k, x) =$

---

[1] We exclude the case where $\triangle k$ is zero because an ideal cipher with a predictable relation in that case would not even be a pseudorandom function.

$E(k \oplus \triangle k, x \oplus \triangle x) \oplus \triangle y$ for all k, x, y. We remark that this would represent a serious defect on any practical cipher, and in many known related-key attacks the above hold only with some probability $\ll 1$ over random choice of k, x, y; this only makes our positive results stronger. On the other hand, the reader can verify that our attacks do not use the fact that the above relationship holds with probability 1.

We begin by introducing an appropriate model in which to undertake our study. In the usual ideal-cipher model, the adversary is given access to an oracle $E : \{0,1\}^\kappa \times \{0,1\}^n \to \{0,1\}^n$ (as well as its inverse E^{-1}), where for each key $k \in \{0,1\}^\kappa$ the function $E(k, \cdot)$ is chosen uniformly from the space of n-bit permutations.[2] Fixing some $\triangle k, \triangle x, \triangle y$ with $\triangle k \neq 0^\kappa$, we model related-key attacks of the form above by instead choosing, for each (unordered) pair $\{k, k \oplus \triangle k\}$, the function $E(k, \cdot)$ uniformly from the space of n-bit permutations and then setting $E(k \oplus \triangle k, x \oplus \triangle x) = E(k, x) \oplus \triangle y$. When we say that a given construction is secure in our model, we mean that it is secure for *every* choice of $\triangle k, \triangle x, \triangle y$; a secure construction is thus expected to be "robust" to block ciphers vulnerable to *any* (linear) related-key attack, regardless of the exact form the attack takes. We suggest this "defective" ideal-cipher model as a general way to better understand the real-world security of constructions analyzed in the (traditional) ideal-cipher model.

We then undertake an analysis in our model of the classical PGV constructions [29] of compression functions from block ciphers. Although these have been the subject of extensive analysis [9,10,32], there has been no previous comprehensive study of their security when instantiated with block ciphers subject to related-key attacks. We find that *none* of the PGV compression functions are collision-resistant in our model; in fact, they do not even offer second-preimage resistance. This stands in contrast to the fact that some of the PGV compression functions are collision-resistant in the (traditional) ideal-cipher model [9,10,32]. On the positive side, we show that it *is* possible to prove collision resistance up to the birthday bound in our model for the *iterated* hash functions obtained by applying the Merkle-Damgård transform to four of the PGV compression functions. (One of these is the Matyas-Meyer-Oseas construction.) These four compression functions share the property that the key to the block cipher depends only on the chaining variable from the previous block, and not on the message being hashed.

We also study preimage resistance of the PGV constructions. Most notable is that the four collision-resistant hash functions we identify, above, can also be proven to be preimage-resistant in our model up to the optimal $\mathcal{O}(q/2^n)$ bound.

Interpreting our Results. Our results do not say anything about the security of the PGV constructions when instantiated with any concrete block cipher, any more than prior results do. Nevertheless, all else being equal, our results suggest using a hash-function construction that is robust to related-key weaknesses in

---

[2] For ease of presentation, we set $\kappa = n$ in our definitions. Our results do not require that the block length and key length be equal unless required by definition of the underlying compression function.

the underlying cipher. Viewed differently, if one uses a hash function secure in our model and then subsequently a related-key attack on the underlying cipher is found, one can make plans to gradually phase out the hash function (based on the expectation that the block cipher might have other, yet-undiscovered weaknesses) without being concerned about an immediate collision attack.

1.2   Related Work

Several previous works have studied the implications of "weakened" ideal models for constructions proven secure in those models [18,23,24,27]. Besides the fact that these works deal with random oracles (and not ideal ciphers), the modeling is also qualitatively different from what we consider here. Specifically, in [18,24, 27], a random oracle is chosen from the correct (uniform) distribution, but the attacker is provided with an extra oracle enabling, e.g., inversion. In contrast, here we model a class of attacks by modifying the distribution from which the ideal object is chosen.

Baecher et al. [1] recently studied *reducibility* between constructions of compression functions from ideal ciphers. As part of this work, they discuss the security of constructions with respect to general (i.e., possibly non-uniform) distributions over ciphers. (Our positive results deal with iterated hash functions, not compression functions, and do not follow from their results.) The distributions they consider are not intended to represent any real-world structural defects in block ciphers, but are instead contrived distributions used to prove separation results. The only other work of which we are aware that studies a weakened ideal-cipher model is by Hirose and Kuwakado [17], who analyze hash-function constructions in a model where the attacker is given a "key-recovery oracle" that, for a given input/output pair x, y, returns a key k (if any) for which $E(k, x) = y$.

Black [8] shows a hash function secure in the ideal-cipher model that is insecure for any real-world instantiation of the cipher. As in other impossibility results, the construction is contrived. Our focus is on positive results, subject to the usual caveats about using idealized models. Hirose [16] shows that for every PGV construction proven to be secure in the ideal cipher model there exists a secure pseudorandom permutation that renders the construction insecure.

Lucks [26] studies the problem of constructing a hash function from a weak compression function. His goal was to achieve properties beyond collision resistance (e.g., k-collision-resistance or second-preimage resistance) even if collisions can be found in the underlying compression function. Zhang et al. [33] study the construction of rate-1 MACs from block ciphers under a weaker security notion than pseudorandomness since the weaker notion is sufficient for secure MACs.

2   Definitions

2.1   Weakened Ideal Ciphers

An *ideal cipher* is an oracle $E : \{0,1\}^n \times \{0,1\}^n \to \{0,1\}^n$ where, for each $k \in \{0,1\}^n$, the function $E_k(\cdot) \stackrel{\text{def}}{=} E(k, \cdot)$ is chosen uniformly from the set of permutations on $\{0,1\}^n$. We let E^{-1} denote the inverse of E; i.e., $E_k^{-1}(y)$ is the unique x such that $E_k(x) = y$.

We now define a cipher that is ideal except for the fact that it has a related-key weakness. By this we mean that the cipher returns related outputs on related keys/inputs. Specifically, there is a shift $\triangle k \neq 0^n$ and shifts $\triangle x, \triangle y \in \{0,1\}^n$ such that $E_k(x) = E_{k \oplus \triangle k}(x \oplus \triangle x) \oplus \triangle y$.[3]

Definition 1 (Ideal cipher vulnerable to related-key attacks). *Let* $\triangle k \in \{0,1\}^n \setminus \{0^n\}$ *and* $\triangle x, \triangle y \in \{0,1\}^n$. *Let* $\mathcal{K} \subset \{0,1\}^n$ *be such that* $(\mathcal{K}, \mathcal{K} \oplus \triangle k)$ *is a partition of* $\{0,1\}^n$. *A* $(\triangle k, \triangle x, \triangle y)$-*ideal* cipher *is an oracle* $E : \{0,1\}^n \times \{0,1\}^n \to \{0,1\}^n$ *where, for each* $k \in \mathcal{K}$, *the function* $E_k(\cdot) = E(k, \cdot)$ *is chosen uniformly from the set of permutations on* $\{0,1\}^n$, *and for* $k \notin \mathcal{K}$ *we define* $E_k(x) \stackrel{\text{def}}{=} E_{k \oplus \triangle k}(x \oplus \triangle x) \oplus \triangle y$.

We let $B(\triangle k, \triangle x, \triangle y)$ denote the set of all functions as in the definition above (i.e., E_k is a permutation for all k, and $E_k(x) = E_{k \oplus \triangle k}(x \oplus \triangle x) \oplus \triangle y$ for all k, x, y). Then $E \stackrel{\$}{\leftarrow} B(\triangle k, \triangle x, \triangle y)$ denotes uniform choice of E from this space.

2.2 Hash Functions and Their Security

A (block-cipher-based) *hash function* is an oracle machine $H : D \to \{0,1\}^c$, where $D \subseteq \{0,1\}^*$. This machine expects to have oracle access to a function $E : \{0,1\}^n \times \{0,1\}^n \to \{0,1\}^n$. In this notation, a *compression function* f is a hash function whose domain D is equal to $\{0,1\}^c \times \{0,1\}^b$, with $b \geq 1$. Fix $h_0 \in \{0,1\}^c$. The *iterated hash* of compression function f is the hash function $H : (\{0,1\}^b)^* \to \{0,1\}^c$ defined by $H^E(\epsilon) \stackrel{\text{def}}{=} h_0$ and $H^E(m_1, \ldots, m_\ell) \stackrel{\text{def}}{=} h_\ell$ with $h_i = f^E(h_{i-1}, m_i)$.

To quantify the collision resistance of a block-cipher-based hash function H in our model, we instantiate the block cipher by a uniform $E \in B(\triangle k, \triangle x, \triangle y)$. An adversary A is given oracles for $E(\cdot, \cdot)$ and $E^{-1}(\cdot, \cdot)$ and aims to find a *collision* for H^E, i.e., messages $M \neq M'$ such $H^E(M) = H^E(M')$.

Definition 2. *Let* H *be a block-cipher-based hash function, and let* A *be an adversary. The advantage of* A *in finding collisions in* H *is*

$$\mathbf{Adv}_{H, \triangle k, \triangle x, \triangle y}^{coll}(A) = \Pr[E \stackrel{\$}{\leftarrow} B(\triangle k, \triangle x, \triangle y); (M, M') \stackrel{\$}{\leftarrow} A^{E, E^{-1}} :$$
$$M \neq M' \wedge H^E(M) = H^E(M')]$$

For $q \geq 1$, we write $\mathbf{Adv}_{H, \triangle k, \triangle x, \triangle y}^{coll}(q) = \max_A \{\mathbf{Adv}_{H, \triangle k, \triangle x, \triangle y}^{coll}(A)\}$ where the maximum is taken over all adversaries that ask at most q queries to the E and E^{-1} oracles.

---

[3] Note that Definition 1 allows only for a single differential. We can easily extend the definition to allow for multiple differentials $\triangle k_1 \neq \triangle k_2 \neq \cdots \neq \triangle k_t \neq 0^n$. Our results hold even for the case of multiple differentials as long as the number of differentials t is a constant.

Definition 3. *The advantage of finding collisions in H, a block-cipher-based hash function, is defined as* $\mathbf{Adv}_H^{coll}(q) = \max_{\triangle k \neq 0^n, \triangle x, \triangle y}\{\mathbf{Adv}_{H,\triangle k,\triangle x,\triangle y}^{coll}(q)\}$ *where the maximum is taken over all* $\triangle k \in \{0,1\}^n \setminus \{0^n\}$ *and* $\triangle x, \triangle y \in \{0,1\}^n$.

We also define the advantage of an adversary in finding collisions in a compression function $f : \{0,1\}^c \times \{0,1\}^b \to \{0,1\}^c$. Here, (h,m) and (h',m') collide under f if they are distinct and $f^E(h,m) = f^E(h',m')$. We also consider finding (h,m) such that $f^E(h,m) = h_0$, for a fixed $h_0 \in \{0,1\}^c$, to be a collision.

Definition 4 (Collision resistance of a compression function when instantiated with a $(\triangle k, \triangle x, \triangle y)$-ideal cipher). *Let f be a block cipher based compression function, $f : \{0,1\}^c \times \{0,1\}^b \to \{0,1\}^c$. Fix a constant $h_0 \in \{0,1\}^c$ and an adversary A. The advantage of A in finding collisions in f is*

$$\mathbf{Adv}_{f,\triangle k,\triangle x,\triangle y}^{coll}(A) = \Pr[E \xleftarrow{\$} B(\triangle k, \triangle x, \triangle y); ((h,m),(h',m')) \xleftarrow{\$} A^{E,E^{-1}} :$$
$$((h,m) \neq (h',m') \wedge f^E(h,m) = f^E(h',m')) \vee f^E(h,m) = h_0]$$

For $q \geq 1$, we write $\mathbf{Adv}_{f,\triangle k,\triangle x,\triangle y}^{coll}(q) = \max_A\{\mathbf{Adv}_{f,\triangle k,\triangle x,\triangle y}^{coll}(A)\}$ *where the maximum is taken over all adversaries that ask at most q queries to the E and E^{-1} oracles.*

Definition 5 (Collision resistance of a compression function instantiated with a weakened ideal cipher). *Let f be a block-cipher based compression function. Then, the advantage of finding collisions in f is defined as* $\mathbf{Adv}_f^{coll}(q) = \max_{\triangle k \neq 0^n, \triangle x, \triangle y}\{\mathbf{Adv}_{f,\triangle k,\triangle x,\triangle y}^{coll}(q)\}$ *where the maximum is taken over all values of $\triangle k \in \{0,1\}^n \setminus \{0^n\}$ and $\triangle x, \triangle y \in \{0,1\}^n$.*

We consider the inversion resistance of the hash function constructions as well. We follow the definition of inversion resistance as in [9] where inversion resistance is defined in terms of inverting a random range point.

Definition 6 (Inversion Resistance of a hash function when instantiated with a $(\triangle k, \triangle x, \triangle y)$-ideal cipher). *Let H be a block cipher based hash function and let A be an adversary. Then the advantage of A in inverting H is the real number*

$$\mathbf{Adv}_{H,\triangle k,\triangle x,\triangle y}^{inv}(A) = \Pr[E \xleftarrow{\$} B(\triangle k, \triangle x, \triangle y); \sigma \xleftarrow{\$} R; M \leftarrow A^{E,E^{-1}}(\sigma) :$$
$$H^E(M) = \sigma]$$

For $q \geq 1$, we write $\mathbf{Adv}_{H,\triangle k,\triangle x,\triangle y}^{inv}(q) = \max_A\{\mathbf{Adv}_{H,\triangle k,\triangle x,\triangle y}^{inv}(A)\}$ *where the maximum is taken over all adversaries that ask at most q queries to the E and E^{-1} oracles.*

Definition 7 (Inversion resistance of a hash function instantiated with a weakened ideal cipher). *The advantage of inverting H, a block-cipher-based hash function, is defined as* $\mathbf{Adv}_H^{inv}(q) = \max_{\triangle k \neq 0^n, \triangle x, \triangle y}\{\mathbf{Adv}_{H,\triangle k,\triangle x,\triangle y}^{inv}(q)\}$ *where the maximum is taken over all values of $\triangle k \in \{0,1\}^n \setminus \{0^n\}$ and $\triangle x, \triangle y \in \{0,1\}^n$.*

2.3   The PGV Constructions

The 12 group-1 and 8 group-2 schemes in [9] are given in Figure 1. This defines
$f_i[n] : \{0,1\}^n \times \{0,1\}^n \rightarrow \{0,1\}^n$ for $i \in [1\dots20]$. The iterated hash of these
compression functions give hash functions $H_i[n]$. We omit writing $[n]$ while referring to the compression and the hash functions.

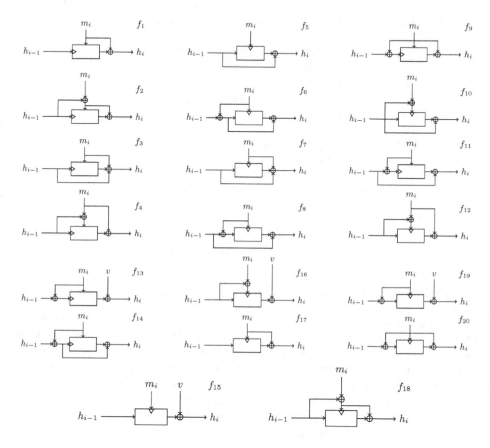

Fig. 1. Compression functions $f_1, \dots, f_{20}$ for the hash functions $H_1, \dots, H_{20}$. The hatch
marks the location of the key.

3   Collision Resistance of the PGV Compression Functions

We show that *none* of the 64 PGV compression functions are collision resistant
when the underlying block cipher is instantiated with a weakened ideal cipher.
This is in contrast to the 12 group-1 compression functions $f_1, \dots, f_{12}$ being
collision-resistant in the ideal-cipher model [9].[4]

---

[4] The remaining compression functions have collisions even in the ideal-cipher model.

Consider an example where E is a weakened ideal cipher as in Definition 1 with $\triangle x = \triangle y = 0^n$ and an arbitrary $\triangle k \neq 0^n$, implying $E_{k \oplus \triangle k}(x) = E_k(x)$. For the Davies-Meyer compression function $f_5(h, m) = E_m(h) \oplus h$, this gives a collision immediately since $f_5(h, m) = f_5(h, m \oplus \triangle k)$ and $\triangle k \neq 0^n$. Similarly, we can find collisions in all the 12 group-1 compression functions for any value of $\triangle k \neq 0^n$ and $\triangle x$, by setting $\triangle y$ as shown in Table 1.

Table 1. Collisions in compression functions $f_1, \ldots, f_{12}$ for any $\triangle k \neq 0^n, \triangle x \in \{0, 1\}^n$

Compression function	$\triangle y$
f_1	$\triangle x$
f_2	$\triangle x$
f_3	$\triangle k \oplus \triangle x$
f_4	$\triangle k \oplus \triangle x$
f_5	$\triangle x$
f_6	$\triangle x$
f_7	$\triangle k \oplus \triangle x$
f_8	$\triangle k \oplus \triangle x$
f_9	$\triangle x$
f_{10}	$\triangle x$
f_{11}	$\triangle k \oplus \triangle x$
f_{12}	$\triangle k \oplus \triangle x$

4   Collision Resistance of the PGV Hash Functions

The group-1 $(H_1, \ldots, H_{12})$ and group-2 $(H_{13}, \ldots, H_{20})$ schemes are collision-resistant in the ideal-cipher model [9]. Somewhat surprisingly, we show that *only hash functions H_1, H_2, H_3 and H_4 are collision-resistant*, in the general case, when instantiated with weakened ideal ciphers as in Definition 1. These four hash functions happen to be those whose key does not depend on the message.

When a construction is such that the key depends on the message, a related-key attack allows us to get a predictable output for some (non-zero) key-shift. Thus we can modify the message (which is part of the key) to produce a collision in the weakened ideal-cipher model. In this section, we prove the collision resistance of $H_1, \ldots, H_4$ and show collisions in the hash functions $H_5, \ldots, H_{20}$.

4.1   Collisions in Hash Functions $H_5, \ldots, H_{20}$

We can find collisions in the hash functions $H_5, \ldots, H_{20}$ when instantiated with a weakened ideal cipher as illustrated in Table 2. The collisions in the hash functions $H_5, \ldots, H_{12}$ are special cases of the collisions found in the corresponding compression functions. In Section 3, we showed that when E is a weakened ideal cipher with $\triangle x = \triangle y = 0^n$ implying $E_{k \oplus \triangle k}(x) = E_k(x)$, we get a collision in the Davies-Meyer compression function $f_5(h, m) = E_m(h) \oplus h$. This leads to a collision in the Davies-Meyer hash function H_5 as well. This is because $H_5{}^E(m_1, \ldots, m_\ell) = H_5{}^E(m_1, \ldots, m_\ell \oplus \triangle k)$ when $E_{k \oplus \triangle k}(x) = E_k(x)$.

Table 2. Collisions in hash functions $H_5, \ldots, H_{20}$

Hash function	$\triangle x$	$\triangle y$
H_5	0^n	0^n
H_6	$\triangle k$	$\triangle k$
H_7	0^n	$\triangle k$
H_8	$\triangle k$	0^n
H_9	$\triangle k$	$\triangle k$
H_{10}	0^n	0^n
H_{11}	$\triangle k$	0^n
H_{12}	0^n	$\triangle k$
H_{13}	$\triangle k$	0^n
H_{14}	$\triangle k$	$\triangle k$
H_{15}	0^n	0^n
H_{16}	0^n	0^n
H_{17}	0^n	$\triangle k$
H_{18}	0^n	$\triangle k$
H_{19}	$\triangle k$	0^n
H_{20}	$\triangle k$	$\triangle k$

4.2   Collision Resistance of Hash Functions H_1, H_2, H_3, and H_4

We prove that the hash functions H_1, H_2, H_3, H_4 (whose key is independent of the message) are collision-resistant. As shown in Table 1, we can easily find collisions in their corresponding compression functions $f_1, \ldots, f_4$. Hence, we can no longer analyze the collision resistance of the hash functions $H_1, \ldots, H_4$ in the Merkle-Dåmgard paradigm. However, the proof technique illustrated in [9] (to prove collision resistance for hash functions whose compression functions are not collision-resistant) can be used here.

Theorem 1 (Collision resistance of hash functions H_1, H_2, H_3, H_4 when instantiated with a weakened ideal cipher). *Fix $n \geq 1$ and $i \in [1 \ldots 4]$. Then $\mathbf{Adv}^{coll}_{H_i[n]}(q) \leq 14q(q+1)/2^n$ for all $q \geq 1$.*

Proof. Fix constant $h_0 \in \{0,1\}^n$. We prove the theorem for H_1 (Matyas-Meyer-Oseas construction).The Matyas-Meyer-Oseas (MMO) construction is $f_1(h,m) = E_h(m) \oplus m$ where E is a block cipher. Let E be a $(\triangle k, \triangle x, \triangle y)$-ideal cipher. The definition of collision resistance considered here is the one in Definition 3. Define a directed graph $G = (V_G, E_G)$ with vertex set $V_G = \{0,1\}^n \times \{0,1\}^n \times \{0,1\}^n$ and an arc $(x,k,y) \to (x',k',y')$ in E_G if and only if $k' = y \oplus x$.[5]

Let $A^{E,E^{-1}}$ be an adversary attacking MMO. We analyze the behaviour of A when its left oracle is instantiated by $E : \{0,1\}^n \times \{0,1\}^n \to \{0,1\}^n$. Since E is a $(\triangle k, \triangle x, \triangle y)$-ideal cipher, E is chosen as follows. Let $\mathcal{K} \subset \{0,1\}^n$ be

---

[5]   The condition for an edge between two vertices depends on the compression function (i.e.) f_1 in this case.

Algorithm 1. SimulateOracles(A, n)

- Initially, $i \leftarrow 0$ and $E_k(x) = $ undefined for all $(k, x) \in \{0,1\}^n \times \{0,1\}^n$
- Run $A^{E, E^{-1}}$, answering oracle queries as follows:
  - When A asks a query (k, x) to its left oracle:
    1. $i \leftarrow i + 1$;
    2. $k_i \leftarrow k$; $x_i \leftarrow x$; $y_i \overset{\$}{\leftarrow} \overline{\text{Range}}(E_k)$; $E_k(x) \leftarrow y_i$;
    3. $\hat{k}_i \leftarrow k \oplus \triangle k$; $\hat{x}_i \leftarrow x \oplus \triangle x$; $\hat{y}_i \leftarrow y_{i-1} \oplus \triangle y$; $E_{k \oplus \triangle k}(x \oplus \triangle x) \leftarrow \hat{y}_i$;
    4. return $(x_i, k_i, y_i), (\hat{x}_i, \hat{k}_i, \hat{y}_i)$ to A;
  - When A asks a query (k, y) to its right oracle:
    1. $i \leftarrow i + 1$;
    2. $k_i \leftarrow k$; $y_i \leftarrow y$; $x_i \overset{\$}{\leftarrow} \overline{\text{Domain}}(E_k)$; $E_k(x_i) \leftarrow y$;
    3. $\hat{k}_i \leftarrow k \oplus \triangle k$; $\hat{y}_i \leftarrow y \oplus \triangle y$; $\hat{x}_i \leftarrow x_{i-1} \oplus \triangle x$; $E_{k \oplus \triangle k}(\hat{x}_i) \leftarrow y \oplus \triangle y$;
    4. return $(x_i, k_i, y_i), (\hat{x}_i, \hat{k}_i, \hat{y}_i)$ to A;

where $\text{Domain}(E_k)$ is the set of points x where $E_k(x)$ is no longer undefined and $\overline{\text{Domain}}(E_k) = \{0,1\}^n - \text{Domain}(E_k)$. $\text{Range}(E_k)$ is the set of points y where $y = E_k(x)$ is no longer undefined and $\overline{\text{Range}}(E_k) = \{0,1\}^n - \text{Range}(E_k)$.

---

such that $(\mathcal{K}, \mathcal{K} \oplus \triangle k)$ is a partition of $\{0,1\}^n$. For each key $k \in \mathcal{K}$, choose a random permutation $E_k(\cdot) : \{0,1\}^n \to \{0,1\}^n$ and for each key $k \notin \mathcal{K}$, $E_k(x) \overset{\text{def}}{=} E_{k \oplus \triangle k}(x \oplus \triangle x) \oplus \triangle y$ for fixed $\triangle k \neq 0^n$, $\triangle x$ and $\triangle y$ where $k \oplus \triangle k \in \mathcal{K}$. A's right oracle is instantiated by E^{-1}, the inverse of E. Assume that A asks at most q total queries.

Run the algorithm SimulateOracles(A, n) described in Algorithm 1. As A executes with its (simulated) oracle, colour the vertices of G as follows.[6] Initially, each vertex of G is *uncoloured*. When A asks an E-query (k, x) (or when A asks an E^{-1} query of (k, y)) and this returns (x, k, y) and $(\hat{x}, \hat{k}, \hat{y})$, then, for each vertex that was returned:

- if $k = h_0$ (if $\hat{k} = h_0$), then vertex (x, k, y) (vertex $(\hat{x}, \hat{k}, \hat{y})$) gets coloured *red*;
- otherwise, vertex (x, k, y) (vertex $(\hat{x}, \hat{k}, \hat{y})$) gets coloured *black*.

Without loss of generality, we assume that the adversary does not ask any oracle query to which the response is already known. Accordingly, every query the adversary asks results in exactly two vertices getting coloured, those two formerly being uncoloured.

A vertex of G is *coloured* when it gets coloured red or black. A path P in G is coloured if all of its vertices are coloured. Vertices (x, k, y) and (x', k', y') are said to *collide* if $y' \oplus x' = y \oplus x$.[7] Distinct paths P and P' are said to collide if all of their vertices are coloured and they begin with red vertices and end with

---

[6]   Note that the vertices and edges of G are fixed. As A's execution proceeds, the vertices of G get coloured depending on A's queries and the results returned.

[7]   The condition for collision between two vertices depends on the compression function (i.e.) f_1 in this case.

colliding vertices. Let C be the event that, as a result of the adversary's queries, two colliding paths are formed in G.

Claim. $\mathbf{Adv}_{H_1[n]}^{\text{coll}}(q) \leq \Pr[C]$.

Claim. $\Pr[C] \leq 14q(q+1)/2^n$.

Proof (Proof Sketch). Let C_i be the event that C occurs by the i-th query. Let C_0 be the null event. Then $\Pr[C] = \sum_{i=1}^{q} \Pr[C_i \mid \overline{C_{i-1}} \wedge \ldots \wedge \overline{C_0}]$. Given $\overline{C_{i-1}} \wedge \ldots \wedge \overline{C_0}$, the event C_i occurs in one of the following ways. In the i-th query, a) a mid vertex (on a path) could get coloured, or b) the start (red) vertex could get coloured, or c) an end vertex (one of the colliding vertices) could get coloured, or d) a start vertex that collides with h_0 could get coloured. Since there are two vertices returned when E is instantiated with a $(\triangle k, \triangle x, \triangle y)$-ideal cipher, any two events listed above can happen in the i-th query leading to C, forming of two colliding paths. The analysis can be found in Appendix A.

Combining the two claims, we show that the MMO construction when instantiated with a weakened ideal cipher is collision resistant. The proofs for H_2, H_3 and H_4 can be obtained by adapting the proof above.

4.3   Additional Results on the Collision Resistance of the PGV Hash Functions

The definition of $(\triangle k, \triangle x, \triangle y)$-ideal cipher in Definition 1 places only one requirement on the values of $\triangle k, \triangle x, \triangle y$, namely, that $\triangle k \neq 0^n$. This requirement is based on the assumption that block ciphers should at least be pseudorandom functions. However, if we allow $\triangle k = 0^n$, we can easily find collisions in H_1, H_2, H_3 and H_4 (that were collision-resistant when $\triangle k \neq 0^n$ by Theorem 1).

In Table 2 of Section 4.1, we show collisions in the hash functions $H_5, \ldots, H_{20}$ when instantiated with a weakened ideal cipher. We claim that the collisions given in Table 2 are the *only* collisions possible in hash functions $H_5, \ldots, H_{20}$.

Theorem 2 (Collision resistance of hash functions $H_5, \ldots, H_{20}$ when instantiated with a weakened ideal cipher). *Fix $n \geq 1$ and $i \in [5 \ldots 20]$. Then we have that $\tilde{\mathbf{Adv}}_{H_i}^{\text{coll}}(q) \leq 14q(q+1)/2^n$ for all $q \geq 1$ where $\tilde{\mathbf{Adv}}_{H_i}^{\text{coll}}(q) = max\{\mathbf{Adv}_{H,\triangle k,\triangle x,\triangle y}^{\text{coll}}(q)\}$ where the maximum is taken over all values of $\triangle k \in \{0,1\}^n \setminus \{0^n\}, \triangle x \in \{0,1\}^n, \triangle y \in \{0,1\}^n$, excluding those $(\triangle k, \triangle x, \triangle y)$ triples given by Row $i - 4$ in Table 2.*

The proof follows along the same lines as the proof in Theorem 1 and is omitted here due to space constraints.

5   Inversion Resistance of the PGV Constructions

Black, Rogaway, and Shrimpton [9] proved that the group-1 and group-2 hash functions are inversion-resistant with better bounds for the group-1 schemes.

We analyze the inversion resistance of the PGV constructions when the underlying block cipher is instantiated with a weakened ideal cipher. Compression functions $f_1, \ldots, f_{12}$ are inversion-resistant in our setting as well. Consequently, their hash functions $H_1, \ldots, H_{12}$ can be proved to be inversion-resistant using the Merkle-Damgård paradigm.

Theorem 3 (Inversion resistance of hash functions $H_1, \ldots, H_{12}$). *Fix $n \geq 1$ and $i \in [1 \ldots 12]$. Then $\mathbf{Adv}_{H_i[n]}^{inv}(q) \leq q/(3 \cdot 2^{n-3})$ for any $q \geq 1$.*

Proof. We prove that the compression functions $f_1, \ldots, f_{12}$ are inversion-resistant and use Merkle-Damgård to prove inversion resistance of the hash functions.

Lemma 1. *Inversion resistance of compression functions $f_1, \ldots, f_{12}$] Fix $n \geq 1$ and $i \in [1 \ldots 12]$. Then $\mathbf{Adv}_{f_i[n]}^{inv}(q) \leq q/(3 \cdot 2^{n-3})$ for any $q \geq 1$.*

Proof. Consider f_1. Fix $h_0 \in \{0, 1\}^n$. The adversary A has access to oracles E, E^{-1} where E is a $(\triangle k, \triangle x, \triangle y)$-ideal cipher and E^{-1} is its inverse. The adversary A is given a range point σ that it tries to invert. Without loss of generality, assume that when A outputs a message M, A has already made the necessary E or E^{-1} queries to compute $H^E(M)$ and that A asks q queries in total to its oracles.

Run SimulateOracles(A, n) as described in Algorithm 1 to get (x_j, k_j, y_j) and $(\hat{x}_j, \hat{k}_j, \hat{y}_j)$ for $j = 1, \ldots, q$. Let I_j be the event that the adversary finds an inversion in the j-th query. Let (x_j, k_j, y_j) and $(\hat{x}_j, \hat{k}_j, \hat{y}_j)$ be the two tuples returned in the j-th query. Either $x_j \oplus y_j = \sigma$ or $\hat{x}_j \oplus \hat{y}_j = \sigma$. If the adversary queried for the tuple (x_j, k_j, y_j), either x_j or y_j was assigned at random from a set of size at least $2^n - (j - 1)$. So, $\Pr[I_j] \leq \frac{2}{2^n - (j-1)}$. Therefore, $\Pr[(h, m) \leftarrow A^{E, E^{-1}}(\sigma) : E(h, m) \oplus m = \sigma] = \Pr[I_1 \vee \ldots \vee I_q] \leq \sum_{j=1}^q \Pr[I_j] \leq \frac{q}{3 \cdot 2^{n-3}}$. Similarly, we can prove this lemma for $f_2, \ldots, f_{12}$ as well.

Lemma 2 (Merkle Damgård for inversion resistance). *Let $f : \{0, 1\}^n \times \{0, 1\}^n \to \{0, 1\}^n$ be a compression function and H, the iterated hash of f. Then, $\mathbf{Adv}_H^{inv}(q) \leq \mathbf{Adv}_f^{inv}(q)$ for all $q \geq 1$.*

Combining Lemmas 1 and 2, we have $\mathbf{Adv}_{H_i[n]}^{inv}(q) \leq q/3 \cdot 2^{n-3}$ for $i \in [1 \ldots 12]$.

To prove the inversion resistance of hash functions $H_{13}, \ldots, H_{20}$, we cannot use Merkle-Damgård because their underlying compression functions are not inversion-resistant. Hence, we use a proof technique similar to that of Theorem 1. However, here, we use it to prove inversion resistance.[8]

---

[8] In order to prove the inversion resistance of the group-2 schemes $H_{13}, \ldots, H_{20}$, Black, Rogaway and Shrimpton use the fact that collision resistance implies inversion resistance. This does not apply here as the group-2 hash functions are no longer collision-resistant as shown in Table 2.

Theorem 4 (Inversion resistance of hash functions $H_{13}, \ldots, H_{20}$). *Fix $n \geq 1$ and $i \in [13 \ldots 20]$. Then $\mathbf{Adv}^{inv}_{H_i[n]}(q) \leq (4q^2 + 16q)/2^{n-1}$ for any $q \geq 1$.*

Proof. Fix constants $h_0, v \in \{0,1\}^n$. We prove the theorem for the case of H_{13} where $f_{13}(h, m) = E_{h \oplus m}(m) \oplus v$. Here, we consider the case when E is a $(\triangle k, \triangle x, \triangle y)$-ideal cipher as in Definition 1. We define a directed graph $G = (V_G, E_G)$ with vertex set $V_G = \{0,1\}^n \times \{0,1\}^n \times \{0,1\}^n$ and an arc $(x, k, y) \to (x', k', y')$ in E_G if and only if $k' \oplus x' = y \oplus v$.

Let $A^{E, E^{-1}}(\sigma)$ be an adversary attacking H_{13}. The adversary is given σ as input and its goal is to invert σ. Assume that A asks at most q total queries. The adversary's queries are answered by using SimulateOracles(A, n) as in Algorithm 1. Initially all the vertices of G are uncoloured. When A asks an E-query (k, x) (or when A asks an E^{-1} query of (k, y)) and this returns (x, k, y) and $(\hat{x}, \hat{k}, \hat{y})$, then, for each vertex (x, k, y): if $x \oplus k = h_0$, then vertex (x, k, y) gets coloured red; otherwise, vertex (x, k, y) gets coloured black.

A vertex of G is *coloured* when it gets coloured red or black. A path P in G is coloured if all of its vertices are coloured. Vertex (x, k, y) is said to *invert* if $y \oplus v = \sigma$. A path is *inverting* if all of its vertices are coloured, it starts with a red vertex and ends in an inverting vertex. Let I be the event that, as a result of the adversary's queries, an inverting path is formed in G.

Claim. $\mathbf{Adv}^{inv}_{H_{13}[n]}(q) \leq \Pr[I]$.

Claim. $\Pr[I] \leq (4q^2 + 16q)/2^{n-1}$.

Proof (Proof Sketch). Let I_j be the event that I occurs by the j-th query. Let I_0 be the null event. Then $\Pr[I] = \sum_{j=1}^{q} \Pr[I_j \mid \overline{I_{j-1}} \wedge \cdots \wedge \overline{I_0}]$. Given $\overline{I_{j-1}} \wedge \cdots \wedge \overline{I_0}$, the event I_j occurs in one of the following ways. In the j-th query, a) the start (red) vertex could get coloured, or b) a mid vertex (on the path) could get coloured, or c) the end vertex (inverting vertex) could get coloured, or d) a vertex that is both a start and an end vertex could get coloured. I could occur in the j-th query due to any of these events.

Using similar techniques as the proof of Theorem 1, we can prove the two claims. The proofs for $H_{14}, \ldots H_{20}$ can be obtained in a similar fashion. The proof is omitted here due to space constraints.

A   Proof of Theorem 1 : Collision Resistance of H_1, H_2, H_3 and H_4

Claim. $\mathbf{Adv}^{coll}_{H_1[n]}(q) \leq \Pr[C]$.

Proof. Suppose that A outputs colliding messages $M = m_1 \ldots m_a$ and $M' = m'_1 \ldots m'_b$, implying that $H^E(M) = H^E(M')$ for the simulated oracle E. Let $P = (x_1, k_1, y_1) \to \ldots \to (x_a, k_a, y_a)$ where, for each $i \in [a]$, $x_i = m_i, k_i = $

$h_{i-1}, y_i = E_{k_i}(x_i)$ and $h_i = y_i \oplus x_i{}^9$. Let $P' = (x'_1, k'_1, y'_1) \rightarrow \ldots \rightarrow (x'_b, k'_b, y'_b)$ where, for each $i \in [b]$, $x'_i = m'_i, k'_i = h'_{i-1}, y'_i = E_{k'_i}(x'_i)$ and $h'_i = y'_i \oplus x'_i$ and $h'_0 = h_0$, a fixed constant. We claim that P and P' are colliding paths.

We assume that A makes all of the queries necessary to compute $H(M)$ and $H(M')$. So, for each $i \in [a]$, A must have made either an E-query (k_i, x_i) or $(k_i \oplus \triangle k, x_i \oplus \triangle x)$ (or an E^{-1}-query (k_i, y_i) or $(k_i \oplus \triangle k, y_i \oplus \triangle y)$). We can then conclude that P and P' are coloured. Moreover, $k_1 = h_0$ and $k'_1 = h_0$, so each of P and P' start with a red node.

If $a \neq b$, then clearly P and P' are distinct. Consider $a = b$ and $M \neq M'$. There is some $i \in [a]$ such that $m_i \neq m'_i$ and so $(x_i, k_i, y_i) \neq (x'_i, k'_i, y'_i)$, implying that P and P' are distinct.

Finally, if M and M' collide, we have $h_a = h'_b$ and hence $y_a \oplus x_a = y'_b \oplus x'_b$. This implies that (x_a, k_a, y_a) and (x'_b, k'_b, y'_b) are colliding vertices. Therefore P and P' are distinct paths that are coloured, start with a red vertex and end with colliding vertices. This completes the proof.

Claim. $\Pr[C] \leq 14q(q+1)/2^n$.

Proof. Let C_i be the event that C occurs by the i-th query and C_0 be the null event. Then $\Pr[C] = \sum_{i=1}^{q} \Pr[C_i | \overline{C_{i-1}} \wedge \ldots \wedge \overline{C_0}]$. Let vertices (x_i, k_i, y_i) and $(\hat{x}_i, \hat{k}_i, \hat{y}_i)$ be the vertices coloured in the i-th query during A's interaction with the oracle. The analysis proceeds by considering the probability of C_i given $\overline{C_{i-1}} \wedge \ldots \wedge \overline{C_0}$. The event C_i can happen in the i-th query if

1. a mid vertex (on a path) gets coloured, or
2. the start (red) vertex gets coloured, or
3. an end vertex (one of the colliding vertices) gets coloured, or
4. a start vertex that collides with h_0 gets coloured.

Note that since two vertices are coloured for every query, any two of the events above can happen in the i-th query leading to C_i. But it is necessary that at least one of them occur in order to form two colliding paths. So,

$$\Pr[C_i | \overline{C_{i-1}} \wedge \ldots \wedge \overline{C_0}] \leq \Pr[\text{Case 1}] + \Pr[\text{Case 2}] + \Pr[\text{Case 3}] + \Pr[\text{Case 4}]$$

Before analyzing the four cases, we define some notation. For $1 \leq a, b \leq q$, let $\mathsf{Arc}(a, b)$ be the event that there exists in G vertices (x_a, k_a, y_a) and (x_b, k_b, y_b) coloured on the a-th and b-th queries respectively, and $k_b = y_a \oplus x_a$. For $1 \leq a \leq q$, let $\mathsf{Start}(a)$ be the event that there exists in G vertex (x_a, k_a, y_a) coloured in the a-th query and $k_a = h_0$. For $1 \leq a, b \leq q$, let $\mathsf{Collide}(a, b)$ be the event that there exists in G vertices (x_a, k_a, y_a) and (x_b, k_b, y_b) coloured in the a-th and b-th queries respectively, and $y_b \oplus x_b = y_a \oplus x_a{}^{10}$. Two vertices (x_a, k_a, y_a) and (x_b, k_b, y_b) are adjacent to each other if either $\mathsf{Arc}(a, b)$ or $\mathsf{Arc}(b, a)$ is true.

---

[9] This again is by the definition of the compression function f_1.

[10] The conditions for defining an arc, a start (red) vertex and collision depend on the compression function f_1.

Case 1. *A mid-vertex gets coloured.* In the i-th query, two vertices (x_i, k_i, y_i) and $(\hat{x}_i, \hat{k}_i, \hat{y}_i)$ are coloured. This event requires that there exists a vertex (x_r, k_r, y_r) such that there exists an arc $(x_r, k_r, y_r) \rightarrow (x_i, k_i, y_i)$ or $(x_r, k_r, y_r) \rightarrow (\hat{x}_i, \hat{k}_i, \hat{y}_i)$, where $r < i$. And there exists a vertex (x_j, k_j, y_j) such that there exists an arc $(x_i, k_i, y_i) \rightarrow (x_j, k_j, y_j)$ or $(\hat{x}_i, \hat{k}_i, \hat{y}_i) \rightarrow (x_j, k_j, y_j)$, where $j < i$.

This event requires that a) $\mathsf{Arc}(r, i) \wedge \mathsf{Arc}(i, j)$ or b) $\mathsf{Arc}(r, \hat{i}) \wedge \mathsf{Arc}(\hat{i}, j)$ or c) $\mathsf{Arc}(r, i) \wedge \mathsf{Arc}(i, \hat{i}) \wedge \mathsf{Arc}(\hat{i}, j)$ or d) $\mathsf{Arc}(r, \hat{i}) \wedge \mathsf{Arc}(\hat{i}, i) \wedge \mathsf{Arc}(i, j)$ be true. So,

$$\Pr[\text{Case 1}] \leq \Pr[\mathsf{Arc}(i, j)] + \Pr[\mathsf{Arc}(\hat{i}, j)] + \Pr[\mathsf{Arc}(i, \hat{i})] + \Pr[\mathsf{Arc}(\hat{i}, i)]$$

Analyzing $\Pr(\mathsf{Arc}(i, j))$: If C_i occurs via an E-query, then the y-value is a random value chosen from a set of size at least $2^n - (i-1)$.[11] Also, note that the (x_j, k_j, y_j) could be any of the $2(i-1)$ vertices coloured in the previous queries. Then,

$$\Pr[\mathsf{Arc}(i, j)] \leq \frac{2(i-1)}{2^n - (i-1)}$$

Alternatively, if C_i occurs via an E^{-1} query, then the x-value is a random value from a set of size at least $2^n - (i-1)$. Then, $\Pr[\mathsf{Arc}(i, j)] \leq \frac{2(i-1)}{2^n - (i-1)}$. So, $\Pr[\mathsf{Arc}(i, j)] \leq \frac{2(i-1)}{2^n - (i-1)}$. Similarly, we can show that $\Pr[\mathsf{Arc}(\hat{i}, j)] \leq \frac{2(i-1)}{2^n - (i-1)}$ and $\Pr[\mathsf{Arc}(i, \hat{i})] = \Pr[\mathsf{Arc}(\hat{i}, i)] \leq \frac{1}{2^n - (i-1)}$. So, $\Pr[\text{Case 1}] \leq \frac{4(i-1)+2}{2^n - (i-1)}$.

Case 2. *A start vertex gets coloured.* In the i-th query, two vertices (x_i, k_i, y_i) and $(\hat{x}_i, \hat{k}_i, \hat{y}_i)$ are coloured. This event requires that either (x_i, k_i, y_i) or $(\hat{x}_i, \hat{k}_i, \hat{y}_i)$ is coloured red and there exists a vertex (x_j, k_j, y_j) such that there exists an arc $(x_i, k_i, y_i) \rightarrow (x_j, k_j, y_j)$ or $(\hat{x}_i, \hat{k}_i, \hat{y}_i) \rightarrow (x_j, k_j, y_j)$, where $j < i$.

This event requires that a) $\mathsf{Start}(i) \wedge \mathsf{Arc}(i, j)$ or b) $\mathsf{Start}(\hat{i}) \wedge \mathsf{Arc}(\hat{i}, j)$ or c) $\mathsf{Start}(i) \wedge \mathsf{Arc}(i, \hat{i}) \wedge \mathsf{Arc}(\hat{i}, j)$ or d) $\mathsf{Start}(\hat{i}) \wedge \mathsf{Arc}(\hat{i}, i) \wedge \mathsf{Arc}(i, j)$ be true. So,

$$\Pr[\text{Case 2}] \leq \Pr[\mathsf{Arc}(i, j)] + \Pr[\mathsf{Arc}(\hat{i}, j)] + \Pr[\mathsf{Arc}(i, \hat{i})] + \Pr[\mathsf{Arc}(\hat{i}, i)]$$

The analysis is the same as case 1. So, the probability of this event is $\frac{4(i-1)+2}{2^n - (i-1)}$.

Case 3. *An end vertex gets coloured.* This case is analyzed in two sub-cases: 1) only one vertex coloured in the i-th query is an end vertex and 2) both vertices coloured in the i-th query are end vertices i.e. the two vertices formed in the i-th query collide with each other.

1) In the i-th query, two vertices (x_i, k_i, y_i) and $(\hat{x}_i, \hat{k}_i, \hat{y}_i)$ are coloured. This event requires that there exists a vertex (x_j, k_j, y_j) such that there exists an arc $(x_j, k_j, y_j) \rightarrow (x_i, k_i, y_i)$ or $(x_j, k_j, y_j) \rightarrow (\hat{x}_i, \hat{k}_i, \hat{y}_i)$, where $j < i$ and there exists a vertex (x_r, k_r, y_r) such that (x_r, k_r, y_r) collides with (x_i, k_i, y_i) or $(\hat{x}_i, \hat{k}_i, \hat{y}_i)$ where $r < i$. This requires that a) $\mathsf{Arc}(j, i) \wedge \mathsf{Collide}(i, r)$ or b)

---

[11] Even though the adversary A learns two triplets for every query, corresponding to a key k, A could have learnt only $(i-1)$ y-values and not $2(i-1)$. This is because the two triplets learnt for each query, due to the related key weakness, are for two different keys since $\triangle k \neq 0^n$.

$\mathsf{Arc}(j,\hat{i}) \wedge \mathsf{Collide}(\hat{i},r)$ or c) $\mathsf{Arc}(j,i) \wedge \mathsf{Arc}(i,\hat{i}) \wedge \mathsf{Collide}(\hat{i},r)$ or d) $\mathsf{Arc}(j,\hat{i}) \wedge \mathsf{Arc}(\hat{i},i) \wedge \mathsf{Collide}(i,r)$ be true.

If C_i occurs via an E-query, then the y-value is a random value chosen from a set of size at least $2^n - (i-1)$. Then,

$$\Pr[\mathsf{Collide}(i,r)] \leq \frac{2(i-1)}{2^n - (i-1)}.$$

Alternatively, if C_i occurs via an E^{-1} query, then the x-value is a random value from a set of size at least $2^n - (i-1)$. Then, $\Pr[\mathsf{Collide}(i,r)] \leq \frac{2(i-1)}{2^n-(i-1)}$. So, $\Pr[\mathsf{Collide}(i,r)] \leq \frac{2(i-1)}{2^n-(i-1)}$. We can show that $\Pr[\mathsf{Collide}(\hat{i},r)] \leq \frac{2(i-1)}{2^n-(i-1)}$ and $\Pr[\mathsf{Arc}(i,\hat{i})] = \Pr[\mathsf{Arc}(\hat{i},i)] \leq \frac{1}{2^n-(i-1)}$. Hence, $\Pr[\text{Case 3.1}] = \frac{4(i-1)+2}{2^n-(i-1)}$.

2) The two vertices coloured in the i-th query, (x_i, k_i, y_i) and $(\hat{x}_i, \hat{k}_i, \hat{y}_i)$ collide with each other. This event requires that there exists a vertex (x_j, k_j, y_j) such that there exists an arc $(x_j, k_j, y_j) \to (x_i, k_i, y_i)$ and vertex (x_p, k_p, y_p) such that there exists an arc $(x_p, k_p, y_p) \to (\hat{x}_i, \hat{k}_i, \hat{y}_i)$, where $p < i$ and (x_i, k_i, y_i) collides with $(\hat{x}_i, \hat{k}_i, \hat{y}_i)$.

Thus, for vertices (x_i, k_i, y_i) and $(\hat{x}_i, \hat{k}_i, \hat{y}_i)$ coloured in the i-th query to collide, we require that $\mathsf{Arc}(j,i) \wedge \mathsf{Arc}(p,\hat{i}) \wedge \mathsf{Collide}(i,\hat{i})$ to be true. Now, $\Pr[\mathsf{Arc}(j,i) \wedge \mathsf{Arc}(p,\hat{i}) \wedge \mathsf{Collide}(i,\hat{i})] \leq \Pr[\mathsf{Arc}(j,i)|\mathsf{Arc}(p,\hat{i})]$.

If C_i occurs via an E-query, then the y-value is random value from a set of size at least $2^n - (i-1)$. Now, if $p \neq j$,

$$\Pr[\mathsf{Arc}(j,i)|\mathsf{Arc}(p,\hat{i})] \leq \frac{2(i-1)}{2^n - (i-1)}$$

If $p = j$,

$$\begin{aligned}
\Pr[\mathsf{Arc}(j,i)|\mathsf{Arc}(p,\hat{i})] &\leq \Pr[k_i = x_j \oplus y_j | k_i \oplus \triangle k = x_p \oplus y_p] \\
&= \Pr[x_p \oplus y_p \oplus \triangle k = x_p \oplus y_p] \\
&= \Pr[\triangle k = 0^n] = 0
\end{aligned}$$

and hence[12],

$$\Pr[\mathsf{Arc}(j,i) \wedge \mathsf{Arc}(p,\hat{i}) \wedge \mathsf{Collide}(i,\hat{i})] \leq \frac{2(i-1)}{2^n - (i-1)}$$

Alternatively, if C_i occurs via an E^{-1}-query, we can still get $\Pr[\mathsf{Arc}(j,i) \wedge \mathsf{Arc}(p,\hat{i}) \wedge \mathsf{Collide}(i,\hat{i})] \leq \frac{2(i-1)}{2^n-(i-1)}$. So, $\Pr[\text{Case 3.2}] = \frac{2(i-1)}{2^n-(i-1)}$. And, hence $\Pr[\text{Case 3}] = \frac{6(i-1)+2}{2^n-(i-1)}$.

Case 4. *A vertex colliding with h_0 gets coloured.* In the i-th query, two vertices (x_i, k_i, y_i) and $(\hat{x}_i, \hat{k}_i, \hat{y}_i)$ are coloured. This event requires (at least) that either (x_i, k_i, y_i) is such that $x_i \oplus y_i = h_0$ or $(\hat{x}_i, \hat{k}_i, \hat{y}_i)$ is such that $\hat{x}_i \oplus \hat{y}_i = h_0$.

---

[12] Note that this requires $\triangle k \neq 0^n$. If $\triangle k = 0^n$, the proof does not hold and in fact, we can find collisions in the hash function.

Consider the probability of $x_i \oplus y_i = h_0$. If this occurs via an E-query, then the y-value is a random value from a set of size $2^n - (i - 1)$. Then, $\Pr[x_i \oplus y_i = h_0] \leq \frac{1}{2^n - (i-1)}$. Alternatively, if C_i occurs in this case via an E^{-1} query, then the x-value is a random value from a set of size at least $2^n - (i - 1)$. Then, $\Pr[x_i \oplus y_i = h_0] \leq \frac{1}{2^n - (i-1)}$. Note that the same analysis works for $(\hat{x}_i, \hat{k}_i, \hat{y}_i)$ as well. So, $\Pr[\text{Case } 4] = \frac{2}{2^n - (i-1)}$.

Combining all four cases, we have that,

$$\Pr[C] \leq \sum_{i=1}^{q} \Pr[C_i | \overline{C_{i-1}} \wedge \ldots \wedge \overline{C_0}] \leq \sum_{i=1}^{q} \frac{14(i-1) + 8}{2^n - (i-1)} \leq \frac{14q(q+1)}{2^n}$$

References

1. Baecher, P., Farshim, P., Fischlin, M., Stam, M.: Ideal-cipher (ir)reducibility for blockcipher-based hash functions. In: Johansson, T., Nguyen, P.Q. (eds.) EURO-CRYPT 2013. LNCS, vol. 7881, pp. 426–443. Springer, Heidelberg (2013)
2. Bellare, M., Rogaway, P.: Random oracles are practical: a paradigm for designing efficient protocols. In: 1st ACM Conf. on Computer and Communications Security, pp. 62–73. ACM Press (1993)
3. Biham, Eli: New types of cryptanalytic attacks using related keys. In: Helleseth, Tor (ed.) EUROCRYPT 1993. LNCS, vol. 765, pp. 398–409. Springer, Heidelberg (1994)
4. Biham, E., Dunkelman, O., Keller, N.: A related-key rectangle attack on the Full KASUMI. In: Roy, B. (ed.) ASIACRYPT 2005. LNCS, vol. 3788, pp. 443–461. Springer, Heidelberg (2005)
5. Biham, E., Dunkelman, O., Keller, N.: A simple related-key attack on the Full SHACAL-1. In: Abe, M. (ed.) CT-RSA 2007. LNCS, vol. 4377, pp. 20–30. Springer, Heidelberg (2006)
6. Biryukov, A., Khovratovich, D.: Related-key cryptanalysis of the Full AES-192 and AES-256. In: Matsui, M. (ed.) ASIACRYPT 2009. LNCS, vol. 5912, pp. 1–18. Springer, Heidelberg (2009)
7. Biryukov, A., Khovratovich, D., Nikolić, I.: Distinguisher and related-key attack on the Full AES-256. In: Halevi, S. (ed.) CRYPTO 2009. LNCS, vol. 5677, pp. 231–249. Springer, Heidelberg (2009)
8. Black, J.A.: The ideal-cipher model, revisited: an uninstantiable blockcipher-based hash function. In: Robshaw, M. (ed.) FSE 2006. LNCS, vol. 4047, pp. 328–340. Springer, Heidelberg (2006)
9. Black, J.A., Rogaway, P., Shrimpton, T.: Black-box analysis of the block-cipher-based hash-function constructions from PGV. In: Yung, M. (ed.) CRYPTO 2002. LNCS, vol. 2442, p. 320. Springer, Heidelberg (2002)
10. Black, J., Rogaway, P., Shrimpton, T., Stam, M.: An analysis of the blockcipher-based hash functions from PGV. Journal of Cryptology 23(4), 519–545 (2010)
11. Canetti, R., Goldreich, O., Halevi, S.: The random oracle methodology, revisited. J. ACM 51(4), 557–594 (2004)
12. Dunkelman, O., Keller, N., Kim, J.-S.: Related-key rectangle attack on the Full SHACAL-1. In: Biham, E., Youssef, A.M. (eds.) SAC 2006. LNCS, vol. 4356, pp. 28–44. Springer, Heidelberg (2007)

13. Dunkelman, O., Keller, N., Shamir, A.: A practical-time related-key attack on the KASUMI cryptosystem used in GSM and 3G telephony. In: Rabin, T. (ed.) CRYPTO 2010. LNCS, vol. 6223, pp. 393–410. Springer, Heidelberg (2010)
14. Even, S., Mansour, Y.: A construction of a cipher from a single pseudorandom permutation. Journal of Cryptology 10(3), 151–162 (1997)
15. Goldreich, O., Goldwasser, S., Micali, S.: How to construct random functions. J. ACM 33(4), 792–807 (1986)
16. Hirose, S.: Secure block ciphers are not sufficient for one-way hash functions in the Preneel-Govaerts-Vandewalle model. In: Nyberg, K., Heys, H.M. (eds.) Selected Areas in Cryptography. LNCS, vol. 2595, pp. 339–352. Springer, Heidelberg (2003)
17. Hirose, S., Kuwakado, H.: Collision resistance of hash functions in a weak ideal cipher model. IEICE Trans. on Fundamentals E95–A(1), 252–255 (2012)
18. Kawachi, A., Numayama, A., Tanaka, K., Xagawa, K.: Security of encryption schemes in weakened random oracle models. In: Nguyen, P.Q., Pointcheval, D. (eds.) PKC 2010. LNCS, vol. 6056, pp. 403–419. Springer, Heidelberg (2010)
19. Kelsey, J., Schneier, B., Wagner, D.: Key-schedule cryptanalysis of IDEA, G-DES, GOST, SAFER, and triple-DES. In: Koblitz, N. (ed.) CRYPTO 1996. LNCS, vol. 1109, pp. 237–251. Springer, Heidelberg (1996)
20. Kelsey, J., Schneier, B., Wagner, D.: Related-key cryptanalysis of 3-WAY, Biham-DES, CAST, DES-X, NewDES, RC2, and TEA. In: Han, Y., Quing, S. (eds.) ICICS 1997. LNCS, vol. 1334, pp. 233–246. Springer, Heidelberg (1997)
21. Knudsen, L.R.: Cryptanalysis of LOKI91. In: Zheng, Yuliang, Seberry, Jennifer (eds.) AUSCRYPT 1992. LNCS, vol. 718, pp. 196–208. Springer, Heidelberg (1993)
22. Knudsen, L.R., Kohno, T.: Analysis of RMAC. In: Johansson, T. (ed.) FSE 2003. LNCS, vol. 2887, pp. 182–191. Springer, Heidelberg (2003)
23. Leurent, G., Nguyen, P.Q.: How risky is the random-oracle model? In: Halevi, S. (ed.) CRYPTO 2009. LNCS, vol. 5677, pp. 445–464. Springer, Heidelberg (2009)
24. Liskov, M.: Constructing an ideal hash function from weak ideal compression functions. In: Biham, E., Youssef, A.M. (eds.) SAC 2006. LNCS, vol. 4356, pp. 358–375. Springer, Heidelberg (2007)
25. Luby, M., Rackoff, C.: How to construct pseudorandom permutations from pseudorandom functions. SIAM Journal on Computing 17(2), 373–386 (1988)
26. Lucks, S.: A failure-friendly design principle for hash functions. In: Roy, B. (ed.) ASIACRYPT 2005. LNCS, vol. 3788, pp. 474–494. Springer, Heidelberg (2005)
27. Numayama, A., Isshiki, T., Tanaka, K.: Security of digital signature schemes in weakened random oracle models. In: Cramer, R. (ed.) PKC 2008. LNCS, vol. 4939, pp. 268–287. Springer, Heidelberg (2008)
28. Phan, R.C.-W.: Related-key attacks on triple-DES and DESX variants. In: Okamoto, T. (ed.) CT-RSA 2004. LNCS, vol. 2964, pp. 15–24. Springer, Heidelberg (2004)
29. Preneel, B., Govaerts, R., Vandewalle, J.: Hash functions based on block ciphers: a synthetic approach. In: Stinson, D.R. (ed.) CRYPTO 1993. LNCS, vol. 773, pp. 368–378. Springer, Heidelberg (1994)
30. Shannon, C.E.: Communication theory of secrecy systems. Bell Systems Technical Journal 28(4), 656–715 (1949)
31. Simon, D.R.: Findings collisions on a one-way street: can secure hash functions be based on general assumptions? In: Nyberg, K. (ed.) EUROCRYPT 1998. LNCS, vol. 1403, pp. 334–345. Springer, Heidelberg (1998)
32. Stam, M.: Blockcipher-based hashing revisited. In: Dunkelman, O. (ed.) FSE 2009. LNCS, vol. 5665, pp. 67–83. Springer, Heidelberg (2009)
33. Zhang, L., Wu, W., Wang, P., Zhang, L., Wu, S., Liang, B.: Constructing rate-1 MACs from related-key unpredictable block ciphers: PGV model revisited. In: Hong, S., Iwata, T. (eds.) FSE 2010. LNCS, vol. 6147, pp. 250–269. Springer, Heidelberg (2010)

Using an Error-Correction Code for Fast, Beyond-Birthday-Bound Authentication

Yusi Zhang[(✉)]

University of California, Davis, 1, Shields Avenue, Davis, CA 95616, USA
yzhangad@gmail.com

Abstract. In this paper, we describe a new variation of PMAC called PMACX. It generalizes PMAC-with-Parity, a prior work of Yasuda. The most unique feature of PMACX is its parallel MDS (Maximum Distance Separating) matrix multiplication on the input message before the authentication. The scheme is parameterized by a generator matrix for an MDS linear code over $GF(2^n)$. PMACX supports any reasonable choice of the matrix's dimension, and this choice of the parameters reflects the trade-off between efficiency and security. For example, if a 14×12 matrix is used, PMACX will be about 14% slower than PMAC, and when $n = 128$, $q = 2^{32}$ and $\rho = 2^{64}$, the best known bound for PMAC, $O(q^2\rho/2^n)$, gives a meaningless result, while our bound, $O(q^2/2^n + q\sigma\rho/2^{2n})$ in this case, is still in the reasonable order of 2^{-64}. ($q^2/2^n + q\sigma\rho/2^{2n} \leq q^2/2^n + q^2\rho^2/2^{2n} = 2^{-64} + 2^{-64} = 2^{-63}$)

We corroborate the above theoretical observation with implementation results. Our comparative experiment shows that a careful choice of the MDS matrix can make PMACX faster than PMAC-with-Parity, yet reducing the number of keys from 4 to 2 and achieving asymptotically the same security level.

Keywords: Block cipher's mode of operation · PMAC · Beyond-birthday-bound security · Long message · Fixed key space

1 Introduction

1.1 MACs as Modes of Operation of Block Ciphers

MACs (Message Authentication Codes) are a class of symmetric cryptographic schemes that can authenticate messages between two users who share a secret key. Common MACs that are standardized and implemented in practice often invoke an underlying block cipher as its building block — the well-known block-cipher based MACs. Popular examples include the CBC family [1],[4],[2],[11],[9] and PMAC [5],[17]. Such MAC schemes are important from an engineering perspective, as the implementations of popular standardized block ciphers, like AES [6], are almost everywhere and this omnipresence implies the possibility of simple add-on implementations and high efficiency for block cipher modes of operations.

© Springer International Publishing Switzerland 2015
K. Nyberg (ed.): CT-RSA 2015, LNCS 9048, pp. 291–307, 2015.
DOI: 10.1007/978-3-319-16715-2_16

1.2   "Birthday Barrier" and the Demand for Going Beyond It

Most popular MAC schemes are provided with proofs of security, and they generally provide the so-called "birthday-bound": the adversarial advantage has the form of $O(q^2\rho^2/2^n)$ or $O(\sigma^2/2^n)$. (Throughout this paper, we use q, ρ, σ to denote the number of queries, the maximum block length of the padded messages, and the sum of the block length of the padded messages.) Even better bounds of the form $O(\rho q^2/2^n)$ have been found for certain schemes like PMAC [15]. However, even though a large amount of work has been done on achieving better security for existing schemes (either by more careful analysis [2],[15] or by adjusting the scheme's specification [17]), the bounding formula will go into void when either ρ or q goes above $2^{n/2}$. This difficulty of providing security over the level of $O(2^{n/2})$ is usually called the "birthday barrier". Going beyond this barrier has a practical significance, provided that there are still a lot of legacy systems deploying 64-bit ciphers (e.g. systems in financial institutions). Furthermore, it would also keep the longevity of the current 128-bit cipher families.

1.3   The Intent of Resisting Long Messages

Among the many works that manage to go beyond the birthday barrier, researchers seem to focus more on the number of queries [19,20]. We believe that one of the practical reasons for such is that most real-world network applications authenticate large number of relatively small messages. Unfortunately, going beyond the birthday barrier in terms of q makes it necessary to introduce qualitative modifications to existing schemes, since there exist general attacks with $O(2^{n/2})$ query complexity for MAC schemes with n-bit intermediate values [16].

On the other hand, there have not been so many works that focus on reducing the effect of message length. From our perspective, this question should be considered the same important as that for number of queries, since quite a few types of application authenticate long messages (e.g. disk authentication). Therefore, we propose the following question:

How to go beyond the birthday barrier in terms of ρ, the maximum message block length, without adding too much complexity and overhead to an existing scheme like PMAC?

1.4   Related Work

Yasuda has presented PMAC-with-Parity [21], which aims to solve the same question we asked. The scheme provides a security bound of the form $O(q^2/2^n + \sigma\rho q/2^{2n})$. From our perspective, this scheme is only of theoretical interest since it requires four independent cipher keys and is at least one and a half times more slowly than the traditional PMAC (The author also proposed variants that have different parameters, which we do not consider here for the sake of brevity).

A pictorial description of PMAC-with-Parity is given in Fig. 1. Loosely speaking, a message is first divided into 2 "sub-messages": one consisting of odd-index blocks and the other consisting of even-index blocks, and a new "sub-message" is obtained by xoring these 2 "sub-messages" (of different parity). Among the four independent keys, three are used in the "PMAC-way" to authenticate the 3 "sub-messages" independently, while the last is used to do the final enciphering, in a similar way to PMAC.

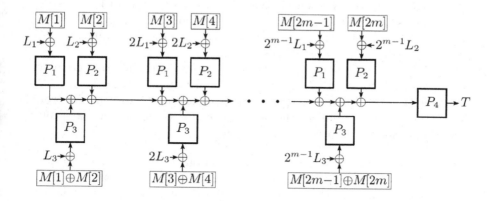

Fig. 1. PMAC-with-Parity: achieve beyond-birthday security at a cost of 4 keys and 2/3-rate

Apart from PMAC-with-Parity, there has been a large amount of related work in going beyond the birthday barrier over almost all kinds of symmetric cryptographic primitives: A general method of providing beyond-birthday-bounds is given in [13], but their methods focus more on reducing the effect of query numbers, and the main contribution is a way to convert PRPs into fixed-length PRFs, instead of MAC schemes. Jaulmes et $al.$ [10] proposed a randomized variant of the plain CBC-MAC that can resist more than $2^{n/2}$ queries. Yasuda designed several beyond-birthday variants of popular MAC algorithms including PMAC [20] and HMAC [18], he also proposed relevant PRF-based solutions [22] as well. For tweakable block ciphers, Minematsu [14] presented a construction based on a modified underlying tweakable block cipher that goes beyond the birthday barrier. A recent work by Landecker et $al.$ [12] solved the problem of restricted tweak space and rekeying in providing beyond-birthday bounds for tweakable block ciphers. Finally, there has been related work on providing beyond-birthday bounds for authenticated encryption as well [7,8].

We remark that almost all related work about beyond-birthday-bounds focuses on the number of queries. To the best of our knowledge, the only work that is relevant to birthday-bounds of message length is Yasuda's PMAC-with-Parity [21].

1.5 Our Contribution

We combined the construction of PMAC-with-Parity and MDS-coding to design PMACX, a new variant of PMAC. It can be viewed as a generalization of

PMAC-with-Parity (and of PMAC as well), whose "parity processing" part is replaced with a general MDS generator matrix multiplication. Our scheme has the following characteristics:

1. PMACX is parameterized by a matrix over $GF(2^n)$. This matrix parameter controls the trade-off between efficiency and security.
2. Theoretically, PMACX can achieve a rate arbitrarily close to 1.
3. PMACX is proved to be secure with a bound of the form: $O(q^2/2^n + q\sigma\rho^{d'-1}/2^{d'n})$, where d' is a positive integer determined by the matrix parameter.
4. PMACX uses only 2 independent keys, regardless of the matrix parameter.
5. Compared to PMAC, the only major structural modification is the introduction of MDS matrix multiplication. A careful instantiation of it would make the overhead minimal relative to the cipher computation. See Table 1 (Section 6) for a comparison of performance.

For a clear illustration of the improvement of our security bound, see Fig. 2. For the sake of simplicity, All the messages are assumed to have the same maximum length, ρ. We plot the values of ρ and q that make the three bounds vacuous: $O(q^2\rho/2^n)$, the best known bound of PMAC, $O(q^2/2^n + q\sigma\rho/2^{2n})$, the bound of PMAC-with-Parity, and $O(q^2/2^n + q\sigma\rho^3/2^{4n})$, one possible bound of PMACX. Note that the last bound corresponds to the case where $d = 7$ or $d = 8$. From the graph it is clear that our security bound provides a larger "security region" of the parameters. In particular, this implies PMACX can theoretically authenticate more messages before its security vanishes. Consider the example of authenticating $2^{9n/8}$ blocks of messages in total: in this case, there is a constraint

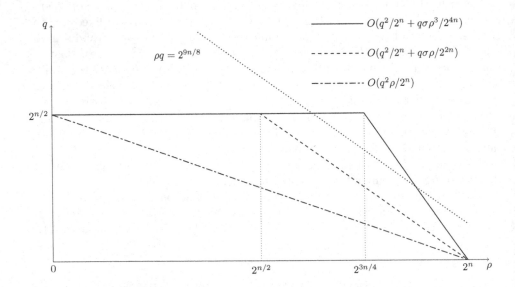

Fig. 2. Values of ρ and q that make the bounds vacuous

on the choice of ρ and q: $q\rho \geq 2^{9n/8}$. This delimiting line is plotted as well, and we can see that both PMAC and PMAC-with-Parity fail to achieve this task, while PMACX can still succeed by choosing q and ρ in the region enclosed by the dotted and the solid line.

Another outstanding advantage of PMACX is its fixed key space. We remark that a much more simple generalization would just use as many independent keys as needed, like the case in PMAC-with-Parity. Such deployment of independent keys would make the analysis much easier, and the problem of reducing the impact of message length could indeed be solved. However, we insist on acquiring better results. We show that although the reduction of the number of keys makes the analysis more involved, the provable security does not go away completely (More concretely, in our analysis the key reduction halves the value of the exponent, d, in the bound's formula).

1.6   Organization of the Paper

Section 2 introduces the terminology and basic definitions used throughout the paper. Section 3 gives the background of the unique notion in PMACX: the MDS generator matrix. Based on these preliminaries, Section 4 presents the detailed specification of PMACX, followed by a security proof in Section 5 . A concrete example of the instantiated generator matrix and the implementation result can be found in Section 6. At last, the whole paper is concluded in Section 7.

2   Preliminary Notion

We use Σ to denote the binary alphabet, $\{0, 1\}$; Σ^n to denote the set of all binary strings of length n; Σ^* to denote the set of all finite binary strings. For a string M, let $|M|$ be its bit-length, $|M|_n := \lceil |M|/n \rceil$ be its n-bit block length (after padding). Let $\mathbf{Func}(m, n)$ be the set of all functions: $\Sigma^m \to \Sigma^n$. Let $\mathbf{Func}(*, n)$ denote the set of all functions: $\Sigma^* \to \Sigma^n$. Let $\mathbf{Perm}(n)$ be the set of all permutations: $\Sigma^n \to \Sigma^n$. When A is a variable and S is a set, the statement: $A \xleftarrow{\$} S$ represents the operation of uniformly sampling an element from S and assigning it to A. The statement $M[1]||M[2]|| \cdots ||M[s] \xleftarrow{}_m M||10^*$ represents the operation as following: first append to M a 1-bit, plus enough many 0's so that its bit-length is an integer multiple of m, next divide it into m-bit blocks and assign them to $M[1], M[2], \cdots, M[s]$ in the natural order. $M[1]||M[2]|| \cdots ||M[s] \xleftarrow{}_m M$ refers to the same operation without padding. In this case, it is assumed that $|M|$ is always a positve integer multiple of m.

We use $GF(2)$ to denote the Galois field with two elements: $\{0, 1\}$ with addition and multiplication modulo 2 as its operation. We treat an element in Σ^n both as an n-bit string and as an element in $GF(2^n) = GF(2)[x]/p(x)$. For the latter case, $p(x)$ is an irreducible degree-n polynomial over $GF(2)$, and an n-bit string, $a = a_{n-1}a_{n-2} \cdots a_0$ is identified as a formal polynomial: $a_{n-1}x^{n-1} + a_{n-2}x^{n-2} + \cdots + a_1 x + a_0$. Throughout the paper we apply these two treatments interchangeably. When a is treated as an element in $GF(2)[x]/p(x)$, we also use the integer representation of it as well, namely $N = a_{n-1} \cdot 2^{n-1} + a_{n-2} \cdot 2^{n-2} + \cdots + a_1 \cdot 2 + a_0$. For example, the integer 2 refers to the formal polynomial $x \in GF(2)[x]/p(x)$.

For the security notions, we apply the convention of "real versus ideal" as our PRP and PRF definitions. Specifically, consider an adversary A, which is a probabilistic Turing machine, given access to either a true oracle of a keyed function (resp., permutation), or an ideal oracle of a compatible idealized random function (resp., permutation). The adversary is restricted with the number of queries q, the time complexity t (with respect to some standard computation model), the maximum queried message's block length (after padding), ρ, and the sum of all queried messages' block lengths (after padding), σ, and he is supposed to differentiate between the two oracles he is interacting with, by outputting a guess bit. We also use the simplified notation: $\rho_l = \rho/l$ and $\sigma_l = \sigma/l$ for sake of tidiness (When such notations are used, it is assumed that ρ and σ are integer multiples of the subscript, l). The PRF-advantage of an adversary A against a keyed function $F_k \colon \Sigma^* \to \Sigma^n$ is:

$$\mathsf{Adv}_F^{\mathrm{prf}}(A) = \mathbf{Pr}[A^{F_k(\cdot)} = 1; k \xleftarrow{\$} K] - \mathbf{Pr}[A^{R(\cdot)} = 1; R \xleftarrow{\$} \mathbf{Func}(*, n)] \, ,$$

and the PRP-advantage against a keyed permutation $E_k \colon \Sigma^n \to \Sigma^n$ is:

$$\mathsf{Adv}_E^{\mathrm{prp}}(A) = \mathbf{Pr}[A^{E_k(\cdot)} = 1; k \xleftarrow{\$} K] - \mathbf{Pr}[A^{P(\cdot)} = 1; P \xleftarrow{\$} \mathbf{Perm}(n)] \, .$$

We then define $\mathsf{Adv}_F^{\mathrm{prf}}(q, t, \rho, \sigma)$ to be the maximum PRF-advantage of all adversaries who ask at most q queries, whose queried message length is at most ρ blocks, whose total queried message length is at most σ blocks and whose time complexity is at most t. A similar definition is made for $\mathsf{Adv}_E^{\mathrm{prp}}(q, t)$. Note that for PRP-advantage we are only interested in the first two arguments, since for an n-bit permutation (the only kind of PRP considered in this work), the single message length is restricted to be n-bit long, and the maximum sum of message lengths are completely determined from q (which is qn).

3   MDS Matrix

We use the well-known MDS (Maximum Distance Separating) notion in constructing our new scheme. Informally speaking, an MDS matrix G of size $m \times n$ $(m > n)$ over a field F, is such that for any non-zero vector in F^n, the multiplication of G and this vector will have as many non-zero elements as possible. In the following sections we will see that this already well-understood, intensively-studied property of linear code generator matrix can help us derive a better bound with respect to the maximum message length. We first formally define what an MDS matrix is:

Definition 1 (MDS Matrix). *An $m \times l$ matrix G over a field F, where $m > l$ is an MDS matrix, if for any non-zero vector $x \in F^l$, the matrix-vector multiplication, $y = G \cdot x \in F^m$, has at least $d = m - l + 1$ non-zero entries. Stated differently* *in terms of coding theory, G is a generator matrix of an MDS $(m, l, m - l + 1)$-linear code.*

It is well-known that an equivalent characterization of MDS-code is a code that achieves the Singleton bound: $d \leq m - l + 1$. It would be clear in our analysis that this property makes the MDS-code an optimal choice for our design scenario.

4   Description of the Mode PMACX

In this section we present the concrete specification of PMACX. The scheme is parameterized by two permutations, $P_1, P_2 \in \mathbf{Perm}(n)$; plus an MDS matrix G. We use PMACX$[G, P_1, P_2]$ to denote the algorithm instantiated with a concrete choice of the three parameters.

The most important parameter unique to PMACX is the MDS matrix $G = (g_{i,j})$, It is an $m \times l$ matrix over $GF(2^n)$, $m > l$. This matrix parameter helps specify three other parameters, which usually are the most direct choices of design from a practical perspective:

- the interval length: l, number of columns of G. This is the number of blocks in an "interval", the atomic unit of parallelizable processing in our scheme.
- the number of masking subkeys: m, number of rows of G.
- the security parameter: $d = m - l + 1$. The larger this value is, the better security bound is achieved. Asymptotically, the bound is in the form: $O(q^2/2^n + q\sigma\rho^{\lfloor(d-1)/2\rfloor}/2^{\lfloor(d+1)/2\rfloor n})$.

Apart from G, the scheme also invokes two permutations: P_1 and P_2. The full specification is shown in Algorithm 1. See Fig. 3 for a graphical illustration.

Input: a message, $M \in \Sigma^*$
Output: a tag, $T \in \Sigma^n$
1   $M[1]||M[2]|| \cdots ||M[s] \leftarrow_{ln} M||10^*$;
2   $S \leftarrow 0^n$;
3   **for** $i = 1$ *to* m **do**
4   $\quad|\quad L_i \leftarrow P_1(i - 1)$;
5   **end**
6   **for** $i = 1$ *to* s **do**
7   $\quad|\quad X_i \leftarrow G \cdot M[i]$;
8   $\quad|\quad X_i[1]||X_i[2]|| \cdots ||X_i[m] \leftarrow_n X_i$;
9   $\quad|\quad$ **for** $j = 1$ *to* m **do**
10 $\quad|\quad\quad XE_i[j] \leftarrow X_i[j] \oplus 2^{i-1}L_j$;
11 $\quad|\quad\quad S \leftarrow S \oplus P_1(XE_i[j])$;
12 $\quad|\quad$ **end**
13 **end**
14 $T \leftarrow P_2(S)$;
15 **return** T

Algorithm 1. PMACX$[G, P_1, P_2]$

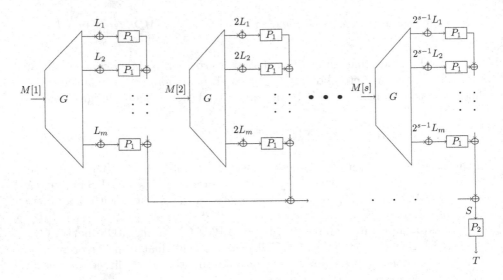

Fig. 3. PMACX$[G, P_1, P_2]$: the message blocks $\{M[i]\}$ are of size ln; the m subkeys are initialized as $L_i = P_1(i - 1)$, and the multiplications are in the field $GF(2)[x]/p(x)$

In practice, P_1 and P_2 are replaced by a block cipher, $E\colon K \times \Sigma^n \to \Sigma^n$, with two independent keys: $k = (k_1, k_2) \in K \times K$, respectively. We use PMACX$[G, E]$ to denote the MAC scheme of which the key generation algorithm randomly chooses (k_1, k_2), and the authentication algorithm computes PMACX$[G, E_{k_1}, E_{k_2}]$ in the above.

5   Security Analysis

We now analyze the security of our new scheme. We prove that PMACX$[G, E]$ is a secure PRF with a security bound of the form $O(q^2/2^n + \rho^{d'-1}\sigma q/2^{d'n})$, where $d' = \lfloor (d+1)/2 \rfloor$:

Theorem 1. *Let $G = (g_{i,j})$ be an $m \times l$ MDS matrix over $GF(2^n)$, $2 \le l < m$, and $E : K \times \Sigma^n \to \Sigma^n$ be a block cipher. Let $d = m - l + 1$ be the Hamming distance of G. Then* PMACX$[G, E]$ *is a good PRF with the following bound:*

$$\mathsf{Adv}^{\mathrm{prf}}_{\mathsf{PMACX}[G,E]}(t, q, \rho, \sigma) \le \frac{m^2 + 3q^2}{2^{n+1}} + \frac{4q(2d\sigma + qm)(2d\rho + m)^{\lfloor (d-1)/2 \rfloor n}}{2^{\lfloor (d+1)/2 \rfloor n}} + 2\mathsf{Adv}^{\mathrm{prp}}_E(t', m+q+m\sigma_l) ,$$

where $m + 2\max\{d, m\}\rho_l \le 2^{n-1}$, $t' = t + O(m + q + m\sigma_l)$.

Remark. The upper bound on the message length in the hypothesis is a reasonable one in the practical scenario where long messages are authenticated.

Proof. We first replace the block cipher calls in PMACX$[G, E]$ with independently uniformly random permutation: P_1 and P_2, and next replace the uniformly random permutation, P_2, with a uniformly random function, F_2. These replacements cost us at most $2\mathsf{Adv}_E^{\mathrm{prp}}(t', m + m\sigma_l + q) + q^2/2^{n+1}$, where $t' = t + O(m + m\sigma_l + q)$. We remark that the whole analysis would be more tidy if we further replace the uniformly random permutation, P_1 as well with a uniformly random function. However, that replacement would incur a loss term of order $m^2\sigma_l^2/2^{n+1}$, which is too much a loss respective to the motivation of reducing the effect of message lengths.

Now consider the transformed algorithm, $\mathsf{PMACX}[G, P_1, F_2]$. We denote the inner procedure of generating the variable S in Algorithm 1 as $\mathsf{inner}[G, P_1, L^m]$, where $L^m = \{L_1, L_2, \cdots, L_m\}$.

Without loss of generality we assume the adversary A never repeats its queries. Consider the two games in Algorithm 2:

```
1  setup
2  |   for i = 1 to m do
3  |   |   L_i ←$ Σ^n;
4  |   |   if L_i ∈ Range(P_1) then
5  |   |   |   CollMask ← true;
6  |   |   |   L_i ←$ Range(P_1);
7  |   |   end
8  |   |   P_1(i − 1) ← L_i;
9  |   end
10 end
11 on the α-th query M^(α) do
12 |   S^(α) ← inner[G, P_1, L^m](M^(α));
13 |   T^(α) ←$ Σ^n;
14 |   if S^(β) = S^(α) for some β ∈ {1, 2, · · · , α − 1} then
15 |   |   if ¬CollS then
16 |   |   |   CollS ← true;
17 |   |   |   CollS^(β,α) ← true;
18 |   |   |   T^(α) ← T^(β);
19 |   |   end
20 |   end
21 |   P_2(S^(α)) ← T^(α);
22 |   return T^(α);
23 end
```

Algorithm 2. Game G_0(with the boxed statement) and Game G_1(without the boxed statement)

It is easy to see that for the two games shown in Algorithm 2, G_0 simulates the real $\mathsf{PMACX}[G, P_1, F_2]$ and G_1 simulates a random oracle that always returns a random n-bit string. Let CollMask, and CollS be the event that the adversary sets the corresponding flag interacting with G_1. We apply the well-known fundamental lemma of game playing [3]:

$$\begin{aligned}
\mathsf{Adv}^{\mathrm{prf}}_{\mathsf{PMACX}[G,P_1,F_2]}(A) &= \mathbf{Pr}[A^{G_0} \text{ outputs } 1] - \mathbf{Pr}[A^{G_1} \text{ outputs } 1] \\
&\leq \mathbf{Pr}_{G_1}[\mathsf{CollMask} \vee \mathsf{CollS}] \\
&\leq \mathbf{Pr}_{G_1}[\mathsf{CollMask}] + \mathbf{Pr}_{G_1}[\mathsf{CollS}] \\
&\leq \mathbf{Pr}_{G_1}[\mathsf{CollMask}] + \sum_{1 \leq \beta < \alpha \leq q} \left(\mathbf{Pr}[A^{G_1} \text{ sets } \mathsf{Coll}^{\beta,\alpha}] \right) .
\end{aligned}$$

It remains to bound the two different kinds of probability terms in the formula above.

We argue that we can without loss of generality assume that the adversary, A, is non-adaptive. This is because in the game G_1, A always gets back a random n-bit string that is independent from the setting of the two random flags. Hence by the technique of *coin fixing* [3], we could eliminate the interaction between the game oracle and the adversary, and let the adversary choose q distinct messages: $M^{(1)}, M^{(2)}, \cdots, M^{(q)}$ all at once at the very beginning of the game, with the intent of setting either of the two flags. Stated differently, the q distinct messages can be assumed to be fixed variables that are not random.

We first bound $\mathbf{Pr}[A^{G_1} \text{ sets } \mathsf{CollS}^{\beta,\alpha}]$. Note that in the game G_1, $L_1, \cdots, L_m$ are independently and uniformly distributed. This is the central part of the whole proof and its analysis is vital in yielding the desired bounding formula.

Lemma 1. *Let $G = (g_{i,j})$ be an $m \times l$ MDS matrix over $GF(2^n)$, $2 \leq l < m$. Let $d = m - l + 1$ be its Hamming distance. For two different messages whose bit lengths are both multiples of ln: M and M', such that $M \neq M', |M| \geq |M'|$, $2\max\{d, m\}|M|_n + m \leq 2^{n-1}$, if the padded messages of A's α-th and β-th queries are M and M', respectively, then*

$$\mathbf{Pr}[A^{G_1} \text{ sets } \mathsf{CollS}^{\beta,\alpha}] \leq 4 \left(\frac{2d|M|_n + m}{2^n} \right)^{\lfloor (d+1)/2 \rfloor} + \frac{2}{2^n} .$$

In the above, the probability is taken over the random choice of G_1.

Note that in the above lemma, the condition on the message length corresponds exactly to that of Theorem 1.

Proof. We let s and s' be the number of l-block intervals of M and M', respectively; let $X_i[j], X_i'[j], XE_i[j], XE_i'[j]$ be as defined according to Algorithm 1.

As $M \neq M'$, by the MDS property of G, $\exists 1 \leq h \leq s$, such that X_h and X_h' differ by at least d blocks. We take the convention that if $h > s'$, namely when X_h' is not defined, X_h and X_h' (undefined) differ by all m blocks. As $m \geq d$, X_h and X_h' always differ by at least d blocks. For the sake of simplicity, we assume that these d indices are $1, 2, \cdots, d$. (The whole following argument will still hold for other index sets by a simple renaming.)

The overall structure of the proof is like the following: We first define AllColl as the event that for all $1 \leq t \leq d$, $XE_h[t]$ collides with some other values in $\{XE_i[j]\}, 1 \leq i \leq s, 1 \leq j \leq m$ or $\{XE_i'[j]\}, 1 \leq i \leq s', 1 \leq j \leq m$, or $\{0, 1, \cdots, m-1\}$. Note that the trivial kind of collision such as $XE_h[j] = XE_h'[j]$ cannot happen since we defined h in such a way that XE_h and XE_h' must differ at all of the d indices. Our main target is to show that this "bad" event happens with a small probability, and unless it happens, there will be at least one fresh sampling of the permutation's image which can help bound the probability of interest within the order of $O(1/2^n)$. The conclusion of lemma would thus naturally follow.

Consider the following experiment: first compute $\{X_i[j]\}$ and $\{X_i'[j]\}$ from M and M'; next fix the masking subkeys: $L_{d+1}, \cdots, L_m$, and compute $\{XE_i[j]\}$, $\{XE_i'[j]\}$ for those $d+1 \leq j \leq m$. We use XE^c to denote these fixed permutation inputs: $XE^c := \{XE_i[j] \text{ or } XE_i'[j] : d+1 \leq j \leq m\}$. Because of the mutual independence among the m masking subkeys, the above fixing of a subset of them will not influence the distribution of the remaining ones. We now focus more on AllColl conditioned on this fixing and we will derive a general bound on it, independent of the concrete choice of fixing. The final bound will be the same one, justified by the conditional probability summation (For the sake of clarity, in the following analysis we do not explicitly include the conditional notation in our formula).

The event AllColl can be further divided into subevents of AllColl_f that are parameterized by a function, $f : \{1, 2, \cdots, d\} \to \{1, 2, \cdots, d, \text{const}\}$. Intuitively, f describes the "concrete behavior" of the d collisions: If $f(j) \neq \text{const}$, $XE_h[j]$ collides with some $XE_i^*[f(j)]$, where the superscript $*$ means either primed or unprimed, and i can be any interval index. On the other hand, if $f(j) = \text{const}$, then $XE_h[j]$ collides with some constant in $\{0, 1, \cdots, m-1\} \bigcup XE^c$. Next, we further divide the set of all functions, $F : \{1, 2, \cdots, d\} \to \{1, 2, \cdots, d, \text{const}\}$, into $d+1$ classes according to the number of "generalized fixed" points: the i-th class F_i ($0 \leq i \leq d$) consists of all functions f such that there are exactly i points in $\{1, 2, \cdots, d\}$ whose image under f equals to either itself or const. From the union bound, $\mathbf{Pr}[\text{AllColl}] \leq \sum_{0 \leq i \leq d} \mathbf{Pr}\left[\bigcup_{f \in F_i} \text{AllColl}_f\right]$. It remains to bound $\mathbf{Pr}\left[\bigcup_{f \in F_i} \text{AllColl}_f\right]$ for each class, F_i. We would use AllColl_i to denote $\bigcup_{f \in F_i} \text{AllColl}_f$.

Under the event AllColl_i, there are i many subkey indices of $j \in \{1, 2, \cdots, d\}, s.t. \ XE_h[j] = XE_t^*[j]$, for some interval index t; or $XE_h[j] = c$, for some c in $\{0, 1, \cdots, m-1\} \cup XE^c$. Since each such equation is a nontrivial equation about L_j (as there is no trivial collision with the same interval index), by the union bound and a simple counting, for each such j the collision takes place with probability at most $\frac{(s+s'-2)+m+(m-d)(s+s')}{2^n} \leq \frac{(m-d+1)(s+s')+m}{2^n} = \frac{l(s+s')+m}{2^n} \leq \frac{2|M|_n+m}{2^n}$. Furthermore, by the mutual independence among $\{L_i\}$, the probability that these i indices collide is at most $\left(\frac{2|M|_n+m}{2^n}\right)^i$.

For the remaining $d-i$ subkey indices, they are mapped under f to a different index, either a larger one or a smaller one. If we further partition these as two different classes, there will be at least $\lceil (d-i)/2 \rceil$ remaining indices such that they are all mapped to some indices larger (or smaller) than them. Assume they are mapped to larger indices (the smaller case would follow exactly the same argument). It can be easily seen that if we fix $\lceil (d-i)/2 \rceil$ many such indices, the joint event of their collisions can be described by a matrix equation: $AL = X$, where A is a matrix of $\lceil (d-i)/2 \rceil$ rows, whose entries are either 0 or 2^k for some nonnegative k (corresponds to the interval index), and each row of which has exactly two nonzero entries; L is the vector of the corresponding masking keys; and X is a constant vector that only depends on M and M'. The key observation is that the matrix A is always in the row-echelon form, since by the choice of these indices there will never be an (i, j)-th nonzero entry in A where $i > j$ (that will imply some index collides with another index smaller than it). Stated differently, if A is an $(a \times b)$-matrix, then for each arbitrary choice of the values of the $a+1$-th, $a+2$-th, $\cdots$, b-th entries in the vector L, there corresponds a unique choice of values of the 1st, 2nd, $\cdots$, a-th entries that satisfies the equation. Hence, again by the union bound and a simple counting [1], the probability of this joint collision is at most $[d(s+s')]^{\lceil (d-i)/2 \rceil} \cdot (1/2^n)^{\lceil (d-i)/2 \rceil} \leq \left(\frac{2d|M|_{nl}}{2^n} \right)^{\lceil (d-i)/2 \rceil}$.

As a conclusion, so far the upper bound for $\mathsf{AllColl}_i$ is at most $\left(\frac{2|M|_n + m}{2^n} \right)^i \cdot \left(\frac{2d|M|_{nl}}{2^n} \right)^{\lceil (d-i)/2 \rceil} \leq \left(\frac{2d|M|_n + m}{2^n} \right)^{i + \lceil (d-i)/2 \rceil}$. Substitute these back:

$$\mathbf{Pr}_{[\mathsf{AllColl}]} \leq \sum_{i=0}^{d} \mathbf{Pr}_{[\mathsf{AllColl}_i]}$$

$$\leq \sum_{i=0}^{d} \left(\frac{2d\,|M|_n + m}{2^n} \right)^{i + \lceil (d-i)/2 \rceil}$$

$$\leq \begin{cases} \left(\frac{2d|M|_n + m}{2^n} \right)^{d/2} + 2\left(\frac{2d|M|_n + m}{2^n} \right)^{d/2+1} + \cdots + 2\left(\frac{2d|M|_n + m}{2^n} \right)^{d} & \text{, if d is even;} \\ 2\left(\frac{2d|M|_n + m}{2^n} \right)^{d/2+1/2} + \cdots + 2\left(\frac{2d|M|_n + m}{2^n} \right)^{d} & \text{, if d is odd.} \end{cases}$$

$$\leq \begin{cases} 3\left(\frac{2d|M|_n + m}{2^n} \right)^{d/2} & \text{, if d is even;} \\ 4\left(\frac{2d|M|_n + m}{2^n} \right)^{(d+1)/2} & \text{, if d is odd.} \end{cases}$$

$$\leq 4\left(\frac{2d\,|M|_n + m}{2^n} \right)^{\lfloor (d+1)/2 \rfloor}.$$

In the above, the last by one inequality utilizes the condition: $2d\,|M|_n + m \leq 2^{n-1}$ (implied by the condition: $2\mathsf{max}\{d, m\}\,|M|_n + m \leq 2^{n-1}$). The inequality derivation is routine and hence omitted.

Finally, if $\mathsf{AllColl}$ does not occur, conditioned on $\overline{\mathsf{AllColl}}$, there will be at least one fresh input for P, and so the probability of $\mathbf{Pr}[A^{G_1} \text{ sets } \mathsf{Coll}^{\beta,\alpha}]$ is at most $1/(2^n - m - \frac{2m|M|_n}{l}) \leq 2/(2^n)$, since $m + \frac{2m|M|_n}{l} \leq m + 2\mathsf{max}\{d, m\}\,|M|_n \leq 2^{n-1}$. The lemma thus follows by the bounding formula: $\mathbf{Pr}[\mathsf{AllColl}] + \mathbf{Pr}[A^{G_1} \text{ sets } \mathsf{Coll}^{\beta,\alpha} | \overline{\mathsf{AllColl}}]$.

$\square$

---

[1] The index of each row can collide with at most d many indexes in any interval, and there are in total $(s+s')$ intervals. Hence, there are at most $[d(s+s')]^{\lceil (d-i)/2 \rceil}$ many possible such matrix equations.

It remains to bound $\mathbf{Pr}[\mathsf{CollMask}]$, which is simple:

$$\mathbf{Pr}[\mathsf{CollMask}] \leq \frac{m^2}{2^{n+1}} \, .$$

The whole proof is complete by substituting the above and the result of Lemma 1 back. We assume that the q queries are sorted in the order of increasing message length. As the summation is over all 2-tuples of the queries, this reordering of the queries will not change the result.

$$\mathsf{Adv}^{\mathrm{prf}}_{\mathsf{PMACX}[G,E]}(t,q,\rho,\sigma) \leq \mathsf{Adv}^{\mathrm{prf}}_{\mathsf{PMACX}[G,P_1,F_2]}(t,q,\rho,\sigma) + 2\mathsf{Adv}^{\mathrm{prp}}_E(t',m+q+m\sigma_l) + \frac{q^2}{2^{n+1}}$$

$$\leq \mathbf{Pr}[\mathsf{CollMask}] + \sum_{1\leq\beta<q}\sum_{\beta<\alpha\leq q} \left(\mathbf{Pr}[A^{G_1} \text{ sets } \mathsf{Coll}^{\beta,\alpha}] \right)$$

$$+ 2\mathsf{Adv}^{\mathrm{prp}}_E(t',m+q+m\sigma_l) + \frac{q^2}{2^{n+1}}$$

$$\leq \frac{m^2}{2^{n+1}} + \frac{q^2}{2} \cdot \frac{2}{2^n} + q\left(\sum_{1\leq\alpha\leq q} 4 \cdot \left(\frac{2d\left|M^{(\alpha)}\right|_n + m}{2^n} \right)^{\left\lfloor \frac{d+1}{2} \right\rfloor} \right)$$

$$+ 2\mathsf{Adv}^{\mathrm{prp}}_E(t',m+q+m\sigma_l) + \frac{q^2}{2^{n+1}}$$

$$\leq \frac{m^2 + 3q^2}{2^{n+1}} + \frac{4q(2d\sigma + qm)(2d\rho+m)^{\lfloor(d-1)/2\rfloor n}}{2^{\lfloor(d+1)/2\rfloor n}}$$

$$+ 2\mathsf{Adv}^{\mathrm{prp}}_E(t',m+q+m\sigma_l) \, .$$

$\square$

6   Concrete Examples and Implementation Results

6.1   On the Choice of the Parameters

We make some general comments on the choice of the matrix parameters. Neglecting the overhead of MDS matrix multiplication, the scheme's efficiency is reflected by the ratio of the MDS matrix's column number and row number. On the other hand, the security level, more specifically, the exponent that appears in the second term in Theorem 1 is in positive relation to $d = m - l + 1$, the difference between the row number and column number (plus 1). The efficiency and the security level, therefore, forms a trade-off that can be controlled by choosing appropriate dimensions for the MDS matrix.

One another remark is that compared to PMAC-with-Parity and its generalizations, our scheme only uses 2 keys and this number of keys is independent from our choice of matrix. We regard this key reduction as the most outstanding superior aspect compared to the prior work. Stated in a qualitative way, our result shows that the many independent permutations are in fact "unnecessary", and can be reduced to the same permutation, except for the last finalization one.

One drawback of this key reduction, however, is that the security level would degrade from $O(q^2/2^n + q\sigma\rho^{d-1}/2^{dn})$ to $O(q^2/2^n + q\sigma\rho^{\lfloor(d-1)/2\rfloor}/2^{\lfloor(d+1)/2\rfloor n})$. [2]

6.2   Implementation Result

In this section we show a comparative implementation result. In our experiment, we measure the performance, in terms of bytes per cycle, of PMACX and PMAC-with-Parity. Our target is to beat PMAC-with-Parity in various aspects, including key space, security, efficiency, etc.. From the above, PMACX already achieves the goal of key space reduction by its fixed number of keys, and the efficiency can be improved by choosing an MDS matrix with row-column ratio close to 1. On the other hand, we would like to maintain the same asymptotic security level, and by Theorem 1, it is easy to see that the minimum required distance of MDS code is $d = 3$, which implies our matrix's row number should be two more than its column number. From an implementation perspective, the simplest ones among such matrices have the form: $G = [I|A]^T$, where I is the $l \times l$ identity matrix and A is the $l \times 2$ redundancy part. It turns out that for G of this form, the MDS property is equivalent to the following condition: every element in A must be nonzero, and every two row vectors of A must be linearly independent.

Based on the above argument, we experiment on MDS matrices of the following sizes: 6×4, 7×5, 8×6, and 14×12. In the experiment, we implement both PMACX and PMAC-with-Parity on a Haswell-family Intel i7 processor, with enough explicit source-level parallelism to fully utilize the AES hardware pipelining. We remark that our implementation of the two modes are not aimed at providing the best performance, but at providing practical comparative results on the two modes. Theoretically speaking, a 6×4 MDS matrix should be enough to achieve the same 2/3-rate as the prior work. However, our implementation result indicates that the overhead of the MDS matrix multiplication cannot be completely overlooked, hence larger matrices are necessary to achieve better rates. See Table 1 for our experimental result (For the sake of completeness, we include the two redundacy rows of each matrix.).

We could see from the last row that the expected outcome is achievable in practice. Indeed, better rates are possible by choosing large enough matrices. The other entries in Table 1, however, exhibit some peculiar behaviors: First, The 7×5-matrix overperforms sharply compared to others. We conjecture that the reason lies in the fact that the aes-encrypt instruction for Haswell-family takes exactly seven cycles. Since our implementation does the block encryption in parallel within each output vector of the MDS matrix multiplication, the very size of a 7-entry output vector shall take the best advantage of the underlying AES hardware's pipelining, and thus achieves a sharp outperformance. Second, contrary to the theoretical rate, the actual processing rate does not increase too much with the size of matrix when the matrix is small (In fact, our result shows

---

[2]   We omit the analysis for the case of independent keys. We remark that it is almost a direct generalization of the same analysis for PMAC-with-Parity [21].

that the larger 8×6 matrix is even more slowly than its smaller 6×4 counterpart). This is because the larger matrix's multiplication takes more time to compute (per byte), counteracting the effect of reducing the average number of block cipher calls. We hence come to the conclusion: when the matrix is relatively small, the MDS matrix multiplication overhead counteracts the improvement of theoretical rate, and that counteraction can be mitigated by choosing large enough matrices (say, a 14×12 one).

Table 1. Comparison of PMAC-with-Parity and PMACX with different matrix dimensions

Mode Name	Rate(Cycle/Byte)	First Redundacy Row	Second Redundacy Row
PMAC-with-Parity	1.77	N/A	N/A
PMACX-6×4	2.04	(1, 1, 1, 2)	(1, 2, 3, 1)
PMACX-7×5	1.75	(1, 1, 1, 2, 2)	(1, 2, 3, 1, 3)
PMACX-8×6	2.10	(1, 1, 1, 2, 2, 3)	(1, 2, 3, 1, 3, 1)
PMACX-14×12	1.60	(1, 1, 1, 1, 2, 2, 2, 3, 3, 3, 5, 5)	(1, 2, 3, 5, 1, 3, 5, 1, 2, 5, 1, 2)

7   Conclusion

We design a new variant of PMAC, PMACX, based on the idea of MDS from coding theory. Our analysis makes it clear that the nice property of MDS: maximizing the number of different output blocks for arbitrarily different inputs can help reduce the impact of message length, and this reduction is in positive relation to the maximum distance of the chosen MDS matrix. Specifically, by choosing MDS matrices with large enough maximum distance, the security level can be made arbitrarily close to 2^n-level for the message length. As a whole, the security level with respect to message length, and the efficiency of the scheme forms a natural trade-off of the design.

Our scheme can also be viewed as a generalization of PMAC-with-Parity, which, by our terminology, is exactly an independently keyed version of PMACX with a (2,3,2)-MDS matrix. We point out that when instantiated with the same MDS matrix, our scheme's security level is worse than PMAC-with-Parity: its security bound is $O(q^2/2^n+q\sigma/2^n)$, while the latter achieves $O(q^2/2^n+q\sigma\rho/2^{2n})$. On the other hand, our scheme reduces the number of keys from 4 to 2, and our analysis illustrates that the 2 keys are enough for any MDS matrix. We regard this reduction of key space size and its fixedness with respect to other parameters another superior property compared to the previous work (In particular, more keys are needed for the generalizations of PMAC-with-Parity in order to reach a higher rate).

We leave it an open question whether it is possible to further reduce the key number from 2 to 1, without making major changes to the scheme's design and the security level.

Acknowledgements. The author would like to thank Dr. Tatsuaki Okamoto for providing the author a summer internship opportunity in Nippon Telegraph and Telephone (NTT), Japan. This internship formed the basis of this work. The author would also like to thank Kan Yasuda, Kazumaro Aoki and Yousuke Toudou for their valuable discussions with the author and kind help in the implementation of the algorithm. At last, the author appreciates the feedback and comments from the CT-RSA 2015 PC reviewers and his advisor, Dr. Phillip Rogaway.

References

1. Bellare, M., Kilian, J., Rogaway, P.: The security of cipher block chaining. In: Desmedt, Y.G. (ed.) CRYPTO 1994. LNCS, vol. 839, pp. 341–358. Springer, Heidelberg (1994)
2. Bellare, M., Pietrzak, K., Rogaway, P.: Improved security analyses for CBC MACs. In: Shoup, V. (ed.) CRYPTO 2005. LNCS, vol. 3621, pp. 527–545. Springer, Heidelberg (2005)
3. Bellare, M., Rogaway, P.: Code-Based Game-Playing Proofs and the Security of Triple Encryption. IACR Cryptology ePrint Archive **2004**, 331 (2004)
4. Black, J.A., Rogaway, P.: CBC MACs for arbitrary-length messages:the three-key constructions. In: Bellare, M. (ed.) CRYPTO 2000. LNCS, vol. 1880, p. 197. Springer, Heidelberg (2000)
5. Black, J.A., Rogaway, P.: A block-cipher mode of operation for parallelizable message authentication. In: Knudsen, L.R. (ed.) EUROCRYPT 2002. LNCS, vol. 2332, p. 384. Springer, Heidelberg (2002)
6. Daemen, J., Rijmen V.: The design of Rijndael: AES-the advanced encryption standard. Springer (2002)
7. Iwata, T.: New blockcipher modes of operation with beyond the birthday bound security. In: Robshaw, M. (ed.) FSE 2006. LNCS, vol. 4047, pp. 310–327. Springer, Heidelberg (2006)
8. Iwata, T.: Authenticated encryption mode for beyond the birthday bound security. In: Vaudenay, S. (ed.) AFRICACRYPT 2008. LNCS, vol. 5023, pp. 125–142. Springer, Heidelberg (2008)
9. Iwata, T., Kurosawa, K.: OMAC: one-key CBC MAC. In: Johansson, T. (ed.) FSE 2003. LNCS, vol. 2887, pp. 129–153. Springer, Heidelberg (2003)
10. Jaulmes, É., Joux, A., Valette, F.: On the security of randomized CBC-MAC beyond the birthday paradox limit: a new construction. In: Daemen, J., Rijmen, V. (eds.) FSE 2002. LNCS, vol. 2365, pp. 237–251. Springer, Heidelberg (2002)
11. Kurosawa, K., Iwata, T.: TMAC: two-key CBC MAC. In: Joye, M. (ed.) CT-RSA 2003. LNCS, vol. 2612, pp. 33–49. Springer, Heidelberg (2003)
12. Landecker, W., Shrimpton, T., Terashima, R.S.: Tweakable blockciphers with beyond birthday-bound security. In: Safavi-Naini, R., Canetti, R. (eds.) CRYPTO 2012. LNCS, vol. 7417, pp. 14–30. Springer, Heidelberg (2012)
13. Lefranc, D., Painchault, P., Rouat, V., Mayer, E.: A generic method to design modes of operation beyond the birthday bound. In: Adams, C., Miri, A., Wiener, M. (eds.) SAC 2007. LNCS, vol. 4876, pp. 328–343. Springer, Heidelberg (2007)
14. Minematsu, K.: Beyond-Birthday-Bound Security Based on Tweakable Block Cipher. In: Dunkelman, O. (ed.) FSE 2009. LNCS, vol. 5665, pp. 308–326. Springer, Heidelberg (2009)

15. Minematsu, K., Matsushima, T.: New bounds for PMAC, TMAC, and XCBC. In: Biryukov, A. (ed.) FSE 2007. LNCS, vol. 4593, pp. 434–451. Springer, Heidelberg (2007)
16. Preneel, B., Van Oorschot, P.C.: MDx-MAC and building fast MACs from hash functions. In: Advances in Cryptology-CRYPT095, pp. 1–14. Springer (1995)
17. Rogaway, P.: Efficient instantiations of tweakable blockciphers and refinements to modes OCB and PMAC. In: Lee, P.J. (ed.) ASIACRYPT 2004. LNCS, vol. 3329, pp. 16–31. Springer, Heidelberg (2004)
18. Yasuda, K.: Multilane HMAC— security beyond the birthday limit. In: Srinathan, K., Rangan, C.P., Yung, M. (eds.) INDOCRYPT 2007. LNCS, vol. 4859, pp. 18–32. Springer, Heidelberg (2007)
19. Yasuda, K.: A one-pass mode of operation for deterministic message authentication— security beyond the birthday barrier. In: Nyberg, K. (ed.) FSE 2008. LNCS, vol. 5086, pp. 316–333. Springer, Heidelberg (2008)
20. Yasuda, K.: A new variant of PMAC: beyond the birthday bound. In: Rogaway, P. (ed.) CRYPTO 2011. LNCS, vol. 6841, pp. 596–609. Springer, Heidelberg (2011)
21. Yasuda, K.: PMAC with parity: minimizing the query-length influence. In: Dunkelman, O. (ed.) CT-RSA 2012. LNCS, vol. 7178, pp. 203–214. Springer, Heidelberg (2012)
22. Yasuda, K.: A parallelizable PRF-based MAC algorithm: Well beyond the birthday bound. IEICE TRANSACTIONS on Fundamentals of Electronics, Communications and Computer Sciences 96(1), 237–241 (2013)

Secure Multiparty Computation

Efficient Leakage Resilient Circuit Compilers

Marcin Andrychowicz[3], Ivan Damgård[1], Stefan Dziembowski[3],
Sebastian Faust[2], and Antigoni Polychroniadou[1]([✉])

[1] Aarhus University, Aarhus, Denmark
{ivan,antigoni}@cs.au.dk
[2] EPFL, Lausanne, Switzerland
sebastian.faust@gmail.com
[3] Warsaw University, Warsaw, Poland
{marcin.andrychowicz,stefan.dziembowski}@crypto.edu.pl

Abstract. In this paper, we revisit the problem of constructing general leakage resilient compilers that can transform any (Boolean) circuit C into a protected circuit C' computing the same functionality as C, which additionally is resilient to certain classes of leakage functions. An important problem that has been neglected in most works on leakage resilient circuits is to minimize the overhead induced by the compiler. In particular, in earlier works for a circuit C of size s, the transformed circuit C' has size at least $\mathcal{O}(sk^2)$, where k is the security parameter. In this work, using techniques from secure Multi-Party Computation, we show that in important leakage models such as bounded independent leakage and leakage from weak complexity classes the size of the transformed circuit can be reduced to $\mathcal{O}(sk)$.

Keywords: Leakage resilience · Multi-party computation · Split-state model · AC^0 · Side channel attacks

1 Introduction

Side channel attacks (SCA) that exploit leakage emitting from a device are among the most severe threats for cryptographic implementations. Since the introduction of timing attacks to the research community in the late 1990s [22],

This is an extended abstract. Further details can be found in the full version.

M. Andrychowicz and S. Dziembowski — Supported by the WELCOME/2010-4/2 grant founded within the framework of the EU Innovative Economy (National Cohesion Strategy) Operational Programme.

S. Faust — Received funding from the Marie Curie IEF/FP7 project GAPS, grant number: 626467.

I. Damgård and A. Polychroniadou — Research supported by the Danish National Research Foundation and the National Science Foundation of China (under the grant 61061130540) for the Sino-Danish Center for the Theory of Interactive Computation and from the Center for Research in Foundations of Electronic Markets (CFEM), supported by the Danish Strategic Research Council.

© Springer International Publishing Switzerland 2015
K. Nyberg (ed.): CT-RSA 2015, LNCS 9048, pp. 311–329, 2015.
DOI: 10.1007/978-3-319-16715-2_17

more sources of side channel leakage have been discovered [14,15,23,28]. To protect cryptographic implementations against these attacks various types of countermeasures have been proposed. One important and particular effective countermeasure already suggested in the early works of Kocher [22] is masking. In a masking scheme the sensitive intermediate data that occurs during the computation of the cryptographic device is encoded with a randomized encoding thereby making leakage of the intermediate values independent of the sensitive values.

The effectiveness of masking as a countermeasure has first been formally studied in the work of Chari *et al.* [3]. While [3] only considered a single masked secret, the concept of *leakage resilient circuit compilers* – pioneered by Ishai *et al.* [19] – studies security guarantees for complicated masked circuits, e.g., a masked AES circuitry. More specifically, a circuit compiler takes as input an arbitrary circuit C computing over some finite field and outputs a protected circuit $\hat{C}$ that has the same functionality as C but comes with built-in security against certain classes of leakages. It is then shown that even given the leakage from the computation of the transformed circuit $\hat{C}$ the adversary learns nothing beyond black-box access. Ishai *et al.* [19] consider an adversary that can learn up to t intermediate values that appear during the computation – so-called t-probing adversaries. A large body of recent work has been conducted on extending the leakage classes beyond t-probing adversaries. This has led to great progress and by now we have developed feasibility results in surprisingly strong leakage models (we review the related work in Section 1.1). Since naturally in feasibility results efficiency plays a secondary role, only little progress has been made in improving the efficiency of circuit compilers.

In this work, we make a step towards closing this gap and propose new leakage resilient circuit compilers for broad classes of leakages that come with significantly improved efficiency. Based on techniques from multiparty computation and new techniques for inner-product based transformations, we propose compilers with provable security for global and computationally weak leakages as introduced in the work of Faust *et al.* [12] and for polynomial-time computable leakages in the split-state model [11,24]. As in earlier works and the ones we improve upon [10,12,16,26], we assume that certain simple parts of the computation are leak-free.

1.1   Previous Works

As already mentioned the circuit compiler of Ishai *et al.* [19] considers an adversary that can learn up to t intermediate values of the computation. Various works [2,8,26,27,27,29] consider extensions of the probing model by either proposing more efficient constructions or developing more practice-oriented models. We notice that for a circuit of size s all the above works result into circuits of size $\mathcal{O}(sk^2)$, where s is the size of the original circuit. In [19] Ishai *et al.* also propose an alternative circuit compiler that asymptotically requires only $\tilde{O}(k)$ blow-up, however, in contrast to the other works mentioned above it only achieves statistical security against non-adaptively chosen probing attacks.

We next review some broader classes of leakage functions that go beyond the probing attacks and will be the main focus of this work.

Computationally Weak Leakages. A severe restriction of the probing model is the fact that the leakage is oblivious to large parts of the circuitry. Faust *et al.* [12] eliminate this restriction by considering *global* leakage functions, i.e., the leakage can depend on all the values that are carried on wires during the computation, but the leakage function is assumed to be computationally bounded (i.e., it cannot evaluate certain decoding functions). One concrete example given by the authors is when the shares are k random bits and the decoding function is the parity. For this setting, [12] shows security with respect to arbitrary global AC^0 leakages. The results for the AC^0 setting were recently improved in [25, 30]. Similar to the probing case the size of the transformed circuit increases *at least* by a factor $\mathcal{O}(k^2)$ where k is the security parameter.

Circuit Compilers in the Split State Model. The most prominent leakage model of leakage resilient cryptography is the so-called bounded leakage model [11]. In the bounded leakage model the adversary can pick a leakage function $f : \{0,1\}^n \rightarrow \{0,1\}^\lambda$ and obtains $f(state)$, where f is efficiently computable and $\lambda \ll n$. The first work that builds circuits resistant to bounded leakages are the works of Juma and Vahlis [21], and Goldwasser and Rothblum [16]. They consider a model where the algorithm is executed by multiple "processors" that leak independently – so-called split-state leakage. The works of [16, 21] use homomorphic encryption and hence rely on computational assumptions. The use of computational assumptions has been eliminated in two recent works [1, 10, 17] using techniques from the randomness extractor and require an overhead of at least $O(k^2)$.

1.2   Our Contribution

Our main contribution is to show how to construct leakage resilient circuit compilers that asymptotically increase the size of the circuit only by a factor of $\tilde{O}(k)$. We give an overview of our main results below.

Efficient Compilers Against Computationally Weak Leakage. An important building-block of leakage resilient circuit compilers are leakage resilient encoding schemes. Our main observation to improve the efficiency of previous compilers for the setting of computationally weak leakages is to use a linear packed secret sharing scheme to encode the computation. In contrast to the standard Shamir secret sharing where for a random polynomial $p(\cdot)$ of degree t we hide the secret at $p(0)$ while $p(1), \ldots, p(t)$ are viewed as shares of $p(0)$, we use some of the points on the polynomial to hide additional secrets. Notice that this technique has also been used in a series of works starting with Franklin and Yung [13] to improve the asymptotic efficiency of information theoretically secure multi-party computation. In particular, our circuit transformation is heavily inspired by the work of Damgård *et al.* [5], and applies two sequentially executed transformations, namely, TR_1 and TR_2 to produce the protected circuit.

The first transformation TR_1 takes as input the circuit C and produces $C' \leftarrow \mathsf{TR}_1(C)$. Its sole use is to make the circuit ready to be encoded with packed secret sharing, and it does not contribute to the actual security. The second transformation $\widehat{C} \leftarrow \mathsf{TR}_2(C')$ takes as input the so prepared C' and protects it by applying packed secret sharing. The transformation uses the same type of gates as in C', and as in several earlier works [10,12,26] a number of leakage-free gates. We notice that the leak-free components that we use enjoy the same properties as the leak-free components used in earlier works [10,12,26]: they are small (linear in the security parameter), stateless and do not take any inputs. Note that we require two different types of leak-free gates.

We show that the compiler is secure against computationally bounded leakages – so-called AC^0 leakages. To this end, we use the framework introduced by Faust et al. [12] to argue about computationally bounded leakages. As a first step, we show that the above encoding based on packed secret sharing is hard to "break" for AC^0 leakages. This requires that the underlying field is of constant size (independent of the security parameter). We use a recent result of Cramer et al. [4] which presents a linear secret sharing scheme that works for constant field size. As a next step, we prove that all our transformed gadgets in $\widehat{C}$ are reconstructible by constant depth circuits, which by applying the composition lemma of [12] can be extended to composed circuits made from the transformed gadgets. The final transformed circuit has size $\mathcal{O}(s \log(s)k)$.

We also show that the above construction is secure in the probing model of Ishai et al. [19]. When we allow t probes per transformed gadget then our security proof relies on the fact that certain parts of the computation are leak-free. If we aim for security of $\mathcal{O}(s \cdot \mathsf{polylog}(t)/n^2)$ probes in the entire circuit, then we eliminate the leak-free assumption for the stateless circuit case. The transformed circuit we obtain has size $\mathcal{O}(s\log(s) \cdot \mathsf{polylog}(k))$. Further details are provided in the full version of this extended abstract. We note that a similar construction using packed-secret sharing has been recently considered in [18].

Efficient Compilers for the Split-State Setting. A second contribution is an efficient compiler for the split-state bounded leakage model. We show that the complexity of the compiler of Dziembowski and Faust [10] can be reduced to $\mathcal{O}(k \log k \log \log k)$, where k is the security parameter. This improves earlier works by at least a *quadratic factor* in the security parameter. We achieve this goal by improving the refreshing scheme of [10] which save a linear factor in complexity compared to earlier work. While this would give us only complexity of $\mathcal{O}(k^2)$, we use the fact that the underlying encoding scheme is secure even if the encoding uses only a small constant number of shares, while we increase the size of the underlying field to sub-exponential size. As multiplication in such fields can be done in complexity $\mathcal{O}(k \log k \log \log k)$, we obtain our result.

1.3 Notation

Across the paper, we use a capital letter C to label a circuit. A circuit C carries values from a finite field $\mathbb{F}$ on its wires and is composed of addition and multiplication gates which compute sums and products in $\mathbb{F}$. The size of C is defined as the number of gates in C and denoted by s. We write $C(x, k)$ for a result of evaluating C on a given input x and the security parameter k. A vector $\mathbf{x}$ is a row vector, and we denote by $\mathbf{x}^\mathsf{T}$ its transposition. We let $\mathbb{F}$ be a finite field and for $m, n \in \mathbb{N}$, let $\mathbb{F}^{m \times n}$ denote the set of $m \times n$-matrices over $\mathbb{F}$. For a matrix $M \in \mathbb{F}^{m \times n}$ and an m bit vector $\mathbf{x} \in \mathbb{F}^m$ we denote by $\mathbf{x} \cdot M$ the n-element vector that results from the matrix vector multiplication of $\mathbf{x}$ and M. For a natural number n let $(0)^n = (0, \ldots, 0)$. We use $\mathbf{x}[i]$ to denote the ith element of a vector $\mathbf{x}$ and $\mathbf{x}[i, \ldots, j]$ to denote the elements $i, i+1, \ldots, j$ of $\mathbf{x}$. In addition, let $[\mathbf{x}]$ denote an encoding which secret shares a block $\mathbf{x}$ of ℓ elements and write the k shares as $[\mathbf{x}] = (x_1, \ldots, x_k)$ where k is the security parameter. Let $[\mathbf{x}]_c$ denote an encoded block secret shared under a linear code c specified by a generator matrix G. A secret sharing scheme is homomorphic if $[\mathbf{x}] + [\mathbf{y}]$ and $[\mathbf{x}][\mathbf{y}]$ are shares of the blocks $\mathbf{x} + \mathbf{y}$ and $\mathbf{xy}$. Moreover, let $\pi(\mathbf{x})$ be a random permutation of the vector $\mathbf{x}$. For two random variables X_0, X_1 over $\mathcal{X}$ we define the statistical distance between X_0 and X_1 as $\Delta(X_0; X_1) = \sum_{x \in \mathcal{X}} 1/2 |\Pr[X_0 = x] - \Pr[X_1 = x]|$.

2   Defining a Circuit Transformation

We consider circuits C with secret state m that operate over some finite field $\mathbb{F}$, take some public input x and produce an output y. We assume that C consists of two types of elementary gates. First, addition and multiplication gates that both input two field elements and compute the corresponding operation in $\mathbb{F}$. Second, the so-called copy-gates that take as input a field element and output two copies of it to handle fan-out of the circuit. One may think of C as an implementation of a block cipher where the state is the key and the public input the plaintext.

A circuit transformation TR compiles any circuit C and the associated initial secret state m_0 into a functionally equivalent circuit $\widehat{C}$ and transformed secret state $\hat{m}_0$ that is resistant to certain leakage attacks characterized by a family of functions $\mathcal{L}$. To model the leakage from $\widehat{C}$ we introduce a leakage game that is executed by an adversary $\mathcal{A}$. In the leakage game, the adversary can submit tuples of the form (x_i, f_i) where x_i denotes an input to the circuit and $f_i \in \mathcal{L}$ is a leakage function. For each query, $\mathcal{A}$ receives the output y_i when using current state m_{i-1} and the corresponding leakage. The exact definition of the leakage depends on the leakage model and will be specified later in this paper. We denote by $\left(\mathcal{A}_\mathcal{L} \rightleftarrows \widehat{C}[\hat{m}_0] \right)$ the output of $\mathcal{A}$ after interacting with the transformed circuit $\widehat{C}$ with initial state $\hat{m}_0$. Moreover, we consider a simulated world where a simulator $\mathcal{S}$ only obtains black-box access to $C[m_0]$, which we denote by $(\mathcal{S} \rightleftarrows C[m_0])$. Security of a circuit transformation guarantees that the output of the adversary in the leakage game is indistinguishable from the output of the simulator in the ideal world. We define the notion of an $\mathcal{L}$-secure circuit transformation below.

Definition 1. *A circuit transformation* TR *is secure with respect to leakages from a family of functions* $\mathcal{L}$ *if the following two properties hold:*

1. Soundness: *For any circuit* C *and any initial state* m_0 *and any input* x_i *we have* $C[m_{i-1}](x_i) = \widehat{C}[\hat{m}_{i-1}](x_i)$.

2. Security: *For any PPT adversary $\mathcal{A}_{\mathcal{L}}$ and any circuit C with initial state m_0, there exists a simulator $\mathcal{S}$ such that for all circuits C with initial state m_0 the following holds:* $\Delta\left((\mathcal{S} \rightleftarrows C[m_0]) ; (\mathcal{A}_{\mathcal{L}} \rightleftarrows \widehat{C}[\hat{m}_0])\right) \leq \mathsf{negl}(k)$.

The transformed circuit $\widehat{C}$ shall use the same types of operations as the underlying circuit C, i.e., if C operates over the binary field, then the elementary operations used in $\widehat{C}$ are Boolean operations. Moreover, for some of our security proofs, we will require so-called *opaque gates*. Similarly, to earlier works [10, 12, 16, 21] on leakage-resilient circuit compilers our leak-free gates do not leak from their internals, but can leak on their outputs. All our leak-free gates do not take any inputs, but merely sample from some efficiently sampable distribution. We will later in this section precisely characterize what operation is carried out by our leak-free gates.

All leakage-resilient circuit transformations follow the same paradigm to transform C into a protected circuit $\widehat{C}$. First, they use a leakage resilient encoding scheme $\Pi = (\mathsf{Enc}, \mathsf{Dec})$ to encode the values carried on the wires of C. More precisely, each wire w in C is represented in $\widehat{C}$ by a wire-bundle carrying the encoding $\mathsf{Enc}(w)$. Notice that also the content of the memory that, e.g., stores the secret key is stored in encoded form in $\widehat{C}$. Clearly, to show that the transformed circuit $\widehat{C}$ is secure against leakage functions from $\mathcal{L}$ our encoding scheme has to be resilient for functions from $\mathcal{L}$.

The next (and more challenging) step is to develop a transformation for the elementary operations of C. For instance, if C is a Boolean circuit, then we need to give secure implementations for NAND gates. Following earlier works, we call these transformed elementary operations *gadgets*. A gadget takes as input encodings and outputs the encoded result, e.g., if the gadget implements a multiplication of two encodings $\mathsf{Enc}(a)$ and $\mathsf{Enc}(b)$, then its output is $\mathsf{Enc}(a \cdot b)$. The difficulty is to design the gadgets in such a way that they guarantee *correctness*, i.e., the output encodes the correct result, while at the same time leakage from the internals of the operations do not reveal any information about the encoded secrets. To this end, we need to ensure that our gadgets operate on encodings, by exploiting some homomorphic property of the underlying encoding scheme. Finally, since our gadgets in the transformed circuit $\widehat{C}$ work on encoded values, we need two additional types of gates: an encoder gate that takes as input a field element x and outputs $\mathsf{Enc}(x)$, and a decoding gadget that takes as input $\mathsf{Enc}(x)$ and returns x. These gates may leak but as shown in earlier works they do not influence the security of transformed circuit and will be ignored for the remainder of this extended abstract.

The above approach of transforming circuits is called a *gate-by-gate transformation*, which allows us to explain circuit transformations in a modular way. That is, given some leakage resilient encoding, we present basic transformations of the gates used in the original circuit C, which by composing these transformed gates results in the transformed circuit $\widehat{C}$. For both of our schemes, we consider circuits C that compute over some finite field $\mathbb{F}$ and assume that the original circuit has multiplication and addition gates that carry out the corresponding operations in the field $\mathbb{F}$.

3   Transformation for Computationally Weak Leakages

Our first transformation achieves security against a family of leakage functions $\mathcal{L}$ that are computable by polynomial-size constant depth circuits (so-called AC^0 circuits). First, we start by defining our general encoding scheme $\Pi_{LPSS} = (\mathsf{Enc}_{LPSS}, \mathsf{Dec}_{LPSS})$, which is an important tool for the transformation. We continue presenting the circuit transformation consisting of the transformations TR^1_{weak} and TR^2_{weak}, where $\mathsf{TR}_{weak} := \mathsf{TR}^2_{weak} \circ \mathsf{TR}^1_{weak}$.

The Encoding Scheme $\Pi_{\mathbf{LPSS}} = (\mathsf{Enc}_{\mathbf{LPSS}}, \mathsf{Dec}_{\mathbf{LPSS}})$. A $(t+1)$-out-of-k secret sharing scheme takes as input a secret x from some input domain and outputs k shares, with the property that it is possible to efficiently reconstruct x from every subset of $t+1$ shares, but every subset of at most t shares reveals nothing about the secret x. Informally, Shamir's secret-sharing scheme [32] is defined by a polynomial $p(\cdot)$ of degree at most t, such that $p(0) = x$. The shares are defined to be $p(a_i)$ for every $i \in 1, \ldots, k$ where $a_1, \ldots, a_k$ are any distinct non-zero elements of $\mathbb{F}$. The reconstruction algorithm of the scheme is based on the fact that any $t+1$ points define exactly one polynomial of degree t. Thus, using Lagrange interpolation, it is possible to efficiently reconstruct the polynomial $p(\cdot)$ given any subset of $t+1$ points and compute $x = p(0)$.

Our underlying leakage resilient encoding scheme is a packed secret sharing scheme. The idea of packed secret sharing dates back to Yung and Franklin [13] who used the technique to reduce the complexity of multiparty computation protocols. The idea is similar to standard Shamir secret-sharing [32] over a field $\mathbb{F}$, but where a block of ℓ different secret values $\mathbf{x} = (x_1, \ldots, x_\ell)$ is shared at once using a single polynomial $p(\cdot)$ of degree d that now evaluates to $(x_1, \ldots, x_\ell)$ in ℓ distinct points. It is easy to see that we can obtain security against a t-probing adversary by choosing $d+1 = t+\ell$.

To obtain security against leakages described by low-depth Boolean circuits, we need a scheme that works over constant size fields such that the underlying operations can be evaluated by small-depth Boolean circuits.[1] Hence, our underlying leakage resilient encoding scheme uses the packed secret sharing scheme of Cramer et al. [4] who showed how packed secret sharing can be combined with techniques from algebraic geometry to make it work for constant field sizes. Since we need a more general model for our purposes rather than the special case of Shamir's scheme, we follow the approach from [4] and define our packed secret sharing scheme in terms of linear codes.

More specifically, a linear packed secret sharing scheme over the finite field $\mathbb{F}$ is defined by the following parameters: number of shares k, secret length $\ell > 1$, randomness length e, privacy threshold t and reconstruction threshold r such that any subset of at most t shares have distribution independent of the secret block and from any set of at least r shares, one can reconstruct the secret block. Also, such a linear secret sharing scheme can define a linear code c with generator

---

[1]   Jumping ahead this is needed to carry out an AC^0 reduction to the hardness of the inner product.

matrix $G \in \mathbb{F}^{k \times (\ell + e)}$, and in this case the set of all encodings $[\mathbf{x}]_c$ form a linear code c. [2]

Formally, our encoding $\Pi_{LPSS} = (\mathsf{Enc}_{LPSS}, \mathsf{Dec}_{LPSS})$, is as follows:

- *Public parameters of the scheme:* Let $G \in \mathbb{F}^{k \times (\ell + e)}$ be a fixed generator matrix of a linear code c. More details on how this matrix will look like are given in [4].
- *Encoding algorithm* $\mathsf{Enc}_{LPSS}(\boldsymbol{x})$: On input the block $\mathbf{x} = (x_1, \ldots, x_\ell)$, choose a random vector $\rho \leftarrow \mathbb{F}^e$ and compute the encoded block under the code c as: $[\mathbf{x}]_c = G \cdot (x_1, \ldots, x_\ell, \rho_1, \ldots, \rho_e)^{\mathsf{T}}$. Output $[\mathbf{x}]_c \in \mathbb{F}^k$.
- *Decoding algorithm* $\mathsf{Dec}_{LPSS}([\boldsymbol{x}]_c)$: On input r shares of $[\boldsymbol{x}]_c$, recover the block $\mathbf{x}$ consisting of the first ℓ values of the computation $(G^{-1} \cdot [\mathbf{x}]_c) \in \mathbb{F}^{\ell + e}$.

Multiplying Shares. If two encodings $[\mathbf{x}]_c$ and $[\mathbf{y}]_c$ are multiplied then $[\mathbf{xy}]_{c^*}$ is obtained where the multiplication yields a codeword under a new code c^* defined considering the derived generator matrix[3] G^*. The code c^* is defined to be the code obtained by taking the linear span of all products of the codewords in c. Hence, the above encoding scheme Π_{LPSS} applies to any generator matrix, e.g. the matrix G^*.

An important feature of the above encoding scheme, which makes it applicable for masking schemes, is the fact that it exhibits homomorphic properties. In particular, any linear combination of encodings corresponds to a linear combinations of the underlying secrets, provided that the *same* secret locations were used in all encodings (in the above case these are the position $(1, \ldots, \ell)$).

The Transformation $C' \leftarrow \mathsf{TR}^1_{weak}(C, k)$. The circuit transformation takes as input the security parameter k and the description of an arbitrary circuit C and compiles it into a transformed circuit C'. The goal of $\mathsf{TR}^1_{weak}(C, k)$ is to prepare the circuit C such that it can efficiently compute on values encoded with Π_{LPSS}. The use of packed secret sharing allows to securely compute addition/multiplication on ℓ values in parallel, at the price of what a single operation would cost using normal secret sharing. To this end, the circuit has to be arranged in such a way that it can operate on blocks of secrets in parallel. The work of [5] achieves this goal with overhead $\mathcal{O}(\log |s|)$, a detailed description can be found in the full version of this extended abstract. Intuitively, the transformation arranges the circuit C such that every layer contains only one type of gates, i.e., either addition or multiplication operations. In addition, sets of shared blocks $S_1, S_2, \ldots$ must be produced such that blocks in S_i contain the i'th input bit to the gates in a given layer, in some fixed order. In order to achieve the above, the values in the computation will have to be permuted between layers

---

[2] For example, in the special case of packed Shamir secret sharing over polynomials of degree d, the set of all encodings $[\mathbf{x}]_d$ forms a linear code, where the generator matrix is formed from a product of two VanderMonde matrices.

[3] Analogously, if packed Shamir secret sharing over polynomials is used, then the multiplication of the shares $[\mathbf{a}]_d$ and $[\mathbf{b}]_d$ under a polynomial of degree d yields a share of $[\mathbf{ab}]_{2d}$ under a polynomial of degree $2d$.

by swap gates in arbitrary ways that depend on the concrete circuit. The basic idea is to handle the arbitrary permutations between blocks using Benes permutation networks. The only non-trivial issue is how to permute the elements *inside* a shared block. For this reason we add permutation block-gadgets which are described in TR^2_{weak}.

Since the resulting circuit C' is compiled to work on packed secret sharing, it can be described by block-gadgets, which operate on blocks of ℓ secrets. More specifically, we have the following block-gadgets: (1) multiplication and addition block gadgets that carry out the respective operation over blocks of ℓ field elements, (2) copy gadgets that handle fan out and output two copies of their inputs, and (3) permutation gadgets (for some fixed number of $\log(k)$ permutations), which take as input a block and output a permutation of the elements. Note that the block-gadgets is just an abstraction to make the exposition in the next step simpler, and all block-gadgets are built out of the elementary multiplication and addition gates that work over the underlying field $\mathbb{F}$.

The Transformation $\widehat{C} \leftarrow \mathsf{TR}^2_{weak}(C', k)$. $\mathsf{TR}^2_{weak}(C', k)$ takes as input a circuit C', prepared by TR^1_{weak} to work on blocks of ℓ secrets, and compiles it into a circuit $\widehat{C}$ that works on encodings of blocks. Recall that C' operates on blocks, so as a first step, $\mathsf{TR}^2_{weak}(C', k)$ encodes blocks using Π_{LPSS}. Moreover, we can replace the block-gadgets by operations that work on encoded blocks. The gadgets are built out of the elementary operations: multiplication, addition and swapping. Moreover, we will use a class of a leak-free gadget which is described in more detail below. The transformation for the different block-gadgets is described in Figure 1. The addition block-gadget directly uses the fact that the encoding scheme is additively homomorphic, and hence to compute the output it suffices to compute component-wise addition of the shares. The transformation for the multiplication block-gadget is more complicated and makes use of a leak-free gate. Specifically, we first compute the component-wise product of the shares. Notice that the resulting shares $[\mathbf{ab}]_{c^*}$, are now shares of the code c^* since once we multiply them the underlying code was changed from c to c^*. Next, we use the opaque gadget $\mathcal{O}_r$, which returns encodings $[\mathbf{r}]_c$ and $[\mathbf{r}]_{c^*}$ of a random block $\mathbf{r}$. We use $[\mathbf{r}]_{c^*}$ to "mask" $[\mathbf{ab}]_{c^*}$, which will allow us to open/decode the random encoding $[\mathbf{ab} + \mathbf{r}]_{c^*}$ to the block $(\mathbf{ab} + \mathbf{r})$. Intuitively, the opening is allowed since the secret data is masked by a random unknown value $\mathbf{r}$. Hence, the opened values does not reveal any information about the secret data. After reconstructing/encoding the block $(\mathbf{ab} + \mathbf{r})$ under the code c, we subtract $[\mathbf{r}]_c$ from it, which results into a random encoding $[\mathbf{ab}]_c$. The reconstruction of $[\mathbf{ab} + \mathbf{r}]_c$ carried out during the multiplication operation can be implemented using a small sub-circuit with linear complexity. Notice that the Permutation block-gadget acts in the same way as the multiplication block-gadget. Moreover, we use a similar leak-free gate, $\mathcal{O}_\pi$, which for some fixed permutation π outputs $[\mathbf{r}]_c$ and $[\mathbf{r}']_c$ for some random block $\mathbf{r} \leftarrow \mathbb{F}^\ell$ and $\mathbf{r}' = \pi(\mathbf{r})$. The leak-free gates do not perform any *heavy* computations, take no inputs and keep no secret internal states, which makes them independent of the computation in the circuit.

Addition block-gadget : $g = a + b \Rightarrow [a + b]_c \leftarrow [a]_c + [b]_c$
$[s]_c = [a]_c + [b]_c = (a_1 + b_1, \ldots, a_k + b_k)$
$[0]_c \leftarrow \mathcal{O}^a$
$[a + b]_c = [s]_c + [0]_c$
Multiply block-gadget : $g = ab \Rightarrow [ab]_c \leftarrow [a]_c[b]_c$
$([r]_c, [r]_{c^*}) \leftarrow \mathcal{O}_r$
$[ab]_{c^*} = [a]_c[b]_c = (a_1 b_1, \ldots, a_k b_k)$
$[ab + r]_{c^*} = [ab]_{c^*} + [r]_{c^*} = (a_1 b_1 + r_1, \ldots, a_k b_k + r_k)$
$(ab + r) \leftarrow \mathsf{Dec}_{LPSS}([ab + r]_{c^*})$
$[ab + r]_c \leftarrow \mathsf{Enc}_{LPSS}(ab + r)$
$[ab]_c = [ab + r]_c - [r]_c$
Permutation block-gadget : Compute $[\pi(\mathbf{x})]_c$ given $[\mathbf{x}]_c$
$([r]_c, [\pi(r)]_c) \leftarrow \mathcal{O}_\pi$
$[\mathbf{x} + \mathbf{r}]_c = [\mathbf{x}]_c + [\mathbf{r}]_c = (x_1 + r_1, \ldots, x_k + r_k)$
$(\mathbf{x} + \mathbf{r}) \leftarrow \mathsf{Dec}_{LPSS}([\mathbf{x} + \mathbf{r}]_c)$
$[\pi(\mathbf{x} + \mathbf{r})]_c \leftarrow \mathsf{Enc}_{LPSS}(\pi(\mathbf{x} + \mathbf{r}))$
$[\pi(\mathbf{x})]_c = [\pi(\mathbf{x} + \mathbf{r})]_c - [\pi(\mathbf{r})]_c$
$\mathcal{O}_\pi$ gate : Compute $[\mathbf{r}]_c$ and $[\pi(\mathbf{r})]_c$
Sample $\mathbf{r} = (r_1, \ldots, r_l) \in_R \mathbb{F}^l$ and compute $\pi(\mathbf{r})$
Sample two random vectors $\boldsymbol{\rho}, \boldsymbol{\rho}'$
Compute $[\mathbf{r}]_c = G(\mathbf{r}, \boldsymbol{\rho})$ and $[\pi(\mathbf{r})]_c = G^*(\pi(\mathbf{r}), \boldsymbol{\rho}')$
$\mathcal{O}_r$ gate : Compute $[\mathbf{r}]_c$ and $[\mathbf{r}]_{c^*}$
Sample $\mathbf{r} = (r_1, \ldots, r_l) \in_R \mathbb{F}^l$ and two random vectors $\boldsymbol{\rho}, \boldsymbol{\rho}'$
Compute $[\mathbf{r}]_c = G(\mathbf{r}, \boldsymbol{\rho})$ and $[\mathbf{r}]_{c^*} = G^*(\mathbf{r}, \boldsymbol{\rho}')$

---

[a] *The gate $\mathcal{O}$ is a special case of the $\mathcal{O}_r$ gate in the sense that the random value* r
is frozen to 0 and only the encoding $[0]_c$ is given as output.

Fig. 1. Multiply, Addition and Permutation block-gadgets for the Π_{LPSS} encoding

Efficiency of TR_{weak}. As already mentioned above, $\mathsf{TR}^1_{weak}(C, k)$ introduces overhead of $\mathcal{O}(\log s)$ resulting into a circuit of size $\mathcal{O}(s \log s)$. Regarding $\mathsf{TR}^2_{weak}(C', k)$, the blow up of the circuit is linear in k because we replace the gates by block-gadgets of cost $\mathcal{O}(k)$. The efficiency of the transformation $\mathsf{TR}^2_{weak}(C', k)$ is achieved by using the packed secret sharing scheme Π_{LPSS} which allows to amortize the cost over many gates. More specifically, our multiplication/permutation block-gadgets have at most quadratic overhead due to the matrix-vector multiplication induced by running $\mathsf{Enc}_{LPSS}, \mathsf{Dec}_{LPSS}$. However, with packed secret sharing we process ℓ blocks in parallel, so amortize the cost over many gates we get linear complexity since $\ell = \Theta(k)$. Therefore, the total size of the transformed circuits is $\mathcal{O}(k \, s \log s)$.

Soundness of TR_{weak}. We show that the input-output functionality of the circuit C is identical to that of $\hat{C}$. The proof of soundness can be found in the full version.

Lemma 1. [Soundness] *The circuit transformation $\mathsf{TR}_{weak}(C, k)$ is sound.*

3.1 Security Against Global and Computational Bounded Leakage

We now show that our leakage-resilient compiler TR_{weak} protects against global, continuous and computationally weak leakages. In particular, we will prove that such circuits protect against leakages that can be computed by circuits of constant depth – so-called AC^0 leakages. The security proof of our transformation follows the general approach presented in the work of Faust et al. [12] which requires two main ingredients, a secure encoding scheme and simulatable gadgets. Informally, given these two ingredients one can apply the composition theorem of Faust et al. [12] and get security for the entire transformation.

We start by showing a general result, working with arbitrary fields, such that the operations of the computation are efficiently simulatable by SHALLOW circuits – in particular, we will require that they can be computed by circuits in the class SHALLOW(d, s) for some constant depth d and size s. We assume that these circuits are deterministic and the only basic operations they are allowed to carry out are additions, permutations and multiplications. Next, in Section 3.2, we consider the case where the shallow functions operate over binary fields and in this case we can show that the class of leakage functions that can be tolerated is in AC^0. For this we need that the size of the field is constant and we need to show that our encoding scheme Π_{LPSS} is secure against AC^0 leakages.

To formalize the notion of shallow simulators we use the formalism of *reconstructors*, defined in [12], for some class $\mathcal{L}$ of leakage functions. A reconstructor takes as input the inputs and outputs of a gadget and is able to simulate its internals in a way that looks indistinguishable for leakages from $\mathcal{L}$. Since we are interested in efficient simulations and reductions, we will explicitly state the complexity of the *reconstructors*. Below, we denote the distribution on the wires of $\widehat{C}$ on input X conditioned on the output being Y by $\mathcal{W}_{\widehat{C}}(X|Y)$.

Definition 2 (Reconstructor for circuits [12]). *Let $\widehat{C}$ be a (transformed) circuit. We say that a pair of strings (X, Y) is plausible for $\widehat{C}$ if $\widehat{C}$ might output Y on input X, i.e., if $\Pr[\widehat{C}(X) = Y] > 0$.*

Consider a distribution $REC_{\widehat{C}}$ over the functions whose input is a pair of strings, and whose output is an assignment to the wires of $\widehat{C}$. Define $REC_{\widehat{C}}(X, Y)$ as the distribution obtained by sampling $R_{\widehat{C}} \leftarrow REC_{\widehat{C}}$ and computing $R_{\widehat{C}}(X, Y)$. Such a distribution is called a $(\mathcal{L}, \epsilon)$-reconstructor for $\widehat{C}$ if for any plausible (X, Y), the following two wire assignment distributions are ϵ close under leakages from $\mathcal{L}$, i.e., for any function $f \in \mathcal{L}$ the following holds:

$$\Delta(f(\mathcal{W}_{\widehat{C}}(X|Y)); f(REC_{\widehat{C}}(X, Y))) \leq \epsilon,$$

where the randomness above is over the randomness of sampling $REC_{\widehat{C}}$ and the internal randomness used by $\widehat{C}$. We say that $\widehat{C}$ is reconstructible by SHALLOW(d, s) if the support of the distribution $REC_{\widehat{C}}$ is computable by circuits in SHALLOW (d, s).

Security and Reconstructibility of Block-gadgets. We show that our transformed Multiply block-gadget is reconstructible by SHALLOW circuits. Moreover, the proofs and the reconstructors of the Permutation and Additon block-gadget can be found in the full version.

Lemma 2 (The Multiply block-gadgets of TR_{weak} are Reconstructible). *Let k be the security parameter. The* Multiply *block-gadget is $(\mathcal{L}, 0)$-reconstructible by* SHALLOW$(2, \mathcal{O}(k))$ *for any $\mathcal{L}$.*

3.2   Security Against AC^0 Leakage

While the above work, in this section, we consider security with respect to AC^0 leakages. To this end, we will first show that the packed secret sharing scheme from Section 2 is secure against AC^0 leakages (see lemma below). Then, we use the composition theorems from [12] together with the fact that all block-gadgets are proven to be reconstructible by shallow circuits. This will show that the transformed circuits are resilient to AC^0 leakages according to Definition 1. In the following, we show that the encoding is secure against AC^0 leakages.

Security of the Π_{LPSS} Encoding. Recall that the circuit compiler TR_{weak} uses the Π_{LPSS} packed secret sharing scheme over a constant size field $\mathbb{F}$. In general, the decoding function Dec_{LPSS} is a function that maps a set of shares to a secret block and the adversary gets to apply an AC^0 function to an encoding. We show that the decoding function is hard to compute in AC^0. The proof of the Lemma can be found in the full version.

Lemma 3. *For $k \in \mathbb{N}_{>0}$, the decoding function Dec_{LPSS}[4] defined by a decoding vector $(\boldsymbol{a}) = (a_1, \ldots, a_k) \in \mathbb{F}^k$ as $\mathsf{Dec}_{LPSS} : (s_1, \ldots, s_k) \mapsto \sum_{i=1}^{k} s_i a_i = \boldsymbol{a}^T \boldsymbol{s}$ does not belong to the AC^0.*

Notice that the above claim proves that the Π_{LPSS} encoding is secure against AC^0 leakages, i.e., for any leakage function f computable by AC^0 circuits and for any two blocks of secrets $\mathbf{x}$ and $\mathbf{x}'$ the following two distributions are statistically close: $\Delta(f(\mathsf{Enc}_{LPSS}(\mathbf{x})); f(\mathsf{Enc}_{LPSS}(\mathbf{x}'))) \leq \mathsf{negl}(k)$.

Security of Circuits. In Section 3.1, we showed that all block-gadgets can be reconstructed by shallow simulators given only the inputs and outputs. Moreover, all gadgets are re-randomizable as the outputs are re-randomized by fresh encodings that are output by leak-free gates. Furthermore, by the claim above the encoding is resilient to AC^0 leakages and all block-gadgets are reconstructible by constant depth circuits, and the composition theorem of [12] combines both terms additively, i.e., the loss in the reduction is only in an additive constant factor in circuit depth. This all together shows that the transformed circuits are secure against AC^0 circuits.

---

[4] We actually encode blocks of elements, but for simplicity of exposition we will assume that we encode single elements.

4   Transformation for Independent Leakages

Dziembowski and Faust [10] proposed a compiler, which transforms arbitrary circuits over some field $\mathbb{F}$ into functionally equivalent circuits secure against any continual leakage assuming that: (i) the memory is divided into sub-computations, which leak independently, (ii) the leakage from each sub-computation is bounded and (iii) the circuit has an access to a leak-free component, which samples random pairs of orthogonal vectors. Their transformation also proceeds in a *gate-by-gate* fashion but the pivotal ingredient of their construction is a protocol for *refreshing* the Leakage-Resilient-Storage used among others in the multiplication gadget protocol.

We present a more efficient and simpler protocol for *refreshing* using the same assumption of a leak-free gadget. Our solution needs $\mathcal{O}(k)$ operations to fully refresh the encoding of the secret in contrast to $\Omega(k^2)$ that was required by earlier works, where k is a security parameter proportional to the bound on the leakage from each sub-computation. More precisely, the blow-up of the circuit's size during compilation with the new refreshing protocol is equal to $\mathcal{O}(k^2)$. It is a significant improvement compared to $\Omega(k^4)$ by Dziembowski and Faust [10], and $\Omega(k^3)$ by Goldwasser and Rothblum [30] where ciphertext-banks are needed.

Moreover, we show that by operating over larger fields (exponential in the security parameter k) and using an efficient field multiplication algorithm, we can achieve even more efficient construction, namely one with a (multiplicative) overhead $\mathcal{O}(k \log k \log \log k)$ regardless whether the new refreshing algorithm is used or not. Although the usage of the more efficient refreshing algorithm does not influence the complexity of the compiler in this case, it is still valuable, because it decreases the size of the transformed circuit by a huge constant factor and is simpler than the original refreshing algorithm.

In contrast, in the previous section we aimed on protecting against low-complexity leakages, in this section we are interested in bounded leakage that occurs independently from two parts of the memory. To this end, we need to use an alternative encoding – the so-called inner-product encoding – that has been used in a series of works [7,10,17]. The inner product encoding scheme, defined by $\Phi_{IP} = (\mathsf{Encode} : \mathcal{M} \to \mathcal{X} \times \mathcal{Y}, \mathsf{Decode} : \mathcal{X} \times \mathcal{Y} \to \mathcal{M})$, works as follows. On an input message $m \in \mathcal{M}$, we choose uniformly at random two vectors $\mathbf{l}$ and $\mathbf{r}$ over the field $\mathbb{F}$ subject to the constraint that their inner product $\langle \mathbf{l}, \mathbf{r} \rangle$ is equal to the message m. The encoding scheme outputs $(\mathbf{l}, \mathbf{r})$. The decoding function is deterministic and takes as input two shares $(\mathbf{l}, \mathbf{r})$ and outputs their inner product $\langle \mathbf{l}, \mathbf{r} \rangle$. In [6,9] it is shown that the above encoding is secure, which means that the adversary learning some partial information $f(\mathbf{l})$ about $\mathbf{l}$ and (independently) $g(\mathbf{r})$ about $\mathbf{r}$ gains no information about the encoded message m. The idea is to keep $\mathbf{l}$ and $\mathbf{r}$ separated (e.g. on different memory chips). We will model this setting assuming that they are kept by different players, which can perform computation and exchange messages. We discuss our encoding more formally in Section 4.2.

4.1   Leakage Model

Our model of leakage is based on [10] and we only recall some important details. The compiler produces a circuit, which is divided into sub-computations. An adversary will be allowed to extract from each sub-computation no more that λ bits of information for some constant λ. For a non-adaptive adversary, it means that it is allowed to adaptively choose any (e.g. polynomially uncomputable) function with range $\{0,1\}^\lambda$, which value depends on all information used in that sub-computation. Except from the above condition, the total amount of leakage during the whole computation is unlimited (in comparison to models, when an adversary can for example obtain values on a fixed number of wires). Because of that, this kind of leakage model is usually called *continual leakage*.

Moreover, we will assume that the sub-computations leak *independently*, that is a leakage function in each observation may only depend on data from one sub-computation. In practice, the separation of sub-computations may be achieved by dividing the memory into parts (e.g. separate RAM chips) and placing the data used in different sub-computations on different memory chips.

We model the execution of such circuit as a protocol executed between ℓ players (denoted $P_1, P_2, \ldots, P_\ell$), where each player performs one of the sub-computations. The adversary can then learn some partial information about the internal states of the players. Informally, an adversary, called λ-*limited leakage adversary* is allowed to extract at most λ bits of information about the internal state of each players. More formal definitions follows in the next paragraphs.

Leakage from Memory. Based on Definition 1 we model independent leakage from memory parts in form of a *leakage game*, where the adversary can *adaptively* learn information from the memory parts. More precisely, for some $u, \ell, \lambda \in \mathbb{N}$ let $M_1, \ldots, M_\ell \in \{0,1\}^u$ denote the contents of the memory parts, then we define a λ-*leakage game* in which a λ-*limited leakage adversary* $\mathcal{A}$, submits (adaptively) tuples of the form $\{(x_i, f_i)\}_{i=1}^m$ where $m \in \mathbb{N}$, $x_i \in \{1, \ldots, \ell\}$ denotes which memory part leaks at the current step and f_i is a leakage function, such that $f_i : \{0,1\}^u \to \{0,1\}^{\lambda'}$ and $\lambda' \leq \lambda$. To each such a query the oracle replies with $f_i(M_{x_i})$ and we say that in this case the adversary $\mathcal{A}$ *retrieved the value* $f_i(M_{x_i})$ *from* M_{x_i}. The only restriction is that in total the adversary does not retrieve more than λ bits from each memory part. In the following, let $(\mathcal{A} \rightleftarrows (M_1, \ldots, M_\ell))$ be the output of $\mathcal{A}$ at the end of this game. Without loss of generality, we assume that $(\mathcal{A} \rightleftarrows (M_1, \ldots, M_\ell)) := (f_1(M_{x_1}), \ldots, f_m(M_{x_m}))$.

Leakage from Computation. We model an execution of the circuit as a protocol executed between players $P_1, P_2, \ldots P_\ell$, where each player corresponds to one of the sub-computations. At the beginning of the game, some of the players (so-called input-players) hold inputs. The execution of the protocol proceeds in rounds. During each round one player is active and can send messages to the other players. The messages can depend on his input (if it is an input-player), the messages he received in previous rounds and his local randomness. An the end of the game, some of the players (called output-players) output the values, which are considered the output of the protocol. Let view_i denote all the information, which were available to P_i, that is all the messages sent or received by P_i, his inputs and his local randomness. After the protocol is executed the adversary plays a game $\mathcal{A} \rightleftarrows (\mathsf{view}_1, \ldots, \mathsf{view}_\ell)$.

4.2   Leakage-Resilient Storage

The notion of leakage-resilient storage $\Phi = (\mathsf{Encode}, \mathsf{Decode})$ was introduced by Davi et al. [7]. An Φ allows to store a secret in an *encoded form* of two *shares* $\mathbf{l}$ and $\mathbf{r}$, such that it should be impossible to learn anything about the secret given independent leakages from both shares. One of the constructions that they propose uses two-source extractors and can be shown to be secure in the independent leakage model.

A Φ scheme is said to be (λ, ϵ)-secure, if for any $\mathbf{s}, \mathbf{s}' \in \mathcal{M}$ and any λ-limited adversary $\mathcal{A}$, we have $\Delta(\mathcal{A} \rightleftarrows (\mathbf{l}, \mathbf{r}); \mathcal{A} \rightleftarrows (\mathbf{l}', \mathbf{r}')) \leq \epsilon$, where $(\mathbf{l}, \mathbf{r}) \leftarrow \mathsf{Encode}(\mathbf{s})$ and $(\mathbf{l}', \mathbf{r}') \leftarrow \mathsf{Encode}(\mathbf{s}')$, for any two secrets $\mathbf{s}, \mathbf{s}' \in \mathcal{M}$. We consider a leakage-resilient storage scheme Φ that allows to efficiently store elements from $\mathcal{M} = \mathbb{F}$. It is a variant of a scheme proposed in [9] and based on the inner-product extractor. For some security parameter $n \in \mathbb{N}$ and a finite field $\mathbb{F}$, $\Phi_\mathbb{F}^n := (\mathsf{Encode}_\mathbb{F}^n, \mathsf{Decode}_\mathbb{F}^n)$ is defined as follows. Security is proven by [10] with the lemma below.

- Encoding algorithm $\mathsf{Encode}_\mathbb{F}^n(\mathbf{s})$: On input the vector $\mathbf{s}$ sample $(\mathbf{l}[2, \ldots, n], \mathbf{r}[2, \ldots, n]) \leftarrow (\mathbb{F}^{n-1})^2$ and set $\mathbf{l}[1] \leftarrow \mathbb{F} \setminus \{0\}$ and
  $\mathbf{r}[1] := \mathbf{l}[1]^{-1} \cdot (\mathbf{s} - \langle(\mathbf{l}[2, \ldots, n], \mathbf{r}[2, \ldots, n])\rangle)$. The output is $(\mathbf{l}, \mathbf{r})$.
- Decoding algorithm $\mathsf{Decode}_\mathbb{F}^n(\mathbf{l}, \mathbf{r})$: On input $(\mathbf{l}, \mathbf{r})$ output $\langle \mathbf{l}, \mathbf{r} \rangle$.

Lemma 4. *Let $n \in \mathbb{N}$ and let $\mathbb{F}$ such that $|\mathbb{F}| = \Omega(n)$. For any $1/2 > \delta > 0, \gamma > 0$ the $\Phi_\mathbb{F}^n$ scheme as defined above is (λ, ϵ)-secure, with $\lambda = (1/2 - \delta)n \log |\mathbb{F}| - \log \gamma^{-1} - 1$ and $\epsilon = 2(|\mathbb{F}|^{3/2 - n\delta} + |\mathbb{F}| \gamma)$.*

Exponentially Large Fields. In the above construction we have two security parameters: n and $|\mathbb{F}|$ (notice that δ and γ are just artifacts of the lemma and do not influence the construction), which influence the leakage bound λ, statistical closeness parameter ϵ and the complexity of the scheme. So far [9,10], n has been treated as a main security parameter and $\mathbb{F}$ was implicitly assumed to be rather small (operations in $\mathbb{F}$ were assumed to take constant time).

To simplify the exposition we introduce a single security parameter k and assume that n and $|\mathbb{F}|$ are functions of k. We are interested in choice of n and $|\mathbb{F}|$ (as functions of k) such that $\lambda = \Omega(k)$ and ϵ is negligible in k. The instantiation from [10] can be viewed as $n = k$ and $|\mathbb{F}| = \Theta(k)$. The fact that length of the shares n was of the same order as k caused overhead $\Omega(k^4)$.

In this paper we propose a different choice of the parameters n and $|\mathbb{F}|$. Namely, we show that by using shares of the *constant* length and an exponentially big (in terms of k) fields $\mathbb{F}$ we get the same security guarantee and a much better efficiency. Namely, taking $n = 24, |\mathbb{F}| = 2^k, \delta = 1/4, \gamma = 2^{-2k}$ in Lemma 4 gives $\lambda = 4k - 1$ and $\epsilon = \mathcal{O}(2^{-k})$. With a constant n each gadget produced by the compiler from [10] performs a constant number of operations over the field $\mathbb{F}$. In [31] they show that multiplication in $GF(2^k)$ can be done in time $\mathcal{O}(k \log k \log \log k)$. Hence, setting $\mathbb{F} = GF(2^k)$ and a constant n we get the compiler with the $\mathcal{O}(k \log k \log \log k)$ overhead. This complexity does not depend whether the new refreshing algorithm is used or not, because in this case all shares have constant lengths independent of k.

In the rest of this section we present the new refreshing algorithm. The only assumption about $\mathbb{F}$, which is necessary for its security is $|\mathbb{F}| \geq 4n$.

Non-zero Flavor of Leakage-Resilient Storage. For technical reasons we slightly change the encoding by assuming that the coordinates of $\mathbf{l}$ and $\mathbf{r}$ are all non-zero (e.i. $\mathbf{l}, \mathbf{r} \in (\mathbb{F} \setminus \{0\})^n$. Therefore, $\mathsf{Encode}_{\mathbb{F}}^n$ procedure can easily be modified to generate only vectors with non-zero coordinates. It is enough to use the already presented $\mathsf{Encode}_{\mathbb{F}}^n$ protocol and check at the end if the computed vectors have all coordinates non-zero. If it is not the case, the protocol is restarted with fresh randomness. It does not influence the efficiency of the construction, because a random vector has at least one coordinate equal to zero with a probability at most $1/4$ regardless of n (but assuming $|\mathbb{F}| \geq 4n$). It is easy to see that this modification changes the security of the Leakage-Resilient Storage only by a negligible factor.

4.3   The Leak-Free Component

As in [10], we assume that the players have access to a leak-free component that samples uniformly random pairs of orthogonal vectors. More specifically, we will assume that we have access to a gate $\mathcal{O}'$ that samples a uniformly random vector $((\mathbf{a}, \tilde{\mathbf{a}}), (\mathbf{b}, \tilde{\mathbf{b}})) \in (\mathbb{F}^n)^4$, subject to the constraint that the following three conditions hold: (i)$\langle \mathbf{a}, \mathbf{b} \rangle + \langle \tilde{\mathbf{a}}, \tilde{\mathbf{b}} \rangle = 0$, (ii) $\{a_i \neq 0\}_{i \in [n]}$ and (iii) $\{\tilde{b}_i \neq 0\}_{i \in [n]}$.

Note that this gate is different from the gate $\mathcal{O}$ used earlier in [9] that simply samples pairs $(\mathbf{a}, \mathbf{b})$ of orthogonal vectors. It is easy to see, however, that this "new" gate $\mathcal{O}'$ can be "simulated" by the players that have access to $\mathcal{O}$ that samples pairs $(\mathbf{c}, \mathbf{d})$ of orthogonal vectors of length $2n$ each. First, observe that $\mathbf{c} \in \mathbb{F}^{2n}$ can be interpreted as a pair $(\mathbf{a}, \tilde{\mathbf{a}}) \in (\mathbb{F}^n)^2$ (where $\mathbf{a}||\tilde{\mathbf{a}} = \mathbf{c}$), and in the same way $\mathbf{d} \in \mathbb{F}^{2n}$ can be interpreted as a pair $(\mathbf{b}, \tilde{\mathbf{b}}) \in (\mathbb{F}^n)^2$ (where $\mathbf{b}||\tilde{\mathbf{b}} = \mathbf{d}$). By the basic properties of the inner product we get that $\langle \mathbf{a}, \mathbf{b} \rangle + \langle \tilde{\mathbf{a}}, \tilde{\mathbf{b}} \rangle = \langle \mathbf{c}, \mathbf{d} \rangle = 0$. Hence, condition (i) is satisfied. Conditions (ii) and (iii) can be simply verified by the players P_l and P_r respectively. If one of these conditions is not satisfied, then the players sample a fresh pair $(\mathbf{c}, \mathbf{d})$ from $\mathcal{O}$ (it happens only with a constant probability, because $|\mathbb{F}| \geq 4n$).

4.4   Leakage-Resilient Refreshing of LRS

Recall than the pivotal element of the compiler from [10] is the protocol for refreshing the encodings of the secrets encoded with $\Phi_{\mathbb{F}}^n$. Such protocol takes an encoding of the secret and produces a fresh encoding of the same secret. However, we can not just decode the secret and then re-encode it with a fresh randomness,

---

Initial state: **Protocol** $\mathsf{Refresh}^n_{\mathbb{F}}(\mathbf{l}, \mathbf{r})$:
- player $P_\mathbf{l}$ holds $\mathbf{l} \in (\mathbb{F} \setminus \{0\})^n$ and player $P_\mathbf{r}$ holds $\mathbf{r} \in (\mathbb{F} \setminus \{0\})^n$.
1. Let $((\mathbf{a}, \tilde{\mathbf{a}}), (\mathbf{b}, \tilde{\mathbf{b}})) \leftarrow \mathcal{O}'$ and give $(\mathbf{a}, \tilde{\mathbf{a}})$ to $P_\mathbf{l}$ and $(\mathbf{b}, \tilde{\mathbf{b}})$ to $P_\mathbf{r}$.

Refreshing the share of $P_\mathbf{r}$:
2. $P_\mathbf{l}$ computes a vector $\mathbf{v}$ such that $\{\mathbf{v}_i := \mathbf{l}_i^{-1} \cdot \mathbf{a}_i\}_{i \in [n]}$ and sends $\mathbf{v}$ to $P_\mathbf{r}$.
3. $P_\mathbf{r}$ computes a vector $\mathbf{x}$ such that $\{\mathbf{x}_i := \mathbf{v}_i \cdot \mathbf{b}_i\}_{i \in [n]}$ and sets $\mathbf{r}' := \mathbf{r} + \mathbf{x}$.
4. If there exists i such that $\mathbf{r}'_i = 0$, then the protocol is restarted from the beginning with new vectors sampled from $\mathcal{O}'$.

Refreshing the share of $P_\mathbf{l}$:
5. $P_\mathbf{r}$ computes a vector $\tilde{\mathbf{v}}$ such that $\{\tilde{\mathbf{v}}_i := \mathbf{r}'^{-1}_i \cdot \tilde{\mathbf{b}}_i\}_{i \in [n]}$ and sends $\tilde{\mathbf{v}}$ to $P_\mathbf{l}$.
6. $P_\mathbf{l}$ computes a vector $\tilde{\mathbf{x}}$ such that $\{\tilde{\mathbf{x}}_i := \tilde{\mathbf{v}}_i \cdot \tilde{\mathbf{a}}_i\}_{i \in [n]}$ and sets $\mathbf{l}' := \mathbf{l} + \tilde{\mathbf{x}}$.
7. If there exists i such that $\mathbf{l}'_i = 0$, then the protocol is restarted from the beginning with new vectors sampled from $\mathcal{O}'$.

Final state:
- player $P_\mathbf{l}$ holds $\mathbf{l}'$ and player $P_\mathbf{r}$ holds $\mathbf{r}'$.

Views: The view $\mathsf{view}_\mathbf{l}$ of player $P_\mathbf{l}$ is $(\mathbf{l}, \mathbf{a}, \mathbf{v}, \tilde{\mathbf{a}}, \tilde{\mathbf{v}})$ and the view $\mathsf{view}_\mathbf{r}$ of player $P_\mathbf{r}$ is $(\mathbf{r}, \mathbf{b}, \mathbf{v}, \tilde{\mathbf{b}}, \tilde{\mathbf{v}})$.

Fig. 2. Protocol $\mathsf{Refresh}^n_{\mathbb{F}}$. Gate $\mathcal{O}'$ samples random vectors $(\mathbf{a}, \tilde{\mathbf{a}}, \mathbf{b}, \tilde{\mathbf{b}}) \in (\mathbb{F} \setminus \{0\})^n \times \mathbb{F}^n \times \mathbb{F}^n \times (\mathbb{F} \setminus \{0\})^n$ such that $\langle \mathbf{t}\mathbf{a}, \mathbf{b} \rangle = -\langle \tilde{\mathbf{a}}, \tilde{\mathbf{b}} \rangle$. Note that the inverses in Steps 2 and 5 always exist, because $\mathbf{l}, \mathbf{r} \in (\mathbb{F} \setminus \{0\})^n$. Steps 4 and 7 guarantee that this condition is preserved under the execution of the protocol $\mathsf{Refresh}^n_{\mathbb{F}}$. The protocol is restarted with a bounded probability regardless of n (but keeping $|\mathbb{F}| \geq 4n$), so it changes the efficiency of the algorithm only by a constant factor.

because an adversary could leak the secret, while it is decoded. Therefore, we need a way to compute a new encoding of a secret without decoding it. The new refreshing protocol performs $\mathcal{O}(n)$ operations over the field $\mathbb{F}$ in comparison to $\Omega(n^2)$ for a protocol from [10].

The refreshing protocol, $\mathsf{Refresh}^n_{\mathbb{F}}$ described in Figure 2 is based on the one proposed in [10] (cf. Section 3), but it is more efficient. The protocol $\mathsf{Refresh}^n_{\mathbb{F}}$ refreshes the secrets encoded with $\Phi^n_{\mathbb{F}}$. $\mathsf{Refresh}^n_{\mathbb{F}}$ is run between two players $P_\mathbf{l}$ and $P_\mathbf{r}$, which initially hold shares $\mathbf{l}$ and $\mathbf{r}$ in $(\mathbb{F} \setminus \{0\})^n$. At the end of the protocol, $P_\mathbf{l}$ holds $\mathbf{l}'$ and $P_\mathbf{r}$ holds $\mathbf{r}'$ such that $\langle \mathbf{l}, \mathbf{r} \rangle = \langle \mathbf{l}', \mathbf{r}' \rangle$. The refreshing scheme is presented in Figure 2. The main idea behind this protocol is as follows. Denote $\alpha := \langle \mathbf{a}, \mathbf{b} \rangle (= -\langle \tilde{\mathbf{a}}, \tilde{\mathbf{b}} \rangle)$. Steps 2 and 3 are needed to refresh the share of $P_\mathbf{r}$. This is done by generating, with the "help" of $(\mathbf{a}, \mathbf{b})$ (coming from $\mathcal{O}'$) a vector $\mathbf{x}$ such that $\langle \mathbf{l}, \mathbf{x} \rangle = \alpha$.

$\langle \mathbf{l}, \mathbf{x} \rangle = \alpha$ comes from the above summation: $\langle \mathbf{l}, \mathbf{x} \rangle = \sum_{i=1}^n \mathbf{l}_i \mathbf{x}_i = \sum_{i=1}^n \mathbf{l}_i \mathbf{v}_i \mathbf{b}_i$ $= \sum_{i=1}^n \mathbf{l}_i \mathbf{l}_i^{-1} \mathbf{a}_i \mathbf{b}_i = \langle \mathbf{a}, \mathbf{b} \rangle = \alpha$. Then, vector $\mathbf{x}$ is added to the share of $P_\mathbf{r}$ by setting (in Step 3) $\mathbf{r}' := \mathbf{r} + \mathbf{x}$. Hence, we get $\langle \mathbf{l}, \mathbf{r}' \rangle = \langle \mathbf{l}, \mathbf{r} \rangle + \langle \mathbf{l}, \mathbf{x} \rangle = \langle \mathbf{l}, \mathbf{r} \rangle + \alpha$. Symmetrically, in Steps 5 and 6 the players refresh the share of $P_\mathbf{l}$, by first generating $\tilde{\mathbf{x}}$ such that $\langle \tilde{\mathbf{x}}, \mathbf{r}' \rangle = -\alpha$, and then setting $\mathbf{l}' := \mathbf{l} + \tilde{\mathbf{x}}$. By similar reasoning as before, we get $\langle \mathbf{l}', \mathbf{r}' \rangle = \langle \mathbf{l}, \mathbf{r}' \rangle - \alpha$, which, in turn is equal to $\langle \mathbf{l}, \mathbf{r} \rangle$. Hence, the following lemma is true. The reconstructor for the $\mathsf{Refresh}^n_{\mathbb{F}}$ and its proof can be found in the full version.

Lemma 5 (Soundness). *For every* $l, r \in (\mathbb{F} \setminus \{0\})^n$ *we have that* $\mathsf{Decode}_{\mathbb{F}}^n(\mathsf{Refresh}_{\mathbb{F}}^n(l, r)) = \mathsf{Decode}_{\mathbb{F}}^n(l, r).$

References

1. Bitansky, N., Dachman-Soled, D., Lin, H.: Leakage-tolerant computation with input-independent preprocessing. In: Garay, J.A., Gennaro, R. (eds.) CRYPTO 2014, Part II. LNCS, vol. 8617, pp. 146–163. Springer, Heidelberg (2014)
2. Castagnos, G., Renner, S., Zémor, G.: High-order masking by using coding theory and its application to AES. In: Stam, M. (ed.) IMACC 2013. LNCS, vol. 8308, pp. 193–212. Springer, Heidelberg (2013)
3. Chari, S., Jutla, C.S., Rao, J.R., Rohatgi, P.: Towards sound approaches to counteract power-analysis attacks. In: Wiener, M. (ed.) CRYPTO 1999. LNCS, vol. 1666, pp. 398–412. Springer, Heidelberg (1999)
4. Cramer, R., Damgård, I., Pastro, V.: On the amortized complexity of zero knowledge protocols for multiplicative relations. In: Smith, A. (ed.) ICITS 2012. LNCS, vol. 7412, pp. 62–79. Springer, Heidelberg (2012)
5. Damgård, I., Ishai, Y., Krøigaard, M.: Perfectly secure multiparty computation and the computational overhead of cryptography. In: Gilbert, H. (ed.) EUROCRYPT 2010. LNCS, vol. 6110, pp. 445–465. Springer, Heidelberg (2010)
6. Davi, F., Dziembowski, S., Venturi, D.: Leakage-resilient storage. Cryptology ePrint Archive, Report 2009/399 (2009)
7. Davì, F., Dziembowski, S., Venturi, D.: Leakage-resilient storage. In: Garay, J.A., De Prisco, R. (eds.) SCN 2010. LNCS, vol. 6280, pp. 121–137. Springer, Heidelberg (2010)
8. Duc, A., Dziembowski, S., Faust, S.: Unifying leakage models: from probing attacks to noisy leakage. In: Nguyen, P.Q., Oswald, E. (eds.) EUROCRYPT 2014. LNCS, vol. 8441, pp. 423–440. Springer, Heidelberg (2014)
9. Dziembowski, S., Faust, S.: Leakage-resilient cryptography from the inner-product extractor. In: Lee, D.H., Wang, X. (eds.) ASIACRYPT 2011. LNCS, vol. 7073, pp. 702–721. Springer, Heidelberg (2011)
10. Dziembowski, S., Faust, S.: Leakage-resilient circuits without computational assumptions. In: Cramer, R. (ed.) TCC 2012. LNCS, vol. 7194, pp. 230–247. Springer, Heidelberg (2012)
11. Dziembowski, S., Pietrzak, K.: Leakage-resilient cryptography. In: Annual IEEE Symposium on Foundations of Computer Science, pp. 293–302 (2008)
12. Faust, S., Rabin, T., Reyzin, L., Tromer, E., Vaikuntanathan, V.: Protecting circuits from leakage: The computationally-bounded and noisy cases. In: Gilbert, H. (ed.) EUROCRYPT 2010. LNCS, vol. 6110, pp. 135–156. Springer, Heidelberg (2010)
13. Franklin, M., Yung, M.: Communication complexity of secure computation (extended abstract). In: STOC, pp. 699–710. ACM, New York (1992)
14. Genkin, D., Pipman, I., Tromer, E.: Get your hands off my laptop: Physical side-channel key-extraction attacks on PCs. In: Batina, L., Robshaw, M. (eds.) CHES 2014. LNCS, vol. 8731, pp. 242–260. Springer, Heidelberg (2014)
15. Genkin, D., Shamir, A., Tromer, E.: RSA key extraction via low-bandwidth acoustic cryptanalysis. In: Garay, J.A., Gennaro, R. (eds.) CRYPTO 2014, Part I. LNCS, vol. 8616, pp. 444–461. Springer, Heidelberg (2014)

16. Goldwasser, S., Rothblum, G.N.: Securing computation against continuous leakage. In: Rabin, T. (ed.) CRYPTO 2010. LNCS, vol. 6223, pp. 59–79. Springer, Heidelberg (2010)
17. Goldwasser, S., Rothblum, G.N.: How to compute in the presence of leakage. Tech. Rep. TR12-010, Electronic Colloquium on Computational Complexity (2012)
18. Grosso, V., Standaert, F.-X., Faust, S.: Masking vs. multiparty computation: How large is the gap for AES? In: Bertoni, G., Coron, J.-S. (eds.) CHES 2013. LNCS, vol. 8086, pp. 400–416. Springer, Heidelberg (2013)
19. Ishai, Y., Sahai, A., Wagner, D.: Private circuits: Securing hardware against probing attacks. In: Boneh, D. (ed.) CRYPTO 2003. LNCS, vol. 2729, pp. 463–481. Springer, Heidelberg (2003)
20. Ishai, Y., Sahai, A., Wagner, D.: Private circuits: Securing hardware against probing attacks (2003). Unpublished manuscript ([19] is a revised and abbreviated version)
21. Juma, A., Vahlis, Y.: Protecting cryptographic keys against continual leakage. In: Rabin, T. (ed.) CRYPTO 2010. LNCS, vol. 6223, pp. 41–58. Springer, Heidelberg (2010)
22. Kocher, P.C.: Timing attacks on implementations of Diffie-Hellman, RSA, DSS, and other systems. In: Koblitz, N. (ed.) CRYPTO 1996. LNCS, vol. 1109, pp. 104–113. Springer, Heidelberg (1996)
23. Kocher, P.C., Jaffe, J., Jun, B.: Differential power analysis. In: Wiener, M. (ed.) CRYPTO 1999. LNCS, vol. 1666, pp. 388–397. Springer, Heidelberg (1999)
24. Micali, S., Reyzin, L.: Physically observable cryptography. In: Naor, M. (ed.) TCC 2004. LNCS, vol. 2951, pp. 278–296. Springer, Heidelberg (2004)
25. Miles, E., Viola, E.: Shielding circuits with groups. In: Proceedings of the 45th Annual ACM Symposium on Symposium on Theory of Computing, STOC 2013, pp. 251–260. ACM, New York (2013)
26. Prouff, E., Rivain, M.: Masking against side-channel attacks: A formal security proof. In: Johansson, T., Nguyen, P.Q. (eds.) EUROCRYPT 2013. LNCS, vol. 7881, pp. 142–159. Springer, Heidelberg (2013)
27. Prouff, E., Roche, T.: Higher-order glitches free implementation of the AES using secure multi-party computation protocols. In: Preneel, B., Takagi, T. (eds.) CHES 2011. LNCS, vol. 6917, pp. 63–78. Springer, Heidelberg (2011)
28. Quisquater, J.-J., Samyde, D.: ElectroMagnetic analysis (EMA): Measures and counter-measures for smart cards. In: Attali, S., Jensen, T. (eds.) E-smart 2001. LNCS, vol. 2140, pp. 200–210. Springer, Heidelberg (2001)
29. Rivain, M., Prouff, E.: Provably secure higher-order masking of AES. In: Mangard, S., Standaert, F.-X. (eds.) CHES 2010. LNCS, vol. 6225, pp. 413–427. Springer, Heidelberg (2010)
30. Rothblum, G.N.: How to compute under AC^0 leakage without secure hardware. In: Safavi-Naini, R., Canetti, R. (eds.) CRYPTO 2012. LNCS, vol. 7417, pp. 552–569. Springer, Heidelberg (2012)
31. Schönhage, A.: Schnelle multiplikation von polynomen über körpern der charakteristik 2. Acta Informatica **7**(4), 395–398 (1977)
32. Shamir, A.: How to share a secret. Commun. ACM **22**(11), 612–613 (1979)

Optimally Efficient Multi-Party Fair Exchange and Fair Secure Multi-Party Computation

Handan Kılınç[1]($\boxtimes$) and Alptekin Küpçü[2]

[1] EPFL, Koç University, Istanbul, Turkey
handan.kilinc@epfl.ch
[2] Koç University, Istanbul, Turkey
akupcu@ku.edu.tr

Abstract. Multi-party fair exchange (MFE) and fair secure multi-party computation (fair SMPC) are under-studied fields of research, with practical importance. We examine MFE scenarios where every participant has some item, and at the end of the protocol, either every participant receives every other participant's item, or no participant receives anything. This is a particularly hard scenario, even though it is directly applicable to protocols such as fair SMPC or multi-party contract signing. We further generalize our protocol to work for any exchange topology. We analyze the case where a trusted third party (TTP) is optimistically available, although we emphasize that the trust put on the TTP is only regarding the *fairness*, and our protocols preserve the *privacy* of the exchanged items even against a malicious TTP.

We construct an *asymptotically optimal* (for the complete topology) multi-party fair exchange protocol that requires a constant number of rounds, in comparison to linear, and $O(n^2)$ messages, in comparison to cubic, where n is the number of participating parties. We enable the parties to efficiently exchange any item that can be efficiently put into a verifiable escrow (e.g., signatures on a contract). We show how to apply this protocol on top of *any* SMPC protocol to achieve a fairness guarantee with very little overhead, especially if the SMPC protocol works with arithmetic circuits. Our protocol guarantees fairness in its strongest sense: even if all $n-1$ other participants are malicious and colluding, fairness will hold.

Keywords: Fair exchange · Optimistic model · Secure and fair computation · Electronic payments

1 Introduction

An exchange protocol allows two or more parties to exchange items. It is *fair* when the exchange guarantees that either all parties receive their desired items or none of them receives any item. Examples of such exchanges include signing electronic contracts, certified e-mail delivery, and fair purchase of electronic goods over the internet. In addition, a fair exchange protocol can be adopted

© Springer International Publishing Switzerland 2015
K. Nyberg (ed.): CT-RSA 2015, LNCS 9048, pp. 330–349, 2015.
DOI: 10.1007/978-3-319-16715-2_18

by secure two- or multi-party computation protocols [7,10,17,26,29,36,45] to achieve fairness [30].

Even in two-party fair exchange scenarios, preventing unfairness completely and efficiently without a trusted third party (TTP) is shown to be impossible [21,41]. The main reason is that one of the parties will be sending the last message of the protocol, regardless of how the protocol looks like, and may choose not to send that message, potentially causing unfairness. In an *optimistic* protocol, the TTP is involved in the protocol *only* when there is a malicious behavior [3,4]. However, it is important not to give a lot of work to the TTP, since this can cause a bottleneck. Furthermore, the TTP is required *only* for *fairness*, and should not learn more about the exchange than is required to provide fairness. In particular, **in our protocols, we show that the TTP does *not* learn the *items*** that are exchanged.

Fair exchange with two parties have been extensively studied and efficient solutions [4,9,32–34] have been proposed, but the multi-party case does not have efficient and general solutions. Multi-party fair exchange (MFE) can be described based on *exchange topologies*. For example, a *ring topology* describes an MFE scenario where each party receives an item from the previous party in the ring [5,27,38,38]. A common scenario with the ring topology is a customer who wants to buy an item offered by a provider: the provider gives the item to the customer, the customer sends a payment authorization to her bank, the customer's bank sends the payment to the provider's bank, and finally the provider's bank credits the provider's account.

Ring topology cannot be used in scenarios like contract-signing and secure multi-party computation (SMPC), since in such scenarios the parties want items from all other parties. In particular, in such settings, **we want that either every participant receives every other participant's item, or no participant receives anything.** This corresponds to the contract being signed only if everyone agrees, or the SMPC output to be revealed only when every participant receives it. We call this kind of topology a *complete topology*. We can think of the parties as nodes in a complete graph and the edges between parties show the exchange links. The complete topology was researched mostly in the contract-signing setting [8,24,25], with one exception [3]. Unfortunately, all these protocols are inefficient compared to ours (see Table 1). Since there was no an efficient MFE protocol that achieves the complete topology, the fairness problem in SMPC protocols still could not be completely solved. Existing fair SMPC solutions either work with inefficient gradual release [23], or require the use of bitcoins [1,11].

Our Contributions: We suggest a new optimistic multi-party fair exchange protocol that guarantees fairness in every topology, including the complete topology, efficiently.

– Our MFE requires only $O(n^2)$ messages and **constant** number of rounds for n parties, being much more efficient than the previous works (see Table 1). These are asymptotically **optimal** for a complete topology, since each party

Table 1. Efficiency comparison with previous works. n is the total number of parties, t is number of dishonest parties, and MPCS means multi-party contract signing protocol.

	Solution for	Topology	Round Complexity	Number of Messages	Broadcast
[25]	MPCS	Complete	$O(n^2)$	$O(n^3)$	Yes
[8]	MPCS	Complete	$O(tn)$	$O(tn^2)$	Yes
[40]	MPCS	Complete	$O(n)$	$O(n^3)$	Yes
[39]	MPCS	Complete	$O(n)$	$O(n^2)$ ✓	Yes
[3]	MFE ✓	Any ✓	$O(1)$ ✓	$O(n^3)$	Yes
Ours	MFE ✓	Any ✓	$O(1)$ ✓	$O(n^2)$ ✓	No ✓

should send his item to all the other parties, even in an unfair exchange. Furthermore, our MFE does *not* necessitate a *broadcast*.

- Our MFE **optimally** guarantees fairness (for honest parties) even when $n-1$ out of n parties are malicious and colluding.
- Our MFE has an easy setup phase, which is employed only **once** for exchanging **multiple** sets of items, thus improving efficiency even further for *repeated exchanges* among the same set of participants.
- The TTP for fairness in our MFE is in the *optimistic* model [4]. The TTP has a very low workload, since the parties only employ efficient discrete-logarithm-based sigma proofs to show their honesty. More importantly, the TTP does *not* learn any exchanged item, so **privacy against the TTP** is preserved.
- We show how to employ our MFE protocol for **any exchange topology**, with the performance improving as the topology gets sparser.
- We formulate MFE as a secure multi-party computation protocol. We then **prove** security and fairness **via ideal-real world simulation** [30]. To the best of our knowledge, no multi-party fair exchange protocol was proven as an SMPC protocol before.
- Based on the definition in [30], we provide an ideal world definition for *fair SMPC*, and prove via simulation that our MFE can be employed **on top of any SMPC protocol** to obtain a *fair* SMPC protocol, with the fairness extension leaking nothing about the inputs, and without necessitating a payment system.

2   Related Works

Multi-party Fair Exchange: Asokan et al. [3] described a generic optimistic fair exchange with a general topology. The parties are restricted to exchange *exchangeable items*, requiring the TTP to be able to replace or revoke the items, greatly decreasing the applicability of their protocol. In addition, broadcast is used to send the items, rendering their protocol inefficient.

Ring Topologies: Bao et al. [6] proposed an optimistic multi-party fair exchange protocol based on the ring topology. In their protocol, one of the participants is

Table 2. Efficiency comparison with previous works in the ring topology. n is number of parties. 'All or None' represents our fairness definition, where either the whole topology is satisfied, or no exchange occurs.

	Number Messages	All or None	TTP-Party Dependency	TTP Privacy
[6]	$O(n)$	No	Yes	Not Private
[27]	$O(n^2)$	No	Yes	Not Private
[38]	$O(n)$	No	Yes	Not Private
Ours	$O(n^2)$	Yes ✓	No ✓	Private ✓

the initiator, who starts the first and second phases of the protocol. The initiator is required to contact the TTP to acknowledge the completion of the first phase of the protocol. Thus, firstly, this is not a strictly optimistic protocol, secondly, there is a necessity of trusting the initiator.

Later, Gonzales-Deleito and Markowitch [27] solved the malicious initiator problem of Bao et al. [6]. But, the problem in their protocol is in the recovery protocol: when one of the participants contacts the TTP, the TTP has to contact the previous participant in the ring. This is not preferable because it is not guaranteed that previous participant will be available. The protocol in [38] have also the problem in the recovery protocol.

Understanding Fairness: There is an important difference between our understanding of fairness, and existing ring-topology protocols' [6,27,38]. According to their definition, in the end, there will be no party such that he does not receive his desired item from the previous party but sends his item to the next party. It means that *there can be some parties who received their desired items and some other parties who did not receive or send anything.* Whereas, **according to our definition, either the whole topology is satisfied (all the necessary exchanges are complete), or no exchange takes place.**

Complete Topologies: Multi-party contract signing indeed corresponds to a complete topology. Garay and Mackenzie [24] proposed the first optimistic multi-party contract signing protocol that requires $O(n^2)$ rounds and $O(n^3)$ messages. Because of its inefficiency, Baum-Waidner and Waidner [8] suggested a more efficient protocol, whose complexity depends on the number of dishonest parties, and if the number of dishonest parties is $n - 1$, its efficiency is the same as [24]. Mukhamedov and Ryan [40] decreased the round complexity to $O(n)$. Lastly, Mauw et al. [39] gave the lower bound of $O(n^2)$ for the number of messages to achieve fairness. Their protocol requires $O(n^2)$ messages, but the round complexity is not constant. **We achieve both lower bounds ($O(n^2)$ messages and constant round) for the first time.**

Fair Secure Multi-party Computation: Secure multi-party computation had an important position in the last decades, but its fairness property did not receive a lot of attention. One SMPC protocol that achieves fairness is designed by Garay et al. [28]. It uses gradual release, which is the drawback of this protocol, because each party broadcasts its output gradually in each round. At each round the number of messages is $O(n^3)$ and there are a lot of rounds due to gradual release.

Another approach is using bitcoin to achieve fairness using a TTP in the optimistic model [1,11]. When one of the parties does not receive the output of the computation, he receives a bitcoin instead. This fairness approach was used by Lindell [35] for the two-party computation case, and by Küpçü and Lysyanskaya [33] and Belenkiy et al. [9] for peer-to-peer systems. However, this approach is not appropriate for multi-party computation since **we do not necessarily know how valuable the output will be before evaluation**. Finally, reputation-based fairness solutions [2] talk about fairness probabilities.

3   Definitions and Preliminaries

3.1   Preliminaries

Threshold Public Key Encryption: In such schemes, encryption is done with a single public key, generated jointly by n decrypters, but decryption requires at least k decrypters to cooperate. It consists of the probabilistic polynomial time (PPT) protocols *Key Generation, Verification, Decryption* and a PPT algorithm for *Encryption* [44]. We describe these via the *ElGamal* $(n, k = n)$ threshold encryption scheme we will employ, as follows:

- *Key Generation:* It generates a list of private keys $SK = \{x_1, ..., x_n\}$, where $x_i \in \mathbb{Z}_p$, public key $PK = (g, h)$, where g is a generator of a large prime p-order subgroup of $\mathbb{Z}_q^*$ with q prime, together with $h = g^{\sum x_i}$, and public verification key $VK = \{vk_1, ..., vk_n\} = \{g^{x_1}, ..., g^{x_n}\}$, where $n \geq 1$. Note that this can be done in a distributed manner [43].
- *Encryption:* It computes the ciphertext for plaintext m as $E = (a, b) = (g^r, mh^r)$ where $r \in \mathbb{Z}_p$.
- *Verification:* It is between a verifier and a prover. Verifier, using VK, E, and the given decryption share of the prover $d_i = g^{rx_i}$, outputs *valid* if prover shows that $\log_g vk_i$ is equal to $\log_a d_i$. Otherwise, it outputs *invalid*.
- *Decryption:* It takes as input n decryption shares $\{d_1, ..., d_n\}$, where $d_i = g^{rx_i}$, VK, and E. Then, it outputs a message m with the following computation (in $\mathbb{Z}_q^*$),

$$\frac{b}{\prod d_i} = \frac{mh^r}{g^{r \sum x_i}} = \frac{mh^r}{h^r} = m$$

  or $\perp$ if the decryption shares are invalid.

Verifiable Encryption: It is an encryption that enables the recipient to verify, using a public key, that the plaintext satisfies some relation, without performing any decryption [14,15]. A public non-malleable label can be attached to a verifiable encryption [44].

Verifiable Escrow: An escrow is a ciphertext under the public key of the TTP. A *verifiable* escrow [4,15] is a *verifiable* encryption under the public key of the TTP. We employ *ElGamal* verifiable encryption scheme [13,20].

Notation. The n parties in the protocol are represented by P_i, where $i \in \{1, ..., n\}$. P_h is to show the honest parties, and P_c is to show the corrupted parties controlled by the adversary $\mathcal{A}$.

VE_i and VS_i is used to show the verifiable encryption and escrow prepared by P_i, respectively. The descriptive notation for verifiable encryption and escrow is $V(E, pk; l)\{(v, \xi) \in R\}$. It denotes the verifiable encryption and escrow for the ciphertext E whereby ξ –whose relation R with the public value v can be verified– is encrypted under the public key pk, and labeled by l. For escrows, pk is the TTP's public key.

$PK(v)\{(v, \xi) \in R\}$ denotes a zero-knowledge proof of knowledge of ξ that has a relation R with the public value v. All relations R in our protocols have an honest-verifier zero-knowledge three-move proof of knowledge [18], so can be implemented very efficiently. ⓩ shows the number z in the Figure 1.

3.2   Definitions

Optimistic Fair Secure Multi-Party Computation: A group of parties with their private inputs w_i desire to compute a function ϕ [8,26]. This computation is *secure* when the parties do not learn anything beyond what is revealed by the output of the computation. It is *fair* if either all of the parties learn the output in the end of the computation, or none of them learns the output. For an *optimistic* protocol, the TTP is involved *only* when there is a dispute about fairness between parties. This is formalized by ideal-real world simulations, defined below.

Ideal World: It consists of an adversary $\mathcal{A}$ that corrupts the set $\mathcal{P}_c$ of m parties where $m \in \{1, ..., n - 1\}$, the set of remaining honest party(s) $\mathcal{P}_h$, and the universal trusted party U (*not the TTP*). The ideal protocol is as follows:

1. U receives inputs $\{w_i\}_{\{i \in \mathcal{P}_c\}}$ or the message ABORT from $\mathcal{A}$, and $\{w_j\}_{\{j \in \mathcal{P}_h\}}$ from the honest party(s). If the inputs are invalid or $\mathcal{A}$ sends the message ABORT, then U sends $\perp$ to all of the parties and halts.
2. Otherwise U computes $\phi(w_1, ..., w_n) = (\phi_1(w_1, ..., w_n), ..., \phi_n(w_1, ..., w_n))$. Let $\phi_i = \phi_i(w_1, ..., w_n)$ be the ith output. Then he sends $\{\phi_i\}_{\{i \in \mathcal{P}_c\}}$ to $\mathcal{A}$ and $\{\phi_j\}_{\{j \in \mathcal{P}_h\}}$ to the corresponding honest party(s).

The outputs of the parties in an ideal execution between the honest party(s) and $\mathcal{A}$ controlling the corrupted parties where U computes ϕ is denoted $\mathsf{IDEAL}_{\phi, \mathcal{A}(aux)}(w_1, w_2, ...w_n, \lambda)$, where $\{w_i\}_{1 \leq i \leq n}$ are the respective private inputs of the parties, aux is an auxiliary input of $\mathcal{A}$, and λ is the security parameter.

Real World: There is no U for a real protocol π to compute the functionality ϕ. There is an adversary $\mathcal{A}$ that controls the set $\mathcal{P}_c$ of corrupted parties and a TTP involved in the protocol when there is an unfair behavior. The pair of outputs of the honest party(s) P_h and $\mathcal{A}$ in the real execution of the protocol π, possibly employing the TTP, is denoted $\mathsf{REAL}_{\pi,\mathbf{TTP},\mathcal{A}(aux)}(w_1, w_2, ...w_n, \lambda)$, where $w_1, w_2, ...w_n, aux$, and λ are like above.

Note that U and TTP are not related to each other. TTP is the part of the real protocol to solve the fairness problem when it is necessary, but U is not real (just an ideal entity).

Definition 1 (Fair Secure Multi-Party Computation). *Let π be a probabilistic polynomial time (PPT) protocol and let ϕ be a PPT multi-party functionality. We say that π computes ϕ **fairly and securely** if for every non-uniform PPT real world adversary $\mathcal{A}$ attacking π, there exists a non-uniform PPT ideal world simulator S so that for every $w_1, w_2, ..., w_n, \lambda \in \{0,1\}^*$, the ideal and real world outputs are computationally indistinguishable:*

$$\{\mathsf{IDEAL}_{\phi,S(aux)}(w_1, w_2, ..., w_n, \lambda)\} \equiv_c \{\mathsf{REAL}_{\pi,\mathsf{TTP},\mathcal{A}(aux)}(w_1, w_2, ..., w_n, \lambda)\}$$

The standard secure multi-party ideal world definition [37] lets the adversary $\mathcal{A}$ to abort *after* learning his output but *before* the honest party(s) learns her output. Thus, proving protocols secure using the old definition would not meet the fairness requirements. Therefore, we prove our protocols' security and fairness under the modified definition above. Canetti [16] gives general definitions for security for multi-party protocols with the same intuition as the security and fairness definition above. Further realize that since the TTP T does not exist in the ideal world, the simulator should also simulate its behavior.

Optimistic Multi-Party Fair Exchange: The participants are $P_1, P_2, ..., P_n$. Each participant P_i has an item f_i to exchange, and wants to exchange his own item f_i with the other parties' items $\{f_j\}_{j\neq i}$, , where $i, j \in \{1, ..., n\}$. Thus, at the end, every participant obtains $\{f_i\}_{1\leq i\leq n}$ in a complete topology, or some subset of it defined by some other exchange topology.

Multi-Party fair exchange is also a multi-party computation where the functionality ϕ is defined via its parts ϕ_i as below (we exemplify using a complete topology):

$$\phi_i(f_1, ..., f_n) = (f_1, f_2, ..., f_{i-1}, f_{i+1}, ..., f_n)$$

The actual ϕ_i would depend on the topology. For example, for the ring topology, it would be defined as $\phi_i(f_1, ..., f_n) = f_{i-1}$ if $i \neq 1$, $\phi_i(f_1, ..., f_n) = f_n$ if $i = 1$. Therefore we can use Definition 1 as the security definition of the multi-party fair exchange, using the ϕ_i representing the desired topology.

Adversarial Model: When there is dispute between the parties, the TTP resolves the conflict *atomically*. We assume that the adversary cannot prevent the honest party(s) from reaching the TTP before the specified time interval. Secure channels are used to exchange the decryption shares and when contacting the TTP. The adversary may control up to $n-1$ out of n parties in the exchange, and is probabilistic polynomial time (PPT).

4   Description of the Protocol

Remember that our aim is to create efficient multi-party fair exchange protocols for every topology. The most important challenges of these kind of protocols are the following:

- Even if there are $n - 1$ colluding parties, the protocol has to guarantee the fairness. Consider a simple protocol for the complete topology: each party first sends the verifiable escrow of the his/her item to the other parties, and after all the verifiable escrows are received, each of them sends the (plaintext) items to each other. If one of the parties comes to the TTP for resolution, the TTP decrypts the verifiable escrow(s) and stores the contacting party's item for the other parties.

  Assume now that P_i and P_j are colluding, and P_i receives verifiable escrow of the honest party P_h. Then P_i contacts the TTP, receives f_h via the decryption of the verifiable escrow of P_h, and gives his item f_i to the TTP. At this moment, if P_i and P_j leave the protocol before P_j sends his verifiable escrow to P_h, then fairness is violated because P_h never gets the item of P_j, whereas, by colluding with P_i, P_j also received f_h.

  Thus, it is important *not* to let a party learn some item *before all the parties are guaranteed* that they will get all the items. We used this intuition while designing our protocols. Therefore, we oblige **parties to depend on some input from every party in every phase of the protocol**. Hence, even if there is only one honest party, the dishonest ones have to contact and provide their correct values to the honest party so that they can continue with the protocol.

- It is desirable and more applicable to use a semi-honest TTP. Hence, privacy against the TTP needs to be satisfied. In the protocol above, the privacy against the TTP is violated since the TTP learns the items of the parties.

- The parties do not receive or send any item to some of the other parties in some topologies (e.g., in the ring topology, P_2 receives an item only from P_1 and sends an item to P_3 only). Yet, a multi-party fair exchange protocol must ensure that either the whole topology is satisfied, or no party obtains any item. Previous protocols fail in this regard, and allow, for example P_2 to receive the item of P_1 as long as she sends her item to P_3, while it may be the case that P_4 did not receive the item of P_3. The main issue here is that, if a multi-party fair exchange protocol lets the topology to be partially satisfied, we might as well replace that protocol with multiple executions of two-party fair exchange protocols. The main goal of MFE is to ensure that either the whole topology is satisfied, or no exchange happens.

We succeed in overcoming the challenges above with our MFE protocol. We first describe the protocol for the complete topology for the sake of simplicity. Then, we show how we can use our MFE protocol for other topologies in Section 5. All zero-knowledge proof of knowledge protocols are executed non-interactively in the random oracle model [12].

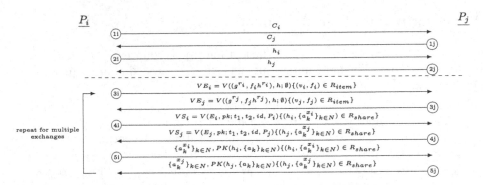

Fig. 1. Our MFE Protocol. Each (i, j) message pair can be performed in any order or in parallel within a step.

4.1 Multi-Party Fair Exchange Protocol (MFE)

There is a trusted third party (TTP) that is involved in the protocol when a dispute happens between the participants about fairness. His public key pk is known to every participant.

Overview: The protocol has three phases. In the first phase, parties jointly generate a public key for the threshold encryption scheme using their private shares. This phase needs to be done only once among the same set of participants. In the second phase, they send to each other the verifiable encryptions of the items that they want to exchange. If anything goes wrong up till here, the protocol is aborted. In the final phase, they exchange decryption shares for each item. If something goes wrong during the final phase, resolutions with the TTP are performed. The details are below (see also Figure 1).

Phase 1 (① and ② in Figure 1): All participants agree on the prime p-order subgroup of $\mathbb{Z}_q^*$, where q is a large prime, and a generator g of this subgroup. Then each P_i does the following [43]:

- P_i randomly selects his share x_i from $\mathbb{Z}_p$ and computes the verification key $h_i = g^{x_i}$. Then he commits to h_i and sends the commitment C_i to other parties [43].
- After receiving all commitments from the other parties, P_i opens C_i and obtains all other parties' h_j.
  Note that this must be done after exchanging all the commitments, since otherwise we cannot claim independence of the shares, and then the threshold encryption scheme's security argument would fail. But with the two steps above, the security proof for threshold encryption holds here.
- After receiving all h_i values successfully, P_i computes the threshold encryption's public key

$$h = \prod_i h_i = \prod_i g^{x_i} = g^{\sum_i x_i} = g^x.$$

Phase 1 is executed only once. Afterward, the same set of parties can exchange as many items as they want by performing only Phase 2 and Phase 3.

Phase 2 (③ in Figure 1): Firstly, parties agree on two time parameters t_1 and t_2, and identification id of the protocol. (Time parameters can also be agreed in Phase 1.) Each participant P_i does the following:

- P_i sends a verifiable encryption of his item f_i as

$$VE_i = V((g^{r_i}, f_i h^{r_i}), h; \emptyset)\{(v, f_i) \in R_{item}\}$$

where r_i is randomly selected from $\mathbb{Z}_p$. For the notation simplicity, we denote $(a_i, b_i) = (g^{r_i}, f_i h^{r_i})$. VE_i includes the encryption of the item f_i with public key h and it can be verified that the encrypted item f_i and the public value v_i has the relation R_{item}. Shortly, P_i proves he encrypts desired item. (e.g., if f_i is a signature on a contract, then v_i contains the signature verification key of P_i together with the contract, and R_{item} is the relation that f_i is a valid signature with respect to v_i.)

Note that without knowing n decryption shares, no party can decrypt any VE_j and learn the items. Thus, if anything goes wrong up to this point, the parties can locally abort the protocol. After this point, they need to obtain all the decryption shares. This is done in the following phase.

Phase 3 (④ and ⑤ in Figure 1): No party begins this phase without completing Phase 2 and receiving all verifiable encryptions VE_j correctly.

- P_i sends to other parties a verifiable escrow VS_i that includes the decryption shares for each verifiable encryption VE_j. VS_i is computed as

$$VS_i = V(E_i, pk; t_1, t_2, id, P_i)\{(h_i, \{a_k^{x_i}\}_{1 \leq k \leq n}) \in R_{share}\}$$

where E_i is the encryption of $a_1^{x_i}, a_2^{x_i}, ..., a_n^{x_i}$ with the TTP's public key pk. The relation R_{share} is:

$$\log_g h_i = \log_{a_k} a_k^{x_i} \text{ for each } k. \tag{1}$$

Simply, the verifiable escrow VS_i includes the encryption of the decryption shares of P_i that will be used to decrypt the encrypted items of all parties. It can be verified that it has the correct decryption shares. In addition, only the TTP can open it. The label t_1, t_2, id, P_i contains the public parameters of the protocol, and P_i is just a name that the participant chooses. Here, we assume that each party knows the other parties' names.

Remark: The name P_i is necessary to show the VS_i belongs him. It is not beneficial to put a wrong name in a verifiable escrow's label, since a corrupted party can convince TTP to decrypt VS_i by showing P_i is dishonest. The other labels id, t_1, t_2 are to show the protocol parameters to the TTP. Exchange identifier id is necessary to prevent corrupted parties to induce TTP to decrypt VS_j for another exchange. Consider that some exchange protocol ended unsuccessfully, which means nobody received any item. The corrupted party can go to the TTP as if VS_j is the verifiable escrow of the next protocol, and have it decrypted, if we were not using exchange identifiers. We will see in our resolution protocols that **cheating in the labels do not provide any advantage to an adversary**. Furthermore, the party names can be random and distinct in each exchange, as long as the parties know each others' names, and so it does not violate the privacy of the parties.

- P_i waits for VS_j from each P_j. If anything is wrong with some VS_j (e.g., verification fails or the label is not as expected), or P_i does not receive the verifiable escrow from at least one participant, he executes **Resolve 1** before t_1. Otherwise, P_i continues with the next step.
- P_i sends his decryption shares $(a_1^{x_i}, a_2^{x_i}, ..., a_n^{x_i})$ to each P_j. In addition, he executes the zero-knowledge proof of knowledge showing that these are the correct decryption shares

$$PK(h_i, \{a_k\}_{k \in N})\{(h_i, \{a_k^{x_i}\}_{1 \le k \le n}) \in R_{share}\}. \tag{2}$$

- P_i waits for $(a_1^{x_j}, a_2^{x_j}, ..., a_n^{x_j})$ from each P_j, together with the same proof that he does. If one of the values that he receives is not as expected or if he does not receive them from some P_j, he performs **Resolve 2** protocol with the TTP, before t_2 and after t_1. Otherwise, P_i continues with the next step.
- After receiving all the necessary values, P_i can decrypt each VE_i and get all the items. The decryption for item f_j is as below:

$$b_j / \prod_k a_j^{x_k} = f_j h^{r_j} / g^{r_j \sum_k x_k} = f_j h^{r_j} / (g^{\sum_k x_k})^{r_j} = f_j h^{r_j} / h^{r_j} = f_j$$

Resolve 1. The goal of Resolve 1 is to *record* the corrupted parties that did *not* send their verifiable escrow in ④. Resolve 1 needs to be done **before t_1**. Parties do *not* learn any decryption shares here. They can just complain about other parties to the TTP. The TTP creates a fresh *complaintList* for the protocol with parameters id, t_1, t_2. The *complaintList* contains the names of pairs of parties having a dispute because of the missing VS. The **complainant** is the party that complains, whose name is saved as the first of the pair, and the **complainee** is saved as the second of the pair. The TTP saves also *complainee's verification key* given by the complainant; in the case that the complainee contacts the TTP, he will be able to prove that he is the complainee. See Algorithm 1.

Algorithm 1. Resolve 1

P_i sends id, t_1, t_2, P_j, h_j to the TTP where P_j is the party that did not send VS_j to P_i. The TTP does the following:
if $currenttime > t_1$ **then**
    send msg "Abort Resolve 1"
else
    $complaintList =$ GetComplaintList(id, t_1, t_2)

    if $complaintList ==$ NULL **then**

        $complaintList =$ EmptyList(id, t_1, t_2)
        // initialize empty list
        $solvedList =$ EmptyList(id, t_1, t_2) //
        will be used in Resolve 2
    end if
    $complaintList$.add$(P_i, (P_j, h_j))$
    send msg "Come after t_1 for Resolve 2"
end if

Resolve 2. Resolve 2 is the resolution protocol where the parties come to the TTP to ask him to decrypt verifiable escrows and the TTP solves the complaint problems recorded in Resolve 1. The TTP does *not* decrypt any verifiable escrow until the *complaintList* is *empty*.

The party P_i, who comes for Resolve 2 **between t_1 and t_2**, gives all verifiable escrows that he has already received from the other parties and his own verifiable escrow to the TTP. The TTP uses these verifiable escrows to save the decryption shares required to solve the complaints in the *complaintList*. If the *complaintList* is not empty in the end, P_i comes after t_2 for Resolve 3. Otherwise, P_i can perform Resolve 3 immediately and get all the decryption shares that he requests.

Algorithm 2. Resolve 2

P_i gives $\mathcal{M}$, which is the set of verifiable escrows that P_i has. The TTP does the following:
$complaintList = $ GetComplaintList(id, t_1, t_2)
for all VS_j in $\mathcal{M}$ **do**
  if $(*, (P_j, h_j)) \in complaintList$ AND
  CheckCorrectness(VS_j, h_j) is true **then**
    $shares_j = $ Decrypt(sk, VS_j)
    $solvedList$.Save$(P_j, shares_j)$
    $complaintList$.Remove$((*, (P_j, h_j)))$
  end if
end for
if *complaintList* is empty **then**
  send msg "Do Resolve 3"
else
  send msg "Come after t_2 for Resolve 3"
end if

CheckCorrectness(VS_j, h_j) returns *true* if the TTP can verify the relation in equation (1) using verifiable escrow VS_j and h_j. Otherwise it returns *false*.

Resolve 3. If the *complaintList* still has parties, even after t_2, the TTP answers each resolving party saying that the protocol is **aborted**, which means nobody is able to learn any item. If the *complaintList* is *empty*, the TTP decrypts any verifiable escrow that is given to him. Besides, if the complainants in the *solvedList* come, he gives the stored decryption shares. See Algorithm 3.

Algorithm 3. Resolve 3

P_i gives $\mathcal{C}$, which is the set of parties that did not perform step ④ or ⑤ with P_i, and $\mathcal{V}$, which is the set of verifiable escrows that belongs to parties in $\mathcal{C}$ who performed step ④. The TTP does the following:
$complaintList = $ GetComplaintList(id, t_1, t_2)

if *complaintList*.isEmpty() **then**
  for all P_j in $\mathcal{C}$ **do**
    if $VS_j \in \mathcal{V}$ **then**
      send Decrypt(sk, VS_j)
    else
      send $solvedList$.GetShares(P_j)
    end if
  end for
else if $currenttime > t_2$ **then**
  send msg "Protocol is aborted"
else
  send msg "Try after t_2"
end if

4.2   Security

Theorem 1. *The MFE protocol above is fair according to Definition 1, assuming that ElGamal threshold encryption scheme is a secure threshold encryption scheme, the associated verifiable escrow scheme is secure, all commitments are hiding and binding, and the discrete logarithm problem is hard (so that the proofs are sound and zero-knowledge).*

Proof Sketch: The proof of Theorem 1 is in the full version of this paper [31]. Assume the worst-case that adversary $\mathcal{A}$ corrupts $n-1$ parties. The simulator S simulates the honest party in the real world and the corrupted parties in the ideal world. S also acts as the TTP in the protocol if any resolution protocol occurs, so S publishes a public key pk as the TTP, and knows the corresponding secret key. Let's assume that S simulates the honest party P_1 without loss of generality in real world.

S behaves the same as in the real protocol for Phase 1. Then in Phase 2, he encrypts random item $\tilde{f}_1$ since he does not know real f_1 and sends the verifiable encryption $\tilde{V}E_1$ to other parties. While he receives other parties' VEs, he learns the other parties' items behaving as the extractor of verifiable encryption.

He behaves as in Phase 3. Additionally he learns decryption shares of the parties that send verifiable escrow using the extractor.

If he receives all verifiable escrows of the other parties, it means it is guaranteed that the real honest party would obtain her desired items, because S in the real world is now able to learn all the decryption shares from the corrupted parties via resolutions. So he sends the items of the other parties to U and receives f_1. Then he calculates Equation 3 to find the appropriate decryption share d_1 such that the other parties can get the item f_1 from a_1, b_1 using d_1. The other decryption shares are calculated as in the real protocol.

$$d_1 = \frac{b_1}{f_1 a_i^{x_2} ... a_i^{x_n}} \tag{3}$$

Otherwise S simulates the resolve protocols and does not send his decryption shares as in real protocol. In the end of t_2, if *complaintList* is empty, S sends items of corrupted parties to U and receives f_1. Then he calculates d_1 from Equation 3. In this point, when some parties come for Resolve 3, S can give every share that they want. If *complaintList* is not empty in the end of t_2, S sends message ABORT to U.

5   All Topologies for MFE

In this section, we adapt our MFE protocol to every topology. Our fairness definition remains the same: either the whole topology is satisfied, or no party learns any item. As an example, consider the ring topology as in Figure 3. Parties want an item from only the previous party. For example, P_2 only wants P_1's item f_1. However, P_2 should contact all other parties because of our all-or-none fairness condition. Besides, we are not limited with a topology that follows a specific pattern such as the number of parties and items being necessarily equal. For example, it is possible to provide fairness in the topology in Figure 5 even though P_2, P_3, and P_4 do not have exchange item with each other.

	f_1	f_2	f_3	f_4
P_1		$\odot$		
P_2			$\odot$	
P_3				$\odot$
P_4	$\odot$			

Fig. 2. Desired items by each parties in matrix form in the ring topology

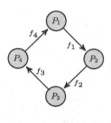

Fig. 3. Graph representation of the ring topology

	f_1	f_2	f_3	f_4	f_5
P_1	$\odot$	$\odot$	$\odot$	$\odot$	$\odot$
P_2	$\odot$				
P_3	$\odot$				
P_4	$\odot$				

Fig. 4. Matrix representation of a topology

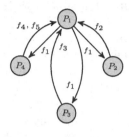

Fig. 5. Graph representation of a topology in Figure 4

Consider some arbitrary topology described by the matrix in Figure 6. If a party desires an item from another party, he should have all the shares of the item as shown in Figure 7. In general, we can say that if a party P_i wants the item f_t he should receive $\{a_t^{x_j}\}_{\{1 \leq j \leq n\}}$ from all the parties $\{P_j\}_{\{1 \leq j \leq n\}}$. Therefore, our MFE can be applied to any topology with the same fairness condition, which is **all parties will receive all their desired items or none of them receives anything** in the end of the protocol.

	f_1	f_2	f_3	f_4	f_5
P_1	$\odot$		$\odot$		
P_2	$\odot$			$\odot$	$\odot$
P_3	$\odot$		$\odot$		
P_4	$\odot$	$\odot$	$\odot$		$\odot$

Fig. 6. Each party wants the marked items corresponding to his/her row. P_i has f_i, except P_4 has both f_4 and f_5.

	f_1	f_2	f_3	f_4	f_5
P_1		$\{a_2^{x_i}\}$	$\{a_3^{x_i}\}$		$\{a_5^{x_i}\}$
P_2	$\{a_1^{x_i}\}$			$\{a_4^{x_i}\}$	$\{a_5^{x_i}\}$
P_3	$\{a_1^{x_i}\}$		$\{a_3^{x_i}\}$		
P_4	$\{a_1^{x_i}\}$	$\{a_2^{x_i}\}$	$\{a_3^{x_i}\}$		$\{a_5^{x_i}\}$

Fig. 7. Necessary shares for each party to get the desired items that are shown in Figure 6. Sets are over $i \in \{1, 2, ..., 5\}$

Our strong fairness condition requires that all parties have to depend each other. Even though P_i does not want an item f_j from P_j, getting his desired item has to also depend on P_j. Therefore we cannot decrease number of messages even in a simpler (e.g., ring) topology.

On the other hand, the size of the verifiable escrow, meaning that the number of shares in the verifiable escrow, decreases in topologies other than the complete one. If we represent the topology in a matrix form as in Figure 6, each party P_i

has to add the number of $\odot$ many shares corresponding to the row of the party P_j to the verifiable escrow that is sent to P_j. We can conclude that the total size of the verifiable escrows that a party sends is $O(\#\odot)$ where $\odot$ is as in Figure 6.

6 Efficient Fair Secure Multi-Party Computation

In this section, we show how to adapt the MFE protocol to **any** secure multi-party computation (SMPC) protocol [7,10,17,26,46] to achieve fairness.

Assume n participants want to compute a function $\phi(w_1,...,w_n) = (\phi_1(w_1,...,w_n),...,\phi_n(w_1,...,w_n))$, where w_i is the input and $\phi_i = \phi_i(w_1,...,w_n)$ is the output of party P_i.

- P_i randomly chooses a share $x_i \in \mathbb{Z}_p$. Then P_i gives his share and w_i to an SMPC protocol that outputs the computation of the functionality ψ where $\psi_i(z_1, z_2, ..., z_n) = (E_i(\phi_i(w_1,...,w_n)), \{g^{x_j}\}_{1 \le j \le n})$ is the output to, and $z_i = (w_i, x_i)$ is the input of P_i. This corresponds to a circuit encrypting the outputs of the original function ϕ using the shares provided as input, and also outputting the verification shares of all parties to everyone. Encryption E_i is done with the key $h = g^{\sum_{j=1}^{n} x_j}$ as follows:

$$E_i(\phi_i(w_1,...,w_n)) = (g^{r_i}, \phi_i h^{r_i})$$

where $r_i \in \mathbb{Z}_p$ are random numbers chosen by the circuit (or they can also be inputs to the circuit), similar to the original MFE protocol.

It is expected that everyone learns the output of ψ before a fair exchange occurs. If some party did not receive his output at the end of the SMPC protocol, then they do not proceed with the fair exchange, and hence no party will be able to decrypt and learn their output.

- If everyone received their output from the SMPC protocol, then they execute the Phase 3 of the MFE protocol above, using g^{x_i} values obtained from the output of ψ as verification shares, and x_i values as their secret shares. Furthermore, the a_i, b_i values are obtained from E_i.

Note that each function output is encrypted with all the shares. But, for party P_i, she need not provide her decryption share for f_i to any other party. Furthermore, instead of providing n decryption shares to each other party as in a complete topology, she needs to provide only one decryption share, $a_j^{x_i}$, to each P_j. Therefore, the Phase 3 of MFE here is a more efficient version. Indeed, the verifiable escrows, the decryption shares, and their proofs each need to be only on a *single* value instead of n values.

Phases 1 and 2 of the fair exchange protocol have already been done during the modified SMPC protocol, since the parties get the encryption of the output that is encrypted by their shares. Since the SMPC protocol is secure, it is guaranteed to output the correct ciphertexts, and we do not need further verification. We also do not need to commit to x_i values, since the SMPC protocol ensures independence of inputs as well. So, the parties only need to perform Phase 3.

In the end of the exchange, each party can decrypt only their own output, because they do not disclose their own decryption shares. Indeed, if a symmetric functionality is desired for SMPC, $\psi(z_1, z_2, ..., z_n) = \{E_i(\phi_i(w_1, ..., w_n)), g^{x_i}\}_{1 \leq i \leq n}$ may be computed, and since P_i does not give the decryption share of f_i to anyone else, each party will still only be able to decrypt their own output. Hence, **a symmetric functionality SMPC protocol may be employed to compute an asymmetric functionality fairly using our modification**. Note also that we view the SMPC protocol as *black box*.

Our overhead over performing *unfair* SMPC is minimal. Even though the input and output sizes are extended additionally by $O(n)$ values and the circuit is extended to perform encryptions, these are minimal requirements, especially if the underlying SMPC protocol works over *arithmetic circuits* (e.g., [7,46]). In such a case, performing ElGamal and creating verification values g^{x_i} are very easy. Afterward, we only add two rounds of interaction for the sake of fairness (i.e., Phase 3 of MFE, with smaller messages). Moreover, all the benefits of our MFE protocol apply here as well.

Theorem 2. *The SMPC protocol above is fair and secure according to Definition 1 for the functionality ϕ, assuming that ElGamal threshold encryption scheme is a secure, the discrete logarithm assumption holds, and the underlying SMPC protocol that computes functionality ψ is secure.*

Proof Sketch: The proof of Theorem 2 is in the full version of this paper [31]. Assume that $\mathcal{A}$ corrupts $n - 1$ parties, which is the worst possible case. The simulator S simulates the honest party in the real world and the corrupted parties in the ideal world. S uses random input and acts as the simulator of underlying SMPC protocol. The only difference between simulator of SMPC and S is that S does not send inputs of the corrupted parties to U directly after learning inputs of them because he needs to be sure that all parties will receive output before sending inputs to U. The output of the simulated SMPC protocol is encryptions of random outputs. Because of the security of ElGamal encryption, these encryptions are indistinguishable from real ones.

In the end, S behaves as the simulator of MFE protocol for Phase 3 to simulate the exchange. If it is guarantee all parties learn outputs, S sends inputs of P_c's to U and receives the output of P_h. Then he calculates each share d_i as in Equation 3. Otherwise he sends the message ABORT to U.

Table 3 compares our fair SMPC solution. Our advantage is in terms of **efficiency**, having **no requirement for an external payment mechanism**, and **proving security and fairness together** via ideal/real simulation.

7 Performance and Privacy Analysis

MFE: Each party P_i in MFE prepares one verifiable encryption and one verifiable escrow, and sends them to $n - 1$ parties. The verification of them are efficient because the relation they show can be proven using discrete-logarithm-based honest-verifier zero-knowledge three-move proofs of knowledge [18]. In the end, P_i sends a message including decryption shares to $n - 1$ parties, again with an efficient proof of knowledge. So, for each party P_i, the number of messages

Table 3. Comparison of our fair SMPC solution with previous works. NFS indicates simulation proof given but not for fairness, FS indicates full simulation proof including fairness, and λ is the security parameter.

Solutions	Technique	TTP	Number of Rounds	Proof Technique
[23]	Gradual Release	No	$O(\lambda)$	NFS
[11]	Bitcoin	Yes	Constant ✓	NFS
[1]	Bitcoin	Yes	Constant ✓	NFS
Ours	MFE	Yes	Constant ✓	FS ✓

that he sends is $O(n)$. Since there are n parties, the total message complexity is $O(n^2)$. Note that there is *no* requirement to have these messages broadcast; just ensuring all previous step's messages are received before moving further is enough for security. Table 1 shows the comparison to the previous works, MFE is much more efficient, obtaining **optimal asymptotic efficiency**.

When there is a malicious party or a party suffering from network failure, MFE protocol ends at the latest, immediately after t_2. In the worst case, n parties contact the TTP, so it is important to reduce his workload. TTP's duties include checking some list from his records, verifying efficient zero-knowledge proofs of knowledge from some number of parties (depending on the size of the *complaintList*), and decrypting verifiable escrows. These actions are all efficient.

Moreover, the **privacy against the TTP is preserved**. He just learns some decryption shares, but he cannot decrypt the encryption of exchanged items, since he never gets the encrypted items.

We used ElGamal threshold encryption for presentation simplicity. Instead, any threshold encryption scheme such as the Pailler cryptosystem [42], Franklin and Haber's cryptosystem [22], or Damgard-Jurik cryptosystem [19] can be used.

Finally, our MFE protocol achieves the intuitive fairness definition of 'either the whole topology is satisfied, or no item is exchanged' for any topology. Such a strong fairness definition necessitates that the exchanges depend on all parties, necessitating quadratic number of messages.

Fair MPC: The overhead of our fairness solution on top of an existing unfair SMPC protocol is increased input/output size, and additional computation of encryptions and verification shares. If an arithmetic circuit is used in the underlying SMPC protocol [7,17,46], then there are only $O(n)$ additional exponentiations required, which does not extend circuit size a lot. If boolean circuits are used, the size of the circuit increases more than arithmetic circuits would have, but it is still tolerable considering in comparison to the related work.

As seen in Table 3, [23] uses gradual release for fairness. However, this brings many extra rounds and messages to the protocol. Each round each party releases his item by broadcasting it. Recent, bitcoin-based approaches [1,11] also require broadcasting in the bitcoin network, which increases message complexity. Our only overhead is a constant number of rounds, and $O(n^2)$ messages. Remember again that these are asymptotically optimal, since fair SMPC necessitates a complete topology.

Acknowledgments. The authors acknowledge the support of TÜBİTAK, the Scientific and Technological Research Council of Turkey, under project number 111E019, as well as European Union COST Action IC1306.

References

1. Andrychowicz, M., Dziembowski, S., Malinowski, D., Mazurek, V.: Secure multiparty computations on bitcoin. In: IEEE Symposium on Security and Privacy (2014)
2. Asharov, G., Lindell, Y., Zarosim, H.: Fair and efficient secure multiparty computation with reputation systems. In: Sako, K., Sarkar, P. (eds.) ASIACRYPT 2013, Part II. LNCS, vol. 8270, pp. 201–220. Springer, Heidelberg (2013)
3. Asokan, N., Schunter, M., Waidner, M.: Optimistic protocols for multi-party fair exchange (1996)
4. Asokan, N., Shoup, V., Waidner, M.: Optimistic fair exchange of digital signatures. IEEE Journal on Selected Areas in Communications, 591–610 (2000)
5. Bao, F., Deng, R.H., Mao, W.: Efficient and practical fair exchange protocols with off-line TTP. In: IEEE Symposium on Security and Privacy (1998)
6. Bao, F., Deng, R.H., Nguyen, K.Q., Varadharajan, V.: Multi-party fair exchange with an off-line trusted neutral party. In: DEXA Workshop (1999)
7. Baum, C., Damgård, I., Orlandi, C.: Publicly auditable secure multi-party computation. Cryptology ePrint Archive, Report 2014/075
8. Baum-Waidner, B., Waidner, M.: Round-optimal and abuse-free optimistic multiparty contract signing. In: Welzl, E., Montanari, U., Rolim, J.D.P. (eds.) ICALP 2000. LNCS, vol. 1853, pp. 524–535. Springer, Heidelberg (2000)
9. Belenkiy, M., Chase, M., Erway, C.C., Jannotti, J., Küpçü, A., Lysyanskaya, A., Rachlin, E.: Making p2p accountable without losing privacy. In: WPES (2008)
10. Ben-Or, M., Goldwasser, S., Wigderson, A.: Completeness theorems for non-cryptographic fault-tolerant distributed computation. In: ACM STOC (1988)
11. Bentov, I., Kumaresan, R.: How to use bitcoin to design fair protocols. In: Garay, J.A., Gennaro, R. (eds.) CRYPTO 2014, Part II. LNCS, vol. 8617, pp. 421–439. Springer, Heidelberg (2014)
12. Blum, M., Feldman, P., Micali, S.: Non-interactive zero-knowledge and its applications. In: ACM STOC (1988)
13. Cachin, C., Camenisch, J.L.: Optimistic fair secure computation. In: Bellare, M. (ed.) CRYPTO 2000. LNCS, vol. 1880, pp. 93–111. Springer, Heidelberg (2000)
14. Camenisch, J., Damgård, I.: Verifiable encryption and applications to group signatures and signature sharing. Technical report (1999)
15. Camenisch, J.L., Shoup, V.: Practical verifiable encryption and decryption of discrete logarithms. In: Boneh, D. (ed.) CRYPTO 2003. LNCS, vol. 2729, pp. 126–144. Springer, Heidelberg (2003)
16. Canetti, R.: Security and composition of multiparty cryptographic protocols. Journal of Cryptology, 143–202 (2000)
17. Cramer, R., Damgård, I.B., Nielsen, J.B.: Multiparty computation from threshold homomorphic encryption. In: Pfitzmann, B. (ed.) EUROCRYPT 2001. LNCS, vol. 2045, pp. 280–300. Springer, Heidelberg (2001)
18. Damgård, I.: On sigma protocols. http://www.daimi.au.dk/ivan/Sigma.pdf
19. Damgård, I.B., Jurik, M.J.: A length-flexible threshold cryptosystem withapplications. In: Safavi-Naini, R., Seberry, J. (eds.) ACISP 2003. LNCS, vol. 2727, pp. 350–364. Springer, Heidelberg (2003)

20. ElGamal, T.: A public-key cryptosystem and a signature scheme based on discrete logarithms. In: Blakley, G.R., Chaum, D. (eds.) Advances in Cryptology — CRYPTO 1984. LNCS, vol. 196, pp. 10–18. Springer, Heidelberg (1985)
21. Even, S., Yacobi, Y.: Relations among public key signature scheme. Technical report, Department of Computer Science, TechUnion (1980)
22. Franklin, M., Haber, S.: Joint encryption and message-efficient secure computation. In: Stinson, D.R. (ed.) Advances in Cryptology — CRYPTO 1993. LNCS, vol. 773, pp. 266–277. Springer, Heidelberg (1994)
23. Garay, J.A., MacKenzie, P.D., Prabhakaran, M., Yang, K.: Resource fairness and composability of cryptographic protocols. In: Halevi, S., Rabin, T. (eds.) TCC 2006. LNCS, vol. 3876, pp. 404–428. Springer, Heidelberg (2006)
24. Garay, J.A., Jakobsson, M., MacKenzie, P.D.: Abuse-free optimistic contract signing. In: Wiener, M. (ed.) CRYPTO 1999. LNCS, vol. 1666, pp. 449–466. Springer, Heidelberg (1999)
25. Garay, J.A., MacKenzie, P.D.: Abuse-free multi-party contract signing. In: Jayanti, P. (ed.) DISC 1999. LNCS, vol. 1693, pp. 151–166. Springer, Heidelberg (1999)
26. Goldreich, O., Micali, S., Wigderson, A.: How to play any mental game. In: STOC (1987)
27. González-Deleito, N., Markowitch, O.: An optimistic multi-party fair exchange protocol with reduced trust requirements. In: Kim, K. (ed.) ICISC 2001. LNCS, vol. 2288, pp. 258–267. Springer, Heidelberg (2002)
28. Gordon, S.D., Katz, J.: Complete fairness in multi-party computation without an honest majority. In: Reingold, O. (ed.) TCC 2009. LNCS, vol. 5444, pp. 19–35. Springer, Heidelberg (2009)
29. Hirt, M., Tschudi, D.: Efficient general-adversary multi-party computation. In: Sako, K., Sarkar, P. (eds.) ASIACRYPT 2013, Part II. LNCS, vol. 8270, pp. 181–200. Springer, Heidelberg (2013)
30. Kılınç, H., Küpçü, A.: Efficiently making secure two-party computation fair. Cryptology ePrint Archive, Report 2014/896
31. Kılınç, H., Küpçü, A.: Optimally efficient multi-party fair exchance and fair secure multi-party computation. Cryptology ePrint Archive, Report 2015/064
32. Küpçü, A., Lysyanskaya, A.: Usable optimistic fair exchange. In: Pieprzyk, J. (ed.) CT-RSA 2010. LNCS, vol. 5985, pp. 252–267. Springer, Heidelberg (2010)
33. Küpçü, A., Lysyanskaya, A.: Usable optimistic fair exchange. Computer Networks (2012)
34. Küpçü, A., Lysyanskaya, A.: Optimistic fair exchange with multiple arbiters. In: Gritzalis, D., Preneel, B., Theoharidou, M. (eds.) ESORICS 2010. LNCS, vol. 6345, pp. 488–507. Springer, Heidelberg (2010)
35. Lindell, A.Y.: Legally-enforceable fairness in secure two-party computation. In: Malkin, T. (ed.) CT-RSA 2008. LNCS, vol. 4964, pp. 121–137. Springer, Heidelberg (2008)
36. Lindell, Y., Pinkas, B.: An efficient protocol for secure two-party computation in the presence of malicious adversaries. In: Naor, M. (ed.) EUROCRYPT 2007. LNCS, vol. 4515, pp. 52–78. Springer, Heidelberg (2007)
37. Lindell, Y., Pinkas, B.: Secure multiparty computation for privacy-preserving data mining. Journal of Privacy and Confidentiality (2009)
38. Liu, Y., Hu, H.: An improved protocol for optimistic multi-party fair exchange. In: EMEIT (2011)
39. Mauw, S., Radomirovic, S., Dashti, M.T.: Minimal message complexity of asynchronous multi-party contract signing. In: CSF (2009)

40. Mukhamedov, A., Ryan, M.D.: Fair multi-party contract signing using private contract signatures. Inf. Comput., 272–290 (2008)
41. Pagnia, H., Gärtner, F.C.: On the impossibility of fair exchange without a trusted third party. Technical report (1999)
42. Paillier, P.: Public-key cryptosystems based on composite degree residuosity classes. In: Stern, J. (ed.) EUROCRYPT 1999. LNCS, vol. 1592, pp. 223–238. Springer, Heidelberg (1999)
43. Pedersen, T.P.: A threshold cryptosystem without a trusted party. In: Davies, D.W. (ed.) EUROCRYPT 1991. LNCS, vol. 547, pp. 522–526. Springer, Heidelberg (1991)
44. Shoup, V., Gennaro, R.: Securing threshold cryptosystems against chosen ciphertext attack. J. Cryptology, 75–96 (2002)
45. Yao, A.C.: Protocols for secure computations. In: FOCS (1982)
46. Zamani, M., Movahedi, M., Saia, J.: Millions of millionaires: Multiparty computation in large networks

Authenticated Encryption

How to Incorporate Associated Data
in Sponge-Based Authenticated Encryption

Yu Sasaki$^{(\boxtimes)}$ and Kan Yasuda

NTT Secure Platform Laboratories, Tokyo, Japan
{sasaki.yu,yasuda.kan}@lab.ntt.co.jp

Abstract. We explore ways to combine associated data A with a sponge-based authenticated encryption (AE) scheme. In addition to the popular "header" and "trailer" methods, this paper investigates two other methods, *concurrent absorption* and *ciphertext translation*. The concurrent absorption is a novel method unique to the sponge construction. The advantage of the concurrent absorption is its efficiency; the number of permutation calls reduces to $\max\{|A|/c, |M|/r\}$ where $|\cdot|$ denotes the bit length, c the capacity size in bits, and r the rate size. In particular, if the size of A is relatively small, i.e. $|A|/c \leq |M|/r$, then there is no need of extra permutation calls for processing A. On the other hand, the ciphertext translation is a generic technique developed by Rogaway (ACM CCS 2002), and in this paper it is concretized as a sponge-based AE scheme. The advantage of the sponge-based ciphertext translation is that it can start encrypting a message M irrespective of the relative arrival time of A. The efficiency of header and trailer methods can also be improved by using a similar technique. Remarkably, all of these methods are highly secure; the key length being denoted by κ, all methods achieve $\min\{2^{(r+c)/2}, 2^c/r, 2^\kappa\}$ security against nonce-respecting adversaries in the ideal model, as recently shown by Jovanovic et al. (Asiacrypt 2014) for the conventional header and trailer methods.

Keywords: CAESAR · AEAD · Sponge · Duplex · Donkey · Monkey · Capacity · Beyond $2^{c/2}$ security

1 Introduction

If one invents a new type of authenticated encryption (AE) scheme, then the scheme might face the problem of handling associated data. The problem is how to efficiently authenticate both associated data A and a message M, where A needs to be sent in the clear and M needs to be encrypted. This would become an easy task if the scheme was of "two-pass" generic composition, say Enc-then-MAC [5]. Then simply the scheme would first encrypt M to get ciphertext C and then authenticate $A \parallel C$ to generate a tag T.

However, several people, including Kaliski [22], noticed that no obvious solution exists for a scheme like OCB [23] where authentication and encryption are tightly integrated in a "one-pass" mechanism. For such schemes Rogaway [22]

© Springer International Publishing Switzerland 2015
K. Nyberg (ed.): CT-RSA 2015, LNCS 9048, pp. 353–370, 2015.
DOI: 10.1007/978-3-319-16715-2_19

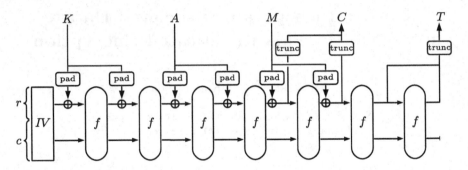

Fig. 1. An illustration of SPONGEWRAP [8] iterating a "monolithic" permutation f. The rate and capacity sizes are denoted by r and c, respectively. The function pad is used for domain separation between A and M, as well as for wrapping the key K and the last blocks of A and M; pad adds a "frame bit" to each block of A and M. The function trunc chops off the frame bits, unwraps the last block of M, and truncates the tag T.

suggested two solutions: *nonce stealing* and *ciphertext translation*. The nonce stealing works when A "fits" in the gap between the acceptable size of nonce input (being larger) and the actual size of the nonce used (being smaller). In such a case one can feed $N \parallel A$ to the nonce input, where N is the original nonce. On the other hand, the ciphertext translation works for A of arbitrary size by using a keyed hash function to compress A and xoring the hash value onto the ciphertext C or onto the tag T.

Today we have another new type of AE scheme which is based on the sponge [7] or more precisely duplex [8] construction. SPONGEWRAP [8] is a primitive AE scheme of this type, and its basic structure is illustrated in Figure 1. SPONGEWRAP iterates a "monolithic" permutation f to perform authentication and encryption in a uniform, single-pass manner. Many engineers consider SPONGEWRAP as an attractive design for realizing AE. Indeed, a number of CAESAR [6] submissions adopt SPONGEWRAP-like modes of operation, e.g. ASCON [13], CBEAM [24], ICE-POLE [20], KEYAK [9], NORX [3], PRIMATEs [2], PRØST-APE [18], and STRIBOB [25].

Moreover, SPONGEWRAP-like AE schemes have turned out to be highly secure. Recently, Jovanovic et al. [16,17] have shown that all of the above CAE-SAR candidates, except APE of PRIMATEs and PRØST-APE, achieve security of $\min\{2^{(r+c)/2}, 2^c/r, 2^\kappa\}$ rather than previously believed $\min\{2^{c/2}, 2^\kappa\}$, where κ, r and c denote the key, rate and capacity sizes, respectively. The older bound was based on the indifferentiability result of the sponge construction [7], which was tight for hashing but not for AE.

As illustrated in Figure 1, SPONGEWRAP handles associated data A as a "header," processing $A \parallel M$ in a single pass, with A in the sponge mode and M in the duplex mode. A special operation is needed between A and M in order to make the "boundary" explicit. Almost all of the above CAESAR candidates

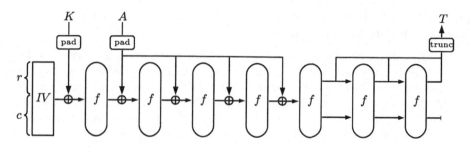

Fig. 2. The donkeySponge construction for message authentication code (MAC)

follow this header approach for handling A. The only exception is NORX, which accepts both header and "trailer," as $A_1 \parallel M \parallel A_2$.

The header method has a potential drawback. The problem is that the entire header A needs to be "available" before starting encryption. Although this issue does not exist in the typical case of packet headers [22], it would be desirable to handle A independent of its relative arrival time. This issue was recently raised by Reyhanitabar and Vizár [21] in the context of authenticated online ciphers, but the observation equally applies to nonce-based, sponge-type AE schemes. The trailer method does not fundamentally resolve this issue. As pointed out by Reyhanitabar and Vizár, the issue does not exist in the ciphertext translation.

Another drawback is inefficiency. The header and trailer methods require roughly $(|A|+|M|)/r$-many invocations of the underlying permutation. This does not seem to be optimal, as is evident from the donkeySponge construction [10] to build a message authentication code (MAC), which is described in Figure 2. The donkeySponge construction suggests that the capacity could "absorb" associated data for the purpose of authentication.

The SPONGEWRAP construction requires a single use of A, i.e. the same A cannot be processed twice under the same K, in order to ensure confidentiality. The monkeyDuplex construction [10] is a reconfiguration of SPONGEWRAP as a nonce-based scheme. The monkeyDuplex construction embeds K and N to the IV and then calls permutation f to mix the state with K and N. As long as a new pair of (K, N) is used, the state gets fully randomized. The monkeyDuplex construction also improves efficiency, because f is called only once for processing (K, N), while the SPONGEWRAP construction calls f at least twice, one for processing K and another for N.

Contributions of this Paper. Given the fact that all existing schemes adopt primarily the header and trailer approach, and also the fact that these two popular methods have potential drawbacks, we would like to explore other possible ways of incorporating associated data into a sponge-based AE scheme. This paper presents three different methods. The aim is to improve the conventional header and trailer methods with respect to either the timing issue or the inefficiency, or both. The key idea is to effectively utilize the capacity for processing A. Fortunately, the resulting AE schemes do not sacrifice security, achieving the latest bound of $\min\{2^{(r+c)/2}, 2^c/r, 2^\kappa\}$.

1. PROPOSING CONCURRENT ABSORPTION METHOD. This is a novel method that essentially removes the permutation calls for processing A in a typical usage. The basic idea is that while r bits of M are absorbed in rate for each block, we absorb c bits of A in capacity. This improves the number of permutation calls from $(|A|+|M|)/r$ to $\max\{|A|/c, |M|/r\}$. In many protocols, $|A|$ is small, say 160 bits [14]. Then, the cost becomes only $|M|/r$ calls of f.

2. CONCRETIZING SPONGE-BASED CIPHERTEXT TRANSLATION. We concretize the ciphertext translation in the sponge-based AE setting. The basic idea is the combination of SPONGEWRAP and donkeySponge, using the latter for hashing associated data A. As pointed out recently [21], this can resolve the arrival timing issue. A straightforward method would require two keys, one for processing M and another for processing A. We devise domain separation so that the whole scheme uses only a single key.

3. PROPOSING DONKEYHEADERTRAILER METHOD. We improve the efficiency of processing the header and trailer in SPONGEWRAP with the idea of donkeySponge. Namely, A is absorbed both in rate and capacity. This reduces the number of permutation calls from $|A|/r$ to $|A|/(r+c)$.

For all the three constructions, we prove the same security bound as the previous work. Note that several sponge-based AE schemes use the frame bit(s) for the separation of A and M. We argue that this is a potential efficiency loss, especially when implementors avoid the bit-wise coding and thus 1 byte per block is occupied for the frame bit. Using K multiple times like GIBBON [2] can avoid the frame bit, but it causes another inefficiency. In this work, we present a new separation method with the doubling operation, which avoids the frame bit only with a single key usage.

Finally, we show comprehensive studies for further optimization of processing A. We apply the nonce stealing [22] to sponge-based AEs. Because the size of IV in permutation based AEs is usually bigger than the one in block-cipher based AEs, the nonce stealing works more efficiently. We then propose a new technique called "key translation" to process more bits of A during the initialization. We survey existing sponge-based AEs and discuss the impact of our methods.

2   New Constructions

This section specifies three constructions. The constructions are: concurrent absorption, ciphertext translation, and donkeyHeaderTrailer.

2.1   The Concurrent Absorption Method

The concurrent absorption is a novel mode of operation unique to the sponge construction. The concurrent absorption is illustrated in Figure 3. Its pseudo-code is given in Figure 4. The basic idea is to absorb associated data A in the capacity part concurrently with absorbing a message M in the rate part.

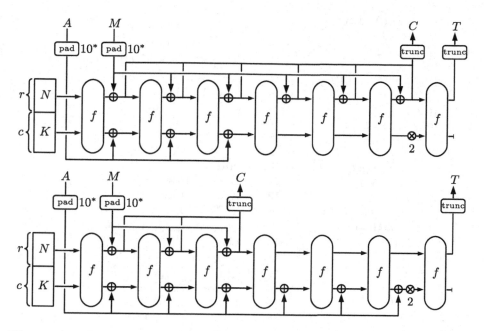

Fig. 3. The *concurrent absorption* mode of operation. **Upper:** case $|A|/c < |M|/r$. **Lower:** case $|A|/c \geq |M|/r$. The multiplication by "2" in the finite field $\mathrm{GF}(2^c)$ (relative to some primitive polynomial) right before outputting the tag T is crucial for security.** The standard 10^* padding is used for both A and M. The ciphertext C is truncated to the length of M. The tag T can be truncated if necessary.

2.2 Sponge-Based Ciphertext Translation

The ciphertext translation is a generic technique developed by Rogaway [22]. We concretize it as a sponge-based construction, as illustrated in Figure 5. The basic idea is to utilize the donkeySponge for "hashing" associated data A, while using the same key for hashing A and for encrypting a message M. The domain separation is realized by using the initial value 0 for hashing A and using a nonce $N \neq 0$ for encrypting M. We omit pseudo-code for the ciphertext translation.

2.3 The donkeyHeaderTrailer Construction

The conventional header and trailer methods can be boosted via donkeySponge construction. It is illustrated in Figure 6. The domain separation is a bit tricky here; we need a special padding 10^*1 for wrapping A' and A'', as well as a multiplication by 2 of the capacity value at the end of encrypting M. We omit pseudo-code of donkeyHeaderTrailer.

** Though an appropriate operation here is crucial, it does not need to be the multiplication by 2 in the large field. A more efficient operation can be used, e.g. a word permutation [15]. The authors are grateful to Tetsu Iwata for pointing this out.

```
1: function ℰ_K(N, A, M)
2:     L ← ⌈(|M| + 1)/r⌉
3:     (M[1], M[2], ⋯ , M[L]) ←ʳ M ∥ 10*
4:     (A[1], A[2], ⋯ , A[L]) ←ᶜ A ∥ 10*
5:     (C[0], Y'[0]) ← (N, K)
6:     for i = 1 to L do
7:         (X[i], Y[i]) ← f(C[i − 1], Y'[i − 1])
8:         C[i] ← X[i] ⊕ M[i]
9:         Y'[i] ← Y[i] ⊕ A[i]
10:    end for
11:    L' ← ⌈(|A| + 1)/c⌉
12:    if L' ≤ L then
13:        (T, Y[L + 1]) ← f(C[L], 2Y'[L])
14:    else
15:        (X[L + 1], Y[L + 1]) ← f(C[L], Y'[L])
16:        for i = L + 1 to L' − 1 do
17:            Y'[i] ← Y[i] ⊕ A[i]
18:            (X[i + 1], Y[i + 1]) ← f(X[i], Y'[i])
19:        end for
20:        Y'[L'+1] ← Y[L']⊕A[L']
21:        (T, Y[L' + 1]) ← f(X[L'], 2Y'[L'])
22:    end if
23:    C ← (C[1] ∥ ⋯ ∥ C[L])|_{|M|}
24:    return (C, T)
25: end function
```

```
1: function 𝒟_K(N, A, C, T)
2:     L ← ⌈(|C| + 1)/r⌉
3:     (C[1], C[2], ⋯ , C[L]) ←ʳ C
4:     (A[1], A[2], ⋯ , A[L]) ←ᶜ A ∥ 10*
5:     (C[0], Y'[0]) ← (N, K)
6:     for i = 1 to L do
7:         (X[i], Y[i]) ← f(C[i − 1], Y'[i − 1])
8:         M[i] ← X[i] ⊕ C[i]
9:         Y'[i] ← Y[i] ⊕ A[i]
10:    end for
11:    L' ← ⌈(|A| + 1)/c⌉
12:    if L' ≤ L then
13:        (T', Y[L + 1]) ← f(C[L]∥X[L]|_{r−|C[L]|}, 2Y'[L])
14:    else
15:        (X[L + 1], Y[L + 1]) ← f(C[L]∥X[L]|_{r−|C[L]|}, Y'[L])
16:        for i = L + 1 to L' − 1 do
17:            Y'[i] ← Y[i] ⊕ A[i]
18:            (X[i + 1], Y[i + 1]) ← f(X[i], Y'[i])
19:        end for
20:        Y'[L' + 1] ← Y[L'] ⊕ A[L']
21:        (T', Y[L' + 1]) ← f(X[L'], 2Y'[L'])
22:    end if
23:    M ← (M[1] ∥ ⋯ ∥ M[L])|_{|C|}
24:    if T' = T then
25:        return (C, T)
26:    else
27:        return ⊥
28:    end if
29: end function
```

Fig. 4. Pseudo-code of the concurrent absorption. The function $\mathcal{E}$ is the encryption algorithm and $\mathcal{D}$ the decryption.

3   Security Definitions

We define adversarial model and security notions. The proofs will be done in the ideal model, regarding the underlying primitive f as a random permutation.

3.1   Adversarial Model

We give adversary $\mathcal{A}$ access to the primitive oracle $f(\cdot), f^{-1}(\cdot)$ as well as to the encryption oracle $\mathcal{E}_K(\cdot, \cdot, \cdot)$ and the decryption oracle $\mathcal{D}_K(\cdot, \cdot, \cdot, \cdot)$. We denote by $q_f, q_\mathcal{E}, q_\mathcal{D}$ the number of queries that $\mathcal{A}$ makes to the oracles, respectively. We also write $\sigma_\mathcal{E}, \sigma_\mathcal{D}$ for the total complexities of the queries made to the oracles,

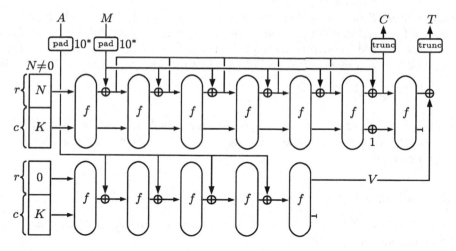

Fig. 5. The ciphertext translation concretized as a sponge-based construction. We require $N \neq 0$. If $A = \varnothing$, then the value $V = 0$ is xored onto the tag. Note the "$\oplus 1$" in the capacity right before outputting the tag T. This $\oplus 1$ is necessary to make a distinction between C and T when $A = \varnothing$.

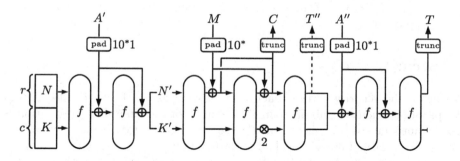

Fig. 6. Boosting the header and trailer methods using donkeySponge. A special padding 10^*1 is used for wrapping A' and A''. If $A' = \varnothing$, then we set $N' \leftarrow N$ and $K' \leftarrow K$. If $A'' = \varnothing$, then $T \leftarrow T''$ is used as a tag. The standard 10^* padding is used for M, including the case $M = \varnothing$. The ciphertext C is truncated to the length of M. The tag T can be truncated if necessary.

respectively. We leave the running time of $\mathcal{A}$ implicit; it does not have to be bounded. The notation $\mathcal{A}^{\mathcal{O}}$ means the value returned by $\mathcal{A}$ after interacting with its oracle $\mathcal{O}(\cdot)$.

3.2 Privacy

The privacy of an AE scheme $\Pi = (\mathcal{E}, \mathcal{D})$ is defined in terms of indistinguishability between the real world and the random world. The real oracle is the encryption algorithm $\mathcal{E}_K(\cdot, \cdot, \cdot)$, and the random one is the oracle $\$(\cdot, \cdot, \cdot)$ which simply returns a fresh, random string of an appropriate length upon a query (N, A, M). In either the world the adversary $\mathcal{A}$ has access to the primitive oracle $f(\cdot)$ and its inverse, where f is regarded as an independent random permutation. We define

$$\mathrm{Adv}_\Pi^{\mathrm{priv}}(\mathcal{A}) := \Pr\big[\mathcal{A}^{\mathcal{E}_K, f, f^{-1}} = 1\big] - \Pr\big[\mathcal{A}^{\$, f, f^{-1}} = 1\big],$$

where $\mathcal{A}$ is assumed to be nonce-respecting with its $\mathcal{E}$-oracle. The probabilities are defined over the choice of key K and the randomness of f and $\$$ and, if any, random coins used by $\mathcal{A}$.

3.3 Authenticity

The authenticity of $\Pi = (\mathcal{E}, \mathcal{D})$ is defined in terms of unforgeability in the above adversarial model. We put

$$\mathrm{Adv}_\Pi^{\mathrm{auth}}(\mathcal{A}) := \Pr\big[\mathcal{A}^{\mathcal{E}_K, \mathcal{D}_K, f, f^{-1}} \text{ forges}\big],$$

where by "forges" we mean the event that oracle $\mathcal{D}_K(\cdot, \cdot, \cdot, \cdot)$ returns something other than the reject symbol $\perp$. Again, we assume that $\mathcal{A}$ is nonce-respecting with its $\mathcal{E}$-oracle. Also, we forbid $\mathcal{A}$ from making a trivial-win query, that is, a query (N, A, C, T) to the $\mathcal{D}$-oracle where (C, T) was a value returned by $\mathcal{E}$-oracle on some previous query (N, A, M).

4   Security Proofs

We prove the security of the concurrent absorption as the basic case. Given the proof of concurrent absorption, the security of the ciphertext translation is almost automatically implied from the generic results given by Rogaway [23]. Also, the security of donkeyHeaderTrailer can be proven via similar techniques.

Our privacy and authenticity bounds are almost identical to those of the original sponge (or more precisely, of NORX) [16,17]. In fact, even the proofs are almost identical; they go through without much modification. The intuition behind the sameness is that xoring associated data onto the capacity does not essentially introduce new types of "bad" events. This fact can be verified by carefully going through each step in the proofs by Jovanovic et al. [16,17].

4.1   Privacy of the Concurrent Absorption

Theorem 1. *Let* $\Pi = (\mathcal{E}, \mathcal{D})$ *be the concurrent absorption. Then we have*

$$\mathrm{Adv}_\Pi^{\mathrm{priv}}(\mathcal{A}) \le \frac{3(q_f + \sigma_\mathcal{E})^2}{2^{r+c+1}} + \left(\frac{8eq_f\sigma_\mathcal{E}}{2^{r+c}}\right)^{1/2} + \frac{(r+1)q_f + \sigma_\mathcal{E}}{2^c},$$

where $e = 2.71\ldots$ *is the base of the natural logarithm.*

Proof. As we have mentioned above, we follow the approach developed by Jovanovic et al. [16,17]. We start with a PRP-PRF switch, in which the random permutation f is replaced with independent random functions g and g^{-1}. We forbid $\mathcal{A}$ from making trivial queries across f-oracle and f^{-1}-oracle. This switch costs us $\binom{q_f + \sigma_\mathcal{E}}{2}/2^{r+c} \leq (q_f + \sigma_\mathcal{E})^2/2^{r+c+1}$.

We call $g^{\pm 1}$-queries made by $\mathcal{A}$ "direct queries." We call g-queries induced by queries to $\mathcal{E}$-oracle "indirect queries." When running $\mathcal{A}^{\mathcal{E},g,g^{-1}}$, consider the following events:

- guess: This corresponds to an indirect query colliding with a direct query, or vice versa.

- hit: This corresponds to a collision between two different indirect queries, including the initial states (N, K).

Then it can be directly verified that unless one of these events occurs, $\mathcal{A}^{\mathcal{E},g,g^{-1}}$ and $\mathcal{A}^{\$,g,g^{-1}}$ are identical. Hence $\mathrm{Adv}_\Pi^{\mathrm{priv}}(\mathcal{A}) \leq \Pr[\text{guess} \vee \text{hit}]$.

It remains to bound $\Pr[\text{guess} \vee \text{hit}]$. Let us introduce two additional events:

- key: This corresponds to a direct query with its capacity part identical to the key value K.

- multi: To define this event, we first set a threshold value ρ. Then multi corresponds to an event where the number of indirect queries having the same rate part exceeds ρ.

Now we use the inequality

$$\Pr[\text{guess} \vee \text{hit}] \leq \Pr[\text{guess} \vee \text{hit} \mid \neg(\text{key} \vee \text{multi})] + \Pr[\text{key} \vee \text{multi}].$$

We first bound $\Pr[\text{guess} \mid \neg(\text{key} \vee \text{multi})]$. By $\neg\text{multi}$ there are at most ρ-many capacity values having a given rate value. Therefore, the probability that any direct query setting guess is at most $\rho q_f/2^c$. On the other hand, for each indirect query, the probability of setting guess is at most $q_f/2^{r+c}$, and hence the probability of any indirect query setting guess is at most $q_f \sigma_\mathcal{E}/2^{r+c}$. So the overall probability is at most $\rho q_f/2^c + q_f \sigma_\mathcal{E}/2^{r+c}$.

We next evaluate $\Pr[\text{hit} \mid \neg(\text{key} \vee \text{multi})]$. This event happening with one of the initial states is at most $\sigma_\mathcal{E}/2^c$. This event happening outside the initial states is at most $\binom{\sigma_\mathcal{E}}{2}/2^{r+c} \leq \sigma_\mathcal{E}^2/2^{r+c+1}$. So the overall probability is at most $\sigma_\mathcal{E}/2^c + \sigma_\mathcal{E}^2/2^{r+c+1}$.

We go on to $\Pr[\text{key}]$. This can be simply bounded by $q_f/2^c$.

Finally we bound $\Pr[\text{multi}]$. For a given rate value, the probability of setting multi with this particular rate value is at most $\binom{\sigma_\mathcal{E}}{\rho}(1/2^r)^\rho \leq (e\sigma_\mathcal{E}/\rho 2^r)^\rho$, using Stirling's approximation. Hence the probability of multi for any rate value is at most $2^r(e\sigma_\mathcal{E}/\rho 2^r)^\rho$.

Summing up all terms gives

$$\Pr[\text{guess} \vee \text{hit}] \leq \frac{q_f \sigma_\mathcal{E} + \sigma_\mathcal{E}^2/2}{2^{r+c}} + \frac{\rho q_f + q_f + \sigma_\mathcal{E}}{2^c} + 2^r\left(\frac{e\sigma_\mathcal{E}}{\rho 2^r}\right)^\rho.$$

By setting $\rho := \max\{r, (2eo_{\mathcal{E}}2^c/q_f2^r)^{1/2}\}$ and assuming $2eq_f\sigma_{\mathcal{E}}/2^{r+c} < 1$, we obtain the desired bound.   □

4.2   Authenticity of the Concurrent Absorption

Theorem 2. *Let $\Pi = (\mathcal{E}, \mathcal{D})$ be the concurrent absorption. Then we have*

$$\mathrm{Adv}_{\Pi}^{\mathrm{auth}}(\mathcal{A}) \leq \frac{(q_f + \sigma_{\mathcal{E}} + \sigma_{\mathcal{D}})^2}{2^{r+c+1}} + \left(\frac{8eq_f\sigma_{\mathcal{E}}}{2^{r+c}}\right)^{1/2}$$
$$+ \frac{(r+1)q_f + \sigma_{\mathcal{E}} + \sigma_{\mathcal{D}}}{2^c} + \frac{(q_f + \sigma_{\mathcal{E}} + \sigma_{\mathcal{D}})\sigma_{\mathcal{D}}}{2^c} + \frac{q_{\mathcal{D}}}{2^r},$$

where $e = 2.71\ldots$ is the base of the natural logarithm.

Proof. We inherit the notation from the privacy proof. Redefining the events guess and hit through not only $\mathcal{E}$-oracle but also $\mathcal{D}$-oracle, we get

$$\Pr[\text{guess} \vee \text{hit}] \leq \frac{(q_f + \sigma_{\mathcal{E}} + \sigma_{\mathcal{D}})^2}{2^{r+c+1}} + \left(\frac{8eq_f\sigma_{\mathcal{E}}}{2^{r+c}}\right)^{1/2} + \frac{(r+1)q_f + \sigma_{\mathcal{E}} + \sigma_{\mathcal{D}}}{2^c},$$

as we have done in the privacy proof. Now since we have

$$\Pr[\mathcal{A}\text{ forges}] \leq \Pr[\mathcal{A}\text{ forges} \mid \neg(\text{guess} \vee \text{hit})] + \Pr[\text{guess} \vee \text{hit}],$$

it remains to bound $\Pr[\mathcal{A}\text{ forges} \mid \neg(\text{guess} \vee \text{hit})]$. If $\mathcal{A}$ succeeds in forgery with a fresh invocation of g (Recall that the permutation f has been already replaced with random functions g and g^{-1}), then such an event occurs with a probability at most $q_{\mathcal{D}}/2^r$. Otherwise, the invocation of g to produce T is "old," meaning that it has collided with some previous direct or indirect queries of g. Such a collision cannot be a trivial one, because of the 10^* padding for M and A and also due to the multiplication by 2 in the finite field $\mathrm{GF}(2^c)$. Therefore, the probability that the invocation of g is old is at most $(q_f + \sigma_{\mathcal{E}} + \sigma_{\mathcal{D}})\sigma_{\mathcal{D}}/2^c$. This completes the proof.   □

5   Comprehensive Studies

5.1   Survey of Existing Schemes

Several sponge based AEs were proposed in CAESAR. Those include ASCON [13], CBEAM [24], ICEPOLE [20], KEYAK [9], NORX [3], PRIMATEs (GIBBON and HANUMAN) [2], and STRIBOB [25]. The parameters, i.e. permutation size, rate size, capacity size, rough ratio of rate to capacity, key size, nonce size, and the number of bits in security are summarized in Table 1.

The ways to incorporate A (including the way of domain separation) and to utilize capacity are our main concerns. Such information is summarized in Table 2. The domain separation is usually achieved by either of the following two ways. First, fix a few bits of each input block for the separation of A and M (frame bits). Second, xor a constant to c for the separation of A and M. For some security purpose, some design xores K to the capacity.

Table 1. Parameters of sponge based AE schemes

Scheme	b	r	c	r/c	$|K|$	$|N|$	Integrity	Confidentiality
Ascon-96	320	128	192	2/3	96	96	96	96
Ascon-128	320	64	256	1/4	128	128	128	128
CBEAM	256	66	190	1/3	128	64	63	127
ICEPOLE-128	1280	1026	254	4	128	128	128	128
ICEPOLE-128a	1280	1026	254	4	128	96	128	128
ICEPOLE-256a	1280	962	318	3	256	96	128	256
RIVER Keyak	800	548	252	2	128 − 224	128	128	128
LAKE Keyak	1600	1348	252	5	128 − 224	128	128	128
NORX 32	512	320	192	5/3	128	64	128	128
NORX 64	1024	640	384	5/3	256	128	256	256
GIBBON/	200	41	159	1/4	80	80	80	80
HANUMAN	280	41	239	1/6	120	120	120	120
STRIBOB	512	256	254	1	192	128	127	191

5.2 Parameter and Design Choices

Choosing the best ratio of r and c. Given a b-bit permutation, what is the best choice of the rate size r and the capacity size c? On one hand, Jovanovic *et al.* proved that the security bound of the sponge based AE was $\min\{2^{b/2}, 2^c/r, 2^\kappa\}$, and suggested to increase r (thus decrease c) to absorb more input bits per block [16,17]. On the other hand, the concurrent absorption method in this paper absorbs A in the capacity. Using a small c makes a process of A slow.

For the donkeyHeaderTrailer and the sponge-based ciphertext translation, A is absorbed in the entire b bits per block. Hence, the ratio of r to c does not affect the performance. They can be chosen to satisfy the suggestion by Jovanovic *et al.* [16,17]. Thus, setting the capacity size equal to the security parameter, i.e. $c = \kappa$, is the best choice.

The concurrent absorption requires a careful analysis. In many cases, $|A|$ is much smaller than $|M|$. For instance, the Internet protocol [14] specifies that a typical Internet header is 20 bytes. Suppose that $|M|$ is 1,000 bytes. Processing the 1,000-byte M requires $8000/r$ blocks, while processing 20-byte A requires $160/c$ blocks. With a practical choice of r and c, processing M is the bottleneck. Thus, minimizing the capacity size ($c = \kappa$) is the best choice.

When $|M|$ is as small as $|A|$, using a bigger c can be optimal. Such a situation may occur for light-weight protocols. Actually several AE schemes, e.g. CLOC [26,27] and SILC [28], were designed to efficiently process short input, though they are block-cipher based schemes.

Let us discuss an example with $|A| = |M| = 160$ processed by Ascon-96 ($b = 320$ and $\kappa = 96$). With the suggestion by [16,17], c is set to $\kappa = 96$ bits, and thus r is $320 - 96 = 224$ bits. Then, 160 bits of M can be absorbed in r only in one block, while 160 bits of A needs two blocks to be absorbed in c. Clearly, processing A is the bottleneck. Let us set c to 160 bits which is bigger

Table 2. Summary of sponge based AE schemes with respect to A and capacity

Scheme	Position of A	Utilization of capacity
ASCON	Header	Capacity is initialized to $K\|N$. $0^*\|K$ and $K\|0^*$ are xored after the initialization and before the finalization. A bit '1' is xored for the separation of A and M.
CBEAM	Header	Several bits are fixed as variant of frame bits termed "multiplex padding."
ICEPOLE	Header	One bit is fixed as the frame bit.
KEYAK	Header/Middle	Two bits are fixed as the frame bits.
NORX	Header/Trailer	Parameter information is xored to capacity during the initialization. Two bits are xored to capacity in all blocks for the domain separation.
GIBBON	Header	IV is initialized to $0^*\|K\|N$. $K\|0^*$ are xored after the first and before the last permutation calls.
HANUMAN	Header	Capacity leaves untouched.
STRIBOB	Header	Several bits are fixed as "multiplex padding."

than the suggestion by [16, 17], and thus r is 160 bits. Then, both of M and A are absorbed in 1 block.

In general, the longer M becomes, the larger r can be. Considering the practical ratio of r to c in Table 1, the smallest one is $1/6$. Hence, if $|M|$ can be supposed to be at least 6 times bigger than $|A|$ ($|M| > 960$ for $|A| = 160$), the size of c can be set to κ. Otherwise, a special attention is needed as the above example of ASCON-96. Note that nonce stealing and key translation schemes explained in the next subsection can also increase the speed of processing A. The size of c should be determined by taking those techniques into account.

Choosing the Best Construction Depending on Applications. The best choice of the three constructions of the donkeyHeaderTrailer, concurrent absorption, and sponge-based ciphertext translation depends on the implementation environment and applications.

- If the scheme is designed to be used in a resource-constraint environment, minimizing the number of permutation calls may be crucial, e.g. for minimizing the energy consumption of the device. In this case, the concurrent absorption can meet the requirement most.

- In the concurrent absorption, A and M need to arrive at the same time. When the scheme is implemented in a high-end environment with sufficient memory amount, firstly arrived A or M can be stored easily until the other one arrives. Then using the concurrent absorption to minimize the number of permutation calls would be the best strategy.

- Suppose that A is a fixed value in the protocol. Then by storing and reusing the intermediate values after A, the performance can be improved. The sponge-based ciphertext translation fits to this scenario by processing A and

(N, M) independently. The donkeyHeaderTrailer can also be used. However, different from the convention, A must be processed prior to N.

- If the construction needs to be chosen before the application is determined, the sponge-based ciphertext translation may be preferred to handle various or unknown locations of A.

5.3 Further Optimization

Nonce Stealing. The nonce stealing was proposed by Rogaway [22]. In the block-cipher based AE with nonce, the nonce is often set to the plaintext, i.e. $E_K(N)$ is computed. Besides, the provable security is often up to the birthday bound. Then, setting $|N|$ to the half of the block size makes a balance. This yields a free space for the other half of the block when $E_K(N)$ is computed. The idea of the nonce stealing is using this free space to process A, i.e. computing $E_K(N\|A)$. The nonce stealing can increase the performance especially when $|A|$ is smaller than the half of the block size.

We point out that the nonce stealing can also be applied to the sponge based schemes. (See Figure 7). As suggested by monkeyDuplex [10], IV can be initialized to $N\|K$ and the padding bits. In the sponge based schemes, the permutation size b is much bigger than the aimed security bits κ. Thus the effect of the nonce stealing is big. Many designs chose to satisfy $c > 2\kappa$ by following the old security bound. Then, by setting $|N| = |K| = \kappa$, $N\|K$ can fit in c, and the entire rate, r bits, can be used for processing A. Note that K must be located in capacity rather than rate, otherwise the security proof will be invalidated. Also note that this constraint can usually be satisfied due to the security bound $\min\{2^{b/2}, 2^c/r, 2^\kappa\}$, which suggests $c = \kappa$ by ignoring a small factor of $1/r$.

Key Translation. The key translation is our new technique to further increase the speed of processing A. In the monkeyDuplex construction, IV is set to $N\|K$ and the padding bits, in which K occupies $|K|$ bits of the capacity part of IV. Then, the permutation is called to mix the state depending on N and K, which makes the scheme secure in the nonce-respecting model.

The idea of the key translation is absorbing $|K|$ bits of A before the initial permutation call, which improves the efficiency only with a small security loss (See Figure 8). The key translation runs contrary to the security goal of the monkeyDuplex, as it absorbs $|K|$-bit input before the first permutation call. However, we can still prove the same security even with the key translation as long as the same (N, K) is never iterated.

The key translation allows a trivial related-key attack.*** Suppose that there are two oracles with K and $K \oplus \Delta$, where Δ is known to the attacker. Then, (N, A) for the oracle with K and $(N, A \oplus \Delta)$ for the oracle with $K \oplus \Delta$ return

---

*** The importance of the related-key nonce-respecting model is unclear and as far as we know, the related-key security has never been discussed for keyed sponge-based constructions before.

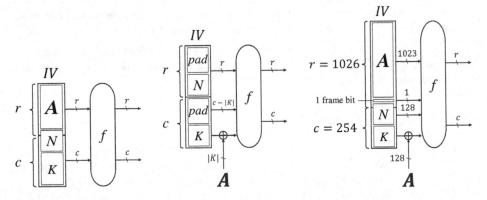

Fig. 7. Nonce stealing.   **Fig. 8.** Key translation.   **Fig. 9.** Two techniques applied to ICEPOLE-128

the same result. Note that this related-key attack can be prevented by ensuring that each nonce is used only once even for different keys, which is likely to be implemented in practice by using a counter as a source of nonce.

Attacks using different key lengths must be avoided carefully. If the scheme supports different key sizes, the key must be padded appropriately in order to prevent the key length extension attack.

The sponge-based AE basically does not provide any confidentiality in the nonce-repeat setting. However, it is worth noting that the key translation offers only $\kappa/2$-bit security with the κ-bit key in the nonce-repeat setting. This is because the key recovery attack proposed by Mendel [19] using a time-memory tradeoff which can recover the κ-bit key with a tradeoff of $TM = 2^\kappa$. In the offline phase of this attack, the attacker fixes all input information but for K and A in the initialization, and run the encryption process by choosing 2^X distinct values of $K \oplus A$. The results are stored in the memory. In the online phase of this attack, the attacker iterates the input value fixed in the offline phase, and make oracle queries by choosing 2^Y distinct values of A, such that $2^X \times 2^Y = 2^\kappa$. One match between offline and online results is expected, which tells the correct value of K. By setting $X = Y = \kappa/2$, the attack cost is minimized to $2^{\kappa/2}$.

Case Study. Let us apply the two techniques to ICEPOLE-128 as an example, in which $b = 1280$, $c = 254$ and $|K| = |N| = 128$. K is set to 128 bits of c and N is set to 126 bits of c and 2 bits of r. ICEPOLE uses 1 bit as the frame bit. The application is illustrated in Figure 9.

With the nonce stealing, up to $1280 - 128 - 128 - 1 = 1023$ bits of A can be processed in IV. We can further add 128 bits of A with the key translation. Thus in total up to 1151 bits of A can be processed. As mentioned before, $|A|$ is usually short. Two techniques have a big impact in practice.

Acknowledgments. The authors are grateful to Florian Mendel for pointing out the key recovery attack on the key translation in the nonce-repeating setting. The authors would also like to thank anonymous reviewers for their helpful comments.

A   Our Techniques from Another Viewpoint: Utilizing Capacity

The goal of this work is to optimize the speed of processing A. This work can be regarded also as part of the series of researches aiming to utilize the capacity of sponge, or more generally, to utilize state bits whose original purpose was meant for security rather than for efficiency. For example, according to the designers, donkeySponge was inspired by the ALRED construction [12] which is a CBC-MAC-based construction optimized with 4-round AES. Similarly, our constructions were inspired by a series of researches, as follows.

A.1   Boosting Merkle-Damgård

The donkey header, donkey trailer and concurrent absorption increase the speed of processing associated data. The similar idea can be seen in the boosted Merkle-Damgård (MD) approach [30] which improves the efficiency of a hash function based MAC, i.e. HMAC [4]. Let H, CF and $trunc$ be a hash function, a compression function and the truncation function, respectively. Also, let n, m and t be the chaining variable size, the message block size, and the tag size ($t < n$), respectively. HMAC computes the tag T for a message $M = M_1\|M_2\|\cdots\|M_L$ under the key K as follows.

$$h_1 \leftarrow CF(IV, K \oplus \texttt{ipad}), \qquad // \text{ initialization}$$
$$h_{i+1} \leftarrow CF(h_i, M_i), \text{ for } i = 1, 2, \ldots, L. \qquad // \text{ main}$$
$$T \leftarrow trunc\Big(H\big((K \oplus \texttt{opad})\|h_{L+1}\big)\Big). \qquad // \text{ finalization}$$

During the main iteration, only m-bit message is processed in each call of CF, while the input size is in each block is $m + n$ bits. In other words, n bits of the state is just used for mixing the compression function, which takes exactly the same role as the capacity in the sponge construction. The boosted MD approach allows xoring (absorbing) n-bits of the message to the chaining variable with a very small loss of security. Its construction is illustrated in Figure 10.

A.2   Absorbing Additional Information in Capacity

When it is focused on the sponge construction, utilizing the capacity in more meaningful ways has been a challenging task. Several constructions made a progress in this direction.

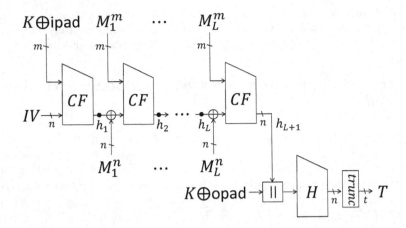

Fig. 10. Boosting Merkle-Damgård construction

- The JH hash function [29] uses the capacity to receive feed-forward from the previous chaining variable. This can contribute to increase security. The JH mode was adopted in a later hash function design SPN-hash [11]. One of the CAESAR candidates Artemia [1] adopted the JH mode for the AEAD.

- The donkeySponge construction [10] for MAC absorbs message bits in capacity as well as rate. There is similarity between the donkeySponge and the boosted MD for improving the performance of the MAC computation.

- The monkeyDuplex construction [10] absorbs the key K in the capacity during the initialization process before the first permutation call, which also improves the performance.

Considering the above previous work, our constructions can be regarded as the utilization of the capacity in order to optimize the computation of associated data in sponge-based AEAD schemes.

References

1. Alizadeh, J., Aref, M.R., Bagheri, N.: Artemia v1. Submission to CAESAR (2014)
2. Andreeva, E., Bilgin, B., Bogdanov, A., Luykx, A., Mendel, F., Mennink, B., Mouha, N., Wang, Q., Yasuda, K.: PRIMATEs v1. Submission to CAESAR (2014)
3. Aumasson, J.P., Jovanovic, P., Neves, S.: NORX V1. Submission to CAESAR (2014)
4. Bellare, M., Canetti, R., Krawczyk, H.: Keying hash functions for message authentication. In: Koblitz, N. (ed.) CRYPTO 1996. LNCS, vol. 1109, pp. 1–15. Springer, Heidelberg (1996)
5. Bellare, M., Namprempre, C.: Authenticated encryption: relations among notions and analysis of the generic composition paradigm. In: Okamoto, T. (ed.) ASIACRYPT 2000. LNCS, vol. 1976, pp. 531–545. Springer, Heidelberg (2000)

6. Bernstein, D.: CAESAR Competition (2013). http://competitions.cr.yp.to/caesar.html

7. Bertoni, G., Daemen, J., Peeters, M., Van Assche, G.: On the indifferentiability of the sponge construction. In: Smart, N.P. (ed.) EUROCRYPT 2008. LNCS, vol. 4965, pp. 181–197. Springer, Heidelberg (2008)

8. Bertoni, G., Daemen, J., Peeters, M., Van Assche, G.: Duplexing the sponge: single-pass authenticated encryption and other applications. In: Miri, A., Vaudenay, S. (eds.) SAC 2011. LNCS, vol. 7118, pp. 320–337. Springer, Heidelberg (2012)

9. Bertoni, G., Daemen, J., Peeters, M., Assche, G.V., Keer, R.V.: CAESAR submission: Keyak v1. Submission to CAESAR (2014)

10. Bertoni, G., Daemen, J., Peeters, M., Assche, G.V.: Permutation-based encryption, authentication and authenticated encryption. In: Workshop Records of DIAC 2012, pp. 159–170 (2012)

11. Choy, J., Yap, H., Khoo, K., Guo, J., Peyrin, T., Poschmann, A., Tan, C.H.: SPN-Hash: improving the provable resistance against differential collision attacks. In: Mitrokotsa, A., Vaudenay, S. (eds.) AFRICACRYPT 2012. LNCS, vol. 7374, pp. 270–286. Springer, Heidelberg (2012)

12. Daemen, J., Rijmen, V.: A new MAC construction ALRED and a specific instance ALPHA-MAC. In: Gilbert, H., Handschuh, H. (eds.) FSE 2005. LNCS, vol. 3557, pp. 1–17. Springer, Heidelberg (2005)

13. Dobraunig, C., Eichlseder, M., Mendel, F., Schläffer, M.: Ascon v1. Submission to CAESAR (2014)

14. Information Sciences Institute University of Southern California: INTERNET PROTOCOL. Internet Engineering Task Force (IETF), RFC 791 (1981). https://www.ietf.org/rfc/rfc791.txt

15. Iwata, T., Minematsu, K.: Generating a fixed number of masks with word permutations and XORs. In: DIAC 2013: Directions in Authenticated Ciphers (2013)

16. Jovanovic, P., Luykx, A., Mennink, B.: Beyond $2^{c/2}$ security in sponge-based authenticated encryption modes. Cryptology ePrint Archive, Report 2014/373 (2014)

17. Jovanovic, P., Luykx, A., Mennink, B.: Beyond $2^{c/2}$ security in sponge-based authenticated encryption modes. In: Sarkar, P., Iwata, T. (eds.) ASIACRYPT 2014. LNCS, vol. 8873, pp. 85–104. Springer, Heidelberg (2014)

18. Kavun, E.B., Lauridsen, M.M., Leander, G., Rechberger, C., Schwabe, P., Yalçın, T.: Prøst v1. Submission to CAESAR (2014)

19. Mendel, F., Mennink, B., Rijmen, V., Tischhauser, E.: A simple key-recovery attack on McOE-X. In: Pieprzyk, J., Sadeghi, A.-R., Manulis, M. (eds.) CANS 2012. LNCS, vol. 7712, pp. 23–31. Springer, Heidelberg (2012)

20. Morawiecki, P., Gaj, K., Homsirikamol, E., Matusiewicz, K., Pieprzyk, J., Rogawski, M., Srebrny, M., Wójcik, M.: ICEPOLE v1. Submission to CAESAR (2014)

21. Reyhanitabar, R., Vizár, D.: Careful with misuse resistance of online AEAD. Posted to CAESAR Mailing List (2014). https://groups.google.com/forum/#!topic/crypto-competitions/o5uMRvi6L74

22. Rogaway, P.: Authenticated-encryption with associated-data. In: Atluri, V. (ed.) ACM CCS 2002, pp. 98–107. ACM (2002)

23. Rogaway, P., Bellare, M., Black, J., Krovetz, T.: OCB: a block-cipher mode of operation for efficient authenticated encryption. In: Reiter, M.K., Samarati, P. (eds.) ACM CCS 2001, pp. 196–205. ACM (2001)

24. Saarinen, M.J.O.: The CBEAMr1 authenticated encryption algorithm. Submission to CAESAR (2014)

25. Saarinen, M.J.O.: The STRIBOBr 1 authenticated encryption algorithm. Submission to CAESAR (2014)
26. Tetsu Iwata, Kazuhiko Minematsu, J.G., Morioka, S.: CLOC: Authenticated encryption for short input. In: Cid, C., Rechberger, C. (eds.) FSE 2014. LNCS. Springer (2014) (to appear)
27. Tetsu Iwata, Kazuhiko Minematsu, J.G., Morioka, S.: CLOC: Compact low-overhead CFB. Submission to CAESAR (2014)
28. Tetsu Iwata, Kazuhiko Minematsu, J.G., Morioka, S., Kobayashi, E.: SILC: Simple lightweight CFB. Submission to CAESAR (2014)
29. Wu, H.: The hash function JH. Submission to NIST SHA-3 Competition (2011)
30. Yasuda, K.: Boosting merkle-damgård hashing for message authentication. In: Kurosawa, K. (ed.) ASIACRYPT 2007. LNCS, vol. 4833, pp. 216–231. Springer, Heidelberg (2007)

Cryptanalysis of Ascon

Christoph Dobraunig[1]($\boxtimes$), Maria Eichlseder[1],
Florian Mendel[1], and Martin Schläffer[2]

[1] IAIK, Graz University of Technology, Graz, Austria
{christoph.dobraunig,maria.eichlseder,florian.mendel}@iaik.tugraz.at
[2] Infineon Technologies AG, Villach, Austria
martin.schlaeffer@gmail.com

Abstract. We present a detailed security analysis of the CAESAR candidate Ascon. Amongst others, cube-like, differential and linear cryptanalysis are used to evaluate the security of Ascon. Our results are practical key-recovery attacks on round-reduced versions of Ascon-128, where the initialization is reduced to 5 out of 12 rounds. Theoretical key-recovery attacks are possible for up to 6 rounds of initialization. Moreover, we present a practical forgery attack for 3 rounds of the finalization, a theoretical forgery attack for 4 rounds finalization and zero-sum distinguishers for the full 12-round Ascon permutation. Besides, we present the first results regarding linear cryptanalysis of Ascon, improve upon the results of the designers regarding differential cryptanalysis, and prove bounds on the minimum number of (linearly and differentially) active S-boxes for the Ascon permutation.

Keywords: Ascon · CAESAR initiative · Cryptanalysis · Authenticated encryption

1 Introduction

The CAESAR competition [20] is an ongoing cryptographic competition, where numerous authenticated encryption schemes are challenging each other with the goal of finding a portfolio of ciphers, suitable for different use-cases. Currently, more than 45 ciphers are still participating in the competition. In the near future, this portfolio will be further reduced to focus the attention of the crypto community on a few candidates. Therefore, analyzing the security of the candidate ciphers is of great importance to enable the committee to judge them adequately.

Ascon is a submission by Dobraunig et al. [11] to the CAESAR competition. In the submission document, the designers discuss the design rationale for the cipher and give first cryptanalytic results, in particular on the differential properties of the Ascon permutation. Since the cipher was only recently presented, results of external cryptanalysis are scarce so far. Jovanovic et al. [15] prove the security of Ascon's mode of operation under idealness assumptions for the permutation.

© Springer International Publishing Switzerland 2015
K. Nyberg (ed.): CT-RSA 2015, LNCS 9048, pp. 371–387, 2015.
DOI: 10.1007/978-3-319-16715-2_20

Our Contribution. We present a detailed security analysis of the CAESAR candidate ASCON-128. Based on the low algebraic degree of ASCON, we are able to construct a zero-sum distinguisher with complexity 2^{130} for the full 12-round ASCON permutation in Section 3. In Section 4, we use similar algebraic properties to construct a distinguisher based on cube testers. We also use cube-like techniques to obtain a key-recovery attack for a round-reduced version of ASCON with 5-round initialization with practical complexity. Theoretical key-recovery attacks are possible for up to 6 rounds of initialization. Moreover, in Section 5, we present the first results on linear cryptanalysis, and improve the results by the designers on differential cryptanalysis. Our results include linear and differential characteristics obtained with heuristic search, as well as a computer-aided proof of security bounds against linear and differential cryptanalysis (minimum number of active S-boxes). Using our results on linear-differential analysis, we present a practical forgery attack for 3 rounds of the finalization and a theoretical forgery attack for 4-round finalization. Our results are summarized in Table 1.

Table 1. Results for ASCON-128. Attacks performed on the initialization or finalization.

type	rounds	time	method	source
permutation distinguisher	12 / 12	2^{130}	zero-sum	Section 3
key recovery	6 / 12	2^{66}	cube-like	Section 4.4
	5 / 12	2^{35}		
	5 / 12	2^{36}	differential-linear	Section 5.4
	4 / 12	2^{18}		
forgery	4 / 12	2^{101}	differential	Section 5.3
	3 / 12	2^{33}		

2   Ascon

ASCON is a submission by Dobraunig et al. [11] to the ongoing CAESAR competition. It is based on a sponge-like construction with a state size of 320 bits (consisting of five 64-bit words $x_0, \ldots, x_4$). ASCON comes in two flavors, ASCON-128 and ASCON-96, with different security levels and parameters, as summarized in Table 2. The analysis in this paper is focused on ASCON-128. In the following, we give a brief overview about the mode of operation and the permutation of ASCON. For a complete description, we refer to the design document [11].

Mode of Operation. ASCON's mode of operation is based on MonkeyDuplex [8]. As illustrated in Fig. 1, the encryption is partitioned into four phases: initialization, processing associated data, processing the plaintext, and finalization. Those phases use two different permutations p^a and p^b. The stronger variant p^a is used for initialization and finalization, while p^b is used in the data processing phases.

Table 2. Parameters for Ascon [11]

name	bit size of				rounds	
	key	nonce	tag	data block	p^a	p^b
Ascon-128	128	128	128	64	12	6
Ascon-96	96	96	96	128	12	8

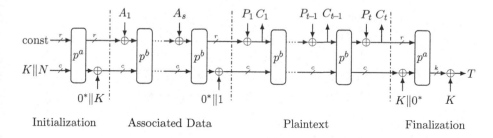

Initialization   Associated Data   Plaintext   Finalization

Fig. 1. The encryption of Ascon [11]

The initialization takes as input the secret key K and the public nonce N. The initialization ensures that we start with a random-looking state at the beginning of the data procession phase for every new nonce. In the subsequent processing of the associated data, r-bit blocks are absorbed by xoring them to the state, separated by invocations of p^b. If no associated data needs to be processed, the whole phase can be omitted. Plaintext is processed in r-bit blocks in a similar manner, with ciphertext blocks extracted from the state right after adding the plaintext. For domain separation between associated data and plaintext, a constant is xored to the secret part of the internal state. After all data is processed, the finalization starts and the k-bit tag T is returned.

Table 3. The S-box of Ascon [11]

x	0	1	2	3	4	5	6	7	8	9	10	11	12	13	14	15
$S(x)$	4	11	31	20	26	21	9	2	27	5	8	18	29	3	6	28

x	16	17	18	19	20	21	22	23	24	25	26	27	28	29	30	31
$S(x)$	30	19	7	14	0	13	17	24	16	12	1	25	22	10	15	23

Permutation. Ascon uses the two permutations p^a and p^b. Both iteratively apply the same round function p: a rounds for p^a, and b rounds for p^b. The round transformation p consists of a constant addition to x_2, followed by the application of a nonlinear substitution layer and a linear layer.

The substitution layer uses a 5-bit S-box (Table 3), which is affine equivalent to the Keccak [2] χ mapping. The ASCON S-box is applied 64 times in parallel on the state. Each bit of the 5 64-bit words $(x_0, \ldots, x_4)$ contributes one bit to each of the 64 S-boxes, where x_0 always serves as most significant bit.

The linear layer is derived from the Σ-function of SHA-2 [19]. The Σ-function is applied to each of the 5 state-words and uses different rotation values for each word:

$$\Sigma_0(x_0) = x_0 \oplus (x_0 \ggg 19) \oplus (x_0 \ggg 28)$$
$$\Sigma_1(x_1) = x_1 \oplus (x_1 \ggg 61) \oplus (x_1 \ggg 39)$$
$$\Sigma_2(x_2) = x_2 \oplus (x_2 \ggg \ \ 1) \oplus (x_2 \ggg \ \ 6)$$
$$\Sigma_3(x_3) = x_3 \oplus (x_3 \ggg 10) \oplus (x_3 \ggg 17)$$
$$\Sigma_4(x_4) = x_4 \oplus (x_4 \ggg \ \ 7) \oplus (x_4 \ggg 41)$$

3   Zero-Sum Distinguishers

In this section, we apply zero-sum distinguishers used in the analysis of Keccak [1,6,7] to ASCON. Zero-sum distinguishers have been used to show non-ideal properties of round-reduced versions for the Keccak permutation. With the help of zero-sum distinguishers, Boura et al. have have been able to distinguish the full 24-round Keccak permutation from a random permutation. Since the core of the ASCON S-box corresponds to the Keccak S-box, we are able to construct distinguishers for the full 12 rounds (or up to 20 rounds) of the ASCON permutation.

Algebraic Model of Ascon. As the name zero-sum distinguishers suggests, we search for a set of inputs and corresponding outputs of an n-bit permutation which sum to zero over $\mathbb{F}_2^n$. To create this set of input-output pairs, we start in the middle of the permutation and compute outwards. Furthermore, we keep a set of $320 - d$ bits constant and vary the other d bits through all possible assignments. Thus, we get 2^d possible intermediate states. For all these 2^d intermediate states, we calculate the respective outputs. If the degree of the function determining the output bits is strictly smaller than d, the resulting outputs will sum to zero over $\mathbb{F}_2^n$ [1,6]. After that, we calculate the input values of the permutation using the 2^d intermediate states. Again, if the degree of the inverse function is smaller than d, the inputs sum to zero over $\mathbb{F}_2^n$. The result is a zero-sum distinguisher, or rather, a family of zero-sum distinguishers.

To apply the technique to ASCON, we have to bound the degree of multiple rounds of the ASCON permutation and its inverse. The algebraic degree of one ASCON S-box is 2, with respect to $\mathbb{F}_2$, and can be easily determined from its algebraic normal form (ANF):

$$y_0 = x_4x_1 + x_3 + x_2x_1 + x_2 + x_1x_0 + x_1 + x_0$$
$$y_1 = x_4 + x_3x_2 + x_3x_1 + x_3 + x_2x_1 + x_2 + x_1 + x_0$$
$$y_2 = x_4x_3 + x_4 + x_2 + x_1 + 1$$
$$y_3 = x_4x_0 + x_4 + x_3x_0 + x_3 + x_2 + x_1 + x_0$$
$$y_4 = x_4x_1 + x_4 + x_3 + x_1x_0 + x_1$$

Here, x_0, x_1, x_2, x_3, x_4, and y_0, y_1, y_2, y_3, y_4 represent the input, and output of an S-box, with x_0/y_0 representing the most significant bit. The S-boxes in one substitution layer are applied in parallel to the state, and the linear layer and constant addition do not increase the algebraic degree. Consequently, the overall degree of one ASCON permutation round is 2, and the degree of r rounds is at most 2^r.

To determine the degree of the inverse permutation, we use the ANF of the inverse ASCON S-box:

$$x_0 = y_4y_3y_2 + y_4y_3y_1 + y_4y_3y_0 + y_3y_2y_0 + y_3y_2 + y_3 + y_2 + y_1y_0 + y_1 + 1$$
$$x_1 = y_4y_2y_0 + y_4 + y_3y_2 + y_2y_0 + y_1 + y_0$$
$$x_2 = y_4y_3y_1 + y_4y_3 + y_4y_2y_1 + y_4y_2 + y_3y_1y_0 + y_3y_1 + y_2y_1y_0$$
$$\quad + y_2y_1 + y_2 + 1 + x_1$$
$$x_3 = y_4y_2y_1 + y_4y_2y_0 + y_4y_2 + y_4y_1 + y_4 + y_3 + y_2y_1 + y_2y_0 + y_1$$
$$x_4 = y_4y_3y_2 + y_4y_2y_1 + y_4y_2y_0 + y_4y_2 + y_3y_2y_0 + y_3y_2 + y_3$$
$$\quad + y_2y_1 + y_2y_0 + y_1y_0$$

The algebraic degree of the ANF of the inverse ASCON S-box is 3. Therefore, the degree for an r-round inverse ASCON permutation is at most 3^r.

Basic Distinguisher for 12 Rounds. To create a zero-sum distinguisher for the 12-round ASCON permutation that is used for the cipher's initialization and finalization, we target the intermediate state after round 5. Thus, we attack 5 backward (inverse) rounds and 7 forward rounds. An upper bound for the degree of the 7-round permutation is $2^7 = 128$, while for the 5 inverse rounds, an upper bound is $3^5 = 243$. So we choose $d = 244$, fix $320 - 244 = 76$ bits of the intermediate state and vary the remaining 244 bits to create a set of 2^{244} intermediate states. For all these states, we calculate 7 rounds forward and 5 rounds backward. The sum of all the resulting input and output values over $\mathbb{F}_2^n$ is zero. A similar attack is possible for $11 = 4 + 7$ rounds (with $d = \max\{81, 128\} + 1 = 129$) and for $13 = 5 + 8$ rounds (with $d = \max\{243, 256\} + 1 = 257$).

Improvement Using Walsh Spectrum Analysis. The complexity of the 12-round distinguisher can be further improved by analyzing the permutation's Walsh spectrum and applying the techniques by Boura and Canteaut [6]: If the Walsh spectrum of a function $F : \mathbb{F}_2^n \rightarrow \mathbb{F}_2^n$ is 2^ℓ-divisible, then for any $G : \mathbb{F}_2^n \rightarrow \mathbb{F}_2^n$, we have

$$\deg(G \circ F) \leq n - \ell + \deg(G).$$

As Boura and Canteaut show, the Walsh spectrum of the Keccak S-box is 2^3-divisible. The affine linear preprocessing and postprocessing that the ASCON S-box adds compared to the Keccak S-box does not change this number. The same holds true for the inverse S-box. The ASCON nonlinear layer applies this S-box 64 times in parallel. The Walsh spectrum of a parallel composition is the multiplication of the individual Walsh spectra [6]. Thus, the Walsh spectrum of the complete nonlinear layer is divisible by $2^{3\cdot 64} = 2^{192}$. Let p denote one round of the ASCON permutation, and p^{-1} its inverse. A closer bound on the degree of 5 rounds of the inverse permutation, p^{-5}, is then obtained by

$$\deg(p^{-5}) = \deg(p^{-4} \circ p^{-1}) \leq 320 - 192 + \deg(p^{-4}) \leq 320 - 192 + 81 = 209.$$

Thus, $d = \max\{209, 128\} + 1 = 210$ is sufficient for $12 = 5 + 7$ rounds of the ASCON permutation.

Adding a Free Round in the Middle. Additionally, as Boura and Canteaut [6] observe, an additional round can be added to the attack (almost) for free as follows: The original attack requires an intermediate state where $n - d$ bits are fixed to a constant, while d bits loop through all possible valuations. Now, we set d to be a multiple of the 5-bit S-box size and furthermore, choose the d variable bits such that they always include complete S-boxes. Then, the inputs (and consequently outputs) of some S-boxes are constant, while the other S-boxes have their inputs (and consequently outputs) loop through all possible values. If we look at the output of the nonlinear layer after this intermediate step, we observe it adheres to the same pattern as the input: $n - d$ bits are fixed and d bits enumerate through all their possible values. We can now use the original intermediate step as the starting point for the backwards rounds, and the output of the nonlinear layer as the starting point for the forward rounds (plus an additional, free linear layer). This way, we can extend the previous attacks by one round each, with the only additional cost of choosing d as a multiple of 5. We get zero-sum distinguishers on 12, 13, and 14 rounds with $d = 130, 210$, and 260, respectively.

More Rounds. Finally, the results of Boura et al. [7, Theorem 2] are also directly applicable to our previous results to distinguish up to 20 permutation rounds with $d = 319$ (using 9 backward rounds with degree ≤ 318 and 11 forward rounds with degree ≤ 317, no free middle round possible).

Using a zero-sum distinguisher, we can show non-random properties for the full 12-round permutation of ASCON. However, the designers already state [11] that the permutation is not ideal and are aware of such distinguishers. The non-ideal properties of the permutation do not seem to affect the security of ASCON. In particular, the complexity of 2^{130} is above the cipher's claimed security level.

4   Cube Attacks

Recently, Dinur et al. [9] published various cube and cube-like attacks on several keyed primitives using the Keccak permutation. Those cube-like attacks include cube testers, which can serve as distinguishers, and also cube-like attacks to recover the secret key. In this section, we apply two attacks presented by Dinur et al. [9] to Ascon.

4.1   Brief Description of Cube Attacks

The cube attack is an algebraic attack developed by Dinur and Shamir [10]. This algebraic attack builds on the fact that for most ciphers, each output bit can be represented as a polynomial over $\mathbb{F}_2^n$ in algebraic normal form (ANF). The variables x_i of this polynomial may be single bits of plaintext, key-bits, or constants. Dinur and Shamir made the following observation: If a carefully chosen set of plaintext bits is varied over all possible values and the other bits are kept constant, the sum of one bit of the output (cube sum) might be the result of a linear polynomial (called superpoly) consisting solely of bits of the secret key. By gathering many of these linear polynomials, the secret key can be found.

To perform such a cube attack on a cipher, two things have to be done. First, an attacker has to find such cubes (variables to vary and the resulting linear key relations). This is done in an offline preprocessing phase. Here, the attacker determines the cubes by selecting the cube variables randomly and check if the resulting superpoly is linear and contains the key. This preprocessing phase has to be carried out once for each cipher. In an online phase, the attacker uses the knowledge of the cubes to recover the secret key of his target. To perform the attack, the attacker has to be able to choose the plaintext according to his needs and obtain the corresponding ciphertext outputs.

4.2   Cube Attack on Ascon

Now we want to investigate the potential threat of cube attacks to Ascon. If we look at the different phases of Ascon, the only phase where a nonce-respecting adversary can easily keep some inputs of the permutation constant and deterministically influence others is the initialization. In this scenario, the key is kept secret and the attacker has the ability to choose the nonce according to his needs.

As evaluated in Section 3, the degree of a 5-round initialization of Ascon is at most 32. Thus, if we search for cubes of 31 variables, the resulting superpoly is definitely linear or constant. Considering 6 rounds of the initialization, we have to look for cubes with at most 63 variables, for 7 rounds with at most 127 variables and so on. So it is likely that a practical cube attack on 6 rounds is already hard to achieve. However, we have not searched for cubes, but instead performed cube-like attacks on Ascon to recover the secret key in Section 4.4.

4.3   Distinguishers Using Cube Testers

Below, we describe a cube tester for 6 rounds of the Ascon permutation with the property that the generated output bits sum to zero over $\mathbb{F}_2$. Moreover, this cube tester has a practical complexity of only 2^{33}, although the expected degree for 6 rounds of the ASCON permutation is about 64. To achieve this, we have to take a closer look at the internal structure of ASCON.

The permutation of ASCON starts with the substitution layer. In this layer, the 5-bit S-box is applied 64 times in parallel to the internal state of ASCON. Each of the five 64-bit words of the internal state contributes exactly one bit to each instantiation of a 5-bit S-box. So if all cube variables lie within the same word of the state, they do not appear together in one term after the application of the S-box layer. Hence, after 5 more rounds, at most 32 variables of one state-word appear together in one term. As a consequence, selecting a cube of 33 variables of the same state-word definitely results in an empty superpoly and all 2^{33} generated outputs sum to zero.

This distinguisher can be used to distinguish the key-stream generated by ASCON-128 in a nonce-misuse scenario, where the attacker can keep the nonce constant while varying the plaintext. For ASCON-128, 64-bit blocks of plaintext are xored with the state-word x_0. Thus, the attacker can vary 33 bits of the first plaintext block, while keeping the remaining 31 bits and the bits of a second plaintext block constant. The resulting 2^{33} second ciphertext blocks will sum to zero. However, the designers of ASCON strictly forbid nonce reuse, and no security claims are made for such a scenario.

Similar cube testers can be applied to reduced versions of ASCON with only 6 rounds (instead of 12 rounds) of initialization. Then, an attacker with control over the nonce can observe the first key-stream block. In contrast to the nonce-misuse scenario, attacks on round-reduced versions of ASCON in a nonce-respecting scenario give insight in the expected security of ASCON and are therefore of more value. Next, we will show how to extend the observations made in this section to a key-recovery attack on round-reduced versions of ASCON.

4.4   Key Recovery Using Cube-Like Attacks

Dinur et al. [9] published a key recovery attack where the superpoly does not necessarily have to be a linear function of the secret key bits, but can also be non-linear. Such attacks are also possible for round-reduced versions of ASCON, with the initialization reduced to 5 or 6 out of 12 rounds. The attack on 5 rounds has practical complexity and has been implemented. We will discuss the working principle of the attack by means of a 5-round version of ASCON-128. For a 6-round initialization, the attack works similarly. The attack itself is divided into two steps, each with an online and an offline phase, and relies on the following two observations.

Observations. The first observation has already been discussed in the context of cube testers: If all cube variables are located within one state-word, they do not appear in the same term of the output polynomial after one application of the substitution layer.

To discuss the second observation, we have to take a look at the ANF of the S-box and consider the positions of the initial values. During the initialization, the constant C is written to x_0, the first word K_1 of the key to x_1, the second key word K_2 to x_2, the first word N_1 of the nonce to x_3, and the second nonce word N_2 to x_4. We use the ANF of the S-box to get the relations for the state words $x_0, \ldots, x_4$ after the first call of the substitution layer. The index i represents the corresponding bit position of the 64-bit word.

$$x_0[i] = N_2[i]K_1[i] + N_1[i] + K_2[i]K_1[i] + K_2[i] + K_1[i]C[i] + K_1[i] + C[i]$$
$$x_1[i] = N_2[i] + N_1[i](K_2[i] + K_1[i]) + N_1[i] + K_2[i]K_1[i] + K_2[i] + K_1[i] + C[i]$$
$$x_2[i] = N_2[i]N_1[i] + N_2[i] + K_2[i] + K_1[i] + 1$$
$$x_3[i] = N_2[i]C[i] + N_2[i] + N_1[i]C[i] + N_1[i] + K_2[i] + K_1[i] + C[i]$$
$$x_4[i] = N_2[i]K_1[i] + N_2[i] + N_1[i] + K_1[i]C[i] + K_1[i]$$

Observe that $N_2[i]$ is only combined nonlinearly with key bit $K_1[i]$, and $N_1[i]$ only with $K_1[i]$ and $K_2[i]$. As demonstrated by Dinur et al. [9], we can make use of this fact to build a so-called borderline cube. For instance, we select $N_2[0..15]$ as our cube variables. The rest of the nonce is kept constant. After round 1, our cube variables only appear with $K_1[0..15]$ in one term and definitely not together with the other bits of the secret key. After 4 more rounds, all of the cube variables may appear together in one term, possibly combined with a selection of the key bits $K_1[0..15]$, but never together with the rest of the key bits. Thus, the cube sum depends on $K_1[0..15]$, but it does not depend on $K_1[16..63]$, or $K_2[0..63]$. This fact leads to the following attack.

Step 1. In the first step, we recover the key-word K_1 in 16-bit chunks. Therefore, we select 4 different borderline cubes with 16 variables in N_2 and probe the online oracle with each of these 4 sets. So we get 4 sums of key-stream blocks, each dependent on 16 different key bits of K_1. In the upcoming offline phase, we use the fact that the sum of the outputs (key-stream blocks) only depends on 16 key bits. So we set the rest of the key bits to a constant and calculate cube sums for every possible 16-bit key part. If such a cube sum corresponds to the cube sum received in the online phase, we get a key candidate. In our experiments, we only received one key candidate per 16-bit block on average. Therefore, we only have one key candidate on average for K_1.

Step 2. In the second step, we recover K_2 in 16-bit chunks. To do so, we use $N_1[i]$ to create our borderline cubes. In contrast to the step before, we have a dependency of the output on bits of K_1, too. So we have to repeat the offline phase for every guess of K_1 received in the previous step. The rest of the procedure works in the same manner as for the recovery of K_1. Again, we only received one key guess for K_2 on average in our implementation of the attack.

The complexity of the described attack depends on the number of key candidates for K_1 and K_2. Since the attack on 5 rounds is practical and we have implemented it, we can state that we only have one key candidate on average. So we estimate that the time complexity is about $8 \cdot 2^{32}$. The attack works similarly for reduced versions of ASCON with only 6 initialization rounds. Here, we need borderline cubes of size 32. If we make the optimistic assumption that we only have one key guess for each recovered key word, the estimated time complexity for the 6 round attack is $4 \cdot 2^{64}$.

5   Differential and Linear Cryptanalysis

Differential [5] and linear [18] cryptanalysis are two standard tools for cryptanalysis. New designs are typically expected to come with some kind of arguments of security against these attacks. For this reason, the designers of ASCON provided security arguments for the individual building blocks (S-box, linear layer), and included first practical results on the differential analysis of ASCON in the design document. In this section, we show some improvements over the existing differential characteristics and present the first linear characteristics for ASCON, including computer-aided proofs on the minimum number of active S-boxes for 3-round characteristics. In addition, we use the combination of differential and linear characteristics to perform practical key-recovery attacks on round-reduced versions of ASCON.

5.1   Linear and Differential Bounds

Beside using heuristic search techniques to find actual characteristics for ASCON (see Section 5.2), we have also used complete search tools (MILP and SAT) to prove bounds on the best possible linear and differential characteristics. The results are given in this section.

Linear Programming. We have first modelled the problem of minimizing the number of active S-boxes in differential characteristics for round-reduced versions of the ASCON permutation as a mixed integer linear program (MILP). The model for R rounds uses the following variables:

- $x_{r,w,b} \in \{0,1\}$ specifies whether bit b of word w of the S-box input in round r is different between the two messages, where $b = 0, \ldots, 63$ and $w = 0, \ldots, 4$.
- $y_{r,w,b} \in \{0,1\}$ specifies whether bit b of word w of the S-box output in round r is different between the two messages, where $b = 0, \ldots, 63$ and $w = 0, \ldots, 4$.
- $d_{r,b} \in \{0,1\}$ specifies if S-box b of round r is active, $b = 0, \ldots, 63$.
- $u_{r,w,b} \in \{0,1,2\}$ is a helper for the linear layer model in word w of round r.

The optimization objective is to minimize the number of active S-boxes,

$$\min \sum_{r=1}^{R} \sum_{b=0}^{63} d_{r,b}.$$

The S-box is modelled only by specifying its branch number, and linking it with the S-box activeness for each $r = 1, \ldots, R$ and $b = 0, \ldots, 63$:

$$d_{r,b} \leq \sum_{w=0}^{63} x_{r,w,b} \leq 5d_{r,b}, \quad \sum_{w=0}^{63} (x_{r,w,b} + y_{r,w,b}) \geq 3d_{r,b}, \quad d_{r,b} \leq \sum_{w=0}^{63} y_{r,w,b} \leq 5d_{r,b}$$

The linear layer is modelled explicitly for $r = 1, \ldots, R$ and $b = 0, \ldots, 63$:

$$y_{r,0,b} + y_{r,0,b+19} + y_{r,0,b+28} + x_{r+1,0,b} = 2 \cdot u_{r,0,b}$$
$$y_{r,1,b} + y_{r,1,b+61} + y_{r,1,b+39} + x_{r+1,1,b} = 2 \cdot u_{r,1,b}$$
$$y_{r,2,b} + y_{r,2,b+1} + y_{r,2,b+6} + x_{r+1,2,b} = 2 \cdot u_{r,2,b}$$
$$y_{r,3,b} + y_{r,3,b+10} + y_{r,3,b+17} + x_{r+1,3,b} = 2 \cdot u_{r,3,b}$$
$$y_{r,4,b} + y_{r,4,b+7} + y_{r,4,b+41} + x_{r+1,4,b} = 2 \cdot u_{r,4,b}$$

Finally, at least one S-box needs to be active:

$$\sum_{w=0}^{4} x_{0,w,0} \geq 1$$

The model for linear cryptanalysis is essentially identical, except for different rotation values. This MILP can then be solved using an off-the-shelf linear optimization tool, such as CPLEX. Unfortunately, it turns out that the highly combinatorial nature of the problem is not well suited for linear solvers, and that SAT solvers are a better fit for this type of problem.

SAT Solvers. For SAT solvers, we can model essentially the same description by using an extended modelling language, as is used by Satisfiability Modulo Theory (SMT) solvers. We used the constraint solver STP by Ganesh et al. [13] to translate a bitvector-based CVC model to conjunctive normal form (CNF). This CNF model can then be solved using a parallel SAT solver, such as Biere's `Treengeling` [3]. Instead of an optimization problem, the problem has to be phrased in terms of satisfiability; i.e., the questions is whether solutions below a specific bound exist.

Modelling the S-box only in terms of its branch number is not very effective for obtaining tight bounds. As a trade-off between the all-too-simplistic branch number model and the complex complete differential description of the S-box (differential distribution table), we chose the following approximation. The linear preprocessing and postprocessing part of the S-box can easily be modelled exactly for both differential and linear cryptanalysis. The nonlinear core (equivalent to the Keccak S-box) is approximated, i.e., the model allows a few transitions that are not possible according to the differential or linear distribution table. For the differential model, we use the following word-wise constraint in terms of input difference words $a_0, \ldots, a_4 \in \mathbb{F}_2^{64}$ and output difference words $b_0, \ldots, b_4 \in \mathbb{F}_2^{64}$:

$$b_i = a_i \oplus ((a_{i+1} \vee a_{i+2}) \wedge t_i), \qquad t_i \in \mathbb{F}_2^{64}, \quad i = 0, \ldots, 4.$$

For the linear model with word-wise linear input mask $a_0, \ldots, a_4 \in \mathbb{F}_2^{64}$ and output mask $b_0, \ldots, b_4 \in \mathbb{F}_2^{64}$, the constraints are similar:

$$a_i = b_i \oplus ((b_{i-1} \vee b_{i-2}) \wedge t_i), \qquad t_i \in \mathbb{F}_2^{64}, \quad i = 0, \ldots, 4.$$

With this model, we can easily prove that the 3-round ASCON permutation has at least 15 differentially active S-boxes (probability $\leq 2^{-30}$), and at least 13 linearly active S-boxes (bias $\leq 2^{-14}$, complexity $\geq 2^{28}$). The bounds on the number of active S-boxes are tight, but not necessarily those on the probability. Using these results, we can prove that the full 12-round initialization or finalization has at least 60 differentially active S-boxes (probability $\leq 2^{-120}$) and at least 52 linearly active S-boxes (bias $\leq 2^{-53}$, complexity $\geq 2^{106}$). These bounds are almost certainly not tight, but we were not able to derive bounds for more than 3 rounds using SAT solvers. This motivates the use of heuristic search tools to find explicit characteristics.

5.2   Differential and Linear Characteristics

In Table 4, we present an overview of our best differential and linear characteristics for different round numbers of the ASCON permutation. We have been able to improve the differential characteristic for 4 rounds of the ASCON permutation compared to the previous best results by the designers [11]. Since the designers included no results on linear cryptanalysis in the submission document, we provide the first linear analysis. When comparing the best differential characteristics with the best linear characteristics, we see that for more than two rounds of the ASCON permutation, the linear characteristics have fewer active S-boxes. This might indicate that ASCON is more vulnerable to linear cryptanalysis. Nevertheless, for 5 rounds of ASCON, the best found linear characteristic has more than 64 active S-boxes. Assuming the best possible bias for all active S-boxes, the attack complexity is already higher than 2^{128}.

Table 4. Minimum number of active S-boxes for the ASCON permutation

result	rounds	differential	linear
proof	1	1	1
	2	4	4
	3	15	13
heuristic	4	44	43
	≥ 5	> 64	> 64

5.3   Forgery Attack on Round-Reduced Ascon

Usually, the characteristics from Section 5.2 cannot be directly used in an attack, since there might be additional requirements that the characteristic has to fulfill. In the case of an attack on the finalization of ASCON-128, suitable characteristics may only contain differences in stateword x_0 at the input of the permutation. The rest of the statewords have to be free of differences. For the output of the finalization, the only requirement is that there is some fixed difference pattern in x_3 and x_4. Knowledge about the expected differences in x_0, x_1, and x_2 at the output of the permutation is not required.

For round-reduced versions of ASCON, we have found suitable characteristics for a reduced 3-round finalization with a probability of 2^{-33} and for 4-round finalization with a probability of 2^{-101}. The used characteristic for the three round attack is given in Table 6 and the differential for the four round attack is given in Table 7 in Appendix A.

5.4 Differential-Linear Cryptanalysis

In differential-linear cryptanalysis, differential and linear characteristics are used together in an attack. This kind of analysis was introduced by Langford and Hellman [17]. Later on, it was demonstrated that this type of analysis is also suitable for cases where the differential and the linear part have a probability different from 1 [4,16]. Differential-linear cryptanalysis is especially useful if the combined success probability of one short differential characteristic and one short linear characteristic is better than the probability of a longer linear or differential characteristic. One reason for such a behavior might be a bad diffusion for fewer rounds. For the attack to work, the individual probabilities of the two used characteristics have to be relatively high. According to Dunkelman et al. [12], the bias at the output of such a differential-linear characteristic is about $2pq^2$, where q is the bias of the linear part and p the probability of the differential characteristic. This results in a data complexity of $\mathcal{O}(p^{-2}q^{-4})$.

Outline of the Attack. For ASCON-128, we can use differential-linear characteristics as key-stream distinguisher. Like for cube-tester (Section 4.3), we can target either the initialization in a nonce-respecting scenario, or the processing of the plaintext in a nonce-misuse scenario. Here, we focus on the initialization. Therefore, differences are only allowed in the nonce (x_3, x_4), whereas the linear active bits have to be observable and therefore must be in x_0.

Analysis of the Initialization. We start with the analysis of a 4-round initialization and create a differential-linear characteristic for it. For the differential part, we place two differences in the same S-box of round 1. With probability 2^{-2}, we have one active bit at the output of this S-box. The linear layer ensures that 3 S-boxes are active in the second round. Those 3 S-boxes have the difference at the same bit-position of their input. All 3 active S-boxes of round 2 have the same output pattern of 2 active bits with probability 2^{-3}. Due to the linear layer, we then have differences on 11 S-boxes of round 3. For the linear characteristic, we use a characteristic with one active S-box in round 4 and 5 active S-boxes in round 3. The bias of the linear characteristic is 2^{-8}. In addition, we place the S-boxes in a way that the linear active S-boxes in round 3 do not overlap with the 11 S-boxes that have differences at their inputs. The bias of the generated differential-linear characteristic is $2pq^2 = 2^{-20}$. In practice, we are only interested in the bias of the output bit for the specific differences at the input. Due to the vast amount of possible combinations of differential and linear characteristics that achieve these requirements, we expect a much better bias.

Practical Evaluation of the Bias. In the best case, we place differences in bit 63 of x_3 and x_4, and get a bias of 2^{-2} in bit 9 of x_0 on the output of the substitution layer of round 4. This is much better than the result of 2^{-20} that we obtained from the theoretical analysis. It is possible to combine multiple characteristics to also get to a bias of 2^{-2} in theory. However, we decided to reduce our differential-linear analysis to statistical tests, where we place differences at the input and try to measure a bias at the output bits. We think that this method is sufficient for practical attacks. For a 5-round initialization, we observe a bias of 2^{-10} on $x_0[16]$ (last substitution layer) for differences in $x_3[63]$, and $x_4[63]$. This bias can be improved to 2^{-9} if we only use nonces with the same sign of the difference (the concrete pairs for both $x_3[63]$ and $x_4[63]$ are either $(0, 1)$ or $(1, 0)$). In the case of a 6-round initialization, we were not able to observe a bias by using a set of 2^{36} inputs. The biases were averaged for randomly-chosen keys.

Observing Key-Dependency of the Bias. As shown by Huang et al. [14], the bias observed at the output depends on the concrete values of secret and constant bits. They used this observation to recover the secret state of ICEPOLE in a nonce-misuse scenario. So we expect that a similar attack is possible on round-reduced versions of ASCON-128. In contrast to Huang et al., we want to recover the secret key directly and attack round-reduced versions of the initialization. This also transfers the attack to a nonce-respecting scenario. For a reduced initalization of 4 out of 12 rounds, we observed the bias patterns shown in Table 5. This table shows that the observable bias depends on the concrete values of two key bits which contribute to the same S-box as the used difference. Moreover, the bias is completely independent of the concrete value of the constant in x_0. This leads to the following straightforward attack.

Table 5. Bias of bit $x_0[i + 1]$ in the S-box outputs of round 4 for differences in input bits $x_3[i]$ and $x_4[i]$ (2^{30} different inputs)

inputs $(x_1[i], x_2[i])$ key-bit pair		(0,0)	(0,1)	(1,0)	(1,1)
output $x_0[i+1]$	sign	+1	−1	+1	−1
	bias	$2^{-2.68}$	$2^{-3.68}$	$2^{-3.30}$	$2^{-2.30}$

Key-Recovery Attack on Round-Reduced Ascon. The target of this attack is a round-reduced version of ASCON-128, where the initialization is reduced to 4 out of 12 rounds. In this setting, the attacker has the ability to choose the nonce and is able to observe the resulting key stream. The attacker performs a sufficient amount of queries, with pairs of nonces which have differences in $x_3[63]$ and $x_4[63]$, and calculates the bias of $x_0[0]$ of the key-stream. With the help of Table 5, the attacker is able to recover two bits of the key by matching the expected bias with his calculated bias. Since the characteristics of

Ascon are rotation-invariant within the 64-bit words, the same method can be used to recover the other key bits by placing differences in bits i and observing the bias at position $i + 1 \mod 64$. Already 2^{12} samples per bit position i are sufficient to get stable results. This results in an expected time complexity of 2^{18} for the key-recovery attack on 4 rounds. However, in practice, we use the bias of all the bits and compute the correlation with the results of a precomputation (fingerprinting) phase to get better results. This way, we were also able to mount a key-recovery attack on the initialization of Ascon-128 reduced to 5 out of 12 rounds. In particular, we can reliably recover all key-bit pairs with values $(0,0)$ and $(1,1)$ with a low complexity of 2^{36}. However, we need to brute-force the other pairs, which results in an additional complexity of 2^{32} on average and 2^{64} in the worst case. Thus, the expected attack complexity is about 2^{36}. The complexities of both attacks on 4 and 5 rounds of the initialization have been practically verified.

Acknowledgments. The authors would like to thank the anonymous reviewers for their valuable comments and suggestions. The work has been supported in part by the Austrian Science Fund (project P26494-N15) and by the Austrian Research Promotion Agency (FFG) and the Styrian Business Promotion Agency (SFG) under grant number 836628 (SeCoS).

A   Differentials to Create Forgery

Table 6 contains the differential characteristic and Table 7 contains the differential used for the forgery attacks of Section 5.3. One column corresponds to the five 64-bit words of the state, and the xor differences are given in hexadecimal notation (truncated in the last round).

Table 6. Differential characteristic to create forgery for round-reduced Ascon-128 with a 3-round finalization. The differential probability is 2^{-33}.

	input difference	after 1 round	after 2 rounds	after 3 rounds
x_0	8000000000000000	8000100800000000	8000000002000080	????????????????
x_1	0000000000000000	8000000001000004	9002904800000000	????????????????
x_2	0000000000000000 $\rightarrow$	0000000000000000 $\rightarrow$	d200000001840006 $\rightarrow$	????????????????
x_3	0000000000000000	0000000000000000	0102000001004084	4291316c5aa02140
x_4	0000000000000000	0000000000000000	0000000000000000	090280200302c084

B   Differential-Linear Key Recovery Attack on 4 Rounds

Fig. 2 illustrates the observed bias in bit $x_0[i]$ in the key-stream for the differential-linear attack of Section 5.4, grouped by the values of the key-bit pair $(x_1[63], x_2[63])$.

Table 7. Differential to create forgery for round-reduced ASCON-128 with a 4-round finalization. The differential probability is 2^{-101}.

input difference	after 4 rounds
x_0 8000000000000000	????????????????
x_1 0000000000000000	????????????????
x_2 0000000000000000 $\rightarrow$	????????????????
x_3 0000000000000000	280380ec6a0e9024
x_4 0000000000000000	eb2541b2a0e438b0

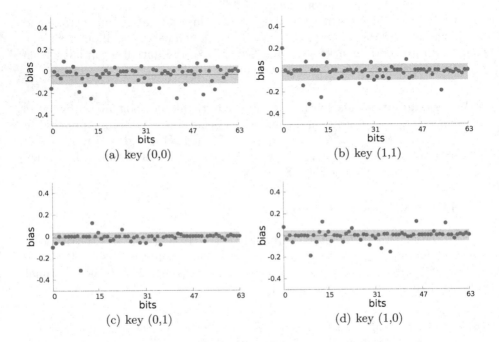

(a) key (0,0)   (b) key (1,1)

(c) key (0,1)   (d) key (1,0)

Fig. 2. Biases for the differential-linear attack on the initialization of ASCON reduced to 4 (out of 12) rounds for the key-bit pair values $(0,0)$, $(0,1)$, $(1,0)$, $(1,1)$

References

1. Aumasson, J.P., Meier, W.: Zero-sum distinguishers for reduced Keccak-f and for the core functions of Luffa and Hamsi. CHES rump session (2009)
2. Bertoni, G., Daemen, J., Peeters, M., Van Assche, G.: Keccak Specifications. Submission to NIST (Round 3) (2011). http://keccak.noekeon.org
3. Biere, A.: Lingeling, Plingeling and Treengeling entering the SAT Competition 2013. In: Balint, A., Belov, A., Heule, M., Järvisalo, M. (eds.) SAT competition 2013. vol. B-2013-1, pp. 51–52 (2013). http://fmv.jku.at/lingeling/
4. Biham, E., Dunkelman, O., Keller, N.: Enhancing Differential-Linear Cryptanalysis. In: Zheng, Y. (ed.) ASIACRYPT 2002. LNCS, vol. 2501, pp. 254–266. Springer, Heidelberg (2002)

5. Biham, E., Shamir, A.: Differential Cryptanalysis of DES-like Cryptosystems. In: Menezes, A., Vanstone, S.A. (eds.) CRYPTO 1990. LNCS, vol. 537, pp. 2–21. Springer, Heidelberg (1991)

6. Boura, C., Canteaut, A.: A zero-sum property for the Keccak-f permutation with 18 rounds. In: IEEE International Symposium on Information Theory, pp. 2488–2492. IEEE (2010)

7. Boura, C., Canteaut, A., De Cannière, C.: Higher-order differential properties of KECCAK and Luffa. In: Joux, A. (ed.) FSE 2011. LNCS, vol. 6733, pp. 252–269. Springer, Heidelberg (2011)

8. Daemen, J.: Permutation-based Encryption. Authentication and Authenticated Encryption, DIAC - Directions in Authenticated Ciphers (2012)

9. Dinur, I., Morawiecki, P., Pieprzyk, J., Srebrny, M., Straus, M.: Cube Attacks and Cube-attack-like Cryptanalysis on the Round-reduced Keccak Sponge Function. IACR Cryptology ePrint Archive 2014, **736** (2014). http://eprint.iacr.org/2014/736

10. Dinur, I., Shamir, A.: Cube Attacks on Tweakable Black Box Polynomials. In: Joux, A. (ed.) EUROCRYPT 2009. LNCS, vol. 5479, pp. 278–299. Springer, Heidelberg (2009)

11. Dobraunig, C., Eichlseder, M., Mendel, F., Schläffer, M.: Ascon. Submission to the CAESAR competition (2014). http://ascon.iaik.tugraz.at

12. Dunkelman, O., Indesteege, S., Keller, N.: A Differential-Linear Attack on 12-Round Serpent. In: Chowdhury, D.R., Rijmen, V., Das, A. (eds.) INDOCRYPT 2008. LNCS, vol. 5365, pp. 308–321. Springer, Heidelberg (2008)

13. Ganesh, V., Dill, D.L.: A decision procedure for bit-vectors and arrays. In: Damm, W., Hermanns, H. (eds.) CAV 2007. LNCS, vol. 4590, pp. 519–531. Springer, Heidelberg (2007)

14. Huang, T., Wu, H., Tjuawinata, I.: Practical State Recovery Attack on ICEPOLE. http://www3.ntu.edu.sg/home/huangtao/icepole/icepole_attack.pdf

15. Jovanovic, P., Luykx, A., Mennink, B.: Beyond $2^{c/2}$ Security in Sponge-Based Authenticated Encryption Modes. In: Sarkar, P., Iwata, T. (eds.) ASIACRYPT 2014. LNCS, vol. 8873, pp. 85–104. Springer, Heidelberg (2014)

16. Langford, S.K.: Differential-linear cryptanalysis and threshold signatures. Ph.D. thesis, Stanford University (1995)

17. Langford, S.K., Hellman, M.E.: Differential-linear cryptanalysis. In: Desmedt, Y.G. (ed.) CRYPTO 1994. LNCS, vol. 839, pp. 17–25. Springer, Heidelberg (1994)

18. Matsui, M., Yamagishi, A.: A New Method for Known Plaintext Attack of FEAL Cipher. In: Rueppel, R.A. (ed.) EUROCRYPT 1992. LNCS, vol. 658, pp. 81–91. Springer, Heidelberg (1993)

19. National Institute of Standards and Technology: FIPS PUB 180–4: Secure Hash Standard. Federal Information Processing Standards Publication 180–4, U.S. Department of Commerce (March 2012). http://csrc.nist.gov/publications/fips/fips180-4/fips-180-4.pdf

20. The CAESAR committee: CAESAR: Competition for authenticated encryption: Security, applicability, and robustness (2014). http://competitions.cr.yp.to/caesar.html

Detecting and Tracing
Malicious Activities

Stronger Security Notions for Decentralized Traceable Attribute-Based Signatures and More Efficient Constructions

Essam Ghadafi[✉]

University College London, London, UK
essam_gha@yahoo.com

Abstract. We revisit the notion of Decentralized Traceable Attribute-Based Signatures (DTABS) introduced by El Kaafarani et al. (CT-RSA 2014) and improve the state-of-the-art in three dimensions: Firstly, we provide a new stronger security model which circumvents some shortcomings in existing models. Our model minimizes the trust placed in attribute authorities and hence provides, among other things, a stronger definition for non-frameability. In addition, our model captures the notion of tracing soundness which is important for many applications of the primitive. Secondly, we provide a generic construction that is secure w.r.t. our strong security model and show two example instantiations in the standard model which are more efficient than existing constructions (secure under weaker security definitions). Finally, we dispense with the need for the expensive zero-knowledge proofs required for proving tracing correctness by the tracing authority. As a result, tracing a signature in our constructions is significantly more efficient than existing constructions, both in terms of the size of the tracing proof and the computational cost required to generate and verify it. For instance, verifying tracing correctness in our constructions requires only 4 pairings compared to 34 pairings in the most efficient existing construction.

Keywords: Attribute-based signatures · Security definitions · Traceability · Standard model

1 Introduction

In Attribute-Based Signatures (ABS) [25,26], messages are signed w.r.t. signing policies expressed as predicates. A signature convinces the verifier that it it was produced by a user with attributes satisfying the signing policy, revealing neither the identity of the user nor the attributes used. Attribute-based signatures have many applications, including trust negotiation, e.g. [12], attribute-based messaging, e.g. [9], and leaking secrets. Refer to [26,29] for more details.

The security of attribute-based signatures [25] requires user's privacy and unforgeability. Informally, user's privacy requires that signatures reveal neither the user's identity nor the attributes used in the signing. On the other hand,

© Springer International Publishing Switzerland 2015
K. Nyberg (ed.): CT-RSA 2015, LNCS 9048, pp. 391–409, 2015.
DOI: 10.1007/978-3-319-16715-2_21

unforgeability requires that a user cannot forge a signature w.r.t. a signing predicate that her attributes do not satisfy, even if she colludes with other users.

Traceable Attribute-Based Signatures (TABS) [11] extend standard attribute-based signatures by adding an anonymity revocation mechanism which allows a tracing authority to recover the identity of the signer. Such a feature is important for enforcing accountability and deterring abuse.

Related Work. Various constructions of attribute-based signatures exist in the literature [13,20,23,24,26,28,29,31]. Those constructions vary in terms of the expressiveness of the policies they support and whether they offer selective or adaptive security. Adaptively secure schemes supporting more expressive policies are preferable since they cover a larger scale of potential applications.

While there exist constructions supporting threshold policies with constant-size signatures, e.g. [13,20], constructions supporting monotonic/non-monotonic policies, e.g. [26,28,29], yield signatures that are linearly dependent on the number of attributes in the policy or the systems' security parameter.

Supporting multiple attribute authorities was first considered by [25,28]. However, it still had the problem of requiring a central trusted authority. Okamoto and Takashima [29] proposed the first fully decentralized construction.

Escala et al. [11] added the traceability feature to standard ABS schemes and proposed a model for the single attribute authority setting. More recently, El Kaafarani et al. [10] proposed a security model and two generic constructions for decentralized traceable attribute-based signatures. They also provided instantiations without random oracles [5]. Besides correctness, the recent model of [10] defines three security requirements: anonymity, full unforgeability and traceability. Informally, anonymity requires that a signature reveals neither the identity of the signer nor the set of attributes used in the signing; full unforgeability requires that users cannot forge signatures w.r.t. signing policies their individual attributes do not satisfy even if they collude, which also captures non-frameability; and traceability requires that the tracing authority is always able to establish the identity of the signer and prove such a claim.

Shortcomings in Existing Models. The unforgeability/non-frameability requirements in all existing models for traceable attribute-based signatures [10, 11] (and even those for standard (i.e. non-traceable) attribute-based signatures, e.g. [25,28,29]) besides placing full trust in attribute authorities, assume the existence of secure means for the delivery of the secret attributes' keys from attribute authorities to users. More specifically, learning the key for any attribute a user owns allows framing the user w.r.t. to those attributes. For instance, the non-frameability definition in the single-authority model of [11] relies on the assumption that the attribute authority is fully honest, whereas the full unforgeability definition (also capturing non-frameability) in the stronger and more recent model of [10] assumes that at least one attribute authority is fully honest.

While this is not an issue in standard attribute-based signatures (since it is infeasible for any party to identify the signer), we emphasize that this could be a serious limitation in the traceable setting. In particular, the innocence of users could be jeopardized by being falsely accused of producing signatures they have not produced. A misbehaving attribute authority or any party intercepting the secret attributes' keys is capable of signing on behalf of the user w.r.t. any predicate satisfied by the compromised subset of attributes.

We believe that the overly strong assumptions upon which the notions in existing models rely is the result of the absence of the assignment of personal keys to the users. Moreover, the absence of users' personal keys further complicates the constructions and degrades the efficiency. For instance, the recent constructions in [10], similarly to [26], rely on the so-called pseudo-attribute technique in order to bind the signature to the message.

Another shortcoming of existing models is the absence of the tracing soundness requirement [30]. This requirement ensures that a valid signature can only trace to a single user even if all entities in the system are fully corrupt. It is vital for many applications, e.g., applications where users get rewarded for signatures they produced or where abusing signing rights might result in legal consequences. In addition, tracing in existing constructions is costly, both in terms of the size of the tracing proof and the cost for producing and verifying it. The most efficient existing construction [10] requires 34 pairings to verify the opening of a single signature.

Our Contribution. We rectify the aforementioned shortcomings in existing models by presenting a stronger security model. Our model is for the dynamic and fully decentralized setting where attributes' management is distributed among different authorities who may not even be aware of one another, and where users and attribute authorities can join the system at any time. Our model offers a stronger definition for non-frameability and captures the useful notion of tracing soundness [30]. In addition, it provides a cleaner definition for traceability.

Our second contribution is a generic construction for the primitive which permits expressive signing policies and meets strong adaptive security requirements. Our generic construction dispenses with the expensive zero-knowledge proofs required by existing constructions for proving tracing correctness by deploying a robust, non-interactive tag-based encryption scheme.

Finally, we provide two example instantiations of the generic framework in the standard model. Besides offering stronger security, our instantiations are more efficient than existing constructions. In addition, our constructions have much smaller computation and communication overhead for tracing.

Paper Organization. In Section 2, we give some preliminary definitions. We present our model in Section 3. We list the building blocks we use in Section 4. In Section 5, we present our generic construction and prove its security. In Section 6, we present instantiations in the standard model.

Notation. A function $\nu(.) : \mathbb{N} \to \mathbb{R}^+$ is negligible in c if for every polynomial $p(.)$ and all sufficiently large values of c, it holds that $\nu(c) < \frac{1}{p(c)}$. Given a probability distribution S, we denote by $y \leftarrow S$ the operation of selecting an element according to S. If A is a probabilistic machine, we denote by $A(x_1, \ldots, x_n)$ the output distribution of A on inputs $(x_1, \ldots, x_n)$. By PPT we mean running in probabilistic polynomial time in the relevant security parameter.

2   Preliminaries

In this section we provide some preliminary definitions.

Bilinear Groups. Let $\mathbb{G}_1 := \langle G \rangle$, $\mathbb{G}_2 := \langle \tilde{G} \rangle$ and $\mathbb{G}_T$ be groups of a prime order p. A bilinear group is a tuple $\mathcal{P} := (\mathbb{G}_1, \mathbb{G}_2, \mathbb{G}_T, p, G, \tilde{G}, e)$ where $e : \mathbb{G}_1 \times \mathbb{G}_2 \longrightarrow \mathbb{G}_T$ is a non-degenerate bilinear map. We will use multiplicative notation for all the groups and let $\mathbb{G}_1^\times := \mathbb{G}_1 \setminus \{1_{\mathbb{G}_1}\}$ and $\mathbb{G}_2^\times := \mathbb{G}_2 \setminus \{1_{\mathbb{G}_2}\}$. We will accent elements from $\mathbb{G}_2$ with ~ for the sake of clarity. We use Type-3 groups [14] where $\mathbb{G}_1 \neq \mathbb{G}_2$ and there is no efficient isomorphism between the groups in either direction. We assume the existence of an algorithm BGrpSetup which on input a security parameter λ outputs a description of bilinear groups.

Complexity Assumptions. We use the following existing assumptions:

SXDH. This assumption requires that the Decisional Diffie-Hellman (DDH) assumption holds in both groups $\mathbb{G}_1$ and $\mathbb{G}_2$.

XDLIN$_{\mathbb{G}_1}$ [1] [1]. Given $\mathcal{P}$ and the tuple $(G^h, G^v, G^u, G^{rh}, G^{sv}, G^{ut}, \tilde{G}^h, \tilde{G}^v, \tilde{G}^u, \tilde{G}^{rh}, \tilde{G}^{sv}) \in \mathbb{G}_1^6 \times \mathbb{G}_2^5$ for unknown $h, r, s, t, u, v \in \mathbb{Z}_p$, it is hard to determine whether or not $t = r + s$.

q-SDH [8]. Given $(G, G^x, \ldots, G^{x^q}, \tilde{G}, \tilde{G}^x)$ for $x \leftarrow \mathbb{Z}_p$, it is hard to output a pair $(c, G^{\frac{1}{x+c}}) \in \mathbb{Z}_p \times \mathbb{G}_1$ for an arbitrary $c \in \mathbb{Z}_p \setminus \{-x\}$.

q-AGHO [3]. Given a uniformly random tuple $(G, \tilde{G}, \tilde{W}, \tilde{X}, \tilde{Y}) \in \mathbb{G}_1 \times \mathbb{G}_2^4$, and q uniformly random tuples $(A_i, B_i, R_i, \tilde{D}_i) \in \mathbb{G}_1^3 \times \mathbb{G}_2$, each satisfying $e(A_i, \tilde{D}_i) = e(G, \tilde{G})$ and $e(G, \tilde{X}) = e(A_i, \tilde{W})e(B_i, \tilde{G})e(R_i, \tilde{Y})$, it is hard to output a new tuple $(A^*, B^*, R^*, \tilde{D}^*)$ satisfying the above equations.

Span Programs. For a field $\mathbb{F}$ and a variable set $\mathcal{A} = \{\alpha_1, \ldots, \alpha_n\}$, a monotone span program [21] is defined by a $\beta \times \gamma$ matrix $\mathbf{S}$ (over $\mathbb{F}$) along with a labeling map ρ which associates each row in $\mathbf{S}$ with an element $\alpha_i \in \mathcal{A}$. The span program accepts a set $\mathcal{A}'$ iff $\mathbf{1} \in \mathrm{Span}(\mathbf{S}_{\mathcal{A}'})$, where $\mathbf{S}_{\mathcal{A}'}$ is the sub-matrix of $\mathbf{S}$ containing only rows with labels $\alpha_i \in \mathcal{A}'$, i.e., the program only accepts $\mathcal{A}'$ if there exists a vector z s.t. $z\mathbf{S}_{\mathcal{A}'} = [1, 0, \ldots, 0]$.

3   Syntax and Security of Decentralized Traceable Attribute-Based Signatures

The entities involved in a DTABS scheme are: a set of attribute authorities, each with a unique identity aid and a pair of secret/verification keys $(\mathsf{ask}_{\mathsf{aid}}, \mathsf{avk}_{\mathsf{aid}})$; a tracing authority TA with a secret tracing key tk that is used to identify the signer of a given signature; a set of users, each with a unique identity uid, a personal

---

[1] It can similarly be defined in $\mathbb{G}_2$.

secret/public key pair ($\mathbf{usk}[\text{uid}]$, $\mathbf{uvk}[\text{uid}]$) and a set of attributes $\mathcal{A} \subseteq \mathbb{A}$ (where $\mathbb{A}$ is the attribute universe). Users and attribute authorities can join the system at any time. Attributes in the system can be distinctly identified by concatenating the identity of the managing authority with the name of the attribute. This way, the identities (and hence the public keys) of attribute authorities managing attributes appearing in the signing policy can be inferred from the predicate itself which eliminates the need for any additional meta-data to be attached.

A DTABS scheme is a tuple of polynomial-time algorithms $\mathcal{DTABS} :=$ (Setup, AKeyGen, UKeyGen, AttKeyGen, Sign, Verify, Trace, Judge). The definition of the algorithms are as follows; to aid notation all algorithms bar the first three take as implicit input the public parameters pp output by Setup.

- Setup(1^λ) is run by some trusted third party. On input a security parameter 1^λ, it outputs public parameters pp and a tracing key tk.
- AKeyGen(pp, aid) is run by attribute authority aid to generate its key pair (ask_{aid}, avk_{aid}). The attribute authority publishes its public key avk_{aid}.
- UKeyGen(pp) generates a personal secret/verification key pair ($\mathbf{usk}[\text{uid}]$, $\mathbf{uvk}[\text{uid}]$) for the user with identity uid. We assume that the public key table $\mathbf{uvk}$ is publicly available (possibly via some PKI) so that anyone can obtain authentic copies of uers' public keys.
- AttKeyGen($\text{ask}_{\text{aid}(\alpha)}$, uid, $\mathbf{uvk}[\text{uid}]$, α) on input the secret key of the attribute authority managing attribute α (i.e. $\text{ask}_{\text{aid}(\alpha)}$), a user's identity uid, a user's personal public key $\mathbf{uvk}[\text{uid}]$ and an attribute $\alpha \in \mathbb{A}$, it outputs a secret key $\text{sk}_{\text{uid},\alpha}$ for attribute α for the user. The key $\text{sk}_{\text{uid},\alpha}$ is given to uid.
- Sign($\{\text{avk}_{\text{aid}(\alpha)}\}_{\alpha \in \mathcal{A}}$, uid, $\mathbf{usk}[\text{uid}]$, $\mathbf{uvk}[\text{uid}]$, $\{\text{sk}_{\text{uid},\alpha}\}_{\alpha \in \mathcal{A}}$, m, $\mathbb{P}$) on input an ordered list of attribute authorities' verification keys $\{\text{avk}_{\text{aid}(\alpha)}\}_{\alpha \in \mathcal{A}}$, a user's identity uid, a user's secret and public keys ($\mathbf{usk}[\text{uid}]$, $\mathbf{uvk}[\text{uid}]$), an ordered list of attributes' secret keys $\{\text{sk}_{\text{uid},\alpha}\}_{\alpha \in \mathcal{A}}$ for attributes $\mathcal{A}$ that user uid owns, a message m and a signing predicate $\mathbb{P}$ such that $\mathbb{P}(\mathcal{A}) = 1$, it outputs a signature Σ on m w.r.t. $\mathbb{P}$.
- Verify($\{\text{avk}_{\text{aid}(\alpha)}\}_{\alpha \in \mathbb{P}}$, m, Σ, $\mathbb{P}$) on input an ordered list of authorities' verification keys $\{\text{avk}_{\text{aid}(\alpha)}\}_{\alpha \in \mathbb{P}}$, a message m, a signature Σ and a predicate $\mathbb{P}$, it verifies whether Σ is valid on m w.r.t. $\mathbb{P}$, outputting a bit accordingly.
- Trace(tk, m, Σ, $\mathbb{P}$, $\mathbf{uvk}$) on input the tracing authority's key tk, a message m, a signature Σ, a signing predicate $\mathbb{P}$, and the public keys table $\mathbf{uvk}$, it outputs an identity uid > 0 of the signer of Σ and a proof π_{Trace} attesting to this claim. If it is unable to trace the signature, it returns $(0, \pi_{\text{Trace}})$.
- Judge($\{\text{avk}_{\text{aid}(\alpha)}\}_{\alpha \in \mathbb{P}}$, m, Σ, $\mathbb{P}$, uid, $\mathbf{uvk}[\text{uid}]$, π_{Trace}) on input an ordered list of attribute authorities' verification keys $\{\text{avk}_{\text{aid}(\alpha)}\}_{\alpha \in \mathbb{P}}$, a message m, a signature Σ, a signing predicate $\mathbb{P}$, a user's identity uid, a user's public verification key $\mathbf{uvk}[\text{uid}]$, and a tracing proof π_{Trace}, it outputs 1 if π_{Trace} is a valid proof that uid has produced Σ or 0 otherwise.

Security of Decentralized Traceble Attribute-Based Signatures. The security properties we require from a DTABS scheme are: correctness, anonymity, unforgeability, non-frameability, traceability, and tracing soundness. Unlike the

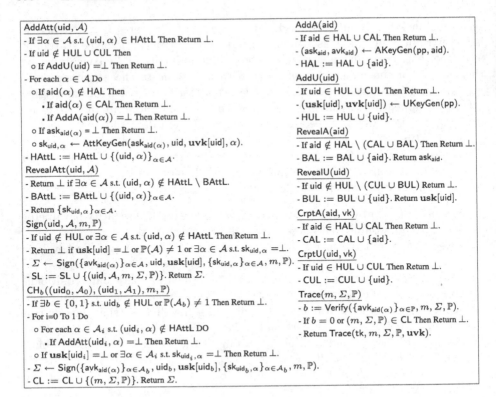

Fig. 1. Oracles used in the security games for DTABS

model of El Kaafrani et al. [10], we split the games of unforgeability and non-frameability in order to strengthen the definition of the latter where we allow for the corruption of all authorities. Even though the games of unforgeability and non-frameability could be combined into one game, separating them preserves simplicity. Also, unlike previous models, our model defines the notion of tracing soundness which was recently proposed in the context of group signatures [30].

In our model, we distinguish between bad entities, i.e. those who were initially honest until the adversary learned their secret keys and corrupt entities whose keys have been chosen by the adversary itself.

The experiments defining the above requirements are in Fig. 2 where the following global lists are maintained: HUL is a list of honest users; HAL is a list of honest attribute authorities; HAttL is a list of honestly created users' attributes and has entries of the form (uid, α); BUL is a list of bad users; BAttL is a list of bad users' attributes whose keys have been revealed to the adversary with entries of the form (uid, α); BAL is a list of bad attribute authorities; CUL is a list of corrupt users; CAL is a list of corrupt attribute authorities; SL is a list of signatures obtained from the Sign oracle; CL is a list of challenge signatures.

The details of the following oracles are given in Fig. 1.

AddA(aid) adds an honest attribute authority with identity aid.

AddU(uid) adds an honest user with identity uid.

AddAtt(uid, $\mathcal{A}$) adds honest attributes $\mathcal{A} \subseteq \mathbb{A}$ for user uid. It can be called multiple times to add more attributes for an existing user.

CrptA(aid, vk) adds a corrupt attribute authority.

CrptU(uid, vk) adds a corrupt user with identity uid.

RevealA(aid) returns the secret key $\mathsf{ask}_{\mathsf{aid}}$ of the honest attribute authority aid.

RevealU(uid) returns the personal secret key $\mathsf{usk}[\mathsf{uid}]$ of user uid.

RevealAtt(uid, $\mathcal{A}$) returns the secret keys $\{\mathsf{sk}_{\mathsf{uid},\alpha}\}_{\alpha \in \mathcal{A}}$ for attributes $\mathcal{A} \subseteq \mathbb{A}$ owned by user uid. It can be called multiple times.

Sign(uid, $\mathcal{A}$, m, $\mathbb{P}$) returns a signature Σ on m using attributes $\mathcal{A}$ belonging to user uid where $\mathbb{P}(\mathcal{A}) = 1$.

$\mathsf{CH}_b((\mathsf{uid}_0, \mathcal{A}_0), (\mathsf{uid}_1, \mathcal{A}_1), m, \mathbb{P})$ on input $(\mathsf{uid}_0, \mathcal{A}_0)$, $(\mathsf{uid}_1, \mathcal{A}_1)$, a message m and a signing policy $\mathbb{P}$ with $\mathbb{P}(\mathcal{A}_0) = \mathbb{P}(\mathcal{A}_1) = 1$, it returns a signature on m using attributes $\mathcal{A}_b$ belonging to user uid_b for $b \leftarrow \{0, 1\}$.

Trace(m, Σ, $\mathbb{P}$) allows the adversary to ask for signatures to be traced.

The details of the security requirements are as follows:

Correctness. This requires that honestly generated signatures verify correctly and trace to the user who produced them. In addition, the Judge algorithm accepts the tracing proof produced by the Trace algorithm. Formally, a DTABS scheme is *correct* if for all $\lambda \in \mathbb{N}$, all PPT adversaries $\mathcal{B}$ have a negligible advantage $\mathsf{Adv}^{\mathrm{Corr}}_{DTABS, \mathcal{B}}(\lambda) := \Pr[\mathsf{Exp}^{\mathrm{Corr}}_{DTABS, \mathcal{B}}(\lambda) = 1]$.

Anonymity. This requires that a signature reveals neither the identity of the user nor the attributes used in the signing. In the game, the adversary chooses a message, a signing policy and two users with two, possibly different, sets of attributes satisfying the signing policy. The adversary gets a signature by either user and wins if it correctly guesses the user. The adversary can fully corrupt all attribute authorities and learn any user's personal secret key/attribute keys including those used for the challenge. Thus, our definition captures full-key exposure attacks. Since the adversary can sign on behalf of any user, it is redundant to provide it with a sign oracle. The only restriction we impose on the adversary is that it may not query the Trace oracle on the challenge signature.

Our definition captures unlinkability since the adversary has access to all users' personal secret keys/attribute keys. Formally, a DTABS scheme is *(fully) anonymous* if for all $\lambda \in \mathbb{N}$, all PPT adversaries $\mathcal{B}$ have a negligible advantage $\mathsf{Adv}^{\mathrm{Anon}}_{DTABS, \mathcal{B}}(\lambda) := \left| \Pr[\mathsf{Exp}^{\mathrm{Anon-1}}_{DTABS, \mathcal{B}}(\lambda) = 1] - \Pr[\mathsf{Exp}^{\mathrm{Anon-0}}_{DTABS, \mathcal{B}}(\lambda) = 1] \right|$.

Unforgeability. This captures unforgeability scenarios where the forgery opens to a particular user. It guarantees that even if all users in the system pool their individual attributes, they cannot output a signature that traces to a user whose individual attributes do not satisfy the signing predicate. In the game, the adversary can adaptively create corrupt attribute authorities and learn some of the honest authorities' secret keys as long as there is at least a single honest attribute authority managing one of the attributes required for satisfying the policy used in the forgery. The adversary can also fully corrupt the tracing authority.

Experiment: $\mathrm{Exp}^{\mathrm{Corr}}_{\mathcal{DTABS},\mathcal{B}}(\lambda)$

- $(\mathrm{pp},\mathrm{tk}) \leftarrow \mathsf{Setup}(1^\lambda)$; HUL, HAttL, HAL := $\emptyset$.
- $(\mathrm{uid}, \mathcal{A}, m, \mathbb{P}) \leftarrow \mathcal{B}(\mathrm{pp} : \mathsf{AddU}(\cdot), \mathsf{AddAtt}(\cdot,\cdot), \mathsf{AddA}(\cdot))$.
- If $\mathbb{P}(\mathcal{A}) \neq 1$ or uid $\notin$ HUL or $\mathbf{usk}[\mathrm{uid}] = \perp$ Then Return 0.
- If $\exists \alpha \in \mathcal{A}$ s.t. $(\mathrm{uid}, \alpha) \notin$ HAttL or $\mathsf{sk}_{\mathrm{uid},\alpha} = \perp$ or aid$(\alpha) \notin$ HAL Then Return 0.
- $\Sigma \leftarrow \mathsf{Sign}(\{\mathsf{avk}_{\mathrm{aid}(\alpha)}\}_{\alpha \in \mathcal{A}}, \mathrm{uid}, \mathbf{usk}[\mathrm{uid}], \mathbf{uvk}[\mathrm{uid}], \{\mathsf{sk}_{\mathrm{uid},\alpha}\}_{\alpha \in \mathcal{A}}, m, \mathbb{P})$.
- If $\mathsf{Verify}(\{\mathsf{avk}_{\mathrm{aid}(\alpha)}\}_{\alpha \in \mathbb{P}}, m, \Sigma, \mathbb{P}) = 0$ Then Return 1.
- $(\mathrm{uid}^*, \pi_{\mathsf{Trace}}) \leftarrow \mathsf{Trace}(\mathrm{tk}, m, \Sigma, \mathbb{P}, \mathbf{uvk})$.
- If $\mathrm{uid}^* \neq \mathrm{uid}$ or $\mathsf{Judge}(\{\mathsf{avk}_{\mathrm{aid}(\alpha)}\}_{\alpha \in \mathbb{P}}, m, \Sigma, \mathbb{P}, \mathrm{uid}, \mathbf{uvk}[\mathrm{uid}], \pi_{\mathsf{Trace}}) = 0$ Then Return 1 Else Return 0.

Experiment: $\mathrm{Exp}^{\mathrm{Anon}\text{-}b}_{\mathcal{DTABS},\mathcal{B}}(\lambda)$

- $(\mathrm{pp},\mathrm{tk}) \leftarrow \mathsf{Setup}(1^\lambda)$; CAL, CUL, HAL, HUL, HAttL, BAL, BUL, BAttL, CL := $\emptyset$.
- $b^* \leftarrow \mathcal{B}\big(\mathrm{pp} : \mathsf{AddU}(\cdot), \mathsf{AddAtt}(\cdot,\cdot), \mathsf{AddA}(\cdot), \mathsf{CrptA}(\cdot,\cdot), \mathsf{CrptU}(\cdot,\cdot), \mathsf{RevealA}(\cdot)$
  $, \mathsf{RevealU}(\cdot), \mathsf{RevealAtt}(\cdot,\cdot), \mathsf{CH}_b((\cdot,\cdot),(\cdot,\cdot),\cdot,\cdot), \mathsf{Trace}(\cdot,\cdot,\cdot)\big)$.
- Return b^*.

Experiment: $\mathrm{Exp}^{\mathrm{Unforge}}_{\mathcal{DTABS},\mathcal{B}}(\lambda)$

- $(\mathrm{pp},\mathrm{tk}) \leftarrow \mathsf{Setup}(1^\lambda)$; CAL, CUL, HAL, HUL, HAttL, BAL, BUL, BAttL, SL := $\emptyset$.
- $(m^*, \Sigma^*, \mathbb{P}^*, \mathrm{uid}^*, \pi^*_{\mathsf{Trace}}) \leftarrow \mathcal{B}\big(\mathrm{pp}, \mathrm{tk} : \mathsf{AddU}(\cdot), \mathsf{AddAtt}(\cdot,\cdot), \mathsf{AddA}(\cdot), \mathsf{CrptA}(\cdot,\cdot), \mathsf{CrptU}(\cdot,\cdot)$
  $, \mathsf{RevealA}(\cdot), \mathsf{RevealU}(\cdot), \mathsf{RevealAtt}(\cdot,\cdot), \mathsf{Sign}(\cdot,\cdot,\cdot,\cdot)\big)$.
- If $\mathsf{Verify}(\{\mathsf{avk}_{\mathrm{aid}(\alpha)}\}_{\alpha \in \mathbb{P}^*}, m^*, \Sigma^*, \mathbb{P}^*) = 0$ Then Return 0.
- If $\mathsf{Judge}(\{\mathsf{avk}_{\mathrm{aid}(\alpha)}\}_{\alpha \in \mathbb{P}^*}, m^*, \Sigma^*, \mathbb{P}^*, \mathrm{uid}^*, \mathbf{uvk}[\mathrm{uid}^*], \pi^*_{\mathsf{Trace}}) = 0$ Then Return 0.
- Let $\mathcal{A}_{\mathrm{uid}^*}$ be the attributes of uid^* managed by dishonest (i.e. $\in$ CAL $\cup$ BAL) attribute authorities.
- If $\exists \mathcal{A}$ s.t. $\{(\mathrm{uid}^*, \alpha)\}_{\alpha \in \mathcal{A}} \subseteq$ BAttL and $\mathbb{P}^*(\mathcal{A} \cup \mathcal{A}_{\mathrm{uid}^*}) = 1$ Then Return 0.
- If $\exists(\mathrm{uid}^*, \cdot, m^*, \Sigma^*, \mathbb{P}^*) \in$ SL Then Return 0 Else Return 1.

Experiment: $\mathrm{Exp}^{\mathrm{NF}}_{\mathcal{DTABS},\mathcal{B}}(\lambda)$

- $(\mathrm{pp},\mathrm{tk}) \leftarrow \mathsf{Setup}(1^\lambda)$; CAL, CUL, HAL, HUL, HAttL, BAL, BUL, BAttL, SL := $\emptyset$.
- $(m^*, \Sigma^*, \mathbb{P}^*, \mathrm{uid}^*, \pi^*_{\mathsf{Trace}}) \leftarrow \mathcal{B}\big(\mathrm{pp}, \mathrm{tk} : \mathsf{AddU}(\cdot), \mathsf{AddAtt}(\cdot,\cdot), \mathsf{AddA}(\cdot), \mathsf{CrptA}(\cdot,\cdot), \mathsf{CrptU}(\cdot,\cdot)$
  $, \mathsf{RevealA}(\cdot), \mathsf{RevealU}(\cdot), \mathsf{RevealAtt}(\cdot,\cdot), \mathsf{Sign}(\cdot,\cdot,\cdot,\cdot)\big)$.
- If $\mathsf{Verify}(\{\mathsf{avk}_{\mathrm{aid}(\alpha)}\}_{\alpha \in \mathbb{P}^*}, m^*, \Sigma^*, \mathbb{P}^*) = 0$ Then Return 0.
- If $\mathsf{Judge}(\{\mathsf{avk}_{\mathrm{aid}(\alpha)}\}_{\alpha \in \mathbb{P}^*}, m^*, \Sigma^*, \mathbb{P}^*, \mathrm{uid}^*, \mathbf{uvk}[\mathrm{uid}^*], \pi^*_{\mathsf{Trace}}) = 0$ Then Return 0.
- If uid $\notin$ HUL \ BUL or $\exists(\mathrm{uid}^*, \cdot, m^*, \Sigma^*, \mathbb{P}^*) \in$ SL Then Return 0 Else Return 1.

Experiment: $\mathrm{Exp}^{\mathrm{Trace}}_{\mathcal{DTABS},\mathcal{B}}(\lambda)$

- $(\mathrm{pp},\mathrm{tk}) \leftarrow \mathsf{Setup}(1^\lambda)$; CUL, HAL, HUL, HAttL, BUL, BAttL, SL := $\emptyset$.
- $(m^*, \Sigma^*, \mathbb{P}^*) \leftarrow \mathcal{B}\big(\mathrm{pp}, \mathrm{tk} : \mathsf{AddU}(\cdot), \mathsf{AddAtt}(\cdot,\cdot), \mathsf{AddA}(\cdot), \mathsf{CrptU}(\cdot,\cdot), \mathsf{RevealU}(\cdot)$
  $, \mathsf{RevealAtt}(\cdot,\cdot), \mathsf{Sign}(\cdot,\cdot,\cdot,\cdot)\big)$.
- If $\mathsf{Verify}(\{\mathsf{avk}_{\mathrm{aid}(\alpha)}\}_{\alpha \in \mathbb{P}^*}, m^*, \Sigma^*, \mathbb{P}^*) = 0$ Then Return 0.
- $(\mathrm{uid}^*, \pi^*_{\mathsf{Trace}}) \leftarrow \mathsf{Trace}(\mathrm{tk}, m^*, \Sigma^*, \mathbb{P}^*, \mathbf{uvk})$.
- If $\mathrm{uid}^* = 0$ or $\mathsf{Judge}(\{\mathsf{avk}_{\mathrm{aid}(\alpha)}\}_{\alpha \in \mathbb{P}^*}, m^*, \Sigma^*, \mathbb{P}^*, \mathrm{uid}^*, \mathbf{uvk}[\mathrm{uid}^*], \pi^*_{\mathsf{Trace}}) = 0$ Then Return 1 Else Return 0.

Experiment: $\mathrm{Exp}^{\mathrm{TS}}_{\mathcal{DTABS},\mathcal{B}}(\lambda)$

- $(\mathrm{pp},\mathrm{tk}) \leftarrow \mathsf{Setup}(1^\lambda)$; CAL, CUL, HAL, HUL, HAttL, BAL, BUL, BAttL := $\emptyset$.
- $(m^*, \Sigma^*, \mathbb{P}^*, \mathrm{uid}_1, \pi_{\mathsf{Trace},1}, \mathrm{uid}_2, \pi_{\mathsf{Trace},2}) \leftarrow \mathcal{B}(\mathrm{pp}, \mathrm{tk} : \mathsf{AddU}(\cdot), \mathsf{AddAtt}(\cdot,\cdot), \mathsf{AddA}(\cdot), \mathsf{CrptA}(\cdot,\cdot)$
  $, \mathsf{CrptU}(\cdot,\cdot), \mathsf{RevealA}(\cdot), \mathsf{RevealU}(\cdot), \mathsf{RevealAtt}(\cdot,\cdot))$.
- If $\mathrm{uid}_1 = \mathrm{uid}_2$ or $\mathsf{Verify}(\{\mathsf{avk}_{\mathrm{aid}(\alpha)}\}_{\alpha \in \mathbb{P}^*}, m^*, \Sigma^*, \mathbb{P}^*) = 0$ Then Return 0.
- If $\exists i \in \{1,2\}$ s.t. $\mathsf{Judge}(\{\mathsf{avk}_{\mathrm{aid}(\alpha)}\}_{\alpha \in \mathbb{P}^*}, m^*, \Sigma^*, \mathbb{P}^*, \mathrm{uid}_i, \mathbf{uvk}[\mathrm{uid}_i], \pi_{\mathsf{Trace},i}) = 0$ Then Return 0.
- Return 1.

Fig. 2. Security experiments for decentralized traceable attribute-based signatures

Our definition is adaptive and allows the adversary to adaptively choose both the signing predicate and the message used in the forgery. Note that we consider the stronger variant of unforgeability, i.e. (strong unforgeability) where the adversary wins even if it forges a new signature on a message/predicate pair that was queried to the sign oracle. It is easy to adapt the definition if the weaker variant of unforgeability is desired. Formally, a DTABS scheme is *unforgeable* if for all $\lambda \in \mathbb{N}$, all PPT adversaries $\mathcal{B}$ have a negligible advantage $\mathsf{Adv}^{\mathrm{Unforge}}_{\mathcal{DTABS},\mathcal{B}}(\lambda) := \Pr[\mathsf{Exp}^{\mathrm{Unforge}}_{\mathcal{DTABS},\mathcal{B}}(\lambda) = 1]$.

Non-Frameability. This ensures that even if all authorities and users collude, they cannot frame an honest user. This guarantees that even if the secret attributes' keys for attributes owned by a user are leaked (for instance, by means of interception or leakage by dishonest attribute authorities), it is still impossible to sign on behalf of the user without knowledge of her personal secret key. Thus, unlike previous models [10,11], ours protects innocent users from being framed by dishonest attribute authorities or parties intercepting the communication between the user and the attribute authorities.

In the game, the adversary can fully corrupt all attribute authorities, the tracing authority and as many users of the system as it wishes. We just require that the forgery is a valid signature and traces to a user whose personal secret key has not been revealed to the adversary. Formally, a DTABS scheme is *non-frameable* if for all $\lambda \in \mathbb{N}$, all PPT adversaries $\mathcal{B}$ have a negligible advantage $\mathsf{Adv}^{\mathrm{NF}}_{\mathcal{DTABS},\mathcal{B}}(\lambda) := \Pr[\mathsf{Exp}^{\mathrm{NF}}_{\mathcal{DTABS},\mathcal{B}}(\lambda) = 1]$.

Traceability. This ensures that the adversary cannot produce a signature that cannot be traced. In the game, the adversary is allowed to corrupt the tracing authority and learn both the personal secret key and attributes' keys of any user. Here we require that all the attribute authorities are honest as knowing the secret key of any attribute authority would allow the adversary to grant attributes to dummy users resulting in untraceable signature. Formally, a DTABS scheme is *traceable* if for all $\lambda \in \mathbb{N}$, all PPT adversaries $\mathcal{B}$ have a negligible advantage $\mathsf{Adv}^{\mathrm{Trace}}_{\mathcal{DTABS},\mathcal{B}}(\lambda) := \Pr[\mathsf{Exp}^{\mathrm{Trace}}_{\mathcal{DTABS},\mathcal{B}}(\lambda) = 1]$.

Tracing Soundness. This new requirement, which was not defined in previous models, ensures that even if all authorities (including the tracing authority) and users in the system are all corrupt and collude, they cannot produce a valid signature that traces to two different users. Among other things, this prevents users from claiming authorship of signatures they did not produce or imputing possibly problematic signatures to other users. Formally, a DTABS scheme satisfies *tracing soundness* if for all $\lambda \in \mathbb{N}$, the advantage $\mathsf{Adv}^{\mathrm{TS}}_{\mathcal{DTABS},\mathcal{B}}(\lambda) := \Pr[\mathsf{Exp}^{\mathrm{TS}}_{\mathcal{DTABS},\mathcal{B}}(\lambda) = 1]$ is negligible for all PPT adversaries $\mathcal{B}$.

4 Building Blocks

In this section we present the building blocks that we use in our constructions.

Digital Signatures. A *digital signature* for a message space $\mathcal{M}_{\mathcal{DS}}$ is a tuple of polynomial-time algorithms $\mathcal{DS} := (\mathsf{KeyGen}, \mathsf{Sign}, \mathsf{Verify})$, where KeyGen outputs a pair of secret/verification keys $(\mathsf{sk}, \mathsf{vk})$; $\mathsf{Sign}(\mathsf{sk}, m)$ outputs a signature σ on the

$\mathcal{DS}.\mathsf{KeyGen}(\mathcal{P})$	$\mathcal{DS}.\mathsf{KeyGen}(\mathcal{P})$
- Choose $x, y \leftarrow \mathbb{Z}_p$ and set $(\tilde{X}, \tilde{Y}) := (\tilde{G}^x, \tilde{G}^y)$.	- Choose $x \leftarrow \mathbb{Z}_p$ and set $\tilde{X} := \tilde{G}^x$.
- Return $\mathsf{sk} := (x, y)$ and $\mathsf{vk} := (\tilde{X}, \tilde{Y})$.	- Return $\mathsf{sk} := x$ and $\mathsf{vk} := \tilde{X}$.
$\mathcal{DS}.\mathsf{Sign}(\mathsf{sk}, m)$	$\mathcal{DS}.\mathsf{Sign}(\mathsf{sk}, m)$
- Choose $r \leftarrow \mathbb{Z}_p$ s.t. $x + r \cdot y + m \neq 0$,	- If $x + m \neq 0$, return $\sigma := G^{\frac{1}{x+m}}$.
set $\sigma := G^{\frac{1}{x+r \cdot y+m}}$. Return (σ, r).	$\mathcal{DS}.\mathsf{Verify}(\mathsf{vk}, m, \sigma)$
$\mathcal{DS}.\mathsf{Verify}(\mathsf{vk}, m, (\sigma, r))$	- Return 1 if $e(\sigma, \tilde{X} \cdot \tilde{G}^m) = e(G, \tilde{G})$.
- Return 1 if $e(\sigma, \tilde{X} \cdot \tilde{Y}^r \cdot \tilde{G}^m) = e(G, \tilde{G})$.	

Fig. 3. The full Boneh-Boyen (Left) and the weak Boneh-Boyen (Right) signatures

$\mathcal{TS}.\mathsf{KeyGen}(\mathcal{P})$	$\mathcal{TS}.\mathsf{KeyGen}(\mathcal{P})$
- $x_1, x_2, y \leftarrow \mathbb{Z}_p$, $\mathsf{sk} := (x_1, x_2, y)$.	- $w, x, \{y_i\}_{i=1}^3 \leftarrow \mathbb{Z}_p$, $(\tilde{W}, \tilde{X}, \tilde{Y}_i) := (\tilde{G}^w, \tilde{G}^x, \tilde{G}^{y_i})$.
- $(X_1, X_2, \tilde{Y}) := (G^{x_1}, G^{x_2}, \tilde{G}^y)$.	- $\mathsf{sk} := (w, x, \{y_i\}_{i=1}^3)$, $\mathsf{vk} := (\tilde{W}, \tilde{X}, \{\tilde{Y}_i\}_{i=1}^3)$.
- $\mathsf{vk} := (X_1, X_2, \tilde{Y})$. Return $(\mathsf{sk}, \mathsf{vk})$.	- Return $(\mathsf{sk}, \mathsf{vk})$.
$\mathcal{TS}.\mathsf{Sign}(\mathsf{sk}, \tilde{\tau}, \tilde{M})$	$\mathcal{TS}.\mathsf{Sign}(\mathsf{sk}, \tau, M)$
- $a \leftarrow \mathbb{Z}_p$, $A := G^a$, $B := A^y$.	- $R \leftarrow \mathbb{G}$, $a \leftarrow \mathbb{Z}_p$, $A := G^a$, $\tilde{D} := \tilde{G}^{\frac{1}{a}}$.
- $\tilde{D} := (\tilde{G} \cdot \tilde{\tau}^{-x_1} \cdot \tilde{M}^{-x_2})^{\frac{1}{a}}$.	- $B := G^{x-aw} \cdot R^{-y_1} \cdot \tau^{-y_2} \cdot M^{-y_3}$.
- Return $\sigma := (A, B, \tilde{D})$.	- Return $\sigma := (A, B, \tilde{D}, R)$.
$\mathcal{TS}.\mathsf{Verify}(\mathsf{vk}, \tilde{\tau}, \tilde{M}, \sigma)$	$\mathcal{TS}.\mathsf{Verify}(\mathsf{vk}, \tau, M, \sigma)$
- Return 1 if $e(A, \tilde{Y}) = e(B, \tilde{G})$ and	- Return 1 if $e(A, \tilde{D}) = e(G, \tilde{G})$ and
$e(A, \tilde{D})e(X_1, \tilde{\tau})e(X_2, \tilde{M}) = e(G, \tilde{G})$.	$e(G, \tilde{X}) = e(A, \tilde{W})e(B, \tilde{G})e(R, \tilde{Y}_1)e(\tau, \tilde{Y}_2)e(M, \tilde{Y}_3)$.

Fig. 4. Two instantiations of tagged signatures

message m; $\mathsf{Verify}(\mathsf{vk}, m, \sigma)$ outputs 1 if σ is a valid signature on m. Existential unforgeability under an adaptive chosen-message attack requires that all PPT adversaries $\mathcal{B}$, which are given the verification key and access to a signing oracle, have a negligible advantage in forging a signature on a new message. A weaker variant of existential unforgeability (i.e. existential unforgeability under a weak chosen-message attack) requires that the adversary sends all its signing queries before seeing the verification key.

We use the full (Fig. 3 (Left)) and weak (Fig. 3 (Right)) Boneh-Boyen signature schemes, where in the figure, $\mathcal{P}$ is the description of an asymmetric bilinear group. Both schemes are secure under the q-SDH assumption. The weaker scheme is only secure under a weak chosen-message attack.

Tagged Signatures. Tagged signatures [10] are digital signatures where the signing and verification algorithms take as an additional input a tag τ. Formally, a tagged signature scheme for a message space $\mathcal{M}_{\mathcal{TS}}$ and a tag space $\mathcal{T}_{\mathcal{TS}}$ is a tuple of polynomial-time algorithms $\mathcal{TS} := (\mathsf{Setup}, \mathsf{KeyGen}, \mathsf{Sign}, \mathsf{Verify})$, where $\mathsf{Setup}(1^\lambda)$ outputs common public parameters param; $\mathsf{KeyGen}(\mathsf{param})$ outputs a pair of secret/verification keys $(\mathsf{sk}, \mathsf{vk})$; the rest of the algorithms are similar to those of standard digital signatures. Besides correctness, the security of a tagged signature [10] requires existential unforgeability under an adaptive chosen-message-tag attack which is similar to the existential unforgeability of digital signatures.

We use two instantiations of tagged signatures based on two structure-preserving signature schemes [2] by Abe et al. [3]. The first instantiation (shown in Fig. 4 (Left)), which we refer to as AGHO1, is based on the re-randomizable signature scheme in [3] which signs messages in $\mathbb{G}_2^2$. Its unforgeability rests on an interactive assumption. See [3] for more details. The second instantiation (shown in Fig. 4 (Right)), which we refer to as AGHO2, is based on the strongly unforgeable signature scheme from [3] whose unforgeability reduces to the non-interactive q-AGHO assumption (cf. Section 2). In both instantiations $\mathcal{TS}$.Setup(1^λ) outputs $\mathcal{P} := (\mathbb{G}_1, \mathbb{G}_2, \mathbb{G}_T, p, G, \tilde{G}, e)$ which is the description of an asymmetric bilinear group.

Strongly Unforgeable One-Time Signatures. A one-time signature scheme is a signature scheme that is unforgeable against an adversary who makes a single signing query. *Strong Unforgeability* requires that the adversary cannot even forge a new signature on a message queried the sign oracle on. Here we use the full Boneh-Boyen signature scheme (Fig. 3) as a one-time signature scheme.

Non-Interactive Zero-Knowledge Proofs. Let $\mathcal{R}$ be an efficiently computable relation on pairs (x, w), where we call x the statement and w the witness. We define the corresponding language $\mathcal{L}$ as all the statements x in $\mathcal{R}$. A Non-Interactive Zero-Knowledge (NIZK) proof system [7] for $\mathcal{R}$ is defined by a tuple of algorithms $\mathcal{NIZK} :=$ (Setup, Prove, Verify, Extract, SimSetup, SimProve). Setup takes as input a security parameter 1^λ and outputs a common reference string crs and an extraction key xk which allows for witness extraction. Prove takes as input (crs, x, w) and outputs a proof π that $(x, w) \in \mathcal{R}$. Verify takes as input (crs, x, π) and outputs 1 if the proof is valid, or 0 otherwise. Extract takes as input (crs, xk, x, π) and outputs a witness. SimSetup takes as input a security parameter 1^λ and outputs a simulated reference string crs$_{\text{Sim}}$ and a trapdoor key tr that allows for proof simulation. SimProve takes as input (crs$_{\text{Sim}}$, tr, x) and outputs a simulated proof π_{Sim} without a witness.

We require: completeness, soundness and zero-knowledge. Completeness requires that honestly generated proofs are accepted; Soundness requires that it is infeasible (but for a small probability) to produce a convincing proof for a false statement; Zero-knowledge requires that a proof reveals no information about the witness used. The formal definitions are in the full version [15].

GROTH-SAHAI PROOFS. Groth-Sahai (GS) proofs [19] are efficient non-interactive proofs in the Common Reference String (CRS) model. In this paper, we will be using the SXDH-based instantiation, which is the most efficient instantiation of the proofs [18]. The language for the system has the form:
$$\mathcal{L} := \{\text{statement} \mid \exists\, \text{witness} : E_{i=1}^n(\text{statement}, \text{witness}) \text{ hold }\},$$
where $E_i(\text{statement}, \cdot)$ is one of the types of equation summarized in Fig. 5, where $\underline{X}_{i=1}^m \in \mathbb{G}_1$, $\underline{\tilde{Y}}_{i=1}^n \in \mathbb{G}_2$, $\underline{x}_{i=1}^m, \underline{\tilde{y}}_{i=1}^n \in \mathbb{Z}_p$ are secret variables (hence underlined), whereas $A_i, T \in \mathbb{G}_1$, $\tilde{B}_i, \tilde{T} \in \mathbb{G}_2$, $a_i, \tilde{b}_i, k_{i,j}, t \in \mathbb{Z}_p$, $t_T \in \mathbb{G}_T$ are public constants. For clarity, we also accent exponents to be mapped to group $\mathbb{G}_2$ with $\tilde{\ }$. The system works by first committing to the elements of the witness and then proving that the commitments satisfy the source equations. The proof system has perfect

- **Pairing Product Equation (PPE):** $\prod_{i=1}^{n} e(A_i, \underline{\tilde{Y}_i}) \prod_{i=1}^{m} e(\underline{X_i}, \tilde{B}_i) \prod_{i=1}^{m} \prod_{j=1}^{n} e(\underline{X_i}, \underline{\tilde{Y}_j})^{k_{i,j}} = t_T.$

- **Multi-Scalar Multiplication Equation (MSME) in** $\mathbb{G}_1$: $\prod_{i=1}^{n} A_i^{\underline{\tilde{y}_i}} \prod_{i=1}^{m} \underline{X_i}^{\tilde{b}_i} \prod_{i=1}^{m} \prod_{j=1}^{n} \underline{X_i}^{k_{i,j}\underline{\tilde{y}_j}} = T.$

- **Multi-Scalar Multiplication Equation (MSME) in** $\mathbb{G}_2$: $\prod_{i=1}^{n} \underline{\tilde{Y}_i}^{a_i} \prod_{i=1}^{m} \tilde{B}_i^{\underline{x_i}} \prod_{i=1}^{m} \prod_{j=1}^{n} \underline{\tilde{Y}_j}^{k_{i,j}\underline{x_i}} = \tilde{T}.$

- **Quadratic Equation (QE) in** $\mathbb{Z}_p$: $\sum_{i=1}^{n} a_i\underline{\tilde{y}_i} + \sum_{i=1}^{m} \underline{x_i}\tilde{b}_i + \sum_{i=1}^{m} \sum_{j=1}^{n} \underline{x_i}\underline{\tilde{y}_j} = t.$

Fig. 5. Types of equations over bilinear groups

$\mathcal{DTBE}.\mathsf{Setup}(1^\lambda, 1)$	$\mathcal{DTBE}.\mathsf{ShareDec}(\mathsf{pk}, \mathsf{sk}, t, C_{\mathrm{dtbe}})$
- $\mathcal{P} \leftarrow \mathsf{BGrpSetup}(1^\lambda)$.	- If $\mathcal{DTBE}.\mathsf{IsValid}(\mathsf{pk}, t, C_{\mathrm{dtbe}}) = 0$ Then Return $\perp$.
- $h, w, z, u, v \leftarrow \mathbb{Z}_p, (H, \tilde{H}) := (G^h, \tilde{G}^h)$.	- Parse C_{dtbe} as $(\tilde{C}_1, \tilde{C}_2, \tilde{C}_3, \tilde{C}_4, \tilde{C}_5)$, sk as (u, v).
- $(U, \tilde{U}) := (H^u, \tilde{H}^u), (V, \tilde{V}) := (U^{\frac{1}{v}}, \tilde{U}^{\frac{1}{v}})$.	- Return $\nu := (\tilde{\eta}_1 := \tilde{C}_1^u, \tilde{\eta}_2 := \tilde{C}_2^v)$.
- $(W, \tilde{W}) := (H^w, \tilde{H}^w), (Z, \tilde{Z}) := (V^z, \tilde{V}^z)$.	$\mathcal{DTBE}.\mathsf{ShareVerify}(\mathsf{pk}, \mathsf{svk}, t, C_{\mathrm{dtbe}}, \nu)$
- sk $:= (u, v)$, svk $:= \perp$.	- Parse ν as $(\tilde{\eta}_1, \tilde{\eta}_2)$.
- pk $:= (\mathcal{P}, H, \tilde{H}, U, \tilde{U}, V, \tilde{V}, W, \tilde{W}, Z, \tilde{Z})$.	- Parse C_{dtbe} as $(\tilde{C}_1, \tilde{C}_2, \tilde{C}_3, \tilde{C}_4, \tilde{C}_5)$.
$\mathcal{DTBE}.\mathsf{Enc}(\mathsf{pk}, t, \tilde{M})$	- If $\mathcal{DTBE}.\mathsf{IsValid}(\mathsf{pk}, t, C_{\mathrm{dtbe}}) = 0$ Then Return 0.
- $r_1, r_2 \leftarrow \mathbb{Z}_p; \tilde{C}_1 := \tilde{H}^{r_1}, \tilde{C}_2 := \tilde{V}^{r_2}$.	- If $e(H, \tilde{\eta}_1) \neq e(U, \tilde{C}_1)$ Or
- $\tilde{C}_3 := \tilde{M} \cdot \tilde{U}^{r_1 + r_2}, \tilde{C}_4 := (\tilde{U}^t \cdot \tilde{W})^{r_1}$.	$\quad e(V, \tilde{\eta}_2) \neq e(U, \tilde{C}_2)$ Then Return 0.
- $\tilde{C}_5 := (\tilde{U}^t \cdot \tilde{Z})^{r_2} \cdot C_{\mathrm{dtbe}} := (\tilde{C}_1, \tilde{C}_2, \tilde{C}_3, \tilde{C}_4, \tilde{C}_5)$.	- Else Return 1.
$\mathcal{DTBE}.\mathsf{Combine}(\mathsf{pk}, \mathsf{svk}, \nu, C_{\mathrm{dtbe}}, t)$	$\mathcal{DTBE}.\mathsf{IsValid}(\mathsf{pk}, t, C_{\mathrm{dtbe}})$
- If $\mathcal{DTBE}.\mathsf{IsValid}(\mathsf{pk}, t, C_{\mathrm{dtbe}}) = 0$ Then Return $\perp$.	- Parse C_{dtbe} as $(\tilde{C}_1, \tilde{C}_2, \tilde{C}_3, \tilde{C}_4, \tilde{C}_5)$.
- Parse C_{dtbe} as $(\tilde{C}_1, \tilde{C}_2, \tilde{C}_3, \tilde{C}_4, \tilde{C}_5)$ and ν as $(\tilde{\eta}_1, \tilde{\eta}_2)$.	- If $e(U^t \cdot W, \tilde{C}_1) \neq e(H, \tilde{C}_4)$ Or
- Return $\perp$ if $\mathcal{DTBE}.\mathsf{ShareVerify}(\mathsf{pk}, \mathsf{svk}, t, C_{\mathrm{dtbe}}, \nu) = 0$.	$\quad e(U^t \cdot Z, \tilde{C}_2) \neq e(V, \tilde{C}_5)$ Then Return 0.
- Return $\tilde{M} := \frac{\tilde{C}_3}{\tilde{\eta}_1 \cdot \tilde{\eta}_2}$.	- Else Return 1.

Fig. 6. The transposed 1-out-of-1 variant of the distributed tag-based encryption scheme in [16]

completeness, (perfect) soundness, composable witness-indistinguishability/zero-knowledge. Refer to [19] for more details.

Robust Non-Interactive Distributed/Threshold Tag-Based Encryption. In distributed tag-based encryption [4,16], the (tag-based) ciphertexts can only be decrypted if all n decryption servers compute their decryption shares correctly. In the threshold variant, at least κ out of n decryption servers must compute their decryption shares correctly for the decryption to succeed. The scheme is *non-interactive* if decrypting a ciphertext involves no interaction among the decryption servers. The scheme is *robust* if invalid decryption shares can be identified by the combiner. If the well-formedness of the ciphertext is publicly verifiable, we say the scheme has *public verifiability*.

Formally, a DTBE scheme for a message space $\mathcal{M}_{\mathcal{DTBE}}$ and a tag space $\mathcal{T}_{\mathcal{DTBE}}$ is a tuple of polynomial-time algorithms (Setup, Enc, IsValid, ShareDec, ShareVerify, Combine), where $\mathsf{Setup}(1^\lambda, n)$ outputs a public key and vectors $\mathbf{svk} = (\mathsf{svk}_1, \ldots, \mathsf{svk}_n)$ and $\mathbf{sk} = (\mathsf{sk}_1, \ldots, \mathsf{sk}_n)$ of verification/secret keys for the decryption servers; $\mathsf{Enc}(\mathsf{pk}, t, m)$ outputs a ciphertext C_{dtbe} on the message m using tag t; $\mathsf{IsValid}(\mathsf{pk}, t, C_{\mathrm{dtbe}})$ outputs 1 if the ciphertext is valid under the tag t w.r.t. pk or 0 otherwise; $\mathsf{ShareDec}(\mathsf{pk}, \mathsf{sk}_i, t, C_{\mathrm{dtbe}})$ outputs the i-th server decryption share ν_i of C_{dtbe} or the symbol $\perp$; $\mathsf{ShareVerify}(\mathsf{pk}, \mathsf{svk}_i, t, C_{\text{dtbe}}, \nu_i)$ verifies the decryption share ν_i and outputs either 0 or 1; $\mathsf{Combine}(\mathsf{pk}, \{\mathsf{svk}_i\}_{i=1}^n, \{\nu_i\}_{i=1}^n, C_{\text{dtbe}}, t)$ outputs either the message m or $\perp$.

Besides correctness, we require *Selective-Tag weak Indistinguishability against Adaptive Chosen Ciphertext Attacks (ST-wIND-CCA)* [22] and *Decryption Consistency (DEC-CON)*. Informally, the former requires that an adversary who gets a decryption oracle for any ciphertext under a tag different from the target tag (which is chosen beforehand), cannot distinguish which challenge message was encrypted. The latter requires that an adversary cannot output two different sets of decryption shares of a ciphertext which open differently. The formal definitions are in the full version [15].

For our purpose, it suffices to have a single decryption server, i.e. 1-out-of-1 scheme. We stress, however, that any variant of distributed/threshold tag-based encryption scheme satisfying the properties above can be used. Besides the original scheme in [16], we also use a variant of [16] (shown in Fig. 6) where we transpose the groups in which the public key and the ciphertext lie. Since here we only consider a single decryption server, the verification key svk is redundant as we include all the public elements in the public key pk. Maintaining it is solely for the sake of consistency with the definition of the algorithms.

5 Our Generic Construction

In this section, we present our generic construction.

Overview of the Construction. We eliminate the need for some of the costly tools required by previous constructions, including the so-called pseudo-attribute technique and the expensive zero-knowledge proofs required for proving tracing correctness. As a result, we obtain more efficient constructions while offering stronger security than previous ones.

Our construction requires a NIZK proof of knowledge proof system $\mathcal{NIZK}$, a selective-tag weakly IND-CCA robust non-interactive (1-out-of-1) distributed tag-based encryption scheme $\mathcal{DTBE}$, a tagged signature scheme $\mathcal{TS}$, an existentially unforgeable signature scheme $\mathcal{WDS}$ secure against a weak chosen-message attack, and a strongly unforgeable one-time signature scheme $\mathcal{OTS}$. Additionally, we require two collision-resistant hash functions $\hat{\mathcal{H}} : \{0,1\}^* \rightarrow \mathcal{T}_{\mathcal{DTBE}}$ and $\mathcal{H} : \{0,1\}^* \rightarrow \mathcal{M}_{\mathcal{OTS}}$. It is sufficient for $\mathcal{WDS}$ to be existentially unforgeable against a weak chosen-message attack as we will use this scheme to sign the verification keys of the one-time signature scheme $\mathcal{OTS}$.

The Setup algorithm generates a common reference string crs for $\mathcal{NIZK}$ and runs $\mathcal{DTBE}.\mathsf{Setup}$ to generate the server's secret esk, the verification key esvk and the public key epk. The public parameters of the system is set to $\mathsf{pp} := (1^\lambda, \mathsf{crs}, \mathsf{epk}, \mathsf{esvk}, \hat{\mathcal{H}}, \mathcal{H})$. The tracing authority's key is set to $\mathsf{tk} := \mathsf{esk}$.

When a new attribute authority joins the system, it creates a verification/secret key pair $(\mathsf{avk}_{\mathsf{aid}}, \mathsf{ask}_{\mathsf{aid}})$ for the tagged signature scheme $\mathcal{TS}$. When a user joins the system, she generates a verification/secret key pair $(\mathbf{uvk}[\mathsf{uid}], \mathbf{usk}[\mathsf{uid}])$ for the digital signature scheme $\mathcal{WDS}$.

Setup(1^λ)
- (crs, xk) $\leftarrow$ $\mathcal{NIZK}$.Setup(1^λ). (epk, esvk, esk) $\leftarrow$ $\mathcal{DTBE}$.Setup($1^\lambda, 1; \rho$).
- Choose collision-resistant hash functions $\hat{\mathcal{H}} : \{0,1\}^* \rightarrow \mathcal{T}_{\mathcal{DTBE}}$ and $\mathcal{H} : \{0,1\}^* \rightarrow \mathcal{M}_{\mathcal{OTS}}$.
- Let tk := esk and pp := (1^λ, crs, epk, esvk, $\hat{\mathcal{H}}, \mathcal{H}$). Return pp.

AKeyGen(pp, aid)
- (avk$_{aid}$, ask$_{aid}$) $\leftarrow$ $\mathcal{TS}$.KeyGen(1^λ). Return (avk$_{aid}$, ask$_{aid}$).

UKeyGen(pp)
- (**uvk**[uid], **usk**[uid]) $\leftarrow$ $\mathcal{WDS}$.KeyGen(1^λ). Return (**uvk**[uid], **usk**[uid]).

AttKeyGen(ask$_{aid(\alpha)}$, uid, **uvk**[uid], α)
- sk$_{uid,\alpha}$ $\leftarrow$ $\mathcal{TS}$.Sign(ask$_{aid(\alpha)}$, **uvk**[uid], α). Return sk$_{uid,\alpha}$.

Sign($\{$avk$_{aid(\alpha)}\}_{\alpha \in \mathcal{A}}$, uid, **usk**[uid], **uvk**[uid], $\{$sk$_{uid,\alpha}\}_{\alpha \in \mathcal{A}}$, $m, \mathbb{P}$)
- Return $\perp$ if $\mathbb{P}(\mathcal{A}) = 0$.
- (otsvk, otssk) $\leftarrow$ $\mathcal{OTS}$.KeyGen(1^λ). C_{dtbe} $\leftarrow$ $\mathcal{DTBE}$.Enc(epk, $\hat{\mathcal{H}}$(otsvk), **uvk**[uid]; μ).
- σ $\leftarrow$ $\mathcal{WDS}$.Sign(**usk**[uid], $\hat{\mathcal{H}}$(otsvk)).
- π $\leftarrow$ $\mathcal{NIZK}$.Prove(crs, $\{$**uvk**[uid], $\mu, z, \{\sigma_{\alpha_i}\}_{i=1}^{|\mathbb{P}|}, \sigma\}$:
$\qquad\qquad\qquad\qquad\qquad\qquad (C_{dtbe}, \hat{\mathcal{H}}$(otsvk), epk, $\{$avk$_{aid(\alpha_i)}\}_{i=1}^{|\mathbb{P}|}, \{\alpha_i\}_{i=1}^{|\mathbb{P}|}) \in \mathcal{L}$).
- σ_{ots} $\leftarrow$ $\mathcal{OTS}$.Sign(otssk, ($\mathcal{H}(m, \mathbb{P}), \pi, C_{dtbe}$, otsvk)).
- Return $\Sigma := (\sigma_{ots}, \pi, C_{dtbe}$, otsvk).

Verify($\{$avk$_{aid(\alpha)}\}_{\alpha \in \mathbb{P}}$, $m, \Sigma, \mathbb{P}$)
- Parse Σ as ($\sigma_{ots}, \pi, C_{dtbe}$, otsvk) and pp as ($1^\lambda$, crs, epk, esvk, $\hat{\mathcal{H}}, \mathcal{H}$).
- Return 1 if all the following verify; otherwise, return 0:
$\qquad$ o $\mathcal{OTS}$.Verify(otsvk, ($\mathcal{H}(m, \mathbb{P}), \pi, C_{dtbe}$, otsvk), σ_{ots}) = 1.
$\qquad$ o $\mathcal{NIZK}$.Verify(crs, π) = 1 $\wedge$ $\mathcal{DTBE}$.IsValid(epk, $\hat{\mathcal{H}}$(otsvk), C_{dtbe}) = 1.

Trace(tk, $m, \Sigma, \mathbb{P}$, **uvk**)
- Parse pp as (1^λ, crs, epk, esvk, $\hat{\mathcal{H}}, \mathcal{H}$). Return ($\perp, \perp$) if Verify($\{avk_{aid(\alpha)}\}_{\alpha \in \mathbb{P}}$, $m, \Sigma, \mathbb{P}$) = 0.
- ν $\leftarrow$ $\mathcal{DTBE}$.ShareDec(epk, tk, $\hat{\mathcal{H}}$(otsvk), C_{dtbe}).
- Return ($\perp, \perp$) if $\mathcal{DTBE}$.ShareVerify(epk, esvk, $\hat{\mathcal{H}}$(otsvk), C_{dtbe}, ν) = 0.
- vk$_{uid}$ $\leftarrow$ $\mathcal{DTBE}$.Combine(epk, esvk, $\nu, C_{dtbe}, \hat{\mathcal{H}}$(otsvk)).
- Return (i, ν) if $\exists i$ s.t. vk$_{uid}$ = **uvk**[i]. Otherwise, return (0, ν).

Judge($\{$avk$_{aid(\alpha)}\}_{\alpha \in \mathbb{P}}$, $m, \Sigma, \mathbb{P}$, uid, **uvk**[uid], π_{Trace})
- Parse pp as (1^λ, crs, epk, esvk, $\hat{\mathcal{H}}, \mathcal{H}$) and π_{Trace} as (uid, ν).
- If (uid, ν) = ($\perp, \perp$) Then Return Verify($\{$avk$_{aid(\alpha)}\}_{\alpha \in \mathbb{P}}$, $m, \Sigma, \mathbb{P}$) = 0.
- Return ($\perp, \perp$) if $\mathcal{DTBE}$.ShareVerify(epk, $\hat{\mathcal{H}}$(otsvk), C_{dtbe}, ν) = 0.
- vk$_{uid}$ $\leftarrow$ $\mathcal{DTBE}$.Combine(epk, esvk, $\nu, C_{dtbe}, \hat{\mathcal{H}}$(otsvk)). If vk$_{uid}$ = **uvk**[uid] Then Return 1 Else Return 0.

Fig. 7. Our generic construction for DTABS

To generate a signing key for attribute $\alpha \in \mathbb{A}$ for user uid, the managing attribute authority signs the user's public key **uvk**[uid] (used as tag) along with the attribute α using her secret tagged signature signing key. The resulting signature σ_α is used as the secret key sk$_{uid,\alpha}$ for that attribute by user uid.

To sign a message m w.r.t. a signing policy $\mathbb{P}$, the user chooses a fresh key pair (otsvk, otssk) for the one-time signature $\mathcal{OTS}$ and encrypts her public key **uvk**[uid] using the distributed tag-based encryption scheme $\mathcal{DTBE}$ (and possibly some randomness μ) using $\hat{\mathcal{H}}$(otsvk) as a tag to obtain a ciphertext C_{dtbe}. She then signs $\hat{\mathcal{H}}$(otsvk) using the digital signature scheme $\mathcal{WDS}$ and her personal secret key **usk**[uid] to obtain a signature σ. Using $\mathcal{NIZK}$, she then computes a proof π that: she encrypted her public key correctly, she has a signature σ

on $\hat{\mathcal{H}}(\text{otsvk})$ that verifies w.r.t. her public key $\mathbf{uvk}[\text{uid}]$, and she has enough attributes on her public key to satisfy the signing predicate $\mathbb{P}$. To prove the latter, we use a span program (see Section 2) represented by the matrix $\mathbf{S}$: the user proves that she knows a secret vector $\mathbf{z} \in \mathbb{Z}_p^{|\mathbb{P}|}$ s.t. $\mathbf{zS} = [1, 0, \ldots, 0]$. She also needs to show that she possesses a valid tagged signature on each attribute in the signing predicate $\mathbb{P}$ for which the corresponding element in $\mathbf{z}$ is non-zero. For attributes appearing in $\mathbb{P}$ that the signer does not own, she chooses random signatures. Finally, she signs $(\mathcal{H}(m, \mathbb{P}), \pi, C_{\text{dtbe}}, \text{otsvk})$ using the one-time signature $\mathcal{OTS}$ to obtain a one-time signature σ_{ots}.

To verify a signature, the proof π and the one-time signature σ_{ots} are verified. We note here that if $\mathcal{TS}$ and/or $\mathcal{WDS}$ are re-randomizable, one can reveal the signature components which are independent of $\mathbf{uvk}[\text{uid}]$ after re-randomizing them. This simplifies the NIZK proof π and thus improves the efficiency.

To trace a signature, the tracing authority uses its secret key to produce the decryption share ν of the ciphertext C_{dtbe} which allows anyone to recover the user's public key vk_{uid} encrypted. It then searches in the public key table $\mathbf{uvk}$ to identify the entry matching vk_{uid}. It returns (uid, ν) if such entry exists, or $(0, \nu)$ otherwise. To verify the tracing correctness, the judge just needs to verify the validity of the decryption share ν and then recovers the plaintext and verifies that it decrypts to the concerned user.

The construction is in Fig. 7. The language associated with the NIZK system is as follows, where for clarity we underline the elements of the witness:

$\mathcal{L} : \Big\{ \big((C_{\text{dtbe}}, \hat{\mathcal{H}}(\text{otsvk}), \text{epk}, \{\text{avk}_{\text{aid}(\alpha_i)}\}_{i=1}^{|\mathbb{P}|}, \{\alpha_i\}_{i=1}^{|\mathbb{P}|}), (\underline{\mathbf{uvk}[\text{uid}]}, \underline{\mu}, \underline{\mathbf{z}}, \{\underline{\sigma_{\alpha_i}}\}_{i=1}^{|\mathbb{P}|}) \big) :$

$\Big(\underline{\mathbf{z}}\mathbf{S} = [1, 0, \ldots, 0] \wedge_{i=1}^{|\mathbb{P}|} \text{ if } \underline{z_i} \neq 0 \Rightarrow \mathcal{TS}.\text{Verify}(\text{avk}_{\text{aid}(\alpha_i)}, \underline{\mathbf{uvk}[\text{uid}]}, \alpha_i, \underline{\sigma_{\alpha_i}}) = 1 \Big) \wedge$

$\mathcal{WDS}.\text{Verify}(\underline{\mathbf{uvk}[\text{uid}]}, \hat{\mathcal{H}}(\text{otsvk}), \underline{\sigma}) = 1 \wedge \mathcal{DTBE}.\text{Enc}(\text{epk}, \hat{\mathcal{H}}(\text{otsvk}), \underline{\mathbf{uvk}[\text{uid}]}; \underline{\mu}) = C_{\text{dtbe}} \Big\}.$

The full proof of the following Theorem is in full version [15]. Next, we present two instantiations in the standard model.

Theorem 1. *The construction in Fig. 7 is a secure decentralized traceable attribute-based signature if the building blocks are secure w.r.t. their requirements.*

6 Instantiations in the Standard Model

Instantiation I. We instantiate $\mathcal{TS}$ using the AGHO1 signature scheme (see Fig. 4 (Left)) and instantiate $\mathcal{WDS}$ and $\mathcal{OTS}$ using the weak and full Boneh-Boyen signature schemes, respectively. We instantiate $\mathcal{NIZK}$ using the Groth-Sahai system, and $\mathcal{DTBE}$ using the scheme in Fig. 6.

Let $\mathbf{S} \in \mathbb{Z}_p^{|\mathbb{P}|, \beta}$ be the span program for $\mathbb{P}$. To sign, proceed as follows:

- To prove that $\mathbf{zS} = [1, 0, \ldots, 0]$, the signer proves the following equations:
$$\sum_{i=1}^{|\mathbb{P}|} (z_i \tilde{S}_{i,1}) = 1 \qquad \sum_{i=1}^{|\mathbb{P}|} (z_i \tilde{S}_{i,j}) = 0, \text{ for } j = 2, \ldots, \beta$$
- To prove if $\underline{z_i} \neq 0 \Rightarrow \mathcal{TS}.\text{Verify}(\text{avk}_{\text{aid}(\alpha_i)}, \underline{\mathbf{uvk}[\text{uid}]}, \alpha_i, \sigma_{\alpha_i}) = 1$, where $\sigma_{\alpha_i} = (A_i', B_i', \tilde{D}_i') \in \mathbb{G}_1^2 \times \mathbb{G}_2$ and $\text{avk}_{\text{aid}(\alpha_i)} = (X_{i,1}, X_{i,2}, \tilde{Y}_i) \in \mathbb{G}_1^2 \times \mathbb{G}_2$.

The signer re-randomizes σ_{α_i} by choosing $a' \leftarrow \mathbb{Z}_p^*$ and computing $\sigma_{\alpha_i} :=$ $(A_i, B_i, \tilde{D}_i) = (A_i'^{a'}, B_i'^{a'}, \tilde{D}_i'^{\frac{1}{a'}})$, and proves the following

$$\breve{D}_i = \tilde{D}_i^{z_i} \qquad \breve{\tilde{Y}}_i = \tilde{Y}_i^{z_i} \qquad \widetilde{\mathsf{vk}}_i = \widetilde{\mathbf{uvk}}[\mathsf{uid}]^{z_i} \qquad \breve{\tilde{G}}_i = \tilde{G}^{z_i}$$

$$e(A_i, \breve{\tilde{Y}}_i) = e(B_i, \breve{\tilde{G}}_i) \qquad e(A_i, \breve{\tilde{D}}_i)e(X_{i,1}, \widetilde{\mathsf{vk}}_i)e(X_{i,2}, \breve{\tilde{G}}_i^{\alpha_i}) = e(G, \breve{\tilde{G}}_i)$$

The verifier can on her own compute a Groth-Sahai commitment to $\breve{\tilde{G}}_i^{\alpha_i}$ by computing $\mathcal{C}_{\breve{\tilde{G}}_i}^{\alpha_i}$, where $\mathcal{C}_{\breve{\tilde{G}}_i}$ is the Groth-Sahai commitment to $\breve{\tilde{G}}_i$. Also, we only need to commit to the vector z in $\mathbb{G}_1$. This improves the efficiency.

- To prove $\mathcal{WDS}.\mathsf{Verify}(\widetilde{\mathbf{uvk}}[\mathsf{uid}], \hat{\mathcal{H}}(\mathsf{otsvk}), \underline{\sigma}) = 1$, the signer proves that

$$e(\underline{\sigma}, \widetilde{\mathbf{uvk}}[\mathsf{uid}])e(\underline{\sigma}, \tilde{G}^{\hat{\mathcal{H}}(\mathsf{otsvk})})e(\underline{G}, \tilde{G}) = 1 \qquad \underline{G} - G = 0$$

- To prove $\mathcal{DTBE}.\mathsf{Enc}(\mathsf{epk}, \hat{\mathcal{H}}(\mathsf{otsvk}), \widetilde{\mathbf{uvk}}[\mathsf{uid}]; (\underline{r_1}, \underline{r_2})) = C_{\mathsf{dtbe}}$, it is sufficient to prove that $\tilde{C}_1$, $\tilde{C}_2$ and $\tilde{C}_3$ were computed correctly and the rest can be verified by checking that $e(H, \tilde{C}_4) = e(U^{\hat{\mathcal{H}}(\mathsf{otsvk})} \cdot W, \tilde{C}_1)$ and $e(V, \tilde{C}_5) = e(U^{\hat{\mathcal{H}}(\mathsf{otsvk})} \cdot Z, \tilde{C}_2)$. Thus, this requires proving $\tilde{C}_1 = \tilde{H}^{\underline{r_1}}$, $\tilde{C}_2 = \tilde{V}^{\underline{r_2}}$ and $\tilde{C}_3 = \tilde{U}^{\underline{r_1}} \cdot \tilde{U}^{\underline{r_2}} \cdot \widetilde{\mathbf{uvk}}[\mathsf{uid}]$.

The total size of the signature is $\mathbb{G}_1^{27 \cdot |\mathbb{P}| + 19} + \mathbb{G}_2^{22 \cdot |\mathbb{P}| + 15} + \mathbb{Z}_p^{\beta+3}$. The proof for the following Theorem follows from that of Theorem 1.

Theorem 2. *The instantiation is secure if the AGHO1 signature scheme is unforgeable and the assumptions* $XDLIN_{\mathbb{G}_2}$, *SXDH, and q-SDH all hold.*

Instantiation II. To get an instantiation that is based on falsifiable assumptions [27], we instantiate $\mathcal{TS}$ using the AGHO2 signature scheme as shown in Fig. 4 (Right). We needed to transpose the groups from which the public key and the signature components of $\mathcal{WDS}$ are chosen. We also transpose the groups in $\mathcal{DTBE}$. The rest of the tools remain the same as in Instantiation I.

The proofs required in the signing are similar to those in Instantiation I with the exception that here z is committed to in $\mathbb{G}_2$, whereas the ciphertext is in $\mathbb{G}_1$. See the full version [15] for details. We detail below how the signer proves she has a signature on an attribute. Here $\sigma_{\alpha_i} = (A_i, B_i, R_i, \tilde{D}_i) \in \mathbb{G}_1^3 \times \mathbb{G}_2$ and $\mathsf{avk}_{\mathsf{aid}(\alpha_i)} = (\tilde{W}_i, \tilde{X}_i, \tilde{Y}_{i,1}, \tilde{Y}_{i,2}, \tilde{Y}_{i,3}) \in \mathbb{G}_2^5$, the signer proves:

$$\breve{A}_i = A_i^{z_i} \qquad \breve{B}_i = B_i^{z_i} \qquad \breve{R}_i = R_i^{z_i} \qquad \breve{G}_i = G^{z_i}$$

$$\breve{\mathsf{vk}}_i = \mathbf{uvk}[\mathsf{uid}]^{z_i} \qquad e(\breve{A}_i, \tilde{D}) = e(\breve{G}_i, \tilde{G})$$

$$e(\breve{G}_i, \tilde{X}_i) = e(\breve{A}_i, \tilde{W}_i)e(\breve{B}_i, \tilde{G})e(\breve{R}_i, \tilde{Y}_{i,1})e(\breve{\mathsf{vk}}_i, \tilde{Y}_{i,2})e(\breve{G}_i^{\alpha_i}, \tilde{Y}_{i,3})$$

The same two efficiency-enhancing observations used in Instantiation I apply but now in the opposite groups. The total size of the signature is $\mathbb{G}_1^{30 \cdot |\mathbb{P}| + 18} + \mathbb{G}_2^{30 \cdot |\mathbb{P}| + 16} + \mathbb{Z}_p^{\beta+3}$. The proof for the following Theorem follows from that of Theorem 1.

Theorem 3. *The instantiation is secure if the assumptions* $XDLIN_{\mathbb{G}_1}$, *q-SDH, q-AGHO, and SXDH all hold.*

Table 1. Efficiency comparison

Scheme	Signature Size	Model	Setting	Tracing		
				Size	Compute	Verify
[11]	$\mathbb{G}^{|\mathbb{P}|+\beta+7}$	ROM	Composite	N/A	N/A	N/A
[10]	$\mathbb{G}_1^{34 \cdot |\mathbb{P}|+28} + \mathbb{G}_2^{32 \cdot |\mathbb{P}|+32} + \mathbb{Z}_p^{\beta+1}$	STD	Prime	$\mathbb{G}_1^3 \times \mathbb{G}_2^4$	$4E_{\mathbb{G}_1} + 6E_{\mathbb{G}_1}$	$34P$
Inst. I	$\mathbb{G}_1^{27 \cdot |\mathbb{P}|+19} + \mathbb{G}_2^{22 \cdot |\mathbb{P}|+15} + \mathbb{Z}_p^{\beta+3}$	STD	Prime	$\mathbb{G}_2^2$	$2E_{\mathbb{G}_2}$	$4P$
Inst. II	$\mathbb{G}_1^{30 \cdot |\mathbb{P}|+18} + \mathbb{G}_2^{30 \cdot |\mathbb{P}|+16} + \mathbb{Z}_p^{\beta+3}$	STD	Prime	$\mathbb{G}_1^2$	$2E_{\mathbb{G}_1}$	$4P$

We end by noting that in both instantiations signature verification can be mode more efficient by batch verifying GS proofs [6,17].

Efficiency Comparison. We compare the efficiency of our instantiations with that of existing constructions in Table 1. In the table, P stands for pairing and E is a multi-scalar exponentiation in the group. Note that the construction in [11] only supports a single attribute authority.

Acknowledgments. The work was done while the author was at the University of Bristol supported by ERC Advanced Grant ERC-2010-AdG-267188-CRIPTO and EPSRC via grant EP/H043454/1.

References

1. Abe, M., Chase, M., David, B., Kohlweiss, M., Nishimaki, R., Ohkubo, M.: Constant-Size Structure-Preserving Signatures: Generic Constructions and Simple Assumptions. In: Wang, X., Sako, K. (eds.) ASIACRYPT 2012. LNCS, vol. 7658, pp. 4–24. Springer, Heidelberg (2012)
2. Abe, M., Fuchsbauer, G., Groth, J., Haralambiev, K., Ohkubo, M.: Structure-Preserving Signatures and Commitments to Group Elements. In: Rabin, T. (ed.) CRYPTO 2010. LNCS, vol. 6223, pp. 209–236. Springer, Heidelberg (2010)
3. Abe, M., Groth, J., Haralambiev, K., Ohkubo, M.: Optimal Structure-Preserving Signatures in Asymmetric Bilinear Groups. In: Rogaway, P. (ed.) CRYPTO 2011. LNCS, vol. 6841, pp. 649–666. Springer, Heidelberg (2011)
4. Arita, S., Tsurudome, K.: Construction of Threshold Public-Key Encryptions through Tag-Based Encryptions. In: Abdalla, M., Pointcheval, D., Fouque, P.-A., Vergnaud, D. (eds.) ACNS 2009. LNCS, vol. 5536, pp. 186–200. Springer, Heidelberg (2009)
5. Bellare, M., Rogaway, P.: Random oracles are practical: A Paradigm for Designing Efficient Protocols. In: ACM-CCS 1993, pp. 62–73. ACM (1993)
6. Blazy, O., Fuchsbauer, G., Izabachène, M., Jambert, A., Sibert, H., Vergnaud, D.: Batch Groth–Sahai. In: Zhou, J., Yung, M. (eds.) ACNS 2010. LNCS, vol. 6123, pp. 218–235. Springer, Heidelberg (2010)
7. Blum, M., Feldman, P., Micali, S.: Non-interactive zero-knowledge and its applications. In STOC **103–112**, 1988 (1988)
8. Boneh, D., Boyen, X.: Short Signatures Without Random Oracles and the SDH Assumption in Bilinear Groups. Journal of Cryptology **21**(2), 149–177 (2008)
9. Bobba, R., Fatemieh, O., Khan, F., Gunter, C.A., Khurana, H.: Using Attribute-Based Access Control to Enable Attribute-Based Messaging. In: ACSAC 2006, pp. 403–413. IEEE Computer Society 3027 (2006)

10. El Kaafarani, A., Ghadafi, E., Khader, D.: Decentralized Traceable Attribute-Based Signatures. In: Benaloh, J. (ed.) CT-RSA 2014. LNCS, vol. 8366, pp. 327–348. Springer, Heidelberg (2014)
11. Escala, A., Herranz, J., Morillo, P.: Revocable Attribute-Based Signatures with Adaptive Security in the Standard Model. In: Nitaj, A., Pointcheval, D. (eds.) AFRICACRYPT 2011. LNCS, vol. 6737, pp. 224–241. Springer, Heidelberg (2011)
12. Frikken, K.B., Li, J., Atallah, M.J.: Trust negotiation with hidden credentials, hidden policies, and policy cycles. In: NDSS 2006, pp. 157–172. The Internet Society (2006)
13. Gagné, M., Narayan, S., Safavi-Naini, R.: Short Pairing-Efficient Threshold-Attribute-Based Signature. In: Abdalla, M., Lange, T. (eds.) Pairing 2012. LNCS, vol. 7708, pp. 295–313. Springer, Heidelberg (2013)
14. Galbraith, S., Paterson, K., Smart, N.P.: Pairings for cryptographers. Discrete Applied Mathematics **156**, 3113–3121 (2008)
15. Ghadafi, E.: Stronger Security Notions for Decentralized Traceable Attribute-Based Signatures and More Efficient Constructions. In: Cryptology ePrint Archive, Report 2014/278. http://eprint.iacr.org/2014/278.pdf
16. Ghadafi, E.: Efficient Distributed Tag-Based Encryption and its Application to Group Signatures with Efficient Distributed Traceability. In: LATINCRYPT 2014. Full Version at http://eprint.iacr.org/2014/833.pdf
17. Ghadafi, E., Smart, N.P., Warinschi, B.: Practical Zero-Knowledge Proofs for Circuit Evaluation. In: Parker, M.G. (ed.) Cryptography and Coding 2009. LNCS, vol. 5921, pp. 469–494. Springer, Heidelberg (2009)
18. Ghadafi, E., Smart, N.P., Warinschi, B.: Groth–Sahai Proofs Revisited. In: Nguyen, P.Q., Pointcheval, D. (eds.) PKC 2010. LNCS, vol. 6056, pp. 177–192. Springer, Heidelberg (2010)
19. Groth, J., Sahai, A.: Efficient non-interactive proof systems for bilinear groups. SIAM Journal on Computing **41**(5), 1193–1232 (2012)
20. Herranz, J., Laguillaumie, F., Libert, B., Ràfols, C.: Short Attribute-Based Signatures for Threshold Predicates. In: Dunkelman, O. (ed.) CT-RSA 2012. LNCS, vol. 7178, pp. 51–67. Springer, Heidelberg (2012)
21. Karchmer, M., Wigderson, A.: On span programs. In: 8th IEEE Structure in Complexity Theory, pp. 102–111 (1993)
22. Kiltz, E.: Chosen-Ciphertext Security from Tag-Based Encryption. In: Halevi, S., Rabin, T. (eds.) TCC 2006. LNCS, vol. 3876, pp. 581–600. Springer, Heidelberg (2006)
23. Li, J., Au, M.H., Susilo, W., Xie, D., Ren, K.: Attribute-based signature and its applications. In: ASIACCS 2010, pp. 60–69. ACM (2010)
24. Li, J., Kim, K.: Attribute-Based Ring Signatures. In: Cryptology ePrint Archive, Report 2008/394. http://eprint.iacr.org/2008/394.pdf
25. Maji, H.K., Prabhakaran, M., Rosulek, M.: Attribute-Based Signatures: Achieving Attribute-Privacy and Collusion-Resistance. In: Cryptology ePrint Archive, Report 2008/328. http://eprint.iacr.org/2008/328.pdf
26. Maji, H.K., Prabhakaran, M., Rosulek, M.: Attribute-Based Signatures. In: Kiayias, A. (ed.) CT-RSA 2011. LNCS, vol. 6558, pp. 376–392. Springer, Heidelberg (2011)
27. Naor, M.: On Cryptographic Assumptions and Challenges. In: Boneh, D. (ed.) CRYPTO 2003. LNCS, vol. 2729, pp. 96–109. Springer, Heidelberg (2003)

28. Okamoto, T., Takashima, K.: Efficient Attribute-Based Signatures for Non-monotone Predicates in the Standard Model. In: Catalano, D., Fazio, N., Gennaro, R., Nicolosi, A. (eds.) PKC 2011. LNCS, vol. 6571, pp. 35–52. Springer, Heidelberg (2011)

29. Okamoto, T., Takashima, K.: Decentralized Attribute-Based Signatures. In: Kurosawa, K., Hanaoka, G. (eds.) PKC 2013. LNCS, vol. 7778, pp. 125–142. Springer, Heidelberg (2013)

30. Sakai, Y., Schuldt, J.C.N., Emura, K., Hanaoka, G., Ohta, K.: On the Security of Dynamic Group Signatures: Preventing Signature Hijacking. In: Fischlin, M., Buchmann, J., Manulis, M. (eds.) PKC 2012. LNCS, vol. 7293, pp. 715–732. Springer, Heidelberg (2012)

31. Shahandashti, S.F., Safavi-Naini, R.: Threshold Attribute-Based Signatures and Their Application to Anonymous Credential Systems. In: Preneel, B. (ed.) AFRICACRYPT 2009. LNCS, vol. 5580, pp. 198–216. Springer, Heidelberg (2009)

Re-Encryption Verifiability:
How to Detect Malicious Activities
of a Proxy in Proxy Re-Encryption

Satsuya Ohata[1,3]($\boxtimes$), Yutaka Kawai[2], Takahiro Matsuda[3],
Goichiro Hanaoka[3], and Kanta Matsuura[1]

[1] The University of Tokyo, Tokyo, Japan
{satsuya,kanta}@iis.u-tokyo.ac.jp
[2] Mitsubishi Electric, Kanagawa, Japan
Kawai.Yutaka@da.MitsubishiElectric.co.jp
[3] National Institute of Advanced Industrial Science and Technology, Ibaraki, Japan
{t-matsuda,hanaoka-goichiro}@aist.go.jp

Abstract. In this paper, we introduce a new functionality for proxy
re-encryption (PRE) that we call *re-encryption verifiability*. In a PRE
scheme with re-encryption verifiability (which we simply call verifiable
PRE, or VPRE), a receiver of a re-encrypted ciphertext can verify
whether the received ciphertext is correctly transformed from an original
ciphertext by a proxy, and thus can detect illegal activities of the proxy.
We formalize the security model for a VPRE scheme, and show that
the single-hop uni-directional PRE scheme by Hanaoka et al. (CT-RSA
2012) can be extended to a secure VPRE scheme.

Keywords: Proxy Re-encryption · Re-encryption verifiability · Soundness

1 Introduction

Proxy re-encryption (PRE) is an interesting extension of traditional public key
encryption (PKE). In addition to the normal operations of PKE, with a dedicated re-encryption key (generated by receiver A), a semi-trusted party called
proxy can turn a class of ciphertexts destined for user A into those for user B.
A remarkable property of PRE is that the proxy carrying out the transform is
totally ignorant of the plaintext. PRE was first formalized by Blaze et al. [5]
and has received much attention in recent years. There are many models as well
as implementations [1,5,7,9,11,13,16,22]. The type of PRE we focus on in this
paper is "single-hop" and "uni-directional", where a ciphertext[1] can be transformed only once, and a re-encryption key used to transform a ciphertext for
user A to that for user B cannot be used to transform for the opposite direction.

---

[1] In the context of single-hop uni-directional PRE, an original ciphertext (which can be
re-encrypted) and a re-encrypted ciphertext (which cannot be re-encrypted further)
are typically called a *second-level* ciphertext and a *first-level* ciphertext, respectively [11,16], and we will also use the names.

© Springer International Publishing Switzerland 2015
K. Nyberg (ed.): CT-RSA 2015, LNCS 9048, pp. 410–428, 2015.
DOI: 10.1007/978-3-319-16715-2_22

In ordinary PRE schemes, a proxy is modeled as a semi-trusted party, and is typically assumed to perform the re-encryption process honestly. This means that we have to put relatively high level of trust on proxies, and it may be undesirable for some applications of PRE, e.g. cloud-based file sharing systems. In this paper, we study a mechanism that enables us to reduce the level of trust on proxies in PRE systems.

To motivate it further, consider a cloud storage service, one of the major applications of PRE, in which users store a (possibly large) encrypted data c. PRE allows an easy way to share the encrypted data in the cloud with another user: if an owner (say user A) of the encrypted data c wants to share it with user B, it can simply give a re-encryption key $rk_{A \to B}$ to the cloud manager, and can go off-line; when later B requests the data for the cloud manager, he/she can transform c into a re-encrypted ciphertext $\widehat{c}$ that can be decrypted by user B. *However, in this situation, can user B be sure if $\widehat{c}$ is actually a re-encryption of c? Can B detect whether the cloud manager (proxy) has misbehaved?* However, an ordinary PRE scheme is not required to support the functionality to check the relation between an original ciphertext c and a re-encrypted ciphertext $\widehat{c}$ (if user A reveals its secret key to user B, then B can check the relation, but it is clearly undesirable). It is therefore desirable if there is a PRE scheme in which the relation between original and re-encrypted ciphertexts can be checked efficiently by a recipient of a re-encrypted ciphertext (user B in this example), without the help of the other entities.

1.1 Our Contribution

In this paper, we introduce a new functionality for PRE that we call *re-encryption verifiability*. In a PRE scheme with re-encryption verifiability (which we simply call verifiable PRE, or VPRE), a receiver of a re-encrypted ciphertext can verify whether the received ciphertext is correctly transformed from an original ciphertext by a proxy, and thus can detect an illegal activity of the proxy. We may even expect that the existence of re-encryption verifiability suppresses proxy's illegal activities, and this functionality enables us to relax the level of trust that we have to put on proxies. We achieve re-encryption verifiability by introducing a new algorithm that we call the *re-encryption verification algorithm*, into the syntax of (single-hop, uni-directional) PRE. This algorithm takes two ciphertexts c and $\widehat{c}$, a secret key sk_B (of the receiver B) and a public key pk_A (of another user A) as input, and can tell whether $\widehat{c}$ is transformed from c using a re-encryption key that transforms a ciphertext from user A to user B. We stress that this algorithm needs not only a re-encrypted ciphertext $\widehat{c}$ but also a (candidate) original ciphertext c (while to normally decrypt a re-encrypted ciphertext, original ciphertext c is not required). *Note that such a situation is natural in the applications of PRE which we explained earlier.*

We formalize the security model for a VPRE scheme. In particular, in order for the re-encryption verification algorithm to be meaningful, in addition to ordinary chosen ciphertext (CCA) security (for both original/transformed ciphertexts), we introduce a new security notion that we call *soundness*. Our security model for CCA security is based on the one used by Hanaoka et al. [11], and is extended to take the existence of the re-encryption verification algorithm into account. For "backward compatibility" with the model of ordinary PRE (without the re-encryption verification algorithm), we show that a VPRE scheme secure in our model is in general secure as a PRE scheme in the model of [11]. Then, we show that the PRE scheme by Hanaoka et al. [11] (which we call "HKK$^+$") can be extended to a VPRE scheme (which we call "eHKK$^+$"), by augmenting the HKK$^+$ scheme with the dedicated re-encryption verification algorithm. To prove the security of the VPRE scheme eHKK$^+$, we need the property that we call *strong smoothness* (which is essentially the same notion as that introduced in [10] with the name γ-*uniformity*) for the underlying threshold PKE scheme. This property is satisfied by natural TPKE schemes, and thus is not a strong assumption at all. For more details, see Section 4.

Naive Approaches and Their Problems. Although one might think that the problem of checking dishonest behaviors of a proxy can be resolved by using a *signature* scheme in a PRE scheme (that is, by considering a proxy re-"signcryption" scheme), we argue that this approach does *not* work. Specifically, consider a situation where a sender holds a key pair of a signature scheme, and consider the typical "Sign-then-Encrypt"-style construction of a proxy re-signcryption scheme, i.e. the construction where a ciphertext is generated by first signing the plaintext, and then the plaintext together with the signature are encrypted by the PRE scheme. Note that what is verified in such a proxy re-signcryption scheme (by a recipient of a re-encrypted ciphertext) is that the original plaintext has not been modified and that it is indeed generated by the sender, but *not* that the transformed ciphertext resulted from re-encryption performed by the proxy. For example, such a construction is vulnerable to the following attack: a sender generates several ciphertexts to the proxy, then the proxy re-encrypts one of them, and sends it to the recipient. The recipient may find that the plaintext recovered from the received ciphertext indeed comes from the sender, but he will not be sure which of the ciphertexts the proxy owns was re-encrypted (and even that whether the received ciphertext is a re-encryption of one of the ciphertexts). In the "Encrypt-then-Sign"-style construction, i.e. the construction where the sender first encrypts a plaintext and then generates a signature on the ciphertext, the situation is worse, because the signature attached to the original ciphertext will not be a valid signature for a re-encrypted ciphertext. Furthermore, these proxy re-signcryption-style approaches also have a potential drawback that the receiver needs to be aware of the sender who generates the original ciphertext, which is not necessary in our VPRE model (and in an ordinary PRE scheme), and may be a barrier for some applications of (V)PRE. In summary, we emphasize that what is achieved by proxy re-signcryption-style approaches and what we achieve in this paper (i.e. verifiability of a dishonest behavior of a proxy) are two very different properties, and one approach cannot be a solution for the other.

On the Choice of Security Models on which Our Security Definitions Are Based. We note that, as mentioned above, our definitions for VPRE are based on those of PRE adopted by Hanaoka et al. [11]. Their security definitions (of chosen ciphertext security) are known to be one of the strongest in the literature of PRE. Notably, besides capturing the chosen ciphertext security (not re-playable variant [8]), the security models in [11] do not assume the so-called *knowledge-of-secret-key* (KOSK) assumption [6], in which an adversary can use any public key for corrupted users, without revealing the corresponding secret key. The KOSK assumption typically appears in security models of cryptographic primitives in which multiple users are inherently involved (e.g. multi-receiver PKE [2,20], multi-signature [4,6,21]). The KOSK assumption does not reflect the reality quite well, and there are several critiques on this assumption (e.g. in the discussions in [4,20,21]). To the best of our knowledge, the Hanaoka et al. model is the only security definitions for PRE that do not assume the KOSK assumption, and thus we base our security definitions on theirs.

As far as we are aware, most popular PRE schemes without random oracles are secure only under the KOSK assumption (e.g. [13,16]). [2] Therefore, we do not think these schemes can be shown to achieve re-encryption verifiability in our model. However, we do not rule out the possibility that these existing PRE schemes can be extended to VPRE schemes that can be shown to be secure in the security models that are appropriately extended from the security models in which the original PRE schemes are proved secure. Especially, the pairing-based schemes (e.g. [13,16]) seem to allow strong validity checking properties between a re-encrypted ciphertext and an original ciphertext, and we think they are good candidates of VPRE schemes. We would like to leave it as our future work whether these existing PRE schemes can be extended to VPRE schemes and can be proven secure in security models appropriately extended from the original security models.

1.2   Related Work

We briefly review the related work. Mambo and Okamoto introduced the concept of proxy decryption [17]. Later, Ivan and Dodis [14] proposed a generic construction of proxy cryptography based on sequential multiple encryption. Blaze, Bleumer and Strauss formulated the concept of PRE cryptosystems [5] and proposed the first bidirectional PRE scheme based on the ElGamal PKE scheme. Subsequently, Ateniese et al. [1], Canetti and Hohenberger [7], Libert and Vergnaud [16], and Chow et al. [9], proposed different PRE schemes with various properties. Shao and Cao [22] proposed a PRE scheme without pairings. Later, however, Zhang et al. [24] pointed out that it is not secure in the Libert-Vergnaud security model [16]; that is, it does not provide master key security.

---

[2] To be more precise, in the security models adopted in these papers, public keys (of even a corrupted user) that can be used in the security games (say, in a re-encryption key generation and/or re-encryption queries) are generated by the challenger, who always generates these keys honestly. Therefore, the KOSK assumption is automatically assumed in these security models.

Subsequently, Matsuda et al. proposed a PRE scheme without pairings [18], but later, Weng, Zhao, and Hanaoka [23] pointed out that their scheme is not chosen-ciphertext secure. Hanaoka et al. [11] proposed a new definition of CCA security in PRE and showed a generic construction of uni-directional PRE. Isshiki et al. [13] proposed a CCA secure PRE scheme. [3] Kirshanova [15] proposed a lattice-based PRE scheme. To the best of our knowledge, none of the previous works considered the re-encryption verifiability.

2   Preliminaries

Basic Notation. $\mathbf{N}$ denotes the set of all natural numbers, and for $n \in \mathbf{N}$, we let $[n] := \{1, \ldots, n\}$. "$x \leftarrow y$" denotes that x is chosen uniformly at random from y if y is a finite set, x is output from y if y is a function or an algorithm, or y is assigned to x otherwise. "$x\|y$" denotes a concatenation of x and y. "$|x|$" denotes the size of the set if x is a finite set or bit length of x if x is a string. "PPT" stands for *probabilistic polynomial-time*. If $\mathcal{A}$ is a probabilistic algorithm then $y \leftarrow \mathcal{A}(x; r)$ denotes that $\mathcal{A}$ computes y as output by taking x as input and using r as randomness. k denotes the security parameter. A function $f(k) : \mathbf{N} \rightarrow [0, 1]$ is said to be *negligible* if for all positive polynomials p and all sufficiently large $k \in \mathbf{N}$, we have $f(k) < 1/p(k)$.

2.1   Re-Splittable Threshold Public Key Encryption

Here, we review the definition of re-splittable threshold PKE [11,19]. This is a special class of TPKE in which a secret key can be split multiple times, and security of the scheme is maintained as long as the number of corrupted secret key shares *under the same splitting* is less than the threshold. The first re-splittable TPKE scheme was proposed by [11]. Recently, Ohata et al. [19] proposed three more schemes. (All schemes so far are based on bilinear maps.)

Formally, a re-splittable TPKE scheme consists of the following six PPT algorithms:

TKG This is the key generation algorithm that takes 1^k, n, and t such that $0 < t \leq n$ as input, and outputs a secret key *tsk* and a public key *tpk*.

TEnc This is the encryption algorithm that takes *tpk* and a plaintext m as input, outputs a ciphertext c.

TSplit This is the key-splitting algorithm that takes *tsk* as input, and outputs n secret key shares $tsk_1, \cdots, tsk_n$ and a verification key *tvk*.

---

[3] Although it is claimed that their security model is stronger than that of [11], they are actually incomparable. The security model for a transformed ciphertext (first-level ciphertext) in [13] allows an adversary a slightly more flexible challenge query than that of [11]. However, all public keys in the security models of [13] that can be used for re-encryption key generation and re-encryption queries must be generated by the challenger, and such restriction is not posed in the model of [11].

TShDec This is the share-decryption algorithm that takes tpk, a secret key share tsk_i ($i \in [n]$) output by $TSplit(tsk)$, and c as input, and outputs a decryption share μ_i (which could be the special symbol $\perp$ meaning that c is invalid).

TShVer This is the share-verification algorithm that takes tpk, tvk, c, an index $i \in [n]$, and a decryption share μ as input, and outputs $\top$ or $\perp$. When the output is $\top$ (resp. $\perp$), we say that μ is a valid (resp. invalid) decryption share of the ciphertext c.

TCom This is the combining algorithm that takes tpk, tvk, c, and t decryption shares (generated under distinct secret key shares) as input, and outputs a decryption result m (which could be the special symbol $\perp$).

For any $k \in \mathbf{N}$, any polynomials t, n such that $0 < t \leq n$, any $(tsk, tpk) \leftarrow TKG(1^k, n, t)$ and any $(tsk_1, \cdots, tsk_n, tvk) \leftarrow TSplit(tsk)$, we require the following two correctness properties: (1) For any ciphertext c, if $\mu = TShDec(tpk, tsk_i, c)$, then we have $TShVer(tpk, tvk, c, i, \mu) = \top$. (2) For any plaintext m, if c is output from $TEnc(tpk, m)$ and $S = \{\mu_{s_1}, \cdots, \mu_{s_t}\}$ is a set of decryption shares (i.e. $\mu_{s_i} = TShDec(tpk, tsk_{s_i}, c)$ for all $i \in [t]$), then we have $TCom(tpk, tvk, c, S) = m$.

Chosen Ciphertext Security. CCA security of a re-splittable TPKE scheme is defined using the following game which is parameterized by two integers t, n with $0 \leq t \leq n$ and is played by the challenger and an adversary $\mathcal{A}$: The challenger first runs $(tsk, tpk) \leftarrow TKG(1^k, n, t)$ and gives tpk to $\mathcal{A}$. Then $\mathcal{A}$ can adaptively make the following types of queries.

Split&corruption query: On input a set of indices $S = \{s_1, \ldots, s_{t-1}\}$, the challenger runs $(tsk_1, \ldots, tsk_n, tvk) \leftarrow TSplit(tsk)$ and returns $(tsk_{s_1}, \ldots, tsk_{s_{t-1}}, tvk)$ to $\mathcal{A}$. The challenger also stores $\{tsk_i\}_{i \in [n]}$ and tvk for later share decryption queries from $\mathcal{A}$.

Share decryption query: On input (tvk, i, c), where tvk is required to be one of the answers to previously asked split&corruption queries, $i \in [n]$, and $c \neq c^*$, the challenger finds tsk_i that is previously generated together with tvk, and returns a decryption share $\mu_i \leftarrow TShDec(tpk, tsk_i, c)$ to $\mathcal{A}$.

Challenge query: This query is asked only once. On input (m_0, m_1), the challenger randomly picks $b \in \{0, 1\}$ and returns $c^* \leftarrow TEnc(tpk, m_b)$ to $\mathcal{A}$.

Finally, $\mathcal{A}$ outputs its guess b' for b, and wins the game if $b = b'$. We define the advantage of $\mathcal{A}$ by $\mathsf{Adv}^{\mathrm{CCA\text{-}TPKE}}_{(\mathcal{A}, n, t)}(k) = |\Pr[b = b'] - 1/2|$. We say that a re-splittable TPKE scheme is *CCA secure*, if for any PPT adversary $\mathcal{A}$ and for any polynomials t and n with $0 < t \leq n$, $\mathsf{Adv}^{\mathrm{CCA\text{-}TPKE}}_{(\mathcal{A}, n, t)}(k)$ is negligible.

Decryption Consistency. Decryption consistency is defined using the game which is defined in the same way as the CCA game, without the challenge query. The adversary $\mathcal{A}$ finally outputs a ciphertext c, a verification key tvk, and two sets of decryption shares $S = \{\mu_{s_1}, \ldots, \mu_{s_t}\}$ and $S' = \{\mu'_{s'_1}, \ldots, \mu'_{s'_t}\}$. $\mathcal{A}$ wins if (a) tvk is one of verification keys returned as a response to one of $\mathcal{A}$'s split&corruption queries. (b) All shares in S and S' are valid for a ciphertext

c under tvk. That is, $\mathsf{TShVer}(tpk, tvk, c, i, \mu_{S_i}) = \mathsf{TShVer}(tpk, tvk, c, i, \mu'_{S'_i}) = \top$ for all $i \in [t]$. (c) S and S' are sets that are distinct regardless of re-ordering the elements. (d) $\mathsf{TCom}(tpk, tvk, c, S) \neq \mathsf{TCom}(tpk, tvk, c, S')$. We let $\mathsf{Adv}^{\mathsf{DC\text{-}TPKE}}_{(\mathcal{A}, n, t)}(k)$ denote the probability of $\mathcal{A}$ winning in this game. We say that a TPKE scheme has *decryption consistency*, if for any PPT adversary $\mathcal{A}$ and for any polynomials t and n such that $0 < t \leq n$, $\mathsf{Adv}^{\mathsf{DC\text{-}TPKE}}_{(\mathcal{A}, n, t)}(k)$ is negligible.

Strong Smoothness. In this paper, we will use the property which we call *strong smoothness*. This is introduced under the name of γ-*uniformity* in [10] for ordinary PKE, and is a stronger version of *smoothness* used in [3]. (We borrow the name from [3] because we believe it describes the property more directly.)

Formally, we say that a re-splittable TPKE scheme has *strong smoothness* if the following quantity

$$\mathsf{Smth}(k) = \max_{\substack{c, m, R, \\ (tpk, tsk) \leftarrow \mathsf{TKG}(1^k; R),}} \Pr_{c' \leftarrow \mathsf{TEnc}(tpk, m)} [c = c']$$

is negligible. Here, R is a randomness used by TKG.

We note that strong smoothness is satisfied if a ciphertext contains an unpredictable component (such as a random group element g^r with a generator g of a cyclic group and a randomness r), and we are not aware of any natural construction of (re-splittable) TPKE based on bilinear maps that does not have strong smoothness. For example, the re-splittable TPKE schemes proposed in [11, 19] have this property unconditionally.

2.2   Other Primitives

Public Key Encryption. A public key encryption scheme (PKE) consists of the following three algorithms $(\mathsf{PKG}, \mathsf{PEnc}, \mathsf{PDec})$. PKG is the key generation algorithm that takes 1^k as input, and outputs a pair of decryption key dk and public key pk. PEnc is the encryption algorithm that takes a public key pk and a plaintext m as input, and outputs a ciphertext c. PDec is the decryption algorithm that takes a decryption key dk and a ciphertext c as input, and outputs a decryption result m (which could be the special symbol $\bot$ meaning that c is invalid). We require the standard correctness for a PKE scheme, namely, for any $(dk, pk) \leftarrow \mathsf{PKG}(1^k)$ and any plaintext m, we have $m = \mathsf{PDec}(dk, \mathsf{PEnc}(pk, m))$. We will use chosen ciphertext security of PKE. The formal definition will be given in the full version.

Signature. A signature scheme consists of the following three algorithms $(\mathsf{SKG}, \mathsf{Sign}, \mathsf{SVer})$. SKG is the key generation algorithm that takes 1^k as input, and outputs a signing key sk and a verification key vk. Sign is the signing algorithm that takes a signing key sk and a message m as input, and outputs a signature σ. SVer is the verification algorithm that takes a verification key vk, a message m, and a signature σ as input, and outputs either $\top$ or $\bot$ (indicating whether the signature is valid or not). We require the standard correctness for a signature scheme, namely, for any $(sk, vk) \leftarrow \mathsf{SKG}(1^k)$ and any message m, we have $\mathsf{SVer}(vk, m, \mathsf{Sign}(sk, m)) = \top$. We will use strong unforgeability of signature. The formal definition will be given in the full version.

3 Proxy Re-Encryption with Re-Encryption Verifiability

In this section, we present the model and the security definitions of VPRE. Note that we only focus on a single-hop uni-directional scheme.

This section is organized as follows: In Section 3.1, we define the syntax of a VPRE scheme. In Section 3.2, based on the definitions given in [11] for (ordinary) PRE, we define three kinds of security definitions of VPRE. In particular, we introduce *soundness*, which plays an important role for VPRE. We also explain the difference between our definitions and those of [11]. Finally, in Section 3.3, we show that a VPRE secure in our definitions is also secure (as an ordinary PRE scheme) in the definitions of [11], and thus our definitions have "backward compatibility" with [11].

3.1 Syntax

Here, we define the syntax of VPRE. As mentioned earlier, the main feature of VPRE is the re-encryption verification algorithm REncVer.

Formally, a VPRE scheme consists of the following seven algorithms:

KG This is the key generation algorithm that takes 1^k as input, and outputs a secret key sk and a public key pk. This process is written as $(\mathsf{sk}, \mathsf{pk}) \leftarrow \mathsf{KG}(1^k)$.

RKG This is the re-encryption key generation algorithm that takes a secret key sk_i of user i and a public key pk_j of user j as input, and outputs a re-encryption key $rk_{i \to j}$. This process is written as $rk_{i \to j} \leftarrow \mathsf{RKG}(\mathsf{sk}_i, \mathsf{pk}_j)$.

Enc This is the encryption algorithm that takes a public key pk and a plaintext m as input, and outputs a *second-level* ciphertext c that can be re-encrypted for another party. This process is written as $c \leftarrow \mathsf{Enc}(\mathsf{pk}, m)$.

REnc This is the re-encryption algorithm that takes a second-level ciphertext c (for user i) and a re-encryption key $rk_{i \to j}$ as input, and outputs a *first-level* ciphertext $\hat{c}$ (for user j) or the special symbol $\bot$ meaning that $(rk_{i \to j}$ or) c is invalid. This process is written as $\hat{c}$ (or $\bot$) $\leftarrow \mathsf{REnc}(rk_{i \to j}, c)$.

REncVer This is the re-encryption verification algorithm that takes a public key pk_i of user i, a secret key sk_j of user j, a second-level ciphertext c, and a first-level ciphertext $\hat{c}$ as input, and outputs $\top$ (meaning that $\hat{c}$ is a valid re-encrypted ciphertext of c_i) or $\bot$. This process is written as $\top$ (or $\bot$) $\leftarrow \mathsf{REncVer}(\mathsf{pk}_i, \mathsf{sk}_j, c, \hat{c})$.

Dec₁ This is the first-level decryption algorithm that takes a secret key sk and a first-level ciphertext $\hat{c}$ as input, and outputs a decryption result m (which could be the special symbol $\bot$ meaning that $\hat{c}$ is invalid). This process is written as $m \leftarrow \mathsf{Dec}_1(\mathsf{sk}, \hat{c})$.

Dec_2 This is the second-level decryption algorithm that takes a secret key sk and a second-level ciphertext c as input, and outputs a decryption result m (which could be $\bot$ as above). This process is written as $m \leftarrow \mathsf{Dec}_2(\mathsf{sk}, c)$.

The REncVer algorithm needs not only a re-encrypted ciphertext $\widehat{c}$ but also a (candidate) original ciphertext c. We again stress that such a situation is natural in the applications of PRE which we explained in Section 1. We remark that as in [11], we do not consider the direct first-level encryption algorithm (that generates a first-level ciphertext that cannot be re-encrypted further), because such a functionality can be realized by just using a CCA secure PKE scheme in addition to a (V)PRE scheme.

We say that a VPRE scheme is *correct* if for all $(\mathsf{sk}_i, \mathsf{pk}_i)$ and $(\mathsf{sk}_j, \mathsf{pk}_j)$ output from $\mathsf{KG}(1^k)$, all plaintexts m, all $rk_{i \to j} \leftarrow \mathsf{RKG}(\mathsf{sk}_i, \mathsf{pk}_j)$, all $c_i \leftarrow \mathsf{Enc}(pk_i, m)$, and all $\widehat{c}_j \leftarrow \mathsf{REnc}(rk_{i \to j}, c_i)$, we have: (1) $\mathsf{Dec}_2(\mathsf{sk}_i, c_i) = m$, (2) $\mathsf{Dec}_1(\mathsf{sk}_j, \widehat{c}_j) = m$, and (3) $\mathsf{REncVer}(\mathsf{pk}_i, \mathsf{sk}_j, c_i, \widehat{c}_j) = \top$.

3.2   Security Definitions

In this subsection, we give the formal security definitions of VPRE.

Soundness. According to the correctness requirement, an algorithm that outputs 1 for any input is "correct" as the re-encryption verification algorithm REncVer. However, this is clearly not what we expect for REncVer. To avoid such triviality and a meaningless definition, here we introduce *soundness* of the REncVer algorithm. Roughly, our soundness definition guarantees that if an adversary who owns a re-encryption key $rk_{i \to j}$ and is given an original (second-level) ciphertext c, it can produce only a re-encrypted ciphertext $\widehat{c}$ that can decrypt to the same value as the decryption result of c. Furthermore, if an adversary does not have the re-encryption key $rk_{i \to j}$, then it cannot produce a valid re-encrypted ciphertext $\widehat{c}$ at all.

Formally, we define the soundness of re-encryption with the following game which is parameterized by an integer $n \in \mathbf{N}$ and is played between the challenger and an adversary $\mathcal{A}$:

Firstly, the challenger generates honest users' key pairs $(\mathsf{sk}_i, \mathsf{pk}_i) \leftarrow \mathsf{KG}(1^k)$ for $i \in [n]$, and sets $\mathcal{PK} = \{\mathsf{pk}_i\}_{i \in [n]}$. Next, the challenger generates a challenge user's key pair $(\mathsf{sk}_{i^*}, \mathsf{pk}_{i^*}) \leftarrow \mathsf{KG}(1^k)$. Then, the challenger gives 1^k and $\mathcal{PK}^* = \mathcal{PK} \cup \{\mathsf{pk}_{i^*}\}$ to $\mathcal{A}$. Then, $\mathcal{A}$ can adaptively make the following types of queries:

Re-encryption key generation (RKG) query: On input $(\mathsf{pk}_i \in \mathcal{PK}^*, \mathsf{pk}_j)$, where pk_j is an arbitrary public key of $\mathcal{A}$'s choice (for which $\mathcal{A}$ is not required to reveal the corresponding secret key), the challenger responds as follows: If $\mathsf{pk}_i = \mathsf{pk}_{i^*}$ and $\mathsf{pk}_j \notin \mathcal{PK}^*$, then the challenger responds with $\bot$. Otherwise, the challenger responds with $\mathsf{RKG}(\mathsf{sk}_i, \mathsf{pk}_j)$.

Re-encryption (REnc) query: On input $(\mathsf{pk}_i \in \mathcal{PK}^*, \mathsf{pk}_j, c)$, where pk_j is an arbitrary public key of $\mathcal{A}$'s choice (for which $\mathcal{A}$ is not required to reveal the corresponding secret key), the challenger responds with $\mathsf{REnc}(\mathsf{RKG}(\mathsf{sk}_i, \mathsf{pk}_j), c)$.

Re-encryption verification (REncVer) query: On input $(\mathsf{pk}_i, \mathsf{pk}_j \in \mathcal{PK}^*, c, \widehat{c})$, where pk_i is an arbitrary public key of $\mathcal{A}$'s choice (for which $\mathcal{A}$ is not required to reveal the corresponding secret key), the challenger responds with $\mathsf{REncVer}(\mathsf{pk}_i, \mathsf{sk}_j, c, \widehat{c})$.

Challenge query: This query is asked only once. On input m^*, the challenger runs $c^* \leftarrow \mathsf{Enc}(\mathsf{pk}_{i^*}, m^*)$, and returns c^* to $\mathcal{A}$.

First-level decryption (Dec$_1$) query: On input $(\mathsf{pk}_j \in \mathcal{PK}^*, \widehat{c})$, the challenger responds with $\mathsf{Dec}_1(\mathsf{sk}_j, \widehat{c})$.

Second-level decryption (Dec$_2$) query: On input $(\mathsf{pk}_i \in \mathcal{PK}^*, c)$, the challenger responds with $\mathsf{Dec}_2(\mathsf{sk}_i, c)$.

Finally, $\mathcal{A}$ outputs $(\mathsf{pk}_j \in \mathcal{PK}^*, \widehat{c}^*)$ and wins the game if they satisfy the following three conditions:

1. $\mathsf{REncVer}(\mathsf{pk}_{i^*}, \mathsf{sk}_j, c^*, \widehat{c}^*) = \top$
2. $\widehat{c}^*$ is not an answer to some of $\mathcal{A}$'s REnc queries of the form $(\mathsf{pk}_{i^*}, \mathsf{pk}_j, c^*)$
3. Either of the following conditions is satisfied:
   - In the case that $\mathcal{A}$ has submitted a RKG query of the form $(\mathsf{pk}_{i^*}, \mathsf{pk}_j)$ and obtained a re-encryption key $rk_{i^* \to j}$: $\mathsf{Dec}_1(\mathsf{sk}_j, \widehat{c}^*) \neq m^*$.
   - Otherwise: $\mathsf{Dec}_1(\mathsf{sk}_j, \widehat{c}^*) \neq \bot$.

We define the advantage of $\mathcal{A}$ by $\mathsf{Adv}^{\mathsf{SND\text{-}VPRE}}_{(\mathcal{A},n)}(k) = \Pr[\mathcal{A} \text{ wins}]$.

Definition 1 (Soundness of Re-encryption). *We say that a VPRE scheme satisfies soundness, if for any PPT adversary $\mathcal{A}$ and for all positive polynomials n, $\mathsf{Adv}^{\mathsf{SND\text{-}VPRE}}_{(\mathcal{A},n)}(k)$ is negligible.*

Second-Level CCA Security. Here, we define the security for second-level ciphertexts (*second-level CCA security*) with the following game which is parameterized by an integer $n \in \mathbf{N}$ and is played between the challenger and an adversary $\mathcal{A}$:

Firstly, the challenger generates honest users' key pairs $(\mathsf{sk}_i, \mathsf{pk}_i) \leftarrow \mathsf{KG}(1^k)$ for $i \in [n]$, and sets $\mathcal{PK} = \{\mathsf{pk}_i\}_{i \in [n]}$. Next, the challenger generates the challenge user's key pair $(\mathsf{sk}_{i^*}, \mathsf{pk}_{i^*}) \leftarrow \mathsf{KG}(1^k)$. Then, the challenger gives 1^k and $\mathcal{PK}^* = \mathcal{PK} \cup \{\mathsf{pk}_{i^*}\}$ to $\mathcal{A}$. Then, $\mathcal{A}$ can adaptively make the following types of queries:

Re-encryption key generation (RKG) and Re-encryption verification (REncVer) queries:
   These are the same as those in the soundness game.

Re-encryption (REnc) query: On input $(\mathsf{pk}_i \in \mathcal{PK}^*, \mathsf{pk}_j, c)$, where pk_j is an arbitrary public key of $\mathcal{A}$'s choice (for which $\mathcal{A}$ is not required to reveal the corresponding secret key), the challenger responds as follows. If $(\mathsf{pk}_i, c) = (\mathsf{pk}_{i^*}, c^*)$ and $\mathsf{pk}_j \notin \mathcal{PK}^*$, then the challenger returns $\bot$ to $\mathcal{A}$. Otherwise, the challenger responds with $\mathsf{REnc}(\mathsf{RKG}(\mathsf{sk}_i, \mathsf{pk}_j), c)$.

Challenge query: This query is asked only once. On input (m_0, m_1), the challenger picks a bit $b \in \{0, 1\}$ uniformly at random, and computes $c^* \leftarrow \mathsf{Enc}(\mathsf{pk}_{i^*}, m_b)$. Then it gives c^* to $\mathcal{A}$.

First-level decryption (Dec_1) query: On input ($\text{pk}_j \in \mathcal{PK}^*, \widehat{c}$), the challenger responds as follow: If $\text{REncVer}(\text{pk}_{i*}, \text{sk}_j, c^*, \widehat{c}) = \top$, then the challenger returns $\bot$ to $\mathcal{A}$. Otherwise, the challenger responds with $\text{Dec}_1(\text{sk}_j, \widehat{c})$.

Second-level decryption (Dec_2) query: On input ($\text{pk}_i \in \mathcal{PK}^*, c$), the challenger responds with $\text{Dec}_2(\text{sk}_i, c)$, except that if $(\text{pk}_i, c) = (\text{pk}_{i*}, c^*)$, then the challenger returns the special symbol $\bot$ to $\mathcal{A}$.

Finally, $\mathcal{A}$ outputs its guess b' for b and wins the game if $b = b'$. We define the advantage of $\mathcal{A}$ by $\text{Adv}_{(\mathcal{A},n)}^{\text{second-VPRE}}(k) = |\Pr[b = b'] - 1/2|$.

Definition 2 (Second-Level CCA Security). *We say that a VPRE scheme is second-level CCA secure, if for any PPT adversary $\mathcal{A}$ and all positive polynomials n, $\text{Adv}_{(\mathcal{A},n)}^{\text{second-VPRE}}(k)$ is negligible.*

First-Level CCA Security. Next, we define the security for first-level ciphertexts (*first-level CCA security*) with the following game between the challenger and an adversary $\mathcal{A}$: Firstly, the challenger generates the challenge key pair (sk^*, pk^*) $\leftarrow \text{KG}(1^k)$, and gives 1^k and pk^* to $\mathcal{A}$. Then, $\mathcal{A}$ can adaptively make the following types of queries:

Re-encryption key generation (RKG) query: On input pk, where pk is an arbitrary public key of $\mathcal{A}$'s choice (for which $\mathcal{A}$ is not required to reveal the corresponding secret key), the challenger responds with $\text{RKG}(\text{sk}^*, \text{pk})$.

Re-encryption verification (REncVer) query: On input ($\text{pk}, c, \widehat{c}$), where pk is an arbitrary public of $\mathcal{A}$'s choice (for which $\mathcal{A}$ is not required to reveal the corresponding secret key), the challenger responds with $\text{REncVer}(\text{pk}, \text{sk}^*, c, \widehat{c})$.

Challenge query: This query is asked only once. On input ($\text{sk}_\mathcal{A}, \text{pk}_\mathcal{A}, m_0, m_1$) where ($\text{sk}_\mathcal{A}, \text{pk}_\mathcal{A}$) is required to be a valid key pair [4], the challenger picks the challenge bit $b \in \{0, 1\}$ randomly and runs $c \leftarrow \text{Enc}(\text{pk}_\mathcal{A}, m_b)$ and $\widehat{c}^* \leftarrow \text{REnc}(\text{RKG}(\text{sk}_\mathcal{A}, \text{pk}^*), c)$. It then returns $\widehat{c}^*$ to $\mathcal{A}$.

First-level decryption (Dec_1) query: On input $\widehat{c}$, the challenger responds with $\text{Dec}_1(\text{sk}^*, \widehat{c})$, except that if $\widehat{c} = \widehat{c}^*$, then the challenger returns the special symbol $\bot$ to $\mathcal{A}$.

Second-level decryption (Dec_2) query: On input c, the challenger responds with $\text{Dec}_2(\text{sk}^*, c)$.

Finally, $\mathcal{A}$ outputs its guess b' for b and wins the game if $b = b'$. We define the advantage of $\mathcal{A}$ by $\text{Adv}_\mathcal{A}^{\text{first-VPRE}}(k) = |\Pr[b = b'] - 1/2|$.

Definition 3 (First-Level CCA Security). *We say that a VPRE scheme is first-level CCA secure, if for any PPT adversary $\mathcal{A}$, $\text{Adv}_\mathcal{A}^{\text{first-VPRE}}(k)$ is negligible.*

---

[4] That is, ($\text{sk}_\mathcal{A}, \text{pk}_\mathcal{A}$) is required to be in the range of $\text{KG}(1^k)$.

Difference with the Definitions (for PRE) in [11]. Soundness is a new security definition for VPRE. Furthermore, regarding the definition of first-level CCA security, we naturally allow REncVer queries for an adversary in addition to queries allowed in the first-level CCA definition of [11, Definition 2].

For the security definition of second-level ciphertexts, we also allow an adversary to make REncVer queries. Furthermore, there is a remarkable difference in the response to Dec_1 queries. The response to Dec_1 queries in the second-level CCA security game defined in [11, Definition1] is as follows (where we *emphasize* the difference).

First-level decryption query (of [11]) : On input $(pk_j \in \mathcal{PK}^*, \widehat{c})$, the challenger responds as follows: *If $\mathcal{A}$ has asked a REnc query of the form $(pk_{i^*}, pk_j \in \mathcal{PK}, c^*)$ and obtained $\widehat{c}_i$ previously, then the challenger returns $\perp$ to $\mathcal{A}$. Else if $\mathcal{A}$ has asked a RKG query of the form $(pk_{i^*}, pk_j \in \mathcal{PK})$ previously and $Dec_1(sk_i, \widehat{c}) \in \{m_0, m_1\}$ holds, then the challenger returns the special symbol* test *to $\mathcal{A}$. Otherwise, the challenger responds with $Dec_1(sk_i, \widehat{c})$.* (We note that here, test is a symbol that is distinguished from $\perp$.)

Note that in a CCA security definition, what we expect is that an adversary can ask any ciphertext that does not trivially allow it to decrypt the challenge ciphertext. The emphasized sentences above are the definitional approach taken in [11] to avoid such "self-broken" definition considered in [11]. On the other hand, our definition of second-level CCA security given in this subsection uses REncVer for deciding "prohibited" decryption queries, and thus is simplified (of course, we additionally need *soundness* in order for REncVer to be meaningful). Our use of REncVer for deciding "prohibited" queries in the CCA security game for an encryption scheme has some similarity with *secretly detectable re-playable CCA security* of [8] and *detectable PKE* of [12], and we believe these connections to be interesting.

3.3 Implications to the Definitions of [11]

Here, we show a "backward compatibility" of our security definitions. Namely, we show that if a VPRE scheme satisfies security definitions given in Section 3.2, then it is also secure as a (V)PRE under the definitions of [11].

Theorem 1. *If a VPRE scheme is first-level CCA secure in the sense of Definition 3, then the VPRE scheme is first-level CCA secure in the sense of [11, Definition 2].*

This is obvious from the definition. In particular, an adversary in our first-level CCA security definition is only more powerful than that of [11, Definition2] (our adversary can make REncVer queries which are not considered in [11]).

Theorem 2. *If a VPRE scheme is second-level CCA secure in the sense of Definition 2 and satisfies soundness (Definition 1), then the VPRE scheme is second-level CCA secure in the sense of [11, Definition1].*

Proof of Theorem 2. Let $n > 0$ be a polynomial, and $\mathcal{A}$ be any PPT adversary that attacks a VPRE scheme in the sense of [11, Definition 1] and makes $Q > 0$ Dec_1 queries. (Since $\mathcal{A}$ is PPT, Q is polynomial.) Consider the following games.

Game 0. The second-level CCA game of [11, Definition 1].

Game 1. Same as Game 0, except that if $\mathcal{A}$ submits a Dec_1 query $(\mathsf{pk}_j, \widehat{c})$ such that (1) $\mathsf{REncVer}(\mathsf{pk}_{i*}, \mathsf{sk}_j, c_{i*}, \widehat{c}) = \top$, and (2) $\widehat{c}$ is not an answer to some of $\mathcal{A}$'s REnc queries of the form $(\mathsf{pk}_{i*}, \mathsf{pk}_j, c^*)$, then the challenger responds as follows:

If $\mathcal{A}$ has submitted a RKG query $(\mathsf{pk}_{i*}, \mathsf{pk}_j)$ before, then the challenger returns test to $\mathcal{A}$. Otherwise, the challenger returns $\bot$ to $\mathcal{A}$.

For $i \in \{0, 1\}$, let Succ_i be the event that in Game i $\mathcal{A}$ succeeds in guessing the challenge bit (i.e. $b' = b$ occurs), and let Bad_i be the event that in Game i, $\mathcal{A}$ submits at least one Dec_1 query $(\mathsf{pk}_j, \widehat{c})$ such that it satisfies the following conditions simultaneously:

1. $\mathsf{REncVer}(\mathsf{pk}_{i*}, \mathsf{sk}_j, c^*, \widehat{c}) = \top$.
2. $\widehat{c}$ has not appeared as an answer to some of $\mathcal{A}$'s previous REnc queries of the form $(\mathsf{pk}_{i*}, \mathsf{pk}_j, c^*)$.
3. Either of the following conditions is satisfied:
   - In the case that $\mathcal{A}$ has submitted a RKG query $(\mathsf{pk}_{i*}, \mathsf{pk}_j)$ and obtained a re-encryption key $rk_{i* \to j}$: $\mathsf{Dec}_1(\mathsf{sk}_j, \widehat{c}) \notin \{m_0, m_1\}$.
   - Otherwise: $\mathsf{Dec}_1(\mathsf{sk}_j, \widehat{c}) \neq \bot$.

$\mathcal{A}$'s advantage (in the second-level CCA definition of [11, Definition1]) is calculated as follows:

$$| \Pr[\mathsf{Succ}_0] - \frac{1}{2} | \leq | \Pr[\mathsf{Succ}_0] - \Pr[\mathsf{Succ}_1] | + | \Pr[\mathsf{Succ}_1] - \frac{1}{2} |.$$

Thus, it suffices to show that each term in the right hand side of the above inequality is negligible.

Firstly, note that Game 0 and Game 1 proceed identically unless Bad_0 or Bad_1 occurs in the corresponding games. Hence, we have $| \Pr[\mathsf{Succ}_0] - \Pr[\mathsf{Succ}_1] | \leq \Pr[\mathsf{Bad}_0] = \Pr[\mathsf{Bad}_1]$. Then, we show that we can construct a soundness adversary $\mathcal{B}$ such that $\mathsf{Adv}^{\mathsf{SND\text{-}VPRE}}_{(\mathcal{B}, n)}(k) \geq (1/Q) \cdot \Pr[\mathsf{Bad}_1]$, which implies that $\Pr[\mathsf{Bad}_1]$ is negligible.

The construction of $\mathcal{B}$ is as follows: First, $\mathcal{B}$ is given public keys $(\mathsf{pk}_1, \cdots, \mathsf{pk}_n, \mathsf{pk}_{i*})$ from the soundness challenger. Then $\mathcal{B}$ forwards them to $\mathcal{A}$.

$\mathcal{B}$ answers to $\mathcal{A}$'s queries (except for the challenge query) exactly as specified in Game 1. This is possible because $\mathcal{B}$ can also query to $\mathcal{B}$'s challenger except for the challenge query. When $\mathcal{A}$ submits the challenge query (m_0, m_1), $\mathcal{B}$ randomly picks $d \leftarrow \{0, 1\}$, submits m_d as $\mathcal{B}$'s challenge to $\mathcal{B}$'s challenger, receives c^*, and returns c^* to $\mathcal{A}$.

When $\mathcal{A}$ terminates, from $\mathcal{A}$'s Dec_1 queries, $\mathcal{B}$ randomly picks one query $(pk_j, \widehat{c})$, and terminates with output $(pk_j, \widehat{c})$.

The above completes the description of $\mathcal{B}$. It is not hard to see that $\mathcal{B}$ simulates Game 1 perfectly for $\mathcal{A}$ until $\mathcal{A}$ submits a Dec_1 query satisfying the conditions of the event Bad_1. Therefore, the probability that $\mathcal{A}$ submits a Dec_1 query satisfying the conditions of Bad_1 in the game simulated by $\mathcal{B}$ is exactly the same as the probability of this event occurring in Game 1. Furthermore, once $\mathcal{A}$ makes such a query, $\mathcal{B}$ can pick it with probability at least $1/Q$. Therefore, we have $\mathsf{Adv}^{\mathsf{SND\text{-}VPRE}}_{(\mathcal{B},n)}(k) \geq (1/Q) \cdot \Pr[\mathsf{Bad}_1]$. Hence, $\Pr[\mathsf{Bad}_1]$ is negligible. This in turn implies that $|\Pr[\mathsf{Succ}_0] - \Pr[\mathsf{Succ}_1]|$ is negligible.

To prove Theorem 2, it remains to show that $|\Pr[\mathsf{Succ}_1] - 1/2|$ is negligible. However, it is straightforward from the definition of the second-level CCA security of the VPRE scheme (in the sense of Definition 2). In particular, a second-level CCA adversary (in the sense of Definition 2) can simulate Game 1 perfectly for $\mathcal{A}$, and such adversary has advantage exactly $|\Pr[\mathsf{Succ}_1] - 1/2|$. □

4 A Concrete VPRE Scheme

In this section, we show a concrete VPRE scheme. Specifically, our VPRE scheme is a simple extension of the PRE scheme by Hanaoka et al. (which we denoted by HKK^+) [11], and we show how to implement the re-encryption verification algorithm for it.

Intuition for Realizing Re-encryption Verification. Consider a situation in which a second-level ciphertext c_A for user A is re-encrypted into a first-level ciphertext $\widehat{c}_B$ for user B. In order to achieve PRE with re-encryption verifiability, one promising approach is to design a PRE scheme with the following properties: (1) When re-encrypting c_A into $\widehat{c}_B$, c_A is somehow embedded into $\widehat{c}_B$ in such a way that when user B decrypts $\widehat{c}_B$, the embedded second-level ciphertext c_A can be extracted. (2) In re-encryption verification (between $\widehat{c}_B$ and a candidate second-level ciphertext c'_A) user B checks whether an extracted ciphertext c_A is equal to the given candidate c'_A. We observe that the HKK^+ scheme has the desirable properties, and this is the reason why we focus on this PRE scheme. We next explain how we extend it into a VPRE scheme.

Extending the Hanaoka et al. PRE [11] to VPRE. Recall that the PRE scheme HKK^+ is a generic construction from a re-splittable TPKE scheme, an (ordinary) PKE scheme, and a signature scheme. We observe that a re-encrypted ciphertext (i.e. first-level ciphertext) $\widehat{c}$ of the HKK^+ scheme contains the information on an original ciphertext (i.e. second-level ciphertext) c which is just a ciphertext of the underlying TPKE scheme. Our re-encryption verification algorithm is thus fairly simple: On input $(\mathsf{pk}_i, \mathsf{sk}_j, c, \widehat{c})$, it executes the first-level decryption algorithm of the HKK^+ scheme partway to recover the "embedded" second-level ciphertext c', and checks whether $c = c'$ holds.

Now, we formally describe the VPRE scheme, which we denote eHKK^+ (which stands for "extended HKK^+"). Let (TKG, TEnc, TSplit, TShDec, TShVer, TCom) be a re-splittable TPKE scheme, (PKG, PEnc, PDec) be a PKE scheme, and (SKG, Sign, SVer) be a signature scheme. Using these as building blocks, the VPRE scheme eHKK$^+$ is constructed as in Fig. 1.

Security. We show that eHKK$^+$ satisfies the three kinds of security of VPRE.

Theorem 3. *If the PKE scheme is CCA secure, the signature scheme is strongly unforgeable, and the re-splittable TPKE scheme has decryption consistency, then the VPRE scheme* eHKK$^+$ *satisfies soundness.*

Intuition. Due to the lack of space, we omit the security proof. Here, we give an intuition of the security proof of soundness. Recall that the third winning condition of an adversary $\mathcal{A}$ who outputs a pair $(\mathsf{pk}_j, \widehat{c}^*)$ in the soundness game is different depending on whether $\mathcal{A}$ has obtained a re-encryption key $rk_{i^* \to j}$ by making a RKG query of the form $(\mathsf{pk}_{i^*}, \mathsf{pk}_j)$. If $\mathcal{A}$ has issued such a RKG query, then the condition is "$\mathsf{Dec}_1(\mathsf{sk}_j, \widehat{c}^*) \neq m^*$", where m^* is the challenge message, while if $\mathcal{A}$ has not done so, then the condition is "$\mathsf{Dec}_1(\mathsf{sk}_j, \widehat{c}^*) \neq \bot$".

We will show that the probability of the adversary $\mathcal{A}$ coming up with the pair $(\mathsf{pk}_j, \widehat{c}^*)$ in the latter case is negligible, mainly due to the strong unforgeability of the signature scheme. Intuitively this can be shown because if $\mathcal{A}$ can output $(\mathsf{pk}_j, \widehat{c}^*)$ such that $\mathsf{Dec}_1(\mathsf{sk}_j, \widehat{c}^*) \neq \bot$ without using a re-encryption key $rk_{i^* \to j}$, (among other things) $\mathcal{A}$ must have generated a forged signature in the plaintext of $\widehat{c}^*$, without relying on RKG queries. However, note that $\mathcal{A}$ may indirectly obtain $rk_{i^* \to j}$ through a REnc query of the form $(\mathsf{pk}_{i^*}, \mathsf{pk}_j, c)$ where c is some second-level ciphertext. Therefore, we also need to use the CCA security of the PKE scheme to guarantee that REnc queries of the above form do not help $\mathcal{A}$ to indirectly obtain $rk_{i^* \to j}$.

To show that the probability of the adversary $\mathcal{A}$ coming up with a ciphertext $\widehat{c}^*$ such that $\mathsf{Dec}_1(\mathsf{sk}_j, \widehat{c}^*) \neq m^*$ in case $\mathcal{A}$ has obtained $rk_{i^* \to j}$ (via a RKG query), we will use the decryption consistency of the re-splittable TPKE scheme. In doing so, as above we have to use the CCA security of the PKE scheme to guarantee that REnc queries do not help, and also to guarantee that the information of $tsk_{i^*.1}$ does not leak from a re-encryption key $rk_{i^* \to j}$ that is obtained by $\mathcal{A}$ through the RKG query that $\mathcal{A}$ issued. Finally, note that the decryption consistency is guaranteed only under an honestly generated verification key tvk_{i^*}, but $\mathcal{A}$ may have generated the ciphertext $\widehat{c}^*$ in such a way that tvk_{i^*} is generated maliciously by $\mathcal{A}$. To prevent it, we will again rely on the strong unforgeability of the signature scheme, which ensures that the only way to generate a valid re-encrypted ciphertext is to use a re-encryption key which is generated honestly (and thus tvk_{i^*} is also honestly generated).

Theorem 4. *If the PKE scheme is CCA secure, the signature scheme is strongly unforgeable, and the re-splittable TPKE scheme is CCA secure, then the VPRE scheme* eHKK$^+$ *is second-level CCA secure.*

Intuition. Due to the lack of space, we omit the security proof. Here, we give an intuition of the security proof of second-level CCA security. The proof follows closely to the above proof of soundness, and the original security proof

$KG(1^k)$:
  $(tsk, tpk) \leftarrow TKG(1^k, 2, 2)$
  $(\widehat{dk}, \widehat{pk}) \leftarrow PKG(1^k)$
  $(dk, pk) \leftarrow PKG(1^k)$
  $(sk, vk) \leftarrow SKG(1^k)$
  $sk \leftarrow (tsk, \widehat{dk}, dk, sk)$
  $pk \leftarrow (tpk, \widehat{pk}, pk, vk)$
  Return (sk, pk).

$Enc(pk_i, m)$:
  $(tpk_i, \widehat{pk}_i, pk_i, vk_i) \leftarrow pk_i$
  Return $c \leftarrow TEnc(tpk_i, m)$.

$RKG(sk_i, pk_j)$:
  $(tsk_i, \widehat{dk}_i, dk_i, sk_i) \leftarrow sk_i$
  $(tpk_j, \widehat{pk}_j, pk_j, vk_j) \leftarrow pk_j$
  $(tsk_{i.1}, tsk_{i.2}, tvk_i) \leftarrow TSplit(tsk_i)$
  $\psi \leftarrow PEnc(pk_j, tsk_{i.1})$
  $\sigma \leftarrow Sign(sk_i, \langle \psi \| tvk_i \| pk_i \| pk_j \rangle)$
  $rk_{i \to j} \leftarrow (pk_i, pk_j, tsk_{i.2}, \psi, tvk_i, \sigma)$
  Return $rk_{i \to j}$.

$Dec_1(sk_j, \widehat{c}_j)$:
  $(tsk_j, \widehat{dk}_j, dk_j, sk_j) \leftarrow sk_j$
  $\widehat{M} \leftarrow PDec(\widehat{dk}_j, \widehat{c}_j)$
  If $\widehat{M} = \bot$ then return $\bot$.
  $\langle pk'_i \| pk'_j \| c_i \| \mu_2 \| \psi \| tvk_i \| \sigma \rangle \leftarrow \widehat{M}$
  If $pk'_j \neq pk_j$ then return $\bot$.
  $(tpk_i, \widehat{pk}_i, pk_i, vk_i) \leftarrow pk'_i$
  If $SVer(vk_i, \langle \psi \| tvk_i \| pk'_i \| pk'_j \rangle, \sigma) = \bot$
    then return $\bot$.
  $tsk_{i.1} \leftarrow PDec(dk_j, \psi)$
  If $tsk_{i.1} = \bot$ then return $\bot$.
  $\mu_1 \leftarrow TShDec(tpk_i, tsk_{i.1}, c_i)$
  If $\mu_1 = \bot$ then return $\bot$.
  If $TShVer(tpk_i, tvk_i, c_i, 2, \mu_2) = \bot$
    then return $\bot$.
  $m \leftarrow TCom(tpk_i, tvk_i, c_i, \{\mu_1, \mu_2\})$
  Return m.

$REnc(rk_{i \to j}, c_i)$:
  $(pk_i, pk_j, tsk_{i.2}, \psi, tvk_i, \sigma) \leftarrow rk_{i \to j}$
  $(tpk_i, \widehat{pk}_i, pk_i, vk_i) \leftarrow pk_i$
  If $SVer(vk_i, \langle \psi \| tvk_i \| pk_i \| pk_j \rangle, \sigma) = \bot$
    then return $\bot$.
  $(tpk_j, \widehat{pk}_j, pk_j, vk_j) \leftarrow pk_j$
  $\mu_2 \leftarrow TShDec(tpk_i, tsk_{i.2}, c_i)$
  If $\mu_2 = \bot$ then return $\bot$.
  $\widehat{M} \leftarrow \langle pk_i \| pk_j \| c_i \| \mu_2 \| \psi \| tvk_i \| \sigma \rangle$
  Return $\widehat{c}_j \leftarrow PEnc(\widehat{pk}_j, \widehat{M})$.

$Dec_2(sk_i, c)$:
  $(tpk_i, \widehat{pk}_i, pk_i, vk_i) \leftarrow pk_i$
  $(tsk_i, \widehat{dk}_i, dk_i, sk_i) \leftarrow sk_i$
  $(tsk_{i.1}, tsk_{i.2}, tvk_i) \leftarrow TSplit(tsk_i)$
  $\mu_1 \leftarrow TShDec(tpk_i, tsk_{i.1}, c)$
  If $\mu_1 = \bot$ then return $\bot$.
  $\mu_2 \leftarrow TShDec(tpk_i, tsk_{i.2}, c)$
  If $\mu_2 = \bot$ then return $\bot$.
  $m \leftarrow TCom(tpk_i, tvk_i, c, \{\mu_1, \mu_2\})$
  Return m.

$REncVer(pk_i, sk_j, c'_i, \widehat{c}_j)$:
  $(tpk_i, \widehat{pk}_i, pk_i, vk_i) \leftarrow pk_i$
  $(tsk_j, \widehat{dk}_j, dk_j, sk_j) \leftarrow sk_j$
  $\widehat{M} \leftarrow PDec(\widehat{dk}_j, \widehat{c}_j)$
  If $\widehat{M} = \bot$ then return $\bot$.
  $\langle pk'_i \| pk'_j \| c_i \| \mu_2 \| \psi \| tvk_i \| \sigma \rangle \leftarrow \widehat{M}$
  If $(pk'_i, pk'_j) \neq (pk_i, pk_j)$ then return $\bot$.
  If $SVer(vk_i, \langle \psi \| tvk_i \| pk'_i \| pk'_j \rangle, \sigma) = \bot$
    then return $\bot$.
  $tsk_{i.1} \leftarrow PDec(dk_j, \psi)$
  If $tsk_{i.1} = \bot$ then return $\bot$.
  $\mu_1 \leftarrow TShDec(tpk_i, tsk_{i.1}, c_i)$
  If $\mu_1 = \bot$ then return $\bot$.
  If $TShVer(tpk_i, tvk_i, c_i, 2, \mu_2) = \bot$
    then return $\bot$.
  If $c'_i = c_i$ then return $\top$ else return $\bot$.

Fig. 1. The VPRE scheme $eHKK^+$ based on the PRE scheme by Hanaoka et al. [11]. Since Dec_2 described above needs to run $TSplit$, it is probabilistic. However, it can be made deterministic by running $(tsk_1, tsk_2) \leftarrow TSplit(tsk)$ in KG (instead of running it in Dec_2) and including (tsk_1, tsk_2) into sk. We do not take this approach in the above so that the description is kept close to the original one shown in [11].

of the HKK$^+$ scheme [11]. More specifically, the difference is that we calculate the (differences of the) probabilities of $\mathcal{A}$ succeeding in guessing the challenge bit (instead of the event that an adversary succeeds in breaking the conditions of soundness). In the final game, we can show that there exists a PPT CCA adversary $\mathcal{B}$ against the re-splittable TPKE scheme such that its advantage $\mathsf{Adv}_{(\mathcal{B},n)}^{\mathsf{CCA-TPKE}}(k)$ is exactly the difference between the success probability of $\mathcal{A}$ in the final game and $1/2$.

Theorem 5. *If the PKE scheme is CCA secure and the re-splittable TPKE scheme has strong smoothness, then the VPRE scheme* eHKK$^+$ *is first-level CCA secure.*

Intuition. Due to the lack of space, we omit the security proof. Here, we give an intuition of the security proof of first-level CCA security. As shown in [11], a first-level ciphertext in the eHKK$^+$ scheme is wrapped entirely by the underlying PKE scheme (regarding $\widehat{pk}$), and thus its CCA security naturally leads to first-level CCA security, if it were not for re-encryption verification queries.

The main difference from the proof in [11] is that we need the strong smoothness of the underlying re-splittable TPKE scheme, which was not necessary in the original proof of [11], in order to deal with REncVer queries. More specifically, recall that in the first-level CCA security game, an adversary $\mathcal{A}$ can choose a key pair $(\mathsf{sk}_\mathcal{A}, \mathsf{pk}_\mathcal{A})$ for the second-level encryption of the challenge query. In particular, $\mathcal{A}$ can know $tsk_\mathcal{A}$. Now, suppose that this TPKE scheme has a "weak plaintext" m_w in the sense that it is easy to find given $tsk_\mathcal{A}$, and its encryption $c_w \leftarrow \mathsf{TEnc}(tpk_\mathcal{A}, m_w)$ is easy to guess. (Such property does not contradict the CCA security of the TPKE scheme, because m_w could be hard to find without $tsk_\mathcal{A}$.) Then $\mathcal{A}$ can choose such m_w as one of the challenge plaintexts, submit it with $(\mathsf{sk}_\mathcal{A}, \mathsf{pk}_\mathcal{A})$ as a challenge query, and obtain the challenge ciphertext $\widehat{c}^*$. Then $\mathcal{A}$ by itself calculates the "easy-to-guess" ciphertext c_w corresponding to m_w, and submits a REncVer query $(\mathsf{pk}_\mathcal{A}, c_w, \widehat{c}^*)$, which by definition reveals the challenge bit (because its answer essentially tells whether "$\widehat{c}^*$ is a re-encryption of c_w"). However, if the underlying re-splittable TPKE scheme is guaranteed to have strong smoothness, such weak plaintexts cannot exist, and hence we can conclude that REncVer queries do not help $\mathcal{A}$.

References

1. Ateniese, G., Fu, K., Green, M., Hohenberger, S.: Improved proxy re-encryption schemes with applications to secure distributed storage. ACM Trans. Inf. Syst. Secur. **9**(1), 1–30 (2006)
2. Bellare, M., Boldyreva, A., Kurosawa, K., Staddon, J.: Multirecipient Encryption Schemes: How to Save on Bandwidth and Computation Without Sacrificing Security. IEEE Trans. on IT. **53**(11), 3927–3943 (2007)
3. Bellare, M., Hofheinz, D., Kiltz, E.: Subtleties in the Definition of IND-CCA: When and How Should Challenge Decryption Be Disallowed? J. Cryptology **28**(1), 29–48 (2015)

4. Bellare, M., Neven, G.: Multi-Signatures in the Plain Public-Key Model and a General Forking Lemma. ACMCCS **2006**, 390–399 (2006)
5. Blaze, M., Bleumer, G., Strauss, M.J.: Divertible Protocols and Atomic Proxy Cryptography. In: Nyberg, K. (ed.) EUROCRYPT 1998. LNCS, vol. 1403, pp. 127–144. Springer, Heidelberg (1998)
6. Boldyreva, A.: Threshold Signatures, Multisignatures and Blind Signatures Based on the Gap-Diffie-Hellman-Group Signature Scheme. In: Desmedt, Y.G. (ed.) Public Key Cryptography – PKC 2003. LNCS, vol. 2567, pp. 31–46. Springer, Heidelberg (2003)
7. Canetti, R., Hohenberger, S.: Chosen-ciphertext secure proxy re-encryption. ACMCCS **2007**, 185–194 (2007)
8. Canetti, R., Krawczyk, H., Nielsen, J.B.: Relaxing Chosen-Ciphertext Security. In: Boneh, D. (ed.) CRYPTO 2003. LNCS, vol. 2729, pp. 565–582. Springer, Heidelberg (2003)
9. Chow, S.S.M., Weng, J., Yang, Y., Deng, R.H.: Efficient Unidirectional Proxy Re-Encryption. In: Bernstein, D.J., Lange, T. (eds.) AFRICACRYPT 2010. LNCS, vol. 6055, pp. 316–332. Springer, Heidelberg (2010)
10. Fujisaki, E., Okamoto, T.: Secure Integration of Asymmetric and Symmetric Encryption Schemes. In: Wiener, M. (ed.) CRYPTO 1999. LNCS, vol. 1666, pp. 537–554. Springer, Heidelberg (1999)
11. Hanaoka, G., Kawai, Y., Kunihiro, N., Matsuda, T., Weng, J., Zhang, R., Zhao, Y.: Generic Construction of Chosen Ciphertext Secure Proxy Re-Encryption. In: Dunkelman, O. (ed.) CT-RSA 2012. LNCS, vol. 7178, pp. 349–364. Springer, Heidelberg (2012)
12. Hohenberger, S., Lewko, A., Waters, B.: Detecting Dangerous Queries: A New Approach for Chosen Ciphertext Security. In: Pointcheval, D., Johansson, T. (eds.) EUROCRYPT 2012. LNCS, vol. 7237, pp. 663–681. Springer, Heidelberg (2012)
13. Isshiki, T., Nguyen, M.H., Tanaka, K.: Proxy Re-Encryption in a Stronger Security Model Extended from CT-RSA2012. In: Dawson, E. (ed.) CT-RSA 2013. LNCS, vol. 7779, pp. 277–292. Springer, Heidelberg (2013)
14. Ivan, A.A., Dodis, Y.: Proxy Cryptography Revisited. NDSS 2003 (2003)
15. Kirshanova, E.: Proxy Re-encryption from Lattices. In: Krawczyk, H. (ed.) PKC 2014. LNCS, vol. 8383, pp. 77–94. Springer, Heidelberg (2014)
16. Libert, B., Vergnaud, D.: Unidirectional Chosen-Ciphertext Secure Proxy Re-Encryption. In: Cramer, R. (ed.) PKC 2008. LNCS, vol. 4939, pp. 360–379. Springer, Heidelberg (2008)
17. Mambo, M., Okamoto, E.: Proxy Cryptosystems: Delegation of the power to decrypt ciphertexts. In: IEICE Trans on Fundamentals of Electronics, Communications and Computer Sciences, E80-A(1), pp. 54–63 (1997)
18. Matsuda, T., Nishimaki, R., Tanaka, K.: CCA Proxy Re-Encryption without Bilinear Maps in the Standard Model. In: Nguyen, P.Q., Pointcheval, D. (eds.) PKC 2010. LNCS, vol. 6056, pp. 261–278. Springer, Heidelberg (2010)
19. Ohata, S., Matsuda, T., Hanaoka, G., Matsuura, K.: More Constructions of Resplittable Threshold Public Key Encryption. In: Yoshida, M., Mouri, K. (eds.) IWSEC 2014. LNCS, vol. 8639, pp. 109–118. Springer, Heidelberg (2014)
20. Pinto, A., Poettering, B., Schuldt, J.C.N.: Multi-recipient Encryption, Revisited. ASIACCS **2014**, 229–238 (2014)
21. Ristenpart, T., Yilek, S.: The Power of Proofs-of-Possession: Securing Multiparty Signatures against Rogue-Key Attacks. In: Naor, M. (ed.) EUROCRYPT 2007. LNCS, vol. 4515, pp. 228–245. Springer, Heidelberg (2007)

22. Shao, J., Cao, Z.: CCA-Secure Proxy Re-encryption without Pairings. In: Jarecki, S., Tsudik, G. (eds.) PKC 2009. LNCS, vol. 5443, pp. 357–376. Springer, Heidelberg (2009)
23. Weng, J., Zhao, Y., Hanaoka, G.: On the Security of a Bidirectional Proxy Re-encryption Scheme from PKC 2010. In: Catalano, D., Fazio, N., Gennaro, R., Nicolosi, A. (eds.) PKC 2011. LNCS, vol. 6571, pp. 284–295. Springer, Heidelberg (2011)
24. Zhang, X., Chen, M., Li, X.: Comments on Shao-Cao's Unidirectional Proxy Re-Encryption Scheme from PKC 2009. Journal of Information Science and Engineering **27**(3), 1153–1158 (2011)

Implementation Attacks
on Exponentiation Algorithms

Exploiting Collisions in Addition Chain-Based Exponentiation Algorithms Using a Single Trace

Neil Hanley[1], HeeSeok Kim[2,3], and Michael Tunstall[4]([✉])

[1] Centre for Secure Information Technologies, ECIT, Queen's University Belfast,
NI Science Park, Queen's Road, Queen's Island, Belfast BT3 9DT, UK
n.hanley@qub.ac.uk
[2] Korea Institute of Science and Technology Information, 245 Daehak-ro,
Yuseong-gu, Daejeon 305-806, South Korea
hs@kisti.re.kr
[3] Korea University of Science and Technology,
217 Gajeong-ro, Yuseong-gu, Daejeon 305-350, South Korea
[4] Cryptography Research, Inc., 425 Market Street, 11th Floor,
San Francisco, CA 94105, USA
michael.tunstall@cryptography.com

Abstract. Public key cryptographic algorithms are typically based on group exponentiation algorithms where the exponent is unknown to an adversary. A collision attack applied to an instance of an exponentiation is typically where an adversary seeks to determine whether two operations in the exponentiation have the same input. In this paper, we extend this to an adversary who seeks to determine whether the output of one operation is used as the input to another. We describe implementations of these attacks applied to a 192-bit scalar multiplication over an elliptic curve that only require a single power consumption trace to succeed with a high probability. Moreover, our attacks do not require any knowledge of the input to the exponentiation algorithm. These attacks would, therefore, be applicable to algorithms, such as EC-DSA, where an exponent is ephemeral, or to implementations where an exponent is blinded. We then demonstrate that a side-channel resistant implementation of a group exponentiation algorithm will require countermeasures that introduce enough noise such that an attack is not practical, as algorithmic countermeasures are not possible. (The work described in this paper was conducted when the last two authors were part of the Cryptography Group at the University of Bristol, United Kingdom.)

1 Introduction

It has been shown in the literature that an adversary can potentially derive a private key used to generate an RSA [1] or EC-DSA [2] signature by observing the power consumption during the computation of a naïvely implemented group exponentiation algorithm. The attack, defined by Kocher et al. [3], targets implementations of group multiplication and squaring operations used in the binary exponentiation algorithm. This vulnerability was present because the

© Springer International Publishing Switzerland 2015
K. Nyberg (ed.): CT-RSA 2015, LNCS 9048, pp. 431–448, 2015.
DOI: 10.1007/978-3-319-16715-2_23

instantaneous power consumption during the computation of a group squaring operation was different to that of a group multiplication, and could, therefore, be distinguished by simply inspecting a power consumption trace. Many group exponentiation algorithms have since been proposed in the literature, designed such that an adversary cannot implement side-channel attacks by inspecting a power consumption trace (see [4] for a survey).

Typically, one would assume that blinding is used such that the input to an exponentiation algorithm is not known to an adversary. Walter [5] observed that one could potentially derive the bits of an exponent by comparing two parts of a consumption trace corresponding to two operations in a group exponentiation and described some simulations. Amiel and Feix [6], and Kim et al. [7] described some attacks and implementations of this strategy applied to the BRIP exponentiation algorithm [8]. A similar attack has been documented by Witteman et al. [9] applicable to Coron's double-and-add-always exponentiation algorithm, and Kim et al. [7] also detail how one could apply such an attack to the Montgomery ladder [10,11].

A typical requirement for the implementations of the attacks described in the literature is that an adversary needs numerous traces with the same input and same exponent to derive an unknown exponent using collisions [6–9,12]. That is, an adversary will take numerous acquisitions and reduce noise in the acquired power consumption traces by computing a mean trace. Clavier et al. [13] defined attacks where one would only require one trace to succeed, although no practical results are given. In this paper we build on the work defined by Clavier et al. and show that these are attacks are practical.

One feature common to the attacks mentioned in the literature is that attacks are based on determining whether the input to two operations is the same. Herein, we extend this to consider an adversary who is able to determine whether the output of one operation is used as the input to another operation, thus allowing an adversary to apply collision attacks to more algorithms, and overcoming the countermeasures described by Kim et al. [7] to protect the Montgomery ladder.

Given that our practical work justifies our extended adversarial model for collision attacks, we define attacks that could be applied to exponentiation algorithms that are considered to be resistant to collision attacks. We prove that it is not possible to define a countermeasure that prevents collision attacks being applied to an addition chain-based exponentiation algorithm.

2   Preliminaries

In this section, we provide some background and notation that we will refer to in later sections.

2.1   Addition Chain-based Exponentiation

Addition chain-based exponentiation methods are used to find a sequence of elements, in a given multiplicative group $\mathbb{G}$, such that the first number is $1_{\mathbb{G}}$

and the last is s^χ for some arbitrary $s \in \mathbb{G}$ and $\chi \in \mathbb{Z}_{>0}$. Each member of the sequence is the product of two previous members of the sequence. More formally,

Definition 1. *An addition chain of length τ in group $\mathbb{G}$ for a group element $s \in \mathbb{G}$ is a sequence of group elements $(\omega_0, \omega_1, \omega_2, \ldots, \omega_\tau)$ such that $\omega_0 = 1_\mathbb{G}$, $\omega_1 = s$ and $\omega_k = \omega_i \otimes \omega_j$, $0 \le i \le j < k \le \tau$, and $\otimes$ is the group operation. The values of i and j are chosen such that ω_k is a chosen power of ω_1.*

Kocher et al. [3] demonstrated that under some circumstances, it is possible to distinguish a multiplication from a squaring operation using some side-channel, thus revealing all or part of an exponent. To counter this, many highly regular exponentiation algorithms have been proposed in the literature [11,14]. We define highly regular as:

Definition 2. *A group $\mathbb{G}$ exponentiation algorithm is defined as highly regular if it consists of an operation on $g \in \mathbb{G}$ that is composed of $g \otimes \cdots \otimes g \otimes g$, where $\otimes$ is the group operation, g occurs $\kappa \in \mathbb{Z}_{>0}$ times, and κ is fixed for an exponent of a given bit length.*

2.2 Elliptic Curves

Let $\mathbb{F}_q$ be a finite field. An elliptic curve $\mathcal{E}$ over $\mathbb{F}_q$ consists of points (x, y), with x, y in $\mathbb{F}_q$, that satisfy the full Weierstraß equation

$$\mathcal{E} : y^2 + \alpha_1 x y + \alpha_3 y = x^3 + \alpha_2 x^2 + \alpha_4 x + \alpha_6$$

with $\alpha_i \in \mathbb{F}_q$ $(1 \le i \le 6)$, and the point at infinity denoted as $\mathcal{O}$. The set $\mathcal{E}(\mathbb{F}_q)$ is defined as

$$\mathcal{E}(\mathbb{F}_q) = \{(x, y) \in \mathcal{E} \mid x, y \in \mathbb{F}_q\} \cup \{\mathcal{O}\},$$

where $\mathcal{E}(\mathbb{F}_q)$ forms an Abelian group under the chord-and-tangent rule and $\mathcal{O}$ is the identity element.

The addition of two points $\boldsymbol{P} = (x_1, y_1)$ and $\boldsymbol{Q} = (x_2, y_2)$ with $\boldsymbol{P} \ne -\boldsymbol{Q}$ is given by $\boldsymbol{P} + \boldsymbol{Q} = (x_3, y_3)$, where

$$x_3 = \lambda^2 + \alpha_1 \lambda - \alpha_2 - x_1 - x_2, \quad y_3 = (x_1 - x_3)\lambda - y_1 - \alpha_1 x_3 - \alpha_3 \quad (1)$$

$$\text{with } \lambda = \begin{cases} \dfrac{y_1 - y_2}{x_1 - x_2} & \text{if } \boldsymbol{P} \ne \boldsymbol{Q}, \\[2mm] \dfrac{3 x_1{}^2 + 2 \alpha_2 x_1 + \alpha_4 - \alpha_1 y_1}{2 y_1 + \alpha_1 x_1 + \alpha_3} & \text{if } \boldsymbol{P} = \boldsymbol{Q}. \end{cases}$$

Provided that the characteristic of the field $\mathbb{F}_q$ is not 2 or 3, we can take $\alpha_1 = \alpha_2 = \alpha_3 = 0$. In the following, we will also assume that $q = p$ is prime. We define the short Weierstraß form over prime field $\mathbb{F}_p$ by the equation

$$y^2 = x^3 + \alpha x + b . \quad (2)$$

Note that the slope λ in the doubling then becomes $\lambda = (3\,x_1{}^2 + \alpha)/(2\,y_1)$, which can be rewritten as $3(x_1 - 1)(x_1 + 1)/(2\,y_1)$ when $\alpha = -3$.

The scalar multiplication of a given point is equivalent to an addition chain-based exponentiation and is a fundamental operation in cryptographic algorithms that use elliptic curve arithmetic, i.e., $k\,\boldsymbol{P}$ for some integer $k < |\mathcal{E}|$. We concentrate on the short Weierstraß form since it is used in standards, such as the FIPS 186-3 [2], WTLS [15], and ANSI X9.62 [16].

3   Previous Work

One would typically assume that an input to a group exponentiation used in a cryptographic algorithm is blinded (or ephemeral) such that the input to an exponentiation algorithm is not known to an adversary. Walter [5] observed that one could potentially derive the bits of an exponent by comparing two parts of the same power consumption trace corresponding to two operations in a group exponentiation without requiring the input. However, Walter only presented results based on simulations.

Amiel and Feix [6], and Kim et al. [7] reported some attacks implementing a collision attack strategy proposed by Okeya and Sakura [12]. They explicated a collision attack on the BRIP exponentiation algorithm [8]. They observed that in the i-th round, the first operation operates on the same value as the last operation in round $(i - 1)$ depending on the value of bits of the exponent. An adversary can then compute the correlation between two power consumption traces taken while computing these operations to determine if the same value was used. A similar attack has been described by Witteman et al. [9] applicable to Coron's double-and-add-always exponentiation algorithm [17]. Witteman et al. demonstrated that this attack works on an ASIC implementation. Kim et al. [7] also determined how one could apply such an attack to the Montgomery ladder [10,11] and how one could prevent these collision attacks by modifying the algorithm (We show how this countermeasure can be overcome in Section 4.5). The practical results described in the literature require numerous acquisitions to be taken to reduce noise to the point where an attack will function.

Clavier et al. have outlined how one could implement these attacks using only one trace [13], although only simulated attacks are described. Recent work by Bauer et al. has also detailed how one could apply such collision attacks to implementations of scalar multiplications over elliptic curves [18]. Again, only simulated results are given. In this paper, we describe how to implement such attacks using a single trace on on both software and hardware platforms.

4   Attacking Addition Chain-based Exponentiation Algorithms

In this section, we describe how one can attack group exponentiation algorithms using collisions between group operations. For each attack, we shall assume that an adversary is obliged to attack individual traces independently rather than build up knowledge from numerous traces. This represents a significant advantage over the implementations of collision attacks described in the literature that typically require numerous traces to succeed [7,9].

Two principle strategies appear in the literature that one could use to protect a group exponentiation algorithm from side-channel analysis.

1. The first countermeasure to protect a group exponentiation algorithm was proposed by Coron [17], where dummy operations are included to provide a regular structure to a group exponentiation algorithm.
2. A set of highly-regular algorithms have been defined where a group exponentiation algorithm is broken up into indistinguishable atomic operations, as first described by Chevallier-Mames et al. [19]. In this paper, we consider unified formulae defined by Brier and Joye [20] as our instance of indistinguishable atomic operations.

We consider one example of each of these strategies to define an attack that an adversary could use, which are applicable to many other algorithms defined in the literature. We also address the Montgomery ladder [10,11], since the version described resists all the collision-based attacks provided in the literature, and describe a novel attack against this version.

In analyzing an implementation of a group exponentiation, the aim of an adversary is to produce a hypothesis that will enable the exponent to be derived in a practical amount of time. This is determined to be less than 2^{54} operations, based on the boundary set for block ciphers by Biryukov et al. [21]. It can only be considered to be an approximate guide because public key algorithms typically require significantly more time to compute than a block cipher. We also define an attack of time complexity less than 2^{40} to be trivial (while not strictly trivial, this represents an arbitrary threshold for what could be achieved with modest resources). We note that these attacks typically cannot determine the first and last bit treated by an exponentiation algorithm, which also impacts the time complexity of the subsequent analysis.

The expected number of operations can be determined using Stinson's algorithm [22], where t-bits have been incorrectly determined in an n-bit hypothesis leads to the scalar in time complexity $\mathcal{O}\left(n \sum_{i=0}^{\lceil t/2 \rceil} \binom{n/2}{i}\right)$ (see Tunstall and Joye for details [23]). Hence, we define $t \leq 21$ to be a practical attack and $t \leq 13$ to be a trivial attack.

4.1 Attack Platforms

We focus on implementations of a scalar multiplication over elliptic curves because of their use in standards, as described in Section 2.2. Specifically, we discuss attacks on the P192 curve defined in the FIPS 186-3 standard [2]. In each implementation, we use projective coordinates [24] where the base point is blinded by replacing the z-coordinate with a 192-bit random value and modifying the x and y-coordinates as required.

For each of three chosen exponentiation algorithms, we describe attack strategies for attacking implementations on two platforms. The purpose of these implementations is to demonstrate the feasibility of the attack on both software and hardware platforms.

The first platform we considered an embedded software implementation on an ARM7TDMI microprocessor, using homogenous projective coordinates and the point addition algorithm proposed by Izu and Takagi [25]. The implementation was based on a series of functions for manipulating large numbers written in the ARM7 assembly language. The multiplication instructions were used such that no change in the execution time would occur for different inputs by using algorithms defined by Großschädl et al. [26].

The power consumption acquisitions were taken with the microprocessor clocked at 7.37 MHz. The entire scalar multiplication generation was recorded at 125 MS/s and then filtered using a low-pass filter with a corner frequency set to 7.37 MHz. Experimentation while conducting the attacks described below determined that this improved the success rate of any subsequent side-channel analysis.

The second platform was a VHDL implementation on a SASEBO-G FPGA board [27], using a Montgomery multiplier based on the CIOS algorithm [28] containing a single 32-bit single-precision multiplier. Homogenous projective coordinates were used in conjunction with the point addition algorithm proposed by Cohen et al. [29], and the doubling algorithm proposed by Bernstein and Lange [30]. The underlying architecture is similar to that presented in [31], with a single ALU containing a modular Montgomery multiplication unit and an addition/subtraction unit, controlled via ROM programmed during synthesis. The power consumption acquisitions were taken with the FPGA clocked at 24 MHz. The entire scalar multiplication algorithm was recorded at 250 MS/s and filtered with both a high-pass filter to remove a DC drift in the traces, and a low-pass filter to remove high frequency noise.

4.2   Implementing the Attacks

In each case described below, we divide the acquired power consumption traces into smaller traces corresponding to individual operations. That is, if we consider a trace T, we can describe the trace as a series of m subtraces

$$T = \{O_1, O_2, O_3, \ldots, O_{m-1}, O_m\},$$

where the exponentiation algorithm consists of m group operations. That is, O_i for $i \in \{1, \ldots, m\}$ will be the power consumption during the i-th group operation in trace T. A group operation is defined as either an addition, a doubling, or a field operation and it should be clear from the context to which we refer. A description of how one achieves this and a description of an attack using these subtraces as a set of traces is given by Clavier et al. [32].

To give an example of how one can extract these subtraces, Figure 1 shows a portion of two power consumption traces, each of which show nine field multiplications visible as a repeating pattern.

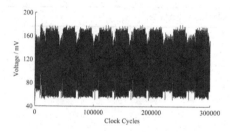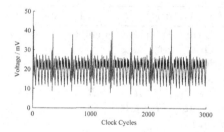

Fig. 1. Example power consumption trace showing the individual field multiplication operations in a group operation for the ARM7 (left) and Virtex-II (right) implementations

The attacks described in the literature typically require an adversary to take a certain number of traces and generate a mean trace by computing the mean power consumption at each point in the set of traces [7,9]. This strategy gives a trace that is representative of the power consumption without high frequency noise, since noise will be removed as one computes the mean. In our implementations, we took a different strategy.

We took all the subtraces $\{O_1, O_2, O_3, \ldots, O_{m-1}, O_m\}$ and computed a mean subtrace $\hat{O}$. This mean trace was then subtracted point-by-point from each element in $\{O_1, O_2, O_3, \ldots, O_{m-1}, O_m\}$ to give $\{O'_1, O'_2, O'_3, \ldots, O'_{m-1}, O'_m\}$. This has the effect of removing instruction dependent power consumption from the resulting set of subtraces, leaving noise and variation caused by the manipulated data.

We discuss our attacks using Pearson's correlation coefficient as a means of detecting collisions, and we also provide results for using the Euclidean distance. A variety of methods are present in the literature, for example, Bauer et al. present results based on simulations using mutual information [18]. The possible choices are too numerous to list all of them, but similar results should be possible.

4.3 Highly-Regular Right-to-Left Scalar Multiplication

In the additive group formed over an elliptic curve, a group exponentiation has been defined by Joye that only uses additions [14] as shown in Algorithm 1. An attack can be defined as a straightforward variant of the attacks described by Kim et al. [7] and Witteman et al. [9]. We note that, in one loop of Algorithm 1, $\mathbf{R}_0$ remains the same when $k_{i+1} = 0$ and $\mathbf{R}_1$ remains the same when $k_{i+1} = 1$. That is, one can observe a collision between the second addition in the loop treating the bit k_i and the first addition in the next loop treating the bit k_{i+1} where $k_{i+1}=1$.

Hence, we wish to compare the power consumption during the second addition of a given round with the first addition of the next round. If we consider the u-point addition traces a_i that make up the power consumption trace A taken

---

Algorithm 1. Joye's Add-Only Scalar Multiplication [14]

Input: P a point on elliptic curve $\mathcal{E}$, an n-bit scalar $k = (k_{n-1}, k_{n-2}, \ldots, k_0)_2$
Output: $Q = kP$
1 $R_0 \leftarrow \mathcal{O}$; $R_1 \leftarrow P$; $R_2 \leftarrow P$;
2 **for** $i \leftarrow 0$ **to** $n-1$ **do**
3 $\quad\quad R_{1-k_i} \leftarrow R_{1-k_i} + R_2$;
4 $\quad\quad R_2 \leftarrow R_0 + R_1$;
5 **end**
6 **return** R_0

---

during the computation of a n-bit scalar multiplication as defined in Algorithm 1, then

$$A = \{a_{1,1} \ldots a_{1,u}, a_{2,1} \ldots a_{2,u}, \ldots, a_{m,1} \ldots a_{m,u}\}$$

using the notation above $O'_i = a_{i,1} \ldots a_{i,u} - \hat{a}_1 \ldots \hat{a}_u = \bar{a}_i$ for all $1 \leq i < m$, i.e., each $\bar{a}_i$ is a trace consisting of u points with the mean subtracted. For a n-bit scaler, m is equal to $2n$ since there are always two point additions per round.

To locate the points in the group addition trace where collisions would occur, one can compute a trace where we assume that a collision always occurs at every possible location, i.e., we assume that the input of the second addition in round ℓ is always equal to the first addition in round $\ell + 1$. This gives

$$C = \rho((\bar{a}_2, \bar{a}_4, \ldots, \bar{a}_{m-2}), (\bar{a}_3, \bar{a}_5, \ldots, \bar{a}_{m-1})),$$

where ρ computes Pearson's correlation coefficient for each of the u points in the group addition trace independently. The correlation trace C consisting of u points will show a significant correlation, where a collision could be detected if present. That is, enough of $(\bar{a}_i, \bar{a}_{i+1})$ will collide, without knowing which, that it will be visible in a correlation trace to find the relevant points in time, which are then used to find the actual collisions. An example trace is shown in Figure 2.

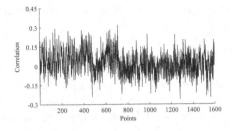

Fig. 2. An example correlation trace showing the correlation across one operation assuming that a collision occurs in every loop of the exponentiation. The example is generated from one power consumption trace taken while a Virtex-II FPGA was computing an exponentiation using Joye's add-only exponentiation algorithm.

A threshold can then be chosen where all points that have a magnitude above this threshold have their index noted, where the choice of threshold depends on the platform one is attacking, which must be decided on a case-by-case basis. Extracting these points, one can form a trace from v-point subtraces by concatenating the points at the selected indices from each $\bar{a}_i$. For example, we can denote:

$$A' = \{a'_{1,1} \ldots a'_{1,v}, a'_{2,1} \ldots a'_{2,v}, \ldots, a'_{m,1} \ldots a'_{m,v}\} = \{\bar{a}'_1, \bar{a}'_2, \ldots, \bar{a}'_m\} \ .$$

This trace is then used to determine whether a collision occurs between individual operations. For example, using Pearson's correlation coefficient to detect a collision, one computes a trace

$$D = d_1 \ldots d_{n-1} = \{\rho(\bar{a}'_2, \bar{a}'_3), \rho(\bar{a}'_4, \bar{a}'_5), \ldots, \rho(\bar{a}'_{m-2}, \bar{a}'_{m-1})\} \ .$$

The correlation coefficients in D can then be converted to hypothetical values for bits of the exponent by observing whether they fall above or below the mean correlation across all d_i for $i \in \{1, \ldots, n-1\}$. Hence, the value of d_i will give a hypothesis for the i-th bit of the exponent for $i \in \{1, \ldots, n-1\}$.

An attack, as described above, was applied independently to each trace in a set of 1000, taken while an ARM7 microprocessor was computing a scalar multiplication, and 8000 taken while a SASEBO board was computing a scalar multiplication using Joye's add-only exponentiation algorithm. The only difference in the way that the attack was applied was in the way that the threshold used to select points from C is chosen. In the application to the SASEBO board, the threshold was set to the mean correlation of $c_1 \ldots c_u$. This approach could not be taken with the implementation of the attack applied to the ARM7 implementation because of the number of points in each trace. An arbitrarily chosen threshold of 0.55 was chosen to select the majority of peaks in the observed traces.

In both cases we studied, an attack can be defined where an adversary can deduce the exponent with a high probability. Indeed, the majority of the values for the time complexity fall well below our defined threshold for a trivial attack. However, the correlation coefficient is less effective than the Euclidean distance. The results are summarized in Table 1 at the end of this section.

4.4   Scalar Multiplication with Dummy Operations

One of the first countermeasures defined to prevent the identification of group operations in an instance of a group exponentiation algorithm was proposed by Coron [17]. In the additive group formed over an elliptic curve, the resulting algorithm is shown in Algorithm 2. Witteman et al. [9] described an attack based on the observation that in the i-th round, the first operation operates on the same value as the last operation in round $(i-1)$ if the output of this operation is discarded under the assumption that the operation is the same. However, their attack was applied to exponentiation in $\mathbb{Z}_n$. When implementing a scalar multiplication, one would use different operations to compute an addition and

---

Algorithm 2. Coron's Double-and-Add-Always Algorithm [17]

Input: P a point on elliptic curve $\mathcal{E}$, an n-bit scalar $k = (k_{n-1}, k_{n-2}, \ldots, k_0)_2$
Output: $Q = kP$
1 $R_0 \leftarrow P$; $R_1 \leftarrow P$;
2 **for** $i \leftarrow n - 2$ **down to** 0 **do**
3      $R_0 \leftarrow 2R_0$;
4      $R_{1-k_i} \leftarrow R_0 + P$;
5 **end**
6 **return** R_0

---

a doubling operation, making a direct comparison problematic. In this section, we show how one could still implement such an attack.

We consider a trace T made up of subtraces corresponding to doubling operations δ_i and additions α_i as follows:

$$T = \{\delta_1, \alpha_1, \delta_2, \alpha_2 \ldots, \delta_{n-1}, \alpha_{n-1}\},$$

where a doubling operation δ_i and addition α_i for $i \in \{1, \ldots, n-1\}$ consist of f and h field multiplications, respectively. We assume that the power consumption taken during one field multiplication consists of u points. One can then compare all of the field multiplications in a doubling operation with all of those in the following addition in a manner similar to that described in Section 4.3, i.e., initially assuming that a collision occurs in every round in order to find the points of interest. This gives the $f \times h$ matrix

$$C = \begin{pmatrix} \bar{c}_{1,1} & \bar{c}_{1,2} & \cdots & \bar{c}_{1,h} \\ \bar{c}_{2,1} & \bar{c}_{2,2} & \cdots & \bar{c}_{2,h} \\ \vdots & \vdots & \ddots & \vdots \\ \bar{c}_{f,1} & \bar{c}_{f,2} & \cdots & \bar{c}_{f,h} \end{pmatrix}$$

where each $\bar{c}_{i,j}$, for $1 \leq i \leq f$ and $1 \leq j \leq h$, is a u-point trace. For convenience, only the field multiplications were considered, with the other field operations discarded.

Two different approaches of using this matrix were explored. In applying the collision attack to traces taken while an ARM7 microprocessor was computing a scalar multiplication using Coron's dummy-and-add-always algorithm, we noted that a significant number of operations that should have no linear relation produced significant correlation coefficients. We, therefore, computed a second matrix where no collisions were possible, i.e., by randomly selecting operations to compare. This matrix was then subtracted from the first matrix point-by-point to remove spurious peaks in the correlation matrix.

As for the attack described in Section 4.3, an arbitrary threshold set to 0.55 was used to determine which points from which operations were selected. As previously, if there are v indices that are selected, then we form one trace from the points indicated on one dimension by extracting the relevant points from each subtrace in T. Then, as in Section 4.3, we define

$$A' = \{a'_{1,1} \dots a'_{1,v}, a'_{2,1} \dots a'_{2,v}, \dots, a'_{2(n-1),1} \dots a'_{2(n-1),v}\}$$
$$= \{\bar{a}'_1, \bar{a}'_2, \dots, \bar{a}'_{2(n-1)}\},$$

from points indicated in one dimension and

$$B' = \{b'_{1,1} \dots b'_{1,v}, b'_{2,1} \dots b'_{2,v}, \dots, b'_{2(n-1),1} \dots b'_{2(n-1),v}\}$$
$$= \{\bar{b}'_1, \bar{b}'_2, \dots, \bar{b}'_{2(n-1)}\},$$

from the other. That is, computing $\rho(\bar{a}'_i, \bar{b}'_i)$ will compute the correlation coefficient between all the combinations of points indicated by C.

As previously mentioned, one can use the indicated points to generate a trace of correlation coefficients,

$$D = d_1 \dots d_{n-1} = \{\rho(\bar{a}'_2, \bar{b}'_3), \rho(\bar{a}'_4, \bar{b}'_5), \dots, \rho(\bar{a}'_{2n-4}, \bar{b}'_{2n-3})\}$$

The mean of these coefficients was used to determine whether a given bit of the exponent is set to 1 or 0, and hence generate a hypothesis for the exponent. The attack was repeated on 1000 power consumption traces as before, with the results summarized in Table 1.

In applying the collision attack to traces taken while a SASEBO board was computing a scalar multiplication using Coron's dummy-and-add-always algorithm, we generated traces by selecting them from matrix C given our knowledge of the algorithms used to compute additions and doubling operations. That is, we concatenated the subtraces of interest from C that should allow a collision to be determined. Given the algorithms used, six field multiplications were compared to allow collisions to be detected, and the mean value of the concatenated subtraces was used as a threshold to extract the points that would be used to generate A' and B'. These traces were then used to generate a series of correlation coefficients D to form hypotheses on the bits of the exponent as described in Section 4.3. The attack was repeated on 8000 power consumption traces, and the results are summarized in Table 1 at the end of this section.

Remark 1. The ARM7 implementation can be attacked readily as the median case is well below our defined threshold for a trivial attack. Contrary to the previous attack, the correlation coefficient provides a better method of detecting collision than using the Euclidean distance when applied to our SASEBO implementation. An adversary using the correlation coefficient would expect to succeed in an attack after examining 280 traces, where each exponent is distinct, to produce a result that can be analyzed with a trivial complexity. That is, if the adversary expended a maximum effort of 2^{40} operations per trace a valid attack will have an overall time complexity of 2^{48} before the key is expected to be broken.

4.5 Montgomery Ladder

Another variant of addition chain-based exponentiation is the Montgomery ladder [10,11], as shown in Algorithm 3. A method of attacking the Montgomery ladder has been described by Kim et al. [7]. However, it requires that Line 3 in Algorithm 3 to be

$$R_{\neg k_i} = R_0 + R_1 .$$

This is because they used the collision between input operands of the addition and doubling operation. In each loop, their implementation computes $R_0 + R_1$ and $R_0 + R_0$ when a bit of the scalar is 0, and $R_0 + R_1$ and $R_1 + R_1$ when a bit of the scalar is 1. That is, the second operands are different when a given bit of a scalar is equal to 0 and equal otherwise.

Algorithm 3. Montgomery Ladder [10,11]

    Input: P a point on elliptic curve $\mathcal{E}$, an n-bit scalar $k = (k_{n-1}, k_{n-2}, \ldots, k_0)_2$
    Output: $Q = kP$
1 $R_0 \leftarrow \mathcal{O}$; $R_1 \leftarrow P$;
2 **for** $i = n - 1$ **down to** 0 **do**
3 | $R_{\neg k_i} \leftarrow R_{k_i} + R_{\neg k_i}$;
4 | $R_{k_i} \leftarrow 2 R_{k_i}$;
5 **end**
6 **return** R_0 ;

This attack described by Kim et al. [7] cannot be applied to Algorithm 3 since Line 3 is

$$R_{\neg k_i} \leftarrow R_{k_i} + R_{\neg k_i} .$$

However, one can still observe collisions between variables:

- In Algorithm 3, if the bits treated in two consecutive loops are the same, then the output of the operation in Line 4 in the first loop will be the input to the operation in Line 4 in the second loop.
- In Algorithm 3, if the bits treated in two consecutive loops are different, then the output of the operation in Line 3 in the first loop will be the input to the operation in Line 4 in the second loop.

An attack is not straightforward since one cannot compare field operations directly. This is because one wishes to compare the input of one operation with the output of another operation. We describe how one can achieve this below.

We consider a trace T made up of subtraces corresponding to doubling operations D_i and additions A_i as follows:

$$T = \{\alpha_1, \delta_1, \alpha_2, \delta_2, \ldots, \alpha_{n-1}, \delta_{n-1}\} .$$

We wish to compare the output of a doubling operations with the input of the subsequent addition and doubling operations. That is, we wish to detect collisions which allow us to determine if two consecutive bits of the exponent are the same.

Then, to evaluate whether a collision occurs, as indicated by our first observation above, we aim to compare the power consumption during the computation of the output of an addition with the power consumption during the processing of the input to a doubling operation. We shall assume that the power consumption corresponding to a group doubling and a group addition operation consists of u_d and u_a points, respectively. We determine a matrix of correlation coefficients C

$$
C = \begin{pmatrix}
\bar{c}_{1,1} & \bar{c}_{1,2} & \cdots & \bar{c}_{1,u_a} \\
\bar{c}_{2,1} & \bar{c}_{2,2} & \cdots & \bar{c}_{2,u_a} \\
\vdots & \vdots & \ddots & \vdots \\
\bar{c}_{u_d,1} & \bar{c}_{u_d,2} & \cdots & \bar{c}_{u_d,u_a}
\end{pmatrix}
$$

where $\bar{c}_{i,j}$ is the correlation of the i-th point from the doubling operation with the j-th point from the addition across, $1 \le i \le u_d$ and $1 \le j \le u_a$, comprising all the pairs of operations that could produce a collision.

As with the attack described in Section 4.4, the correlation coefficients generated in the matrix contained many spurious, yet seemingly significant, correlation coefficients. A second matrix was again generated, where no collisions were possible, and was subtracted from the matrix to remove the spurious correlation coefficients. From this differential matrix, we chose all indices where the correlation coefficient was greater than an arbitrarily chosen threshold of 0.15. As previously, if there are v indices that are selected, then we form one trace from the points indicated on one dimension by extracting the relevant points from each subtrace in T, giving

$$
\begin{aligned}
A' &= \{a'_{1,1} \ldots a'_{1,v}, a'_{2,1} \ldots a'_{2,v}, \ldots, a'_{2\,(n-1),1} \ldots a'_{2\,(n-1),v}\} \\
&= \{\bar{a}'_1, \bar{a}'_2, \ldots, \bar{a}'_{2\,(n-1)}\},
\end{aligned}
$$

and another trace from points indicated on the other dimension

$$
\begin{aligned}
B' &= \{b'_{1,1} \ldots b'_{1,v}, b'_{2,1} \ldots b'_{2,v}, \ldots, b'_{2\,(n-1),1} \ldots b'_{2\,(n-1),v}\} \\
&= \{\bar{b}'_1, \bar{b}'_2, \ldots, \bar{b}'_{2\,(n-1)}\}.
\end{aligned}
$$

Hence, computing $\rho(\bar{a}'_i, \bar{b}'_i)$ will compute the correlation coefficient between all the combinations of points indicated by C.

One can then use these reduced traces to generated a series of correlation coefficients

$$
D = d_1 \ldots d_{n-1} = \{\rho(\bar{a}'_2, \bar{b}'_3), \rho(\bar{a}'_4, \bar{b}'_5), \ldots, \rho(\bar{a}'_{2n-4}, \bar{b}'_{2n-3})\}
$$

as described in Section 4.3, and the mean of these coefficients are used to generate hypotheses for the exponent.

This can be repeated to compare a doubling operation with the following doubling operation to evaluate the collisions. This analysis produces two traces of correlation coefficients that can be used to produce hypotheses for each bit of the exponent. Where the hypotheses differ, we selected the hypothesis with the largest difference from the mean correlation coefficient under the assumption that this will be the strongest distinguisher.

However, once an estimation for the exponent used in an implementation of the Montgomery ladder is determined, one cannot directly apply Stinson's algorithm. This is because each time one wishes to flip a bit, all the bits that are less significant also need to be flipped. However, adapting the algorithm is straightforward, and the expected time complexity of an attack will be the same.

This attack applied to the ARM7 implementation can be readily conducted as the median case is well below our defined threshold for a trivial attack when the correlation coefficient is used. The results of the attack applied to 1000 traces are summarized in Table 1.

No practical attack was derived for for our SASEBO implementation. We assume that the leakage required to conduct this attack is not present. That is, the data does not leak in a similar fashion at two different points in time.

Table 1. The probability of successfully attacking an implementation of the add-only exponentiation algorithm on an ARM7 microprocessor given $1k$ observations and a Virtex-II FPGA given $8k$ observations. Where Pr(triv.) and Pr(prac.) are the probability of a successful attack with a trivial and practical attack complexity, respectively.

Platform	Algorithm	Matching Method	E (#Errors)	σ	Pr(triv.)	Pr(prac.)
ARM7	Add-only	Euclidean distance	5.78	4.30	0.926	0.991
		Correlation Coefficient	5.52	4.96	0.935	0.993
	Dummy	Euclidean distance	6.10	7.10	0.894	0.968
		Correlation Coefficient	8.40	8.66	0.820	0.920
	Montgomery	Euclidean distance	14.7	4.35	0.306	0.926
		Correlation Coefficient	21.7	4.74	0.0110	0.409
SASEBO	Add-only	Euclidean distance	7.69	2.68	0.955	1
		Correlation Coefficient	24.8	4.93	0.00338	0.190
	Dummy	Euclidean distance	37.7	5.88	0.00188	0.00225
		Correlation Coefficient	24.4	4.88	0.00525	0.207

5 Extending the Attack

To resist the attacks described in Section 4, one would need to use an exponentiation algorithm that is highly regular, see Definition 2. If values are reused once created, then, to resist our attacks, the order they are used should not reveal any information to an adversary. That is, an adversary should not be able to find meaningful collisions based on comparing the input or output of one operation with the input or output of another operation. Hence, we define the following property:

Definition 3. *An exponentiation is defined as to be totally regular if it consists of operations $g_1, g_2, \ldots, g_\kappa$, that are composed $g_\kappa \circ \cdots \circ g_2 \circ g_1$, where $\kappa \in \mathbb{Z}$ is fixed for an exponent of a given bit length and each g_i is of the form $z_i = g_i(x_i, y_i)$ for $i \in \{1, \ldots, \kappa\}$. Given the function $\mathcal{H} = g_i$ for $i \in \{1, \ldots, \kappa\}$ and some function $\mathcal{H}$, the address is fixed for each x_i, y_i, z_i for $i \in \{1, \ldots, \kappa\}$.*

However, such an exponentiation algorithm is not possible.

Lemma 1. *A totally regular addition chain-based exponentiation algorithm that can compute s^χ for any $s, \chi \in \mathbb{Z}_{>0}$, assuming χ has a fixed bit length, does not exist.*

Proof. Let $\mathbf{A}$ be an addition chain that can be used to compute s^χ from n for some arbitrary $s, \chi \in \mathbb{Z}_{>0}$. That is, there will exist some function

$$\mathcal{F} : \mathbb{Z}_{>0} \longrightarrow \mathbb{Z}_{>0} : s \longmapsto s^\chi,$$

that uses addition chain $\mathcal{A}$ to compute $\mathcal{F}(n)$ for some arbitrary χ of a given bit length. If $\mathcal{F}$ is totally regular, this would imply that $\mathbf{A}$ would remain unchanged for all possible exponents that have the same bit length as χ. However, by Definition 1, the last element of $\mathcal{A}$ is s^χ, and we note that χ cannot be changed by modifying s_0, s_1. Hence,

$$\mathcal{F} \Longleftrightarrow \mathcal{A}$$

and a totally regular addition chain-based exponentiation algorithm is not possible. $\qquad\qquad\square$

Given the attacks described above, it is straightforward to define attacks applicable to exponentiation algorithms that have been previously considered resistant to collision attacks. Hence, if one wishes to resist the attacks in this paper, one needs to ensure that such a side-channel analysis produces results that are sufficiently noisy, that subsequent analysis would be computationally infeasible.

6   Conclusion

We describe attacks based on collisions of arbitrarily chosen variables manipulated in group operations to determine an unknown exponent and demonstrate that they can be applied to a single trace without requiring any profiling. This represents a significant advantage over practical attacks described in the literature that typically require numerous traces to be acquired [7,9].

   We show that collision attacks can be applied to instances of exponentiation algorithms, where only a single trace can be analyzed by an attacker (i.e., the exponent is blinded or ephemeral). We demonstrated that it is possible to compare the input or output of one operation with the input or output of another operation. This leads to a very strong attack model, and we prove that it is not possible to construct an algorithm to resist these attacks. In implementing an exponentiation algorithm sufficient countermeasures need to be included to reduce the accuracy of the hypotheses made by an adversary, such that any subsequent analysis would be prohibitively time consuming. This can range from inserting noise into the implementation through hardware countermeasures [33] to a random ordering of group operations in an exponentiation algorithm [34]. We refer the reader to Fan and Verbauwhede [35] for a thorough treatment of this topic.

Acknowledgments. The authors would like to thank Georg Fuchsbauer, Seokhie Hong and Elisabeth Oswald for their helpful comments. This research was supported by "Construction and Operation of Science & Technology Security Center" Program funded by the Ministry of Science, ICT & Future Planning (G-15-GM-CR03). The work described in this paper has also been supported in part the European Commission through the ICT Programme under Contract ICT-2007-216676 ECRYPT II and the EPSRC via grant EP/I005226/1.

References

1. Rivest, R., Shamir, A., Adleman, L.M.: Method for obtaining digital signatures and public-key cryptosystems. Communications of the ACM **21**, 120–126 (1978)
2. National Institute of Standards and Technology (NIST): Recommended elliptic curves for federal government use. In the appendix of FIPS 186-3, available from http://csrc.nist.gov/publications/fips/fips186-3/fips_186-3.pdf (2009) (online; accessed January 2015)
3. Kocher, P.C., Jaffe, J., Jun, B.: Differential Power Analysis. In: Wiener, M. (ed.) CRYPTO 1999. LNCS, vol. 1666, pp. 388–397. Springer, Heidelberg (1999)
4. Joye, M., Tunstall, M.: Exponent Recoding and Regular Exponentiation Algorithms. In: Preneel, B. (ed.) AFRICACRYPT 2009. LNCS, vol. 5580, pp. 334–349. Springer, Heidelberg (2009)
5. Walter, C.D.: Sliding Windows Succumbs to Big Mac Attack. In: Koç, Ç.K., Naccache, D., Paar, C. (eds.) CHES 2001. LNCS, vol. 2162, pp. 286–299. Springer, Heidelberg (2001)
6. Amiel, F., Feix, B.: On the BRIP Algorithms Security for RSA. In: Onieva, J.A., Sauveron, D., Chaumette, S., Gollmann, D., Markantonakis, K. (eds.) WISTP 2008. LNCS, vol. 5019, pp. 136–149. Springer, Heidelberg (2008)
7. Kim, H., Kim, T.H., Yoon, J.C., Hong, S.: Practical second-order correlation power analysis on the message blinding method and its novel countermeasure for RSA. ETRI Journal **32**, 102–111 (2010)
8. Mamiya, H., Miyaji, A., Morimoto, H.: Efficient Countermeasures against RPA, DPA, and SPA. In: Joye, M., Quisquater, J.-J. (eds.) CHES 2004. LNCS, vol. 3156, pp. 343–356. Springer, Heidelberg (2004)
9. Witteman, M.F., van Woudenberg, J.G.J., Menarini, F.: Defeating RSA Multiply-Always and Message Blinding Countermeasures. In: Kiayias, A. (ed.) CT-RSA 2011. LNCS, vol. 6558, pp. 77–88. Springer, Heidelberg (2011)
10. Montgomery, P.: Speeding the Pollard and elliptic curve methods of factorization. Mathematics of Computation **48**, 243–264 (1987)
11. Joye, M., Yen, S.M.: The montgomery powering ladder. In: Kaliski Jr., B.S., Ç. K. Koç, Paar, C., (eds.) CHES 2002. LNCS, vol. 2523, 291–302. Springer, Heidelberg (2003)

12. Okeya, K., Sakurai, K.: A Second-Order DPA Attack Breaks a Window-Method Based Countermeasure against Side Channel Attacks. In: Chan, A.H., Gligor, V.D. (eds.) ISC 2002. LNCS, vol. 2433, pp. 389–401. Springer, Heidelberg (2002)
13. Clavier, C., Feix, B., Gagnerot, G., Giraud, C., Roussellet, M., Verneuil, V.: ROSETTA for Single Trace Analysis. In: Galbraith, S., Nandi, M. (eds.) INDOCRYPT 2012. LNCS, vol. 7668, pp. 140–155. Springer, Heidelberg (2012)
14. Joye, M.: Highly Regular Right-to-Left Algorithms for Scalar Multiplication. In: Paillier, P., Verbauwhede, I. (eds.) CHES 2007. LNCS, vol. 4727, pp. 135–147. Springer, Heidelberg (2007)
15. Wireless Application Protocol (WAP) Forum: Wireless transport layer security (WTLS) specification. http://www.wapforum.org
16. X9.62, A.: Public key cryptography for the financial services industry, the elliptic curve digital signature algorithm (ECDSA) (1999)
17. Coron, J.-S.: Resistance against Differential Power Analysis for Elliptic Curve Cryptosystems. In: Koç, Ç.K., Paar, C. (eds.) CHES 1999. LNCS, vol. 1717, pp. 292–302. Springer, Heidelberg (1999)
18. Bauer, A., Jaulmes, E., Prouff, E., Wild, J.: Horizontal Collision Correlation Attack on Elliptic Curves. In: Lange, T., Lauter, K., Lisoněk, P. (eds.) SAC 2013. LNCS, vol. 8282, pp. 553–570. Springer, Heidelberg (2014)
19. Chevallier-Mames, B., Ciet, M., Joye, M.: Low-cost solutions for preventing simple side-channel analysis: Side-channel atomicity. IEEE Transactions on Computers 53, 760–768 (2004)
20. Brier, E., Joye, M.: Weierstraßelliptic curve and side-channel attacks. In: Naccache, D., Paillier, P. (eds.) PKC 2002. LNCS, vol. 2274, pp. 335–345. Springer, Heidelberg (2002)
21. Biryukov, A., Dunkelman, O., Keller, N., Khovratovich, D., Shamir, A.: Key Recovery Attacks of Practical Complexity on AES-256 Variants with up to 10 Rounds. In: Gilbert, H. (ed.) EUROCRYPT 2010. LNCS, vol. 6110, pp. 299–319. Springer, Heidelberg (2010)
22. Stinson, D.: Some baby-step giant-step algorithms for the low hamming weight discrete logarithm problem. Mathematics of Computation 71, 379–391 (2002)
23. Tunstall, M., Joye, M.: The distributions of individual bits in the output of multiplicative operations. Cryptography and Communications 7, 71–90 (2015)
24. De Win, E., Mister, S., Preneel, B., Wiener, M.: On the Performance of Signature Schemes Based on Elliptic Curves. In: Buhler, J.P. (ed.) ANTS 1998. LNCS, vol. 1423, pp. 252–266. Springer, Heidelberg (1998)
25. Izu, T., Takagi, T.: Fast elliptic curve multiplications resistant against side channel attacks. IEICE Transactions 88-A, 161–171 (2005)
26. Großschädl, J., Oswald, E., Page, D., Tunstall, M.: Side-Channel Analysis of Cryptographic Software via Early-Terminating Multiplications. In: Lee, D., Hong, S. (eds.) ICISC 2009. LNCS, vol. 5984, pp. 176–192. Springer, Heidelberg (2010)
27. Research Center for Information Security: Side-channel Attack Standard Evaluation Board (SASEBO). http://www.risec.aist.go.jp/project/sasebo/ (2002) (Online; accessed January 2015)
28. Koc, C.K., Acar, T., Kaliski Jr., B.S.: Analyzing and comparing montgomery multiplication algorithms. IEEE Micro 16, 26–33 (1996)
29. Cohen, H., Miyaji, A., Ono, T.: Efficient Elliptic Curve Exponentiation Using Mixed Coordinates. In: Ohta, K., Pei, D. (eds.) ASIACRYPT 1998. LNCS, vol. 1514, pp. 51–65. Springer, Heidelberg (1998)

30. Bernstein, D.J., Lange, T.: Faster Addition and Doubling on Elliptic Curves. In: Kurosawa, K. (ed.) ASIACRYPT 2007. LNCS, vol. 4833, pp. 29–50. Springer, Heidelberg (2007)
31. Keller, M., Byrne, A., Marnane, W.P.: Elliptic curve cryptography on fpga for low-power applications. TRETS 2 (2009)
32. Clavier, C., Feix, B., Gagnerot, G., Roussellet, M., Verneuil, V.: Horizontal Correlation Analysis on Exponentiation. In: Soriano, M., Qing, S., López, J. (eds.) ICICS 2010. LNCS, vol. 6476, pp. 46–61. Springer, Heidelberg (2010)
33. Mangard, S., Oswald, E., Popp, T.: Power Analysis Attacks – Revealing the Secrets of Smart Cards. Springer (2007)
34. Oswald, E., Aigner, M.: Randomized Addition-Subtraction Chains as a Countermeasure against Power Attacks. In: Koç, Ç.K., Naccache, D., Paar, C. (eds.) CHES 2001. LNCS, vol. 2162, pp. 39–50. Springer, Heidelberg (2001)
35. Fan, J., Verbauwhede, I.: An Updated Survey on Secure ECC Implementations: Attacks, Countermeasures and Cost. In: Naccache, D. (ed.) Cryphtography and Security: From Theory to Applications. LNCS, vol. 6805, pp. 265–282. Springer, Heidelberg (2012)

Cold Boot Attacks
in the Discrete Logarithm Setting

Bertram Poettering[1] and Dale L. Sibborn[2]([✉])

[1] Ruhr University Bochum, Bochum, Germany
[2] Royal Holloway, University of London, London, UK
dale.sibborn.2011@live.rhul.ac.uk

Abstract. In a cold boot attack a cryptosystem is compromised by analysing a noisy version of its internal state. For instance, if a computer is rebooted the memory contents are rarely fully reset; instead, after the reboot an adversary might recover a noisy image of the old memory contents and use it as a stepping stone for reconstructing secret keys. While such attacks were known for a long time, they recently experienced a revival in the academic literature. Here, typically either RSA-based schemes or blockciphers are targeted.

We observe that essentially no work on cold boot attacks on schemes defined in the discrete logarithm setting (DL) and particularly for elliptic curve cryptography (ECC) has been conducted. In this paper we hence consider cold boot attacks on selected wide-spread implementations of DL-based cryptography. We first introduce a generic framework to analyse cold boot settings and construct corresponding key-recovery algorithms. We then study common in-memory encodings of secret keys (in particular those of the wNAF-based and comb-based ECC implementations used in OpenSSL and PolarSSL, respectively), identify how redundancies can be exploited to make cold boot attacks effective, and develop efficient dedicated key-recovery algorithms. We complete our work by providing theoretical bounds for the success probability of our attacks.

1 Introduction

Cold boot attacks. Since they were reported in the literature by Halderman *et al.* in 2008 [4], cold boot attacks have received a great deal of attention. The attacks rely on the fact that computer memory typically retains information when going through a power-down power-up cycle; this might allow an adversary to get access to confidential information such as cryptographic keys. Unfortunately (for the attacker), while the power is cut the bits in memory will decay over time, which means that any information obtained is likely to be 'noisy'. The focus of cold boot attacks resides in modelling quality and quantity of noise and applying intelligent algorithms to extracted memory images in order to fully recover keys.

The amount of time for which information is retained without power depends on the particular memory type (modern technologies imply a quicker decay) and the environment temperature (information degrades more quickly at higher temperatures). After power is switched off, the decay proceeds in a quite predictable

© Springer International Publishing Switzerland 2015
K. Nyberg (ed.): CT-RSA 2015, LNCS 9048, pp. 449–465, 2015.
DOI: 10.1007/978-3-319-16715-2_24

pattern [3,20]. More precisely, memory is partitioned into regions, and each region has a 'ground state' which is either 0 or 1. In a 0 ground state, the 1 bits will eventually decay to a 0. The probability of a 0 bit decaying to a 1 is very small, but not vanishing (a typical probability is 0.001 [4]). When the ground state is 1, the opposite is true.

Previous cold boot key-recovery algorithms. The general possibility of using cold boot attacks to recover data from memory chips has been known since at least the 1970s. However, in the academic literature it was not until 2008 that Halderman *et al.* became the first to focus on reconstructing cryptographic private keys from information obtained via this type of attack. There is now an abundance of literature concerning the cold boot recovery of private keys. RSA key-recovery algorithms are without doubt the most popular [4,7,8,11–13,16,19], whilst symmetric-key cryptographic schemes have received less attention [1,4,10,21]. One area that remains comparatively unexplored is the discrete logarithm setting. As far as we are aware, this issue has only been discussed in [13].

Published cold boot analyses almost ubiquitously assume that attackers can obtain a (noisy) copy of a private key that was stored with some form of redundancy. For instance, in the case of RSA, while in principle it is only necessary for the private key to contain the prime factors p and q, the PKCS#1 standard [9] suggests storing several extra values (such as d, d_p, d_q, and q_p^{-1}) in order to increase the efficiency of decryption and signing operations. It is this redundancy that was exploited by previous authors to recover private keys even when they were subjected to very high noise levels. In contrast, the discrete logarithm analysis of Lee *et al.* [13] assumes that an attacker only has access to the public key $X = g^x$ and a decayed version of the private key x. Consequently, given that there is no further redundancy, their proposed algorithm would be unable to efficiently recover keys that were affected by high noise levels.

Our contributions. Given the above discussion it is natural to ask whether in practical discrete logarithm-based software implementations there are any private key representations that contain redundancy that can be used to improve cold boot key-recovery algorithms. It turns out that such cases are indeed the rule, and they will form the basis of this paper. The scenarios we consider are taken from two wide-spread ECC implementations found in TLS libraries: the windowed non-adjacent form (wNAF) representation used in OpenSSL, and the PolarSSL comb-based approach. By exploiting redundancies in the respective in-memory representations of private keys we are able to vastly improve upon the results from [13].

Our techniques are based on a novel statistical test that allows a trade-off between success rate and execution speed. We stress that this test is not only applicable to the discrete logarithm setting, but is applicable to all types of key. In particular, it complements the framework of Paterson *et al.* [16] for the RSA setting. We observe that the statistical test proposed in [16] has a bounded running-time, but no lower bound on the success of the algorithm is provided in the scenario where keys are subjected to asymmetric errors. In contrast, for our algorithm we succeed in lower-bounding the success rate. Although we provide no bound on the running time of our primary algorithm, we note that various modifications allow an attacker to seek her own compromise between a preferred success rate and a desired running-time.

2   Multinomial Distributions and the Multinomial Test

The general strategy behind key-recovery procedures for cold boot attacks is to only consider small parts of the targeted key at a time. For instance, RSA-based reconstruction procedures usually start with the least significant bits (LSB) [7, 8,12,13,16,19], but it is also possible to begin with the most significant bits (MSB) [18]. It is typical to use an iterative process to guess a couple of bits of the key and assess the plausibility of the guess on the basis of both a model of the decay process and the available redundancy in the encoding. Previous cold boot papers have proposed various methods by which the plausibility of the guess is ascertained. Examples are the Hamming distance approach of [7] and the maximum-likelihood method of [16]. The theoretical success of the algorithm is usually based on assumptions that are typically only true for a specific key being considered, and are possibly not easy to generalise. In this section we propose a general statistical test that can be used in various scenarios. The test is based on multinomial distributions and works well for scenarios when the distribution of private key bits is known (such as RSA), but can also be modified to work even when the attacker knows nothing of the distribution of the private key.

We will now study the multinomial distribution and its associated test. Multinomial distributions are a generalisation of the binomial distribution. The distribution has k mutually exclusive events with probabilities $p = (p_1, \ldots, p_k)$, where $\sum_{i=1}^{k} p_i = 1$ and for all i we have $p_i \neq 0$. If there are n trials, we let the random variables $X_1, \ldots, X_k$ denote the amount of times the ith event occurs and say that $X = (X_1, \ldots, X_k)$ follows a multinomial distribution with parameters n and p. Given a set of observed values, $x = (x_1, \ldots, x_k)$, we can use a multinomial test to see if these values are consistent with the probability vector p (which is the null hypothesis, denoted H_0). The alternative hypothesis (denoted H_1) for the probability vector is $\pi = (x_1/n, \ldots, x_k/n)$, where each component is the maximum-likelihood estimate for each probability. The two hypotheses can be compared via the calculation $-2 \sum_{i=1}^{k} x_i \ln(p_i/\pi_i)$, which is called the *multinomial test statistic*. When the null hypothesis is true, the distribution of this statistic converges to the chi-squared distribution with $k - 1$ degrees of freedom as $n \to \infty$.

We will now see how the multinomial test statistic may be applied in cold boot key recovery algorithms. Let s_i denote a (partial) candidate solution for the private key (including the redundant representation) across a (partial) section of bits. When comparing a partial candidate solution s_i to the noisy information r we define n_{01}^i to be the number of positions at which there is a 0 in the candidate solution and a 1 in the corresponding position in the noisy information r. We define n_{00}^i, n_{10}^i, and n_{11}^i correspondingly, so $n = n_{00} + n_{01} + n_{11} + n_{10}$. Crucially, this count only considers the newly-guessed bits generated at the relevant phase of the algorithm, while all previous guesses are ignored. It is clear that these counts follow a multinomial distribution. Let $\alpha := \mathbb{P}(0 \to 1)$ denote the probability that a 0 bit flips to a 1 in the execution of the cold boot attack, and let $\beta := \mathbb{P}(1 \to 0)$ denote the probability that a 1 flips to a 0. For the correct candidate solution, s_c, the probability of observing each of the four values $(n_{00}^c, n_{01}^c, n_{11}^c, n_{10}^c)$ is precisely $H_0 : p = (p_0(1 - \alpha), p_0\alpha, p_1(1 - \beta), p_1\beta)$, where p_b, $b \in \{0,1\}$, is the probability of a b-bit appearing in the correct candidate solution. Notice that we require $\alpha, \beta \neq 0$ since each component of the probability vector must be non-zero. The test may be modified to cover the case when α or β is zero, but we defer this discussion to the full version [17]. For each candidate solution we could use the previous set of probabilities as the null hypothesis of the multinomial test. We would like to test whether our guessed candidate solution is consistent with this probability vector. The alternative hypothesis is that the set of probabilities for the four bit-pairs is equal to the maximum-likelihood estimates for each category. That is, $H_1 : p = (n_{00}^i/n, n_{01}^i/n, n_{11}^i/n, n_{10}^i/n)$ for each candidate i. We define our first statistical test, which we call Correlate′, to be

$$\text{Correlate}'(s_i, r) := -2n_{00}^i \ln\left(\frac{np_0(1 - \alpha)}{n_{00}^i}\right) - 2n_{01}^i \ln\left(\frac{np_0\alpha}{n_{01}^i}\right)$$
$$-2n_{11}^i \ln\left(\frac{np_1(1 - \beta)}{n_{11}^i}\right) - 2n_{10}^i \ln\left(\frac{np_1\beta}{n_{10}^i}\right) , \quad (1)$$

where the values in brackets are the null hypothesis values divided by the alternative hypothesis values. Correlate′ outputs a numerical value (≥ 0) for each candidate. We now need to discuss when we consider this test to pass or fail. It is well known that when the null hypothesis is correct the distribution of the right-hand side of equation (1) converges to a chi-squared distribution with $k-1$ degrees of freedom as $n \to \infty$. In our analysis we have $k = 4$, hence the test statistic converges to a chi-squared distribution with three degrees of freedom. We can therefore set a threshold C such that any candidate whose test statistic is less than C is retained, otherwise the candidate is discarded. We therefore define

$$\text{Correlate}_C(s_i, r) = \text{pass} \quad \Leftrightarrow \quad \text{Correlate}'(s_i, r) < C ,$$

where C would be an additional (user-chosen) input to the algorithm. The chi-squared distribution can tell us how to set the threshold C to achieve any desired success rate. If we set the threshold C such that $\int_0^C \chi_3^2(x)dx = \gamma$, we know that, asymptotically, the probability that the correct candidate's correlation value Correlate′(s_c, r) is less than C is equal to γ. Recall that the Correlate′ test only considers the newly generated bits at each stage of the algorithm, and all previous bits are ignored. This eases the success analysis of the algorithm since the probability of passing each Correlate test is independent in this case. Therefore, if the private key has been parsed into m distinct parts, and the attacker applies a Correlate test to each of the m parts, the probability that the correct private key is recovered is γ^m, assuming the same threshold C is used for each Correlate test.

The only issue yet to be addressed is specifying the values that p_0 and p_1 should take. If the distribution of the private key is known, then it is easy to assign values to these parameters. For example, in the RSA setting, the analyses of [8, 16] assume that the entire private key would have approximately an equal number of zeros and ones. Therefore, if we were to use the Correlate' test (equation (1)) in the RSA setting we would set $p_0 = p_1 = 1/2$. Notice that this immediately gives us a threshold-based approach for recovering noisy RSA private keys that have been degraded according to an asymmetric binary channel (i.e., $\alpha \neq \beta$), and such an approach is currently lacking in the literature.

In other settings it may not be possible to accurately assign values to these parameters. The approach we use to overcome this issue is to conduct two separate multinomial tests: one for the 0 bits and another for the 1s. The advantage of using two separate tests is that we do not need to estimate the values of p_0 and p_1, and hence our algorithm's success will not be harmed by a poor estimation of these parameters. For the correct solution, each 0 can flip to a 1 with probability α or it can remain a 0 with probability $1 - \alpha$. Hence, if there are n_0 zeros in the correct solution, then (n_{01}, n_{00}) follows a multinomial distribution with parameters n_0 and $p = (\alpha, 1 - \alpha)$. Similarly, if there are n_1 ones in the correct solution, then (n_{10}, n_{11}) follows a multinomial distribution with parameters n_1 and $p = (\beta, 1 - \beta)$. We may now use the multinomial test to examine each candidate solution without having to estimate p_0 and p_1. Specifically, we define

$$\text{Correlate}^0(s_i, r) := -2n_{00}^i \ln \left(\frac{n_0(1 - \alpha)}{n_{00}^i} \right) - 2n_{01}^i \ln \left(\frac{n_0 \alpha}{n_{01}^i} \right) \qquad (2)$$

and

$$\text{Correlate}^1(s_i, r) := -2n_{11}^i \ln \left(\frac{n_1(1 - \beta)}{n_{11}^i} \right) - 2n_{10}^i \ln \left(\frac{n_1 \beta}{n_{10}^i} \right) . \qquad (3)$$

Then we define $\text{Correlate}_C(s_i, r)$ such that

$$\text{Correlate}_C(s_i, r) = \text{pass} \Leftrightarrow \text{Correlate}^0(s_i, r) < C \wedge \text{Correlate}^1(s_i, r) < C . \qquad (4)$$

Notice now that Correlate^0 and Correlate^1 are functions with one degree of freedom. Therefore the probability that $\text{Correlate}^0 < C$ is $\gamma = \int_0^C \chi_1^2(x)\mathrm{d}x$. The same holds for the probability that $\text{Correlate}^1 < C$.

3   Exponentiation Algorithms

As all discrete log keys considered in this paper are defined over elliptic curves we use the additive notation $Q = aP$ to denote a public key Q, where P is the base point and scalar a is the private key. We write $\mathcal{O}$ for the point at infinity, i.e., the neutral element in that group.

A core part of any DLP-based cryptosystem realised in the elliptic curve setting is a point multiplication routine. Here, a curve point P, also refered to as base point, is multiplied with a scalar $a \in \mathbb{N}$ to obtain another curve point $Q = aP$. The overall performance of this operation depends on various factors, including the representation of field elements, the availability of optimised formulas for basic group operations like point addition and doubling, the representation of curve points, and the scheduler that specifies how the basic group operations are combined to achieve a full point multiplication algorithm (see [2] for a recent survey on available options and trade-offs in all these categories). In the context of cold boot attacks particularly the scheduler seems to be an interesting target to analyse: in ECC-based cryptosystems, secret keys typically correspond with scalars, i.e., with precisely the information the scheduler works with. In the following we give a brief overview over the most relevant such algorithms [5]. We analyse the resilience of specific instances against cold book attacks in later sections of this paper.

The textbook method for performing point multiplication is the *double-and-add* algorithm. Given scalar $a \in \mathbb{N}$ and an appropriate length parameter $\ell \in \mathbb{N}$, it requires that a is represented by its *binary expansion* $[a]_1 = (a_\ell, \ldots, a_0)$, where $a = \sum_{i=0}^{\ell} a_i 2^i$ and $a_\ell, \ldots, a_0 \in \{0, 1\}$. Given $[a]_1$, and denoting 'right-shifting' a by k positions with $a \gg k$, we observe

$$aP = \left(\sum_{i=0}^{\ell} a_i 2^i \right) P = 2 \left(\sum_{i=0}^{\ell-1} a_{i+1} 2^i \right) P + a_0 P = 2(a \gg 1)P + a_0 P \ .$$

This recursion can be unrolled to

$$aP = 2(2(2(\ldots + a_3 P) + a_2 P) + a_1 P) + a_0 P \ . \tag{5}$$

The double-and-add algorithm for computing $Q = aP$ is now immediate: it initializes Q with $\mathcal{O}$ and iteratively updates $Q \leftarrow 2Q + a_i P$, where the a_i are considered 'left-to-right' (i.e., i counts backwards from ℓ down to 0).

3.1   (Windowed) Signed-Digit Representations

A common property of most encodings used to represent elliptic curve points is that group negation is a cheap operation [2,5] and hence point subtraction performs as efficient as point addition. This is exploited in point multiplication algorithms that are based on the *signed-digit representation* of scalars.

Formally, for fixed window size w we denote with $[a]_{\pm w} = (a_\ell, \ldots, a_0)$ any decomposition of $a \in \mathbb{N}$ such that $a = \sum_{i=0}^{\ell} a_i 2^i$ and $a_i \in [-2^{w-1} \mathinner{..} 2^{w-1} - 1]$. As equation (5) still holds if the coefficients a_i are negative or greater than 1, a 'double-and-add-or-subtract' algorithm that operates on such signed-digit representations is readily derived. The key idea is that the extra freedom obtained by allowing coefficients to be large or negative will make it possible to find particularly sparse scalar representations, i.e., representations for which only a minimum number of group additions/subtractions is required.

We describe three common signed-digit normal forms for representing scalars $a \in \mathbb{N}$. The first one, *non-adjacent form* (NAF), limits the digit set to $\{0, \pm 1\}$ and requires that no two consecutive coefficients are non-zero. The second and third are defined in respect to a window size w. Specifically, while the *fixed-window NAF* is an encoding of the form $[a]_{\pm w}$ that requires $a_i = 0$ for all $i \not\equiv 0 \pmod{w}$, the *sliding-window NAF* (wNAF) ensures that all non-zero a_i are odd and all w-length subsequences of $[a]_{\pm w}$ contain at most one such element. All three types of encoding are unique. Note that storing a NAF or wNAF might require one extra digit over the plain binary expansion. For instance, consider that the binary expansion of the decimal number 15 is the sequence $(1, 1, 1, 1)$, while its NAF is $(1, 0, 0, 0, \bar{1})$, where we write $\bar{1}$ for -1.

Algorithm 1 gives instructions on how to derive the wNAF of a scalar $a \in \mathbb{N}$. Observe that the computation is conducted in a greedy right-to-left fashion, with a $(w-1)$-look-ahead. As the latter property will become relevant in our later analyses, we state it formally.

Fact 1 (Suffix property of wNAF). *Fix a scalar $a \in \mathbb{N}$ and a window size w. Denote a's binary expansion with $(a_\ell, \ldots, a_0)$ and its wNAF with $(b_\ell, \ldots, b_0)$, for an appropriate length parameter ℓ. Then for all $0 \le t \le \ell - w + 1$ it holds that $(b_t, \ldots, b_0)$ is fully determined by $(a_{t+w-1}, \ldots, a_0)$.*

Algorithm 1 Textbook wNAF encoding	**Algorithm 2** PolarSSL's comb encoding
Input: scalar a, length parameter ℓ, window size w	**Input:** odd scalar a, parameters w, d
Output: wNAF $(b_\ell, \ldots, b_0)$	**Output:** coefficients $K^d, (\sigma^{d-1}, K^{d-1}), \ldots, (\sigma^0, K^0)$
1: **for** $i \leftarrow 0$ to ℓ **do**	1: **for** $i \leftarrow 0$ to $d-1$ **do**
2: **if** a is odd **then**	2: $\bar{K}^i \leftarrow (a_{i+(w-1)d}, \ldots, a_{i+d}, a_i)$
3: $b_i \leftarrow a \operatorname{smod} 2^w$	3: $K^0 \leftarrow \bar{K}^0$ and $c \leftarrow (0, \ldots, 0)$
4: **else**	4: **for** $i \leftarrow 1$ to $d-1$ **do**
5: $b_i \leftarrow 0$	5: **if** $\bar{K}_0^i = 0$ **then**
6: $a \leftarrow (a - b_i) \gg 1$	6: $(c, K^i) \leftarrow \bar{K}^i \boxplus K^{i-1} \boxplus c$ and $\sigma^{i-1} \leftarrow -1$
7: **return** $(b_\ell, \ldots, b_0)$	7: **else**
	8: $(c, K^i) \leftarrow \bar{K}^i \boxplus c$ and $\sigma^{i-1} \leftarrow +1$
	9: **return** $c, (+1, K^{d-1}), \ldots, (\sigma^0, K^0)$

Fig. 1. In Algorithm 1, operator 'smod' computes signed remainders of integer divisions by powers of two. Precisely, for integers a, b we have $b = a \operatorname{smod} 2^w$ iff $\exists k : a = k2^w + b \wedge b \in [-2^{w-1} .. 2^{w-1} - 1]$. In Algorithm 2, for same-size bit-vectors $\alpha, \beta, \gamma, \delta, \epsilon$ we write $(\alpha, \beta) = \gamma \boxplus \delta$ iff $2\alpha_i + \beta_i = \gamma_i + \delta_i$ for all i. Correspondingly we write $(\alpha, \beta) = \gamma \boxplus \delta \boxplus \epsilon$ iff $2\alpha_i + \beta_i = \gamma_i + \delta_i + \epsilon_i$. That is, the addition is bit-wise and the sum is stored in β_i, with α_i taking the carry.

3.2 Point Multiplication in OpenSSL

We give details about the elliptic curve point multiplication routine used in OpenSSL. Specifically, we studied the code from file `crypto/ec/ec_mult.c` of

OpenSSL version 1.0.1h from March 2012, which is the latest stable release. Relevant for this work is particularly the function `compute_wNAF` defined in line 193, which computes a so-called *modified wNAF*. In brief, while a regular wNAF requires every w-length subsequence of digits to contain at most one non-zero element, in modified wNAFs [15] this requirement is relaxed for the most significant non-zero position, in order to potentially allow saving a final doubling operation (see the full version [17] for further details). OpenSSL's `compute_wNAF` function computes the modified wNAF with default window size $w = 4$ (see line 816). The resulting coefficients $b_i \in [-2^{w-1} .. 2^{w-1} - 1]$ are encoded into an array of octets (data type '`signed char`'), using a standard two-complement in-memory representation. For instance, we have $-3 \mapsto$ `11111101` and $+1 \mapsto$ `00000001`.

3.3   Comb-Based Methods

The wNAF method for point multiplication aims at requiring less point additions than the double-and-add technique; the number of doubling operations, however, remains invariant (or is even increased). In contrast, comb-based methods [14] get along with significantly fewer doublings—at the expense of some precomputation dependent on the base point. In the following we give a rudimentary introduction to comb-based multiplication techniques. See [5] for further details.

Fix a base point P and parameters $w, d \in \mathbb{N}$. For any scalar $a \in \mathbb{N}$ with $0 \leq a < 2^{wd}$ let $[a]_1 = (a_{wd-1}, \ldots, a_0)$ denote its binary expansion. For all $i \in [0 .. d - 1]$ let $K^i = (K^i_{w-1}, \ldots, K^i_0)$ where $K^i_j = a_{i+jd}$ as illustrated in Figure 2. That is, as values $K^i_j \in \{0, 1\}$ are assigned such that

$$a = \sum_{i=0}^{wd-1} 2^i a_i = \sum_{i=0}^{d-1} \sum_{j=0}^{w-1} 2^{i+jd} K^i_j = \sum_{i=0}^{d-1} 2^i \sum_{j=0}^{w-1} 2^{jd} K^i_j \ ,$$

we have that

$$aP = \sum_{i=0}^{d-1} 2^i T(K^i_{w-1}, \ldots, K^i_0) \quad \text{where} \quad T: (k_{w-1}, \ldots, k_0) \mapsto \sum_{j=0}^{w-1} 2^{jd} k_j P \ .$$

The fundamental idea behind comb-based point multiplication is to precompute table T; as we have seen, the remaining part of the operation can then be conducted with not more than d additions and doublings.

As first observed by Hedabou *et al.* [6], implementations of the described point multiplication method might offer only limited resilience against side-channel attacks based on simple power analysis (SPA). This comes from the fact that adding neutral element $T(0, \ldots, 0) = \mathcal{O}$ to an accumulator is an event that is likely recognizable by analysing power traces.

To mitigate the threat, [6] proposes a comb-based scheduler where situation $K^i = (0, \ldots, 0)$ does not occur. In a nutshell, it (a) considers only odd scalars (this guarantees $K^0 \neq (0, \ldots, 0)$), (b) introduces for each $i \in [0 .. d - 1]$ a flag $\sigma^i \in \{\pm 1\}$ that defaults to $\sigma^i = +1$ and indicates whether the corresponding K^i should be considered 'positive' or 'negative', and (c) examines

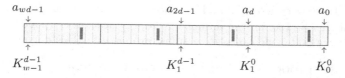

Fig. 2. Visualization of the comb method, for parameters $(w, d) = (4, 10)$. The cells represent the bits of the scalar, the bold rectangles mark the prongs of a comb positioned at offset $i = 2$.

vectors $K^1, \ldots, K^{d-1}$ (in that order) and for each particular K^i that is equal to $(0, \ldots, 0)$ it updates $K^i \leftarrow K^{i-1}$ and $\sigma^{i-1} \leftarrow -1$. Observe that restriction (a) does not impose a real limitation in groups of prime order q because $aP = -(-aP) = -(q-a)P$ and either a or $q-a$ is odd. Observe also that the steps introduced in (c) do not affect the overall outcome of the point multiplication as for all integers x we have $x = 2 \cdot x + (-1) \cdot x$.

3.4   Point Multiplication in PolarSSL

We analysed the source code of the point multiplication routine deployed in PolarSSL[1] version 1.3.8, published on July 11 2014. The scheduler (function `ecp_comb_fixed` in file `library/ecp.c`) is comb-based, and comments in the code give explicit credit to the results of [6]. However, as a matter of fact the actually implemented algorithm significantly improves on the referred-to work, as we detail below. We believe that this is the first description of this point multiplication method in the academic literature.

PolarSSL borrows from [6] both the restriction to handle only odd scalars and the introduction of flags $\sigma^i \in \{\pm 1\}$ that indicate whether corresponding K^i are considered 'positive' or 'negative'. Novel is that the iteration over $K^1, \ldots, K^{d-1}$ that before was solely concerned about fixing the $K^i = (0, \ldots, 0)$ condition is now replaced by an iteration over the same values where action is taken roughly every second time, namely whenever $K_0^i = 0$. Concretely, in this case the algorithm sets $\sigma^{i-1} \leftarrow -1$ (similarly to [6]) and replaces K^i by $K^i \boxplus K^{i-1}$, where addition '$\boxplus$' is understood position-wise, carrying over into K^{i+1}. This method ensures that all K^i have $K_0^i = 1$, and effectively makes precomputed table T half-size. On the downside, for recording the carries of the final '$\boxplus$' step, vector $K^{d-1}, \ldots, K^0$ has to be extended by an auxiliary component K^d. The details on the procedure are given in Algorithm 2.

We conclude by describing how resulting sequence $K^d, (\sigma^{d-1}, K^{d-1}), \ldots, (\sigma^0, K^0)$ is encoded in computer memory. PolarSSL imposes the requirement $w \in [2 .. 7]$ (in practice $w \in \{4, 5\}$ is used, see line 1382 of `ecp.c`) and can hence store each K^i in a separate octet (data type 'unsigned char'). The remaining eighth bit is used to store the corresponding sign indicator; precisely, $\sigma^i = +1$

---

[1] Available at https://polarssl.org.

and $\sigma^i = -1$ are encoded as 0 and 1, respectively. For example, if $w = 3$ and $\sigma^i = -1$ and $K^i = (1, 0, 1)$, the in-memory representation is 10000101.

Similarly to Fact 1 we can state a suffix property for this encoding.

Fact 2 (Suffix property of PolarSSL's comb encoding). *Fix a scalar $a \in \mathbb{N}$ and parameters w, d. Denote a's binary expansion with $(a_{wd-1}, \ldots, a_0)$, its comb encoding with $(\bar{K}^{d-1}, \ldots, \bar{K}^0)$ where $\bar{K}^i_j = a_{i+jd}$, and its PolarSSL comb encoding with $(K^d, \sigma^{d-1}, K^{d-1}, \ldots, \sigma^0, K^0)$. Then it holds for all $1 \le t \le d$ that $(K^{t-1}, \sigma^{t-2}, K^{t-2}, \ldots, \sigma^0, K^0)$ is fully determined by $(\bar{K}^{t-1}, \ldots, \bar{K}^0)$.*

4   General Procedures for Recovering Noisy Keys

We present next our algorithms that recover the private keys of DL-based cryptosystems from noisy memory images. Separate algorithms are proposed for OpenSSL and PolarSSL and, thus, each will have its own analysis of success probability. We start with specifying the attack model.

4.1   Attack Model

Both in OpenSSL and PolarSSL, discrete log secret keys and their NAF or comb encodings reside in computer memory simultaneously, at least for a short period of time. Our cold boot attack model hence assumes that the adversary can obtain noisy versions of the original private key and its encoding, and aims at recovering the private key. We assume that a 0 bit will flip with probability $\alpha = \mathbb{P}(0 \to 1)$ and a 1 bit will flip with probability $\beta = \mathbb{P}(1 \to 0)$. Furthermore, we assume that the attacker knows the values of α and β. Such an assumption is possible because an adversary can easily estimate using an analysis similar to [7]. We refer the reader to that paper for the details.

4.2   NAF Encodings

Algorithm 3 attempts to recover a key that has been encoded with either the textbook wNAF or the modified NAF of OpenSSL. It takes several inputs: the public key, $Q = aP$; the noisy memory image, $\mathcal{M}^*$; the length of the private key, ℓ; the window size, w; a variable parameter, t; a constant k. We first discuss the textbook NAF, for which $k = 0$. The algorithm will output either a (the private key) or $\bot$, which represents failure. The recovery procedure begins by initialising a set $CandSet$ to be empty. The set $CandSet$ will store (partial) candidate solutions for the private key a. At each stage of the algorithm we wish to compute t new wNAF digits for each candidate solution. To be certain of outputting the first t signed digits of the wNAF, the algorithm requires knowledge of the least $t + w - 1$ bits of the binary representation (cf. Fact 1). Hence, the first stage of the algorithm (cf. lines 1–5) takes all bit strings of length $t + w - 1$ (giving us the ability to calculate the least t signed digits of the wNAF), converts them to integers, then calculates their corresponding wNAFs for positions

$b_{t-1}, \ldots, b_0$ (prepending zeros if necessary, and ignoring any b_j for $j \geq t$ if they exist). The algorithm then compares each bit string and its corresponding wNAF against $\mathcal{M}^*$ via the Correlate function (see Section 2). If the candidate passes the Correlate test, then the candidate solution is added to the set $CandSet$, otherwise it is discarded. Once all bit strings of length $t + w - 1$ have been checked, we move on to the second stage of the algorithm (cf. lines 6–12). We first initialise a set $CandSet'$ to be empty. For each string x in $CandSet$, we prepend all bit strings of length t to x (giving us the ability to compute the next t signed digits of the wNAF). We then calculate the wNAFs of (the integer conversions of) all the strings. Again, we prepend zeros to the wNAF if necessary, and we ignore any b_j for $j \geq 2t$. Then the algorithm compares each bit string and its corresponding wNAF against $\mathcal{M}^*$ via the Correlate function. If the candidate solution passes the test it is added to $CandSet'$. When all appropriate strings have been checked, we overwrite $CandSet \leftarrow CandSet'$. If we let ℓ' denote the length of the partial candidates, then we repeat the previous stage of the algorithm until $\ell' > \ell - t$ (because, at this point, prepending t bits to the candidate solutions would result in them having a greater length than the private key a). At this juncture the algorithm will prepend all bit-strings of length $\ell - \ell'$ to all the strings in $CandSet$ (cf. lines 13–16). Each of these new strings x is then compared against the public key $Q = aP$, via the calculation xP. If there is a match with $Q = aP$, then the algorithm outputs x, otherwise the algorithm outputs $\perp$.

Algorithm 3 Generic key-recovery for textbook and OpenSSL wNAF.

Input: noisy memory image $\mathcal{M}^*$, reference public key $Q = aP$, parameters ℓ, w, t, k;
    use $k = 0$ for textbook wNAF recovery, and $k > 0$ otherwise.
Output: secret key a or $\perp$

1: $CandSet \leftarrow \emptyset$	10: if Correlate($\mathcal{M}_x, \mathcal{M}^*$) = pass **then**
2: **for all** $x \in \{0,1\}^{t+w-1}$ **do**	11: add x to $CandSet'$
3: calculate partial representation $\mathcal{M}_x$ of x	12: $CandSet \leftarrow CandSet'$
4: if Correlate($\mathcal{M}_x, \mathcal{M}^*$) = pass **then**	13: **for all** $x \in \{0,1\}^{k + (\ell - k - w + 1 \bmod t)} \times CandSet$ **do**
5: add x to $CandSet$	14: $a \leftarrow \sum_{i=0}^{\ell-1} 2^i x_i$
6: **for** $i \leftarrow 2$ **to** $\lfloor (\ell - k + 1 - w)/t \rfloor$ **do**	15: if $Q = aP$ **then**
7: $CandSet' \leftarrow \emptyset$	16: **return** a
8: **for all** $x \in \{0,1\}^t \times CandSet$ **do**	17: **return** $\perp$
9: calculate partial representation $\mathcal{M}_x$ of x	

We will now discuss the modifications that we make for the OpenSSL implementation of the wNAF encoding. First, we will discuss how the textbook wNAF is converted to the modified wNAF used in OpenSSL. If the most significant $w+1$ digits of the standard wNAF (excluding leading zeros) are a 1, followed by $w - 1$ zeros, followed by a negative signed-digit $\bar{b}$, then we apply a transformation to the leading $w + 1$ digits as follows:

$$1 \underbrace{0 \ldots 0}_{w-1} \bar{b} \quad \mapsto \quad 01 \underbrace{0 \ldots 0}_{w-2} \beta \ ,$$

where $\beta := 2^{w-1} - b$. Hence, the textbook wNAF is only affected in (at most) the most significant $w + 1$ digits (excluding leading zeros). Algorithm 3 relies on the fact that textbook wNAFs can be built up in a bit-by-bit fashion from the least significant bit (cf. Fact 1), but this is no longer possible with the modified wNAF. Therefore, when dealing with the OpenSSL NAF, we include an extra parameter $k > 0$ in Algorithm 3, where $k \in \mathbb{N}^{>0}$. The only difference is that instead of entering the final stage of the algorithm when $\ell' > \ell - t$, we now enter the final stage when $\ell' > \ell - t - k$. That is, we stop k bits earlier than with $k = 0$, and then the final stage appends $\ell - \ell'$ bits to each string in $CandSet$ and checks whether any of these new strings matches the private key, a. The reasoning behind this is that if the bit representation of an integer has a leading 1 in position i, then the standard wNAF will only be affected in positions $i + 1$ to $i - w + 1$. In Algorithm 3, at most we compute $\ell - k - w + 1$ signed digits for each candidate solution. For a uniformly random private key a, the higher we set k, the more likely it is that the textbook wNAF and modified wNAF of a agree in the positions our algorithm computes (since a uniformly random key is more likely to have a leading 1 in bit positions $\ell - 1$ to $\ell - k - 1$, meaning the first $\ell - k - w + 1$ signed digits remain unaffected). This will be discussed in more detail in Section 4.4. However, there is a trade-off between running-time and success. A higher k results in a higher success, but the last stage of Algorithm 3 appends bit-strings of at least length k to all surviving candidates. Hence, the greater k is, the longer the running-time of this final phase. A typical value for k would be below 10.

4.3   Comb Encodings

In this section we consider key-recovery for comb-based methods. The textbook comb encoding together with the original key represents merely a repetition code, and there are standard techniques to recover the key for such a code. Hence, we shall proceed straight to the discussion of PolarSSL combs. To prevent side-channel attacks (cf. Section 3.3), the PolarSSL comb uses a lookahead algorithm, so we will need a more sophisticated algorithm than the standard techniques used for repetition codes. The pseudocode for our algorithm can be found in Algorithm 4. The inputs are: the noisy memory image, $\mathcal{M}^*$; the public key, $Q = aP$; the length of the comb (i.e., the number of prongs), w; the number of comb positions, d; and a variable parameter t. To calculate component K^0 of the comb requires knowledge of bits $a_{(w-1)d}, a_d, \ldots, a_0$ (and only these bits). If we want to calculate K^1 and σ^0, we additionally need bits $a_{1+(w-1)d}, a_{1+d}, \ldots, a_1$, and so on (cf. Fact 2). Our algorithm considers t-many comb components at each stage. During the first stage (cf. lines 1–9) we wish to compute $K^{t-1}, (\sigma^{t-2}, K^{t-2}), \ldots, (\sigma^0, K^0)$ for each candidate solution. To calculate these components only requires knowledge of tw bits (in the appropriate positions of the key). Since PolarSSL only handles odd scalars, there are 2^{tw-1} candidate solutions across these tw bits. For each of these candidate strings, we compare the bits of the string x and its comb with the noisy versions via the Correlate function. If the candidate passes the Correlate test, the string is added to $\mathcal{C}andSet$ (which we initialize to empty), otherwise it is discarded. We then (cf. lines 10–20) repeat the procedure by combining each surviving candidate with all possible bit combinations in the tw positions that will allow us to compute the next t comb components, which are $K^{2t-1}, (\sigma^{2t-2}, K^{2t-2}), \ldots, (\sigma^t, K^t)$. If ℓ' denotes the length of the current candidates, the algorithm exits this particular For loop when $dw - \ell' \leq tw$ (i.e., when adding t more $\bar{K}^j$ would result in there being more $\bar{K}^j$ than exist for the private key). At this point, the algorithm fills in all the missing bits with all possible combinations (cf. lines 21–26). Then the algorithm checks whether any of the strings is a match for the private key (by using the public information $Q = aP$). If there is a match, the algorithm outputs the string, otherwise it outputs $\perp$.

Algorithm 4 Generic key-recovery algorithm for PolarSSL comb method.

Input: noisy memory image $\mathcal{M}^*$, reference public key $Q = aP$, parameters d, w, t
Output: secret key a or $\perp$

1: $\mathcal{C}andSet \leftarrow \emptyset$
2: **for all** $x \in \{0,1\}^{tw-1} \times \{1\}$ **do**
3:     **for** $j \leftarrow 0$ to $t - 1$ **do**
4:         $\bar{K}^j \leftarrow (x_{(j+1)w-1}, \ldots, x_{jw})$
5:     compute $K^{t-1}, (\sigma^{t-2}, K^{t-2}), \ldots, (\sigma^0, K^0)$
6:     using lines 3–8 of Algorithm 2
7:     calculate partial representation $\mathcal{M}_x$
8:     **if** Correlate$(\mathcal{M}_x, \mathcal{M}^*)$ = pass **then**
9:         add x to $\mathcal{C}andSet$
10: **for** $i \leftarrow 2$ to $\lceil d/t \rceil - 1$ **do**
11:     $\mathcal{C}andSet' \leftarrow \emptyset$
12:     **for all** $x \in \{0,1\}^{tw} \times \mathcal{C}andSet$ **do**
13:         **for** $j \leftarrow 0$ to $it - 1$ **do**
14:             $\bar{K}^j \leftarrow (x_{(j+1)w-1}, \ldots, x_{jw})$
15:         compute $K^{it-1}, (\sigma^{it-2}, K^{it-2}), \ldots, (\sigma^0, K^0)$
16:         using lines 3–8 of Algorithm 2
17:         calculate partial representation $\mathcal{M}_x$
18:         **if** Correlate$(\mathcal{M}_x, \mathcal{M}^*)$ = pass **then**
19:             add x to $\mathcal{C}andSet'$
20:     $\mathcal{C}andSet \leftarrow \mathcal{C}andSet'$
21: **for all** $x \in \{0,1\}^{wd-(\lceil d/t \rceil-1)tw} \times \mathcal{C}andSet$ **do**
22:     **for** $j \leftarrow 0$ to $d - 1$ **do**
23:         $\bar{K}^j \leftarrow (x_{(j+1)w-1}, \ldots, x_{jw})$
24:     $a \leftarrow \sum_{j=0}^{d-1} \sum_{i=0}^{w-1} 2^{j+id} \bar{K}_i^j$
25:     **if** $Q = aP$ **then**
26:         **return** a
27: **return** $\perp$

Remark 1. We note that in some cases there is a simple way to slightly increase the efficiency of Algorithm 4. If ℓ is the length of the private key, but $\ell \neq wd$, then the private key will have to be prepended with $wd - \ell$ zero bits. Algorithm 4 can be improved by utilising this information and only considering candidate solutions with zeros in these particular positions. However, as in practice $w = 4$ or $w = 5$ is used and we consider $\ell = 160$ in our simulations, there will be no need for prepended zeros and our algorithm will run exactly as presented in Algorithm 4.

Remark 2 (Optimality of Algorithms 3 and 4). We do not claim that Algorithms 3 or 4 are the optimal procedures for recovering keys in their respective scenarios. However, these algorithms are appealing because we are able to provide a theoretical analysis of the success rate (cf. Section 2). Furthermore, the experimental results we obtain from these algorithms are good in practice, as we shall see in the coming sections.

4.4   Success Analysis of OpenSSL Implementation

We now analyse the success probability of Algorithm 3 when combined with the Correlate test from Section 2. The success probability is relatively straightforward to calculate if the input is an image of a textbook wNAF: The correct candidate will pass the Correlate test (equation (4)) with probability γ^2, where $\gamma = \int_0^C \chi_1^2(x)\mathrm{d}x$. Hence, the probability of recovering the correct key would be $\gamma^{2 \cdot \lfloor (\ell+1-w)/t \rfloor}$ because there are $\lfloor (\ell + 1 - w)/t \rfloor$ Correlate tests to pass and the probability of passing each test is independent (because Correlate considers only the newly computed bits at each stage). However, since a modified NAF is used in OpenSSL, the corresponding analysis of success will differ slightly. Fortunately, the difference between textbook NAF and modified NAF is only in the most significant $w + 1$ bits (and sometimes there is no difference at all): If the leading 1 bit of the discrete logarithm key is in position i then, at most, only signed digits $i - w + 1$ to $i + 1$ of the standard wNAF will be affected by the transformation to the modified wNAF. Therefore the standard and modified wNAFs will agree up to position $i - w$. Algorithm 3 only computes the least significant $j = \ell - k - w + 1 - (\ell - k - w + 1 \bmod t)$ digits of the wNAF, i.e., $b_{j-1}, \ldots, b_0$. Therefore, we must now bound the probability that a randomly chosen private key's standard wNAF is equal to its modified NAF up to digit b_{j-1}. If the private key has a 1 bit anywhere between positions $j + w - 1$ and $\ell - 1$ then the computed NAF digits will be identical to the modified wNAF digits up to position $j - 1$, and then the multinomial test will behave exactly as expected (having probability γ of passing each test). The probability of a 1 bit appearing in any of these positions is precisely

$$1 - 2^{-k-(\ell-k-w+1 \bmod t)} \ .$$

If we let M-NAF denote the modified wNAF, and wNAF_{j-1} (resp. M-NAF_{j-1}) denote digits 0 to $j - 1$ of wNAF (resp. M-NAF), then it follows that

$$\begin{aligned}
\mathbb{P}(\text{success}) &= \mathbb{P}(\text{success}|w\text{-NAF}_{j-1} = \text{M-NAF}_{j-1}) \cdot \mathbb{P}(w\text{-NAF}_{j-1} = \text{M-NAF}_{j-1}) \\
&\quad + \mathbb{P}(\text{success}|w\text{-NAF}_{j-1} \neq \text{M-NAF}_{j-1}) \cdot \mathbb{P}(w\text{-NAF}_{j-1} \neq \text{M-NAF}_{j-1}) \\
&\geq \left(1 - 2^{-k-(\ell-k-w+1 \bmod t)}\right) \cdot \gamma^{2 \cdot \lfloor (\ell-k+1-w)/t \rfloor} \ .
\end{aligned}$$

Thus, by setting the thresholds k and C (and, hence, γ) appropriately, we can achieve any desired success rate (potentially at the expense of a long running time).

   If either $\alpha = 0$ or $\beta = 0$ our algorithm has a slightly different analysis. Since neither α nor β will be zero in practice, we have relegated this analysis to the full version [17].

4.5   Success Analysis of PolarSSL Implementation

Given the previous discussion regarding the success of recovering keys of the NAF algorithms, it is now very easy to analyse the success of Algorithm 4. It is clear from the algorithm that there are $\lceil d/t \rceil - 1$ Correlate tests to pass. The correlate function is in equation (4), and the correct candidate has probability γ^2 of passing the test, where $\gamma = \int_0^C \chi_1^2(x)\mathrm{d}x$. Since each Correlate test only considers the newly calculated bits, the probability of passing each Correlate test is independent, so we have $\mathbb{P}(\text{success}) = \gamma^{2 \cdot (\lceil d/t \rceil - 1)}$.

5   Implemented Simulations of Key Recovery

We present the results of some simulations of Algorithms 3 and 4 using the Correlate test from equation (4). Unless otherwise stated, we ran 100 tests for each set of parameters. The results for OpenSSL can be seen in Table 1a and those for PolarSSL in Table 1b. The values displayed in these tables are merely to support the validity of our theoretical analysis, and they do not represent the practical limits of our algorithms. However, it is clear that any algorithm attempting key recovery in the PolarSSL and OpenSSL settings will not be able to match the performance of the RSA algorithms. We discuss the reasons why in the full version [17]. For each set of parameters, the table shows the predicted theoretical success of the algorithms and the success rate we achieved with our 100 simulations. Note that as the noise rate increases the success rate will slowly decline. However, for OpenSSL, the success rate for $\beta = 0.15$ was higher than for $\beta = 0.10$, despite all other parameters being the same. This is merely an outlier, which is a result of the limited number of simulations we ran. If we were to perform a much larger number of simulations, we expect this outlier to disappear. All values we have used for α and β are practical, but higher values of β are much rarer in practice. For small values of β (which are most common) our algorithms have a good success rate. For example, for OpenSSL we have a success rate of 45% when $\beta = 0.05$. Furthermore, for small values such as this we could significantly improve the success by increasing theshold C. For such small values of β this would not greatly affect the running time. We note that the practical success is generally much higher than the predicted success. There is an easy explanation for this, which we will defer to the full version [17].

6   Conclusions

We propose key-recovery algorithms for various discrete log cryptosystems, with particular emphasis on the widely deployed PolarSSL and OpenSSL implementations. These algorithms represent a large improvement over previous key-recovery algorithms for discrete-log cold boot attacks. We provide a theoretical analysis that lower-bounds the success of our algorithms. Furthermore, the statistical test we use in our framework provides an avenue to obtain arbitrary success rates in the RSA setting when the errors are asymmetric. Such results were only previously available in the symmetric setting. We provide results of several key-recovery simulations, both for PolarSSL and OpenSSL, that fully support our theoretical analyses and show that our attacks are practical.

Table 1. Results from simulations of cold boot attacks against the point multipliers of OpenSSL and PolarSSL. All simulations used a 160-bit key. The estimated success, based on the convergence to the chi-squared distribution, is in the columns labelled 'χ^2 est.'

w	α	β	t	C	k	χ^2 est.	prac. suc.
2	0.001	0.01	7	6	3	0.51	0.92
2	0.001	0.05	10	3.5	3	0.15	0.45
2	0.001	0.10	10	3.5	3	0.15	0.17
2	0.001	0.15	10	3.5	3	0.15	0.20
2	0.001	0.20	14	2	3	0.02	0.07
2	0.001	0.25	12	2	3	0.01	0.06
2	0.001	0.30	12	2	3	0.01	0.04
2	0.001	0.35	14	0.75	3	0	0.02

(a) OpenSSL

w	d	α	β	t	C	χ^2 est.	prac. suc.
4	40	0.001	0.01	2	7	0.73	0.81
4	40	0.001	0.02	2	5	0.38	0.65
4	40	0.001	0.03	2	4	0.17	0.60
4	40	0.001	0.05	2	3.5	0.09	0.58
4	40	0.001	0.06	2	3	0.04	0.55
4	40	0.001	0.07	2	3	0.04	0.52
4	40	0.001	0.08	2	2.5	0.01	0.37
4	40	0.001	0.10	2	2.5	0.01	0.08

(b) PolarSSL

Acknowledgments. The authors were supported by EPSRC Leadership Fellowship EP/H005455/1. The first author was also supported by a Sofja Kovalevskaja Award of the Alexander von Humboldt Foundation, and the German Federal Ministry for Education and Research.

References

1. Albrecht, M., Cid, C.: Cold boot key recovery by solving polynomial systems with noise. In: Lopez, J., Tsudik, G. (eds.) ACNS 2011. LNCS, vol. 6715, pp. 57–72. Springer, Heidelberg (2011)
2. Bos, J.W., Costello, C., Longa, P., Naehrig, M.: Selecting elliptic curves for cryptography: An efficiency and security analysis. Cryptology ePrint Archive, Report 2014/130 (2014). http://eprint.iacr.org/2014/130
3. Gutmann, P.: Data remanence in semiconductor devices. In: 10th USENIX Security Symposium USENIX, Washington. D.C., USA, August 13–17, 2001
4. Halderman, J.A., Schoen, S.D., Heninger, N., Clarkson, W., Paul, W., Calandrino, J.A., Feldman, A.J., Appelbaum, J., Felten, E.W.: Lest we remember: cold-boot attacks on encryption keys. Commun. ACM **52**(5), 91–98 (2009)
5. Hankerson, D., Menezes, A., Vanstone, S.: Guide to Elliptic Curve Cryptography. Springer (2004)
6. Hedabou, M., Pinel, P., Bénéteau, L.: A comb method to render ECC resistant against side channel attacks. Cryptology ePrint Archive, Report 2004/342 (2004). http://eprint.iacr.org/2004/342
7. Henecka, W., May, A., Meurer, A.: Correcting errors in RSA private keys. In: Rabin, T. (ed.) CRYPTO 2010. LNCS, vol. 6223, pp. 351–369. Springer, Heidelberg (2010)
8. Heninger, N., Shacham, H.: Reconstructing RSA private keys from random key bits. In: Halevi, S. (ed.) CRYPTO 2009. LNCS, vol. 5677, pp. 1–17. Springer, Heidelberg (2009)

9. Jonsson, J., Kaliski, B.S.: Public-Key Cryptography Standards (PKCS) #1: RSA Cryptography Specifications Version 2.1 (RFC 3447) (2003). https://www.ietf.org/rfc/rfc3447.txt

10. Kamal, A.A., Youssef, A.M.: Applications of SAT solvers to AES key recovery from decayed key schedule images. Cryptology ePrint Archive, Report 2010/324 (2010). http://eprint.iacr.org/2010/324

11. Kunihiro, N., Honda, J.: RSA meets DPA: Recovering RSA secret keys from noisy analog data. In: Batina, L., Robshaw, M. (eds.) CHES 2014. LNCS, vol. 8731, pp. 261–278. Springer, Heidelberg (2014)

12. Kunihiro, N., Shinohara, N., Izu, T.: Recovering RSA secret keys from noisy key bits with erasures and errors. In: Kurosawa, K., Hanaoka, G. (eds.) PKC 2013. LNCS, vol. 7778, pp. 180–197. Springer, Heidelberg (2013)

13. Lee, H.T., Kim, H.T., Baek, Y.-J., Cheon, J.H.: Correcting errors in private keys obtained from cold boot attacks. In: Kim, H. (ed.) ICISC 2011. LNCS, vol. 7259, pp. 74–87. Springer, Heidelberg (2012)

14. Lim, C.H., Lee, P.J.: More flexible exponentiation with precomputation. In: Desmedt, Y.G. (ed.) CRYPTO 1994. LNCS, vol. 839, pp. 95–107. Springer, Heidelberg (1994)

15. Möller, B.: Improved techniques for fast exponentiation. In: Lee, P.J., Lim, C.H. (eds.) ICISC 2002. LNCS, vol. 2587, pp. 298–312. Springer, Heidelberg (2003)

16. Paterson, K.G., Polychroniadou, A., Sibborn, D.L.: A coding-theoretic approach to recovering noisy RSA keys. In: Wang, X., Sako, K. (eds.) ASIACRYPT 2012. LNCS, vol. 7658, pp. 386–403. Springer, Heidelberg (2012)

17. Poettering, B., Sibborn, D.: Cold boot attacks in the discrete logarithm setting. Cryptology ePrint Archive, Report 2015/057 (2015). http://eprint.iacr.org/2015/057

18. Sarkar, S., Gupta, S.S., Maitra, S.: Reconstruction and error correction of RSA secret parameters from the MSB side. In: WCC 2011 - Workshop on Coding and Cryptography, pp. 7–16. Paris, France, April 2011

19. Sarkar, S., Maitra, S.: Side channel attack to actual cryptanalysis: Breaking CRT-RSA with low weight decryption exponents. In: Prouff, E., Schaumont, P. (eds.) CHES 2012. LNCS, vol. 7428, pp. 476–493. Springer, Heidelberg (2012)

20. Scheick, L.Z., Guertin, S.M., Swift, G.M.: Analysis of radiation effects on individual DRAM cells. Nuclear Science, IEEE Transactions on $47(6)$, 2534–2538 (2000)

21. Tsow, A.: An improved recovery algorithm for decayed AES key schedule images. In: Jacobson Jr., M.J., Rijmen, V., Safavi-Naini, R. (eds.) sac 2009. lncs, vol. 5867, pp. 215–230. Springer, Heidelberg (2009)

Homomorphic Encryption
and Its Applications

Communication Optimal Tardos-Based Asymmetric Fingerprinting

Aggelos Kiayias[1], Nikos Leonardos[2], Helger Lipmaa[3],
Kateryna Pavlyk[3], and Qiang Tang[1,4(✉)]

[1] National and Kapodistrian University of Athens, Athens, Greece
aggelos@di.uoa.gr
[2] Université Paris Diderot – Paris 7, Paris, France
nleon@liafa.univ-paris-diderot.fr
[3] University of Tartu, Tartu, Estonia
helger.lipmaa@gmail.com, kateryna.pavlyk@ut.ee
[4] University of Connecticut, Storrs, USA
qiang@cse.uconn.edu

Abstract. Asymmetric fingerprinting schemes — introduced by Pfitzmann and Schunter in Eurocrypt 1996 — enable the transmission of a file stored in a server to a set of users so that each user obtains a variation of the file. The security considerations of these schemes are as follows: if any (appropriately bounded) subset of users collude to produce a "pirate" copy of the file, it is always possible for the server to prove to a third party judge the implication of at least one of them, while a malicious server can never implicate innocent users.

Given that asymmetric fingerprinting is supposed to distribute files of substantial size (e.g., media files including video and audio) any communication rate (defined as the size of the file over the total transmission length) less than 1 would render them practically useless. The existence of such schemes is currently open. Building on a rate close to 1 oblivious transfer (constructed from recently proposed rate optimal homomorphic encryption), we present the first asymmetric fingerprinting scheme that is *communication optimal*, i.e., its communication rate is arbitrarily close to 1 (for sufficiently large files) thus resolving this open question. Our scheme is based on Tardos codes, and we prove our scheme secure in an extended formal security model where we also deal with the important but previously unnoticed (in the context of asymmetric fingerprinting) security considerations of *accusation withdrawal* and *adversarial aborts*.

Keywords: Asymmetric fingerprinting · Tardos Code · Rate optimal · Group accusation

1 Introduction

In a fingerprinting scheme, cf. [4], a server (or service provider SP) distributes a file to a set of users. The server has the flexibility to furnish a different version

---

N. Leonardos—Work done while the second author was at University of Athens.

K. Nyberg (ed.): CT-RSA 2015, LNCS 9048, pp. 469–486, 2015.
DOI: 10.1007/978-3-319-16715-2_25

of the file to each user. This is done by splitting the file into segments and offering at least two variations per segment. Given these segments, the file can be assembled in a *fingerprinted* fashion: at each segment the variation obtained corresponds to a symbol over an alphabet. Therefore, each user's file determines a string over that alphabet - the user's fingerprint (e.g., the data M is divided into n blocks, for each block i, there are two versions m_i^0, m_i^1, a user assigned with a binary codeword $b_1, \ldots, b_n$ will receive his versions as $m_1^{b_1} || \ldots || m_n^{b_n}$). The objective here is that if the users collude to produce a "pirate" version of the file by combining their segments, the server is still capable of discovering (at least some) of the identities of the colluding users.

If the SP alone generates the fingerprints for users and directly transmits them the fingerprinted files, we have what is known as a symmetric fingerprinting scheme. As the server is fully trusted in this setting, the security requirement is that malicious users cannot collude to frame any innocent user or evade the tracing algorithm. The subtle issue in this case is that the server and the user are both able to produce a pirate file so when a pirate copy is brought to light, an honest SP cannot provide an "undeniable" proof that a user is at fault and symmetrically an honest user cannot defend herself against a malicious SP that frames her (say, due to e.g., an insider attack on the SP side).

In order to resolve the above issue, [21] introduced asymmetric fingerprinting schemes in which no one (even the server) should be capable to implicate an innocent user. Thus when a dispute happens, the server can provide a convincing proof that a guilty user is at fault. It follows that the server should not be fully aware of the fingerprint of each user (otherwise it is capable of impersonating them) and hence this suggests that the download of the fingerprinted file should be performed in an oblivious manner from the servers' point of view. Now in this case, the Judge could resolve the dispute between the server and a user (i.e., guilty users will be found guilty by the judge while the server will not be able to implicate an innocent user in the eyes of the judge).

In the original papers [21–23] the file transfer stage was treated generically as an instance of secure two party computation. Unfortunately, even with "communication efficient" secure two-party computation [8,10,14,20] the communication overhead of the resulting protocol is prohibitively high (e.g., even with the most communication efficient generic protocols, [10,14], the communication rate — the size of the file over total number of bits transmitted — will be at most 0.5 and their use will impose the additional cost of a prohibitively large CRS which needs to be known a-priori to both client and server). With the discovery of optimal length binary fingerprinting codes by Tardos [26], Charpentier et al. [6] observed that oblivious transfer could be used as a building block for a Tardos-based asymmetric fingerprinting. Their proposed solution however is sub-optimal (it has a rate still at most 0.5) and in order to achieve the fingerprint generation it relies on *commutative encryption*, a primitive not known to be constructible in a way that the resulting scheme can be shown provably secure. Furthermore no complete security analysis is provided in [6] which leaves a number of important security issues unaddressed (specifically "accusation withdrawals" and "selective aborts" – see below).

Achieving rate close to 1 is the most critical open question in the context of asymmetric fingerprinting from an efficiency point of view. Indeed, any asymmetric fingerprinting is particularly sensitive to its communication overhead: the file to be transmitted by the sender can be quite large (e.g., a movie file) and thus any scheme whose communication rate is not close to 1 is likely to be useless in a practical setting. We note that efficient asymmetric fingerprinting schemes can enable more complex applications; e.g., as building blocks for "anonymous buyer-seller watermarking" [24,25]; these systems rely on asymmetric fingerprinting schemes to enable copyright protection (but they do not consider the implementation of such fingerprinting schemes explicitly).

Furthermore, analyzing the security of an asymmetric fingerprinting scheme is involved as the security requirements require that the SP cannot frame an innocent user, while at the same time the malicious users should still not be able to escape from tracing. The analysis should rely both on the security of the protocol and on the property of the code, specifically, no user should be able to produce a pirate file that makes the SP and the judge disagree. Given that Tardos tracing accuses a subset of the users (based on a threshold condition) it is possible for the judge and the SP to disagree on some users. This type of attack has not been considered before; we call it accusation withdrawal as it forces the SP to withdraw an originally made accusation since the judge cannot support it. Ensuring that no accusation withdrawal happens protects the SP from starting accusation procedures that are not going to succeed with high probability. Finally, during the file transfer stage the user may abort. Given that these file transfer procedures can be lengthy (due to the large size of the files to be downloaded) the possibility of an adversary exploiting aborting and restarting as an attack strategy is important to be included in the security model (and in fact we show an explicit attack if many aborts are permitted — see below).

1.1 Our Contributions

Rate-Optimality. We propose the first rate-optimal (rate is defined as the size of the actual data over the size of total communication) asymmetric fingerprinting scheme. Our scheme is based on Tardos codes [26]. To achieve this property, we use a rate optimal 1-out-of-2 oblivious transfer ((2,1)-OT), and a new rate-optimal 1-out-of-2 strong conditional oblivious transfer ((2, 1)-SCOT, [3]). Both are constructed in [16], and they are built on the rate-optimal homomorphic encryption scheme developed in the same paper. Based on these rate optimal protocols, we propose a rate-optimal fingerprinted data transfer protocol (tailored specifically for bias-based codes including Tardos codes).

More precisely, in a fingerprinted data transfer protocol, the sender has as private input two pairs of messages and biases. The sender and the receiver simulate two private biased coin tosses using SCOT and the receiver obtains one message from each pair (which one of the two it receives, is determined by the outcome of the biased coin flip). The actual message transmission is based on the rate optimal OT protocol. Furthermore the sender selects randomly one of the two SCOT-s and revokes its receiver security, i.e., the sender will learn which one of the two versions the receiver has obtained in this SCOT. This partial revocation of receiver-security will enable the sender to correlate "pirate" files that are generated by coalitions of malicious users. Our final scheme inherits the communication efficiency of the underlying SCOT and OT protocols and thus it is communication-optimal: the rate of each data transfer is asymptotically 1.

A Complete Security Analysis in the (extended) Pfitzmann-Schunter Model: we analyze the security of our construction in an *extended* version of the Pfitzmann-Schunder model [22]. The extension we present is two-fold: first we extend the model to capture the setting of multiple accusations. In the original modeling only a single colluder was required to be accused. In the extended model we allow a set of users to be accused. This accommodates accusation algorithms based on Tardos fingerprinting [26] that have this capability. Group accusation in asymmetric schemes needs special care from a security point of view: it makes the system prone to *accusation withdrawal*, the setting where the server will have to withdraw an accusation because the judge is unable to verify it. We demonstrate (through actual implementation experiments, see Fig 2) that the straightforward application of Tardos identification (as may naively be inferred from the description of [6]) does not preclude accusation withdrawal. We subsequently show how to modify the accusation algorithm between judge and server so that no accusation withdrawal can take place. Our second model extension concerns the explicit treatment of the abort operation within the security model: all known asymmetric fingerprinting schemes rely on two-party coin tossing. Given that *fair* coin tossing is known to be unattainable [7] it follows that it may be possible for an adversarial set of users to exploit this weakness and utilize a transmission abort strategy with the purpose of evading detection. We demonstrate that an explicit treatment of this in the security model is essential as if one enables users to restart after an abort, it is possible to completely break server security! (this fact went entirely unnoticed before). By properly controlling aborts and restarts we show how security can be maintained.

2   Rate-Optimal OT and SCOT Protocols

We recall that an OT protocol and a strong conditional OT (SCOT, [3]) protocol for predicate Q (s.t. $Q(x,y) \in \{0,1\}$) implement securely the following functionalities respectively (W.l.o.g., assume $|m_0| = |m_1|$):

$$f_{OT}(b, (m_0, m_1)) = (m_b, \bot), \ f_{Q-SCOT}(x, (y, m_0, m_1)) = (m_{Q(x,y)}, \bot) \ .$$

Here, we will use the rate optimal OT and SCOT protocols derived in [16] from their recently developed rate optimal large-output branching program homomorphic encryption (LHE) scheme. We recall that their LHE scheme enables the receiver to compute on ciphertexts the value $f(x,y)$, where x is his input, y is sender input, and f is an arbitrary function that can be evaluated by a polynomial-size (integer-valued) branching program. In the LHE scheme of [16], the receiver encrypts (by using a variant of the Damgård-Jurik cryptosystem [9]) his input x, and sends the ciphertext $\mathsf{Enc}_r(x)$ to the sender. The sender evaluates privately large-output branching programs like in [15,19], but does it in a communication-preserving manner. Let the output of the evaluation be denoted as $\mathsf{Eval}(P, \mathsf{Enc}_r(x))$, where P is a large-output branching program that evaluates $f(\cdot, y)$ on input x. The sender returns a single "ciphertext" to the receiver, who then (multiple-)decrypts it as in [15,19]. The rate of the LHE scheme is defined as $r = (|x| + |P(x)|)/(|\mathsf{Enc}_r(x)| + |\mathsf{Enc}_r(P(x))|)$. Assuming $|f(x,y)|$ is large, [16] showed by using an intricate analysis how to achieve a rate $1 - o(1)$. We refer to [16] for more information.

Rate-optimal OT. As shown in [16], one can define a rate-optimal $(2, 1)$-oblivious transfer protocol as follows. Let the server have a database (m_0, m_1) and assume that $P[x, (m_0, m_1)] = m_x$ for $x \in \{0, 1\}$. Thus, the size of P is 1. Since rate-optimal $(2, 1)$-OT has many applications, we will call it *oblivious download* (OD). Let $\mathsf{OD}_s[\mathsf{Enc}_r(x), (m_0, m_1)]$ denote the server side computation in this protocol, given client ciphertext $\mathsf{Enc}_r(x)$ and server input (m_0, m_1).

Rate-optimal SCOT. Also, as shown in [16], one can use the LHE of to construct an efficient SCOT protocol for the functionality $f_{Q-\mathsf{SCOT}}(x, (y, m_0, m_1))$, where Q has a polynomial-size branching program (i.e., $Q \in \mathbf{L/poly}$), as follows. Let P' be an efficient branching program that evaluates the predicate $Q(x, y)$. Let P be a large-value branching program, obtained from P' by just replacing the leaf value 0 with m_0 and 1 with m_1. The LHE scheme (and thus also the resulting SCOT protocol) will have computation, linear in the size of P', and communication $(1 + o(1))(|x| + |m_0|)$ and thus rate $1 - o(1)$. In the rest of the paper we will need the next instantiation of a new rate-optimal SCOT protocol.

Rate-optimal SCOT for the LEQ Predicate. Denote $\mathsf{LEQ}(x, y) := [x \leq y]$. It is easy to see that LEQ can be evaluated by a branching program of size and length $\ell := \max(|x|, |y|)$. Thus, one can implement $f_{\mathsf{LEQ}-\mathsf{SCOT}}$ securely in time $\Theta(\ell)$ and rate $1 - o(1)$. Let us denote server computation in this protocol as $\mathsf{LEQ}_s[\mathsf{Enc}_r(x), (y, m_0, m_1)]$.

Remark. The security of the $\mathsf{OD}, \mathsf{SCOT}$ protocols are simple corollaries of the security proofs from [15,16]. Also, one can also use an arbitrary efficient — with communication $o(|m_i|)$ — millionaire's protocol, like the one in [3,12,18] to find out $b = [x < y]$, and then use the oblivious download protocol to implement an optimal-rate SCOT protocol for the LEQ predicate. However, we think that the use of optimal-rate LHE from [16] (instead of composing a millionaire's protocol and an OD protocol) is more elegant.

3   Fingerprinted Data Transfer for Bias-Based Codes

In this section, we will introduce the main building block of our Tardos-based asymmetric fingerprinting scheme, which we call fingerprinted data transfer.

As our fingerprinting scheme relies on the properties of fingerprinting codes (we only focus on binary codes here), let us first recall the basics about fingerprinting codes. A *binary fingerprinting code* [17] is a pair of algorithms (gen, trace), where gen is a probabilistic algorithm taking a number N, an optional number (upper-bound on the detected coalition size) $t \in [N] = \{1, \ldots, N\}$ and security parameter ϵ as input and outputs N bit-strings $\mathcal{C} = \{C_1, \ldots, C_N\}$ (called codewords), where $C_i = c_1^i \ldots c_n^i$ for $i \in [N]$ and a tracing key tk. trace is a deterministic algorithm inputting the tracing key tk and a "pirate" codeword C^*, and outputting a subset $\mathcal{U}_{acc} \subseteq [N]$ of accused users. A code is called *bias-based* [2] if each codeword $C_j = c_1^j \ldots c_n^j$ is sampled according to a vector of biases $\langle p_1, \ldots, p_n \rangle$, where $\forall j \in [N], \forall i \in [n], \Pr[c_i^j = 1] = p_i$, and $p_i \in [0, 1]$.

A fingerprinting code is called $t-collusion$ *resistant* (*fully collusion resistant if $t = N$*) if for any adversary $\mathcal{A}$ who corrupts up to t users (whose indices form a set $\mathcal{U}_{cor} \subset \{1, \cdots, N\}$), and outputs a pirate codeword $C^* = c_1^* \ldots c_n^*$ (which satisfies the marking assumption, i.e., for each $i \in [n], c_i^* = c_i^j$ for some $j \in \mathcal{U}_{cor}$), $\Pr[\mathcal{U}_{acc} = \emptyset$ or $\mathcal{U}_{acc} \not\subseteq \mathcal{U}_{cor} : \mathcal{U}_{acc} \leftarrow \mathsf{trace}(tk, C^*)] \leq \epsilon$ (i.e., the probability that no users are accused or an innocent user is accused is bounded by ε).

We also recall the Tardos code [26] $F_{nt\epsilon}$ here, it has length $n = 100t^2k$, with $k = \log \frac{1}{\epsilon}$. The gen algorithm generates a codeword as follows. For each segment index $j \in [n]$, it chooses a bias $p_j \in [0, 1]$ according to a distribution μ (see [26] for the definition of μ). Each bias satisfies $\frac{1}{300t} \leq p_j \leq 1 - \frac{1}{300t}$, where t is the collusion size. For each codeword $C = c_1 \ldots c_n$ outputted by gen, $\Pr[c_j = 1] = p_j$, and $\Pr[c_j = 0] = 1 - p_j$ for all $j \in [n]$. Regarding security, there is a trace algorithm such that, for any coalition of size at most t, with probability at least $1 - \epsilon^{t/4}$ accuses a member of the coalition, while any non-member is accused with probability at most ϵ.

3.1   Definitions of Fingerprinted Data Transfer

Now we define our main building block of fingerprinted data transfer (FDT for short). Recall that each user should receive a fingerprinted copy of the file according to his codeword. In the case of asymmetric fingerprinting, the segments of the file will be transferred in an oblivious fashion so that the server should be aware of only half of the user fingerprinting code. To be more specific, all segments are transmitted using oblivious transfer to enable the user to receive one of the versions, and for each pair of segments $(2i - 1, 2i)$, where $i \in [n]$, the server will know one of the segments, the version that the user receives.

Intuitively, if we double the length of the fingerprinting code (dividing the file into $2n$ segments), each user is essentially assigned two codewords, one is known to the server, thus the trace algorithm can be executed to identify malicious users; the other one is unknown to the server, and will be revealed to the judge only when dispute happens. A user will be accused only when both codewords are considered contributing to a pirate file. In this way, a malicious SP $\mathcal{S}$ frames an honest user unless innocent users may be accused in the fingerprinting code.

We also need to be careful that if malicious users know which half of the codeword is known to the server, they may collude in a way that every codeword in the collusion only contribute to half of the file thus no one will be accused on both fingerprints. Thus for the segments $(2i - 1, 2i)$ for $i \in [n]$, the index that the segment version is revealed to the server is also oblivious to the user.

The asymmetric fingerprinting scheme will essentially be running FDT (defined below) in parallel for all pairs of the segments $(2i - 1, 2i)$, thus it is enough for us to illustrate the idea by considering only the sub-protocol for one pair of segments. As Tardos code is binary, there are only two versions for each segment. Consider two parties, a sender $\mathcal{S}$ and a receiver $\mathcal{R}$. The sender has two pairs of messages, two rational valued "biases" in $[0, 1]$ and one bit c as inputs. The receiver has no input. After the execution of the FDT protocol, $\mathcal{R}$ will sample one message from each of the two pairs following the binary probability distribution defined by the two biases and $\mathcal{S}$ will learn the output of the receiver for the c-th pair. This describes the ideal operation of the primitive for the case of one pair of segments. It is straightforward to extend to an arbitrary number of pairs. The following is the formal definition of the fingerprinted data transfer for bias-based codes including our main target Tardos code [26]. And following the standard simulation base paradigm [13], we can also define the security of the FDT protocol, and we defer it to the full version.

Definition 1. *A fingerprinted data transfer functionality Π involves two parties, a sender $\mathcal{S}$ and a receiver $\mathcal{R}$. The sender inputs two biases $p_0, p_1 \in [0, 1]$, four messages $(m_0^0, m_0^1), (m_1^0, m_1^1)$, and a bit $c \in \{0, 1\}$; at the end of the protocol, $\mathcal{R}$ outputs $\{m_i^{b_i}\}$ for $i, b_i \in \{0, 1\}$ such that $\Pr[b_i = 1] = p_i$; while $\mathcal{S}$ outputs b_c. We can express this (probabilistic) functionality as:*

$$\Pi[\perp, ((p_0, p_1), (m_0^0, m_0^1, m_1^0, m_1^1), c)] = [(m_0^{b_0}, m_1^{b_1}), b_c], \text{where } \Pr[b_i = 1] = p_i$$

Somewhat similar functionalities have been used for completely different applications, see, e.g. [1,11]. The FDT protocol of Sect. 3.2 might be modified so as to be used in these applications; we omit further discussions.

3.2   A Communication-Optimal Fingerprinted Data Transfer

On the receiver $\mathcal{R}$ side, for each pair of messages, say pair 0, FDT will enable an oblivious sampling of one message from (m_0^0, m_0^1) according to the bias p_0, i.e., $\mathcal{R}$ receives m_0^1 with probability p_0. To enable efficient oblivious sampling, suppose $p_0 \approx t_0/T$ for some t_0, where $T = 2^\ell$ and ℓ is the precision level (this provides an exponentially good approximation). To run a coin tossing protocol to generate a random coin u, $\mathcal{R}$ and the SP $\mathcal{S}$ can utilize a SCOT protocol (e.g., [3]) to transmit the data in a way that the user receives m_0^1 iff $u \le t_0$. Doing this will allow the receiver to get m_0^1 with probability close to $p_0 = t_0/T$. Furthermore, they can run such procedure twice for the two pairs, and then run a $(2, 1)$-OT protocol to reveal one of the bit to the SP.

Unfortunately, directly applying the SCOT protocol from, e.g, [3] will result in a communication rate as low as $1/\ell$, as the sender has to send ℓ ciphertexts with similar size to m_i^0. Moreover, a malicious user may abort after receiving the file without revealing half of his bits. To deal with these concerns, our protocol will be divided into two phases, the first (the handshake phase) samples only the codewords according to the biases that are specified by the sender; the second (the content-transfer phase) transfers the actual content according to the codewords that have been drawn. In our implementation, we will only use the SCOT protocol to sample the distribution (transfer only short messages) and then employ a rate-optimal OT protocol (we call oblivious download, OD for short)to execute the content-transfer after the OT protocol is run in which the SP is the receiver and the SP sees one of the bits. We assume that during the hand-shake phase, the sender and receiver exchange their public keys with the corresponding certificates.

Now we proceed to construct the new fingerprinted data transfer protocol. Suppose the sender has $p_0 = \frac{t_0}{T}$, $p_1 = \frac{t_1}{T}$; these determine two distributions over $\{0,1\}$. The sender also has two pairs of messages as inputs $(m_0^0, m_0^1), (m_1^0, m_1^1)$, and prepares another two pairs of $(h_0^0, h_0^1), (h_1^0, h_1^1)$, where $h_i^b = H(m_i^b)|i|b$ for $i, b \in \{0,1\}$. We assume that H is a collision resistant hash function shared by the sender and the receiver, and Com is a secure (binding and hiding) commitment scheme. We choose Enc_r and Enc_s to be good rate additive homomorphic encryption schemes (e.g. using the Damgard-Jurik [9] encryption to encrypt the message bit by bit as in [16]). Here, $\mathcal{R}$ knows the secret key of Enc_r and $\mathcal{S}$ knows the secret key of Enc_s. Recall that $\mathsf{LEQ}_s[\mathsf{Enc}_r(x), (y, m_0, m_1)]$ denotes the sender computation in a concrete SCOT protocol that implements $f_{\mathsf{LEQ-SCOT}}$, and $\mathsf{OD}_s[\mathsf{Enc}_r(x), (m_0, m_1)]$ denote the computation of the server in this protocol, given client ciphertext $\mathsf{Enc}_r(x)$ and server input (m_0, m_1) (defined in Section 2). The full protocol of FDT is presented in Fig 1.

We can estimate the communication rate α of our FDT protocol as follows:

$$\frac{1}{\alpha} \approx \frac{2(|\mathsf{Com}(r_0)| + |\mathsf{Enc}_r(s_0)| + |\mathsf{Enc}_r(h_0^{b_0})|) + |\mathsf{Enc}_s(c)| + |\mathsf{Enc}_s(h_c^{b_c})| + 2|\mathsf{Enc}_r(m_0^{b_0})|}{2|m_0^{b_0}| + 1}$$

$$\approx \frac{o(|m_0^{b_0}|)}{2|m_0^{b_0}|} + \frac{|\mathsf{Enc}_r(b_0)| + |\mathsf{Enc}_r(m_0^b)|}{|b_0| + |P[b_0, (m_0^0, m_0^1)]|} \to \frac{1}{r}, \text{when } m \to \infty ,$$

where m is the message size and r is the rate as defined in Sect. 2. We can group several terms into $o(|m_0^{b_0}|)$ as all those are encryptions (or commitments) of fixed size short messages. Thus, when the LHE scheme is rate optimal as [16], our FDT protocol (and further our asymmetric fingerprinting scheme, see next section) is also rate optimal.

Security Analysis. We briefly explain the properties of our protocol in the semi-honest model. Correctness follows from the coin tossing and the property of the LHE [16]. For instance, $\overline{\mu_0} = \mathsf{Enc}_r(h_0^1), C_0 = \mathsf{Enc}_r(m_0^1)$, if $r_0 \oplus s_0 \leq t_0$, in this case, $\Pr[b_0 = 1] = t_0/T = p_0$. For security, as we are working in the semi-honest model for now, the sender and receiver views can be simulated easily to preserve the consistency with the output. For detailed proofs, we refer to the full version.

Receiver $\mathcal{R}$	Sender $\mathcal{S}$
	$\mathcal{S}$ selects $r_0, r_1 \leftarrow_r Z_T$, and
$\xleftarrow{\quad \mathsf{Com}(r_0), \mathsf{Com}(r_1) \quad}$	computes commitments $\mathsf{Com}(r_0), \mathsf{Com}(r_1)$
$\mathcal{R}$ selects $s_0, s_1 \leftarrow_r$ $\xrightarrow{\quad \mathsf{Enc}_r(s_0), \mathsf{Enc}_r(s_1) \quad}$	
Z_T	
	$\mathcal{S}$ computes $c_0 = \mathsf{Enc}_r(r_0 \oplus s_0)$
	$\mathcal{S}$ computes $c_1 = \mathsf{Enc}_r(r_1 \oplus s_1)$
	$\mathcal{S}$ computes $\overline{\mu_0} = \mathsf{LEQ}_s[c_0, (t_0, h_0^1, h_0^0)]$
$\xleftarrow{\quad \overline{\mu_0}, \overline{\mu_1}, \mathsf{Enc}_s(c) \quad}$	$\mathcal{S}$ computes $\overline{\mu_1} = \mathsf{LEQ}_s[c_1, (t_1, h_1^1, h_1^0)]$
$\mathcal{R}$ retrieves $h_0^{b_0}, h_1^{b_1}$	
and computes $u_c =$	
$\mathsf{OD}_s[\mathsf{Enc}_s(c), (h_0^{b_0}, h_1^{b_1})]$ $\xrightarrow{\quad u_c \quad}$	
	$\mathcal{S}$ decrypts u_c and checks the validity
	$\mathcal{S}$ computes $\mathsf{Enc}_r(b_0) = \mathsf{LEQ}_s[c_0, (t_0, 1, 0)]$
	$\mathcal{S}$ computes $\mathsf{Enc}_r(b_1) = \mathsf{LEQ}_s[(c_1, (t_1, 1, 0)]$
	$\mathcal{S}$ computes $C_0 = \mathsf{OD}_s[\mathsf{Enc}_r(b_0), (m_0^0, m_0^1)]$
$\xleftarrow{\quad C_0, C_1 \quad}$	$\mathcal{S}$ computes $C_1 = \mathsf{OD}_s[\mathsf{Enc}_r(b_1), (m_1^0, m_1^1)]$
$\mathcal{R}$ checks the validity,	
outputs: $m_0^{b_0}, m_1^{b_1}$	$\mathcal{S}$ outputs b_c (as inferred by $h_c^{b_c}$)

Fig. 1. Fingerprinted Data Transfer. $\{(m_b^0, m_b^1), p_b = \frac{t_b}{T})\}_{b=0,1}, c$ are inputs of $\mathcal{S}$.

Lemma 1. *Our protocol shown in Fig. 1 securely implements the fingerprinted data transfer functionality. Specifically, it is correct; and it satisfies receiver security if the underlying encryption Enc_r is IND-CPA secure; it satisfies sender security if the underlying commitment scheme $\mathsf{Com}(\cdot)$ is computationally hiding, and the encryption Enc_s is IND-CPA secure.*

Work in the Malicious Model. Ultimately, we would like to design protocols to defend against malicious adversaries who may arbitrarily deviate from the protocol. The general method that in every step, both parties deploy zero-knowledge proofs to show that they follow the protocol, could be inefficient. Note that our protocol is highly structured, user misbehaviors can be easily detected by the SP with some routine checks about the consistency in the transcripts. In the 2nd round in coin tossing phase, the user could not learn any extra information by not following protocol, as simulation for malicious user is not influenced by the choices of s_0, s_1. While in the 4th round, the SP checks the validity of $h_c^{b_c} = H(m_c^{b_c})||c||b_c$, if u_c is not calculated as in the protocol and passes the checking, it means the malicious user finds a value equal to $H(m_c^{1-b_c})$. As the message segment $m_c^{1-b_c}$ has sufficient entropy thus $h_c^{1-b_c}$ is also unpredictable, otherwise, the user could easily find a collision by randomly sample messages from the distribution of $m_c^{1-b_c}$. To be more specific, suppose M is the space of $m_c^{1-b_c}$ and $\mathcal{D}$ is its distribution, and $H(M) = \{H(m) : m \in M\}$, $\mathcal{D}$ will induce a distribution $\mathcal{H}$ on $H(M)$. Suppose the sender can predict $h(m_c^{1-b_c})$ with probability δ, then the maximum probability of $\mathcal{H}$ is no less than δ. Let us use h_0 to denote the most probable value in $H(M)$. The adversary $\mathcal{A}$ simply sample m_i randomly according to $\mathcal{D}$, and computes the hash value. Following the Chernoff bound, using $O(\frac{1}{\delta^2})$ many samples, $\mathcal{A}$ will almost certainly reach h_0 twice. At the same time, the probability that there are two same messages appear in the sampled messages is exponentially small, as the most probable message from $\mathcal{D}$ appears with negligible probability. Based on these two facts, $\mathcal{A}$ found a collision.

Regarding malicious SP, the user can also do some simple checks of the consistency of the hash values. Note that there is a trusted judge that makes the final decision about the set of accused users. We will show in next section (as the judge is not involved with the FDT protocol) how we can take advantage of this third-party to "force" the SP to follow the protocol, by adding some simple and efficient "proofs of behavior". We require the SP signs on each round of messages she sends together with the user identity, and the user also signs on each round of messages he sends. We also let user store part of the transcripts and reveal them to the judge in case of dispute. Through a careful analysis of Tardos code property together with these simple mechanisms, we can argue security of our asymmetric fingerprinting scheme in the malicious model.

4   An Optimal Asymmetric Fingerprinting Scheme Based on Tardos Code

Pfitzmann and Schunter [22] define an asymmetric fingerprinting scheme to be a collection of four protocols $\langle \mathsf{key\_gen}, \mathsf{fing}, \mathsf{identify}, \mathsf{dispute} \rangle$. The algorithm $\mathsf{key\_gen}$ can be used by a user to produce a public and a secret-key. The protocol fing is a two-party protocol between a user and an SP that will result in the user obtaining the fingerprinted copy of the file and the SP receiving some state of the user codeword. The algorithm $\mathsf{identify}$ is an algorithm that, given a pirate copy and the state of the SP, outputs a non-empty set of public keys (corresponding to the accused user identities). Finally the algorithm $\mathsf{dispute}$ is a 3-party protocol between the judge (or arbiter as it is called in [22]), the user and the SP that either accepts the SP's accusation or rejects it (depending on the evidence presented by the involved parties). For brevity we refer to [22] for the full syntax of the scheme. Regarding the security model, an asymmetric fingerprinting scheme should satisfy two security properties: (i) *security for the SP*, that states that no malicious coalition of less than t users can escape the accusation of one of its members from the $\mathsf{identify}$ algorithm as well as the validation of this accusation by the $\mathsf{dispute}$ protocol, and (ii) *security for the user*, that states that an innocent user cannot be implicated by a malicious SP (who can also corrupt other users) in being responsible for a certain pirate copy. For formal definitions of an asymmetric fingerprinting scheme, we refer to the full version.

In addition to the above basic requirements, we put forth two additional properties that will be of interest.

Communication efficiency. The communication rate of an asymmetric fingerprinting scheme is measured as the ratio of the length of the file that is distributed to the users over the total communication complexity of the fing protocol. In a communication optimal asymmetric fingerprinting scheme it holds that the rate approaches 1 as the length of the file becomes larger. All known schemes in the literature [6, 21–23] have rate at most 0.5.

Security for the SP under group accusations. In [22] the algorithm identify is responsible for producing a single colluder whose implication is guaranteed to be validated by the dispute algorithm. In [6] this is extended to group accusation, i.e., the identify algorithm produces a set of accused users as output (this is possible given that the underlying fingerprinting code enables such group accusation). For SP security to be preserved under group accusations however, it should be the case that for each accused user, its implication to the construction of the pirate copy is validated by the dispute protocol. In the other case, the SP will have to withdraw at least one accusation (something that may lead to problems in a practical deployment). Therefore a protocol solution should guarantee in the setting of group accusation no accusation withdrawal can occur with non-negligible probability. We refer the formal definitions to the full version.

4.1   Our Construction

We next describe our construction which satisfies the original security requirements of [22] as well as the two properties that we described above. Specifically it is the first asymmetric fingerprinting scheme with both optimal communication complexity and code length. And one can easily adapt our construction to other asymmetric fingerprinting scheme from any bias-based code.

Recall the definition of Tardos code as explained in section 3, the main task is the fing protocol, which will be constructed from our fingerprinted data transfer protocol (see Fig 1) with some extra checks to achieve security in the malicious model in which the adversary may not follow the protocol. To describe the generation of the fingerprinted copy of each user in more detail, let us abstract each variant of a segment m_i^b with a value in $\{0,1\}$, where $i \in [2n], b \in \{0,1\}$ and $2n$ is the length of the fingerprint. Thus, the fingerprinted file of each user is a $2n$-bit string, where each bit signifies which variant of the corresponding segment the user received. It will be generated so that n bits from a set $L \subseteq [2n]$ will be known to the SP, while the other n bits (from $[2n] \setminus L$) will only be known by the user. The user, however, will not know if a given location belongs to L or not. Each of the parts L and $[2n] \setminus L$ is an instance of the Tardos code [26]. The two parts are produced by generating two segments at a time, using the functionality achieved by the protocol in Figure 1, i.e., for the i-th pair of segments $(2i-1, 2i)$, where $i \in [n]$, the user and the server runs the fingerprinted data transfer with the SP taking $[(p_{2i-1}, p_{2i}), (m_{2i-1}^0, m_{2i-1}^1), (m_{2i}^0, m_{2i}^1), c_i]$ as inputs. Based on the security properties of this protocol, the user receives two variants of two different segments, while the SP does not know one of them and the user is oblivious regarding which one the SP knows. Our asymmetric fingerprinting scheme proceeds as follows:

Key generation. The key_gen for the user is simply the generation of two public-secret key pairs $(pk_1, sk_1), (pk_2, sk_2)$. The first is for a digital signature scheme (which we use as black-box), and the second is for the additively homomorphic encryption Enc_r used in the fingerprinted data transfer.

The fing protocol. The user has as input its public and secret keys while the SP has as input SP public keys, and system parameters, e.g., the level of precision ℓ. Furthermore, the protocol is stateful from the point of view of the SP. The state of the SP contains the definition of the Tardos code parameters (e.g., probabilities $\{p_i\}$). Also, the SP has as private inputs a set $L = \{c_1, \ldots, c_n\}$, and a file that is divided in $2n$ segments for each one of which there are two variations. The i-th segment, b-th variant is denoted by m_i^b.

The fing protocol proceeds as follows: the SP and the user first carry out a handshake protocol to prepare the system parameters including the exchange of the public keys of each other; then for each i-th pair of segments with indices $(2i-1, 2i)$ where $i \in [n]$, the user and the server runs the FDT with the SP taking $[(p_{2i-1}, p_{2i}), (m_{2i-1}^0, m_{2i-1}^1), (m_{2i}^0, m_{2i}^1), c_i]$ as inputs, and these n protocols are run in parallel. Also in each round, if the SP sends out a message, she signs on the message together with the user's identity; if the user sends a message, he signs it as well. During protocol execution each party verifies that the messages they receive are proper and if they are not they will abort the protocol.

Furthermore some additional checks are in place to detect the malicious behavior within fing as explained at the end of section 3.2. These are as follows: The user checks after receiving the actual data segments (in the last round) whether they are consistent with the hash values (see Remark in section 3.2) he received in the 3-rd round. The SP, checks the validity of the hash value she received in the 4-th round. Also, both parties will store some information for input to the dispute protocol. The user keeps the commitments received from the first round and the hashed values and the encrypted bits of $\{\mathsf{Enc}_s c_i\}$ for $i \in L$, received in the 4-th round; the SP keeps the encrypted random coins of the user received in the 2nd round. Note that these checks do not enforce semi-honest behavior - nevertheless we will show (see Theorem 1,2) they are sufficient for security against malicious parties in the presence of the judge (which is assumed honest).

We see that our fing protocol essentially runs out FDT protocol in parallel with only some extra signatures, thus it inherits the rate optimality from FDT.

The identify algorithm. This algorithm takes a pirate file M, and all users' half codeword $X_1, \ldots, X_N$ together with the location indices $L_1, \ldots, L_N$ and the vector of biases $\langle p_1, \ldots, p_{2n} \rangle$ as inputs. It first extracts a codeword $Y = y_1 \ldots y_{2n} \in \{0,1\}^{2n}$ from M (as we assume each bit is publicly computable from the segment). For the ease of presentation, we describe the algorithm for one user with stored codeword $X = x_{c_1} \ldots x_{c_n}$ and $L = \{c_1, \ldots, c_n\}$. For each $j \in L$, it computes:

$$U_j = \begin{cases} \sqrt{\frac{1-p_j}{p_j}}, & \text{if } x_j = 1; \\ -\sqrt{\frac{p_j}{1-p_j}}, & \text{if } x_j = 0 \end{cases}$$

as in [26]. The service provider calculates the score of the user over the locations in L; $S = \sum_{j \in L} y_j U_j$, and if $S > Z$, where $Z = 20tk$, the SP reports this user to the judge. This is repeated for every user and a list of accused users is compiled and reported to the judge.

The dispute protocol. This is a protocol among the SP, the judge and a user. The two parties first submit to the judge the protocol transcript they stored. In more detail, the user submits SP's commitments sent in the 1st round and the hash values; also, the SP submits the biases and the encryptions from the user in the 2nd round as well as openings of her commitments. The judge first verifies the code parameters, then does the following checks, (1). the validity of the segments, i.e., they should be one of the versions. (2). the validity of all signatures, if any signature is invalid, accuse the party who submits it. (3). Otherwise, the judge checks whether the user codeword is generated properly, i.e., each bit of the codeword is consistent with the coin-tosses – whether $b_i = [r_i + s_i \leq t_i]$ where b_i is the i-th bit, r_i, s_i, t_i are as in the FDT (the notation $[\cdot]$ here denotes a predicate). To finish this check, the judge requires the SP to open her commitments, and the user to reveal his coins in the ciphertext $\{\mathsf{Enc}_r(s_i)\}$ and prove their validity. (4). Furthermore, the judge requests from the user to submit the encrypted locations $\{\mathsf{Enc}_s(c_i)\}$ and requests the SP to decrypt it and prove a correct decryption, so that the judge calculates the set of locations L. Any party failed to prove the correct decryption will be accused.

If all the checks pass, the judge will recover user's fingerprint x' from the bits $\{b_i\}$, also he inspects the pirate content and extracts the fingerprint y'. Then he computes the U' as in the *identify* algorithm for locations $L' = [2n] \backslash L$ using x', y' as inputs. Finally, for any user reported, the judge calculates his score over the locations in L'; $S' = \sum_{j \in L'} y'_j U'_j$, and make decisions if $S' > Z'$, where $Z' = Z/2 = 10tk$, he validates the accusation; otherwise, the user is acquitted.

Note that we are using a lower threshold on the judge-side, to counter-balance the probability that a user is accused over L, but not over $[2n] \backslash L$. In fact this is an essential feature of our scheme to ensure security for the SP under group accusations. We in fact show that if $Z' = Z$ it can happen with high probability that the SP will have to withdraw an accusation; in Fig 2, we explore this experimentally by having a coalition of 40 users where the pirate strategy is as follows: the pirate content is formed via a majority strategy by the segments available to the coalition of size t. For each segment with probability p (a parameter of the strategy) the pirate segment is determined with probability p to be the majority of the segments of all t users or with probability $1 - p$ the segment of the first user. We variate the parameter p of the strategy and we demonstrate from experimental data that for suitable choice of p the number of accusation withdrawals can be as high as as a quarter of the coalition. One would expect that in practice, such high level of accusation withdrawal would impact seriously the credibility of the SP. In our construction, by appropriately differentiating the tracing algorithm between the judge and the SP we circumvent this problem entirely. It should be noted that this issue was not addressed in [6] where the Tardos tracing algorithm was also used for determining the implication of users.

Remark: There are two phases when the judge requests one of the two parties to prove a valid decryption of a bit. As we are using a variant of DJ

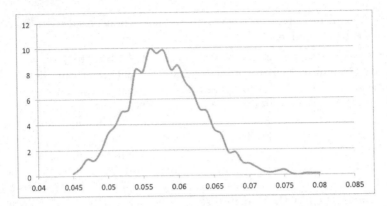

Fig. 2. The vertical axis represents the number of accusation withdrawals (i.e., for how many users the service provider has to abandon its accusation); the total number of colluding users is 40. The horizontal access is the parameter of the colluding strategy p; for a suitably choice of p the accusation withdrawals reach 25% of colluders.

encryption [9], the prover can simply reveal the message together with the random coins used in encryption as it decodes uniquely in this form. Specifically, if a message m is encrypted with random coin r, it results in a ciphertext $c = (n+1)^m r^{n^s} \mod n^{s+1}$, the prover can decrypts c to recover m and then obtains $r = d^{n^{-s} \mod \phi(n)} \mod n$, where $d = r^{n^s} \mod n$ is computed from $c \cdot (n+1)^{-m} \mod (n^{s+1})$.

4.2 Security Analysis

We give here explain the intuitions about the security analysis of our asymmetric fingerprinting scheme, for the details of the proofs, we refer to the full version.

Security for the innocent user. We will show that no innocent user will be framed. In the case of a semi-honest SP, she follows the fingerprinted data transfer protocol and the accusation procedure, but will try to make a pirate copy to frame some innocent user. As the FDT protocol satisfies the simulation based definition, from the composition lemma [5], A semi-honest SP will have the similar behavior interacting with only an oracle which returns her half of the codeword. In this case, the SP wins only when she is able to break the innocent user security of Tardos code as shown in Theorem 2.1 in [26] that an innocent user will be framed with a probability no bigger than ϵ regardless of what biases are used and what is the pirate copy.

Lemma 2. *An innocent user will be accused with negligible probability by a semi-honest service provider if the encryption* Enc_r *used is IND-CPA secure.*

Now we consider a malicious SP who may arbitrarily deviate from the protocol. With the simple checks, there is only one class of deviations left (which is not yet clear whether always detectable): the malicious SP submits different biases to the judge with those used during fing; This includes many subtle attacks, e.g., in one instance of FDT, the malicious SP uses the same messages in each pair to do the transmission, i.e., SP inputs $(m_0^{b_0}, m_0^{b_0}), (m_1^{b_1}, m_1^{b_1})$ (same for the hash values). Doing this the malicious SP will know the complete codeword of the user. Similarly, the SP could swap the messages in each pair, i.e., transmit version $1 - b_i$ if the code is b_i. Both of these behavior can be seen as special case of the above deviation. In the first case, the user codeword is essentially generated using a vector of probabilities $\langle p_1, \ldots, p_{2n} \rangle$, where each $p_i \in \{0, 1\}$, while the latter case is that each $p_i = 1 - p_i'$ where p_i' is the reported bias. As the judge will check the constancy of the codeword with the coin tossing, the more indices the SP reports different biases, the hight the probability she got caught. Through a careful analysis, we manage to show that the probability of accusing an innocent user and the probability of reporting different biases without being detected can never be non-negligible simultaneously, which further implies that either the malicious SP deviates without hurting the innocent user security, or the deviation will be almost always detected by the judge.

Theorem 1. *A malicious service provider can frame an innocent user without being detected by the judge with negligible probability if the underlying encryption Enc_r is IND-CPA secure, the commitment scheme is computationally binding, the digital signature scheme we use as black-box is existentially unforgeable, and the hash function is collision resistant.*

Security for the SP under group accusations. The analysis for the effectiveness of the accusation procedure will also proceed in two steps. We first deal with semi-honest users who will follow the fing protocol and the accusation procedure, but they will try to make a pirate copy and avoid being accused. From the half fingerprint known to the SP, the SP can always identify colluders. As the FDT satisfies the simulation based security, the behavior of the adversary is essentially the same as the one interacting with only an oracle returning the codewords of corrupted users, while no information about which half of the codewords are known to the SP is leaked. Further we can show that by relaxing the threshold on the judge side, whoever accused by the SP using the half fingerprint will also be accused by the judge using another half fingerprint.

Lemma 3. *Suppose $\mathcal{U}_{cor}$, with $|\mathcal{U}_{cor}| \leq t$, is a coalition of users. If all users are semi-honest during the fing protocol execution. The probability that no user is accused or an accused user is acquitted by the judge is $\epsilon^{1/16} + \epsilon^{t/4} + \epsilon_0$, where ϵ is the parameter from the Tardos code, ϵ_0 is negligible (to the security parameter), if the underlying commitment scheme $\mathsf{Com}(\cdot)$ is computationally hiding, and the encryption Enc_s is IND-CPA secure.*

The case that malicious users can arbitrarily deviate from the protocol are easier to analyze than Theorem 1 due to the simple checks. It is easy to see that in each round, the user is forced to be behave honestly, otherwise the deviation will be detected with overwhelming probability.

Theorem 2. *Suppose $\mathcal{U}_{cor}$, with $|\mathcal{U}_{cor}| \leq t$, is a coalition of users. Assuming Enc_s is IND-CPA secure, the commitment scheme $\mathsf{Com}(\cdot)$ is computationally hiding and the signature scheme used is existentially unforgeable, and the hash function is collision resistent. Then the probability that no user is accused or an accused user is acquitted by the judge is $\epsilon^{1/16} + \epsilon^{t/4} + \epsilon_0$, where ϵ is the error probability from the Tardos code, ϵ_0 is negligible (to the security parameter).*

5   Security Implications of Protocol Restarts

In the following, we consider the original Tardos code with length $m = 100t^2k$ and threshold $Z = 20tk$, where c is the number of colluders and $k = \log \frac{1}{\epsilon}$ the security parameter. For simplicity, we take t equal to the number of users n.

If the colluders are allowed restarts, they can act as follows. They do $(\mu - 1)$ restarts each to receive a total of $\mu m n$ bits. For the pirate codeword, they output a zero whenever they can. Formally, for any $j \in [m]$, let x be the number of ones the pirates have received collectively at location j. They set y_j, the bit of the pirate copy at j, as follows.

$$y_j = \begin{cases} 1 & \text{if } x = \mu n; \\ 0 & \text{otherwise.} \end{cases}$$

We are going to show that with this simple strategy, each pirate escapes with high probability. Let p denote the bias-vector, X the codeword of an arbitrary pirate, Y the pirate copy generated by the aforementioned strategy, and

$$U_j = \begin{cases} \sqrt{\frac{1-p_j}{p_j}}, & if\, X_j = 1; \\ -\sqrt{\frac{p_j}{1-p_j}}, & if\, X_j = 0. \end{cases}$$

The score of the pirate can be expressed as $S = \sum_{j \in [m]} Y_j U_j$. Our task is to upper-bound $\Pr[S > Z]$. We'll use $e^x \leq 1 + x + x^2$, valid for $x \leq 1$. Since $|U_j| < \sqrt{300n}$, choosing $\alpha < \frac{1}{10n}$ we have

$$\mathrm{E}[e^{\alpha S}] = \mathrm{E}[\prod e^{\alpha Y_j U_j}] = \prod \mathrm{E}[e^{\alpha Y_j U_j}] \leq \prod \mathrm{E}[1 + \alpha Y_j U_j + \alpha^2 Y_j^2 U_j^2]$$

$$\leq \prod (1 + \alpha \mathrm{E}[Y_j U_j] + \alpha^2 \mathrm{E}[U_j^2]) = \prod (1 + \alpha \mathrm{E}[Y_j U_j] + \alpha^2).$$

For any $j \in [m]$ we have

$$\mathrm{E}[Y_j U_j] = \mathrm{E}_{p_j}\left[p_j^{\mu n}\sqrt{\frac{1-p_j}{p_j}}\right] = \frac{1}{\pi/2 - 2t'} \int_{t'}^{\pi/2-t'} \sin^{2\mu n - 1} r \cos r \, dr$$

$$= \frac{1}{\pi/2 - 2t'} \cdot \frac{1}{2\mu n} \cdot \sin^{2\mu n} r \Big|_{t'}^{\pi/2-t'} = \frac{(1-t)^{\mu n} - t^{\mu n}}{(\pi - 4t')\mu n} \leq \frac{1}{3\mu n}.$$

Putting things together, and using $1 + x \leq e^x$, we obtain $\mathrm{E}[e^{\alpha S}] \leq \prod (1 + \alpha/(3\mu n) + \alpha^2) \leq e^{\alpha^2 m + \alpha m/(3\mu n)}$. An application of Markov's inequality now gives that: $\Pr[S > Z] < \frac{E[e^{\alpha S}]}{e^{\alpha Z}} \leq e^{\alpha^2 m + \alpha m/(3\mu n) - \alpha Z}$. For $m = 100n^2 k$, $Z = 20nk$, $k = \log(1/\epsilon)$, $\alpha = \frac{1}{10n}(1 - \frac{5}{3\mu})$, $\mu > 1$, we conclude that:

$$\Pr[S > Z] < \epsilon^{(1 - \frac{5}{3\mu})^2}.$$

Thus, even allowing a single restart per user, is sufficient for the pirates to escape with high probability. Another way to view this, is that an instantiation of Tardos code that can handle a coalition of size t, is not secure against a coalition of size $2t$. The simple way around this, is to instantiate the code so as to handle coalition size μt, and allow each user at most $\mu - 1$ restarts.

6   Conclusion

In this paper, we constructed the first communication optimal asymmetric fingerprinting scheme, (i.e., the total number of bits transmitted in the protocol is almost the same as the length of the files), based on Tardos code. This is an appealing feature, especially for fingerprinting schemes in which large data (like movies) are transmitted. Besides rate optimality, we also considered two properties: security against accusation withdrawal and security under adversarial aborts, which are overlooked in previous asymmetric fingerprinting schemes.

Acknowledgments. The first, second and the fifth authors were supported by the ERC project CODAMODA. The third author was supported by the Estonian Research Council, and European Union through the European Regional Development Fund. The fourth author was supported by institutional research funding IUT20-57 of the Estonian Ministry of Education and Research.

References

1. Ambainis, A., Jakobsson, M., Lipmaa, H.: Cryptographic Randomized Response Techniques. In: Bao, F., Deng, R., Zhou, J. (eds.) PKC 2004. LNCS, vol. 2947, pp. 425–438. Springer, Heidelberg (2004)
2. Amiri, E., Tardos, G.: High Rate Fingerprinting Codes And the Fingerprinting Capacity. In: Mathieu, C. (ed.) SODA 2009, pp. 336–345. SIAM, New York, January 4–6 (2009)
3. Blake, I.F., Kolesnikov, V.: Strong Conditional Oblivious Transfer and Computing on Intervals. In: Lee, P.J. (ed.) ASIACRYPT 2004. LNCS, vol. 3329, pp. 515–529. Springer, Heidelberg (2004)
4. Boneh, D., Shaw, J.: Collusion-Secure Fingerprinting for Digital Data. In: Coppersmith, D. (ed.) CRYPTO 1995. LNCS, vol. 963, pp. 452–465. Springer, Heidelberg (1995)
5. Canetti, R.: Security and composition of multiparty cryptographic protocols. J. Cryptology **13**(1), 143–202 (2000)
6. Charpentier, A., Fontaine, C., Furon, T., Cox, I.: An asymmetric fingerprinting scheme based on tardos codes. In: Proceedings of the 13th International Conference on Information Hiding, IH 2011, pp. 43–58 (2011)

7. Cleve, R., Limits on the security of coin flips when half the processors are faulty (extended abstract). In: STOC, pp. 364–369 (1986)
8. Damgård, I., Faust, S., Hazay, C.: Secure Two-Party Computation with Low Communication. In: Cramer, R. (ed.) TCC 2012. LNCS, vol. 7194, pp. 54–74. Springer, Heidelberg (2012)
9. Damgård, I., Jurik, M.: A generalisation, a simplification and some applications of paillier's probabilistic public-key system. In: Public Key Cryptography, pp. 119–136 (2001)
10. Damgård, I., Zakarias, S.: Constant-Overhead Secure Computation of Boolean Circuits using Preprocessing. In: Sahai, A. (ed.) TCC 2013. LNCS, vol. 7785, pp. 621–641. Springer, Heidelberg (2013)
11. Dodis, Y., Halevi, S., Rabin, T.: A Cryptographic Solution to a Game Theoretic Problem. In: Bellare, M. (ed.) CRYPTO 2000. LNCS, vol. 1880, pp. 112–130. Springer, Heidelberg (2000)
12. Fischlin, M.: A Cost-Effective Pay-Per-Multiplication Comparison Method for Millionaires. In: Naccache, D. (ed.) CT-RSA 2001. LNCS, vol. 2020, pp. 457–472. Springer, Heidelberg (2001)
13. Goldreich, O.: The Foundations of Cryptography, vol. 2, Basic Applications. Cambridge University Press (2004)
14. Ishai, Y., Kushilevitz, E., Meldgaard, S., Orlandi, C., Paskin-Cherniavsky, A.: On the Power of Correlated Randomness in Secure Computation. In: Sahai, A. (ed.) TCC 2013. LNCS, vol. 7785, pp. 600–620. Springer, Heidelberg (2013)
15. Ishai, Y., Paskin, A.: Evaluating Branching Programs on Encrypted Data. In: Vadhan, S.P. (ed.) TCC 2007. LNCS, vol. 4392, pp. 575–594. Springer, Heidelberg (2007)
16. Kiayias, A., Leonardos, N., Lipmaa, H., Pavlyk, K., Tang, Q.: Near Optimal Rate Homomorphic Encryption for Branching Programs. Technical Report 2014 (2014). http://eprint.iacr.org/2014/851
17. Kiayias, A., Pehlivanoglu, S.: Encryption for Digital Content, vol. 52. Advances in Information Security. Springer, US (October 2010)
18. Laur, S., Lipmaa, H.: A New Protocol for Conditional Disclosure of Secrets and Its Applications. In: Katz, J., Yung, M. (eds.) ACNS 2007. LNCS, vol. 4521, pp. 207–225. Springer, Heidelberg (2007)
19. Lipmaa, H.: First CPIR Protocol with Data-Dependent Computation. In: Lee, D., Hong, S. (eds.) ICISC 2009. LNCS, vol. 5984, pp. 193–210. Springer, Heidelberg (2010)
20. Naor, M., Nissim, K.: Communication preserving protocols for secure function evaluation. In: STOC, pp. 590–599 (2001)
21. Pfitzmann, B.: Trials of traced traitors. In: Information Hiding, pp. 49–64 (1996)
22. Pfitzmann, B., Schunter, M.: Asymmetric Fingerprinting. In: Maurer, U.M. (ed.) EUROCRYPT 1996. LNCS, vol. 1070, pp. 84–95. Springer, Heidelberg (1996)
23. Pfitzmann, B., Waidner, M.: Asymmetric fingerprinting for larger collusions. In: ACM Conference on Computer and Communications Security, pp. 151–160 (1997)
24. Rial, A., Balasch, J., Preneel, B.: A privacy-preserving buyer-seller watermarking protocol based on priced oblivious transfer. IEEE Transactions on Information Forensics and Security 6(1), 202–212 (2011)
25. Rial, A., Deng, M., Bianchi, T., Piva, A., Preneel, B.: A provably secure anonymous buyer-seller watermarking protocol. IEEE Transactions on Information Forensics and Security 5(4), 920–931 (2010)
26. Tardos, G.: Optimal probabilistic fingerprint codes. J. ACM 55(2) (2008)

Linearly Homomorphic Encryption from DDH

Guilhem Castagnos[1]([✉]) and Fabien Laguillaumie[2]

[1] Institut de Mathématiques de Bordeaux UMR 5251, Université de Bordeaux,
351, cours de la Libération, 33405 Talence cedex, France
`guilhem.castagnos@math.u-bordeaux.fr`

[2] CNRS/ENSL/INRIA/UCBL LIP Laboratoire de l'Informatique du Parallélisme,
Université Claude Bernard Lyon 1, 46 Allée d'Italie, 69364 Lyon, France
`fabien.laguillaumie@ens-lyon.fr`

Abstract. We design a linearly homomorphic encryption scheme whose security relies on the hardness of the decisional Diffie-Hellman problem. Our approach requires some special features of the underlying group. In particular, its order is unknown and it contains a subgroup in which the discrete logarithm problem is tractable. Therefore, our instantiation holds in the class group of a non maximal order of an imaginary quadratic field. Its algebraic structure makes it possible to obtain such a linearly homomorphic scheme whose message space is the whole set of integers modulo a prime p and which supports an unbounded number of additions modulo p from the ciphertexts. A notable difference with previous works is that, for the first time, the security does not depend on the hardness of the factorization of integers. As a consequence, under some conditions, the prime p can be scaled to fit the application needs.

1 Introduction

A widely deployed kind of encryption scheme has an "algebraic" property which precludes it to reach the highest level of security. It is called *homomorphic*, because an operation on the ciphertexts translates into an operation on the underlying plaintexts. This homomorphic property is actually very important for many applications, like e-voting for instance. Indeed, an *additively* homomorphic encryption makes it possible to obtain an encryption of the sum of all the ballots (which consists in 0 or 1 in the case of a 2-choice referendum for instance) from their encryption, so that a single decryption will reveal the result of the election, saving a lot of computational resources which would have been necessary to decrypt all the ciphertexts one by one. A tremendous breakthrough related to homomorphic encryption was Gentry's theoretical construction of a *fully* homomorphic encryption scheme [Gen09], which actually allows to evaluate any function on messages given their ciphertexts.

Currently, no linearly homomorphic encryption scheme is secure under a discrete logarithm related assumption. This theoretical question has been open for thirty years. In this paper, we provide the first construction of such a scheme.

© Springer International Publishing Switzerland 2015
K. Nyberg (ed.): CT-RSA 2015, LNCS 9048, pp. 487–505, 2015.
DOI: 10.1007/978-3-319-16715-2_26

Related Work. The story of homomorphic encryption begins with the first probabilistic encryption scheme [GM84], which was also homomorphic, improved in [Ben88, NS98, OU98]. One of the most achieved system was actually designed by Paillier [Pai99]. Its semantic security relies on the decisional composite residuosity assumption. Paillier's scheme has then been generalized by Damgård and Jurik [DJ01], allowing to encrypt larger messages. This family of practical linearly homomorphic schemes is still growing with the recent work of Joye and Libert [JL13]. The security of these schemes is based on the problem of factoring RSA integers (including the elliptic curve variant of Paillier [Gal02]).

To design a linearly homomorphic encryption based on the Discrete Logarithm problem (DL), a folklore solution consists in encoding the message in the exponent of an Elgamal encryption, *i.e.*, in encrypting m as $(g^r, h^r g^m)$ where g is a generator of a cyclic group $G = \langle g \rangle$ and $h = g^x$ is the public key. Unfortunately, to decrypt, one has to recover m from g^m and as the DL problem in G must be intractable, m has to be small enough to ensure a fast decryption. As a result, only a logarithmic number of additions is possible. There have been some attempts to reach a fully additive homomorphy based on the DL problem, with a variant of Elgamal modulo p^2 ([CPP06]) or with messages encoded as a small smooth number ([CC07]); both solutions still have a partial homomorphy. In [W+11], the map $m \mapsto g_0^m \bmod p_0$ is used with the plain Elgamal, where p_0 is a prime such that $p_0 - 1$ is smooth and g_0 is a primitive root modulo p_0. Unfortunately, although not clearly stated, this scheme only supports a limited number of additions, and it is not semantically secure as the set of encoded messages does not belong to a proper subgroup of $(\mathbf{Z}/p\mathbf{Z})^\times$ where the Decisional Diffie-Hellman assumption (DDH) holds.

A full solution was proposed by Bresson *et al.* in [BCP03]. However, their scheme is not only based on the DL problem but also on the factorization problem. It is less efficient than [Pai99] but has an additional property: it has a double trapdoor. The idea is to use the same setting as Paillier: In $(\mathbf{Z}/N^2\mathbf{Z})^\times$, the DL problem in basis $f = 1 + N$ is easy. Bresson *et al.* use an Elgamal encryption of the message m as $(g^r, f^m \cdot h^r)$ modulo N^2, where N is an RSA integer.

To our knowledge, designing a linearly homomorphic scheme based on the sole hardness of the DL problem is an open problem, as stated in [CPP06]. Some other schemes allow more homomorphic operations, like [BGN05] or [CL12]. As already mentioned, a fully homomorphic encryption (FHE) scheme appeared in 2009 [Gen09]. Its security relies on hard problems related to lattices. The latest developments of FHE [BV14] are getting more and more efficient and might become operational soon for applications that need a complex treatment over ciphertexts. Meanwhile, for applications that need only to add ciphertexts, protocols that rely on "classical" algorithmic assumptions are still more competitive, in particular in terms of compactness.

Our Contributions. Our contribution has both a theoretical and a practical impact. On one hand, we propose a linearly homomorphic encryption scheme whose security relies on the hardness of the decisional Diffie-Hellman problem. In particular it is the first time that the security of such a scheme does not depend on the hardness of the factorization of integers. On the other hand, we provide an efficient implementation within some specific group, namely the class group of orders in imaginary quadratic fields.

The design of our scheme is somehow similar to the one of [BCP03]. We use a group $G = \langle g \rangle$ such that the DDH assumption holds in G and such that there exists a subgroup $\langle f \rangle$ of G where the DL problem is easy (called a DDH group with an easy DL subgroup). Then the core of the protocol is an Elgamal encryption of the message m as $(g^r, f^m \cdot h^r)$ for a random r. In our case, the message space will be $(\mathbf{Z}/p\mathbf{Z})^*$, where p is a prime. Compared to some other linearly homomorphic schemes, ours allows some flexibility as p can be chosen (with some restrictions) independently from the security parameter.

To reach this unnatural feature without involving the factorization problem, we had to use the particular algebraic structure of class groups of imaginary quadratic fields, which have some specificities which seem hard to find in other groups. We designed a method to compute a group of unknown[1] order (to insure the hardness of a partial discrete logarithm assumption) which contains an easy DL subgroup (of known order). The interest of class group of orders in imaginary (or real) quadratic fields in cryptography decreased after critical attacks by Castagnos et al. [CL09, CJLN09] on some specific cryptosystems such as NICE [HPT99, PT00] and its real variant [JSW08]. These attacks will not apply in our setting. Indeed, these attacks recover the secret key by exposing the factorization of the discriminant of the field, thanks to the structure of the kernel of the surjection between the class group of a non maximal order to the class group of the maximal order. In our case, the factorization of the discriminant will be public and we will use constructively the ideas of [CL09]: the subgroup with an easy DL will be precisely the kernel of this surjection. The security of our scheme is proved to rely only on the hardness of the DDH problem in the class group of a non maximal order and on the hardness of computing class numbers. Several systems that adapt either Diffie-Hellman or Elgamal in class groups are already based on the DL problem and the DDH assumption in class groups of maximal order ([BW88, BDW90, SP05, BH01, BV07]) of discriminant Δ_K. The current best known algorithms to solve these problems have a sub-exponential complexity of complexity $L_{|\Delta_K|}(1/2, o(1))$ (cf. [BJS10]). It means that the factorization problem (or the discrete logarithm problem in a finite field) can be solved asymptotically *faster* than the discrete logarithm in the class group.[2] Moreover, arithmetic operations in class groups are very efficient, since the reduction and composition of quadratic forms have a quadratic time complexity (and even quasi linear using fast arithmetic).

As a result, our scheme is very competitive. With a straightforward implementation and using an underlying arithmetics very favorable to [Pai99, BCP03],

---

[1] There have been some use of groups of unknown order [Bre00, CHN99, DF02].
[2] Note that it is well known (see [HM00] for instance) that computing the class number of a quadratic field of discriminant Δ allows to factor Δ. However for our scheme, the factorization of the discriminant Δ will be public or Δ will be a prime, so we will not rely on the hardness of the factorization problem.

it compares very well with these linearly homomorphic protocols. With a similar level of security, it is faster than [BCP03] with a 2048 bits modulus, and the decryption process is faster than Paillier's for a 3072 bits modulus.

A very nice application of our protocol is that it can be used directly in Catalano and Fiore's linearly homomorphic encryption transformation to evaluate degree-2 computations on ciphertexts [CF14]. Their technique requires the message space to be a public ring in which it is possible to sample elements uniformly at random. Our scheme has this feature naturally, contrary to some of the other additively homomorphic schemes. It is therefore a very competitive candidate in 2-server delegation of computation over encrypted data (see [CF14] for more details).

2   DDH Group with an Easy DL Subgroup

In this section, we introduce and formalize the concept of a group in which the decisional Diffie-Hellman problem is hard, whereas it contains a subgroup in which the discrete logarithm problem is easy. This problem has already been used to design cryptosystems, including, for instance, Bresson *et al.*'s encryption scheme [BCP03]. It will be adjusted to build our new encryption protocol.

2.1   Definitions and Reductions

Definition 1. *We define a* DDH *group with an easy* DL *subgroup as a pair of algorithms* (Gen, Solve). *The* Gen *algorithm is a group generator which takes as input two parameters* λ *and* μ *and outputs a tuple* (B, n, p, s, g, f, G, F). *The integers* B, n, p *and* s *are such that* s *is a* λ-*bit integer,* p *is a* μ-*bit integer,* $\gcd(p, s) = 1$, $n = p \cdot s$ *and* B *is an upper bound for* s. *The set* $(G, \cdot)$ *is a cyclic group of order* n *generated by* g, *and* $F \subset G$ *is the subgroup of* G *of order* p *and* f *is a generator of* F. *The upper bound* B *is chosen such that the distribution induced by* $\{g^r, r \xleftarrow{\$} \{0, \ldots, Bp-1\}\}$ *is statistically indistinguishable from the uniform distribution on* G. *We assume that the canonical surjection* $\pi : G \to G/F$ *is efficiently computable from the description of* G, H *and* p *and that given an element* $h \in G/F$ *one can efficiently lift* h *in* G, *i.e., compute an element* $h_\ell \in \pi^{-1}(h)$. *We suppose moreover that:*

1. *The* DL *problem is easy in* F. *The* Solve *algorithm is a deterministic polynomial time algorithm that solves the discrete logarithm problem in* F:
$$\Pr[x = x^\star : (B, n, p, s, g, f, G, F) \xleftarrow{\$} \mathsf{Gen}(1^\lambda, 1^\mu), x \xleftarrow{\$} \mathbf{Z}/p\mathbf{Z}, X = f^x,$$
$$x^\star \leftarrow \mathsf{Solve}(B, p, g, f, G, F, X)] = 1$$

2. *The* DDH *problem is hard in* G *even with access to the* Solve *algorithm:*
$$\left| \Pr[b = b^\star : (B, n, p, s, g, f, G, F) \xleftarrow{\$} \mathsf{Gen}(1^\lambda, 1^\mu), x, y, z \xleftarrow{\$} \mathbf{Z}/n\mathbf{Z}, \right.$$
$$X = g^x, Y = g^y, b \xleftarrow{\$} \{0, 1\}, Z_0 = g^z, Z_1 = g^{xy},$$
$$\left. b^\star \xleftarrow{\$} \mathcal{A}(B, p, g, f, G, F, X, Y, Z_b, \mathsf{Solve}(.))] - \frac{1}{2} \right|$$
is negligible for all probabilistic polynomial time attacker $\mathcal{A}$.

The bound B for the order s in Definition 1 can be chosen as $B = 2^{2\lambda}$. Indeed, the statistical distance of $\{g^r, r \xleftarrow{\$} \{0, \ldots, Bp - 1\}\}$ to the uniform distribution can be shown to be upper bounded by $n/(4pB) = s/2^{2\lambda+2} \leqslant 2^{-\lambda-2}$ which a negligible function of λ.

It is fundamental to note that in this definition, the order n of the group G is *not* an input of the adversary or of the Solve algorithm: Only the bound Bp is implicitly given. Indeed, if n or s were efficiently computable from the description of G, a DDH group with an easy DL subgroup would not exist since it would be possible to partially compute discrete logarithms. More formally, let us define the following partial discrete logarithm problem initially introduced by Paillier in [Pai99], in the context of the group $(\mathbf{Z}/N^2\mathbf{Z})^\times$.

Definition 2 (Partial Discrete Logarithm (PDL) Problem). *Let us denote by* (Gen, Solve) *a* DDH *group with an easy* DL *subgroup. Let* (B, n, p, s, g, f, G, F) *be an output of* $\mathrm{Gen}(1^\lambda, 1^\mu)$, $x \xleftarrow{\$} \mathbf{Z}/n\mathbf{Z}, X = g^x$. *The* Partial Discrete Logarithm Problem *consists in computing* x *modulo* p; *given* (B, p, g, f, G, F, X) *and access to the* Solve *algorithm.*

The proofs of the two following lemmas can be found in the full version of this article [CL15].

Lemma 1. *Let* (Gen, Solve) *be a* DDH *group with an easy* DL *subgroup and let the tuple* (B, n, p, s, g, f, G, F) *be an output of* $\mathrm{Gen}(1^\lambda, 1^\mu)$. *The knowledge of* n *makes the* PDL *problem easy.*

Lemma 2. *Let G be a* DDH *group with an easy* DL *subgroup. The* DDH *problem in G reduces to the* PDL *problem.*

Remark 1. Combining Lemmas 1 and 2 we get that as previously mentioned, with the notation of Definition 1, if n is easily computable from the description of G, then the DDH problem in G is easy so, G can not be a DDH group with an easy DL subgroup.

The following problem was introduced in [BCP03] in $(\mathbf{Z}/N^2\mathbf{Z})^\times$. It is a variant of the Diffie-Hellman problem, that we adapt to our general context.

Definition 3 (Lift Diffie-Hellman (LDH) Problem). *Let* (Gen, Solve) *be a* DDH *group with an easy* DL *subgroup. Let* $(B, n, p, s, g, f, G, F) \xleftarrow{\$} \mathrm{Gen}(1^\lambda, 1^\mu)$. *Let* $x, y \xleftarrow{\$} \mathbf{Z}/n\mathbf{Z}, X = g^x, Y = g^y$ *and* $Z = g^{xy}$ *and* $\pi : G \to G/F$ *be the canonical surjection. The* Lift Discrete Logarithm Problem *consists in computing Z, given the tuple* $(B, p, g, f, G, F, X, Y, \pi(Z))$ *and access to the* Solve *algorithm.*

In the following theorem we prove that this problem is equivalent to the PDL problem. Curiously only one implication was proved in [BCP03].

Theorem 1. *In a* DDH *group with an easy* DL *subgroup, the* LDH *and* PDL *are equivalent.*

Proof. In all the proof, we implicitly set $s = n/p$ and $\alpha \in (\mathbf{Z}/p\mathbf{Z})^{\times}$ such that $g^s = f^{\alpha}$ and denote $\beta \equiv \alpha^{-1} \pmod{p}$. Let us first prove that the PDL problem reduces to the LDH problem, which is a direct generalization of the proof of [BCP03, Theorem10]. Let (B, p, g, f, G, F, X) be a PDL challenge and let denote $X = g^x$ where $x = x_1 + x_2 p$ with $x_1 = x \bmod p$. The adversary draws $r_1 \overset{\$}{\leftarrow} \{0, \ldots, B-1\}$, $r_2 \overset{\$}{\leftarrow} \{0, \ldots, p-1\}$ and sets $Y = g^{r_1} f^{r_2}$. Note that $Y = g^{r_1 + s\beta r_2}$. Let us prove that the random variable Y is statistically indistinguishable from the uniform distribution in G.

The distance between Y and the uniform distribution in G is the same than the distance between $Y' = r_1 + s\beta r_2 \bmod n$ with r_1 uniformly drawn in $\{0, \ldots, B-1\}$ and r_2 independently uniformly drawn in $\{0, \ldots, p-1\}$ and the uniform distribution in $\{0, \ldots, n-1\}$. Let y be an element of $\{0, \ldots, n-1\}$, we denote $y = y_1 + y_2 s$ with $y_1 \in \{0, \ldots, s-1\}$ and $y_2 \in \{0, \ldots, p-1\}$ the euclidean division of y by s. We have

$$\Pr[Y' = y] = \Pr[Y' = y_1 + y_2 s] = \Pr[r_1 + s\beta r_2 \equiv y_1 + y_2 s \pmod{n}] =$$

$$\Pr[r_1 \equiv y_1 \pmod{s}] \Pr[r_2 \beta \equiv y_2 \pmod{p}] = \Pr[r_1 \equiv y_1 \pmod{s}]/p$$

as $\beta \not\equiv 0 \pmod{p}$. Now let $B = qs + r$ with $0 \leqslant r < s$ be the euclidean division of B by s. We proceed as in the proof of [CL15, Lemma 4, Appendix C]. For $y_1 < r$, $\Pr[r_1 \equiv y_1 \pmod{s}] = (q+1)/B > \frac{1}{s}$ and for $y_1 \geqslant r$, $\Pr[r_1 \equiv y_1 \pmod{s}] = q/B \leqslant \frac{1}{s}$. Eventually, $\Delta(X, Y) = r\left(\frac{q+1}{Bp} - \frac{1}{n}\right) = \frac{r(s-r)}{Bn} = \frac{r(n-pr)}{pBn} \leqslant \frac{r(n-r)}{pBn}$. This last quantity is the statistical distance of $\{g^r, r \overset{\$}{\leftarrow} \{0, \ldots, Bp-1\}\}$ to the uniform distribution in G which is suppose to be negligible. This proves that Y is statistically indistinguishable from the uniform distribution in G.

The adversary then compute $Z' = \pi(X^{r_1}) = \pi(X^{r_1 + s\beta r_2})$ and queries the LDH oracle with $(B, p, g, f, G, F, X, Y, Z')$. Then the oracle provides with non negligible probability $Z = X^{r_1 + s\beta r_2} = X^{r_1}(g^x)^{s\beta r_2} = X^{r_1} g^{(x_1 + x_2 p)(s\beta r_2)} = X^{r_1} g^{x_1 s\beta r_2} = X^{r_1} f^{x_1 r_2}$. Then, $Z/X^{r_1} = f^{x_1 r_2}$ and running the Solve algorithm on this value gives $x_1 r_2 \pmod{p}$ to the adversary from which he can get x_1, the answer to the PDL instance.

Now, let us prove that the LDH problem reduces to the PDL problem. Let us consider $X = g^x, Y = g^y, Z = g^{xy}$ for random x and y, such that the LDH challenge writes as $(B, p, g, f, G, F, X, Y, Z' = \pi(Z))$. The adversary makes two queries to the PDL oracle relative to X and Y, from which he obtains $x \pmod{p}$ and $y \pmod{p}$. The adversary draws $r_1 \overset{\$}{\leftarrow} \{0, \ldots B-1\}$ and $r_2 \overset{\$}{\leftarrow} \{0, \ldots, p-1\}$ and sets $U = g^{r_1} f^{r_2}$, which is as before statistically indistinguishable from the uniform distribution in G. The adversary queries the PDL oracle with U, which gives $r_1 + s\beta r_2 \pmod{p}$ as $U = g^{r_1 + s\beta r_2}$. From this answer, the adversary can compute $s\beta \pmod{p}$. From the definition of a DDH group with an easy DL subgroup, the adversary can compute $Z'_{\ell} \in \pi^{-1}(Z')$. He then draws $r \overset{\$}{\leftarrow} \mathbf{Z}/p\mathbf{Z}$ and computes $V = f^r Z'_{\ell}$. The random variable V is uniformly distributed in G. As $\pi(V) = Z' = \pi(Z)$, there exists $\gamma \in \mathbf{Z}/p\mathbf{Z}$ such that $V = f^{\gamma} Z = g^{s\beta\gamma + xy}$. From a last call to the PDL oracle, the adversary can get $s\beta\gamma + xy \pmod{p}$ from which he can compute γ since $\gcd(s\beta, p) = 1$. Eventually, the adversary deduces Z from $V = f^\gamma Z$. □

We now further analyze the relations between the problems in G/F and G. We first give a lemma that shows that we can define a morphism in order to lift the elements from G/F to G. The proofs can be found in the full version of this article [CL15].

Lemma 3. *Let* $(B, n, p, s, g, f, G, F) \xleftarrow{\$} \mathsf{Gen}(1^\lambda, 1^\mu)$ *where* $(\mathsf{Gen}, \mathsf{Solve})$ *is a* DDH *group with an easy* DL *subgroup. Denote* $\pi : G \to G/F$ *the canonical surjection. The map* $\psi : G/F \to G$ *s.t.* $h \mapsto h_\ell^p$, *where* $h_\ell \in \pi^{-1}(h)$, *is an effective injective morphism.*

Theorem 2. *Let* $(B, n, p, s, g, f, G, F) \xleftarrow{\$} \mathsf{Gen}(1^\lambda, 1^\mu)$ *where* $(\mathsf{Gen}, \mathsf{Solve})$ *is a* DDH *group with an easy* DL *subgroup. The* DL *problem in* G/F *reduces to the* DL *problem in* G.

Unfortunately, it seems unlikely that a similar reduction of the DDH problem in G/F to the DDH problem in G exists. Indeed, a DDH challenge in G/F can be lifted into $\psi(G/F) \subset G$. But $G = \psi(G/F) \times F$, so the reduction has to fill the F−part to keep the DDH challenge's form. This seems impossible with a non-negligeable advantage.

2.2   A Generic Linearly Homomorphic Encryption Scheme

From a DDH group with an easy DL subgroup, we can devise generically a linearly homomorphic encryption scheme. An Elgamal type scheme is used in G, with plaintext message $m \in \mathbf{Z}/p\mathbf{Z}$ mapped to $f^m \in F$. The resulted scheme is linearly homomorphic. Thanks to the Solve algorithm, the decryption does not need a complex DL computation. We depict this scheme in Fig. 1. Note that the outputs n and s of Gen are not used in the algorithms.

Let us prove the homomorphic property of the scheme. Let us consider an output of the EvalSum algorithm on an input corresponding to encryptions of m and m'. Due to Elgamal's multiplicativity, the first line of the decryption algorithm applied on this output gives $M = f^m f^{m'} = f^{m+m'} \bmod p$ as f as multiplicative order p. As a consequence, the decryption process indeed returns $m + m' \bmod p$, and the EvalSum algorithm gives a random encryption of $m + m'$ (mod p) (in the sense that it has the same output distribution than the encryption algorithm on the input $m + m'$ (mod p)). The same argument works for the EvalScal algorithm, with any scalar $\alpha \in \mathbf{Z}/p\mathbf{Z}$.

2.3   Security

The total break of our scheme (tb − cpa attack) consists in finding x from (B, p, g, g^x, f), *i.e.*, in computing a discrete logarithm in G. From Theorem 2, this is harder than computing a discrete logarithm in G/F.

KeyGen(1^λ)

1. $(B, n, p, s, g, f, G, F) \xleftarrow{\$} \text{Gen}(1^\lambda, 1^\mu)$
2. Pick[a] $x \xleftarrow{\$} \{0, \ldots, Bp - 1\}$, set $h \leftarrow g^x$
3. Set $pk \leftarrow (B, p, g, h, f)$ and $sk \leftarrow x$.
4. Return (pk, sk)

Encrypt($1^\lambda, pk, m$)

1. Pick $r \xleftarrow{\$} \{0, \ldots, Bp - 1\}$
2. Compute $c_1 \leftarrow g^r$
3. Compute $c_2 \leftarrow f^m h^r$
4. Return (c_1, c_2)

---

[a] As n will be unknown in the sequel, x is picked at random in $\{0, \ldots, Bp - 1\}$

Decrypt($1^\lambda, pk, sk, (c_1, c_2)$)

1. Compute $M \leftarrow c_2/c_1^x$
2. $m \leftarrow \text{Solve}(p, g, f, G, F, M)$
3. Return m

EvalSum($1^\lambda, pk, (c_1, c_2), (c_1', c_2')$)

1. Compute $c_1'' \leftarrow c_1 c_1'$, $c_2'' \leftarrow c_2 c_2'$
2. Pick $r \xleftarrow{\$} \{0, \ldots, Bp - 1\}$
3. Return $(c_1'' g^r, c_2'' h^r)$

EvalScal($1^\lambda, pk, (c_1, c_2), \alpha$)

1. Compute $c_1' \leftarrow c_1^\alpha$ and $c_2' \leftarrow c_2^\alpha$
2. Pick $r \xleftarrow{\$} \{0, \ldots, Bp - 1\}$
3. Return $(c_1' g^r, c_2' h^r)$

Fig. 1. A generic linearly homomorphic encryption scheme

Theorem 3. *The scheme described in Fig. 1 is one-way under chosen plaintext attack* (ow − cpa) *if and only if the Lift Diffie-Hellman* (LDH) *problem is hard (so if and only if the partial discrete logarithm problem* (PDL) *is hard).*

Proof. See [CL15].

Theorem 4. *The scheme described in Fig. 1 is semantically secure under chosen plaintext attacks* (ind−cpa) *if and only the decisional Diffie-Hellman problem is hard in G.*

Proof. Let's construct a reduction $\mathcal{R}$ that solve the DDH assumption using an efficient ind − cpa adversary $\mathcal{A}$. $\mathcal{R}$ takes as input $(B, p, g, f, G, F, X, Y, Z)$, a DDH instance, and sets $pk = (B, p, g, X, f)$. When $\mathcal{A}$ requests an encryption of one of his choice of challenge messages m_0 and m_1, $\mathcal{R}$ flips a bit b encrypts m_b as $(Y, f^{m_b} Z)$ and sends this ciphertext as its answer to $\mathcal{A}$. If Z was not a random element, this ciphertext would be indistinguishable from a true encryption of m_b because of the choice of the bound B, and $\mathcal{A}$ will correctly answer with its (non-negligeable) advantage ϵ. Otherwise, the encryption is independent of the message and $\mathcal{A}$'s advantage to distinguish is $1/2$. Therefore, the reduction returns one if and only $\mathcal{A}$ correctly guessed b and has advantage $\epsilon/2$ to solve the DDH assumption. $\square$

3   A Linearly Homomorphic Encryption from DDH

We prove that, somewhat like in Paillier's encryption scheme [Pai99] within $\mathbf{Z}/N^2\mathbf{Z}$, a subgroup with an easy discrete logarithm problem exists in class groups of imaginary quadratic fields, and it allows to design a new linearly homomorphic encryption scheme. We refer the reader to Appendix A for background on class groups of imaginary quadratic fields and their use in Discrete Logarithm based cryptography.

3.1   A Subgroup with an Easy DL Problem

The next proposition, inspired by [CL09, Theorem2], establish the existence of a subgroup of a class group of an imaginary quadratic fields where the DL problem is easy.

Proposition 1. *Let Δ_K be a fundamental discriminant with $\Delta_K \equiv 1$ (mod 4) of the form $\Delta_K = -pq$ where p is an odd prime and q a non-negative integer prime to p such that $q > 4p$. Let $= (p^2, p)$ be an ideal of $\mathcal{O}_{\Delta_p}$, the order of discriminant $\Delta_p = \Delta_K p^2$. Denote by $f = [\ ]$ the class of in $C(\mathcal{O}_{\Delta_p})$. For $m \in \{1, \ldots, p-1\}$, $\mathrm{Red}(f^m) = (p^2, L(m)p)$ where $L(m)$ is the odd integer in $[-p, p]$ such that $L(m) \equiv 1/m$ (mod p). Moreover, f is a generator of the subgroup of order p of $C(\mathcal{O}_{\Delta_p})$.*

Proof. We consider the surjection $\bar{\varphi}_p : C(\mathcal{O}_{\Delta_p}) \longrightarrow C(\mathcal{O}_{\Delta_K})$. From [CL09, Lemma1] and [Cox99, Prop. 7.22 and Th. 7.24], the kernel of $\bar{\varphi}_p$ is isomorphic to $(\mathcal{O}_{\Delta_K}/p\mathcal{O}_{\Delta_K})^\times/(\mathbf{Z}/p\mathbf{Z})^\times$. As $p \mid \Delta_K$, the group $(\mathcal{O}_{\Delta_K}/p\mathcal{O}_{\Delta_K})^\times$ is isomorphic to $(\mathbf{F}_p[X]/(X^2))^\times$. This group contains $p(p-1)$ elements of the form $a + b\sqrt{\Delta_K}$ where $a \in (\mathbf{Z}/p\mathbf{Z})^\times$ and $b \in \mathbf{Z}/p\mathbf{Z}$. Now let us consider the quotient group $(\mathcal{O}_{\Delta_K}/p\mathcal{O}_{\Delta_K})^\times/(\mathbf{Z}/p\mathbf{Z})^\times$ where $[x] = [y]$ with $x, y \in (\mathcal{O}_{\Delta_K}/p\mathcal{O}_{\Delta_K})^\times$ if and only if there exists $\lambda \in (\mathbf{Z}/p\mathbf{Z})^\times$ such that $x = \lambda y$. This quotient is cyclic of order p and a system of representatives is $[1]$ and $[a + \sqrt{\Delta_K}]$ where a is an element of $(\mathbf{Z}/p\mathbf{Z})^\times$. Let $g = [1 + \sqrt{\Delta_K}]$, one has $g^m = [1 + m\sqrt{\Delta_K}] = [L(m) + \sqrt{\Delta_K}]$ for all $m \in \{1, \ldots, p-1\}$ and $g^p = [1]$. Let $\alpha_m = \frac{L(m) + \sqrt{\Delta_K}}{2} \in \mathcal{O}_{\Delta_K}$. Then α_m is a representative of the class g^m. The element g^m maps to the class $[\varphi_p^{-1}(\alpha_m \mathcal{O}_{\Delta_K})]$ of the kernel of $\bar{\varphi}_p$. From [BTW95, Prop.2.9], one can see that $\alpha_m \mathcal{O}_{\Delta_K} = (N(\alpha_m), -L(m) \mod 2N(\alpha_m))$ where the remainder is computed from the centered euclidean division. Now, $\varphi_p^{-1}(\alpha_m \mathcal{O}_{\Delta_K}) = (N(\alpha_m), -L(m)p \mod 2N(\alpha_m))$. As $N(\alpha_m) = \frac{L(m)^2 - \Delta_K}{4}$ and $q > 4p$, it follows that $p^2 < N(\alpha_m)$ and that $-L(m)p \mod 2N(\alpha_m) = -L(m)p$. As a consequence, $\varphi_p^{-1}(\alpha_m \mathcal{O}_{\Delta_K})$ corresponds to the form $(\frac{L(m)^2 - \Delta_K}{4}, -L(m)p, p^2)$, of discriminant Δ_p which is equivalent to $(p^2, L(m)p, \frac{L(m)^2 - \Delta_K}{4})$ which corresponds to the ideal $(p^2, L(m)p)$. Finally, this ideal of $\mathcal{O}_{\Delta_p}$ is reduced as $|L(m)p| < p^2 < \sqrt{|\Delta_p|}/2$, where the second inequality holds because $q > 4p$. Consequently, if $= (p^2, p)$, then $[\ ]$ generates the kernel of $\bar{\varphi}_p$ as $[\ ] = [\varphi_p^{-1}(\alpha_1 \mathcal{O}_{\Delta_K})]$. Moreover, $[\ ]^m = [\varphi_p^{-1}(\alpha_m \mathcal{O}_{\Delta_K})]$ so $\mathrm{Red}([\ ]^m) = (p^2, L(m)p)$, for $m \in \{1, \ldots, p-1\}$. $\square$

We devise, in Fig. 2, a new DDH group with an easy DL subgroup in class groups of imaginary quadratic fields, by assuming the difficulty of the DDH problem. In the Gen algorithm, we first construct a fundamental discriminant

$\Delta_K = -pq$ such that the 2-Sylow subgroup of $C(\Delta_K)$ is of order 2 (cf. Appendix A). Then, using [HJPT98, Subsection 3.1]'s method, we construct an ideal of $\mathcal{O}_{\Delta_K}$ of norm r, where r is a prime satisfying $\left(\frac{\Delta_K}{r}\right) = 1$. We then assume, as in the previous implementations of Elgamal (cf. Appendix A) that the class $[\,^2]$ will be of order s, an integer of the same order of magnitude than the odd part, $h(\Delta_K)/2$. Due to our choice of p and q, pq is 2λ-bit integer, and as s is close to $\sqrt{|\Delta_K|}$ (cf. Appendix A), it will be a λ-bit integer.

If $\mu > 80$, following the Cohen-Lenstra heuristics, the probability that p divides $h(\Delta_K)$ and s is negligible. Therefore, we can assume that $\gcd(p, h(\Delta_K)) = 1$. We consider the non-maximal order $\mathcal{O}_{\Delta_p}$ of discriminant $p^2\Delta_K$ as in Proposition 1. The fact that $\lambda \geqslant \mu + 2$ ensures that $q > 4p$. As a result, the subgroup F generated by f gives an easy DL subgroup. The morphism $\bar{\varphi}_p$ defined in Appendix A plays the role of the surjection π between $C(\mathcal{O}_{\Delta_p})$ and $C(\mathcal{O}_{\Delta_p})/F \simeq C(\mathcal{O}_{\Delta_K})$, which is computable in polynomial time, knowing p (cf. [HJPT98, Algorithm3]). Moreover, still with the knowledge of p, it is possible to lift elements of $C(\mathcal{O}_{\Delta_K})$ in $C(\mathcal{O}_{\Delta_p})$, using [HPT99, Algorithm 2]. We can then apply the injective morphism of Lemma 3 on $[\,^2]$ to get a class of $C(\Delta_p)$ with the same order s and multiply this class by f^k where $k \xleftarrow{\$} \{1, p-1\}$. As $\gcd(p, s) = 1$ the result, g is of order ps (this procedure to get an element of order ps was also used in the proof of Theorem 2). Note that g is still a square of $C(\Delta_p)$: as the map of Lemma 3 is a morphism, the lift of $[\,^2]$ gives a square of $C(\Delta_p)$. Moreover, F is a subgroup of the squares: $f = (f^{2^{-1} \bmod p})^2$ as p is odd. As a consequence, g is a square as it is a product of two squares.

Eventually, we take $B = \lceil |\Delta_K|^{3/4} \rceil$. The statistical distance of $\{g^r, r \xleftarrow{\$} \{0, \ldots, Bp-1\}\}$ to the uniform distribution can be shown to be upper bounded by $ps/(4pB) = s/(4\lceil|\Delta_K|^{3/4}\rceil)$. By Eq. 1 in Appendix A, this is less than $\frac{\log|\Delta_K|}{4\pi\lceil|\Delta_K|^{1/4}\rceil} \in \tilde{\mathcal{O}}(2^{-\lambda/2})$ which is a negligible function of λ. As a consequence, the distribution $\{g^r, r \xleftarrow{\$} \{0, \ldots, Bp-1\}\}$ is statistically indistinguishable from the uniform distribution in $G = \langle g \rangle$. For performance issue, one can take a better bound for B, for instance $B = 2^{80}\lceil\log(|\Delta_K|)|\Delta_K|^{1/2}/(4\pi)\rceil$, which makes the statistical distance less than 2^{-80}.

3.2   The New Protocol

The DDH group with an easy DL subgroup of Fig. 2 gives rise to a linearly homomorphic encryption scheme in quadratic fields, using the generic construction of Fig. 1. Compared to previous solutions based on a similar construction ([BCP03]), this scheme is only based on the difficulty of the discrete logarithm in G, and does not rely on the difficulty of factorization.

In practice, the best attack against the scheme consists in retrieving the private key, i.e., in computing a discrete logarithm. As said in Appendix A, the problems of computing discrete logarithm in $C(\mathcal{O}_{\Delta_K})$ and computing $h(\mathcal{O}_{\Delta_K})$ have similar complexity. Given oracle for both problems, one can compute discrete logarithm in $C(\mathcal{O}_{\Delta_p})$ and totally break the scheme. Indeed, if $s = h(\mathcal{O}_{\Delta_K})$,

$\mathsf{Gen}(1^\lambda, 1^\mu)$

1. Pick p a random μ-bits prime and q a random $(2\lambda - \mu)$ prime such that $pq \equiv -1$ (mod 4) and $(p/q) = -1$.
2. $\Delta_K \leftarrow -pq$, $\Delta_p \leftarrow p^2 \Delta_K$, $B \leftarrow \lceil |\Delta_K|^{3/4} \rceil$, $f \leftarrow [(p^2, p)]$ in $C(\Delta_p)$ and $F = \langle f \rangle$
3. Let r be a small prime, with $r \neq p$ and $\left(\frac{\Delta_K}{r}\right) = 1$, set   an ideal lying above r.
4. Let $k \xleftarrow{\$} \{1, p-1\}$ and set $g \leftarrow [\varphi_p^{-1}(\ ^2)]^p f^k$ in $C(\Delta_p)$ and $G \leftarrow \langle g \rangle$
5. Return $(B, \emptyset, p, \emptyset, g, f, G, F)$

$\mathsf{Solve}(B, p, g, f, G, F, X)$

1. Parse $\mathsf{Red}(X)$ as $(p^2, \tilde{x}p)$
2. If fails Return $\perp$ Else Return $\tilde{x}^{-1}$ (mod p)

Fig. 2. A new DDH Group with an Easy DL Subgroup

given g and $h = g^x$, we can compute $\bar{\varphi}_p(g)$ and $\bar{\varphi}_p(h) = \bar{\varphi}_p(g)^{x \bmod s}$. The oracle for discrete logarithm in $C(\mathcal{O}_{\Delta_K})$ gives x mod s. As shown in Lemma 1, if s is known the PDL problem is easy, so one can compute x mod p and we get x as $\gcd(p, s) = 1$ with the Chinese remainder theorem. Moreover, finding $h(\mathcal{O}_{\Delta_K})$ or the multiplicative order of g can be sufficient: knowing $s = h(\mathcal{O}_{\Delta_K})$ breaks the PDL problem (cf. Lemma 1) and the one wayness of the scheme by Theorem 3.

4   Extensions

Removing the Condition on the Relative Size of p and q. To have a polynomial Solve algorithm, we impose $q > 4p$, so that the reduced elements of $\langle f \rangle$ are ideals of norm p^2. For a large message space, e.g. with a 2048-bit p (as in [Pai99] or [BCP03] with a 2048 bit RSA integer), $|\Delta_p| = p^3 q > 4p^4$ has more than 8194 bits and $|\Delta_K| = pq > 4p^2$ has more than 4098 bits. So we loose our advantage over factoring based schemes, as we only need a discriminant Δ_K of 1348 bits to have the same security than a 2048 bit RSA integer (cf. Appendix A). Suppose that we work with $\Delta_K = -p$. In the order $\mathcal{O}_{\Delta_p}$ of discriminant $\Delta_p = p^2 \Delta_K = -p^3$, the ideals of norm p^2 are no longer reduced. However, we can still have a polynomial time algorithm to solve the discrete logarithm in $\langle f \rangle$ where $f = [(p^2, p)]$. From the proof of Proposition 1, f still generate the subgroup of order p, and for $k \in \{1, \ldots, p-1\}$, the class f^k still contains a non reduced ideal $(p^2, L(k)p)$ where $L(k)$ is defined as in Proposition 1. We can use the main result of [CL09] constructively to find this non reduced ideal that will disclose the discrete logarithm k given the reduced element of the class f^k. The idea is to lift this reduced element in a class group of a suborder where the ideals of norm p^2 are reduced. Let $\Delta_{p^2} = p^4 \Delta_K$. For $p > 4$, we have $p^2 < \sqrt{|\Delta_{p^2}|}/2$ so the ideals of norm p^2 are reduced. We lift an element of $\mathcal{O}_{\Delta_p}$ in $\mathcal{O}_{\Delta_{p^2}}$ by computing $[\varphi_p^{-1}(\cdot)]^p$ on a representative ideal prime to p (we can use

[HJPT98, Algorithm1] to find an ideal prime to p in a given class). This map is injective, so applied on f we get a class f_ℓ of order p in $C(\mathcal{O}_{\Delta_{p^2}})$. Moreover, this class is in the kernel of the map $\bar{\varphi}_{p^2}$ from $C(\mathcal{O}_{\Delta_{p^2}})$ to $C(\mathcal{O}_{\Delta_K})$, and an easy generalization of Proposition 1 shows that the subgroup of $C(\mathcal{O}_{\Delta_{p^2}})$ generated by f_ℓ is also generated by $[(p^2,p)]$. As a result, if $h = f^x$ in $C(\mathcal{O}_{\Delta_p})$, we have $h_\ell = [\varphi_p^{-1}([h])]^p = ([\varphi_p^{-1}([f])]^p)^x = f_\ell^x$ and x can be computed as $x = y/z$ where y is the discrete logarithm of h_ℓ in basis $[(p^2,p)]$ and y is the discrete logarithm of f_ℓ in basis $[(p^2,p)]$. Both logarithms can be computed as in $C(\mathcal{O}_{\Delta_p})$. This variant also works with $\Delta_K = -pq$ and $q < 4p$, so p can be chosen independently from the security level, with the restriction that p must have at least 80 bits.

A Faster Variant. We can change the KeyGen algorithm as follows: g is now in the class group of the maximal order (i.e., g is the class of ^{2}) and we set $h = g^x$ where x is the secret key and the computation is done in $C(\mathcal{O}_{\Delta_K})$. Let us denote by $\psi : C(\mathcal{O}_{\Delta_K}) \to C(\mathcal{O}_{\Delta_p})$ the injective morphism of Lemma 3, that computes $[\varphi_p^{-1}(\cdot)]^p$ on a representative ideal prime to p.

To encrypt $m \in \mathbf{Z}/p\mathbf{Z}$, we compute $c_1 = g^r$ and $c_2 = f^m\psi(h^r)$ in $C(\mathcal{O}_{\Delta_p})$. To decrypt, we first compute c_1^x and lift it, by computing $c_1' = \psi(c_1^x)$ in $C(\mathcal{O}_{\Delta_p})$. Then we retrieve $f^m = c_2/c_1'$. This variant can be viewed as a mix of an Elgamal cryptosystem in $C(\mathcal{O}_{\Delta_K})$ (lifted in $C(\mathcal{O}_{\Delta_p})$ by applying ψ) and of a cryptosystem based on the subgroup decomposition problem using the direct product between $\psi(\langle g \rangle)$ and $\langle f \rangle$. The advantage of this variant is that ciphertexts are smaller (c_1 is in $C(\mathcal{O}_{\Delta_K})$ instead of $C(\mathcal{O}_{\Delta_p})$) and that computations are faster: encryption performs two exponentiations in $C(\mathcal{O}_{\Delta_K})$ instead of $C(\mathcal{O}_{\Delta_p})$ and one lift (which computational cost is essentially the exponentiation to the power p). Decryption similarly involves one exponentiation in $C(\mathcal{O}_{\Delta_K})$ instead of $C(\mathcal{O}_{\Delta_p})$ and a lift. However, the semantic security is now based on a non standard problem. Let g be a generator of a subgroup of $C(\mathcal{O}_{\Delta_K})$ of order s. After having chosen m, the adversary is asked to distinguished the following distributions: $\{(g^x, g^y, \psi(g^{xy})), x,y \xleftarrow{\$} \mathbf{Z}/s\mathbf{Z}\}$ and $\{(g^x, g^y, \psi(g^{xy})f^m), x,y \xleftarrow{\$} \mathbf{Z}/s\mathbf{Z}\}$. The total break is equivalent to the DL problem in $C(\mathcal{O}_{\Delta_K})$.

Other improvements than those we presented are possible: we can gain efficiency using the Chinese Remainder Theorem using discriminant of the form $\Delta_K = -(\prod_{i=1}^n p_i)q$, and generalizing à la Damgård and Jurik (cf. [DJ01]), with discriminants of the form $\Delta_{p^t} = p^{2t}\Delta_K$, with $\Delta_K = -pq$ and $t \geqslant 1$ to enlarge the message space to $\mathbf{Z}/p^t\mathbf{Z}$ without losing the homomorphic property. A non-trivial adaptation may also be possible with real quadratic fields.

5 Performances and Comparisons

We now compare the efficiency of our cryptosystem with some other linearly homomorphic encryptions schemes, namely the system of Paillier and the one from [BCP03]. The security of the Paillier cryptosystem is based on the factorization problem of RSA integers, while [BCP03] is based on both the factorization and the DL problems. For our scheme, the best attack consists in computing DL in $C(\mathcal{O}_{\Delta_K})$ or in computing $h(\mathcal{O}_{\Delta_K})$ and both problems have similar complexity.

In [BJS10], the DL problem with a discriminant Δ_K of 1348 (resp. 1828 bits) is estimated as hard as factoring a 2048 (resp. 3072 bits) RSA integer n. In Fig. 1, we give the timings in ms of the time to perform an encryption and decryption for the three schemes. Concerning Paillier, for encryption and decryption, the main operation is an exponentiation of the form $x^k \bmod n^2$ where k has the same bit length as n. Concerning [BCP03], which has an Elgamal structure, two exponentiations of the form $x^k \bmod n^2$ with k an integer of the same bit length as n^2 are used for encryption and one for decryption. Our scheme has also this structure with two exponentiations for encryption and one for decryption. Decryption also involves an inversion modulo p. The exponentiations are made in $C(\mathcal{O}_{\Delta_p})$ with $\Delta_p = p^2 \Delta_K$. The size of the exponent is bounded by Bp where we have seen that B can be chosen roughly of the bit size of $\sqrt{\Delta_K}$ plus 80 bits. For a same security level, our scheme is thus more efficient for a small p.

The timings where performed with Sage 6.3 on a standard laptop with a straightforward implementation. The exponentiation in class group uses a PARI/GP function (qfbnupow). We must stress that *this function is far less optimized than the exponentiation in* $\mathbf{Z}/n\mathbf{Z}$, *so there is a huge bias in favor of BCP and Paillier*. A more optimized implementation would give much better results for our system. Nevertheless, we see that for a 2048 bits modulus, our cryptosystem is already faster than the protocol from [BCP03]. Moreover, for stronger securities, our system will be faster, as asymptotically, the factorization algorithms have complexity $L(1/3, \cdot)$ whereas the algorithms for class groups of quadratic fields have complexity $L(1/2, \cdot)$. Moreover the multiplication modulo n and the composition of quadratic forms have both quasi linear complexity [Sch91]. As shown in Table 1, already with a 3072 bits modulus our cryptosystem is competitive: faster than Paillier for decryption. For a very high security level (7680 bits modulus), our system would be twice as fast as Paillier for encryption, for messages of 512 bits. We also give timings of our faster variant of Subsection 4. For a same security level, this variant becomes more interesting when the message space grows. In Table 1, we see that even with a naive implementation, our system is competitive for message space up to 256 bits (resp. 912 bits) for 2048 bits security (resp. for 3072 bits security).

Note that a medium size message space can be sufficient for applications. For example, our system may be used as in [CGS97] to design a voting scheme. For a yes/no pool, a voter encrypts 0 (resp. 1) to vote no (resp. to vote yes). By combining all the ciphertexts, the election manager would get an encryption of the sum of the vote modulo p. Decryption allows to decide the result if the number of voters ℓ satisfies $\ell < p$. So a 80-bit p is largely sufficient as $2^{80} \approx 10^{24}$. With Elgamal, in [CGS97], the discrete logarithm in decryption involves a baby-step giant-step computation of time $\mathcal{O}(\sqrt{\ell})$ (so a very low number of voters can be handled) whereas a single inversion modulo p is needed for our scheme. For a multi-candidate election system with m candidates and ℓ voters, one votes for the ith candidate by encrypting ℓ^i. The tally is decrypted with a decomposition in base ℓ, so we must have $\ell^m < p$. With a 256-bit integer, we can have 2^{16} voters and 16 candidates, which is the good order of magnitude for real life elections, for which there are around a thousand registered voters by polling stations.

Table 1. Efficiency Comparison of Linearly Homomorphic Encryption Schemes

Cryptosystem	Parameter	Message Space	Encrypt (ms)	Decrypt (ms)
Paillier	2048 bits modulus	2048 bits	**28**	**28**
BCP03	2048 bits modulus	2048 bits	107	54
New Proposal	1348 bits Δ_K	80 bits	93	49
Variant Subsec. 4	1348 bits Δ_K	80 bits	82	45
Variant Subsec. 4	1348 bits Δ_K	256 bits	105	68
Paillier	3072 bits modulus	3072 bits	**109**	109
BCP03	3072 bits modulus	3072 bits	427	214
New Proposal	1828 bits Δ_K	80 bits	179	91
Variant Subsec. 4	1828 bits Δ_K	80 bits	145	**78**
Variant Subsec. 4	1828 bits Δ_K	512 bits	226	159
Variant Subsec. 4	1828 bits Δ_K	912 bits	340	271

Acknowledgments. This work has been supported in part by ERC Starting Grant ERC-2013-StG-335086-LATTAC and by the financial support from the French State, managed by the French National Research Agency (ANR) in the frame of the "Investments for the future" Programme IdEx Bordeaux (ANR-10-IDEX-03-02), Cluster of excellence CPU.

A   Background on Imaginary Quadratic Fields

Let $D < 0$ be a squarefree integer and consider the quadratic imaginary field $K = \mathbf{Q}(\sqrt{D})$. The *fundamental discriminant* Δ_K of K is defined as $\Delta_K = D$ if $D \equiv 1 \pmod 4$ and $\Delta_K = 4D$ otherwise. The ring $\mathcal{O}_{\Delta_K}$ of algebraic integers in K is the *maximal* order of K. If $\mathcal{O}_{\Delta_f}$ is a sub-ring of $\mathcal{O}_{\Delta_K}$, it is characterized by its *finite* index in $\mathcal{O}_{\Delta_K}$, called its *conductor*. Its discriminant $\Delta_f = f^2 \Delta_K$. Every (primitive) ideal of $\mathcal{O}_\Delta$ can be written as $\left(a\mathbf{Z} + \frac{-b+\sqrt{\Delta}}{2}\mathbf{Z} \right)$ with $a \in \mathbf{N}$ and $b \in \mathbf{Z}$ such that $b^2 \equiv \Delta \pmod{4a}$, and denoted by (a, b) for short. The *ideal class group* of $\mathcal{O}_\Delta$ is $C(\mathcal{O}_\Delta) = I(\mathcal{O}_\Delta)/P(\mathcal{O}_\Delta)$, where $I(\mathcal{O}_\Delta)$ is the group of invertible fractional ideals of $\mathcal{O}_\Delta$ and $P(\mathcal{O}_\Delta)$ the subgroup consisting of principal ideals. Its cardinality is the *class number* of $\mathcal{O}_\Delta$ denoted by $h(\mathcal{O}_\Delta)$. A canonical representative of the class of the ideal is denoted by Red( ). There exists a computable surjection $\bar{\varphi}_f : C(\mathcal{O}_{\Delta_f}) \twoheadrightarrow C(\mathcal{O}_{\Delta_K})$, when f is known. Additional material can be found in [CL15, AppendixB] and [Cox99].

In 2000, Jacobson has described an index-calculus method to solve the DL problem in class group of imaginary quadratic field of discriminant Δ_K [Jac00]. Various improvements have been proposed to this algorithm: In [BJS10], it is conjecture that a state of the art implementation has conjectured complexity $L_{|\Delta_K|}[1/2, o(1)]$. Moreover, the best known algorithm to compute class numbers of fundamental discriminant are again index-calculus method with the same complexity. In [HM00], Hamdy and Möller discuss the selection of a discriminant

Δ_K such that the DL problem in $C(\mathcal{O}_{\Delta_K})$ is as hard as in finite fields: It is advised to construct a fundamental discriminant Δ_K and to minimize to 2-Sylow subgroup of the class group. In our case, by construction Δ_K will be the product of two odd primes. If we take $\Delta_K = -pq$ with p and q such that $p \equiv -q$ (mod 4) then Δ_K is a fundamental discriminant. Moreover the 2-Sylow subgroup will be isomorphic to $\mathbf{Z}/2\mathbf{Z}$ if we choose p and q such that $(p/q) = (q/p) = -1$ (cf. [Kap78, p.598]). In that case, we will work with the odd part, which is the group of squares of $C(\mathcal{O}_{\Delta_K})$. Following the Cohen-Lenstra heuristics, cf. [Coh00, Chapter 5.10.1], the probability that the odd part of the class group is cyclic is 97.757% and the probability that an odd prime r divides $h(\mathcal{O}_{\Delta_K})$ is approximately $1/r + 1/r^2$. As a result, we can not guarantee that the order of the odd part is not divisible by small primes. Nevertheless, as indicated in [HM00], this does not lead to a weakness on the DL problem, as there is no efficient algorithm to compute $h(\mathcal{O}_{\Delta_K})$ or odd multiples or factors of $h(\mathcal{O}_{\Delta_K})$, hence an adaptation of the Pohlig-Hellman Algorithm is not possible. On average, $h(\mathcal{O}_{\Delta_K})$ is in the order of $\sqrt{|\Delta_K|}$, see [Coh00, Theorem 4.9.15 (Brauer-Siegel)]. Moreover (cf. [Coh00, p.295]),

$$h(\Delta_K) < \frac{1}{\pi} \log |\Delta_K| \sqrt{|\Delta_K|}. \tag{1}$$

Since index-calculus algorithms for solving the DL problem are asymptotically much slower than index-calculus algorithms to solve the integer factorization problem, the discriminant can be taken smaller than RSA modulus. In [BJS10], the DL problem with a discriminant of 1348 bits (resp. 1828 bits) is estimated as hard as factoring a 2048 bits (resp. 3072 bits) RSA integer.

Elgamal Cryptosystem Adaptations in Class Group. Buchmann and Williams ([BW88]) have proposed an adaptation of the Diffie-Hellman key exchange in imaginary quadratic fields and briefly described an adaptation of the Elgamal cryptosystem in the same setting. Efficient implementations of these cryptosystems are discussed in [BDW90, SP05, BH01] and [BV07]. At a high level, the key generation process of these adaptations of Elgamal can be sketched as follows. First, generate Δ_K a fundamental negative discriminant, such that $|\Delta_K|$ is large enough to thwart the computation of discrete logarithm (cf. previous subsection). Then choose g a class of $C(\mathcal{O}_{\Delta_K})$ of even order (from the discussion of the previous subsection, the order of g will be close to $h(\Delta_K) \approx \sqrt{|\Delta_K|}$ with high probability). Finally, the private key is $x \xleftarrow{\$} \{0, \ldots, \lfloor \sqrt{|\Delta_K|} \rfloor\}$ and the public key is (g, h), where $h = g^x$. To implement Elgamal, it remains the problem of the embedding of a message. In [BW88], an integer m is encrypted as $(g^r, m + N(h^r))$ where $N(h^r)$ denotes the norm of the reduced ideal of the class h^r. As a result, the scheme is not based on the traditional DDH assumption. Another solution is given in [SP05, Section2]. An integer message $m \leq \sqrt{|\Delta|}/2$ is mapped to the class M of an ideal above p where p is the first prime with $p > m$ such that Δ is a quadratic residue modulo p. If $d = m - p$, the message m is encrypted as (g^r, Mh^r, d): The distance d seems to be public, in order to recover m from M. This can be a problem for semantic security: the first stage adversary can choose two messages m_0, m_1 such that $d_0 \neq d_1$ and easily win the indistinguishability game with probability one by recognizing the message thanks to the distance. In [BH01], a "hashed" version is used, a bit-string m is encrypted as $(g^r, m \oplus H(h^r))$ where H is a cryptographic hash function. In [BV07], an adaptation of DHIES is described. An variant of the Elgamal cryptosystem in a non maximal order of discriminant $\Delta_q = q^2 \Delta_K$ is presented in [HJPT98]. A traditional setup of Elgamal is done in $C(\mathcal{O}_{\Delta_q})$, $h = g^x$. A ciphertext is (g^r, mh^r) in $C(\mathcal{O}_{\Delta_q})$ where m is an ideal of norm smaller than $\sqrt{\Delta_K}/2$. To decrypt, the ciphertext is moved in the maximal order with the trapdoor q where a traditional decryption is made to recover the message in $C(\mathcal{O}_{\Delta_K})$. Eventually, the message is lifted back in $C(\mathcal{O}_{\Delta_q})$. This variant can be seen as an Elgamal with a CRT decryption procedure: its advantage is that most of the decryption computation is done in $C(\mathcal{O}_{\Delta_K})$ and Δ_K can be chosen relatively small (big enough such the factorization of Δ_q is intractable, the discrete logarithm problem can be easy in $C(\mathcal{O}_{\Delta_K})$). The problem of the embedding of the plaintext in an ideal is not addressed in this paper. A chosen-ciphertext attack against this cryptosystem has been proposed in [JJ00]. In [KM03], an adaptation of the Diffie-Hellman key exchange and of the Elgamal cryptosystem are given using class semigroup of an imaginary non-maximal quadratic order. Unfortunately a cryptanalysis of this proposal has been presented in [Jac04]. A final important remark on the adaptation of the Elgamal cryptosystem is that it is necessary to work in the group of squares, *i. e.*, the *principal genus*. We didn't find this remark in previous works: in the whole class group, the DDH problem is easy. Indeed, it is well known that in $(\mathbf{Z}/p\mathbf{Z})^\times$, one can compute Legendre symbols and defeats the DDH assumption. As a consequence, it is necessary to work in the group of squares. In a class group, for example if the discriminant $\Delta = - \prod_{i=1}^{k} p_i$ is odd and the p_i are distinct primes numbers, we can associate to a class the value of the generic characters, the Legendre symbols (r, p_i) for i from 1 to k where r is an integer represented by the class (see [Cox99] for details on genus theory). It is easy to see that the previous attack in $(\mathbf{Z}/p\mathbf{Z})^\times$ can be adapted in class groups with the computation of the generic characters. As a result, it is necessary to work in the group of squares, which is the principal genus (cf. [Cox99, Theorem 3.15]), *i. e.*, the set of classes such that the generic characters all equal 1.

References

[BCP03] Bresson, E., Catalano, D., Pointcheval, D.: A Simple Public-Key Cryptosystem with a Double Trapdoor Decryption Mechanism and Its Applications. In: Laih, C.-S. (ed.) ASIACRYPT 2003. LNCS, vol. 2894, pp. 37–54. Springer, Heidelberg (2003)

[BDW90] Buchmann, J., Düllmann, S., Williams, H.C.: On the Complexity and Efficiency of a New Key Exchange System. In: Quisquater, J.-J., Vandewalle, J. (eds.) EUROCRYPT 1989. LNCS, vol. 434, pp. 597–616. Springer, Heidelberg (1990)

[Ben88] Benaloh, J. C.: Verifiable Secret-Ballot Elections. PhD thesis, Yale University (1988)

[BGN05] Boneh, D., Goh, E.-J., Nissim, K.: Evaluating 2-DNF Formulas on Ciphertexts. In: Kilian, J. (ed.) TCC 2005. LNCS, vol. 3378, pp. 325–341. Springer, Heidelberg (2005)

[BH01] Buchmann, J., Hamdy, S.: A survey on IQ-cryptography, Public-Key Cryptography and Computational Number Theory, de Gruyter, 1–15 (2001)

[BJS10] Biasse, J.-F., Jacobson Jr., M.J., Silvester, A.K.: Security Estimates for Quadratic Field Based Cryptosystems. In: Steinfeld, R., Hawkes, P. (eds.) ACISP 2010. LNCS, vol. 6168, pp. 233–247. Springer, Heidelberg (2010)

[Bre00] Brent, R.P.: Public Key Cryptography with a Group of Unknown Order. Technical Report. Oxford University (2000)

[BTW95] Buchmann, J., Thiel, C., Williams, H.C.: Short Representation of Quadratic Integers. In: Proc. of CANT 1992, Math. Appl., vol. 325. pp. 159–185. Kluwer Academic Press (1995)

[BV07] Buchmann, J., Vollmer, U.: Binary Quadratic Forms. Springer, An Algorithmic Approach (2007)

[BV14] Brakerski, Z., Vaikuntanathan, V.: Efficient Fully Homomorphic Encryption from (Standard) LWE. SIAM J. Comput. **43**(2), 831–871 (2014)

[BW88] Buchmann, J., Williams, H.C.: A Key-Exchange System Based on Imaginary Quadratic Fields. J. Cryptology **1**(2), 107–118 (1988)

[CC07] Castagnos, G., Chevallier-Mames, B.: Towards a DL-Based Additively Homomorphic Encryption Scheme. In: Garay, J.A., Lenstra, A.K., Mambo, M., Peralta, R. (eds.) ISC 2007. LNCS, vol. 4779, pp. 362–375. Springer, Heidelberg (2007)

[CF14] Catalano, D., Fiore, D.: Boosting Linearly-Homomorphic Encryption to Evaluate Degree-2 Functions on Encrypted Data. Cryptology ePrint Archive, report 2014/813 (2014). http://eprint.iacr.org/2014/813

[CGS97] Cramer, R., Gennaro, R., Schoenmakers, B.: A Secure and Optimally Efficient Multi-authority Election Scheme. In: Fumy, W. (ed.) EUROCRYPT 1997. LNCS, vol. 1233, pp. 103–118. Springer, Heidelberg (1997)

[CJLN09] Castagnos, G., Joux, A., Laguillaumie, F., Nguyen, P.Q.: Factoring pq^2 with Quadratic Forms: Nice Cryptanalyses. In: Matsui, M. (ed.) ASIACRYPT 2009. LNCS, vol. 5912, pp. 469–486. Springer, Heidelberg (2009)

[CL09] Castagnos, G., Laguillaumie, F.: On the Security of Cryptosystems with Quadratic Decryption: The Nicest Cryptanalysis. In: Joux, A. (ed.) EUROCRYPT 2009. LNCS, vol. 5479, pp. 260–277. Springer, Heidelberg (2009)

[CL12] Castagnos, G., Laguillaumie, F.: Homomorphic Encryption for Multiplications and Pairing Evaluation. In: Visconti, I., De Prisco, R. (eds.) SCN 2012. LNCS, vol. 7485, pp. 374–392. Springer, Heidelberg (2012)

[CL15] Castagnos, G., Laguillaumie, F.: Linearly Homomorphic Encryption from DDH, Extended version, Cryptology ePrint Archive, report 2015/047 (2015). http://eprint.iacr.org/2015/047

[CPP06] Chevallier-Mames, B., Paillier, P., Pointcheval, D.: Encoding-Free ElGamal Encryption Without Random Oracles. In: Yung, M., Dodis, Y., Kiayias, A., Malkin, T. (eds.) PKC 2006. LNCS, vol. 3958, pp. 91–104. Springer, Heidelberg (2006)

[CHN99] Coron, J.-S., Handschuh, H., Naccache, D.: ECC: Do We Need to Count? In: Lam, K.-Y., Okamoto, E., Xing, C. (eds.) ASIACRYPT 1999. LNCS, vol. 1716, pp. 122–134. Springer, Heidelberg (1999)

[Coh00] Cohen, H.: A Course in Computational Algebraic Number Theory. Springer (2000)

[Cox99] Cox, D.A.: Primes of the form $x^2 + ny^2$. John Wiley & Sons (1999)

[DF02] Damgård, I.B., Fujisaki, E.: A Statistically-Hiding Integer Commitment Scheme Based on Groups with Hidden Order. In: Zheng, Y. (ed.) ASIACRYPT 2002. LNCS, vol. 2501, pp. 125–142. Springer, Heidelberg (2002)

[DJ01] Damgård, I., Jurik, M.J.: A Generalisation, a Simplification and some Applications of Paillier's Probabilistic Public-Key System. In: Kim, K. (ed.) Proc. of PKC 2001. LNCS, vol. 1992, pp. 119–136. Springer, Heidelberg (2001)

[Gal02] Galbraith, S.D.: Elliptic Curve Paillier Schemes. J. Cryptology 15(2), 129–138 (2002)

[Gen09] Gentry, C.: Fully homomorphic encryption using ideal lattices. In: Proc. of STOC 2009, pp. 169–178. ACM (2009)

[GM84] Goldwasser, S., Micali, S.: Probabilistic Encryption. JCSS 28(2), 270–299 (1984)

[HJPT98] Hühnlein, D., Jacobson Jr., M.J., Paulus, S., Takagi, T.: A Cryptosystem Based on Non-maximal Imaginary Quadratic Orders with Fast Decryption. In: Nyberg, K. (ed.) EUROCRYPT 1998. LNCS, vol. 1403, pp. 294–307. Springer, Heidelberg (1998)

[HM00] Hamdy, S., Möller, B.: Security of Cryptosystems Based on Class Groups of Imaginary Quadratic Orders. In: Okamoto, T. (ed.) ASIACRYPT 2000. LNCS, vol. 1976, pp. 234–247. Springer, Heidelberg (2000)

[HPT99] Hartmann, M., Paulus, S., Takagi, T.: NICE - New Ideal Coset Encryption -. In: Koç, Ç.K., Paar, C. (eds.) CHES 1999. LNCS, vol. 1717, pp. 328–339. Springer, Heidelberg (1999)

[Jac00] Jacobson Jr., M.J.: Computing discrete logarithms in quadratic orders. J. Cryptology 13, 473–492 (2000)

[Jac04] Jacobson Jr., M.J.: The Security of Cryptosystems Based on Class Semigroups of Imaginary Quadratic Non-maximal Orders. In: Wang, H., Pieprzyk, J., Varadharajan, V. (eds.) ACISP 2004. LNCS, vol. 3108, pp. 149–156. Springer, Heidelberg (2004)

[JJ00] Jaulmes, É., Joux, A.: A NICE Cryptanalysis. In: Preneel, B. (ed.) EUROCRYPT 2000. LNCS, vol. 1807, pp. 382–391. Springer, Heidelberg (2000)

[JL13] Joye, M., Libert, B.: Efficient Cryptosystems from 2^k-th Power Residue Symbols. In: Johansson, T., Nguyen, P.Q. (eds.) EUROCRYPT 2013. LNCS, vol. 7881, pp. 76–92. Springer, Heidelberg (2013)

[JSW08] Jacobson Jr., M.J., Scheidler, R., Weimer, D.: An Adaptation of the NICE Cryptosystem to Real Quadratic Orders. In: Vaudenay, S. (ed.) AFRICACRYPT 2008. LNCS, vol. 5023, pp. 191–208. Springer, Heidelberg (2008)

[Kap78] Kaplan, P.: Divisibilité par 8 du nombre des classes des corps quadratiques dont le 2-groupe des classes est cyclique, et réciprocité biquadratique. J. Math. Soc. Japan 25(4), 547–733 (1976)

[KM03] Kim, H., Moon, S.: Public-key cryptosystems based on class semigroups of imaginary quadratic non-maximal orders. In: Safavi-Naini, R., Seberry, J. (eds.): ACISP 2003. LNCS, vol. 2727. Springer, Heidelberg (2003)

[NS98] Naccache, D., Stern, J.: A New Public Key Cryptosystem Based on Higher Residues. In: Proc. of ACM CCS 1998, pp. 546–560 (1998)

[OU98] Okamoto, T., Uchiyama, S.: A New Public-Key Cryptosystem as Secure as Factoring. In: Nyberg, K. (ed.) EUROCRYPT 1998. LNCS, vol. 1403, pp. 308–318. Springer, Heidelberg (1998)

[Pai99] Paillier, P.: Public-Key Cryptosystems Based on Composite Degree Residuosity Classes. In: Stern, J. (ed.) EUROCRYPT 1999. LNCS, vol. 1592, pp. 223–238. Springer, Heidelberg (1999)

[PT00] Paulus, S., Takagi, T.: A New Public-Key Cryptosystem over a Quadratic Order with Quadratic Decryption Time. J. Cryptology 13(2), 263–272 (2000)

[SP05] Schielzeth, D., Pohst, M.E.: On Real Quadratic Number Fields Suitable for Cryptography. Experiment. Math. 14(2), 189–197 (2005)

[Sch91] Schönhage, A.: Fast reduction and composition of binary quadratic forms. In: Proc. of ISSAC 1991, pp. 128–133. ACM (1991)

[W+11] Wang, L., Wang, L., Pan, Y., Zhang, Z., Yang, Y.: Discrete Logarithm Based Additively Homomorphic Encryption and Secure Data Aggregation. Information Sciences 181(16), 3308–3322 (2011)

Author Index